standard catalog of®

LIONEL TRAINS

1970-2000

Edited by
Justin Moen

ACKNOWLEDGMENTS

When this project began, it was suggested that it would be a life's work because of the huge volume of product it would cover. It was also suggested that it would take a hand truck to move the completed volume. Production constraints solved the latter problem and, more significantly, a generous outpouring of help from contributors, collectors and businesses reduced a lifetime of work into only a couple of years.

Space considerations have limited the number of contributor comments included in this volume, leaving the photos to speak largely for themselves. However, the guidance of these collectors as to what to photograph, and essential variations to include, were critical to assembling this book.

Rob English opened his collection of scale-proportioned locomotives and rolling stock to photograph. Joel Fugazzotto provided photographs of each of the vat and ore cars from the modern era. The trains on the cover, and at the beginning of many of the chapters, are from the collection of Dave Martiny, who hosted photographer Kris Kandler for two days as these photos were taken. The guru of Lionel catalogs, Bob Osterhoff (www.trainpaper.com), supplied several of the catalogs shown herein. Stuart Rankin (www.LionelNation.com), spent days unpacking each of the items in his collection to photograph—and surely spent more days repacking thereafter! This book's coverage of uncataloged items would be much lighter without Stu's help. As has seemingly been done with previoius Lionel Trains titles, a trip was made to the home of Bob Tschopp. There, in a reversal of past experiences, the extensive MPC collection of teenager Bobby was unpacked and photographed, with his mom and dad doing the manual labor and Bobby pointing out the pertinent details of variations.

Scott Griggs of www.trainz.com has maintained a digital library of his inventory through the years, which he opened for this project, saving thousands of miles of driving in search of obscure items.

Greg Stout of Stout Auctions, who arguably sells more trains than anyone in the country, including some of the largest collections, also provided unlimited access to his studio-grade photographs, as well as a database of actual prices realized for trains. Greg's knowledge of the hobby and hobbyists were a tremendous help for this project.

A handful of collectors chose to remain anonymous. Their anonymity, however, does not lessen the value of their contributions of photographs and information to this work. To them, and those reading this book, a special thank you is at hand.

This book would not have been possible without the groundbreaking efforts of Paul V. Ambrose. Paul is one of the foremost experts on Lionel postwar trains and has been instrumental in creating the format used for writing books about toy trains.

Enjoy Coca-Cola
CCBX
9745
Enjoy
FANTA

CONTENTS

Happy
LIONEL
Holidays!

LIONEL
TRAINS

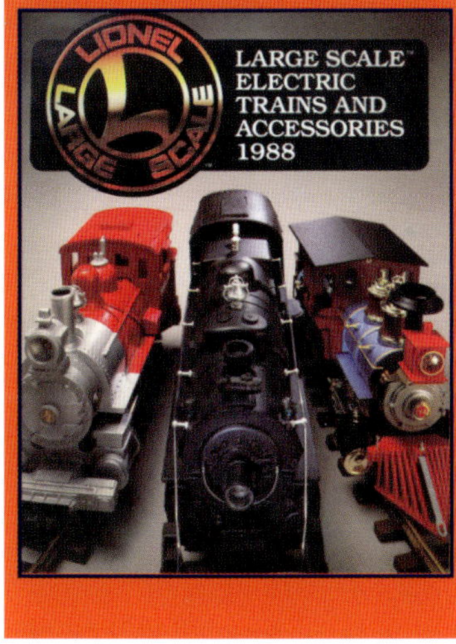
LIONEL
LARGE SCALE
LARGE SCALE
ELECTRIC
TRAINS AND
ACCESSORIES
1988

Chapter 1

Modern-era Lionel Trains & the Collecting Hobby

LIONEL TRAINS-STANDARD OF THE WORLD

Lionel—a brand name so powerful that even today—50 years after what was widely considered the company's heyday, few people in this country don't immediately associate the name with "electric trains."

Joshua Lionel Cohen, along with Harry Grant, founded the company on Sept. 5, 1900—and gave it Cohen's middle name. Cohen, the 23-year-old son of immigrants, had a lucrative contract to produce fuses for U.S. Navy mines. Ever an experimenter, Cohen sought to expand the company's business. In 1901, seeking to create an animated window display for merchants, he installed a small electric motor on the underside of a wooden gondola car and set the car on a circle of steel rails. Powered by dry cell batteries, the window display was a success, but not in the way intended. Onlookers didn't want to buy the merchandise the gondola was hauling; they wanted to buy the display itself—the "electric train."

This gondola, as well as the other early trains, ran on track with rails spaced 2-7/8-inches apart, or 2-7/8-inch-gauge. This size would remain the norm for Lionel until 1906 when the slightly smaller "Standard Gauge" was introduced, followed in 1915 by "O-Gauge"—a size created by another firm, but ultimately the size most commonly associated with Lionel (O-Gauge trains are the subject of this volume). Changes were being made in Cohen's personal life in this time period as well, and in 1910, he changed his last name to Cowen for reasons unknown today.

The firm continued to flourish and expand during the years prior to WWII, but America's entry into the war would forever change the look of Lionel trains. War production and materials rationing brought a complete halt to the production of Lionel trains in June 1942. With the Japanese signing of surrender papers on Sept. 2, 1945, an all-out effort was made to have O-Gauge Lionel trains on the market in time for Christmas 1945.

The company succeeded in this effort, but the trains were much different looking than the prewar trains. Realistic operating knuckle couplers were used throughout the line, as were newly designed trucks, and while several of the items in the fledgling line were based on prewar offerings, the gondola car was all new—and featured a molded plastic body. This new material would come to dominate the manufacture of car bodies throughout the postwar era, and into the modern era as well.

The 1950s are considered the golden age of Lionel trains, and the marketplace was willing, and Lionel employed a pool of creative talent that designed many of the products still gracing the pages of Lionel catalogs today. However, by the 1960s, trains—both real and toy—no longer had the mystique they once had, and the company's fortunes began to decline. Because he possibly foresaw these changes, in 1958, Joshua Cowen resigned as Chairman of the Board. The following year he sold his stock—the controlling interest—in the company to his great-nephew—the famous, or infamous, Roy Cohn. Cohn promptly discharged the company's design and production team—the men who had led the company to its peak a few years earlier. Seeking to diversify, fewer and fewer company resources were devoted to the manufacture or sale of electric trains, concentrating instead on electronics, fasteners and other products.

In the ultimate move in this diversification, in 1969, The Lionel Toy Corp. (as it had become in 1965) exited the toy train business by licensing the name and selling the tooling to Model Products Corp. (MPC), a division of General Mills. Some production was moved to Michigan immediately and, by the mid-1970s, Lionel trains were no longer a presence in the huge Hillside plant. In 1973, MPC gave way to Fundimensions, and the MPC logo was dutifully removed from the side of Lionel rolling stock, although General Mills remained the owner. In 1985, General Mills spun of its toy and hobby operations, and the manufacture of Lionel trains went along with it, becoming part of Kenner-Parker. The following year Detroit real estate developer Richard Kughn bought the Lionel operations from Kenner-Parker. Kughn, already an avid train collector, brought with him a direct knowledge of the customer base, and the customer's point of view, and immediately put in place a number of changes. Kughn named his company Lionel Trains, Inc., and sought to improve the quality and diversity of the trains offered. Also during this time an entirely new control system, known as Trainmaster, which had been developed by rock legend Neil Young, was introduced, along with the revolutionary "RailSounds" sound system. In 1993, Kughn was able to buy outright the name "Lionel Corporation" when the original firm was finally liquidated. This ended 24 years of paying licensing fees and royalties.

In 1995, Kughn sold the bulk of his interest in Lionel Trains, Inc. Neil Young acquired 20 percent of the company, with the bulk of the business owned by Wellspring Associates, led by former Paramount chairman Martin Davis.

While Lionel has contracted some production offshore since 1966—or even prior to WWII if you consider that some of the prewar tooling was made in Italy—in the modern era increasing use of offshore contract manufacturers have been made. In fact, in 2001, Lionel closed its last U.S. production facility.

COLLECTING

Toy train collecting and operation is a hobby well suited to sharing with others. Toy train enthusiasts love to get together with others of the same ilk, swapping not only stories and information, but the trains as well. Fellow collectors are a tremendous source of information, and no book or Web site can compare to the wealth of knowledge that can be gleaned by sharing a pot of coffee and stories with other train buffs. Holding an example of an item in your hands, studying the detail, and having a more experienced collector point out the differences, major and subtle, is the best learning opportunity. The piece not for sale can be examined unhurried, and questions answered honestly—an excellent preparation for seeking an item in the marketplace.

While Internet auctions have provided access to even the scarcest of trains to collectors, no matter how remote their location, there is no substitute for rubbing shoulders with fellow collectors in hobby shops and train shows. Particularly when seeking variations involving subtle differences in paint and plastic shading, examining the item personally is the best way to go.

Toy trains have been collected almost as long as they have been produced, and in any hobby, collectors tend to form groups. The oldest successful national organization for train collectors is the aptly named Train Collectors Association, or TCA. Also the largest collector's organization in this hobby, the TCA was founded in Yardley, Pa., in 1954. The organization has various regional divisions and chapters, many of which have commissioned Lionel to produce special items for them, as does the national organization. One of the regional groups, the Eastern Division, hosts the largest toy train show in the world twice annually in York, Pa.

The National Headquarters of the TCA includes the Toy Train Museum, which is open to the public. The organization can be contacted via their Web site, www.traincollectors.org, or by writing to:

TRAIN COLLECTORS ASSOCIATION
P.O. Box 248
300 Paradise Lane
Strasburg, PA 17579
(717) 687-8623

Founded in 1966, the Toy Train Operating Society was formed on the West Coast at a time when it was felt that the TCA was primarily an East Coast collector oriented organization. Although both groups are national organizations, even today most TTOS members and events are found on the West Coast. The TTOS can be contacted at:

TOY TRAIN OPERATING SOCIETY
25 W. Walnut St., Suite 308
Pasadena, CA 91103
(626) 578-0673
www.ttos.org

While Lionel enthusiasts dominate the two groups above today, they are open to fans of all makes. Seeking an all-Lionel organization all the time, in 1970, Jim Gates of Des Moines, Iowa, founded the Lionel Collector's Club of America. The organization has grown steadily since, and has commissioned Lionel to produce a number of special items for them, some of which have become highly collectible. The club's mailing address is:

LCCA BUSINESS OFFICE
P.O. Box 479
La Salle, IL 61301-0479
www.lionelcollectors.org

While the emphasis of the clubs listed above is collecting, the trains were designed for operating. Feeling there was a need for a club to emphasize this, in 1979, Larry Keller of Cincinnati, OH, formed the Lionel Operating Train Society, or LOTS. As with the other clubs listed here, LOTS publishes its own magazine and swap lists. LOTS can be reached at:

LOTS BUSINESS OFFICE
6376 West Fork Road
Cincinnati, OH 45247-5704
www.lots-trains.org

HOW TO USE THIS STANDARD CATALOG

The shear number of items produced by Lionel since 1970 is staggering. The diversity of items produced from 1970 through 2000, the scope of this book, far exceeds the number of items Lionel produced in the 70 years prior. For this reason, some painful choices had to be made in the preparation of this volume. Due to space limitations, accessories have been omitted entirely. Also, when compared to previous Standard Catalogs, you will see that the descriptions are not nearly so detailed, again the result of space concerns. Also, it is somewhat redundant to say a given boxcar is yellow when that information is printed below a color photo of the boxcar!

In the 1970s, Lionel realized that much of its production was going to collectors, rather than families who would be playing with them. Thus, their manufacturing methods adjusted accordingly. They were not just making toys; rather they were making collector's items. Hence, considerable emphasis was placed on product uniformity. The result of this is that while there are many, many items in this book, there are relatively few variations—the last 19608 tank car off the assembly line is exactly like the first one off the assembly line.

In order to serve the novice, as well as the experienced train collector, this book has been divided into chapters by body type: tank cars, steam locomotives, etc. Within each chapter the listings are arranged numerically by Lionel's assigned product number. In many cases, this is the number stamped on the side of the car. However, this is not always the case. In recent years Lionel has had a trend of putting eiher a prototypical number on the sides of their products, or a foreshortened catalog number.

REFERENCE EXAMPLE

1.→ 

3.→

2.→ **[8150] PENNSYLVANIA**: 1981, green GG1 with five gold

4.→ stripes numbered "4935."

5.→

EX-C7	LN-C8	Scarcity
150	200	4
↑ A.	↑ B.	↑ C.

1.) Photo: In some listings, photos are supplied to better help identify and verify what Model and Type you possess.

2.) Listing Name/Type: Items will be listed by Model number and Variation number (Type).

3.) Photo Indicator: Items with a icon indicates that this listing is accompanied by a photo. If the image is not directly above its given listing, it will more times than not be in an enlarged two-column format or on the following page.

4.) Listing Description: Located directly after the Listing Name/Type is a brief description of the listing, giving vital information to better help identification.

5.) Values Table: Below the Listing Description is the Values Table. Values for each condition are in U.S. Dollars.

- **A.) EX-C7=*Excellent:*** Minute scratches or nicks, no dents or rust, all original, less than average wear.
- **B.) LN-C8=*Like New:*** Only the slightest signs of handling and wheel wear, brilliant colors and crisp markings; literally like new. As a rule, Like New trains must have their original boxes in comparable condition to realize the prices listed in this guide.
- **C.) Scarcity:** On a scale of 1-8, this system will assess the accessibility and scarcity of the particular listing. On occasion, an item may be so rare that there is not enough reference to place a price or scarcity.

CONDITION AND RARITY

To the collector condition is everything, and the Train Collectors Association, the world's oldest and largest train collector group has established very precise language for describing the condition of collectable trains in order to protect both the buyer and the seller. All reputable dealers and collectors use this terminology. In fact, failure to properly use these terms in transactions between members can result in expulsion from the organization.

These grading standards are as follows:

Fair or C4: Well-scratched, chipped, dented, rusted, warped.

Good or C5: Small dents, scratches, dirty.

Very Good or C6: Few scratches, exceptionally clean, no major dents or rust.

Excellent or C7: Minute scratches or nicks, no dents or rust, all original, less than average wear.

Like New or C8: Only the slightest signs of handling and wheel wear, brilliant colors and crisp markings; literally like new. As a rule, Like New trains must have their original boxes in comparable condition to realize the prices listed in the guide.

Mint or C10: Brand new, absolutely unmarred, all original and unused. Items dusty or faded from display, or with fingerprints from handling, cannot be considered mint. Although Lionel test ran their locomotives briefly at the factory, items "test run" by consumers cannot be considered mint. Most collectors expect mint items to come with all associated packaging with which they were originally supplied.

In the modern era, only trains in Mint and Like New condition are considered collectible. Trains in these conditions are simply too abundant, too plentiful and, as a rule, too inexpensive for lesser grade trains to command any attention.

Demand is one of the key factors influencing values. Many collectors hope to add an 18005 Hudson to their collection. Even though this item is not difficult to find, it still commands a hefty price. Another factor affecting demand is the ongoing production of Lionel trains. Today, an increasing number of trains are being sold to high-end operators. As locomotives of a given type with improved control systems come out, demand for their now outdated predecessors drops—they simply become old, used trains. Similarly, when a new locomotive is produced, some operators and collectors seek to build "matching" trains—drawing on cars previously produced, increasing demand for those items.

Rarity, or scarcity, is also a factor influencing the value of trains. Because most of the trains produced in the modern era have been marketed as collectibles, there has been little attrition due to damage from playwear. Because of the successful pre-sell programs of Lionel and its dealer network, virtually everything the company produces is made to order. There is no need to cut production runs because of lackluster sales. Similarly, stringent quality controls have reduced the number of scarce variations. Further, many individuals purchased trains from the late '70s into the '80s as investments (a poor choice), and these trains are now finding their way to the marketplace. As with most things produced as "collectibles," very few of the trains of the modern era can be considered rare, or even scarce.

Supply, as a short-term extension of rarity, whether actual or temporary, also affects price. If only one example of a sought after item is available at an auction, the price was driven to a higher level than would be the case if there was multiple examples of identical items being offered.

Buyer's intent is the final factor driving prices. A dealer, buying for resale, must buy an item at a low enough price that they can in turn sell it at a profit. An operator, who intends to take a car home and run it on their layout, will pay no more for a Mint condition car than they will for a Like New car—because a Like New car is what they will have shortly after arriving home regardless of which one they buy! The collector, seeking to add a Mint condition item to their permanent collection is the individual likely to pay the most for a given item.

The values listed in this volume were compiled based in part on monitoring activities, train shows and auctions. These prices represent what trains have been trading for, not the asking price, nor the cataloged price. They represent values collectors and operators have been paying to add items to their collections. If contemplating a sale to a dealer, you should expect to receive about half of the amounts listed in the given conditions.

It is ***important*** however that you remember these values serve only as a ***guide***. What you consider an item to be worth is of far greater importance than the opinion of this, or any other author or collector. It is your money you are spending, or your train you are selling. Beyond the factors listed above, prices can be and are affected by region of the country, time of the year, and personal factors. Hence, the values printed should only be used as an approximation; prices slightly higher, or lower, are not at all unreasonable. It should be noted also that the publisher does not sell trains. **This is NOT a mail-order catalog.** And you should not expect a dealer to "price match" or a collector to pay "book value."

Scale vs. Gauge, and What Is Standard-0?

Almost all toy train enthusiasts and even model railroaders use the terms "scale" and "gauge" interchangeably, but this is not correct. *Scale* is a numeric ratio representing the relative size of a model to that of the full-sized, or prototype, item. A 1/48-scale model is 1/48 the size of the real train. Many of Lionel's trains approximate 1/48-scale, although considerable liberties have been taken, particularly on items designed when Lionel's trains were toys, not collectibles. *Gauge* is the distance between the rail heads—most full-sized railroads in the United States operate on track that is 4-foot 8-1/2-inch-gauge.

Lionel O, 027, 072, Super 0, and Fast Track are all truly the same gauge—1-1/4 inches—by the industry standard, all these are O-Gauge. Incidentally, some other early toy train gauges were Number 1-Gauge, with a rail width of 1-3/4 inches and Number 2-Gauge, with a width of two inches. The prewar "Standard Gauge" had a rail-to-rail width of 2-1/8 inches. Despite this seeming standardization, Lionel has chosen to confuse things by creating their own terminology using some of these same words.

Lionel's O-Gauge track stands 11/16 inches tall, and a circle of standard curved sections forms a circle with a 31-inch outside diameter. Track designated 072 has the same cross-section as O, but forms a circle 72 inches center to center (or 74 inches outside diameter).

The popular 027 shares the 1-1/4-inch gauge with O, but is less expensive to produce, standing only 7/16 inches tall. A circle of this track forms a circle 27 inches in outside diameter. Because it was less expensive to produce, 027 track has been used in entry-level trade sets for decades. These sets typically included other components that were less expensive to produce (and frequently somewhat smaller) than those found in Lionel's premium "O-Gauge" line. The locomotives, freight cars and other items associated with these sets have also been referred to as "027." Occasional reference in this text is made to various items being the "traditional 027 size." This is to distinguish them from the bulk of the trains, which are the slightly larger traditional O size.

"Standard 0" was a term created by Lionel's marketing department in 1973. That year Lionel purchased the tooling to produce a number of different types of freight cars that were very nearly true 1/48-scale from Pola. These cars towered over both the O- and 027-gauge counterparts. Because the Pola trucks and couplers were not compatible with Lionel's own, a new truck was created. Die-with functioning coil springs, these were the most realistic trucks produced by Lionel since the full-scale trucks of the 1940 700-series cars. The scale-sized cars, and their remarkable new trucks, were dubbed "Standard 0." The cars had lackluster sales—at least initially—though that size has flourished since the 1990s. The trucks, however, were a tremendous success and were used on Lionel's premium freight cars, regardless of proportion. Few continue to associate the term "Standard 0" with the trains themselves, which are referred to in this text as "1/48-scale." "Standard 0" is now most commonly used when describing the die-cast sprung truck.

CHAPTER 2
STEAM LOCOMOTIVES

The steam locomotive has long been the visual image associated with Lionel trains. Typically made of die-cast metal, the long, black heavy locomotives have a nostalgic, and long-lasting look.

In the United States, steam locomotives are described using the Whyte classification system, which is related to the locomotive's wheel arrangement. A locomotive classified by Whyte as a 4-6-4 has a four-wheel leading, or pilot truck, six rigidly coupled driving wheels mounted on three axles, and four trailing wheels. From the side, an observer would see two front wheels, three center wheels, and two rear wheels.

While on Lionel's replicas the leading and trailing trucks are mounted loosely and move easily, this is not the case with a real locomotive. The leading truck is designed to begin the locomotive's turn in curves, or lead it in. The trailing truck is used to support the great weight of the firebox above it. Steam switchers, operating at low speeds, do not require a massive firebox, nor do they attain such speeds as to need guidance through curves, and accordingly typically have neither pilot nor trailing trucks. The larger the locomotive, the larger the trailing truck normally has to be to support the firebox weight—although there are some exceptions to this rule. The faster the locomotives are intended to operate, conventionally the greater number of wheels on the pilot truck.

Accordingly, a 4-8-4 is generally considered passenger and fast freight locomotive, while a 2-8-5 tends to be thought of as freight locomotive. Advances in locomotive design from the 1920s onward tended to blur these distinctions.

Various Whyte classifications, or wheel arrangements, are frequently referred to by names—a 2-8-4 arrangement is typically called a "Berkshire." While in most cases these names were universally applied across railroads, in some cases a particular railroad may use a unique name. For example, a 4-8-2 locomotive was almost universally known as a "Mountain," but on the New York Central railroad they were known as "Mohawk."

Steam locomotives were part of the initial offerings by Lionel during the modern era. At first, the offerings were almost exclusively inexpensive plastic or die-cast models based on postwar designs. Near the end of the first decade of the modern era more and more of the high quality steam locomotives of the postwar era began to appear in the catalog, often wearing realistic and brightly colored paint schemes rather than the mundane all-black finish of previous years. In 1989, Lionel issued the first totally new large steam locomotive that the company had produced in decades—a scale-sized replica of Reading T-1 4-8-4 Northern 2100. No doubt this particular locomotive was chosen because the actual locomotive was owned by Lionel owner Richard Kughn, along with Ross Rowland (of American Freedom Train fame) and restored by a team led by Bill Benson. Kughn invested over one million dollars in the restoration of the actual locomotive. The model was massive, measuring 27 inches long, and equipped with every Lionel innovation of the time. In 1990, Lionel took the bold step of reincarnating the legendary scale-detailed prewar 700E scale Hudson, with some features the original lacked, including an operating smoke unit.

Perhaps the success of these two detailed, scale-sized locomotives was the catalyst for greater developments. Since that time Lionel has issued a steady stream of scale-sized, beautifully detailed steam locomotives. Most of these have been equipped with Lionel's revolutionary wireless digital control system "TrainMaster."

3100 GREAT NORTHERN: 1981, 4-8-4 Northern locomotive, Famous American Railroads number three.

EX-C7	LN-C8	Scarcity
125	150	5

8001 NICKEL PLATE ROAD: 1980, uncataloged 2-6-4 locomotive.

EX-C7	LN-C8	Scarcity
20	30	3

8002 UNION PACIFIC: 1980, 2-8-4 Berkshire locomotive, Famous American Railroads number two.

EX-C7	LN-C8	Scarcity
125	175	5

8003 CHESSIE STEAM SPECIAL: 1980, 2-8-4 Berkshire locomotive.

EX-C7	LN-C8	Scarcity
120	150	5

8004 ROCK ISLAND: 1980-82, 4-4-0 American locomotive.

EX-C7	LN-C8	Scarcity
50	75	4

8005 SANTA FE: 1980-82, 4-4-0 American locomotive.

EX-C7	LN-C8	Scarcity
20	30	4

8006 ATLANTIC COAST LINE: 1980, uncataloged JCPenney 4-6-4 Hudson locomotive.

EX-C7	LN-C8	Scarcity
125	175	6

8007 NYNH & H: 1980-81, 2-6-4 locomotive.

EX-C7	LN-C8	Scarcity
35	50	5

8008 CHESSIE SYSTEM: 1980, 4-4-2 Atlantic locomotive.

EX-C7	LN-C8	Scarcity
20	35	3

8040 NICKEL PLATE ROAD: 1970-72, 2-4-2 Columbia locomotive.

EX-C7	LN-C8	Scarcity
20	30	2

8040 CANADIAN NATIONAL: 1971, uncataloged 2-4-2 Columbia locomotive.

EX-C7	LN-C8	Scarcity
30	50	5

8041 NEW YORK CENTRAL: 1970, 2-4-2 Columbia locomotive.

EX-C7	LN-C8	Scarcity
20	30	2

8041 PENNSYLVANIA: 1971, uncataloged 2-4-2 Columbia locomotive.

EX-C7	LN-C8	Scarcity
20	30	2

8042 GRAND TRUNK WESTERN: Cataloged in 1970, uncataloged from 1971-73, 2-4-2 Columbia locomotive.

8042 GRAND TRUNK WESTERN (Type I): The floor of cab was a thin casting on some of the locomotives.

EX-C7	LN-C8	Scarcity
20	30	2

8042 GRAND TRUNK WESTERN (Type II): The floor of cab was a thick casting on other locomotives.

EX-C7	LN-C8	Scarcity
20	30	2

8043 NICKEL PLATE ROAD: 1970, uncataloged 2-4-2 Columbia locomotive.

EX-C7	LN-C8	Scarcity
20	30	2

8062 GREAT NORTHERN: 1970, 4-6-4 Hudson locomotive.

EX-C7	LN-C8	Scarcity
Cataloged, but not produced.		

[8100] NORFOLK AND WESTERN: 1981, Class J 4-8-4 Northern locomotive numbered "611."

EX-C7	LN-C8	Scarcity
150	200	5

[8101] CHICAGO AND ALTON: 1981, 4-6-4 Hudson locomotive numbered "659."

EX-C7	LN-C8	Scarcity
125	175	5

8102 UNION PACIFIC: 1981-82, 4-4-2, Atlantic locomotive.

EX-C7	LN-C8	Scarcity
25	40	3

[8104] UNION PACIFIC: 1981, uncataloged 4-4-0 American locomotive numbered "3."

EX-C7	LN-C8	Scarcity
60	85	4

8140 SOUTHERN: 1971, uncataloged 2-4-0 locomotive.

EX-C7	LN-C8	Scarcity
12	18	2

8141 PENNSYLVANIA: 1971-72, 2-4-2 Columbia locomotive.

8141 PENNSYLVANIA (Type I): Some of the locomotives and tenders are lettered in white.

EX-C7	LN-C8	Scarcity
15	20	3

8141 PENNSYLVANIA (Type II): Other locomotives and tenders are lettered in red.

EX-C7	LN-C8	Scarcity
15	20	3

8142 CHESAPEAKE AND OHIO: 1971-72, 4-4-2 die-cast Atlantic locomotive with the Sound of Steam.

8142 CHESAPEAKE AND OHIO (Type I): As described above.

EX-C7	LN-C8	Scarcity
20	28	3

8142 CHESAPEAKE AND OHIO (Type II): Some units were equipped with an electronic whistle in addition to the Sound of Steam.

EX-C7	LN-C8	Scarcity
20	28	3

8200 "KICKAPOO": 1972, Dockside 0-4-0T locomotive.

EX-C7	LN-C8	Scarcity
10	15	5

8203 PENNSYLVANIA: Cataloged in 1972, available but uncataloged in 1974, cataloged again in 1975, 2-4-2 locomotive.

EX-C7	LN-C8	Scarcity
12	20	3

8204 CHESAPEAKE AND OHIO: 1972, 4-4-2 Atlantic locomotive.

EX-C7	LN-C8	Scarcity
15	20	3

8206 NEW YORK CENTRAL: 1972-75, 4-6-4 Hudson locomotive.

8206 NEW YORK CENTRAL (Type I): Gloss black paint.

EX-C7	LN-C8	Scarcity
60	80	4

8206 NEW YORK CENTRAL (Type II): Flat black paint.

EX-C7	LN-C8	Scarcity
60	80	4

8209: 1972, Dockside switcher 0-4-0T with tender.

EX-C7	LN-C8	Scarcity
20	30	3

8209: 1973-76, Dockside switcher 0-4-0T without tender.

EX-C7	LN-C8	Scarcity
20	30	3

8210 JOSHUA L. COWEN: 1982, 4-6-4 Hudson locomotive.

EX-C7	LN-C8	Scarcity
125	175	4

8212 BLACK CAVE: 1982, 0-4-0 locomotive.

EX-C7	LN-C8	Scarcity
10	15	2

8213 DENVER & RIO GRANDE WESTERN: Cataloged from 1982-83, available but uncataloged from 1984-91, 2-4-2 Columbia locomotive.

EX-C7	LN-C8	Scarcity
20	30	2

8214 PENNSYLVANIA: 1982-83, 2-4-2 Columbia locomotive.

EX-C7	LN-C8	Scarcity
20	30	2

[8215] NICKEL PLATE ROAD: 1982, uncataloged 2-8-4 Berkshire locomotive numbered "779."

EX-C7	LN-C8	Scarcity
25	175	5

8300 SANTA FE: 1973-74, 2-4-0 locomotive.

EX-C7	LN-C8	Scarcity
10	15	3

8302 SOUTHERN: 1973-76, 2-4-0 locomotive.

EX-C7	LN-C8	Scarcity
10	20	2

8303 JERSEY CENTRAL: 1973-74, 2-4-2 Columbia locomotive.

EX-C7	LN-C8	Scarcity
15	25	2

8304 ROCK ISLAND: 1973-75, 4-4-2 Atlantic locomotive and tender with Sound of Steam.

EX-C7	LN-C8	Scarcity
20	35	3

8304 PENNSYLVANIA: 1974-75, 4-4-2 Atlantic locomotive and tender with Sound of Steam.

EX-C7	LN-C8	Scarcity
20	35	3

8304 BALTIMORE AND OHIO: 1975, 4-4-2 Atlantic locomotive and tender with Sound of Steam.

EX-C7	LN-C8	Scarcity
20	35	3

8304 CHESAPEAKE AND OHIO: 1975-77, 4-4-2 Atlantic locomotive and tender with Sound of Steam.

EX-C7	LN-C8	Scarcity
20	35	3

8305 MILWAUKEE ROAD: 1973, 4-4-2 Atlantic locomotive and tender with Sound of Steam.

EX-C7	LN-C8	Scarcity
25	40	3

[8307] SOUTHERN PACIFIC: 1983, class GS-4 4-8-4 Northern locomotive numbered "4449."

EX-C7	LN-C8	Scarcity
250	325	6

8308 JERSEY CENTRAL: 1973-74, uncataloged 2-4-2 Columbia locomotive.

EX-C7	LN-C8	Scarcity
36	43	2

[8309] SOUTHERN: 1983, 2-8-2 Mikado locomotive numbered "4501," Famous American Railroads number four.

EX-C7	LN-C8	Scarcity
150	200	5

8310 NICKEL PLATE ROAD: 1973, uncataloged 2-4-0 locomotive.

EX-C7	LN-C8	Scarcity
10	15	2

8310 SANTA FE: 1974-75, uncataloged 2-4-0 locomotive.

EX-C7	LN-C8	Scarcity
10	15	2

8310 JERSEY CENTRAL: 1974-75, uncataloged 2-4-0 locomotive.

EX-C7	LN-C8	Scarcity
10	15	2

8311 SOUTHERN: 1973, uncataloged 0-4-0 switcher.

EX-C7	LN-C8	Scarcity
10	15	2

8313 SANTA FE: 1983-84, 0-4-0 switcher.

EX-C7	LN-C8	Scarcity
10	15	2

8314 SOUTHERN: 1983-85, 2-4-0 locomotive.

EX-C7	LN-C8	Scarcity
10	15	2

8315 BALTIMORE AND OHIO: 1983-84, 4-4-0 American locomotive.

EX-C7	LN-C8	Scarcity
35	55	4

8402 READING: 1984-85, 4-4-2 Atlantic locomotive.

EX-C7	LN-C8	Scarcity
15	20	4

8403 CHESSIE SYSTEM: 1984-85, 4-4-2 Atlantic locomotive.

EX-C7	LN-C8	Scarcity
20	25	4

[8404] PENNSYLVANIA: 1984-85, 6-8-6 S2 steam turbine locomotive numbered "6200," Famous American Railroads number five.

EX-C7	LN-C8	Scarcity
100	140	5

[8406] NEW YORK CENTRAL: 1984, 4-6-4 Hudson locomotive numbered "783."

EX-C7	LN-C8	Scarcity
175	225	5

8410 REDWOOD VALLEY EXPRESS: 1984-85, 4-4-0 American locomotive.

EX-C7	LN-C8	Scarcity
20	30	4

[8476] TCA: 1985, uncataloged 4-6-4 Hudson locomotive numbered "5484."

EX-C7	LN-C8	Scarcity
125	200	6

8500 PENNSYLVANIA: 1975-76, 2-4-0 locomotive.

EX-C7	LN-C8	Scarcity
10	20	3

8502 SANTA FE: 1975, 2-4-0 locomotive.

EX-C7	LN-C8	Scarcity
10	20	3

8506 PENNSYLVANIA: 1975-77, 0-4-0 switcher.

EX-C7	LN-C8	Scarcity
40	55	4

8507 SANTA FE: 1975, uncataloged 2-4-0 locomotive.

EX-C7	LN-C8	Scarcity
10	20	3

8512 SANTA FE: 1985-86, 0-4-0T locomotive.

EX-C7	LN-C8	Scarcity
15	20	3

8516 NEW YORK CENTRAL: 1985-86, 0-4-0 switcher.

EX-C7	LN-C8	Scarcity
35	55	4

8600 NEW YORK CENTRAL: 1976, 4-6-4 Hudson locomotive.

EX-C7	LN-C8	Scarcity
100	125	4

8601 ROCK ISLAND: 1976-77, 0-4-0 locomotive.

EX-C7	LN-C8	Scarcity
10	15	2

8602 DENVER & RIO GRANDE WESTERN: 1976-78, 2-4-0 locomotive.

EX-C7	LN-C8	Scarcity
10	15	2

8603 CHESAPEAKE & OHIO: 1976-77, 4-6-4 Hudson locomotive.

8603 CHESAPEAKE & OHIO (Type I): Locomotive with driver rims buffed.

EX-C7	LN-C8	Scarcity
65	100	4

8603 CHESAPEAKE & OHIO (Type II): Locomotive with driver rims painted white.

EX-C7	LN-C8	Scarcity
65	100	4

8604 JERSEY CENTRAL: 1976, uncataloged 2-4-2 Columbia locomotive.

EX-C7	LN-C8	Scarcity
15	20	3

[8606] BOSTON & ALBANY: 1986, uncataloged "784" 4-6-4 Hudson locomotive.

EX-C7	LN-C8	Scarcity
500	650	6

[8610] WABASH: 1986-87, 4-6-2 Pacific steam locomotive numbered "672," Fallen Flags number one.

EX-C7	LN-C8	Scarcity
250	325	5

[8615] LOUISVILLE AND NASHVILLE: 1986, uncataloged 2-8-4 M-1 Berkshire locomotive numbered "1970."

EX-C7	LN-C8	Scarcity
350	425	5

8616 SANTA FE: 1986, 4-4-2 Atlantic locomotive.

EX-C7	LN-C8	Scarcity
25	35	3

8617 NICKEL PLATE ROAD: 1986-91, 4-4-2 Atlantic locomotive.

EX-C7	LN-C8	Scarcity
25	35	3

8625 PENNSYLVANIA: 1986-90, 2-4-0 locomotive.

EX-C7	LN-C8	Scarcity
15	20	2

[8630] W. & A.R.R.: 1986, uncataloged "3" 4-4-0 "General" locomotive.

EX-C7	LN-C8	Scarcity
60	75	5

8635 SANTA FE: 1986, 0-4-0 locomotive Service Station Special item.

EX-C7	LN-C8	Scarcity
40	60	5

[8701]W. & A.R.R.: 1977-79, "3," "General" 4-4-0 American locomotive.

EX-C7	LN-C8	Scarcity
70	90	4

8702 SOUTHERN: 1977-78, 4-6-4 Hudson locomotive.

EX-C7	LN-C8	Scarcity
150	200	4

8703 WABASH: 1977, 2-4-2 Columbia locomotive.

EX-C7	LN-C8	Scarcity
15	20	2

8800 LIONEL LINES: 1975, 4-4-2 Atlantic locomotive.

EX-C7	LN-C8	Scarcity
40	50	5

8801 BLUE COMET: 1978-80, 4-6-4 Hudson locomotive.

EX-C7	LN-C8	Scarcity
300	400	5

8803 SANTA FE: 1978, 0-4-0 locomotive.

EX-C7	LN-C8	Scarcity
15	20	2

8900 SANTA FE: 1979, 4-6-4 Hudson locomotive, Famous American Railroads number one.

EX-C7	LN-C8	Scarcity
150	175	5

8902 ATLANTIC COAST LINE: Cataloged from 1979-82, uncataloged in 1986, cataloged again from 1987-90, 2-4-0 locomotive.

EX-C7	LN-C8	Scarcity
10	15	1

8903 DENVER & RIO GRANDE WESTERN: 1979-81, 2-4-2 Columbia locomotive.

EX-C7	LN-C8	Scarcity
10	15	1

8904 WABASH: Cataloged in 1979, available but uncataloged in 1981, 2-4-2 Columbia locomotive.

EX-C7	LN-C8	Scarcity
15	20	2

8905 "SMOKEY MOUNTAIN": 1979, Dockside 0-4-0T locomotive.

EX-C7	LN-C8	Scarcity
10	15	1

[16655] "1993": 1993, tender with RailSounds numbered "1993."

EX-C7	LN-C8	Scarcity
80	110	4

[16673] LIONEL LINES: 1994-97, tender only with air whistle.

EX-C7	LN-C8	Scarcity
20	25	4

[18000] PENNSYLVANIA: 1989 and 1991, "8977" 0-6-0 B-6 switcher.

EX-C7	LN-C8	Scarcity
300	375	4

[18001] ROCK ISLAND: 1987, "5100" 4-8-4 Northern locomotive.

EX-C7	LN-C8	Scarcity
175	225	4

[18002] NEW YORK CENTRAL: 1987, uncataloged "785" 4-6-4 Hudson locomotive.

EX-C7	LN-C8	Scarcity
300	350	5

[18003] DELAWARE, LACKAWANNA & WESTERN: 1988, "1501" 4-8-4 Northern locomotive.

EX-C7	LN-C8	Scarcity
150	180	4

[18004] READING: 1989, "8004" 4-6-2 Pacific locomotive.

EX-C7	LN-C8	Scarcity
125	175	4

[18005] NEW YORK CENTRAL: 1990, "5340" 4-6-4 Hudson locomotive with display case.

EX-C7	LN-C8	Scarcity
600	750	5

[18006] READING: 1989, uncataloged "2100" 4-8-4 T-1 Northern locomotive.

EX-C7	LN-C8	Scarcity
250	300	4

[18007] SOUTHERN PACIFIC: 1991, Class GS-2 4-8-4 Northern locomotive numbered "4410."

EX-C7	LN-C8	Scarcity
250	300	4

[18008] DISNEYLAND 35TH ANNIVERSARY: 1990, "4" 4-4-0 American locomotive with display case.

EX-C7	LN-C8	Scarcity
150	175	4

[18009] NEW YORK CENTRAL: Uncataloged in 1990, cataloged in 1991, "3000" 4-8-2 Mountain locomotive.

EX-C7	LN-C8	Scarcity
300	350	4

[18010] PENNSYLVANIA: 1991-92, "6200" 6-8-6 S-2 turbine.

EX-C7	LN-C8	Scarcity
800	1,200	6

[18011] CHESSIE SYSTEM: 1991, class T-1 4-8-4 Northern steam locomotive numbered "2101."

EX-C7	LN-C8	Scarcity
300	350	4

[18011] CARAIL SYSTEM: 1992, class T-1 4-8-4 Northern steam locomotive numbered "1994."

EX-C7	LN-C8	Scarcity
700	1,200	8

[18012] NEW YORK CENTRAL: 1990, 4-6-4 Hudson locomotive numbered "5340."

EX-C7	LN-C8	Scarcity
500	700	4

[18013] DISNEYLAND 35TH ANNIVERSARY: 1990, "4" 4-4-0 American locomotive.

EX-C7	LN-C8	Scarcity
150	200	4

[18014] LIONEL LINES: 1991, "8014" 2-6-4 locomotive.

EX-C7	LN-C8	Scarcity
60	75	4

[18016] NORTHERN PACIFIC: 1992, "2626" 4-8-4 Northern locomotive.

EX-C7	LN-C8	Scarcity
175	200	4

[18018] SOUTHERN: 1992, "4501" 2-8-2 Mikado locomotive.

EX-C7	LN-C8	Scarcity
700	800	5

[18022] PERE MARQUETTE: 1993, "1201" 2-8-4 Berkshire locomotive.

EX-C7	LN-C8	Scarcity
300	350	4

[18023] WESTERN MARYLAND: 1992, "6" Shay locomotive.

EX-C7	LN-C8	Scarcity
1,000	1,350	5

[18024] TEXAS & PACIFIC: 1992, uncataloged "907" 4-8-2 Mountain locomotive with display case, made for Sears.

EX-C7	LN-C8	Scarcity
400	450	4

[18025] TEXAS & PACIFIC: 1992, uncataloged "907" 4-8-2 Mountain locomotive with display case, made for Sears.

EX-C7	LN-C8	Scarcity
400	450	4

[18026] NEW YORK CENTRAL: 1992, uncataloged "5450" two-rail Smithsonian Dreyfuss 4-6-4 Hudson locomotive.

EX-C7	LN-C8	Scarcity
2,100	2,500	7

[18027] NEW YORK CENTRAL: 1993, uncataloged "5450" three-rail Dreyfuss 4-6-4 Hudson locomotive.

EX-C7	LN-C8	Scarcity
1,600	1,800	7

[18028] PENNSYLVANIA: 1993, uncataloged "3768" two-rail Smithsonian 4-6-2 Pacific locomotive.

EX-C7	LN-C8	Scarcity
2,100	2,500	7

[18029] NEW YORK CENTRAL: 1993, uncataloged three-rail Dreyfuss 4-6-4 Hudson steam locomotive numbered "5454" with operating roller base.

EX-C7	LN-C8	Scarcity
1,900	2,100	7

[18030] FRISCO: 1993, uncataloged 2-8-2 Mikado locomotive numbered "4100."

EX-C7	LN-C8	Scarcity
500	600	5

[18031] BUNDESBAHN: 1993, uncataloged 1/48-scale BR-50 2-10-0 locomotive, two-rail.

EX-C7	LN-C8	Scarcity
Too rarely traded to establish accurate pricing.		

[18034] SANTA FE: 1994, 2-8-2 Mikado locomotive numbered "3158."

EX-C7	LN-C8	Scarcity
450	500	5

[18035] REICHSBAHN: 1993, uncataloged 1/48-scale BR-50 2-10-0 locomotive, two-rail.

EX-C7	LN-C8	Scarcity
Too rarely traded to establish accurate pricing.		

[18036] FRENCH: 1993, uncataloged 1/48-scale BR-50 2-10-0 locomotive, two-rail.

EX-C7	LN-C8	Scarcity
Too rarely traded to establish accurate pricing.		

[18040] NORFOLK AND WESTERN: 1995, "612" Class J 4-8-4 Northern locomotive.

EX-C7	LN-C8	Scarcity
400	450	4

[18041] BOSTON & ALBANY: 1995, "619" 4-6-4 Hudson locomotive.

EX-C7	LN-C8	Scarcity
Cataloged, but not produced.		

[18042] BOSTON & ALBANY: 1995, "618" 4-6-4 Hudson locomotive.

EX-C7	LN-C8	Scarcity
175	200	4

[18043] CHESAPEAKE & OHIO: 1995, "490" 4-6-4 Hudson locomotive.

EX-C7	LN-C8	Scarcity
600	700	4

[18044] SOUTHERN: 1996, "1390" 4-6-2 Pacific locomotive.

EX-C7	LN-C8	Scarcity
175	225	4

[18045] NEW YORK CENTRAL: 1996, "777" Commodore Vanderbilt 4-6-4 Hudson locomotive.

EX-C7	LN-C8	Scarcity
400	500	4

[18046] WABASH: 1996, "700" 4-6-4 Hudson locomotive.

EX-C7	LN-C8	Scarcity
275	325	4

[18049] NORFOLK AND WESTERN: 1996, "600" Warhorse series Class J 4-8-4 Northern.

EX-C7	LN-C8	Scarcity
275	325	4

[18050] PENNSYLVANIA: 1996, "2055" JCPenney 4-6-2 Pacific locomotive.

EX-C7	LN-C8	Scarcity
250	275	5

[18052] PENNSYLVANIA: 1997, Torpedo "238E" locomotive.

EX-C7	LN-C8	Scarcity
300	400	5

[18053] BERKSHIRE: 1997, "726" 2-8-4 Century Club Berkshire locomotive.

EX-C7	LN-C8	Scarcity
600	700	5

[18054] NEW YORK CENTRAL: 1997, 0-4-0 switcher black numbered "1665."

EX-C7	LN-C8	Scarcity
75	100	4

[18056] NEW YORK CENTRAL: 1997, J1-e 4-6-4 Hudson locomotive numbered "5344" and Vanderbilt tender.

EX-C7	LN-C8	Scarcity
400	500	4

[18057] LIONEL LINES: 1997, Century Club S-2 turbine 6-8-6 numbered "671."

EX-C7	LN-C8	Scarcity
400	500	6

[18058] HUDSON: 1997, "773" 4-6-4 Hudson locomotive.

EX-C7	LN-C8	Scarcity
700	800	6

[18059] WESTERN MARYLAND: 1998, "209" Pacific 4-6-2 locomotive.

EX-C7	LN-C8	Scarcity
Cataloged, but not produced.		

[18062] SANTA FE: 1997, "3447" 4-6-4 Hudson locomotive.

EX-C7	LN-C8	Scarcity
500	600	6

[18063] NEW YORK CENTRAL: 1999, dark gray/black scale Commodore Vanderbilt 4-6-4 Hudson locomotive.

EX-C7	LN-C8	Scarcity
750	800	6

[18064] NEW YORK CENTRAL: 1998, "3000" 4-8-2 Mohawk L-3A locomotive.

EX-C7	LN-C8	Scarcity
600	700	4

[18067] NEW YORK CENTRAL: 1997, factory weathered scale Commodore Vanderbilt 4-6-4 Hudson locomotive.

EX-C7	LN-C8	Scarcity
800	850	7

[18070] WESTERN MARYLAND: 1998, "208" 4-6-2 Pacific locomotive.

EX-C7	LN-C8	Scarcity
Cataloged, but not produced.		

[18071] SOUTHERN PACIFIC: 1998, "4449" Daylight 4-8-4 Northern locomotive.

EX-C7	LN-C8	Scarcity
475	550	5

[18072] LIONEL LINES: 1998, Torpedo locomotive.

EX-C7	LN-C8	Scarcity
250	300	4

[18079] NEW YORK CENTRAL: 1999, "1967" 2-8-2 Mikado locomotive.

EX-C7	LN-C8	Scarcity
475	550	5

[18080] DENVER & RIO GRANDE WESTERN: 1999, "1210" 2-8-2 Mikado locomotive.

EX-C7	LN-C8	Scarcity
475	550	5

[18082] NEW YORK CENTRAL: 1999, "5404" 4-6-4 Hudson locomotive.

EX-C7	LN-C8	Scarcity
150	175	4

[18083] CHESAPEAKE AND OHIO: 1999, "305" 4-6-4 Hudson locomotive.

EX-C7	LN-C8	Scarcity
150	175	4

[18084] SANTA FE: 1999, "305" 4-6-4 Hudson locomotive.

EX-C7	LN-C8	Scarcity
150	175	4

[18085] NEW HAVEN: 1999, "1334" 4-6-2 Pacific locomotive.

EX-C7	LN-C8	Scarcity
200	225	4

[18086] NEW YORK CENTRAL: 1999, "4929" 4-6-2 Pacific locomotive.

EX-C7	LN-C8	Scarcity
200	225	4

[18087] SANTA FE: 1999, "3448" 4-6-2 Pacific locomotive.

EX-C7	LN-C8	Scarcity
200	225	4

[18088] SOUTHERN: 1999, "1407" 4-6-2 Pacific locomotive.

EX-C7	LN-C8	Scarcity
225	250	4

[18089] JERSEY CENTRAL: 1999, "771" 4-6-0 Camelback locomotive.

EX-C7	LN-C8	Scarcity
300	350	4

[18090] DENVER & RIO GRANDE WESTERN: 1990, uncataloged "1990" LCCA 4-6-2 Pacific locomotive.

EX-C7	LN-C8	Scarcity
250	300	6

[18091] PENNSYLVANIA: 1999, "821" 4-6-0 Camelback locomotive.

EX-C7	LN-C8	Scarcity
300	350	4

[18092] SOUTHERN PACIFIC: 1999, "2283" 4-6-0 Camelback locomotive.

EX-C7	LN-C8	Scarcity
300	350	4

[18093] CHICAGO & NORTHWESTERN: 1999, "3006" 4-6-0 Camelback locomotive.

EX-C7	LN-C8	Scarcity
300	350	4

[18094] BALTIMORE AND OHIO: 1999-2000, E6 4-4-2 Atlantic locomotive, command control-equipped.

EX-C7	LN-C8	Scarcity
300	350	4

[18095] PENNSYLVANIA: 1999-2000, E6 4-4-2 Atlantic locomotive, command control-equipped.

EX-C7	LN-C8	Scarcity
275	325	4

[18096] SANTA FE: 1999-2000, E6 4-4-2 Atlantic locomotive, command control-equipped.

EX-C7	LN-C8	Scarcity
325	375	4

[18097] JERSEY CENTRAL: 1999, "770" 4-6-0 Camelback locomotive.

EX-C7	LN-C8	Scarcity
275	325	4

[18098] PENNSYLVANIA: 1999, "820" 4-6-0 Camelback locomotive.

EX-C7	LN-C8	Scarcity
275	325	4

[18099] SOUTHERN PACIFIC: 1999, "2282" 4-6-0 Camelback locomotive.

EX-C7	LN-C8	Scarcity
300	350	4

[18600] ATLANTIC COAST LINE: 1987, uncataloged 4-4-2 Atlantic locomotive numbered "8600."

EX-C7	LN-C8	Scarcity
35	40	3

[18601] GREAT NORTHERN: 1988, 4-4-2 Atlantic locomotive numbered "8601."

EX-C7	LN-C8	Scarcity
35	40	3

[18602] PENNSYLVANIA: 1987, 4-4-2 Atlantic locomotive numbered "8602."

EX-C7	LN-C8	Scarcity
35	40	3

[18604] WABASH: 1988-91, 4-4-2 Atlantic locomotive numbered "8604."

[18604] WABASH (Type I): From 1988 through 1990, the boiler casting did not include a feedwater heater.

EX-C7	LN-C8	Scarcity
35	40	3

[18604] WABASH (Type II): In 1991, the boiler casting was modified to include a feedwater heater.

EX-C7	LN-C8	Scarcity
35	40	3

[18605] MOPAR EXPRESS: 1987-88, uncataloged 4-4-2 Atlantic locomotive numbered "1987."

EX-C7	LN-C8	Scarcity
75	100	6

[18606] NEW YORK CENTRAL: 1989, "8606" 2-6-4 locomotive.

EX-C7	LN-C8	Scarcity
75	85	4

[18607] UNION PACIFIC: 1989, "8607" 2-6-4 locomotive.

EX-C7	LN-C8	Scarcity
65	75	4

[18608] DENVER & RIO GRANDE WESTERN: 1989, "8608" 2-6-4 locomotive, Service Station Special item.

EX-C7	LN-C8	Scarcity
80	100	5

[18609] NORTHERN PACIFIC: 1990, "8609" 2-6-4 locomotive.

EX-C7	LN-C8	Scarcity
75	100	4

[18610] ROCK ISLAND: 1990, "8610" 0-4-0 locomotive.

EX-C7	LN-C8	Scarcity
60	75	4

[18611] LIONEL LINES: 1990, "8611" 2-6-4 locomotive, Service Station Special item.

EX-C7	LN-C8	Scarcity
80	100	5

[18612] CHICAGO & NORTHWESTERN: 1989, 4-4-2 Atlantic locomotive numbered "8612."

EX-C7	LN-C8	Scarcity
40	50	4

[18613] NEW YORK CENTRAL: 1989, uncataloged 4-4-2 Atlantic locomotive numbered "8613."

EX-C7	LN-C8	Scarcity
40	50	4

[18614] CIRCUS TRAIN: 1989, uncataloged 4-4-2 Atlantic locomotive numbered "1989."

EX-C7	LN-C8	Scarcity
60	80	5

[18615] GRAND TRUNK WESTERN: 1990, 4-4-2 Atlantic locomotive numbered "8615."

EX-C7	LN-C8	Scarcity
40	50	4

[18616] NORTHERN PACIFIC: 1990, uncataloged 4-4-2 Atlantic locomotive numbered "8616."

EX-C7	LN-C8	Scarcity
60	80	5

[18617] ADOLPHUS III: 1989-92, uncataloged 4-4-2 Atlantic locomotive.

[18617] ADOLPHUS III (Type I): In 1989 and 1990, the boiler casting did not include a feedwater heater.

EX-C7	LN-C8	Scarcity
80	100	6

[18617] ADOLPHUS III (Type II): In 1991, the boiler casting was modified to include a feedwater heater.

EX-C7	LN-C8	Scarcity
80	100	6

[18618] BALTIMORE AND OHIO: 1991, 4-4-2 Atlantic locomotive numbered "8618."

EX-C7	LN-C8	Scarcity
Cataloged, but not produced.		

[18620] ILLINOIS CENTRAL: 1991, 2-6-2 locomotive numbered "8620."

EX-C7	LN-C8	Scarcity
80	100	5

[18621] WESTERN PACIFIC: 1992, 0-4-0 locomotive numbered "8621."

EX-C7	LN-C8	Scarcity
Cataloged, but not produced.		

[18622] UNION PACIFIC: 1990-91, uncataloged 4-4-2 Atlantic locomotive numbered "8622."

EX-C7	LN-C8	Scarcity
40	50	4

[18623] TEXAS AND PACIFIC: 1992, 4-4-2 Atlantic locomotive numbered "8623."

EX-C7	LN-C8	Scarcity
60	80	5

[18625] ILLINOIS CENTRAL: 1991, uncataloged 4-4-2 Atlantic locomotive numbered "8625."

EX-C7	LN-C8	Scarcity
40	50	4

[18626] DELAWARE AND HUDSON: 1992, 2-6-2 locomotive numbered "8626."

EX-C7	LN-C8	Scarcity
80	100	5

[18627] CHESAPEAKE AND OHIO: Cataloged in 1992, available but uncataloged in 1993, cataloged again in 1994, uncataloged but available again in 1995, 4-4-2 Atlantic locomotive numbered "8627" or "8633."

EX-C7	LN-C8	Scarcity
40	50	4

[18628] MISSOURI-KANSAS-TEXAS: Cataloged in 1992, available but uncataloged in 1993, 4-4-2 Atlantic locomotive numbered "8628."

EX-C7	LN-C8	Scarcity
40	50	4

[18630] CHICAGO & NORTHWESTERN: 1993, 4-6-2 Pacific locomotive numbered "2903."

EX-C7	LN-C8	Scarcity
175	200	4

[18632] NEW YORK CENTRAL: 1993-95, 4-4-2 Atlantic locomotive numbered "8632."

EX-C7	LN-C8	Scarcity
40	50	4

[18632] CHESAPEAKE AND OHIO: 1997-99, 4-4-2 Atlantic locomotive numbered "8632."

EX-C7	LN-C8	Scarcity
40	50	4

[18633] CHESAPEAKE AND OHIO: 1994-95, 4-4-2 Atlantic locomotive numbered "8633."

EX-C7	LN-C8	Scarcity
40	50	4

[18633] UNION PACIFIC: 1993-95, 4-4-2 Atlantic locomotive numbered "8633."

EX-C7	LN-C8	Scarcity
40	50	4

[18635] SANTA FE: 1993, "8625" 2-6-4 locomotive.

EX-C7	LN-C8	Scarcity
65	75	4

[18636] BALTIMORE & OHIO: 1994, 4-6-2 Pacific locomotive numbered "5300."

EX-C7	LN-C8	Scarcity
175	200	4

[18637] UNITED AUTO WORKERS: 1993, uncataloged 4-4-2 Atlantic locomotive numbered "8633."

EX-C7	LN-C8	Scarcity
40	50	4

[18638] NORFOLK AND WESTERN: 1994, "638" 2-6-4 locomotive.

EX-C7	LN-C8	Scarcity
85	110	4

[18639] READING: 1995, "639" 4-6-2 Pacific locomotive.

EX-C7	LN-C8	Scarcity
100	125	4

[18640] UNION PACIFIC: 1995, "8640" 4-6-2 Pacific locomotive.

EX-C7	LN-C8	Scarcity
100	125	4

[18641] FORD: 1994, "8641" uncataloged 4-4-2 Atlantic locomotive.

EX-C7	LN-C8	Scarcity
60	80	5

[18642] LIONEL LINES: 1995, "8642" 4-6-2 Pacific locomotive.

EX-C7	LN-C8	Scarcity
75	100	4

[18644] SANTA FE: 1996-99, "8644" 4-4-2 Atlantic locomotive.

EX-C7	LN-C8	Scarcity
40	50	4

[18648] SEARS ZENITH: 1996, "8632" uncataloged 4-4-2 Atlantic locomotive.

EX-C7	LN-C8	Scarcity
80	100	6

[18649] CHEVROLET: 1996, "USA-1" uncataloged 4-4-2 Atlantic locomotive.

EX-C7	LN-C8	Scarcity
80	100	6

[18650] LIONEL LINES: 1996-99, "X-1110" 4-4-2 Atlantic locomotive.

EX-C7	LN-C8	Scarcity
50	60	4

[18653] BOSTON AND ALBANY: 1997, "2044" 4-6-2 Pacific locomotive.

EX-C7	LN-C8	Scarcity
80	100	4

[18654] SOUTHERN PACIFIC: 1997, "2044" 4-6-2 Pacific locomotive.

EX-C7	LN-C8	Scarcity
80	100	4

[18656] BLOOMINGDALES: 1996, "8632" 4-4-2 Atlantic locomotive.

EX-C7	LN-C8	Scarcity
80	100	6

[18657] SEARS ZENITH: 1996, "8632" 4-4-2 Atlantic locomotive.

EX-C7	LN-C8	Scarcity
80	100	6

[18658] LIONEL LINES: 1997, Little League 4-4-2 Atlantic locomotive numbered "X-1110."

EX-C7	LN-C8	Scarcity
50	60	4

[18660] CANADIAN NATIONAL: 1998, "2044" 4-6-2 Pacific locomotive.

EX-C7	LN-C8	Scarcity
80	100	4

[18661] NORFOLK AND WESTERN: 1998, "2044" 4-6-2 Pacific locomotive.

EX-C7	LN-C8	Scarcity
80	100	4

[18662] PENNSYLVANIA: 1998, 0-4-0 switcher.

EX-C7	LN-C8	Scarcity
100	125	4

[18666] SPOKANE, PORTLAND AND SEATTLE: 1997, "2044" 4-6-2 Pacific locomotive.

EX-C7	LN-C8	Scarcity
100	125	4

[18668] BLOOMINGDALES: 1997, "8632" 4-4-2 Atlantic locomotive.

EX-C7	LN-C8	Scarcity
80	100	6

[18669] ILLINOIS CENTRAL: 1998, JCPenney "2099" 4-6-2 Pacific locomotive.

EX-C7	LN-C8	Scarcity
175	200	6

[18670] DELAWARE AND HUDSON: 1998, 4-4-2 "1400" Atlantic locomotive.

EX-C7	LN-C8	Scarcity
35	45	4

[18671] NORFOLK AND WESTERN: 1998, 4-4-2 "1201" Atlantic locomotive.

EX-C7	LN-C8	Scarcity
35	45	4

[18678] QUAKER OATS: 1998, 4-4-2 "8632" Atlantic locomotive.

EX-C7	LN-C8	Scarcity
100	125	6

[18679] TEXAS & PACIFIC: 1999-2000, uncataloged JCPenney 4-6-2 Pacific "721," traditionally controlled.

EX-C7	LN-C8	Scarcity
175	200	6

[18680] LIONEL RAILROADER CLUB: 2000, uncataloged "Century Celebration" "2000" 4-6-4 Hudson steam locomotive, traditionally controlled.

EX-C7	LN-C8	Scarcity
200	250	6

[18681] PENNSYLVANIA: 1999, "460" 4-4-2 Atlantic locomotive.

EX-C7	LN-C8	Scarcity
30	40	3

[18682] SANTA FE: 2000-01, "524" 4-4-2 Atlantic locomotive, traditionally controlled.

EX-C7	LN-C8	Scarcity
30	40	3

[18684] LIONEL RAILROADER CLUB: 1999, uncataloged "1999" 4-6-2 Pacific locomotive.

EX-C7	LN-C8	Scarcity
175	200	6

[18700] ROCK ISLAND: 1987-88, "8700" 0-4-0T locomotive.

EX-C7	LN-C8	Scarcity
20	25	3

[18702] VIRGINIA AND TRUCKEE: 1988, "8702" 4-4-0 American locomotive, Service Station Special item.

EX-C7	LN-C8	Scarcity
125	150	5

[18704] LIONEL LINES: 1989, uncataloged "8704" 2-4-0 locomotive.

EX-C7	LN-C8	Scarcity
20	25	3

[18705] "NEPTUNE": 1990-91, "8705" 0-4-0T locomotive.

EX-C7	LN-C8	Scarcity
20	25	3

[18706] SANTA FE: 1991, "8706" 2-4-0 locomotive.

EX-C7	LN-C8	Scarcity
20	25	3

[18707] MICKEY'S WORLD TOUR: 1991-92, "8707" uncataloged 2-4-0 locomotive.

EX-C7	LN-C8	Scarcity
40	50	5

[18709] LIONEL EMPLOYEE LEARNING CENTER "BLUE ENGINE": 1992, uncataloged 0-4-0T locomotive.

EX-C7	LN-C8	Scarcity
80	100	6

[18710] SOUTHERN: 1993, 2-4-0 locomotive numbered "2000."

EX-C7	LN-C8	Scarcity
15	20	2

[18711] SOUTHERN: 1993, 2-4-0 locomotive numbered "2000."

EX-C7	LN-C8	Scarcity
15	20	2

[18712] JERSEY CENTRAL: 1993, 2-4-0 locomotive numbered "2000."

EX-C7	LN-C8	Scarcity
15	20	2

[18713] CHESSIE SYSTEM: 1994-95, 2-4-0 locomotive numbered "1993."

EX-C7	LN-C8	Scarcity
15	20	2

[18716] LIONELVILLE: 1990-91, Circus 4-4-0 American locomotive numbered "8716."

EX-C7	LN-C8	Scarcity
75	85	4

[18718] LIONEL LINES: 1997-98, 0-4-0 Dockside switcher numbered "8200."

EX-C7	LN-C8	Scarcity
15	20	2

[18719] THOMAS THE TANK: 1997, Engine 0-6-0 numbered "1."

EX-C7	LN-C8	Scarcity
100	125	4

[18720] UNION CAVALRY: 1999, 4-4-0 American locomotive numbered "1865."

EX-C7	LN-C8	Scarcity
100	125	4

[18721] CONFEDERATE STATES: 1999, 4-4-0 American locomotive numbered "1861."

EX-C7	LN-C8	Scarcity
100	125	4

[18722] PERCY THE TANK ENGINE: 1999, locomotive numbered "6."

EX-C7	LN-C8	Scarcity
100	125	4

[19820]: 1995-96, die-cast tender with RailSounds II.

EX-C7	LN-C8	Scarcity
100	125	4

[19833]: 1997, RailSounds II tender numbered "2426RS."

EX-C7	LN-C8	Scarcity
150	175	4

[28000] CHICAGO & ILLINOIS MIDLAND: 1999, 4-6-4 Hudson locomotive.

EX-C7	LN-C8	Scarcity
125	150	4

[28004] BALTIMORE AND OHIO: 1999-2000, E6 4-4-2 Atlantic locomotive, traditionally controlled.

EX-C7	LN-C8	Scarcity
275	325	4

[28005] PENNSYLVANIA: 1999-2000, E6 4-4-2 Atlantic locomotive, traditionally controlled.

EX-C7	LN-C8	Scarcity
250	300	4

[28006] SANTA FE: 1999-2000, E6 4-4-2 Atlantic locomotive, traditionally controlled.

EX-C7	LN-C8	Scarcity
200	225	4

[28007] NEW YORK CENTRAL: 1999, 4-6-4 Hudson locomotive numbered "5406."

EX-C7	LN-C8	Scarcity
300	325	4

[28008] CHESAPEAKE & OHIO: 1999, 4-6-4 Hudson locomotive numbered "306."

EX-C7	LN-C8	Scarcity
275	300	4

[28009] SANTA FE: 1999, 4-6-4 Hudson locomotive numbered "3463."

EX-C7	LN-C8	Scarcity
275	300	4

[28011] CHESAPEAKE & OHIO: 1999, 2-6-6-6 Allegheny locomotive numbered "1601."

EX-C7	LN-C8	Scarcity
1,600	1,800	4

[28012] NEW YORK CENTRAL: 2000, uncataloged Commodore Vanderbilt 4-6-4 Hudson locomotive, red.

EX-C7	LN-C8	Scarcity
1,600	1,800	6

[28013] NEW HAVEN: 1999, 4-6-2 Pacific locomotive numbered "1335."

EX-C7	LN-C8	Scarcity
200	250	4

[28014] NEW YORK CENTRAL: 1999, 4-6-2 Pacific locomotive numbered "4930."

EX-C7	LN-C8	Scarcity
200	250	4

[28015] SANTA FE: 1999, 4-6-2 Pacific locomotive numbered "3449."

EX-C7	LN-C8	Scarcity
200	250	4

[28016] SOUTHERN: 1999, 4-6-2 Pacific locomotive numbered "1408."

EX-C7	LN-C8	Scarcity
200	250	4

[28017] CASE CUTLERY: 1999, uncataloged 4-6-2 Pacific locomotive.

EX-C7	LN-C8	Scarcity
225	275	6

[28020] LIONEL LINES: 1999, 4-6-2 Pacific locomotive numbered "3344."

EX-C7	LN-C8	Scarcity
175	200	4

[28022] WEST SIDE LUMBER: 1999, Shay locomotive numbered "800."

EX-C7	LN-C8	Scarcity
900	1,050	4

[28023] PENNSYLVANIA: 1999, K4 Pacific 4-6-2 locomotive numbered "1361," command control-equipped.

EX-C7	LN-C8	Scarcity
250	275	4

[28024] NEW YORK CENTRAL: 2000, uncataloged Commodore Vanderbilt 4-6-4 Hudson locomotive, blue.

EX-C7	LN-C8	Scarcity
1,600	1,800	6

[28025] PENNSYLVANIA: 1999, K4 Pacific 4-6-2 locomotive, traditionally controlled.

EX-C7	LN-C8	Scarcity
250	275	4

[28026] LIONEL LINES: 1999, Pacific 4-6-2 locomotive numbered "1999," command control-equipped.

EX-C7	LN-C8	Scarcity
250	275	4

[28027] NEW YORK CENTRAL: 2000, 4-6-4 Hudson locomotive numbered "5413."

EX-C7	LN-C8	Scarcity
425	475	4

[28028] VIRGINIAN: 1999, 2-6-6-6 Allegheny locomotive numbered "1601."

EX-C7	LN-C8	Scarcity
1,100	1,200	5

[28029] UNION PACIFIC: 1999-2000, Big Boy 4-8-8-4 Articulated locomotive numbered "4006."

EX-C7	LN-C8	Scarcity
1,100	1,200	5

[28030] NEW YORK CENTRAL: 2000, 4-6-4 Hudson locomotive numbered "5450," gray, command control-equipped.

EX-C7	LN-C8	Scarcity
250	275	4

[28031] NEW YORK CENTRAL: 2000, 4-6-4 Hudson locomotive numbered "5451," gray.

EX-C7	LN-C8	Scarcity
Cataloged, but not produced.		

[28032] BALTIMORE AND OHIO: 2000, 4-6-2 Pacific locomotive, command control-equipped.

EX-C7	LN-C8	Scarcity
250	275	4

[28033] BALTIMORE AND OHIO: 2000, Pacific 4-6-2 locomotive, traditionally controlled.

EX-C7	LN-C8	Scarcity
150	175	4

[28034] UNION PACIFIC: 2000, 4-6-2 Pacific locomotive, command control-equipped.

EX-C7	LN-C8	Scarcity
250	275	4

[28035] UNION PACIFIC: 2000, 4-6-2 Pacific locomotive, traditionally controlled.

EX-C7	LN-C8	Scarcity
150	175	4

[28036] SOUTHERN PACIFIC: 2000-01, 2-8-0 Consolidation "2685" locomotive, command control-equipped.

EX-C7	LN-C8	Scarcity
325	350	4

[28037] SOUTHERN PACIFIC: 2000-01, 2-8-0 Consolidation "2686" locomotive, traditionally controlled.

EX-C7	LN-C8	Scarcity
200	225	4

[28038] UNION PACIFIC: 2000-01, 2-8-0 Consolidation "324" locomotive, command control-equipped.

EX-C7	LN-C8	Scarcity
325	350	4

[28039] UNION PACIFIC: 2000-01, 2-8-0 Consolidation "326" locomotive, traditionally controlled.

EX-C7	LN-C8	Scarcity
200	225	4

[28051] BALTIMORE AND OHIO: 2000, EM-1 2-8-8-4 Articulated locomotive numbered "7617."

EX-C7	LN-C8	Scarcity
800	900	4

[28052] NORFOLK AND WESTERN: 2000, Class A 2-6-6-4 Articulated locomotive numbered "1218."

EX-C7	LN-C8	Scarcity
900	975	4

[28055] GREAT NORTHERN: 2000-01, 4-6-4 Hudson "1725" locomotive, traditionally controlled.

EX-C7	LN-C8	Scarcity
125	150	4

[28057] SOUTHERN: 2000, 4-8-2 Mountain locomotive numbered "1491," command control-equipped.

EX-C7	LN-C8	Scarcity
700	750	4

[28058] NEW HAVEN: 2000, 4-8-2 Mountain locomotive numbered "3310," command control-equipped.

EX-C7	LN-C8	Scarcity
600	700	4

[28059] WESTERN PACIFIC: 2000, 4-8-2 Mountain locomotive numbered "179," command control-equipped.

EX-C7	LN-C8	Scarcity
700	750	4

[28062] LIONEL LINES: 2000, gold-plated 700E J-1E 4-6-4 Hudson locomotive numbered "1900" with case.

EX-C7	LN-C8	Scarcity
1,000	1,150	5

[28063] PENNSYLVANIA: 2000, T-1 4-4-4-4 Duplex locomotive numbered "5511," command control-equipped.

EX-C7	LN-C8	Scarcity
600	700	4

[28064] UNION PACIFIC: 2000, uncataloged 4-6-6-4 Challenger locomotive with coal tender numbered "3985," command control-equipped.

EX-C7	LN-C8	Scarcity
1,400	1,600	5

[28065] NEW YORK CENTRAL: 2000, 4-6-4 Hudson locomotive with RailSounds numbered "5412."

EX-C7	LN-C8	Scarcity
200	250	4

[28069] NEW YORK CENTRAL: 2000, uncataloged Lionel Century Club Niagara 4-8-4 steam locomotive numbered "6024."

EX-C7	LN-C8	Scarcity
800	900	5

[28089] PENNSYLVANIA: 2000, T-1 4-4-4-4 Duplex locomotive numbered "5511," two-rail.

EX-C7	LN-C8	Scarcity
900	1,000	6

[28090] UNION PACIFIC: 2000, uncataloged 4-6-6-4 Challenger locomotive with oil tender numbered "3977," two-rail.

EX-C7	LN-C8	Scarcity
1,400	1,600	6

[28099] UNION PACIFIC: 2000, uncataloged 4-6-6-4 Challenger locomotive with oil tender numbered "3977," command control-equipped.

EX-C7	LN-C8	Scarcity
1,400	1,600	5

[52060] VIRGINIA TRAIN COLLECTORS: 1994, uncataloged tender with whistle numbered "7694."

EX-C7	LN-C8	Scarcity
45	50	6

[52175] DEPT. 56: 1999, uncataloged 4-6-4 Hudson locomotive.

EX-C7	LN-C8	Scarcity
325	350	5

[52189] MONOPOLY: 1999, 4-6-4 Hudson locomotive numbered "1999."

EX-C7	LN-C8	Scarcity
375	400	6

[52219] MONOPOLY: 2000, uncataloged 4-6-4 Bronze Hudson locomotive numbered "2000."

EX-C7	LN-C8	Scarcity
475	525	6

[Unnumbered] LIONEL LINES: 1976-77, uncataloged LCCA tender only.

EX-C7	LN-C8	Scarcity
20	25	5

[Unnumbered] TCA SACRAMENTO-SIERRA LIONEL LINES: 1984, uncataloged tender, shell only.

EX-C7	LN-C8	Scarcity
Too rarely traded to establish accurate pricing.		

Chapter 3

DIESEL LOCOMOTIVES

Modern-era Lionel motive power has been dominated by replicas of diesel locomotives. There are several reasons, and advantages, to this. First, the diesel locomotive is what most of the train-buying public is familiar with on a day-to-day basis. Second, Lionel in most instances makes the diesel body from plastic and the frame from sheet metal. While tooling for injection-molded plastic is expensive, it is nowhere nearly as expensive as die-casting tooling—and molds for plastic have a longer life to boot. And lastly, whereas steam locomotives as a rule were custom made to each railroad's specification—limiting the number of railroad markings that can reasonably be applied to a locomotive of a given style, diesels tend to be more of an assembly line type of operation. This means a greater variety of railroad motifs can be applied to bodies produced from a given mold—lowering manufacturing costs.

The initial offerings under General Mills ownership consisted primarily of modest and mid-priced locomotives, particularly the Electro Motive Division (EMD) GP-7, GP-9 and NW-2 models, as well as the American Locomotive Co. (Alco) FA units. Rapidly, the celebrated EMD F-3 joined these offerings. Of these locomotives, only the F-3 had a die-cast chassis, the other locomotives utilizing a stamped steel chassis.

In 1974, Fundimensions issued a replica of their own design. Patterned after the General Electric (GE) U36B. These models utilized the same trucks as the GP-7, but had entirely new body and frame designs.

In 1979, the long awaited return of Lionel's dual-motored replica of the Fairbanks-Morse H24-66 "Trainmaster" occurred. Collectors quickly snapped up the initial offerings, Southern Pacific and Virginian, and they were rapidly followed by other road names.

In 1989, die-cast frames returned to some models of the NW-2 switchers for the first time since the early 1950s, and a similar improvement was made to selected models of the Alco FA four years later.

In the late-1970s, Lionel began experimenting with minor modifications to old favorites to create new looking locomotives. This included installation of six-wheel trucks rather than four-wheel, and using mold inserts to create low hood versions of the EMD road switchers. Perhaps inspired by the success of these efforts, throughout the 1990s, and beyond, Lionel has introduced a plethora of totally new locomotives. Many of these have been 1/48-scale proportioned, a nod toward increasing interest in what is called "high rail" operation. Additionally, increasingly sophisticated sound and control systems have been incorporated as well. Many of these features have also been carried over into Lionel's replica of the Union Pacific gas turbines, which are included in this chapter because they resemble diesel locomotives—although they're a unique breed.

634 SANTA FE: 1970, uncataloged NW-2 switcher.

EX-C7	LN-C8	Scarcity
30	60	7

[1203] BOSTON AND MAINE: 1972, uncataloged New England Division of Train Collectors Association NW-2 switcher, shell only.

EX-C7	LN-C8	Scarcity
20	45	6

1776 SEABOARD COAST LINE: 1974-76, GE U36B locomotive.

1776 SEABOARD COAST LINE (Type I): With white "SEABOARD COAST LINE" lettering stamped on edge of black frame.

EX-C7	LN-C8	Scarcity
50	80	4

1776 SEABOARD COAST LINE (Type II): Some locomotives were produced without the lettering on the frame. These were not factory errors, but rather deliberate production due to the difficulty in stamping lettering on the frame.

EX-C7	LN-C8	Scarcity
50	80	4

1976 TCA SEABOARD: 1976, uncataloged GE U36B locomotive.

EX-C7	LN-C8	Scarcity
100	150	7

[1976] FLORIDA EAST COAST: 1976, F-3 A-B-A TCA Southern Division, uncataloged locomotive bodies only.

EX-C7	LN-C8	Scarcity
125	200	6

[7500] LIONEL 75TH ANNIVERSARY: 1975-77, GE U36B locomotive.

EX-C7	LN-C8	Scarcity
60	110	4

[7686] VIRGINIA TRAIN COLLECTORS: 1986, uncataloged EMD GP-7 locomotive.

EX-C7	LN-C8	Scarcity
50	80	5

8010 SANTA FE: Cataloged in 1970, uncataloged in 1971, NW-2 switcher.

EX-C7	LN-C8	Scarcity
25	50	5

8020 SANTA FE: 1970-72 and 1974-76, Alco FA locomotive.

EX-C7	LN-C8	Scarcity
20	30	2

8020 SANTA FE: 1970, Alco FA dummy locomotive.

EX-C7	LN-C8	Scarcity
20	30	2

8021 SANTA FE: 1971-72 and 1974-76, Alco FB locomotive.

EX-C7	LN-C8	Scarcity
20	30	2

8022 SANTA FE: 1971, uncataloged Alco FA locomotive.

8022 SANTA FE (Type I): Some of the locomotives had the yellow Santa Fe nose herald applied via a decal.

EX-C7	LN-C8	Scarcity
30	60	4

8022 SANTA FE (Type II): Other locomotives lacked the yellow Santa Fe nose herald decal.

EX-C7	LN-C8	Scarcity
30	60	4

8025 CANADIAN NATIONAL: 1971-73, uncataloged Alco FA locomotive.

8025 CANADIAN NATIONAL (Type I): Powered unit.

EX-C7	LN-C8	Scarcity
30	60	4

8025 CANADIAN NATIONAL (Type II): Non-powered Alco FA dummy locomotive.

EX-C7	LN-C8	Scarcity
20	30	4

8030 ILLINOIS CENTRAL: 1970-72, EMD GP-9 locomotive.

8030 ILLINOIS CENTRAL (Type I): As first produced, the handrails along the long hood were made from wire supported by metal posts that were derived from the postwar 2411-4 log car stakes.

EX-C7	LN-C8	Scarcity
30	50	4

8030 ILLINOIS CENTRAL (Type II): In later production the wire handrail supports were delicately molded plastic parts.

EX-C7	LN-C8	Scarcity
30	50	4

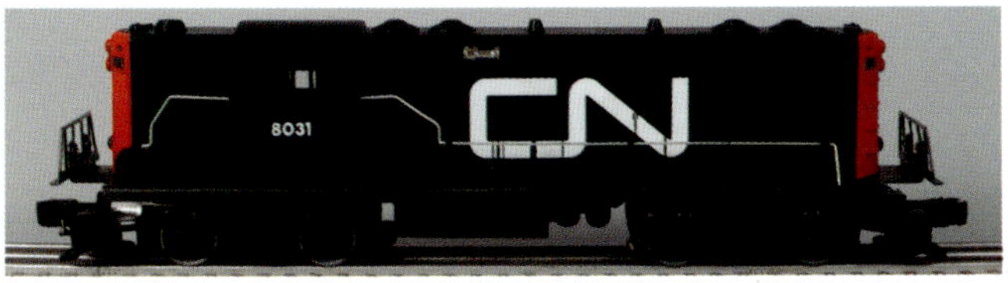

8031 CANADIAN NATIONAL: 1971-73, uncataloged EMD GP-7 locomotive.

8031 CANADIAN NATIONAL (Type I): As first produced, the handrails along the long hood were made from wire supported by metal posts that were derived from the postwar 2411-4 log car stakes.

EX-C7	LN-C8	Scarcity
40	70	5

8031 CANADIAN NATIONAL (Type II): In later production the wire handrail supports were delicately molded plastic parts.

EX-C7	LN-C8	Scarcity
40	70	5

8031 ILLINOIS CENTRAL: 1970, EMD GP-9 dummy locomotive.

EX-C7	LN-C8	Scarcity
Cataloged, but not produced.		

8050 DELAWARE & HUDSON: 1980, GE U36C locomotive.

EX-C7	LN-C8	Scarcity
50	100	4

8051 DELAWARE & HUDSON: 1980, GE U36C dummy locomotive.

EX-C7	LN-C8	Scarcity
40	60	4

8054/8055 BURLINGTON: 1980, F-3 A-A locomotive set.

EX-C7	LN-C8	Scarcity
150	400	5

8056 CHICAGO & NORTHWESTERN: 1980, Fairbanks-Morse Trainmaster locomotive.

EX-C7	LN-C8	Scarcity
100	150	4

8057 BURLINGTON: 1980, NW-2 switcher.

EX-C7	LN-C8	Scarcity
40	60	4

8059 PENNSYLVANIA: 1980, uncataloged F-3 B locomotive.

EX-C7	LN-C8	Scarcity
90	125	5

8060 PENNSYLVANIA: 1980, uncataloged F-3 B locomotive.

EX-C7	LN-C8	Scarcity
120	200	6

8061 CHESSIE SYSTEM: 1980, GE U36C locomotive.

EX-C7	LN-C8	Scarcity
50	70	4

8062 BURLINGTON: 1980, uncataloged F-3 B locomotive.

EX-C7	LN-C8	Scarcity
70	200	5

8063 SEABOARD: 1980, EMD SD-9 locomotive.

EX-C7	LN-C8	Scarcity
50	65	4

8064 FLORIDA EAST COAST: 1980, EMD GP-9 locomotive.

EX-C7	LN-C8	Scarcity
60	80	5

8065 FLORIDA EAST COAST: 1980, EMD GP-9 dummy locomotive.

EX-C7	LN-C8	Scarcity
50	70	5

8066 TP & W: Cataloged from 1980-81, uncataloged in 1983, EMD GP-20 locomotive.

EX-C7	LN-C8	Scarcity
40	60	4

8067 TEXAS AND PACIFIC: 1980, Alco FA locomotive.

EX-C7	LN-C8	Scarcity
Cataloged, but not produced.		

[8068] ROCK ISLAND: 1980, uncataloged LCCA EMD GP-20 locomotive numbered "1980."

EX-C7	LN-C8	Scarcity
50	75	6

8071 VIRGINIAN: 1980, uncataloged EMD SD-18 locomotive.

EX-C7	LN-C8	Scarcity
60	75	4

8072 VIRGINIAN: 1980, uncataloged EMD SD-18 dummy locomotive.

EX-C7	LN-C8	Scarcity
50	60	4

8111 DT & I: 1971-74, NW-2 switcher.

8111 DT & I (Type I): Furnished with two green marker lights on the front.

EX-C7	LN-C8	Scarcity
30	40	3

8111 DT & I (Type II): Furnished with two red marker lights on the front.

EX-C7	LN-C8	Scarcity
30	40	3

8151 BURLINGTON: 1981, EMD SD-28 locomotive.

EX-C7	LN-C8	Scarcity
50	75	4

8152 CANADIAN PACIFIC: 1987, EMD SD-24 locomotive.

EX-C7	LN-C8	Scarcity
50	80	4

8153 READING: 1981-82, NW-2 switcher.

EX-C7	LN-C8	Scarcity
40	50	4

8154 ALASKA RAILROAD: 1981-82, NW-2 switcher.

EX-C7	LN-C8	Scarcity
40	50	4

8155 MONON: 1981-82, GE U36B locomotive.

EX-C7	LN-C8	Scarcity
50	70	4

8156 MONON: 1981-82, GE U36B dummy locomotive.

EX-C7	LN-C8	Scarcity
40	60	4

8157 SANTA FE: 1981, Fairbanks-Morse Trainmaster locomotive.

EX-C7	LN-C8	Scarcity
100	150	5

8158 DM & IR: 1981-82, EMD GP-35 locomotive.

EX-C7	LN-C8	Scarcity
40	55	4

8159 DM & IR: 1981-82, EMD GP-35 dummy locomotive.

EX-C7	LN-C8	Scarcity
30	45	4

8160 BURGER KING: 1981-82, EMD GP-20 locomotive.

EX-C7	LN-C8	Scarcity
30	45	4

8161 L.A.S.E.R.: 1981-82, switcher.

EX-C7	LN-C8	Scarcity
15	20	3

8162 ONTARIO NORTHLAND: 1981, uncataloged EMD SD-18 locomotive.

EX-C7	LN-C8	Scarcity
40	60	5

8163 ONTARIO NORTHLAND: 1981, uncataloged EMD SD-18 dummy locomotive.

EX-C7	LN-C8	Scarcity
30	45	5

8164 PENNSYLVANIA: 1981, uncataloged F-3 B locomotive.

EX-C7	LN-C8	Scarcity
125	175	6

8182 NIBCO EXPRESS: 1982, uncataloged NW-2 switcher.

EX-C7	LN-C8	Scarcity
50	90	6

[8190] DIESEL HORN: 1981, uncataloged kit.

EX-C7	LN-C8	Scarcity
5	20	4

8250 SANTA FE: 1972, 1974-75, EMD GP-9 locomotive.

EX-C7	LN-C8	Scarcity
30	45	4

8252 DELAWARE AND HUDSON: 1972, Alco FA locomotive.

EX-C7	LN-C8	Scarcity
35	55	4

8253 DELAWARE AND HUDSON: 1972, Alco FB unit.

EX-C7	LN-C8	Scarcity
30	45	4

8254 ILLINOIS CENTRAL: 1972, EMD GP-9 dummy locomotive.

EX-C7	LN-C8	Scarcity
25	35	4

8255 SANTA FE: 1972, EMD GP-9 dummy locomotive.

EX-C7	LN-C8	Scarcity
25	35	4

8258 CANADIAN NATIONAL: 1972-73, uncataloged EMD GP-7 dummy locomotive.

EX-C7	LN-C8	Scarcity
25	35	4

8260/8262 SOUTHERN PACIFIC: 1982, F-3 A-A locomotive set.

EX-C7	LN-C8	Scarcity
150	200	5

8261 SOUTHERN PACIFIC: 1982, uncataloged F-3 B-unit.

EX-C7	LN-C8	Scarcity
200	250	5

8263 SANTA FE: 1982, EMD GP-7 locomotive.

EX-C7	LN-C8	Scarcity
30	50	4

8265 SANTA FE: 1982, SD-40 locomotive.

EX-C7	LN-C8	Scarcity
100	130	5

8266 NORFOLK AND WESTERN: 1982, SD-24 locomotive.

EX-C7	LN-C8	Scarcity
60	80	4

8268 TEXAS AND PACIFIC: 1982-83, Alco FA locomotive.

8268 TEXAS AND PACIFIC (Type I): Locomotive without ballast weight, or with Service Station-installed weights.

EX-C7	LN-C8	Scarcity
30	40	3

8268 TEXAS AND PACIFIC (Type II): Locomotive with factory installed weights.

EX-C7	LN-C8	Scarcity
30	40	3

8269 TEXAS AND PACIFIC: 1982-83, Alco FA locomotive dummy.

EX-C7	LN-C8	Scarcity
25	35	3

8350 U.S. STEEL: 1973-75, switcher.

EX-C7	LN-C8	Scarcity
10	15	2

8351 SANTA FE: 1973-75, Alco FA locomotive.

EX-C7	LN-C8	Scarcity
15	20	2

8352 SANTA FE: 1973-75, EMD GP-20 locomotive.

EX-C7	LN-C8	Scarcity
15	30	4

8353 GRAND TRUNK WESTERN: 1973-75, EMD GP-7 locomotive.

EX-C7	LN-C8	Scarcity
40	55	4

8354 ERIE: 1973 and 1975, NW-2 switcher.

EX-C7	LN-C8	Scarcity
40	55	4

8355 SANTA FE: 1973-74, EMD GP-20 dummy locomotive.

EX-C7	LN-C8	Scarcity
40	55	4

8356 GRAND TRUNK WESTERN: 1973-75, EMD GP-7 dummy locomotive.

EX-C7	LN-C8	Scarcity
35	45	4

8357 PENNSYLVANIA: 1973-75, EMD GP-9 locomotive.

EX-C7	LN-C8	Scarcity
45	60	5

8358 PENNSYLVANIA: 1973-75, EMD GP-9 dummy locomotive.

EX-C7	LN-C8	Scarcity
40	50	5

[8359] CHESSIE SYSTEM: 1973, EMD GP-7 "GM50" locomotive.

EX-C7	LN-C8	Scarcity
40	50	5

8360 LONG ISLAND: 1973-74, EMD GP-20 locomotive.

EX-C7	LN-C8	Scarcity
35	45	4

8361 WESTERN PACIFIC: 1973-75, Alco FA locomotive.

EX-C7	LN-C8	Scarcity
35	45	4

8362 WESTERN PACIFIC: 1973-75, Alco FB locomotive.

EX-C7	LN-C8	Scarcity
35	45	4

8363 BALTIMORE AND OHIO: 1973-75, F-3 locomotive A-unit.

EX-C7	LN-C8	Scarcity
100	150	5

8364 BALTIMORE AND OHIO: 1973-75, F-3 locomotive dummy A-unit.

EX-C7	LN-C8	Scarcity
60	75	5

8365/8366 CANADIAN PACIFIC: 1973, F-3 locomotive A-A set Service Station Special item.

EX-C7	LN-C8	Scarcity
175	225	5

8367 LONG ISLAND: 1973-75, EMD GP-20 dummy locomotive.

EX-C7	LN-C8	Scarcity
40	50	4

8369 ERIE-LACKAWANNA: 1983-85, EMD GP-20 locomotive.

EX-C7	LN-C8	Scarcity
60	75	4

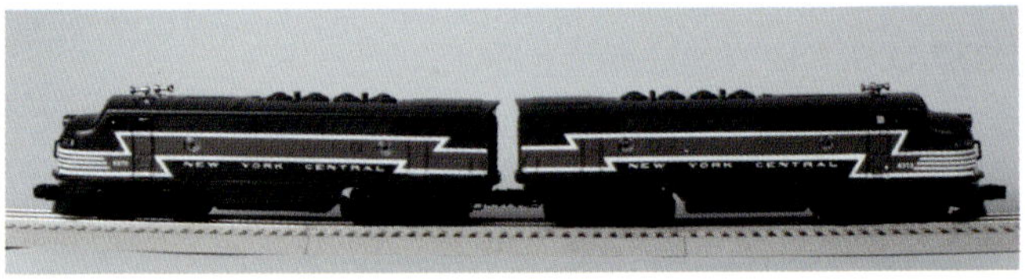

8370/8372 NEW YORK CENTRAL: 1983, F-3 locomotive A-A set.

EX-C7	LN-C8	Scarcity
150	200	5

8371 NEW YORK CENTRAL: 1983, F-3 locomotive B-unit.

EX-C7	LN-C8	Scarcity
50	75	5

8374 BURLINGTON NORTHERN: 1983-85, NW-2 switcher.

EX-C7	LN-C8	Scarcity
40	60	4

8375 CHICAGO & NORTHWESTERN: 1983-85, EMD GP-7 locomotive.

EX-C7	LN-C8	Scarcity
55	80	4

8376 UNION PACIFIC: 1983, SD-40 locomotive.

EX-C7	LN-C8	Scarcity
70	110	4

8377 U.S. DIESEL: 1983-84, switcher.

EX-C7	LN-C8	Scarcity
55	65	3

[8378] WABASH: 1983, uncataloged Fairbanks-Morse Trainmaster locomotive numbered "550."

EX-C7	LN-C8	Scarcity
375	475	6

8380 LIONEL LINES: 1983, uncataloged SD-28 locomotive.

EX-C7	LN-C8	Scarcity
50	70	4

8452 ERIE: 1974-75, Alco A locomotive.

EX-C7	LN-C8	Scarcity
25	35	4

8453 ERIE: 1974-75, Alco B locomotive.

EX-C7	LN-C8	Scarcity
25	35	4

8454 DENVER & RIO GRANDE WESTERN: 1974-75, EMD GP-7 locomotive.

EX-C7	LN-C8	Scarcity
30	40	4

8455 DENVER & RIO GRANDE WESTERN: 1974-75, EMD GP-7 dummy locomotive.

EX-C7	LN-C8	Scarcity
25	35	4

8458 ERIE-LACKAWANNA: 1984, SD-40 locomotive.

EX-C7	LN-C8	Scarcity
100	150	4

8460 MISSOURI-KANSAS-TEXAS: 1974-75, NW-2 switcher.

EX-C7	LN-C8	Scarcity
25	35	4

8463 CHESSIE SYSTEM: 1974, uncataloged EMD GP-20 locomotive.

EX-C7	LN-C8	Scarcity
45	60	5

8464/8465 DENVER & RIO GRANDE WESTERN

8464/8465 DENVER & RIO GRANDE WESTERN: 1974, F-3 locomotive A-A set Service Station Special item.

EX-C7	LN-C8	Scarcity
80	110	5

8466 AMTRAK: 1974-76, F-3 locomotive A-unit.

EX-C7	LN-C8	Scarcity
70	85	4

8467 AMTRAK: 1974-76, F-3 A locomotive unit dummy.

EX-C7	LN-C8	Scarcity
40	60	4

8468 BALTIMORE AND OHIO: 1974-75, F-3 locomotive B-unit.

EX-C7	LN-C8	Scarcity
45	65	5

8469 CANADIAN PACIFIC: 1974, F-3 locomotive B-unit Service Station Special item.

EX-C7	LN-C8	Scarcity
50	70	6

8470 CHESSIE SYSTEM: 1974, GE U36B locomotive.

EX-C7	LN-C8	Scarcity
35	45	4

8471 PENNSYLVANIA: 1974-76, NW-2 switcher.

EX-C7	LN-C8	Scarcity
50	75	5

8473 COCA-COLA: Uncataloged in 1974, cataloged in 1975, EMD NW-2 switcher.

8473 COCA-COLA (Type I): Locomotive with three steps on frame.

EX-C7	LN-C8	Scarcity
30	45	4

8473 COCA-COLA (Type II): Locomotive with two steps on frame.

EX-C7	LN-C8	Scarcity
30	45	4

8473 COCA-COLA (Type III): Locomotive with one step on frame.

EX-C7	LN-C8	Scarcity
30	45	4

8474 DENVER & RIO GRANDE WESTERN: 1974, F-3 locomotive B-unit Service Station Special item.

EX-C7	LN-C8	Scarcity
50	65	6

8467/8466 AMTRAK

8475 AMTRAK: 1974, F-3 locomotive B-unit.

EX-C7	LN-C8	Scarcity
40	55	5

8477 NEW YORK CENTRAL: 1984, uncataloged EMD GP-9 locomotive.

EX-C7	LN-C8	Scarcity
70	90	5

8480/8482 UNION PACIFIC: 1984, F-3 locomotive A-A set.

EX-C7	LN-C8	Scarcity
100	140	5

8481 UNION PACIFIC: 1984, F-3 locomotive B-unit.

EX-C7	LN-C8	Scarcity
100	140	5

8485 U.S. MARINES: 1984-85, NW-2 switcher.

EX-C7	LN-C8	Scarcity
40	55	4

[8507]/[8508] CANADIAN NATIONAL: 1985, Lionel Collectors Association of Canada, uncataloged F-3 locomotive A-A set, shells only.

EX-C7	LN-C8	Scarcity
200	250	6

8550 JERSEY CENTRAL: 1975-76, EMD GP-9 locomotive.

EX-C7	LN-C8	Scarcity
40	70	4

8552/8553/8554 SOUTHERN PACIFIC: 1975-76, Alco locomotive A-B-A set.

EX-C7	LN-C8	Scarcity
100	125	5

8555/8557 MILWAUKEE ROAD: 1975, F-3 locomotive A-A set Service Station Special item.

EX-C7	LN-C8	Scarcity
125	150	5

8556 CHESSIE SYSTEM: 1975-76, NW-2 switcher.

EX-C7	LN-C8	Scarcity
60	85	4

[8559] NORFOLK AND WESTERN: 1975, EMD GP-9 locomotive numbered "1776."

EX-C7	LN-C8	Scarcity
40	65	4

8560 CHESSIE SYSTEM: 1975, GE U36B locomotive dummy.

8560 CHESSIE SYSTEM (Type I): Non-illuminated.

EX-C7	LN-C8	Scarcity
30	50	4

8560 CHESSIE SYSTEM (Type II): Illuminated.

EX-C7	LN-C8	Scarcity
30	50	4

8561 JERSEY CENTRAL: 1975-76, EMD GP-9 locomotive dummy.

EX-C7	LN-C8	Scarcity
30	50	4

8562 MISSOURI PACIFIC: 1975-76, EMD GP-20 locomotive.

EX-C7	LN-C8	Scarcity
40	70	5

8563 ROCK ISLAND: 1975-76, uncataloged Alco FA locomotive.

EX-C7	LN-C8	Scarcity
25	35	4

8564 UNION PACIFIC: 1975, GE U36B locomotive.

EX-C7	LN-C8	Scarcity
35	50	4

8480/8482 UNION PACIFIC

8565 MISSOURI PACIFIC: 1975-76, EMD GP-20 dummy locomotive.

EX-C7	LN-C8	Scarcity
35	45	4

8566 SOUTHERN: 1975-77, F-3 locomotive A-unit.

EX-C7	LN-C8	Scarcity
125	175	4

8567 SOUTHERN: 1975-77, F-3 A locomotive unit dummy.

EX-C7	LN-C8	Scarcity
55	75	4

8568 PREAMBLE EXPRESS: 1975, uncataloged F-3 locomotive A-unit.

EX-C7	LN-C8	Scarcity
40	60	4

8569 SOO LINE: 1975-77, NW-2 switcher.

EX-C7	LN-C8	Scarcity
30	40	4

8570 LIBERTY SPECIAL: 1975, uncataloged Alco FA locomotive.

EX-C7	LN-C8	Scarcity
40	60	5

8571 FRISCO: 1975-76, GE U36B locomotive.

EX-C7	LN-C8	Scarcity
40	55	4

8572 FRISCO: 1975-76, GE U36B dummy locomotive.

EX-C7	LN-C8	Scarcity
30	40	4

8555/8557 MILWAUKEE ROAD

DIESEL LOCOMOTIVES

8573 UNION PACIFIC: 1975, uncataloged GE U36B dummy locomotive.

EX-C7	LN-C8	Scarcity
75	100	4

8575 MILWAUKEE ROAD: 1975, F-3 locomotive B-unit Service Station Special item.

EX-C7	LN-C8	Scarcity
50	75	6

8576 PENN CENTRAL: Uncataloged in 1975, cataloged in 1976-77, EMD GP-7.

EX-C7	LN-C8	Scarcity
45	60	5

8580/8582 ILLINOIS CENTRAL: 1985 and 1987, F-3 locomotive A-A set.

EX-C7	LN-C8	Scarcity
200	250	4

8581 ILLINOIS CENTRAL: 1985 and 1987, F-3 locomotive B-unit.

EX-C7	LN-C8	Scarcity
70	100	4

8585 BURLINGTON NORTHERN: 1985, SD-40 locomotive.

EX-C7	LN-C8	Scarcity
175	225	4

[8587]WABASH: 1985, uncataloged EMD GP-9 locomotive numbered "484."

EX-C7	LN-C8	Scarcity
150	200	5

8650 BURLINGTON NORTHERN: 1976-77, GE U36B locomotive.

EX-C7	LN-C8	Scarcity
55	75	4

8651 BURLINGTON NORTHERN: 1976-77, GE U36B dummy locomotive.

EX-C7	LN-C8	Scarcity
35	55	4

8652 SANTA FE: 1976-77, F-3 locomotive A-unit.

EX-C7	LN-C8	Scarcity
175	225	4

8653 SANTA FE: 1976-77, F-3 locomotive A-unit dummy.

EX-C7	LN-C8	Scarcity
65	90	4

8654 BOSTON AND MAINE: 1976-77, EMD GP-9 locomotive.

EX-C7	LN-C8	Scarcity
60	80	4

8655 BOSTON AND MAINE: 1976-77, dummy EMD GP-9 locomotive.

EX-C7	LN-C8	Scarcity
45	55	4

8656 CANADIAN NATIONAL: 1976, Alco FA locomotive.

EX-C7	LN-C8	Scarcity
75	100	5

8657 CANADIAN NATIONAL: 1976, Alco FB locomotive.

EX-C7	LN-C8	Scarcity
30	40	5

8658 CANADIAN NATIONAL: 1976, dummy Alco FA locomotive.

EX-C7	LN-C8	Scarcity
40	85	5

8660 CP RAIL: 1976-77, NW-2 switcher.

EX-C7	LN-C8	Scarcity
50	70	4

8661 SOUTHERN: 1976, F-3 locomotive B-unit.

EX-C7	LN-C8	Scarcity
60	75	5

8662 BALTIMORE AND OHIO: 1986, EMD GP-7 locomotive.

EX-C7	LN-C8	Scarcity
45	79	4

8664 AMTRAK: 1976-77, Alco FA locomotive.

EX-C7	LN-C8	Scarcity
30	40	4

8665 BANGOR AND AROOSTOOK: 1976, uncataloged EMD GP-9 locomotive numbered "1776" and named "Jeremiah O'Brien."

EX-C7	LN-C8	Scarcity
40	60	4

8652 SANTA FE

8666 NORTHERN PACIFIC: 1976, Service Station Special item, EMD GP-9 locomotive.

EX-C7	LN-C8	Scarcity
60	90	6

8667 AMTRAK: 1976-77, Alco FB locomotive.

EX-C7	LN-C8	Scarcity
30	40	4

8668 NORTHERN PACIFIC: 1976, Service Station Special item, EMD dummy GP-9 locomotive.

EX-C7	LN-C8	Scarcity
55	80	6

8669 ILLINOIS CENTRAL GULF: 1976-77, GE U36B locomotive.

EX-C7	LN-C8	Scarcity
50	60	5

8670 CHESSIE SYSTEM: 1976, switcher.

EX-C7	LN-C8	Scarcity
15	20	2

8679 NORTHERN PACIFIC: 1986, EMD GP-20 locomotive.

EX-C7	LN-C8	Scarcity
55	65	4

8687 JERSEY CENTRAL: 1986, Fairbanks-Morse Trainmaster locomotive.

EX-C7	LN-C8	Scarcity
175	225	4

8750 ROCK ISLAND: 1977-78, EMD GP-7 locomotive.

EX-C7	LN-C8	Scarcity
40	60	4

8751 ROCK ISLAND: 1977-78, dummy EMD GP-7 locomotive.

EX-C7	LN-C8	Scarcity
30	40	4

8755 SANTA FE: 1977-78, GE U36B locomotive.

EX-C7	LN-C8	Scarcity
35	50	4

8756 SANTA FE: 1977-78, GE U36B dummy locomotive.

EX-C7	LN-C8	Scarcity
25	35	4

8757 CONRAIL: Uncataloged in 1976, cataloged from 1977-78, EMD GP-9 locomotive.

8757 CONRAIL (Type I): White frame and rails.

EX-C7	LN-C8	Scarcity
35	50	4

8757 CONRAIL (Type II): Black frame and rails.

EX-C7	LN-C8	Scarcity
35	50	4

8758 SOUTHERN: Uncataloged in 1977, cataloged in 1978, EMD dummy GP-7 locomotive.

EX-C7	LN-C8	Scarcity
30	40	4

8759 ERIE-LACKAWANNA: 1977-79, EMD GP-9 locomotive.

EX-C7	LN-C8	Scarcity
50	65	4

8760 ERIE-LACKAWANNA: 1977-79, dummy EMD GP-9 locomotive.

EX-C7	LN-C8	Scarcity
40	55	4

8761 GRAND TRUNK WESTERN: 1977-78, NW-2 switcher.

EX-C7	LN-C8	Scarcity
35	55	4

8763 NORFOLK AND WESTERN: Uncataloged in 1976, cataloged from 1977-78, EMD GP-9 locomotive.

EX-C7	LN-C8	Scarcity
40	55	4

8769 REPUBLIC STEEL: 1977-78, switcher.

EX-C7	LN-C8	Scarcity
10	15	2

8770 EMD: 1977-78, NW-2 switcher.

EX-C7	LN-C8	Scarcity
35	45	3

8771 GREAT NORTHERN: 1977, GE U36B locomotive.

EX-C7	LN-C8	Scarcity
50	65	4

8772 GULF, MOBILE AND OHIO: 1977, EMD GP-20 locomotive.

EX-C7	LN-C8	Scarcity
50	65	4

8773 MICKEY MOUSE: 1977-78, GE U36B locomotive.

EX-C7	LN-C8	Scarcity
300	400	5

8774 SOUTHERN: Uncataloged in 1977, cataloged in 1978, EMD GP-7 locomotive.

EX-C7	LN-C8	Scarcity
50	65	4

8775 LEHIGH VALLEY: Uncataloged in 1977, cataloged in 1978, EMD GP-9 locomotive.

EX-C7	LN-C8	Scarcity
50	65	4

8776 CHICAGO & NORTHWESTERN: Uncataloged in 1977, cataloged in 1978, EMD GP-20 locomotive.

EX-C7	LN-C8	Scarcity
50	65	4

8777 SANTA FE: 1977, F-3 locomotive B-unit Service Station Special item.

EX-C7	LN-C8	Scarcity
65	75	5

8778 LEHIGH VALLEY: Uncataloged in 1977, cataloged in 1978, EMD GP-9 dummy locomotive.

EX-C7	LN-C8	Scarcity
50	65	4

8779 CHICAGO & NORTHWESTERN: Uncataloged in 1977, cataloged in 1978, EMD GP-20 dummy locomotive.

EX-C7	LN-C8	Scarcity
55	70	4

8851/8852 NEW HAVEN: Uncataloged in 1978, cataloged in 1979, F-3 locomotive A-A set.

EX-C7	LN-C8	Scarcity
150	200	4

8854 CP RAIL: 1978-79, EMD GP-9 locomotive.

EX-C7	LN-C8	Scarcity
50	60	4

8855 MILWAUKEE ROAD: 1978, SD-18 locomotive.

EX-C7	LN-C8	Scarcity
50	60	4

8857 NORTHERN PACIFIC: 1978-80, GE U36B locomotive.

EX-C7	LN-C8	Scarcity
55	70	4

8858 NORTHERN PACIFIC: 1978-80, GE U36B dummy locomotive.

EX-C7	LN-C8	Scarcity
35	45	4

8860 ROCK ISLAND: 1978-79, NW-2 switcher.

EX-C7	LN-C8	Scarcity
30	40	4

8861 SANTA FE: 1978-79 Alco FA locomotive.

EX-C7	LN-C8	Scarcity
25	35	3

8862 SANTA FE: 1978-79, Alco FB locomotive.

EX-C7	LN-C8	Scarcity
20	25	3

8864 NEW HAVEN: 1978, F-3 B locomotive.

EX-C7	LN-C8	Scarcity
45	65	5

8866 MINNEAPOLIS & ST. LOUIS: 1978, Service Station Special item, EMD GP-9 locomotive.

EX-C7	LN-C8	Scarcity
50	65	5

8867 MINNEAPOLIS & ST. LOUIS: 1978, EMD dummy GP-9 locomotive Service Station Special item.

EX-C7	LN-C8	Scarcity
45	60	5

8872 SANTA FE: Uncataloged in 1978, cataloged in 1979, SD-18 locomotive.

EX-C7	LN-C8	Scarcity
50	60	4

8873 SANTA FE: Uncataloged in 1978, cataloged in 1979, dummy SD-18 locomotive.

EX-C7	LN-C8	Scarcity
40	50	4

8950 VIRGINIAN: 1979, Fairbanks-Morse Trainmaster locomotive.

EX-C7	LN-C8	Scarcity
160	200	4

8951 SOUTHERN PACIFIC: 1979, Fairbanks-Morse Trainmaster locomotive.

EX-C7	LN-C8	Scarcity
200	240	5

8952/8953 PENNSYLVANIA: 1979, F-3 A-A locomotive set.

EX-C7	LN-C8	Scarcity
250	300	5

8955 SOUTHERN: 1979, GE U36B locomotive.

EX-C7	LN-C8	Scarcity
50	75	4

8956 SOUTHERN: 1979, GE U36B dummy locomotive.

EX-C7	LN-C8	Scarcity
40	60	4

8957 BURLINGTON NORTHERN (Type I): 1979, EMD GP-20 locomotive.

EX-C7	LN-C8	Scarcity
40	50	4

8957 BURLINGTON NORTHERN (Type II): 1980, uncataloged Detroit-Toledo TCA EMD GP-20 locomotive.

EX-C7	LN-C8	Scarcity
100	150	6

8958 BURLINGTON NORTHERN (Type I): 1979, EMD GP-20 dummy locomotive.

EX-C7	LN-C8	Scarcity
35	45	4

8958 BURLINGTON NORTHERN (Type II): 1980, uncataloged Detroit-Toledo TCA, EMD GP-20 dummy locomotive.

EX-C7	LN-C8	Scarcity
80	125	5

8960 SOUTHERN PACIFIC: 1979, uncataloged GE U36C locomotive.

EX-C7	LN-C8	Scarcity
50	65	5

8961 SOUTHERN PACIFIC: 1979, uncataloged GE U36C dummy locomotive.

EX-C7	LN-C8	Scarcity
40	50	5

8962 READING: 1979, GE U36B locomotive.

EX-C7	LN-C8	Scarcity
35	45	4

8970/8971 PENNSYLVANIA: Uncataloged in 1979, cataloged in 1980, Tuscan EMD F-3 locomotive A-A set.

EX-C7	LN-C8	Scarcity
200	250	5

[11711] SANTA FE: 1991, F-3 locomotive A-B-A set numbered "8100," "8101" and "8102."

EX-C7	LN-C8	Scarcity
250	300	4

[11713] SANTA FE: 1990, Dash 8-40B locomotive set.

EX-C7	LN-C8	Scarcity
175	200	4

[11724] GREAT NORTHERN: 1992, F-3 locomotive A-B-A set numbered "366A," "370B" and "351C."

EX-C7	LN-C8	Scarcity
400	525	5

[11734] ERIE: 1993, Alco FA-FB-FA locomotive set numbered "725A," "725B" and "736a," part of Fallen Flags number seven.

EX-C7	LN-C8	Scarcity
175	225	4

[11737] TCA: 1993, uncataloged F-3 A-B-A locomotive set numbered "40."

EX-C7	LN-C8	Scarcity
350	400	6

[11843] BOSTON AND MAINE: 1998, EMD GP-9 A-B-A locomotive set.

EX-C7	LN-C8	Scarcity
350	400	5

[11863] SOUTHERN PACIFIC: 1998, EMD GP-9 locomotive numbered "2383."

EX-C7	LN-C8	Scarcity
150	175	4

[11864] NEW YORK CENTRAL: 1998, EMD GP-9 locomotive numbered "2383."

EX-C7	LN-C8	Scarcity
150	175	4

[11865] ALASKA RAILROAD: 1998-99, EMD GP-7 locomotive numbered "1802."

EX-C7	LN-C8	Scarcity
80	100	4

[11903] ATLANTIC COAST LINE: 1996, F-3 A-B-A locomotive set numbered "342," "342B" and "343."

EX-C7	LN-C8	Scarcity
450	525	5

[11956] UNION PACIFIC: 1997, EMD GP-9 numbered "2380" and "2381," powered and dummy locomotive set.

EX-C7	LN-C8	Scarcity
200	250	4

[14532] PENNSYLVANIA: 2000, uncataloged Lionel Century Club Sharknose A-A locomotive numbered "9744," command control-equipped.

EX-C7	LN-C8	Scarcity
400	500	6

[18100] SANTA FE: F-3 locomotive A-unit numbered "8100" (see 11711).

[18101] SANTA FE: F-3 locomotive B-unit numbered "8101" (see 11711).

[18102] SANTA FE: F-3 dummy locomotive A-unit numbered "8102" (see 11711).

[18103] SANTA FE: 1991, F-3 dummy locomotive B-unit numbered "8103," uncataloged.

EX-C7	LN-C8	Scarcity
175	200	4

[18104] GREAT NORTHERN: F-3 A locomotive dummy unit numbered "366a" (see 11724).

[18105] GREAT NORTHERN: F-3 B locomotive dummy unit numbered "370b" (see 11724).

[18106] GREAT NORTHERN: F-3 A locomotive dummy unit numbered "351c" (see 11724).

[18107] DENVER & RIO GRANDE WESTERN: 1992, Alco PA-1 PA-PB-PA locomotive set numbered "6001" and "6002."

EX-C7	LN-C8	Scarcity
600	700	5

[18108] GREAT NORTHERN: 1993, F-3 locomotive B-unit numbered "371B."

EX-C7	LN-C8	Scarcity
75	100	4

[18109] ERIE: Alco FA locomotive numbered "725a" (see 11734).

[18110] ERIE: Alco FB locomotive numbered "725b" (see 11734).

[18111] ERIE: Alco FA locomotive dummy numbered "736a" (see 11734).

[18112] TCA: F-3 locomotive A-unit numbered "40" (see 11737).

[18113] TCA: F-3 locomotive B-unit (see 11737).

[18114] TCA: F-3 locomotive A-unit dummy numbered "40" (see 11737).

[18115] SANTA FE: 1993, F-3 locomotive B-unit.

EX-C7	LN-C8	Scarcity
75	100	4

[18116] ERIE-LACKAWANNA: 1993, Alco PA-1 PA-PA locomotive set numbered "858" and "859."

EX-C7	LN-C8	Scarcity
400	450	4

[18117]/[18118] SANTA FE: 1993, F-3 A-A locomotive set numbered "200."

EX-C7	LN-C8	Scarcity
250	300	4

[18119]/[18120] UNION PACIFIC: 1994, Alco A-A locomotive set numbered "8119" and "8120."

EX-C7	LN-C8	Scarcity
175	225	4

[18121] SANTA FE: 1994, F-3 locomotive B-unit numbered "200A."

EX-C7	LN-C8	Scarcity
60	75	4

[18122] SANTA FE: 1995, F-3 locomotive B-unit numbered "200B."

EX-C7	LN-C8	Scarcity
150	175	4

[18123] ATLANTIC COAST LINE: F-3 locomotive A-unit numbered "342" (see 11903).

[18124] ATLANTIC COAST LINE: F-3 locomotive B-unit numbered "342b" (see 11903).

[18125] ATLANTIC COAST LINE: F-3 locomotive A-unit dummy numbered "343" (see 11903).

[18128] SANTA FE: 1996, F-3 locomotive A-unit numbered "2343."

EX-C7	LN-C8	Scarcity
300	350	4

[18129] SANTA FE: 1996, F-3 locomotive B-unit with RS II.

EX-C7	LN-C8	Scarcity
225	250	4

[18130] SANTA FE: 1996, F-3 locomotive A-B set.

EX-C7	LN-C8	Scarcity
400	600	4

[18131] NORTHERN PACIFIC: 1997, F-3 locomotive A-B set numbered "2390A" and "2390C."

EX-C7	LN-C8	Scarcity
300	350	4

[18132] SANTA FE: F-3 locomotive A-unit powered (see 18130).

[18133] SANTA FE: F-3 locomotive dummy A-unit (see 18130).

[18134] SANTA FE: 1997, F-3 locomotive A-unit dummy numbered "2343."

EX-C7	LN-C8	Scarcity
150	175	4

[18135] NEW YORK CENTRAL: 1997, F-3 A-A locomotive numbered "2333."

EX-C7	LN-C8	Scarcity
500	600	4

[18136] SANTA FE: 1997, F-3 locomotive B-unit with RailSounds numbered "2343C."

EX-C7	LN-C8	Scarcity
175	200	4

[18138] MILWAUKEE ROAD: 1998, F-3 locomotive A-unit numbered "75A" (see 18140).

EX-C7	LN-C8	Scarcity
Too rarely traded to establish accurate pricing.		

[18139] MILWAUKEE ROAD: 1998, F-3 locomotive B-unit numbered "2378B."

EX-C7	LN-C8	Scarcity
Too rarely traded to establish accurate pricing.		

[18140] MILWAUKEE ROAD: 1998, F-3 A-B locomotive numbered "75A."

EX-C7	LN-C8	Scarcity
275	325	4

[18145] NORTHERN PACIFIC: 1997, F-3 locomotive A-unit numbered "2390A."

EX-C7	LN-C8	Scarcity
250	300	5

[18146] NORTHERN PACIFIC: 1997, F-3 locomotive B-unit numbered "2390C."

EX-C7	LN-C8	Scarcity
125	150	5

[18147] NORTHERN PACIFIC: 1997, F-3 locomotive A-B units numbered "2390A" and "2390C."

EX-C7	LN-C8	Scarcity
375	450	5

[18149] UNION PACIFIC: 1998, Veranda Gas Turbine locomotive numbered "61."

EX-C7	LN-C8	Scarcity
700	800	6

[18154] DELUXE SANTA FE: 1998-2000, FT A-A locomotive numbered "167-168."

EX-C7	LN-C8	Scarcity
250	300	4

[18155] DELUXE SANTA FE: FT A locomotive (see 18154).

[18156] DELUXE SANTA FE: FT A dummy locomotive (see 18154).

[18157] SANTA FE: 1998-2000, FT A-A locomotive pair numbered "158."

EX-C7	LN-C8	Scarcity
175	200	4

[18158] SANTA FE: FT A powered locomotive (see 18157).

[18159] SANTA FE: FT A dummy locomotive (see 18157).

[18160] NEW YORK CENTRAL: 1998-2000, deluxe FT locomotive A-A numbered "1603" and "2403."

EX-C7	LN-C8	Scarcity
275	300	4

[18163] NEW YORK CENTRAL: 1998-2000, FT locomotive A-A units numbered "1600" and "2400."

EX-C7	LN-C8	Scarcity
200	225	4

[18166] BALTIMORE AND OHIO: 1999-2000, FT locomotive A-A, command control-equipped.

EX-C7	LN-C8	Scarcity
250	300	4

[18169] BALTIMORE AND OHIO: 1999-2000, FT locomotive A-A, traditionally controlled.

EX-C7	LN-C8	Scarcity
175	200	4

[18178] NEW YORK CENTRAL: 1998, uncataloged F-3 locomotive B-unit Century Club.

EX-C7	LN-C8	Scarcity
150	175	6

[18191] WESTERN PACIFIC: 1998, F-3 locomotive A-A units.

EX-C7	LN-C8	Scarcity
550	600	4

[18192] WESTERN PACIFIC: 1998, F-3 A locomotive powered (see 18191).

EX-C7	LN-C8	Scarcity
Too rarely traded to establish accurate pricing.		

[18193] WESTERN PACIFIC: F-3 A locomotive dummy (see 18191).

[18197] WESTERN PACIFIC: 1999, F-3 locomotive B-unit numbered "2355C."

EX-C7	LN-C8	Scarcity
175	200	4

[18198] WESTERN PACIFIC: 1999, F-3 locomotive B-unit numbered "2355c" command control-equipped.

EX-C7	LN-C8	Scarcity
250	275	5

[18200] CONRAIL: 1987, SD-40 locomotive numbered "8200."

EX-C7	LN-C8	Scarcity
175	200	4

[18201] CHESSIE SYSTEM: 1988, SD-40 locomotive numbered "8201."

EX-C7	LN-C8	Scarcity
200	225	4

[18202] ERIE-LACKAWANNA: 1989, uncataloged SD-40 dummy numbered "8459."

EX-C7	LN-C8	Scarcity
75	100	4

[18203] CP RAIL: 1989, SD-40 numbered "8203."

EX-C7	LN-C8	Scarcity
175	200	4

[18204] CHESSIE SYSTEM: 1990, uncataloged SD-40 dummy locomotive numbered "8204."

EX-C7	LN-C8	Scarcity
100	125	5

[18205] UNION PACIFIC: 1989, Dash 8-40C locomotive numbered "9100."

EX-C7	LN-C8	Scarcity
175	200	4

[18206] SANTA FE: 1990, Dash 8-40B locomotive numbered "8206."

EX-C7	LN-C8	Scarcity
175	200	4

[18207] NORFOLK SOUTHERN: 1992, Dash 8-40C locomotive numbered "8689."

EX-C7	LN-C8	Scarcity
175	200	4

[18208] BURLINGTON NORTHERN: 1991, uncataloged SD-40 dummy locomotive numbered "8586."

EX-C7	LN-C8	Scarcity
100	125	5

[18209] CP RAIL: 1992, uncataloged SD-40 dummy locomotive numbered "8209."

EX-C7	LN-C8	Scarcity
125	150	5

[18210] ILLINOIS CENTRAL: 1993, SD-40 locomotive numbered "6006."

EX-C7	LN-C8	Scarcity
125	150	4

[18211] SUSQUEHANNA: 1993, Dash 8-40B locomotive numbered "4002."

EX-C7	LN-C8	Scarcity
125	150	4

[18212] SANTA FE: 1993, Dash 8-40B dummy locomotive numbered "8212."

EX-C7	LN-C8	Scarcity
100	125	4

[18213] NORFOLK SOUTHERN: 1994, Dash 8-40C locomotive numbered "8688."

EX-C7	LN-C8	Scarcity
125	150	4

[18214] CSX: 1994, Dash 8-40C locomotive numbered "7500."

EX-C7	LN-C8	Scarcity
200	225	4

[18215] CSX: 1994, Dash 8-40C locomotive numbered "7643."

EX-C7	LN-C8	Scarcity
200	225	4

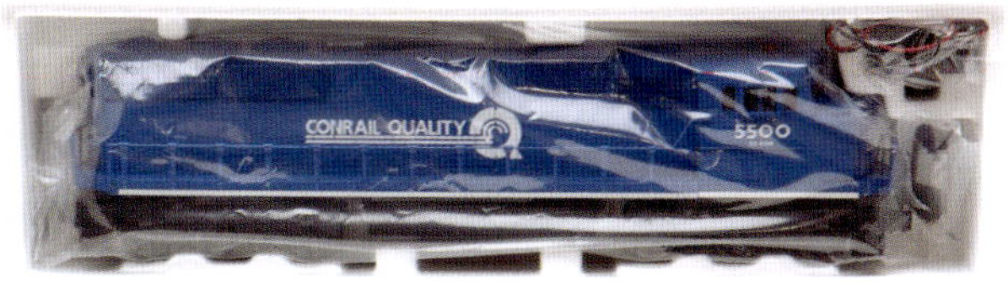

[18216] CONRAIL: 1994, SD-60M locomotive numbered "5500."

EX-C7	LN-C8	Scarcity
225	250	4

[18217] ILLINOIS CENTRAL: 1994, SD-40 locomotive numbered "6007."

EX-C7	LN-C8	Scarcity
150	175	4

[18218] SUSQUEHANNA: 1994, Dash 8-40B locomotive numbered "4004."

EX-C7	LN-C8	Scarcity
150	175	4

[18219] CHICAGO & NORTHWESTERN: 1995, Dash 8-40C locomotive numbered "8501."

EX-C7	LN-C8	Scarcity
175	200	4

[18220] CHICAGO & NORTHWESTERN: 1995, Dash 8-40C locomotive numbered "8502."

EX-C7	LN-C8	Scarcity
125	150	4

[18221] DENVER & RIO GRANDE WESTERN: 1995, SD-50 locomotive numbered "5512."

EX-C7	LN-C8	Scarcity
225	250	4

[18222] DENVER & RIO GRANDE WESTERN: 1995, SD-50 locomotive numbered "5517."

EX-C7	LN-C8	Scarcity
150	175	4

[18223] MILWAUKEE ROAD: 1995, SD-40 locomotive numbered "154."

EX-C7	LN-C8	Scarcity
175	200	4

[18224] MILWAUKEE ROAD: 1995, SD-40 locomotive numbered "155."

EX-C7	LN-C8	Scarcity
125	150	4

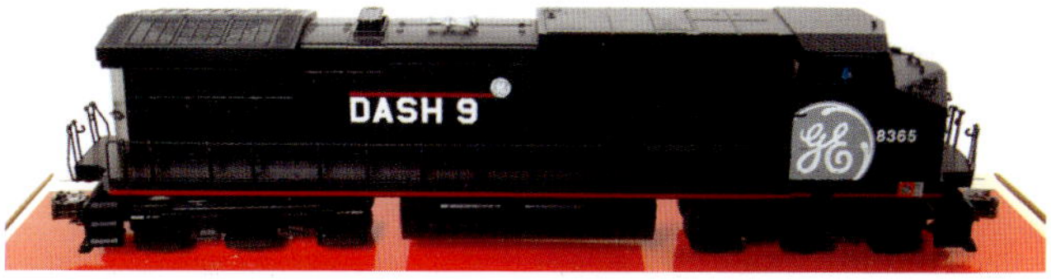

[18226] GE: 1997, Dash 9 locomotive.

EX-C7	LN-C8	Scarcity
150	175	5

DIESEL LOCOMOTIVES

[18228] SOUTHERN PACIFIC: 1997 Dash 9 locomotive numbered "8228," gray, red nose.

EX-C7	LN-C8	Scarcity
150	175	4

[18229] SOUTHERN PACIFIC: 1998, SD40 locomotive "Warhorse" series numbered "7333."

EX-C7	LN-C8	Scarcity
150	200	4

[18231] BNSF: 1998, Dash 9 locomotive deluxe numbered "739."

EX-C7	LN-C8	Scarcity
175	225	4

[18232] SOO LINE: 1997, SD-60 locomotive numbered "5500."

EX-C7	LN-C8	Scarcity
150	200	4

[18233] BNSF: 1998, Dash 9 locomotive numbered "745."

EX-C7	LN-C8	Scarcity
150	175	4

[18234] BNSF: 1998-99, Dash 9 locomotive numbered "740," command control-equipped.

EX-C7	LN-C8	Scarcity
175	200	4

[18235] BNSF: 1998, Dash 9 locomotive two-pack numbered "739" and "740."

EX-C7	LN-C8	Scarcity
350	375	4

[18238] CONRAIL: 1999-2000, SD70 locomotive numbered "4145."

EX-C7	LN-C8	Scarcity
150	175	4

[18240] CONRAIL: 1998, Dash 8-40B locomotive numbered "5065," command control-equipped.

EX-C7	LN-C8	Scarcity
150	175	4

[18241] BURLINGTON NORTHERN: 1999-2000, SD70 locomotive numbered "9413."

EX-C7	LN-C8	Scarcity
200	225	4

[18245] PENNSYLVANIA: 1999, Alco PA-1 locomotive A-A numbered "5750."

EX-C7	LN-C8	Scarcity
250	300	4

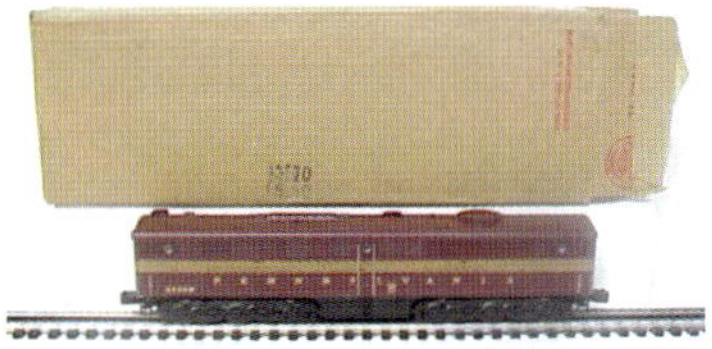

[18248] PENNSYLVANIA: 1999, Alco PB-1 locomotive numbered "5750B."

EX-C7	LN-C8	Scarcity
175	200	4

[18249] ERIE: 2000, Alco PB-1 locomotive numbered "850B."

EX-C7	LN-C8	Scarcity
175	200	4

[18250] BNSF: 1999-2000, SD70 locomotive numbered "9870."

EX-C7	LN-C8	Scarcity
175	200	4

[18251] CSX: 1999-2000, SD60 locomotive numbered "8701."

EX-C7	LN-C8	Scarcity
175	200	4

[18252] AMTRAK: 1999, Dash 9 locomotive, command control-equipped.

EX-C7	LN-C8	Scarcity
150	175	4

[18253] BNSF: 1999, Dash 9 locomotive, command control-equipped.

EX-C7	LN-C8	Scarcity
175	200	4

[18254] SANTA FE: 1999, Dash 9 locomotive, command control-equipped.

EX-C7	LN-C8	Scarcity
175	200	4

[18255] NS: 1999, Dash 9 locomotive, command control-equipped.

EX-C7	LN-C8	Scarcity
175	200	4

[18256] AMTRAK: 1999, Dash 9 locomotive, traditionally controlled.

EX-C7	LN-C8	Scarcity
125	150	4

[18257] BNSF: 1999, Dash 9 locomotive, traditionally controlled.

EX-C7	LN-C8	Scarcity
125	150	4

[18258] SANTA FE: 1999, Dash 9 locomotive, traditionally controlled.

EX-C7	LN-C8	Scarcity
125	150	4

[18259] NORFOLK SOUTHERN: 1999, Dash 9 locomotive, traditionally controlled.

EX-C7	LN-C8	Scarcity
125	150	4

[18260] CONRAIL: 1999-2000, SD70 locomotive numbered "4144."

EX-C7	LN-C8	Scarcity
150	175	4

[18261] BURLINGTON NORTHERN: 1999-2000, SD60 locomotive numbered "9412."

EX-C7	LN-C8	Scarcity
150	175	4

[18262] BNSF: 1999-2000, SD70 locomotive numbered "9869."

EX-C7	LN-C8	Scarcity
150	175	4

[18263] CSX: 1999-2000, SD60 locomotive numbered "8700."

EX-C7	LN-C8	Scarcity
150	175	4

[18264] SOUTHERN PACIFIC: 1999-2000, SD70M locomotive numbered "8238."

EX-C7	LN-C8	Scarcity
150	175	4

[18265] SOUTHERN PACIFIC: 1999-2000, SD70M locomotive numbered "9803."

EX-C7	LN-C8	Scarcity
175	200	4

[18268] LIONEL CENTENNIAL: 2000, SD90MAC locomotive numbered "2000," command control-equipped.

EX-C7	LN-C8	Scarcity
175	200	4

[18269] UNION PACIFIC: 2000, SD90MAC locomotive numbered "8006," command control-equipped.

EX-C7	LN-C8	Scarcity
175	200	4

[18270] UNION PACIFIC: 2000, SD90MAC numbered "8007" locomotive traditionally controlled.

EX-C7	LN-C8	Scarcity
Too rarely traded to establish accurate pricing.		

[18271] CANADIAN PACIFIC: 2000, SD90MAC locomotive numbered "9129," command control-equipped.

EX-C7	LN-C8	Scarcity
175	200	4

[18272] CANADIAN PACIFIC: 2000, SD90MAC locomotive numbered "9130" traditionally controlled.

EX-C7	LN-C8	Scarcity
Too rarely traded to establish accurate pricing.		

[18273] UNION PACIFIC: 1999-2000, SD40MAC locomotive numbered "8071."

EX-C7	LN-C8	Scarcity
175	200	4

[18280] MAERSK: 2000, SD70 locomotive, command control-equipped.

EX-C7	LN-C8	Scarcity
175	200	4

[18281] BNSF: 2000, Dash 9-44CW locomotive numbered "788," command control-equipped.

EX-C7	LN-C8	Scarcity
175	200	4

[18282] BNSF: 2000, Dash 9-44CW locomotive numbered "789," traditionally controlled.

EX-C7	LN-C8	Scarcity
100	125	4

[18283] CSX: 2000, Dash 9-44CW locomotive numbered "9019," command control-equipped.

EX-C7	LN-C8	Scarcity
175	200	4

[18284] CSX: 2000, Dash 9-44CW locomotive numbered "9020," traditionally controlled.

EX-C7	LN-C8	Scarcity
125	150	4

[18288] BURLINGTON NORHTERN: 2000, uncataloged "Odyssey System" SD70 locomotive, command control-equipped.

EX-C7	LN-C8	Scarcity
300	350	5

[18301] SOUTHERN: 1988, Fairbanks-Morse Trainmaster locomotive numbered "8301."

EX-C7	LN-C8	Scarcity
150	175	4

[18307] PENNSYLVANIA: 1994, Fairbanks-Morse Trainmaster locomotive numbered "8699."

EX-C7	LN-C8	Scarcity
150	175	4

[18309] READING: 1993, Fairbanks-Morse Trainmaster locomotive numbered "863."

EX-C7	LN-C8	Scarcity
150	175	4

[18321] JERSEY CENTRAL: 1999, Trainmaster locomotive numbered "2341."

EX-C7	LN-C8	Scarcity
275	300	4

[18322] LACKAWANNA: 1999, Trainmaster locomotive numbered "2321."

EX-C7	LN-C8	Scarcity
375	400	4

[18327] VIRGINIAN: 1999-2000, "2331" Fairbanks-Morse Trainmaster locomotive.

EX-C7	LN-C8	Scarcity
300	350	4

[18340] FAIRBANKS-MORSE: 2000, uncataloged Lionel Century Club II Demo FM Trainmaster locomotives, numbered "TM-1" and "TM-2."

EX-C7	LN-C8	Scarcity
800	850	5

[18500] MILWAUKEE ROAD: 1987, EMD GP-9 locomotive numbered "8500," Fallen Flags number two.

EX-C7	LN-C8	Scarcity
125	150	5

[18501] WESTERN MARYLAND: 1989, NW-2 switcher numbered "8501," Fallen Flags number four.

EX-C7	LN-C8	Scarcity
125	150	4

[18502] LIONEL LINES: 1990, 90th Anniversary EMD GP-9 locomotive numbered "1900."

EX-C7	LN-C8	Scarcity
100	125	4

[18503] SOUTHERN PACIFIC: 1990, NW-2 switcher numbered "8503."

EX-C7	LN-C8	Scarcity
125	150	4

[18504] FRISCO: 1991, EMD GP-7 locomotive numbered "504," Fallen Flags number five.

EX-C7	LN-C8	Scarcity
75	100	5

[18505] NICKEL PLATE ROAD: 1992, EMD GP-7 locomotive powered and dummy set numbered "400" and "401," Fallen Flags number six.

EX-C7	LN-C8	Scarcity
150	175	4

[18513] NEW YORK CENTRAL: 1994, EMD GP-7 locomotive numbered "7420."

EX-C7	LN-C8	Scarcity
100	125	4

[18514] MISSOURI PACIFIC: 1995, EMD GP-7 locomotive numbered "4124."

EX-C7	LN-C8	Scarcity
150	175	4

[18550] MILWAUKEE ROAD: 1987, uncataloged JCPenney EMD GP-9 locomotive numbered "8500," with display case.

EX-C7	LN-C8	Scarcity
100	125	6

[18551] SUSQUEHANNA: 1989, uncataloged JCPenney Alco RS-3 locomotive numbered "8809," with display case.

EX-C7	LN-C8	Scarcity
100	125	6

[18552] DM & IR: 1990, uncataloged JCPenney SD-18 locomotive numbered "8813," with display case.

EX-C7	LN-C8	Scarcity
100	125	6

[18553] UNION PACIFIC: 1991, uncataloged Sears EMD GP-9 locomotive numbered "150," with display case.

EX-C7	LN-C8	Scarcity
125	150	6

[18554] GULF, MOBILE & OHIO: 1992-93, uncataloged JCPenney Alco RS-3 locomotive numbered "721," with display case.

EX-C7	LN-C8	Scarcity
125	150	6

[18555] CHICAGO & ILLINOIS MIDLAND: 1992, uncataloged Sears SD-9 locomotive numbered "52."

EX-C7	LN-C8	Scarcity
100	125	6

[18558] MISSOURI-KANSAS-TEXAS: 1994, uncataloged JCPenney EMD GP-9 locomotive numbered "91," with display case.

EX-C7	LN-C8	Scarcity
100	125	6

[18562] SOUTHERN PACIFIC: 1996, EMD GP-9 locomotive numbered "2380."

EX-C7	LN-C8	Scarcity
100	125	4

[18563] NEW YORK CENTRAL: 1996, EMD GP-9 locomotive numbered "2380."

EX-C7	LN-C8	Scarcity
100	125	4

[18564] CANADIAN PACIFIC: 1997, EMD GP-9 locomotive numbered "2380."

EX-C7	LN-C8	Scarcity
100	125	4

[18565] MILWAUKEE ROAD: 1997, EMD GP-P locomotive numbered "2338."

EX-C7	LN-C8	Scarcity
100	125	4

[18566] CONRAIL: 1997, EMD SD-20 locomotive numbered "8495," Service Station Special item.

EX-C7	LN-C8	Scarcity
75	100	5

[18567] PENNSYLVANIA: 1997, EMD GP-9 locomotive numbered "2028."

EX-C7	LN-C8	Scarcity
100	125	4

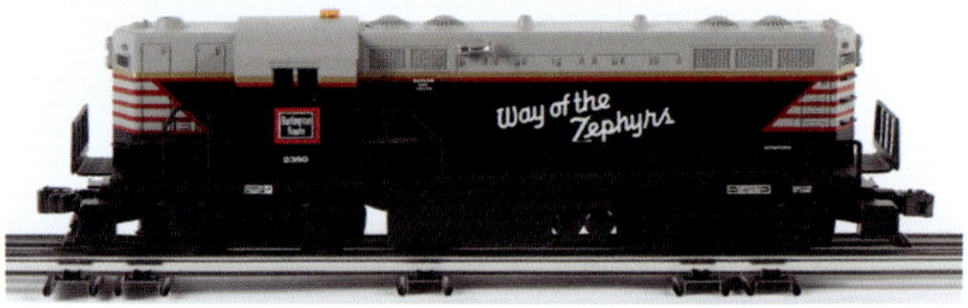

[18569] BURLINGTON: 1998, EMD GP-9 locomotive numbered "2380."

EX-C7	LN-C8	Scarcity
100	125	4

[18573] SANTA FE: 1998, EMD GP-9 locomotive numbered "2380."

EX-C7	LN-C8	Scarcity
125	150	4

[18574] MILWAUKEE ROAD: 1998, EMD GP20 locomotive numbered "975."

EX-C7	LN-C8	Scarcity
100	125	4

[18575] CUSTOM SERIES I: 1998, EMD GP-9 locomotive numbered "2398."

EX-C7	LN-C8	Scarcity
175	200	5

[18576] SOUTHERN PACIFIC: 1998, EMD GP-9 dummy locomotive B-unit numbered "2385."

EX-C7	LN-C8	Scarcity
75	100	4

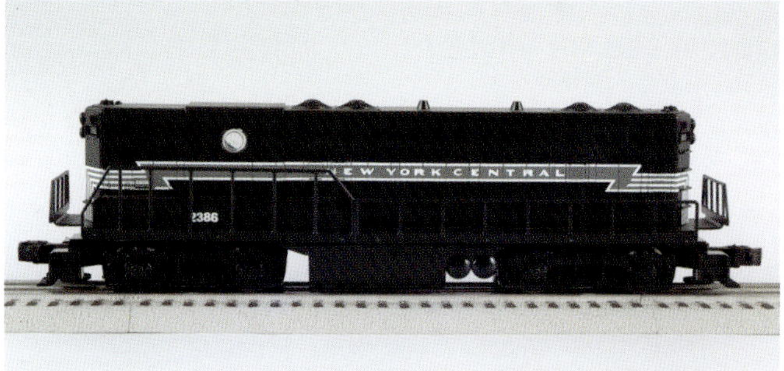

[18577] NEW YORK CENTRAL: 1998, EMD GP-9 dummy locomotive B-unit numbered "2385."

EX-C7	LN-C8	Scarcity
75	100	4

[18579] MILWAUKEE ROAD: 1999, EMD GP-9 dummy locomotive numbered "2384."

EX-C7	LN-C8	Scarcity
75	100	4

[18580] PENNSYLVANIA: 1998, EMD GP-9 locomotive B-unit numbered "2027."

EX-C7	LN-C8	Scarcity
75	100	4

[18582] SEABOARD: 1998, NW-2 switcher numbered "6250."

EX-C7	LN-C8	Scarcity
225	250	4

[18585]: 1999, Centennial SD-40 locomotive numbered "1999."

EX-C7	LN-C8	Scarcity
400	450	4

[18587] NICKEL PLATE ROAD: 1999-2001, Alco C-420 locomotive numbered "577," command control-equipped.

EX-C7	LN-C8	Scarcity
150	175	4

[18588] DELAWARE AND HUDSON: 1999-2001, Alco C-420 locomotive numbered "412," command control-equipped.

EX-C7	LN-C8	Scarcity
150	175	4

[18589] LEHIGH VALLEY: 1999-2001, Alco C-420 locomotive numbered "409," command control-equipped.

EX-C7	LN-C8	Scarcity
175	200	4

[18590] NICKEL PLATE ROAD: 1999-2001, Alco C-420 locomotive numbered "578," traditionally controlled.

EX-C7	LN-C8	Scarcity
100	125	4

[18591] DELAWARE AND HUDSON: 1999-2001, Alco C-420 locomotive numbered "411," traditionally controlled.

EX-C7	LN-C8	Scarcity
75	100	4

[18592] LEHIGH VALLEY: 1999-2001, Alco C-420 locomotive numbered "410," traditionally controlled.

EX-C7	LN-C8	Scarcity
75	100	4

[18595] DELAWARE AND HUDSON: 1999-2000, Alco RS-11 locomotive, traditionally controlled, numbered "5002."

EX-C7	LN-C8	Scarcity
Cataloged, but not produced.		

[18596] DELAWARE AND HUDSON: 1999-2001, Alco RS-11 locomotive numbered "5001," command control-equipped.

EX-C7	LN-C8	Scarcity
275	300	5

[18597] NEW YORK CENTRAL: 1999-2000, Alco RS-11 locomotive, traditionally controlled, numbered "8011."

EX-C7	LN-C8	Scarcity
Cataloged, but not produced.		

[18598] NEW YORK CENTRAL: 1999-2001, Alco RS-11 locomotive numbered "8010," command control-equipped.

EX-C7	LN-C8	Scarcity
275	300	5

[18599] CHESAPEAKE AND OHIO: 1999-2000, EMD GP-38 locomotive numbered "3855."

EX-C7	LN-C8	Scarcity
100	125	4

18799 BETHLEHEM STEEL: 1999, switcher numbered "44."

EX-C7	LN-C8	Scarcity
50	60	3

[18800] LEHIGH VALLEY: 1987, EMD GP-9 locomotive numbered "8800."

EX-C7	LN-C8	Scarcity
60	75	4

[18801] SANTA FE: 1987, GE U36B locomotive numbered "8801."

EX-C7	LN-C8	Scarcity
60	75	4

[18802] SOUTHERN: 1987, EMD GP-9 locomotive numbered "8802," Service Station Special item.

EX-C7	LN-C8	Scarcity
75	90	5

[18803] SANTA FE: 1988, Alco RS-3 locomotive numbered "8803."

EX-C7	LN-C8	Scarcity
60	75	4

[18804] SOO LINE: 1988, Alco RS-3 locomotive numbered "8804."

EX-C7	LN-C8	Scarcity
60	75	4

[18805] UNION PACIFIC: 1989, Alco RS-3 locomotive numbered "8805."

EX-C7	LN-C8	Scarcity
60	75	4

[18806] NEW HAVEN: 1989, EMD SD-18 locomotive numbered "8806."

EX-C7	LN-C8	Scarcity
60	75	4

[18807] LEHIGH VALLEY: 1990, Alco RS-3 locomotive numbered "8807."

EX-C7	LN-C8	Scarcity
60	75	4

[18808] ATLANTIC COAST LINE: 1990, EMD SD-18 locomotive numbered "8808."

EX-C7	LN-C8	Scarcity
75	90	4

[18809] SUSQUEHANNA: 1989, uncataloged Alco RS-3 locomotive numbered "8809."

EX-C7	LN-C8	Scarcity
85	110	5

[18810] CSX: 1990, EMD SD-18 locomotive numbered "8810."

EX-C7	LN-C8	Scarcity
60	75	4

[18811] ALASKA RAILROAD: 1991, EMD SD-9 locomotive numbered "8811."

EX-C7	LN-C8	Scarcity
80	100	4

[18812] KANSAS CITY SOUTHERN: 1991, EMD GP-38 locomotive numbered "4000."

EX-C7	LN-C8	Scarcity
60	75	4

[18814] DELAWARE AND HUDSON: 1991, Alco RS-3 locomotive numbered "8814," Service Station Special item.

EX-C7	LN-C8	Scarcity
75	100	4

[18815] AMTRAK: Cataloged in 1991, uncataloged in 1992, Alco RS-3 locomotive numbered "1815."

EX-C7	LN-C8	Scarcity
50	60	4

[18816] CHICAGO & NORTHWESTERN: 1992, EMD GP-38-2 locomotive numbered "4600."

EX-C7	LN-C8	Scarcity
50	60	4

[18817] UNION PACIFIC: 1991, uncataloged EMD GP-9 locomotive numbered "150" (see 18553).

EX-C7	LN-C8	Scarcity
60	75	4

[18818] LIONEL RAILROADER CLUB: 1992, uncataloged EMD GP-38-2 locomotive numbered "1992."

EX-C7	LN-C8	Scarcity
100	125	6

[18819] LOUISVILLE AND NASHVILLE: 1992, EMD GP-38-2 locomotive numbered "4136."

EX-C7	LN-C8	Scarcity
100	125	4

[18820] WESTERN PACIFIC: 1992, EMD GP-9 locomotive numbered "8820," Service Station Special item.

EX-C7	LN-C8	Scarcity
75	100	6

[18821] CLINCHFIELD: 1993, EMD GP-38-2 locomotive numbered "6005."

EX-C7	LN-C8	Scarcity
60	75	4

[18824] MONTANA RAIL LINK: 1993, EMD SD-9 locomotive numbered "600."

EX-C7	LN-C8	Scarcity
75	90	4

[18825] SOO LINE: 1993, EMD GP-38-2 locomotive numbered "4000," Service Station Special item.

EX-C7	LN-C8	Scarcity
60	75	4

[18826] CONRAIL: 1993, EMD GP-7 locomotive numbered "5808."

EX-C7	LN-C8	Scarcity
60	75	4

[18827] "HAPPY HOLIDAYS": 1993, Alco RS-3 locomotive numbered "8827."

EX-C7	LN-C8	Scarcity
125	150	5

[18830] BUDWEISER: 1993-94, uncataloged EMD GP-9 locomotive numbered "1947."

EX-C7	LN-C8	Scarcity
125	150	5

[18831] SOUTHERN PACIFIC: 1994, EMD GP-20 locomotive numbered "4060."

EX-C7	LN-C8	Scarcity
60	75	4

[18832] PENNSYLVANIA: 1995, Alco RSD-4 locomotive numbered "8446."

EX-C7	LN-C8	Scarcity
60	75	4

[18833] MILWAUKEE ROAD: 1994, Alco RS-3 locomotive numbered "2487."

EX-C7	LN-C8	Scarcity
60	75	4

[18834] CHESAPEAKE AND OHIO: 1994, EMD SD-28 locomotive numbered "8834."

EX-C7	LN-C8	Scarcity
60	75	4

[18835] NEW YORK CENTRAL: 1994, Alco RS-3 locomotive numbered "8223," Service Station Special item.

EX-C7	LN-C8	Scarcity
100	125	5

[18836] CANADIAN NATIONAL/GRAND TRUNK WESTERN: 1994, EMD GP-38-2 locomotive numbered "5800."

EX-C7	LN-C8	Scarcity
80	100	4

[18837] "HAPPY HOLIDAYS": 1994-95, Alco RS-3 locomotive numbered "8837."

EX-C7	LN-C8	Scarcity
80	100	4

[18838] SEABOARD: 1995, Alco RSC-3 locomotive numbered "1538."

EX-C7	LN-C8	Scarcity
60	75	4

[18840] U.S. ARMY: 1995, EMD GP-7 locomotive numbered "1821."

EX-C7	LN-C8	Scarcity
60	75	4

[18841] WESTERN MARYLAND: 1995, EMD GP-20 locomotive numbered "27," Service Station Special item.

EX-C7	LN-C8	Scarcity
60	75	4

[18842] B & LE: 1995, uncataloged JCPenney EMD SD-38 locomotive numbered "868."

EX-C7	LN-C8	Scarcity
175	200	6

[18843] GREAT NORTHERN: 1996, Alco RS-3 locomotive numbered "197."

EX-C7	LN-C8	Scarcity
60	75	4

[18844] NDEM: 1996, EMD GP-38 locomotive numbered "9288."

EX-C7	LN-C8	Scarcity
Cataloged, but not produced.		

[18845] DENVER & RIO GRANDE WESTERN: 1997, Alco RS-3 locomotive numbered "5204."

EX-C7	LN-C8	Scarcity
60	75	4

[18846] 1997 LIONEL TRAINS: 1998, Centennial series EMD GP-9 locomotive.

EX-C7	LN-C8	Scarcity
175	200	5

[18847] SANTA FE: 1999, Fairbanks-Morse H-12-44 switcher numbered "9087."

EX-C7	LN-C8	Scarcity
300	350	4

[18848] PENNSYLVANIA: 1999, Fairbanks-Morse H-12-44 switcher numbered "502."

EX-C7	LN-C8	Scarcity
300	350	4

[18853] SANTA FE: 1997, uncataloged JCPenney EMD GP-9 locomotive numbered "2370."

EX-C7	LN-C8	Scarcity
100	125	5

[18854] UNION PACIFIC: 1997, EMD GP-9 locomotive set numbered "2380" and "2387," dummy.

EX-C7	LN-C8	Scarcity
350	400	4

[18855] UNION PACIFIC: EMD GP-9 dummy locomotive (see 18854).

[18856] NEW JERSEY TRANSIT: 1999, EMD GP-38-2 locomotive numbered "4303."

EX-C7	LN-C8	Scarcity
200	250	4

[18857] UNION PACIFIC: 1997, EMD GP-9 locomotive numbered "2397."

EX-C7	LN-C8	Scarcity
100	125	4

[18858] 1998 LIONEL TRAINS: 1998, EMD GP20 locomotive numbered "1998."

EX-C7	LN-C8	Scarcity
200	225	4

[18859] THE PHANTOM II: 1999.

EX-C7	LN-C8	Scarcity
275	300	5

[18860] THE PHANTOM: 1998, The Pratt's Hollow Collection.

EX-C7	LN-C8	Scarcity
275	300	5

[18864] SOUTHERN PACIFIC: 1998, EMD GP-9 locomotive B-unit.

EX-C7	LN-C8	Scarcity
60	75	4

[18865] NEW YORK CENTRAL: 1998, EMD GP-9 locomotive B-unit.

EX-C7	LN-C8	Scarcity
75	100	4

[18866] MILWAUKEE ROAD: 1998, EMD GP-9 locomotive.

EX-C7	LN-C8	Scarcity
125	150	4

[18868] NEW JERSEY TRANSIT: 1998, uncataloged EMD GP-38-2 locomotive numbered "4300."

EX-C7	LN-C8	Scarcity
60	75	4

[18870] PENNSYLVANIA: 1998, EMD GP-9 locomotive numbered "2029."

EX-C7	LN-C8	Scarcity
125	150	4

[18872] WABASH: 1999, EMD GP-7 three-unit locomotive "lash-up" set numbered "453," "454" and "455."

EX-C7	LN-C8	Scarcity
375	425	4

[18876] CHICAGO & NORTHWESTERN: 1999, Fairbanks-Morse H-12-44 switcher numbered "1053."

EX-C7	LN-C8	Scarcity
300	350	4

[18877] UNION PACIFIC: 1999, EMD GP-9 B-unit dummy locomotive numbered "2399."

EX-C7	LN-C8	Scarcity
100	125	4

[18878] ALASKA RAILROAD: 1999, EMD GP-7 locomotive numbered "1803."

EX-C7	LN-C8	Scarcity
60	75	4

[18879] BALTIMORE AND OHIO: 1999, EMD GP-9 locomotive numbered "5616."

EX-C7	LN-C8	Scarcity
175	200	5

[18881] CUSTOM: 1999, EMD GP-9 locomotive numbered "5616."

EX-C7	LN-C8	Scarcity
175	200	5

[18890] UNION PACIFIC: 1989, uncataloged LOTS Alco RS-3 locomotive numbered "8805."

EX-C7	LN-C8	Scarcity
100	125	6

[18892] BURLINGTON: 1999, EMD GP-9 locomotive numbered "2328."

EX-C7	LN-C8	Scarcity
175	200	5

[18897] CHRISTMAS: 1999, EMD GP-7 locomotive numbered "1999."

EX-C7	LN-C8	Scarcity
125	150	4

[18900] PENNSYLVANIA: Uncataloged in 1988, cataloged in 1989, switcher numbered "8900."

EX-C7	LN-C8	Scarcity
20	25	2

[18901]/[18902] PENNSYLVANIA: 1988, Alco FA-FA locomotive set numbered "8901" and "8902."

EX-C7	LN-C8	Scarcity
75	100	4

[18903]/[18904] AMTRAK: 1988-89, Alco FA-FA locomotive set numbered "8903" and "8904."

EX-C7	LN-C8	Scarcity
75	100	4

[18906] ERIE-LACKAWANNA: 1991, uncataloged Alco RS-3 locomotive numbered "8906."

EX-C7	LN-C8	Scarcity
70	85	4

[18907] ROCK ISLAND: 1993, 44-ton switcher numbered "371."

EX-C7	LN-C8	Scarcity
40	50	3

[18908]/[18909] NEW YORK CENTRAL: 1993, Alco FA-FA locomotive set numbered "8908" and "8909."

EX-C7	LN-C8	Scarcity
50	60	4

[18910] CSX: 1993, switcher numbered "8910."

EX-C7	LN-C8	Scarcity
25	30	2

[18911] UNION PACIFIC: 1993, switcher numbered "8911."

EX-C7	LN-C8	Scarcity
25	30	2

[18912] AMTRAK: 1993, switcher numbered "8912."

EX-C7	LN-C8	Scarcity
25	30	2

[18913] SANTA FE: 1993-94, Alco FA locomotive numbered "8913."

EX-C7	LN-C8	Scarcity
25	30	2

[18915] WESTERN MARYLAND: 1993, Alco FA locomotive numbered "8915."

EX-C7	LN-C8	Scarcity
30	35	4

[18916] WESTERN MARYLAND: 1993, Alco FA dummy locomotive with horn numbered "8916."

EX-C7	LN-C8	Scarcity
20	25	4

18917 SOO LINE: 1993, NW-2 switcher.

EX-C7	LN-C8	Scarcity
35	40	4

[18918] BOSTON & MAINE: 1993, NW-2 switcher numbered "8918."

EX-C7	LN-C8	Scarcity
35	40	4

[18919] SANTA FE: 1993-94, Alco FA locomotive dummy with horn numbered "8919."

EX-C7	LN-C8	Scarcity
20	25	2

[18920] FRISCO: 1994, NW-2 switcher numbered "254."

EX-C7	LN-C8	Scarcity
35	40	4

[18921] CHICAGO & NORTHWESTERN: 1994, NW-2 switcher numbered "1017."

EX-C7	LN-C8	Scarcity
50	60	4

[18922] NEW HAVEN: 1994, Alco FA locomotive numbered "8922."

EX-C7	LN-C8	Scarcity
50	60	4

[18923] NEW HAVEN: 1994, Alco FA dummy locomotive numbered "8923."

EX-C7	LN-C8	Scarcity
30	40	4

[18924] ILLINOIS CENTRAL: 1994-95, switcher numbered "8924."

EX-C7	LN-C8	Scarcity
20	25	3

[18925] DENVER & RIO GRANDE WESTERN: 1994-95, switcher numbered "8925."

EX-C7	LN-C8	Scarcity
20	25	3

[18926] READING: 1994-95, switcher numbered "8926."

EX-C7	LN-C8	Scarcity
20	25	3

[18927] U.S. NAVY: 1994-95, NW-2 switcher numbered "65-00637."

EX-C7	LN-C8	Scarcity
40	50	3

[18928] CHICAGO & NORTHWESTERN: 1995, NW-2 switcher calf.

EX-C7	LN-C8	Scarcity
25	30	4

[18929] BOSTON & MAINE: 1995, NW-2 switcher calf.

EX-C7	LN-C8	Scarcity
25	30	4

[18930] CRAYOLA: Uncataloged in 1994, cataloged in 1995, switcher.

EX-C7	LN-C8	Scarcity
15	20	2

[18931] CHRYSLER: 1994, uncataloged Mopar NW-2 switcher numbered "1818."

EX-C7	LN-C8	Scarcity
50	60	6

[18932] JERSEY CENTRAL: 1996, NW-2 switcher numbered "8932."

EX-C7	LN-C8	Scarcity
30	35	4

[18933] JERSEY CENTRAL: 1996, NW-2 switcher calf numbered "8933."

EX-C7	LN-C8	Scarcity
25	30	4

[18934]/[18935] READING: 1995, Alco FA-FA locomotive set numbered "300" and "304."

EX-C7	LN-C8	Scarcity
50	60	4

[18936] AMTRAK: 1995, Alco FA locomotive numbered "8936."

EX-C7	LN-C8	Scarcity
25	30	4

[18937] AMTRAK: 1995-97, Alco FA-2 locomotive dummy.

EX-C7	LN-C8	Scarcity
20	25	4

[18938] U.S. NAVY: 1995, NW-2 switcher calf.

EX-C7	LN-C8	Scarcity
25	30	4

[18939] UNION PACIFIC: 1996, NW-2 switcher set.

EX-C7	LN-C8	Scarcity
75	100	4

[18943] GEORGIA POWER: 1995, uncataloged NW-2 switcher numbered "1960."

EX-C7	LN-C8	Scarcity
100	125	4

[18946] U.S.C.G: 1996, NW-2 switcher numbered "8946."

EX-C7	LN-C8	Scarcity
40	50	4

[18947] PORT OF LIONEL CITY: 1997, Alco FA-2 locomotive numbered "2030."

EX-C7	LN-C8	Scarcity
35	40	4

Diesel Locomotives

[18948] PORT OF LIONEL CITY: 1997, Alco FB-2 locomotive numbered "2030B."

EX-C7	LN-C8	Scarcity
30	35	4

[18949] NEW YORK CENTRAL: 1997, NW-2 switcher numbered "622."

EX-C7	LN-C8	Scarcity
Cataloged, but not produced.		

[18951] ERIE: 1997, NW-2 switcher numbered "6220."

EX-C7	LN-C8	Scarcity
Cataloged, but not produced.		

[18952] SANTA FE: 1997, Alco PA-1 locomotive numbered "2000."

EX-C7	LN-C8	Scarcity
150	175	4

[18953] NEW YORK CENTRAL: 1997, Alco PA-1 locomotive numbered "2000."

EX-C7	LN-C8	Scarcity
150	175	4

[18954] SANTA FE: 1997-99, powered Alco FA-2 locomotive numbered "212."

EX-C7	LN-C8	Scarcity
35	40	4

[18955] NEW JERSEY TRANSIT: 1996, uncataloged NW-2 switcher numbered "500."

EX-C7	LN-C8	Scarcity
50	60	6

[18956] DODGE MOTORSPORTS: 1996, uncataloged "8956" NW-2 switcher.

EX-C7	LN-C8	Scarcity
100	125	6

[18959] NEW YORK CENTRAL: 1997, NW-2 switcher numbered "622."

EX-C7	LN-C8	Scarcity
300	350	4

[18961] ERIE: 1995, Alco PA-1 locomotive numbered "850."

EX-C7	LN-C8	Scarcity
200	225	5

[18965] SANTA FE: 1998, Alco PB-1 locomotive.

EX-C7	LN-C8	Scarcity
150	175	4

[18966] NEW YORK CENTRAL: 1998, Alco PB-1 locomotive numbered "2000B."

EX-C7	LN-C8	Scarcity
150	175	4

[18971]: 1998, Alco dummy locomotive A-unit.

EX-C7	LN-C8	Scarcity
35	40	4

[18972] ROCK ISLAND: 1998, Alco FA A-A locomotive.

EX-C7	LN-C8	Scarcity
Cataloged, but not produced.		

[18973] ROCK ISLAND: 1998-99, Alco FA-2 locomotive numbered "2031."

EX-C7	LN-C8	Scarcity
Too rarely traded to establish accurate pricing.		

[18974] ROCK ISLAND: 1998-99, Alco FA-2 dummy locomotive.

EX-C7	LN-C8	Scarcity
Too rarely traded to establish accurate pricing.		

[18975] SOUTHERN: 1999, 44-ton switcher numbered "1955."

EX-C7	LN-C8	Scarcity
100	125	4

[18978] CHESAPEAKE & OHIO: 1999-2000, NW-2 switcher numbered "624."

EX-C7	LN-C8	Scarcity
200	225	4

[21780] SANTA FE: 2000, F-3 A-B-B-A locomotive passenger set numbered "200."

EX-C7	LN-C8	Scarcity
1,500	1,600	4

[28500] MISSOURI PACIFIC: 1999-2000, EMD GP-20, "2274," command upgradeable.

EX-C7	LN-C8	Scarcity
125	150	4

[28501] SANTA FE: 1999-2000, Merger EMD GP-9 locomotive numbered "2924," command upgradeable.

EX-C7	LN-C8	Scarcity
125	150	4

[28502] SANTA FE: 1999-2000, Merger EMD GP-9 locomotive numbered "2925," command control-equipped.

EX-C7	LN-C8	Scarcity
175	200	4

[28503] ATLANTIC COAST LINE: 2000, EMD GP-7 locomotive, command control-equipped.

EX-C7	LN-C8	Scarcity
175	200	4

[28504] ATLANTIC COAST LINE: 2000, EMD GP-7 locomotive, traditionally controlled.

EX-C7	LN-C8	Scarcity
125	150	4

[28505] MONON: 2000-01, Alco C-420 locomotive numbered "505," command control-equipped.

EX-C7	LN-C8	Scarcity
175	200	4

[28506] MONON: 2000-01, Alco C-420 locomotive numbered "506," traditionally controlled.

EX-C7	LN-C8	Scarcity
125	150	4

[28507] NEW HAVEN: 2000-01, Alco C-420 locomotive numbered "2556," command control-equipped.

EX-C7	LN-C8	Scarcity
200	250	4

[28508] NEW HAVEN: 2000-01, Alco C-420 locomotive numbered "2557," traditionally controlled.

EX-C7	LN-C8	Scarcity
175	225	4

[28509] FLORIDA EAST COAST: 1999, EMD GP-7 locomotive Triple Lashup: "607/608/609."

EX-C7	LN-C8	Scarcity
400	450	4

[28514] BALTIMORE AND OHIO: 2000, EMD GP-9 locomotive numbered "6590."

EX-C7	LN-C8	Scarcity
60	70	4

28515 LIONEL SERVICE STATION: 2000, Alco C-420 locomotive, command control-equipped.

EX-C7	LN-C8	Scarcity
100	125	5

[28517] CHICAGO & NORTHWESTERN: 2000-01, EMD GP-7 locomotive numbered "1518," command control-equipped.

EX-C7	LN-C8	Scarcity
200	250	4

[28800] NORFOLK AND WESTERN: 1999-2000, EMD GP-7 locomotive numbered "507."

EX-C7	LN-C8	Scarcity
40	55	4

[28801] LIONEL LINES: 1999, 44-ton switcher.

EX-C7	LN-C8	Scarcity
40	55	4

[28821] SANTA FE: 2000, FT dummy locomotive numbered "172."

EX-C7	LN-C8	Scarcity
Cataloged, but not produced.		

[28826] PIONEER SEED: 2000, uncataloged EMD GP-7 locomotive numbered "2001" traditionally controlled.

EX-C7	LN-C8	Scarcity
Too rarely traded to establish accurate pricing.		

[29122] ERIE-LACKAWANNA: 1999, F-3 A-B locomotive set.

EX-C7	LN-C8	Scarcity
725	775	4

[38100] TEXAS SPECIAL: 1999, F-3 A-B locomotive set numbered "2245."

EX-C7	LN-C8	Scarcity
700	750	5

[38103] TEXAS SPECIAL: 1999, F-3 locomotive numbered "2245."

EX-C7	LN-C8	Scarcity
350	400	5

[38114] SANTA FE: 1999-2000, FT locomotive B-unit.

EX-C7	LN-C8	Scarcity
100	125	4

[38115] NEW YORK CENTRAL: 1999-2000, FT locomotive B-unit.

EX-C7	LN-C8	Scarcity
100	125	4

[38116] BALTIMORE AND OHIO: 1999-2000, FT locomotive B-unit.

EX-C7	LN-C8	Scarcity
100	125	4

[38144] CHESAPEAKE AND OHIO: 2000, F-3 A-A locomotive set numbered "7019" and "7021."

EX-C7	LN-C8	Scarcity
500	600	4

[38150] PLATINUM GHOST: 1999, "2333" locomotive.

EX-C7	LN-C8	Scarcity
450	500	4

[38153] SPIRIT OF THE CENTURY: 1999, "2333" locomotive.

EX-C7	LN-C8	Scarcity
850	950	4

[38188] SOUTHERN: 2000, F-3 A-B-A "2356" locomotive set.

EX-C7	LN-C8	Scarcity
600	650	4

[38196] SANTA FE: 2000, FT A-unit locomotive numbered "171."

EX-C7	LN-C8	Scarcity
Too rarely traded to establish accurate pricing.		

[38197] SOUTHERN PACIFIC: 2000, F-3 A-B-A locomotive set numbered "2387."

EX-C7	LN-C8	Scarcity
550	600	4

[52005] CANADIAN NATIONAL: 1993, uncataloged Lionel Collectors Association of Canada F-3 B-unit numbered "9517."

EX-C7	LN-C8	Scarcity
Too rarely traded to establish accurate pricing.		

[52007] LONG ISLAND: 1992, uncataloged NLOE Alco RS-3 locomotive numbered "1552."

EX-C7	LN-C8	Scarcity
125	150	6

[52035] TCA YORKRAIL: 1994, uncataloged EMD GP-9 locomotive numbered "1750," shell only.

EX-C7	LN-C8	Scarcity
35	40	6

[52037] TCA YORKRAIL: 1994, uncataloged EMD GP-9 locomotive numbered "1754."

EX-C7	LN-C8	Scarcity
125	175	6

[52078] SOUTHERN PACIFIC: 1996, uncataloged TTOS EMD SD-9 locomotive numbered "5366."

EX-C7	LN-C8	Scarcity
200	225	6

52173 LONG ISLAND RR: 2000, F-3 locomotive, A-A shells.

EX-C7	LN-C8	Scarcity
Too rarely traded to establish accurate pricing.		

[52197] ARTRAIN: 2000, uncataloged EMD GP38 locomotive numbered "2380."

EX-C7	LN-C8	Scarcity
225	250	6

[NO NUMBER] PACIFIC NORTHWEST TCA: 📷 1974, uncataloged F-3 A-A locomotive, shells only.

EX-C7	LN-C8	Scarcity
Too rarely traded to establish accurate pricing.		

[NO NUMBER] TCA LONE STAR TEXAS SPECIAL: 1981, uncataloged F-3 A-unit, shell only.

EX-C7	LN-C8	Scarcity
Too rarely traded to establish accurate pricing.		

[NO NUMBER] TCA LONE STAR TEXAS SPECIAL: 1982, uncataloged F-3 B-unit, shell only.

EX-C7	LN-C8	Scarcity
Too rarely traded to establish accurate pricing.		

[NO NUMBER] PACIFIC NORTHWEST TCA

CHAPTER 4

ELECTRIC LOCOMOTIVES

Electric locomotives began to grace the pages of modern-era catalogs in 1975 with the return of the postwar locomotive styled after the GE EP-5 rectifier. This streamlined locomotive was quite a contrast to the next locomotive reintroduced—the boxy E-33 rectifier—another GE product—which returned to the line in 1976. But the crown jewel of Lionel's electric locomotive line has long been their die-cast, dual motor, Magne-traction-equipped replicas of the famed Pennsylvania GG1 electric. The GG1 rejoined the line in 1977, and like the other electrics, has been produced sporadically since.

Except for the GG1, the reintroduced electric locomotives lacked Magne-traction, but by the mid-1980s, this feature returned to most of the locomotives. And by 1997, Lionel's remarkable "Trainmaster" control and realistic RailSounds systems began to be installed in electrics, regardless of style.

[8150] PENNSYLVANIA: 1981, green GG1 with five gold stripes numbered "4935."

EX-C7	LN-C8	Scarcity
150	200	4

8272 PENNSYLVANIA: 1982, uncataloged GE EP-5 rectifier.

EX-C7	LN-C8	Scarcity
75	100	4

8551 PENNSYLVANIA: 1975-76, GE EP-5 rectifier.

EX-C7	LN-C8	Scarcity
60	80	4

8558 MILWAUKEE ROAD: 1976-77, GE EP-5 rectifier.

EX-C7	LN-C8	Scarcity
60	80	4

8659 VIRGINIAN: 1976-77, GE E33 rectifier.

8659 VIRGINIAN (Type I): Some locomotives had a light yellow nose decal.

EX-C7	LN-C8	Scarcity
70	90	4

8659 VIRGINIAN (Type II): Other locomotives had a dark yellow nose decal.

EX-C7	LN-C8	Scarcity
70	90	4

8762 GREAT NORTHERN: 1977-78, GE EP-5 rectifier.

EX-C7	LN-C8	Scarcity
70	700	4

8753 PENNSYLVANIA: 1977, uncataloged Tuscan GG1.

EX-C7	LN-C8	Scarcity
175	225	4

8754 NEW HAVEN: 1977-78, GE E33 rectifier.

EX-C7	LN-C8	Scarcity
45	60	4

8850 PENN CENTRAL: Uncataloged in 1978, cataloged in 1979, GG1.

EX-C7	LN-C8	Scarcity
175	225	4

8859 CONRAIL: 1978-82, GE E33 rectifier.

EX-C7	LN-C8	Scarcity
60	90	4

[18300] PENNSYLVANIA: 1987, gold-painted GG1 numbered "8300."

EX-C7	LN-C8	Scarcity
225	275	4

[18302] GREAT NORTHERN: 1988, GE EP-5 rectifier numbered "8302." Fallen Flags number three.

EX-C7	LN-C8	Scarcity
175	200	5

[18303] AMTRAK: 1989, GG1 numbered "8303."

EX-C7	LN-C8	Scarcity
175	225	4

[18308] PENNSYLVANIA: 1992, GG1 numbered "4866."

EX-C7	LN-C8	Scarcity
175	200	4

[18311] DISNEY: 1994, GE EP-5 rectifier numbered "8311."

EX-C7	LN-C8	Scarcity
125	175	4

[18313] PENNSYLVANIA: 1996, GG1 with single gold stripe numbered "4907."

EX-C7	LN-C8	Scarcity
150	175	4

[18314] PENNSYLVANIA: 1997, GG1 with five gold stripes numbered "2332."

EX-C7	LN-C8	Scarcity
400	500	5

[18315] VIRGINIAN: 1997, GE E33 rectifier numbered "2329."

EX-C7	LN-C8	Scarcity
175	200	5

[18319] NEW HAVEN: 1999, GE EP-5 rectifier numbered "2350."

EX-C7	LN-C8	Scarcity
150	175	4

[18326] PENNSYLVANIA: 2000, GG1 Congressional.

EX-C7	LN-C8	Scarcity
450	500	4

[28518] PENNSYLVANIA: 2000, EP-5 GE rectifier numbered "2352," command control-equipped.

EX-C7	LN-C8	Scarcity
350	375	4

Chapter 5
MOTORIZED

During the 1950s, motorized units provided inexpensive animation to many Lionel railroads, and lucrative profits for the company as well. While it is not surprising that many of these type units have been made in the modern era—it is surprising that these were not revived until 1982 when the 8264 Canadian Pacific snowplow was introduced. This was followed by succession of other motorized trolleys, cranes, maintenance cars, and handcars.

Particularly broad was a range of handcars featuring not just workmen, but an ongoing parade of cartoon characters, as well of course as the ever-popular Santa Claus. These were all based on modifications of the postwar #65 handcar.

Until mid-90s the motorized units of the modern era were based on those of the postwar era, although in many cases minor redesign work was done to accommodate less-expensive and cooler-running DC can motors.

In 1995, two all-new motorized units arrived in the Lionel lineup. The on-track step van and on-track pickup truck both featured operating headlights and colorful bodies.

Although some enthusiasts consider Budd RDC cars to be "motorized units" in this volume they, like the MU cars, are considered passenger equipment and are so located in the appropriate chapter.

8264 CANADIAN PACIFIC: 1982, Vulcan switcher with snowplow.

EX-C7	LN-C8	Scarcity
40	55	4

8379 PENNSYLVANIA: 1983, uncataloged fire car.

EX-C7	LN-C8	Scarcity
45	60	4

8368 ALASKA RAILROAD: 1983, Vulcan switcher.

EX-C7	LN-C8	Scarcity
45	65	4

8459 DENVER & RIO GRANDE WESTERN: 1984, Vulcan rotary snowplow.

EX-C7	LN-C8	Scarcity
50	70	4

8578 NEW YORK CENTRAL: 1985 and 1987, Ballast Tamper.

EX-C7	LN-C8	Scarcity
50	65	4

8690 LIONEL LINES: 1986, trolley.

EX-C7	LN-C8	Scarcity
35	45	4

[11988] NEW YORK CENTRAL: 1999, fire car numbered "18444" and firefighting instruction car (numbered "19853") set.

EX-C7	LN-C8	Scarcity
100	125	4

[18400] SANTA FE: 1987, Vulcan rotary snowplow numbered "8400."

EX-C7	LN-C8	Scarcity
100	125	4

[18401] OPERATING HANDCAR: 1987.

[18401] OPERATING HANDCAR (Type I): Dark orange body molding, and no ballast weight.

EX-C7	LN-C8	Scarcity
20	25	4

[18401] OPERATING HANDCAR (Type II): Light orange body molding, and ballast weight included for improved traction.

EX-C7	LN-C8	Scarcity
20	25	4

18402 LIONEL LINES: 1988, burro crane.

EX-C7	LN-C8	Scarcity
35	45	4

[18403] SANTA CLAUS: 1988, green handcar.

EX-C7	LN-C8	Scarcity
15	20	3

[18404] SAN FRANCISCO: 1988, trolley numbered "8404."

EX-C7	LN-C8	Scarcity
40	50	4

18405 SANTA FE: 1989, burro crane.

EX-C7	LN-C8	Scarcity
40	50	4

18406 LIONEL: 1989 and 1991, Track Maintenance car.

EX-C7	LN-C8	Scarcity
25	30	4

[18407] SNOOPY AND WOODSTOCK: 1990-91, handcar.

EX-C7	LN-C8	Scarcity
35	45	4

[18408] SANTA CLAUS: 1989, white handcar.

EX-C7	LN-C8	Scarcity
20	25	4

18410 PENNSYLVANIA: 1990, burro crane.

EX-C7	LN-C8	Scarcity
60	75	5

18411 CANADIAN PACIFIC: 1980, fire car.

EX-C7	LN-C8	Scarcity
50	60	4

18412 UNION PACIFIC: 1991, fire car.

EX-C7	LN-C8	Scarcity
Cataloged, but not produced.		

[18413] CHARLIE BROWN AND LUCY: 1991, handcar.

EX-C7	LN-C8	Scarcity
35	45	4

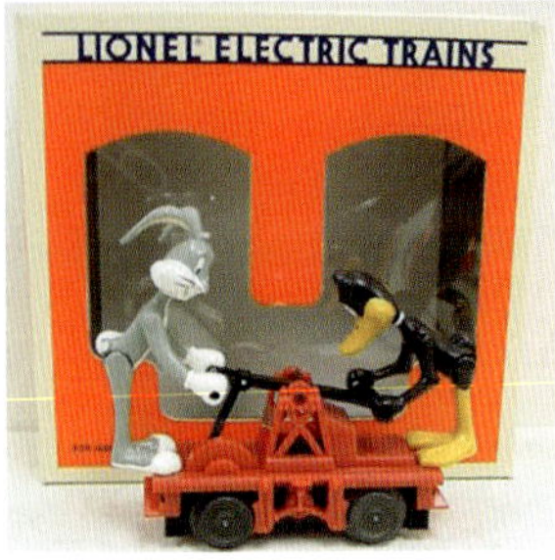

[18416] BUGS BUNNY AND DAFFY DUCK: 1992-93, handcar.

EX-C7	LN-C8	Scarcity
60	75	5

18417 LIONEL: 1993, gang car.

EX-C7	LN-C8	Scarcity
30	40	4

[18419] LIONELVILLE: 1994, electric trolley numbered "8419."

EX-C7	LN-C8	Scarcity
50	60	4

[18421] SYLVESTER AND TWEETY: 1994, handcar.

EX-C7	LN-C8	Scarcity
30	35	4

[18422] SANTA AND SNOWMAN: 1994, handcar.

EX-C7	LN-C8	Scarcity
20	25	3

[18423] LIONEL TRACK TESTING EQUIPMENT: 1995, on-track step van.

EX-C7	LN-C8	Scarcity
15	20	4

[18424] LIONEL: 1995, on-track pickup truck.

EX-C7	LN-C8	Scarcity
15	20	4

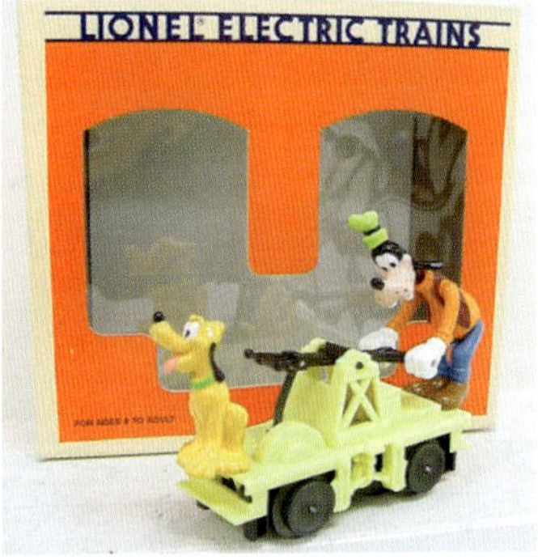

[18425] GOOFY AND PLUTO: 1995, handcar.

EX-C7	LN-C8	Scarcity
25	30	4

[18426] SANTA AND SNOWMAN: 1995, handcar.

EX-C7	LN-C8	Scarcity
15	20	4

[18427] TIE-JECTOR: 1997, numbered "55."

EX-C7	LN-C8	Scarcity
40	50	4

[18429]: 1996, handcar.

EX-C7	LN-C8	Scarcity
25	30	4

[18430] NEW YORK CENTRAL: 1996, crew car.

EX-C7	LN-C8	Scarcity
25	30	4

[18431] LIONEL TRANSIT: 1996-97, trolley car.

EX-C7	LN-C8	Scarcity
30	40	4

[18433] MICKEY AND MINNIE: 1996-97, handcar.

EX-C7	LN-C8	Scarcity
35	45	5

[18434] PORKY AND PETUNIA: 1996, handcar.

EX-C7	LN-C8	Scarcity
25	30	4

[18436] DODGE RAM: 1997, track inspection vehicle.

EX-C7	LN-C8	Scarcity
25	30	4

[18438] PENNSYLVANIA: 1998, high-rail vehicle numbered "49."

EX-C7	LN-C8	Scarcity
25	30	4

[18439] UNION PACIFIC: 1998, high-rail maintenance vehicle.

EX-C7	LN-C8	Scarcity
25	30	4

[18440] NEW JERSEY TRANSIT: 1998, high-rail inspection vehicle.

EX-C7	LN-C8	Scarcity
30	35	4

[18444] LIONELVILLE: 1998, fire car, Service Station Special item.

EX-C7	LN-C8	Scarcity
100	125	5

[18445] NEW YORK CENTRAL: 1998, fire car.

EX-C7	LN-C8	Scarcity
60	75	4

[18446] GREAT NORTHERN: 1999, rotary snowplow numbered "58."

EX-C7	LN-C8	Scarcity
100	125	4

[18447]: 1999, executive inspection vehicle.

EX-C7	LN-C8	Scarcity
75	100	4

[18452] BOSTON MASS TRANSIT: 1999-2000, trolley numbered "3321."

EX-C7	LN-C8	Scarcity
35	40	4

[18454]: 2000, blue #68 executive inspection car.

EX-C7	LN-C8	Scarcity
70	80	4

[18455] NEW YORK CENTRAL: 2000-01, Tie-Jector "X-2."

EX-C7	LN-C8	Scarcity
50	60	4

[18457]: 2000-01, postwar handcar numbered "65."

EX-C7	LN-C8	Scarcity
40	45	4

[18458] DENVER & RIO GRANDE WESTERN: 2000, snowplow numbered "53."

EX-C7	LN-C8	Scarcity
100	125	4

[18515] LIONEL STEEL: 1996, Vulcan switcher numbered "57," Service Station Special item.

EX-C7	LN-C8	Scarcity
100	125	4

[18583] AEC: 1998, switcher #57.

EX-C7	LN-C8	Scarcity
175	200	4

[19854] LIONELVILLE: 1998, fire car #1, Service Station Special item.

EX-C7	LN-C8	Scarcity
25	30	4

[52088] DESERT TCA 25TH ANNIVERSARY: 1996, uncataloged on-track step van.

EX-C7	LN-C8	Scarcity
75	100	6

[52107] LCCA: 1996, uncataloged pickup truck.

EX-C7	LN-C8	Scarcity
35	40	6

[52108] LCCA: 1996, uncataloged step van.

EX-C7	LN-C8	Scarcity
35	40	6

CHAPTER 6

CABOOSES

As the new owners of Lionel began producing trains in 1970, the caboose was still considered a key component of the freight train. Naturally, production of these "crummies" began immediately, utilizing the original Lionel tooling for the Pennsylvania N5c "porthole" cabooses, as well as the traditional 027-sized offset-cupola caboose often referred to by collectors as the "SP-type." This designation was bestowed on these cabooses because when Lionel created the tooling in 1947, the cabooses produced were decorated with the Southern Pacific "SP" abbreviation.

In 1976, this pair was joined by a third returning postwar design, the bay window caboose. By 1982, these three designs were looking dated, and Lionel-maker Fundimensions created a new style caboose. Drawing from the style of caboose dominating prototype railroads at the time, the new Extended Vision caboose was created. The boxy cupola of these cabooses extended beyond the side walls of the caboose, combining the best qualities of cupola and bay-window cabooses, and affording the conductor an outstanding field of vision. In 1988, this caboose was further modified when a smoke unit was introduced in the 19807 Pennsylvania caboose. Since that time this style caboose has been built both with and without the smoke generator.

In 1986, another new style of caboose joined the Lionel lineup when a Standard 0 caboose was created. This large caboose was molded with simulated wooden siding. The following year a new, taller cupola was created to fit this car body and was introduced on the 17602 Conrail. Since then both styles of cupolas have appeared on various models. In 1990, another similar appearing Standard 0 caboose was introduced, this one molded with simulated steel sides. From 1992 onward, certain of the Standard 0 cabooses, both the wood and steel side cabooses have occasionally been equipped with smoke generators.

The cabooses mentioned above have been the staples of Lionel's caboose offerings in the modern era—but they are by no means the only styles built. An exquisite reproduction of the prewar semi-scale cast caboose was built in 1991, and the following year a scale brass representation of a Pennsylvania N-8 cabin car was produced as a companion for the scale S-2 turbine offered that year. At the opposite end of the spectrum from these two spectacular cabooses is the four-wheel "bobber" caboose introduced in 1972 and included in only the most inexpensive of sets. Another staple of entry-level sets, especially in the early modern era is the work caboose. Intended originally to be used in conjunction with a crane car, these cabooses have a cabin on one end, and the other end features a low tool storage area over which the boom of the crane projects. Based on a flatcar, in the early modern era, these cars were almost entirely plastic and made of snap-together construction. In 1981, this design was modified to create the transfer caboose, with the cabin centered on the flatcar, creating two large platforms, one on either end. In 1989, a die-cast chassis returned to the work caboose, marking the return of the work caboose to the premium status it enjoyed in the late 1940s and early 1950s.

[1980] IETCA: 1980, uncataloged, with a traditionally sized offset cupola.

EX-C7	LN-C8	Scarcity
10	20	5

[1986] LCOL: 1986, uncataloged, with a shell only.

EX-C7	LN-C8	Scarcity
5	10	6

6401 VIRGINIAN: 1981, with a blue and yellow bay window.

6401 VIRGINIAN (Type I): As described above.

EX-C7	LN-C8	Scarcity
20	25	4

6401 VIRGINIAN (Type II): 1984, uncataloged, with a Sacramento-Sierra TCA bay window.

EX-C7	LN-C8	Scarcity
25	30	6

6420 READING: 1981-82, transfer.

EX-C7	LN-C8	Scarcity
10	15	4

6421 JOSHUA L. COWEN: 1982, with a bay window.

EX-C7	LN-C8	Scarcity
20	25	5

6422 DM & IR: 1981, with a bay window.

EX-C7	LN-C8	Scarcity
20	25	5

6425 ERIE-LACKAWANNA: 1983-84, with a bay window.

EX-C7	LN-C8	Scarcity
20	25	5

6426 READING: 1982-83, transfer.

EX-C7	LN-C8	Scarcity
10	15	3

6427 BURLINGTON NORTHERN: 1983-84, transfer.

EX-C7	LN-C8	Scarcity
10	15	3

6428 CHICAGO & NORTHWESTERN: 1983-85, transfer.

EX-C7	LN-C8	Scarcity
10	15	3

6430 SANTA FE: 1983-89, with a traditionally sized offset cupola.

EX-C7	LN-C8	Scarcity
2	5	2

6431 SOUTHERN: 1983, with a bay window, Famous American Railroads number four.

EX-C7	LN-C8	Scarcity
20	30	5

6432 UNION PACIFIC: 1981-82, with a traditionally sized offset cupola.

EX-C7	LN-C8	Scarcity
2	5	2

6433 CANADIAN PACIFIC: 1981, with a bay window.

EX-C7	LN-C8	Scarcity
30	40	6

6435 U.S. TRANSFER: 1983-84.

EX-C7	LN-C8	Scarcity
5	10	3

6438 GREAT NORTHERN: 1981, with a bay window, Famous American Railroads number three.

EX-C7	LN-C8	Scarcity
20	30	5

6439 READING: 1984-85, with a bay window.

EX-C7	LN-C8	Scarcity
10	15	4

6441 ALASKA RAILROAD: 1982-85, with a bay window.

EX-C7	LN-C8	Scarcity
20	25	4

6449 WENDY'S: 1981-82, N5c porthole.

EX-C7	LN-C8	Scarcity
25	30	4

[6478] BLACK CAVE: 1982, with a traditionally sized offset cupola.

EX-C7	LN-C8	Scarcity
3	5	2

6482 NIBCO EXPRESS: 1982, uncataloged, with a traditionally sized offset cupola.

EX-C7	LN-C8	Scarcity
25	35	6

6483 JERSEY CENTRAL: 1982, uncataloged, with a LCCA traditionally sized offset cupola.

EX-C7	LN-C8	Scarcity
15	25	5

6485 CHESSIE SYSTEM: 1984-85, with a traditionally sized offset cupola.

EX-C7	LN-C8	Scarcity
3	5	2

6486 SOUTHERN: 1983-85, with a traditionally sized offset cupola.

EX-C7	LN-C8	Scarcity
2	5	2

6491 ERIE-LACKAWANNA: 1985-86, transfer.

EX-C7	LN-C8	Scarcity
5	10	3

CABOOSES

6493 LANCASTER AND CHESTER: 1986-87, with a bay window.

EX-C7	LN-C8	Scarcity
15	25	4

6494 SANTA FE: 1985-86, bobber.

EX-C7	LN-C8	Scarcity
1	5	4

6496 SANTA FE: 1986, Service Station Special item.

EX-C7	LN-C8	Scarcity
10	20	5

[6506] L.A.S.E.R.: 1981-82, Security Car.

EX-C7	LN-C8	Scarcity
10	15	3

6900 NORFOLK AND WESTERN: 1982, extended vision.

EX-C7	LN-C8	Scarcity
30	40	4

6901 ONTARIO NORTHLAND: 1982, uncataloged, extended vision.

EX-C7	LN-C8	Scarcity
20	25	3

6903 SANTA FE: 1983, extended vision.

EX-C7	LN-C8	Scarcity
50	60	5

6904 UNION PACIFIC: 1983, extended vision.

EX-C7	LN-C8	Scarcity
50	60	5

6905 NICKEL PLATE: 1983, uncataloged, extended vision.

EX-C7	LN-C8	Scarcity
20	25	4

6906 ERIE-LACKAWANNA: 1984, extended vision caboose.

EX-C7	LN-C8	Scarcity
35	50	5

6907 NEW YORK CENTRAL: 1986, uncataloged, wood-sided with 1/48-scale proportions.

EX-C7	LN-C8	Scarcity
35	45	5

6908 PENNSYLVANIA: 1984-85, N5c porthole, Famous American Railroads number five.

EX-C7	LN-C8	Scarcity
25	35	5

6910 NEW YORK CENTRAL: 1984, uncataloged, extended vision.

EX-C7	LN-C8	Scarcity
20	25	4

[6912] REDWOOD VALLEY EXPRESS: 1984-85, with a traditionally sized offset cupola.

EX-C7	LN-C8	Scarcity
5	10	3

6913 BURLINGTON NORTHERN: 1985, extended vision.

EX-C7	LN-C8	Scarcity
35	50	5

6916 NEW YORK CENTRAL: 1985-86.

EX-C7	LN-C8	Scarcity
10	20	3

6917 JERSEY CENTRAL: 1986, extended vision.

EX-C7	LN-C8	Scarcity
25	30	3

6918 BALTIMORE AND OHIO: 1986, with a traditionally sized offset cupola.

EX-C7	LN-C8	Scarcity
5	10	2

6919 NICKEL PLATE ROAD: 1986-91, with a traditionally sized offset cupola.

EX-C7	LN-C8	Scarcity
2	5	1

6920 BOSTON & ALBANY: 1986, uncataloged wood-sided with 1/48-scale proportions.

EX-C7	LN-C8	Scarcity
30	50	5

CABOOSES

6921 PENNSYLVANIA: 1986-90, with a traditionally sized offset cupola.

EX-C7	LN-C8	Scarcity
2	5	1

6926 TCA NEW ORLEANS: 1986, uncataloged, extended vision.

EX-C7	LN-C8	Scarcity
20	30	6

7508 LIONEL 75TH ANNIVERSARY: 1975-77, N5c porthole.

EX-C7	LN-C8	Scarcity
15	20	4

7600 FRISCO (Type I): 1974-76, "Spirit of 76," N5c porthole.

EX-C7	LN-C8	Scarcity
20	30	4

7600 FRISCO (Type II): 1976, uncataloged, "Spirit of 76," N5c Midwest TCA porthole, numbered "00003."

EX-C7	LN-C8	Scarcity
25	35	6

[7681] VIRGINIA TRAIN COLLECTORS: 1981, uncataloged, N5c porthole.

EX-C7	LN-C8	Scarcity
15	20	5

9021 SANTA FE: 1970-71 and 1973-75.

9021 SANTA FE (Type I): Most of these work cabooses had red cabs.

EX-C7	LN-C8	Scarcity
5	10	2

9021 SANTA FE (Type II): Some had orange cabs.

EX-C7	LN-C8	Scarcity
15	25	5

8341 ATLANTIC COAST LINE: Uncataloged in 1986, cataloged from 1987-90, with a traditionally sized offset cupola.

EX-C7	LN-C8	Scarcity
2	4	1

9025 DT & I: 1971-74 and 1977-78.

EX-C7	LN-C8	Scarcity
3	5	1

9027 SOO LINE: 1975-76.

EX-C7	LN-C8	Scarcity
3	5	1

9057 CP RAIL: 1978-79, with a traditionally sized offset cupola.

EX-C7	LN-C8	Scarcity
5	10	4

9058 LIONEL LINES: 1978-79 and 1983, with a traditionally sized offset cupola.

EX-C7	LN-C8	Scarcity
3	5	2

9059 LIONEL LINES: 1979 and 1981, uncataloged, with a traditionally sized offset cupola.

EX-C7	LN-C8	Scarcity
5	10	3

9060 NICKEL PLATE ROAD: 1970-72, with a traditionally sized offset cupola.

9060 NICKEL PLATE ROAD (Type I): The bodies of some of the cabooses were brown.

EX-C7	LN-C8	Scarcity
3	5	2

9060 NICKEL PLATE ROAD (Type II): Other cabooses were maroon.

EX-C7	LN-C8	Scarcity
3	5	2

9061 SANTA FE: 1970-76, with a traditionally sized offset cupola-type red.

9061 SANTA FE (Type I): The earliest of these cabooses rode on AAR trucks.

EX-C7	LN-C8	Scarcity
5	10	4

9061 SANTA FE (Type II): Later cabooses rode on Symington-Wayne trucks.

EX-C7	LN-C8	Scarcity
5	10	4

9062 PENN CENTRAL: 1970-72 and 1974-76, with a traditionally sized offset cupola.

9062 PENN CENTRAL (Type I): The earliest of these cabooses rode on AAR trucks.

EX-C7	LN-C8	Scarcity
5	10	4

9062 PENN CENTRAL (Type II): Later cabooses rode on Symington-Wayne trucks.

EX-C7	LN-C8	Scarcity
5	10	4

9063 GRAND TRUNK WESTERN: 1970-73, uncataloged, with a traditionally sized offset cupola.

9063 GRAND TRUNK WESTERN (Type I): Most of these cabooses were orange.

EX-C7	LN-C8	Scarcity
10	15	3

9063 GRAND TRUNK WESTERN (Type II): Some were maroon.

EX-C7	LN-C8	Scarcity
15	20	5

9064 CHESAPEAKE AND OHIO: 1971-72 and 1975-77, with a traditionally sized offset cupola.

EX-C7	LN-C8	Scarcity
5	10	4

9065 CANADIAN NATIONAL: 1971-73, uncataloged with a traditionally sized offset cupola.

EX-C7	LN-C8	Scarcity
15	20	4

9066 SOUTHERN: 1973-76, with a traditionally sized offset cupola.

EX-C7	LN-C8	Scarcity
5	10	4

[9067] KICKAPOO VALLEY: 1972, bobber.

[9067] KICKAPOO VALLEY (Type I): Green body.

EX-C7	LN-C8	Scarcity
5	10	4

[9067] KICKAPOO VALLEY (Type II): Yellow body.

EX-C7	LN-C8	Scarcity
5	10	4

[9067] KICKAPOO VALLEY (Type III): Red body.

EX-C7	LN-C8	Scarcity
5	10	4

9068 READING: 1973-76, green bobber.

9068 READING (Type I): As described above.

EX-C7	LN-C8	Scarcity
3	5	3

9068 READING (Type II): 1976, uncataloged, Gateway TCA bobber.

EX-C7	LN-C8	Scarcity
10	15	6

9069 JERSEY CENTRAL: Cataloged from 1973-74, uncataloged from 1975-76, with a traditionally sized offset cupola.

EX-C7	LN-C8	Scarcity
5	10	4

9070 ROCK ISLAND: 1973-74, with a traditionally sized offset cupola.

EX-C7	LN-C8	Scarcity
10	15	4

9071 SANTA FE: Uncataloged in 1974, cataloged from 1977-78, bobber.

EX-C7	LN-C8	Scarcity
5	10	4

9073 COCA-COLA: Cataloged in 1974, uncataloged in 1975, with a traditionally sized offset cupola.

EX-C7	LN-C8	Scarcity
10	15	4

9075 ROCK ISLAND: 1975-76, uncataloged, with a traditionally sized offset cupola.

EX-C7	LN-C8	Scarcity
10	15	4

9076 "WE THE PEOPLE": 1975, uncataloged, with a traditionally sized offset cupola.

EX-C7	LN-C8	Scarcity
20	25	5

9077 DENVER & RIO GRANDE WESTERN: Cataloged from 1976-83, uncataloged from 1984-91, with a traditionally sized offset cupola.

EX-C7	LN-C8	Scarcity
3	5	3

9078 ROCK ISLAND: 1976-77, bobber.

EX-C7	LN-C8	Scarcity
3	5	3

9080 WABASH: 1977, with a traditionally sized offset cupola.

EX-C7	LN-C8	Scarcity
5	10	4

9085 SANTA FE: 1979-82.

EX-C7	LN-C8	Scarcity
3	5	3

9160 ILLINOIS CENTRAL: 1970-72, orange N5c porthole.

9160 ILLINOIS CENTRAL (Type I): The earliest of these cars rode on AAR trucks and were painted light orange.

EX-C7	LN-C8	Scarcity
15	20	4

9160 ILLINOIS CENTRAL (Type II): Later cabooses rode on Symington-Wayne trucks and were painted slightly darker orange.

EX-C7	LN-C8	Scarcity
15	20	4

9161 CANADIAN NATIONAL: 1972-74, N5c porthole.

EX-C7	LN-C8	Scarcity
15	20	4

9162 PENNSYLVANIA: 1972-76, N5c porthole.

EX-C7	LN-C8	Scarcity
15	20	4

CABOOSES

9163 SANTA FE: 1973-76, N5c porthole.

EX-C7	LN-C8	Scarcity
15	20	4

9165 CANADIAN PACIFIC: 1973, N5c porthole, Service Station Special item.

EX-C7	LN-C8	Scarcity
15	20	4

9166 DENVER & RIO GRANDE WESTERN: 1974-75, with a traditionally sized offset cupola, Service Station Special item.

EX-C7	LN-C8	Scarcity
15	20	5

9167 CHESSIE SYSTEM: 1974-76, N5c porthole.

EX-C7	LN-C8	Scarcity
20	25	4

9168 UNION PACIFIC: 1975-77, N5c porthole.

EX-C7	LN-C8	Scarcity
15	20	4

9169 MILWAUKEE ROAD: 1975, with a traditionally sized offset cupola, Service Station Special item.

EX-C7	LN-C8	Scarcity
20	25	4

[9170] NORFOLK AND WESTERN: 1975, N5c porthole, numbered "1776."

EX-C7	LN-C8	Scarcity
20	25	4

9171 MISSOURI PACIFIC: Uncataloged in 1975, cataloged from 1976-77, with a traditionally sized offset cupola.

EX-C7	LN-C8	Scarcity
15	20	4

9172 PENN CENTRAL: Uncataloged in 1975, cataloged from 1976-77, with a traditionally sized offset cupola.

EX-C7	LN-C8	Scarcity
20	25	4

9173 JERSEY CENTRAL: Uncataloged in 1975, cataloged from 1976-77, with a traditionally sized offset cupola.

EX-C7	LN-C8	Scarcity
20	25	4

9174 NEW YORK CENTRAL: 1976, with a P & E bay window.

EX-C7	LN-C8	Scarcity
40	60	5

9175 VIRGINIAN: 1976-77, N5c porthole.

EX-C7	LN-C8	Scarcity
20	25	4

9176 BANGOR AND AROOSTOOK: 1976, uncataloged, N5c porthole.

EX-C7	LN-C8	Scarcity
15	25	4

9177 NORTHERN PACIFIC: 1976, bay window, Service Station Special item.

EX-C7	LN-C8	Scarcity
25	30	4

9178 ILLINOIS CENTRAL GULF: 1976-77, with a traditionally sized offset cupola.

EX-C7	LN-C8	Scarcity
15	20	5

9179 CHESSIE SYSTEM: 1976, bobber.

EX-C7	LN-C8	Scarcity
3	7	2

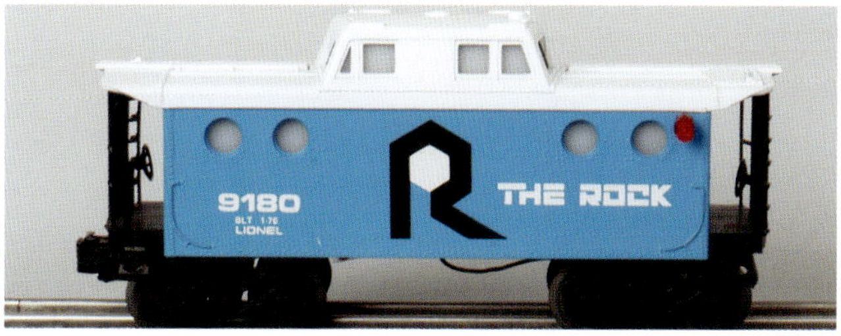

9180 ROCK ISLAND: 1977-78, N5c porthole.

EX-C7	LN-C8	Scarcity
12	20	4

9181 BOSTON AND MAINE (Type I): 1976, uncataloged, 1977, N5c porthole.

EX-C7	LN-C8	Scarcity
15	20	4

9181 BOSTON AND MAINE (Type II): 1977, uncataloged, New England Division of Train Collectors Association N5c porthole.

EX-C7	LN-C8	Scarcity
20	25	6

9182 NORFOLK AND WESTERN: Uncataloged in 1976, cataloged from 1977-80, N5c porthole.

EX-C7	LN-C8	Scarcity
15	20	4

9183 MICKEY MOUSE: 1977-78, N5c porthole.

EX-C7	LN-C8	Scarcity
22	30	5

9184 ERIE: 1977-78, red bay window.

9184 ERIE (Type I): As described above.

EX-C7	LN-C8	Scarcity
15	20	4

9184 ERIE (Type II): 1977, uncataloged, overstamped North Texas TCA.

EX-C7	LN-C8	Scarcity
15	20	6

9184 ERIE (Type III): 1982, uncataloged, overstamped LCOL.

EX-C7	LN-C8	Scarcity
15	20	6

9185 GRAND TRUNK WESTERN: 1977, N5c porthole.

EX-C7	LN-C8	Scarcity
15	20	4

9186 CONRAIL: Uncataloged in 1976, cataloged from 1977-78, blue N5c porthole.

9186 CONRAIL (Type I): As described above.

EX-C7	LN-C8	Scarcity
15	20	5

9186 CONRAIL (Type II): 1979, uncataloged, overstamped Atlantic TCA.

EX-C7	LN-C8	Scarcity
15	20	6

9187 GULF, MOBILE & OHIO: 1977, with a traditionally sized offset cupola.

EX-C7	LN-C8	Scarcity
10	20	4

9188 GREAT NORTHERN: 1977, with a bay window.

EX-C7	LN-C8	Scarcity
15	20	4

9231 READING: 1979, with a bay window.

EX-C7	LN-C8	Scarcity
20	25	4

9239 LIONEL LINES: 1983, uncataloged, N5c porthole.

EX-C7	LN-C8	Scarcity
30	35	6

X9259 SOUTHERN: 1977, uncataloged, with an LCCA bay window.

EX-C7	LN-C8	Scarcity
30	35	6

9268 NORTHERN PACIFIC: 1977, uncataloged, with a bay window.

EX-C7	LN-C8	Scarcity
15	20	4

9269 MILWAUKEE ROAD: 1978, with a bay window.

EX-C7	LN-C8	Scarcity
20	25	4

9270 NORTHERN PACIFIC: 1978, N5c porthole.

EX-C7	LN-C8	Scarcity
12	18	4

9271 MINNEAPOLIS AND ST. LOUIS: 1978-79, with a bay window, Service Station Special item.

EX-C7	LN-C8	Scarcity
20	25	5

9272 NEW HAVEN: 1978-80, with a red bay window.

9272 NEW HAVEN (Type I): As described above.

EX-C7	LN-C8	Scarcity
15	20	4

9272 NEW HAVEN (Type II): 1979, uncataloged, overstamped Metropolitan Division of Train Collectors Association.

EX-C7	LN-C8	Scarcity
15	20	6

9272 NEW HAVEN (Type III): 1979, uncataloged, overstamped Detroit-Toledo TCA.

EX-C7	LN-C8	Scarcity
15	20	6

9273 SOUTHERN: 1978, uncataloged, with a bay window.

EX-C7	LN-C8	Scarcity
25	30	6

9274 SANTA FE: 1978, uncataloged, with a bay window.

EX-C7	LN-C8	Scarcity
25	30	6

9287 SOUTHERN: Uncataloged in 1977, cataloged in 1978, red N5c porthole.

9287 SOUTHERN (Type I): As described above.

EX-C7	LN-C8	Scarcity
10	15	4

9287 SOUTHERN (Type II): 1977, uncataloged, overstamped TCA Southern Division.

EX-C7	LN-C8	Scarcity
10	15	6

9288 LEHIGH VALLEY: Uncataloged in 1977, cataloged in 1978, 1980 N5c porthole.

EX-C7	LN-C8	Scarcity
18	25	5

9289 CHICAGO & NORTHWESTERN: Uncataloged in 1977 and 1979, cataloged in 1978 and 1980 N5c porthole caboose.

9289 CHICAGO & NORTHWESTERN (Type I): As described above.

EX-C7	LN-C8	Scarcity
15	20	4

9289 CHICAGO & NORTHWESTERN (Type II): 1980, uncataloged, overstamped Midwest TCA Museum Express.

EX-C7	LN-C8	Scarcity
15	20	6

9309 TP & W: Cataloged from 1980-81, uncataloged in 1983, with a bay window.

EX-C7	LN-C8	Scarcity
10	15	4

9316 SOUTHERN PACIFIC: 1979, uncataloged, with a bay window.

EX-C7	LN-C8	Scarcity
30	40	5

9317 SANTA FE: 1979, with a bay window.

EX-C7	LN-C8	Scarcity
20	25	4

9323 SANTA FE: 1979, with a bay window, Famous American Railroads number one.

EX-C7	LN-C8	Scarcity
20	25	5

9326 BURLINGTON NORTHERN: 1979-80, with a green bay window.

9326 BURLINGTON NORTHERN (Type I): As described above.

EX-C7	LN-C8	Scarcity
15	20	4

9326 BURLINGTON NORTHERN (Type II): 1982, uncataloged, overstamped TTOS.

EX-C7	LN-C8	Scarcity
15	20	6

9328 CHESSIE SYSTEM: 1980, with a bay window.

EX-C7	LN-C8	Scarcity
20	25	4

9341 ATLANTIC COAST LINE: Cataloged from 1979-82, uncataloged in 1986, cataloged again from 1987-90, with a traditionally sized offset cupola.

EX-C7	LN-C8	Scarcity
3	5	2

9346 WABASH: 1979, traditionally sized offset cupola.

EX-C7	LN-C8	Scarcity
3	5	2

9355 DELAWARE & HUDSON: 1980, with a blue and gray bay window.

9355 DELAWARE & HUDSON (Type I): As described above.

EX-C7	LN-C8	Scarcity
15	20	4

9355 DELAWARE & HUDSON (Type II): In 1982, some cars were overstamped to create this uncataloged TTOS bay window caboose.

EX-C7	LN-C8	Scarcity
20	25	6

9357 SMOKEY MOUNTAIN LINE: 1979, bobber.

9357 SMOKEY MOUNTAIN LINE (Type I): Red body.

EX-C7	LN-C8	Scarcity
3	5	2

9357 SMOKEY MOUNTAIN LINE (Type II): Green body.

EX-C7	LN-C8	Scarcity
3	5	2

9357 SMOKEY MOUNTAIN LINE (Type III): Yellow body.

EX-C7	LN-C8	Scarcity
3	5	2

9361 CHICAGO & NORTHWESTERN: 1980, with a yellow bay window.

9361 CHICAGO & NORTHWESTERN (Type I): As described above.

EX-C7	LN-C8	Scarcity
30	35	4

9361 CHICAGO & NORTHWESTERN (Type II): 1982, uncataloged, overstamped TTOS.

EX-C7	LN-C8	Scarcity
30	35	4

9368 UNION PACIFIC: 1980, with a bay window, Famous American Railroads number two.

EX-C7	LN-C8	Scarcity
15	20	4

9372 SEABOARD: 1980, with a bay window.

EX-C7	LN-C8	Scarcity
15	20	4

9376 TEXAS AND PACIFIC: 1980, with a traditionally sized offset cupola.

EX-C7	LN-C8	Scarcity
Cataloged, but not produced.		

9380 NYNH & H: 1980-81, with a traditionally sized offset cupola.

EX-C7	LN-C8	Scarcity
5	8	2

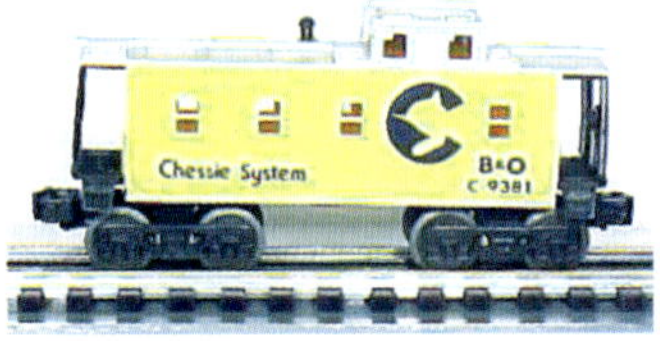

9381 CHESSIE SYSTEM: 1980, with a traditionally sized offset cupola.

EX-C7	LN-C8	Scarcity
5	8	2

9382 FLORIDA EAST COAST: 1980, with a red and yellow bay window.

9382 FLORIDA EAST COAST (Type I): As described above.

EX-C7	LN-C8	Scarcity
25	30	4

9382 FLORIDA EAST COAST (Type II): 1982, uncataloged, with a TTOS bay window.

EX-C7	LN-C8	Scarcity
30	35	6

9387 BURLINGTON NORTHERN: 1981, with a bay window.

EX-C7	LN-C8	Scarcity
20	25	4

16500 ROCK ISLAND: 1987-88, bobber.

EX-C7	LN-C8	Scarcity
5	10	2

16501 LEHIGH VALLEY: 1987, with a traditionally sized offset cupola.

EX-C7	LN-C8	Scarcity
15	20	4

16503 NEW YORK CENTRAL: 1987, transfer.

EX-C7	LN-C8	Scarcity
10	15	4

16504 SOUTHERN: 1987, N5c porthole, Service Station Special item.

EX-C7	LN-C8	Scarcity
15	20	4

16505 WABASH: 1988-91, with a traditionally sized offset cupola.

EX-C7	LN-C8	Scarcity
5	10	2

16506 SANTA FE: 1988, with a bay window.

EX-C7	LN-C8	Scarcity
20	25	3

[16507] MOPAR EXPRESS: 1987-88, uncataloged, with a traditionally sized offset cupola, numbered "1987."

EX-C7	LN-C8	Scarcity
35	40	6

[16508] LIONEL LINES: 1989, uncataloged, with a traditionally sized offset cupola, numbered "6508."

EX-C7	LN-C8	Scarcity
8	12	4

16509 DENVER & RIO GRANDE WESTERN: 1989, with a traditionally sized offset cupola, Service Station Special item.

EX-C7	LN-C8	Scarcity
15	20	5

16510 NEW HAVEN: 1989, with a bay window.

EX-C7	LN-C8	Scarcity
15	20	4

16511 PENNSYLVANIA: Uncataloged in 1988, cataloged in 1989, bobber.

EX-C7	LN-C8	Scarcity
5	10	2

16513 UNION PACIFIC: 1989, with a traditionally sized offset cupola.

EX-C7	LN-C8	Scarcity
10	15	2

16515 LIONEL LINES: 1989, RailScope with a traditionally sized offset cupola.

EX-C7	LN-C8	Scarcity
15	20	5

16516 LEHIGH VALLEY: 1990, with a traditionally sized offset cupola.

EX-C7	LN-C8	Scarcity
15	20	4

16517 ATLANTIC COAST LINE: 1990, with a bay window.

EX-C7	LN-C8	Scarcity
15	20	4

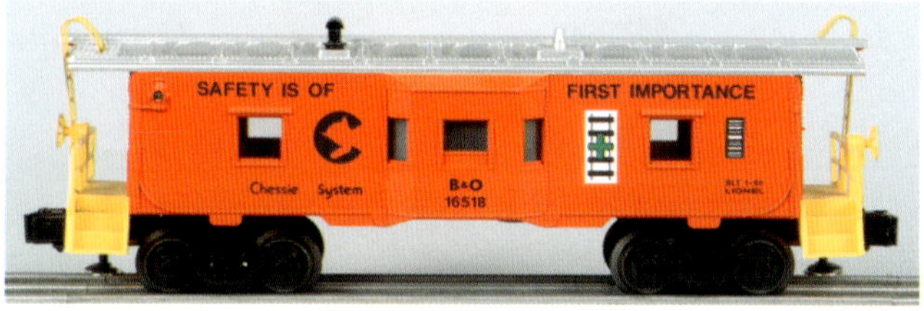

16518 CHESSIE SYSTEM: 1990, with a bay window.

EX-C7	LN-C8	Scarcity
30	35	4

16519 ROCK ISLAND: 1990, transfer.

EX-C7	LN-C8	Scarcity
10	15	2

[16520] "WELCOME TO THE SHOW" CIRCUS: 1989, uncataloged, with a traditionally sized offset cupola.

EX-C7	LN-C8	Scarcity
10	15	5

16521 PENNSYLVANIA: 1990-91, traditionally sized offset cupola.

EX-C7	LN-C8	Scarcity
5	8	3

16522 "CHILLS & THRILLS" CIRCUS: 1990-91, N5c porthole.

EX-C7	LN-C8	Scarcity
5	8	5

16523 ALASKA RAILROAD: 1991, with a traditionally sized offset cupola.

EX-C7	LN-C8	Scarcity
20	25	4

[16524] ANHEUSER-BUSCH: 1989-92, uncataloged, with a traditionally sized offset cupola.

EX-C7	LN-C8	Scarcity
25	30	5

16525 DELAWARE & HUDSON: 1991, with a bay window, Service Station Special item.

EX-C7	LN-C8	Scarcity
25	30	5

16526 KANSAS CITY SOUTHERN: 1991, with a traditionally sized offset cupola.

EX-C7	LN-C8	Scarcity
10	15	4

16527 WESTERN PACIFIC: 1992.

EX-C7	LN-C8	Scarcity
Cataloged, but not produced.		

[16528] UNION PACIFIC: 1990-91, uncataloged, with a traditionally sized offset cupola, numbered "6528."

EX-C7	LN-C8	Scarcity
10	15	4

[16529] SANTA FE: 1991, traditionally sized offset cupola, numbered "16829."

EX-C7	LN-C8	Scarcity
8	10	4

[16530] MICKEY'S WORLD TOUR: 1991-92, uncataloged, with a traditionally sized offset cupola, numbered "16830."

EX-C7	LN-C8	Scarcity
10	15	3

16531 TEXAS AND PACIFIC: 1992, with a traditionally sized offset cupola.

EX-C7	LN-C8	Scarcity
15	20	3

16533 CHICAGO & NORTHWESTERN: 1992, with a bay window.

EX-C7	LN-C8	Scarcity
20	25	4

16534 DELAWARE AND HUDSON: 1992, with a traditionally sized offset cupola.

EX-C7	LN-C8	Scarcity
10	15	4

16535 ERIE-LACKAWANNA: 1991, uncataloged, with a bay window.

EX-C7	LN-C8	Scarcity
25	30	5

16536 CHESSIE SYSTEM: Cataloged in 1992, uncataloged in 1993, and again uncataloged from 1994-99, traditionally sized caboose with an offset cupola.

16536 CHESSIE SYSTEM (Type I): A yellow, four-window-per-side caboose was produced through 1996.

EX-C7	LN-C8	Scarcity
10	15	4

16536 CHESSIE SYSTEM (Type II): When production began in 1997, the caboose was red, and had only two windows on each side of the body.

EX-C7	LN-C8	Scarcity
10	15	4

16537 MISSOURI-KANSAS-TEXAS: Cataloged in 1992, uncataloged in 1993, with a traditionally sized offset cupola.

EX-C7	LN-C8	Scarcity
10	15	4

[16538] LOUISVILLE AND NASHVILLE: 1992, uncataloged, with a bay window numbered "1041."

EX-C7	LN-C8	Scarcity
20	25	4

16538 LOUISVILLE AND NASHVILLE: 1992, Family Lines Steelside with smoke and 1/48-scale proportions.

EX-C7	LN-C8	Scarcity
Cataloged, but not produced.		

[16539] WESTERN PACIFIC: 1992, Steelside with smoke, numbered "539" with 1/48-scale proportions. This was a Service Station Special item.

EX-C7	LN-C8	Scarcity
35	40	5

[16541] MONTANA RAIL LINK: 1993, extended vision with smoke numbered "10131."

EX-C7	LN-C8	Scarcity
35	40	4

[16543] NEW YORK CENTRAL: 1993-99, with a traditionally sized offset cupola.

[16543] NEW YORK CENTRAL (Type I): Initially the caboose had four windows per side of the body.

EX-C7	LN-C8	Scarcity
10	15	4

[16543] NEW YORK CENTRAL (Type II): Beginning in 1998, the caboose had only two windows on each side of the body.

EX-C7	LN-C8	Scarcity
10	15	4

16544 UNION PACIFIC: 1993-95, with a traditionally sized offset cupola.

EX-C7	LN-C8	Scarcity
15	20	4

16546 CLINCHFIELD: 1993, with a traditionally sized offset cupola.

EX-C7	LN-C8	Scarcity
15	20	4

16547 HAPPY HOLIDAYS: 1993-95, with a traditionally sized offset cupola, produced in both two- and four-window variations.

EX-C7	LN-C8	Scarcity
30	35	4

16548 CONRAIL: 1993, with a traditionally sized offset cupola.

EX-C7	LN-C8	Scarcity
15	20	4

16549 SOO LINE: 1993.

EX-C7	LN-C8	Scarcity
15	20	4

16550 U.S. NAVY: 1994-95, searchlight.

EX-C7	LN-C8	Scarcity
10	15	4

16551 BUDWEISER: 1993-94, uncataloged, with a traditionally sized offset cupola.

16551 BUDWEISER (Type I): Initially the caboose had four windows per side of the body.

EX-C7	LN-C8	Scarcity
25	30	6

16551 BUDWEISER (Type II): In 1994, the caboose had only two windows on each side of the body.

EX-C7	LN-C8	Scarcity
25	30	6

16552 FRISCO: 1994, searchlight.

EX-C7	LN-C8	Scarcity
20	25	4

16553 UNITED AUTO WORKERS: 1993, uncataloged, with a traditionally sized offset cupola.

EX-C7	LN-C8	Scarcity
20	25	5

[16554] GRAND TRUNK WESTERN: 1994, extended vision caboose with smoke numbered "79052."

EX-C7	LN-C8	Scarcity
25	30	4

16555 CHESAPEAKE AND OHIO: 1994, with a traditionally sized offset cupola.

EX-C7	LN-C8	Scarcity
15	20	4

16557 FORD: 1994, uncataloged, with a traditionally sized offset cupola.

EX-C7	LN-C8	Scarcity
15	20	5

[16558] CRAYOLA: Uncataloged in 1994, cataloged in 1995, with a traditionally sized offset cupola.

[16558] CRAYOLA (Type I): Initially the caboose had four windows per side of the body.

EX-C7	LN-C8	Scarcity
10	15	4

[16558] CRAYOLA (Type II): In 1995, the caboose had only two windows on each side of the body.

EX-C7	LN-C8	Scarcity
10	15	4

[16559] SEABOARD: 1995, command control-equipped, numbered "5658."

EX-C7	LN-C8	Scarcity
15	20	4

16560 CHRYSLER: 1994, uncataloged, Mopar.

EX-C7	LN-C8	Scarcity
15	20	5

[16561] UNION PACIFIC: 1995, command control-equipped, numbered "25766."

EX-C7	LN-C8	Scarcity
20	25	4

16562 READING: 1995, command control-equipped.

EX-C7	LN-C8	Scarcity
20	25	4

[16563] LIONEL LINES: 1995, with a traditionally sized offset cupola.

EX-C7	LN-C8	Scarcity
15	20	4

16564 WESTERN MARYLAND: 1995, command control-equipped, Service Station Special item.

EX-C7	LN-C8	Scarcity
20	25	4

16565 MILWAUKEE ROAD: 1995, with a bay window.

EX-C7	LN-C8	Scarcity
40	45	4

[16566] U.S. ARMY: 1995, traditionally sized offset cupola numbered "907."

EX-C7	LN-C8	Scarcity
15	20	4

[16568] SANTA FE: 1996-99, with a traditionally sized offset cupola.

EX-C7	LN-C8	Scarcity
15	20	4

16569 UNION PACIFIC: 1997.

EX-C7	LN-C8	Scarcity
17	25	4

16570 NDEM: 1996, extended vision.

EX-C7	LN-C8	Scarcity
Cataloged, but not produced.		

[16571] GEORGIA POWER: 1995, uncataloged, with a traditionally sized offset cupola numbered "52789."

EX-C7	LN-C8	Scarcity
40	50	6

[16575] SEARS ZENITH: 1995, with a traditionally sized offset cupola.

EX-C7	LN-C8	Scarcity
25	30	4

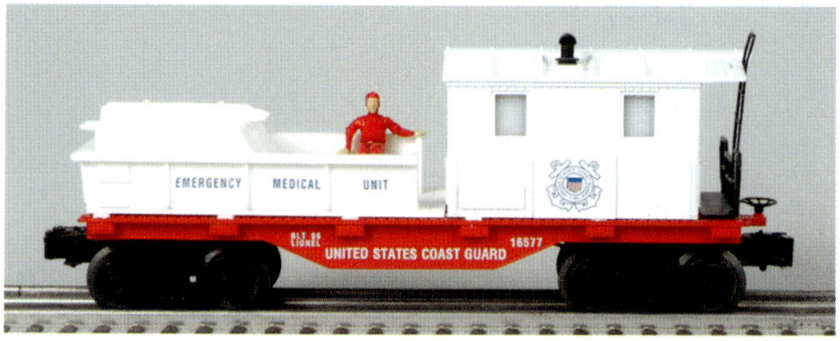

[16577] U.S. COAST GUARD: 1996.

EX-C7	LN-C8	Scarcity
15	20	4

16578 LIONEL LINES: 1995, uncataloged, with a traditionally sized offset cupola.

EX-C7	LN-C8	Scarcity
10	15	4

[16579] GM/AC DELCO: 1995, with a traditionally sized offset cupola.

EX-C7	LN-C8	Scarcity
20	25	6

[16580] LIONEL: 1996-99, with a traditionally sized offset cupola.

EX-C7	LN-C8	Scarcity
4	8	4

[16581] UNION PACIFIC: 1996, illuminated.

EX-C7	LN-C8	Scarcity
20	25	4

[16585] LIONEL LINES: 1997, illuminated, numbered "6257."

EX-C7	LN-C8	Scarcity
Cataloged, but not produced.		

[16586] SOUTHERN PACIFIC: 1997, illuminated, numbered "6357."

EX-C7	LN-C8	Scarcity
15	20	4

[16590] DODGE MOTORSPORTS: 1996, with a traditionally sized offset cupola, numbered "6950."

EX-C7	LN-C8	Scarcity
25	30	4

[16591] LITTLE LEAGUE BASEBALL: 1997, with a traditionally sized offset cupola, numbered "6397."

EX-C7	LN-C8	Scarcity
20	25	4

[16593] LIONEL BELT LINE: 1998, numbered "6257."

EX-C7	LN-C8	Scarcity
20	25	4

[16594] LIONEL: 1998, numbered "6357."

EX-C7	LN-C8	Scarcity
20	25	4

16645 AMTRAK: Cataloged in 1991, uncataloged in 1992, searchlight.

EX-C7	LN-C8	Scarcity
20	25	4

16804 LIONEL RAILROADER CLUB: 1991, uncataloged, with a bay window.

EX-C7	LN-C8	Scarcity
20	25	6

17600 NEW YORK CENTRAL: 1987, uncataloged, wood-sided with 1/48-scale proportions.

EX-C7	LN-C8	Scarcity
40	45	4

17601 SOUTHERN: 1988, wood-sided with 1/48-scale proportions.

EX-C7	LN-C8	Scarcity
40	45	4

17602 CONRAIL: 1987, wood-sided with 1/48-scale proportions.

EX-C7	LN-C8	Scarcity
90	120	4

17603 ROCK ISLAND: 1988, wood-sided with 1/48-scale proportions.

EX-C7	LN-C8	Scarcity
35	45	4

17604 LACKAWANNA: 1988, wood-sided with 1/48-scale proportions.

EX-C7	LN-C8	Scarcity
35	45	4

17605 READING: 1989, wood-sided with 1/48-scale proportions.

EX-C7	LN-C8	Scarcity
35	45	4

17606 NEW YORK CENTRAL: 1990, steel-side with smoke and 1/48-scale proportions.

EX-C7	LN-C8	Scarcity
50	60	4

17607 READING: 1990, steelside with smoke and 1/48-scale proportions.

EX-C7	LN-C8	Scarcity
50	60	4

17608 CHESAPEAKE AND OHIO: 1991, steelside with smoke and 1/48-scale proportions.

EX-C7	LN-C8	Scarcity
50	60	4

17610 WABASH: 1991, steelside caboose with smoke and 1/48-scale proportions.

EX-C7	LN-C8	Scarcity
50	60	4

[17611] NEW YORK CENTRAL: Uncataloged in 1990, cataloged in 1991, wood-sided, numbered "6003" with 1/48-scale proportions.

EX-C7	LN-C8	Scarcity
50	60	4

17612 NICKEL PLATE ROAD: 1992, steelside with smoke, Fallen Flags number six with 1/48-scale proportions.

EX-C7	LN-C8	Scarcity
50	60	4

[17613] SOUTHERN: 1992, steelside with smoke, numbered "7613" with 1/48-scale proportions.

EX-C7	LN-C8	Scarcity
50	60	4

17615 NORTHERN PACIFIC: 1992, wood-sided with smoke and 1/48-scale proportions.

EX-C7	LN-C8	Scarcity
50	60	4

17617 DENVER & RIO GRANDE WESTERN: 1995, steelside caboose with 1/48-scale proportions.

EX-C7	LN-C8	Scarcity
50	60	4

17618 FRISCO: 1995, wood-sided with 1/48-scale proportions.

EX-C7	LN-C8	Scarcity
50	60	4

[17620] NORTHERN PACIFIC: 1998, wood-sided, numbered "1746."

EX-C7	LN-C8	Scarcity
50	60	4

[17623] FARMRAIL: 1999, extended vision.

EX-C7	LN-C8	Scarcity
50	60	5

[17624] CONRAIL: 1999, extended vision, numbered "6900."

EX-C7	LN-C8	Scarcity
45	50	4

[17625] BURLINGTON NORTHERN: 1999, steelside, numbered "7606."

EX-C7	LN-C8	Scarcity
50	60	4

[17626] SERVICE CENTER: 2000, extended vision. Service Station Special item.

EX-C7	LN-C8	Scarcity
20	25	5

[17630] 100TH ANNIVERSARY: 2000, die-cast gold caboose "2000."

EX-C7	LN-C8	Scarcity
290	325	5

[17635] 100TH ANNIVERSARY: 2000, gold-plated, numbered "2000."

EX-C7	LN-C8	Scarcity
325	350	5

[17636] NEW YORK CENTRAL: 2000-01, die-cast semi-scale, numbered "18096."

EX-C7	LN-C8	Scarcity
90	100	4

[17637] NEW YORK CENTRAL/P & LE: 2000, die-cast semi-scale, numbered "21."

EX-C7	LN-C8	Scarcity
90	100	4

17880 DENVER & RIO GRANDE WESTERN: 1990, uncataloged, LCCA, wood-sided with 1/48-scale proportions.

EX-C7	LN-C8	Scarcity
60	65	6

[18556] CHICAGO & ILLINOIS MIDLAND: 1992, uncataloged, Sears caboose and freight car set.

EX-C7	LN-C8	Scarcity
95	120	6

19700 CHESSIE SYSTEM: 1988, extended vision.

EX-C7	LN-C8	Scarcity
50	60	4

19701 MILWAUKEE ROAD: 1988, N5c porthole. Fallen Flags number two.

EX-C7	LN-C8	Scarcity
50	60	5

19702 PENNSYLVANIA: 1987, N5c porthole.

EX-C7	LN-C8	Scarcity
40	50	4

CABOOSES

19703 GREAT NORTHERN: 1988, extended vision. Fallen Flags number three.

EX-C7	LN-C8	Scarcity
40	50	5

19704 WESTERN MARYLAND: 1989, extended vision with smoke. Fallen Flags number four.

EX-C7	LN-C8	Scarcity
35	45	5

19705 CP RAIL: 1989, extended vision with smoke.

EX-C7	LN-C8	Scarcity
30	40	4

[19706] UNION PACIFIC: 1989, extended vision with smoke, numbered "9706."

EX-C7	LN-C8	Scarcity
30	40	4

19707 SOUTHERN PACIFIC: 1990, with searchlight and smoke.

EX-C7	LN-C8	Scarcity
60	65	5

[19708] LIONEL LINES: 1990, with a bay window, numbered "1990."

EX-C7	LN-C8	Scarcity
30	40	4

19709 PENNSYLVANIA: 1989 and 1991, with smoke.

EX-C7	LN-C8	Scarcity
60	65	5

19710 FRISCO: 1991, extended vision with smoke, Fallen Flags number five.

EX-C7	LN-C8	Scarcity
30	40	5

19711 NORFOLK SOUTHERN: 1992, extended vision with smoke.

EX-C7	LN-C8	Scarcity
40	50	4

19712 PENNSYLVANIA: 1991, N5c porthole.

EX-C7	LN-C8	Scarcity
30	40	4

19714 NEW YORK CENTRAL: 1992, with searchlight and smoke.

EX-C7	LN-C8	Scarcity
60	80	4

[19715] DM & IR: 1992, uncataloged, extended vision, numbered "C-217."

EX-C7	LN-C8	Scarcity
45	50	4

[19716] ILLINOIS CENTRAL: 1993, extended vision with smoke, numbered "9405."

EX-C7	LN-C8	Scarcity
60	70	4

[19717] SUSQUEHANNA: 1993, with a bay window, numbered "0121."

EX-C7	LN-C8	Scarcity
30	40	4

[19718] CHICAGO & ILLINOIS MIDLAND: 1992, uncataloged, extended vision, numbered "74."

EX-C7	LN-C8	Scarcity
30	40	5

[19719] ERIE: 1993, with a bay window, numbered "C-300," Fallen Flags number seven.

EX-C7	LN-C8	Scarcity
25	30	5

19720 SOO LINE: 1983, extended vision, Service Station Special item.

EX-C7	LN-C8	Scarcity
25	30	5

[19721] GULF, MOBILE & OHIO: 1993, uncataloged, extended vision, numbered "2956."

EX-C7	LN-C8	Scarcity
25	30	5

19723 DISNEY: 1994, extended vision.

EX-C7	LN-C8	Scarcity
30	35	4

[19724] MISSOURI-KANSAS-TEXAS: 1994, uncataloged, JCPenney extended vision, numbered "125."

EX-C7	LN-C8	Scarcity
25	30	5

19726 NEW YORK CENTRAL: 1995, with a bay window, Service Station Special item.

EX-C7	LN-C8	Scarcity
25	30	5

[19727] PENNSYLVANIA: 1996, N5c porthole, numbered "477938."

EX-C7	LN-C8	Scarcity
15	20	4

[19728] NORFOLK AND WESTERN: 1996, with a bay window.

EX-C7	LN-C8	Scarcity
35	40	4

[19732] SANTA FE: 1996, with a bay window, numbered "6517."

EX-C7	LN-C8	Scarcity
35	40	4

[19733] NEW YORK CENTRAL: 1996, numbered "6357."

EX-C7	LN-C8	Scarcity
10	15	3

[19734] SOUTHERN PACIFIC: 1996, numbered "6357."

EX-C7	LN-C8	Scarcity
10	15	3

[19736] PENNSYLVANIA: 1997, Tuscan N5c porthole, numbered "6417," "Buffalo Zone."

EX-C7	LN-C8	Scarcity
15	20	4

[19737] LACKAWANNA: 1997, searchlight, numbered "2420."

EX-C7	LN-C8	Scarcity
35	40	4

[19738] CONRAIL: 1997, N5c porthole, numbered "6417," Service Station Special item.

EX-C7	LN-C8	Scarcity
35	40	5

[19739] NEW YORK CENTRAL: 1997, wood-sided, numbered "6907."

EX-C7	LN-C8	Scarcity
30	35	4

[19740] VIRGINIAN: 1997, uncataloged, N5c porthole, numbered "6427."

EX-C7	LN-C8	Scarcity
30	35	4

[19741] PENNSYLVANIA: 1998, N5c porthole, numbered "6417."

EX-C7	LN-C8	Scarcity
25	30	4

[19742] ERIE: 1998, with a bay window, with caboose Talk "C301."

EX-C7	LN-C8	Scarcity
35	40	5

[19748] SPOKANE, PORTLAND AND SEATTLE: 1997, uncataloged, bay window, numbered "6517."

EX-C7	LN-C8	Scarcity
20	25	5

[19749] SOUTHERN PACIFIC: 1998, bay window, numbered "6517."

EX-C7	LN-C8	Scarcity
50	60	5

[19750] 1998 HOLIDAY MUSIC: 1998, bay window.

EX-C7	LN-C8	Scarcity
100	125	4

[19751] PENNSYLVANIA: 1998 N5c porthole, numbered "492418."

EX-C7	LN-C8	Scarcity
20	25	4

[19752] NORTHERN PACIFIC: 1998, bay window, numbered "407."

EX-C7	LN-C8	Scarcity
25	30	4

[19753] UNION PACIFIC: 1998, extended vision, numbered "25641."

EX-C7	LN-C8	Scarcity
25	30	4

[19754] NEW YORK CENTRAL: 1998, numbered "20112."

EX-C7	LN-C8	Scarcity
25	30	4

[19755]: 1999, Centennial N5c porthole.

EX-C7	LN-C8	Scarcity
25	30	4

[19756] LIONEL LINES: 1999, with a bay window.

EX-C7	LN-C8	Scarcity
20	25	4

[19758] DL & W: 1999, numbered "6419."

EX-C7	LN-C8	Scarcity
25	30	4

[19759] CORVETTE: 1999, N5c porthole.

EX-C7	LN-C8	Scarcity
25	30	4

[19774] LIONEL RAILROADER CLUB: 1999, uncataloged, N5c porthole, numbered "1999."

EX-C7	LN-C8	Scarcity
25	30	5

[19778] SOUTHERN/CASE CUTLERY: 1999, uncataloged, wood-sided, numbered "1889" with 1/48-scale proportions.

EX-C7	LN-C8	Scarcity
Too rarely traded to establish accurate pricing.		

[19779] SOUTHERN PACIFIC: 1999, with a bay window, numbered "1908."

EX-C7	LN-C8	Scarcity
25	30	5

[19780] LEHIGH VALLEY: 1999-2000, N5c porthole, numbered "641751."

EX-C7	LN-C8	Scarcity
25	30	5

[19781] VAPOR RECORDS: 1999-2000, Holiday N5c porthole, numbered "6417."

EX-C7	LN-C8	Scarcity
20	25	4

[19782] NEW YORK CENTRAL: 2000, bay window, numbered "21719."

EX-C7	LN-C8	Scarcity
35	40	4

[19785] SOUTHERN PACIFIC: 2000, bay window, numbered "6517."

EX-C7	LN-C8	Scarcity
25	30	4

[19786] PENNSYLVANIA: 2000, uncataloged, extended vision.

EX-C7	LN-C8	Scarcity
20	25	4

19807 PENNSYLVANIA: 1988, extended vision with smoke.

EX-C7	LN-C8	Scarcity
20	25	4

[19889] PENNSYLVANIA: 2000, with a bay window with Crewtalk, numbered "477719."

EX-C7	LN-C8	Scarcity
100	125	4

[19890] SANTA FE: 2000, with a bay window with Crewtalk, numbered "999211."

EX-C7	LN-C8	Scarcity
100	125	4

[19957] AMBASSADOR: 1997, uncataloged, numbered "1997."

EX-C7	LN-C8	Scarcity
275	350	6

[19958] AMBASSADOR: 1998, uncataloged, silver, numbered "1998" with 1/48-scale proportions.

EX-C7	LN-C8	Scarcity
350	500	7

[19959] AMBASSADOR: 1998, uncataloged, gold, numbered "1998" with 1/48-scale proportions.

EX-C7	LN-C8	Scarcity
550	800	8

[21719] MAINE CENTRAL: 1999, bay window.

EX-C7	LN-C8	Scarcity
40	50	4

[26502] UNION PACIFIC: 1997, with a bay window, numbered "6517."

EX-C7	LN-C8	Scarcity
30	35	4

[26503] SANTA FE: 1997, high-cupola, numbered "7606R."

EX-C7	LN-C8	Scarcity
55	65	4

[26504] MOBIL OIL: 1997, uncataloged, square window, numbered "6257."

EX-C7	LN-C8	Scarcity
15	20	4

[26505] LIONELVILLE FIRE CO.: 1998.

EX-C7	LN-C8	Scarcity
25	30	4

[26506] NORFOLK AND WESTERN: 1998, square window, numbered "562748."

EX-C7	LN-C8	Scarcity
10	15	3

[26507] DELAWARE AND HUDSON: 1998, square window, numbered "35707."

EX-C7	LN-C8	Scarcity
10	15	3

[26508] ALASKA RAILROAD: 1998, square window, numbered "1081."

EX-C7	LN-C8	Scarcity
15	20	4

[26511] QUAKER OATS: 1998, uncataloged, square window.

EX-C7	LN-C8	Scarcity
30	35	5

[26513] NEW YORK CENTRAL: 1999, emergency, numbered "26505."

EX-C7	LN-C8	Scarcity
20	25	4

[26515] LIONEL LINES: 1999, bobber.

EX-C7	LN-C8	Scarcity
3	8	2

[26516] SAFARI RR: 1999, uncataloged, bobber.

EX-C7	LN-C8	Scarcity
3	8	2

[26519] CHRISTMAS: 1999, numbered "6496."

EX-C7	LN-C8	Scarcity
20	25	4

[26520] BETHLEHEM STEEL: 1999, numbered "6130," Service Station Special item.

EX-C7	LN-C8	Scarcity
25	30	5

[26523] KEEBLER CHEEZIT: 1999, uncataloged, square window.

EX-C7	LN-C8	Scarcity
Too rarely traded to establish accurate pricing.		

[26524] NEW YORK CENTRAL: 1999, uncataloged, square window, numbered "295."

EX-C7	LN-C8	Scarcity
10	15	4

[26528] PENNSYLVANIA: 1999, square window, numbered "6257."

EX-C7	LN-C8	Scarcity
10	15	4

CABOOSES

[26530] LIONEL LINES: 1999, square window, numbered "6257."

EX-C7	LN-C8	Scarcity
10	15	4

[26532] NEW YORK CENTRAL: 2000, square window, numbered "296."

EX-C7	LN-C8	Scarcity
10	15	4

[26533] SOUTHERN PACIFIC: 2000, square window.

EX-C7	LN-C8	Scarcity
10	15	4

[26534] PENNSYLVANIA: 2000, square window, numbered "6257."

EX-C7	LN-C8	Scarcity
10	15	4

[26535] FRISCO: 2000, square window, numbered "1700."

EX-C7	LN-C8	Scarcity
10	15	4

[26536] CENTENNIAL EXPRESS: 2000, square window.

EX-C7	LN-C8	Scarcity
Too rarely traded to establish accurate pricing.		

[26537] LIONEL MINES: 2000, uncataloged, square window.

EX-C7	LN-C8	Scarcity
25	30	5

[26539] WHIRLPOOL: 2000, uncataloged, square window.

EX-C7	LN-C8	Scarcity
Too rarely traded to establish accurate pricing.		

[26543] GREAT NORTHERN: 2000-01, square window, "X66."

EX-C7	LN-C8	Scarcity
15	20	4

[26545] SNAP-ON: 2000, uncataloged, square window.

EX-C7	LN-C8	Scarcity
Too rarely traded to establish accurate pricing.		

[26548] PIONEER SEED: 2000, uncataloged, square window.

EX-C7	LN-C8	Scarcity
Too rarely traded to establish accurate pricing.		

[26552] MONOPOLY SHORT LINE: 2000, uncataloged, square window.

EX-C7	LN-C8	Scarcity
Too rarely traded to establish accurate pricing.		

26572: 2000, uncataloged, Lionel 20th Century square window.

EX-C7	LN-C8	Scarcity
15	20	4

51701 NEW YORK CENTRAL: 1991, semi-scale, numbered "19400."

EX-C7	LN-C8	Scarcity
100	125	5

[51702] PENNSYLVANIA: 1991-92, N-8, numbered "478039."

EX-C7	LN-C8	Scarcity
250	300	5

[52020] LONG ISLAND NLOE: 1993, uncataloged, with a bay window, numbered "8393."

EX-C7	LN-C8	Scarcity
50	60	6

[52036] TCA 40TH ANNIVERSARY: 1994, uncataloged.

EX-C7	LN-C8	Scarcity
35	40	6

[52047] COTTON BELT: 1993-94, uncataloged, Southwest TTOS wood-sided with smoke, numbered "1921" with 1/48-scale proportions.

EX-C7	LN-C8	Scarcity
50	60	6

[52050] SCHUYLKILL HAVEN BOROUGH DAY: 1994, uncataloged, with a traditionally sized offset cupola, numbered "1994."

EX-C7	LN-C8	Scarcity
25	30	6

[52079] SOUTHERN PACIFIC: 1996, uncataloged, TTOS bay window, numbered "1996."

EX-C7	LN-C8	Scarcity
35	40	6

[52102] SANTA FE: 1996, uncataloged, Chicagoland RR Club extended vision, numbered "999758."

EX-C7	LN-C8	Scarcity
55	65	6

[52103] SANTA FE: 1996, uncataloged, Chicagoland RR Club extended vision, numbered "999556."

EX-C7	LN-C8	Scarcity
55	65	6

[52139] DEPT. 56: 1997, uncataloged, square window, numbered "6256."

EX-C7	LN-C8	Scarcity
55	60	5

[52161] MONOPOLY: 1998, with a traditionally sized offset cupola, "M-1006."

EX-C7	LN-C8	Scarcity
40	50	6

[52165] ARTRAIN: 1997, uncataloged, square window, numbered "6256."

EX-C7	LN-C8	Scarcity
60	75	6

52206 LCCA SD40: 2000, uncataloged, with extended vision, numbered "2000."

EX-C7	LN-C8	Scarcity
Too rarely traded to establish accurate pricing.		

[52208] LIONEL LINES: 2000, uncataloged, extended vision.

EX-C7	LN-C8	Scarcity
125	150	5

[88011] CANADIAN NATIONAL: 1988, uncataloged, Lionel Collectors Association of Canada, wood-sided with 1/48-scale proportions.

EX-C7	LN-C8	Scarcity
300	325	6

[99002] LOONEY TUNES: 1999, uncataloged, square window.

EX-C7	LN-C8	Scarcity
Too rarely traded to establish accurate pricing.		

[99009] MICKEY'S HOLIDAY EXPRESS: 1999, uncataloged, S/W.

EX-C7	LN-C8	Scarcity
Too rarely traded to establish accurate pricing.		

CABOOSES

Chapter 7
CRANE CARS

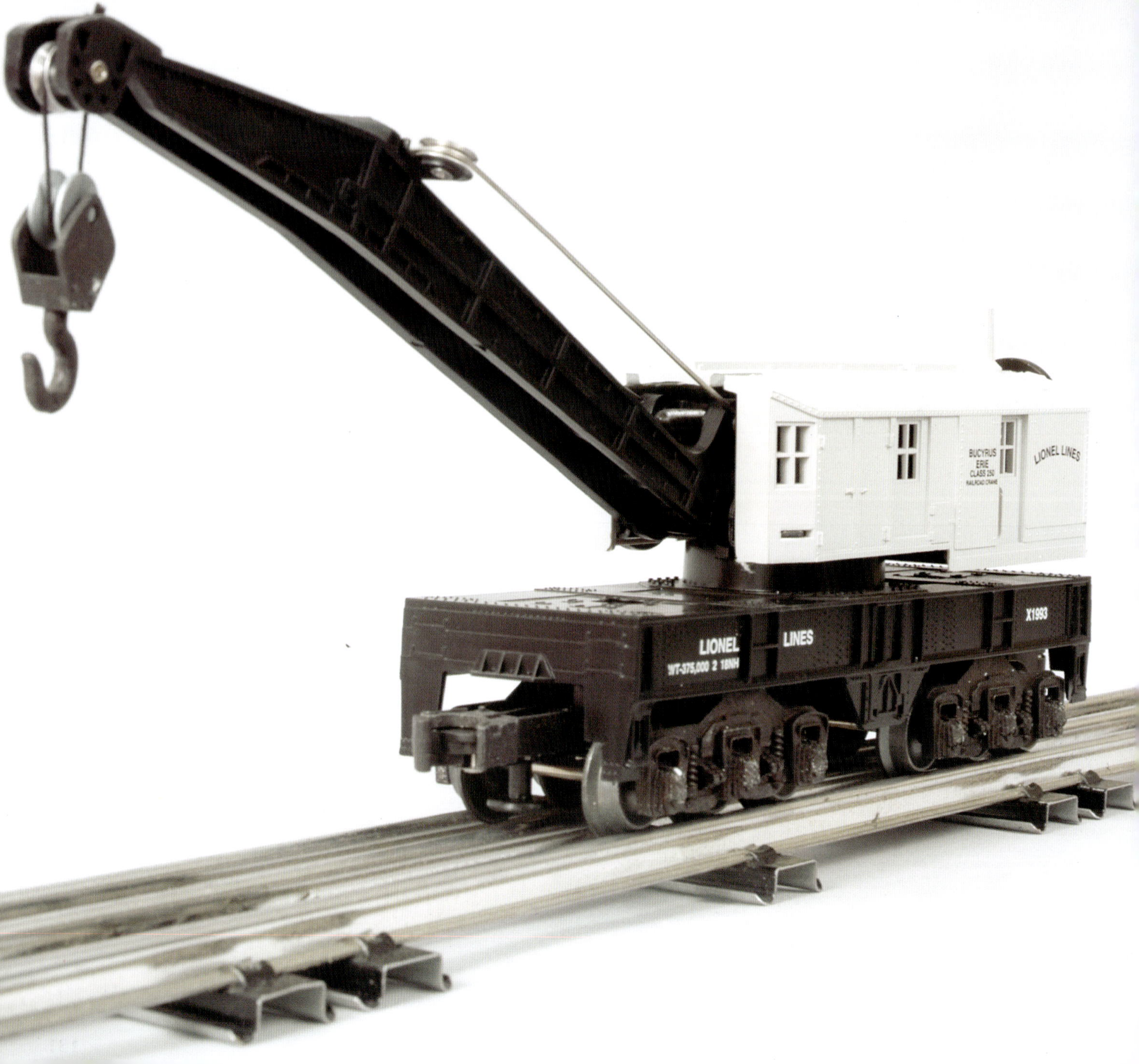

For real railroads, the wrecking crane or "big hook" is an expensive piece of equipment that the firms hope to rarely use. For a child with a train set, the crane adds a new dimension of play—lifting wrecked cars, unloading "Erector" bits from a gondola car, or relocating a line side block signal.

The first modern era crane was actually the last postwar crane. In 1971, MPC assembled, marketed and shipped 6560 Bucyrus Erie wrecking cranes made primarily, if not entirely, from surplus Lionel Corp. repair parts.

Since then, steady streams of cranes have been produced in a variety of colors. In 1981, six-wheel trucks returned to the crane car after an almost 30-year absence when Lionel began installing their new trucks designed for use on the 9500-series passenger cars.

But the Bucyrus-Erie crane was not the only postwar crane revived in the modern era. In 1981, the relatively simple derrick car was reintroduced as the 9378. It was such a faithful reproduction of the postwar 6670 that the latter masqueraded as the new car for the catalog illustration.

In 1988, the postwar 3360 Burro crane also returned to the product line, wearing a new number—18402. The diminutive motorized crane was an immediate hit with collectors as well as operators, and has been cataloged in a variety of colors and markings since then.

Lionel has not relied solely on postwar-derived cranes. In 1984, a newly created, short, and very inexpensive crane was introduced as a component of the 1403 Redwood Valley Express set. It has appeared only sporadically since, probably due to its relatively low quality.

6508 CANADIAN PACIFIC: 1981, 12-wheel crane car with maroon base and gray cab.

6508 CANADIAN PACIFIC (Type I): As described above.

EX-C7	LN-C8	Scarcity
30	45	5

6508 CANADIAN PACIFIC (Type II): In 1983, some cranes were overstamped to create this uncataloged LCOL crane car.

EX-C7	LN-C8	Scarcity
35	50	6

6510 UNION PACIFIC: 1982, yellow 12-wheel crane car.

EX-C7	LN-C8	Scarcity
30	35	5

6524 ERIE: 1984, 12-wheel crane car with yellow base and maroon cab.

EX-C7	LN-C8	Scarcity
25	35	5

6560 BUCYRUS ERIE: 1971, crane car.

EX-C7	LN-C8	Scarcity
60	95	6

[6567] ILLINOIS CENTRAL GULF: 1985, uncataloged LCCA 12-wheel crane car "100408."

EX-C7	LN-C8	Scarcity
25	35	5

[6574] REDWOOD VALLEY EXPRESS: 1984-85, flatcar with crane in the traditional 027/Scout size.

EX-C7	LN-C8	Scarcity
5	10	2

6576 SANTA FE: Cataloged in 1985-86, uncataloged in 1992, flatcar with crane in the traditional 027/Scout size.

EX-C7	LN-C8	Scarcity
3	6	1

6579 NEW YORK CENTRAL: 1985-86, eight-wheel crane car.

EX-C7	LN-C8	Scarcity
20	30	4

6593 SANTA FE: 1986, eight-wheel crane car, Service Station Special item.

EX-C7	LN-C8	Scarcity
25	35	6

9235 UNION PACIFIC: 1983-84, derrick car.

EX-C7	LN-C8	Scarcity
12	18	4

9236 CHICAGO & NORTHWESTERN: 1983-85, derrick car.

EX-C7	LN-C8	Scarcity
15	20	4

9245 ILLINOIS CENTRAL: 1985, derrick car.

EX-C7	LN-C8	Scarcity
Cataloged, but not produced.		

9329 CHESSIE SYSTEM: 1980, 12-wheel crane car.

EX-C7	LN-C8	Scarcity
30	35	5

9332 READING: 1979, eight-wheel crane car.

EX-C7	LN-C8	Scarcity
30	35	5

9348 SANTA FE: 1979, uncataloged eight-wheel crane car, Famous American Railroads number 1.

EX-C7	LN-C8	Scarcity
30	35	5

[9364] NORFOLK AND WESTERN: 1979, flatcar with crane "9325" in the traditional 027/Scout size.

EX-C7	LN-C8	Scarcity
3	5	1

9378 LIONEL: 1980-82, derrick car.

EX-C7	LN-C8	Scarcity
10	15	3

16609 LEHIGH VALLEY: 1987, derrick car.

EX-C7	LN-C8	Scarcity
20	25	4

16644 AMTRAK: Cataloged in 1991, uncataloged in 1992, eight-wheel crane car.

EX-C7	LN-C8	Scarcity
35	40	5

16653 WESTERN PACIFIC: 1992, 12-wheel crane car, Service Station Special item.

EX-C7	LN-C8	Scarcity
45	55	5

16658 ERIE-LACKAWANNA: 1993, 12-wheel crane car.

EX-C7	LN-C8	Scarcity
35	45	5

16684 U.S. NAVY: 1994-95, crane car.

EX-C7	LN-C8	Scarcity
25	30	4

16709 NEW YORK CENTRAL: 1995, derrick car.

EX-C7	LN-C8	Scarcity
20	25	4

16717 JERSEY CENTRAL: 1996, eight-wheel crane car.

EX-C7	LN-C8	Scarcity
20	25	4

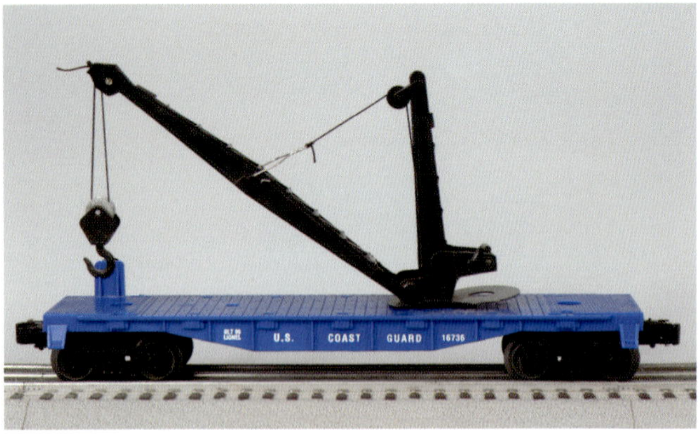

16736 U.S.C.G.: 1996, derrick car.

EX-C7	LN-C8	Scarcity
20	25	4

[16746] PORT OF LIONEL CITY: 1997, derrick car.

EX-C7	LN-C8	Scarcity
15	20	4

[16997] LIONEL LINES RECOVERY: 1999, 12-wheel crane car.

EX-C7	LN-C8	Scarcity
30	40	4

18402 LIONEL LINES: 1988, Burro Crane.

EX-C7	LN-C8	Scarcity
35	45	4

18405 SANTA FE: 1989, Burro Crane.

EX-C7	LN-C8	Scarcity
40	50	4

18410 PENNSYLVANIA: 1990, Burro Crane.

EX-C7	LN-C8	Scarcity
60	75	5

19402 GREAT NORTHERN: 1988, 12-wheel crane car, Fallen Flags number three.

EX-C7	LN-C8	Scarcity
25	30	5

19405 SOUTHERN: 1991, 12-wheel crane car.

EX-C7	LN-C8	Scarcity
50	60	4

19412 FRISCO: 1992, 12-wheel crane car.

EX-C7	LN-C8	Scarcity
40	50	5

[19834] LIONEL LINES: 1997, gray-cab 12-wheel crane car "2460."

EX-C7	LN-C8	Scarcity
25	30	4

[19837] LIONEL LINES: 1999, red-cab 12-wheel crane car "2460."

EX-C7	LN-C8	Scarcity
25	30	4

[19883] LIONEL LINES: 1999, Bucyrus Erie crane car "64608."

EX-C7	LN-C8	Scarcity
Too rarely traded to establish accurate pricing		

[52008] BUCYRUS ERIE: 1993, uncataloged gray-cab 12-wheel TCA crane car "1993X."

EX-C7	LN-C8	Scarcity
35	45	6

[52192] SOUTHERN PACIFIC: 2000, uncataloged TTOS crane and gondola two-pack.

EX-C7	LN-C8	Scarcity
60	75	6

[52193] SOUTHERN PACIFIC: 2000, uncataloged TTOS crane.

EX-C7	LN-C8	Scarcity
40	50	6

CRANE CARS

Chapter 8

FLATCARS AND INTERMODAL CARS

During the postwar era Lionel produced a huge variety of cars based on flatcars because they were not only interesting with their loads, they were also inexpensive to produce. While these two factors are still relevant during the modern era, there is one other factor that is perhaps even more important. During the 1940s, '50s and '60s, a huge amount of goods were moved in boxcars, today there is increasing reliance on intermodal transportation. Long trains of flatcars (or their derivatives) hauling seemingly endless streams of containers and semi-trailers have supplanted the boxcar of the past.

Over 15 basic body types of flatcars have been produced in the modern era. These range from the revived 1940s 2411-style die-cast flatcar, to the plastic 6511-type flatcar that was the mainstay of the postwar era, to totally new exciting designs such as the F-9 Well Car, center-beam flatcars as well as the intermodal-oriented TTUX and Maxi-stack cars.

Searchlight cars, log cars, maintenance cars and a host of other variations of the traditional flatcar continue to be produced as well. A collection of modern-era flatcars would be second in size only to a collection of house cars, and would certainly be more diverse.

The 1/48-scale proportioned, or "Standard 0" flatcars introduced in the mid-1970s are not to be forgotten either. Like the rest of the series, these cars suffered from lackluster sales, in recent years the increased interest in scale-like replicas has boosted their standing.

Lionel has packaged many of their flatcars with loads produced by outside vendors, including such collectible producers as Ertl. The values of the cars listed in this chapter are predicated on the original loads—and restraints (if applicable) to be present.

0781 LIONEL RAILROADER CLUB: 1983, uncataloged with trailers.

EX-C7	LN-C8	Scarcity
25	35	5

[1980] ATLANTIC TCA: 1980, uncataloged with trailers.

EX-C7	LN-C8	Scarcity
20	30	6

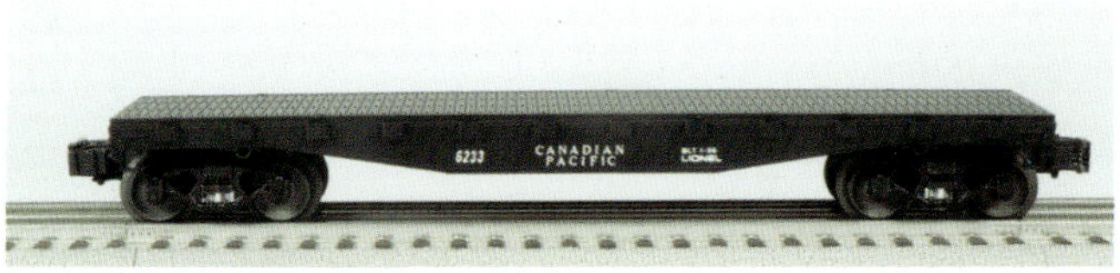

6233 CANADIAN PACIFIC: 1986, uncataloged with stakes with 1/48-scale proportions.

EX-C7	LN-C8	Scarcity
40	50	5

[6504] L.A.S.E.R.: 1981-82, with helicopter in the traditional 027/Scout size.

EX-C7	LN-C8	Scarcity
10	15	3

[6505] L.A.S.E.R.: 1981-82, Radar Car.

EX-C7	LN-C8	Scarcity
5	12	3

[6506] L.A.S.E.R.: 1981-82, Security Car.

EX-C7	LN-C8	Scarcity
10	15	3

[6507] L.A.S.E.R.: 1981-82, with cruise missile.

EX-C7	LN-C8	Scarcity
5	12	3

[6509] LIONEL: 1981, depressed center with girders.

EX-C7	LN-C8	Scarcity
30	35	5

6515 UNION PACIFIC: 1983-84 and 1986, in the traditional 027/Scout size.

EX-C7	LN-C8	Scarcity
3	5	3

6521 NEW YORK CENTRAL: 1984-85, with stakes with 1/48-scale proportions.

EX-C7	LN-C8	Scarcity
20	25	5

6522 CHICAGO & NORTHWESTERN: 1983-85, searchlight car.

EX-C7	LN-C8	Scarcity
15	20	4

6526 U.S. MARINES: 1984-85, searchlight car.

EX-C7	LN-C8	Scarcity
15	20	3

6529 NEW YORK CENTRAL: 1985-86, searchlight car.

EX-C7	LN-C8	Scarcity
15	20	3

6531 EXPRESS MAIL: 1985-86, with trailers.

EX-C7	LN-C8	Scarcity
20	25	3

[6561]: 1983-84, with cruise missile in the traditional 027/Scout size.

EX-C7	LN-C8	Scarcity
10	15	3

[6562]: 1983-84, with fences in the traditional 027/Scout size.

EX-C7	LN-C8	Scarcity
10	15	3

[6564]: 1983-84, with two U.S.M.C. tanks in the traditional 027/Scout size.

EX-C7	LN-C8	Scarcity
10	15	3

[6573] REDWOOD VALLEY EXPRESS: 1984-85, with dump bin in the traditional 027/Scout size.

EX-C7	LN-C8	Scarcity
5	10	2

[6574] REDWOOD VALLEY EXPRESS: 1984-85, with crane in the traditional 027/Scout size.

EX-C7	LN-C8	Scarcity
5	10	2

[6575] REDWOOD VALLEY EXPRESS: 1984-85, with fences in the traditional 027/Scout size.

EX-C7	LN-C8	Scarcity
5	10	2

6576 SANTA FE: Cataloged from 1985-86, uncataloged in 1992, with crane in the traditional 027/Scout size.

EX-C7	LN-C8	Scarcity
3	6	1

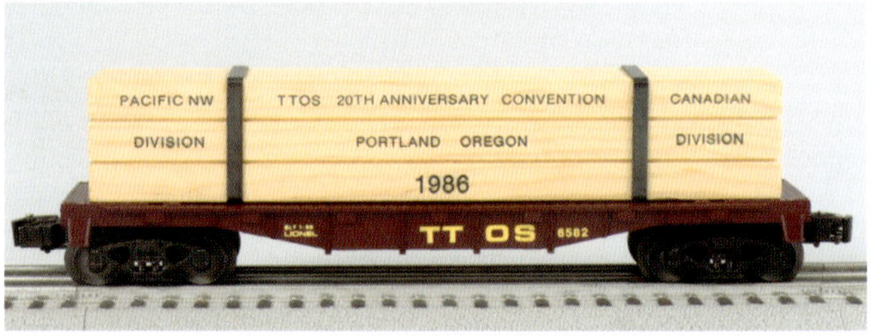

6582: 1986, uncataloged TTOS Portland with wood load.

EX-C7	LN-C8	Scarcity
30	50	5

6585 PENNSYLVANIA: 1986-90, with fences in the traditional 027/Scout size.

EX-C7	LN-C8	Scarcity
3	6	1

6587 W & ARR: 1986, uncataloged with horses.

EX-C7	LN-C8	Scarcity
10	15	1

9014 TRAILER TRAIN: 1978-79, in the traditional 027/Scout size.

EX-C7	LN-C8	Scarcity
Cataloged, but not produced.		

[9019]: 1978, unlettered in the traditional 027/Scout size.

EX-C7	LN-C8	Scarcity
2	4	1

9020 UNION PACIFIC: 1970-78, in the traditional 027/Scout size.

9020 UNION PACIFIC (Type I): Most of these cars were produced in various shades of yellow.

EX-C7	LN-C8	Scarcity
2	4	1

9020 UNION PACIFIC (Type II): A few of these cars were produced with Tuscan bodies.

EX-C7	LN-C8	Scarcity
15	20	6

9022 SANTA FE: 1970-72 and 1975-79, bulkhead in the traditional 027/Scout size.

9022 SANTA FE (Type I): Most of these cars were produced with red bodies.

EX-C7	LN-C8	Scarcity
5	10	2

9022 SANTA FE (Type II): Some of these cars were produced with black bodies.

EX-C7	LN-C8	Scarcity
8	15	4

9023 MISSOURI-KANSAS-TEXAS: 1973-74, bulkhead in the traditional 027/Scout size.

EX-C7	LN-C8	Scarcity
5	10	2

9024 CHESAPEAKE AND OHIO: 1973-75, in the traditional 027/Scout size.

EX-C7	LN-C8	Scarcity
3	5	1

9026 REPUBLIC STEEL: 1975-82, in the traditional 027/Scout size.

EX-C7	LN-C8	Scarcity
3	5	1

9120 NORTHERN PACIFIC: 1970-71, with trailers.

9120 NORTHERN PACIFIC (Type I): As first produced these cars were equipped with AAR trucks.

EX-C7	LN-C8	Scarcity
20	25	4

9120 NORTHERN PACIFIC (Type II): Later cars rode on Symington-Wayne trucks.

EX-C7	LN-C8	Scarcity
20	25	4

9121 LOUISVILLE & NASHVILLE: 1971-79, with bulldozer and scraper.

9121 LOUISVILLE & NASHVILLE (Type I): Some of these cars had bodies molded of maroon plastic.

EX-C7	LN-C8	Scarcity
35	45	5

9121 LOUISVILLE & NASHVILLE (Type II): Most of the cars had brown-molded bodies.

EX-C7	LN-C8	Scarcity
25	35	4

9122 NORTHERN PACIFIC: 1972-75, with trailers.

9122 NORTHERN PACIFIC (Type I): Some of these cars had molded green bodies similar to that of the 9120.

EX-C7	LN-C8	Scarcity
35	45	5

9122 NORTHERN PACIFIC (Type II): Most of these cars had molded Tuscan bodies.

EX-C7	LN-C8	Scarcity
20	25	4

9123 CHESAPEAKE AND OHIO: Uncataloged in 1972, cataloged from 1973-74, tri-level auto carrier.

EX-C7	LN-C8	Scarcity
15	20	4

[9123] TCA DEARBORN: 1973, uncataloged tri-level auto carrier numbered "1973."

EX-C7	LN-C8	Scarcity
25	30	6

9124 P & LE: 1973-74, with log load.

EX-C7	LN-C8	Scarcity
15	18	4

9125 NORFOLK AND WESTERN: 1973-77, bi-level auto carrier.

EX-C7	LN-C8	Scarcity
15	20	4

9126 CHESAPEAKE AND OHIO: 1973-75, tri-level auto carrier.

EX-C7	LN-C8	Scarcity
15	20	4

9129 NORFOLK AND WESTERN: 1975-76, tri-level auto carrier.

EX-C7	LN-C8	Scarcity
15	20	4

9133 BURLINGTON NORTHERN: 1976-77 and 1980, with trailers.

EX-C7	LN-C8	Scarcity
20	25	4

9139 PENN CENTRAL: 1976-77, tri-level auto carrier.

EX-C7	LN-C8	Scarcity
18	25	4

9145 ILLINOIS CENTRAL GULF: 1977-80, tri-level auto carrier.

EX-C7	LN-C8	Scarcity
15	20	4

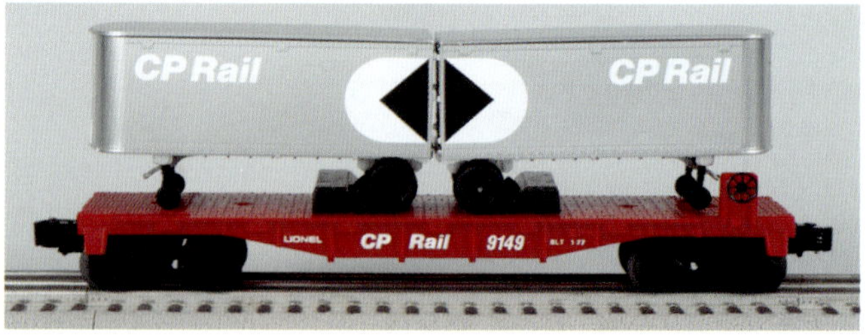

9149 CP RAIL: 1977-78, with trailers.

EX-C7	LN-C8	Scarcity
20	30	4

9157 CHESAPEAKE AND OHIO: 1976-78 and 1981-82, with crane.

EX-C7	LN-C8	Scarcity
25	35	4

9158 PENN CENTRAL: 1976-77 and 1980, with shovel.

EX-C7	LN-C8	Scarcity
25	35	4

9212 SEABOARD COAST LINE: 1976, uncataloged LCCA with trailers.

EX-C7	LN-C8	Scarcity
10	20	6

9216 GREAT NORTHERN: 1978, tri-level auto carrier.

EX-C7	LN-C8	Scarcity
20	25	4

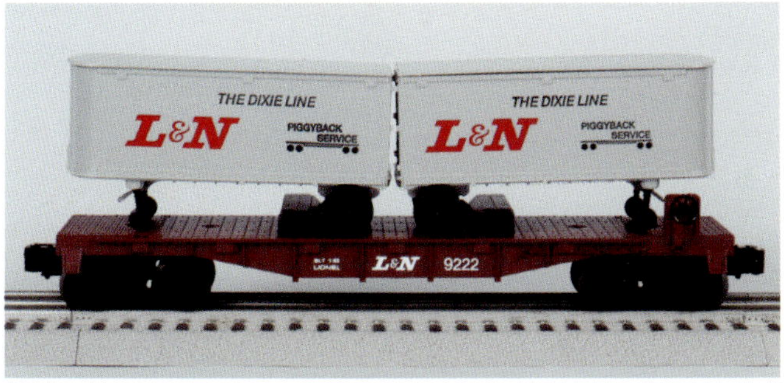

9222 LOUISVILLE & NASHVILLE: 1983-84, with trailers.

EX-C7	LN-C8	Scarcity
20	25	4

9226 DELAWARE & HUDSON: 1984-85, with trailers.

EX-C7	LN-C8	Scarcity
20	25	4

9232 ALLIS-CHALMERS: Cataloged from 1980-81, uncataloged in 1983, condenser car.

EX-C7	LN-C8	Scarcity
25	30	6

9233 DEPRESSED: 1980, center with transformer.

EX-C7	LN-C8	Scarcity
35	45	6

9234 LIONEL: 1980, Radioactive Waste car.

EX-C7	LN-C8	Scarcity
35	45	6

9235 UNION PACIFIC: 1983-84, derrick car.

EX-C7	LN-C8	Scarcity
12	18	4

9236 CHICAGO & NORTHWESTERN: 1983-85, derrick car.

EX-C7	LN-C8	Scarcity
15	20	4

9238 NORTHERN PACIFIC: 1984, log dump car.

EX-C7	LN-C8	Scarcity
12	18	4

9241 PENNSYLVANIA: 1985-86, log dump car.

EX-C7	LN-C8	Scarcity
12	18	4

9245 ILLINOIS CENTRAL: 1985, derrick car.

EX-C7	LN-C8	Scarcity
Cataloged, but not produced.		

9281 SANTA FE: 1978-80, tri-level auto carrier.

EX-C7	LN-C8	Scarcity
15	20	4

9282 GREAT NORTHERN: 1978-79 and 1981-82, with trailers.

EX-C7	LN-C8	Scarcity
15	20	4

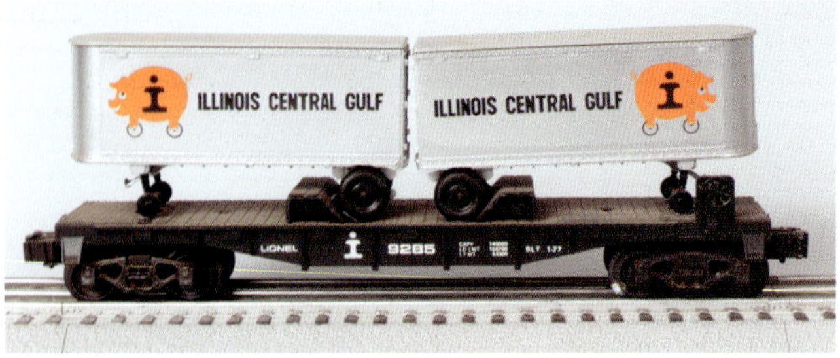

9285 ILLINOIS CENTRAL GULF: 1977, with trailers.

EX-C7	LN-C8	Scarcity
20	25	4

9300 PENN CENTRAL: 1970-75 and 1977, operating dump car.

9300 PENN CENTRAL (Type I): Some of these cars came with silver-painted turned wood helium tank loads.

EX-C7	LN-C8	Scarcity
8	14	3

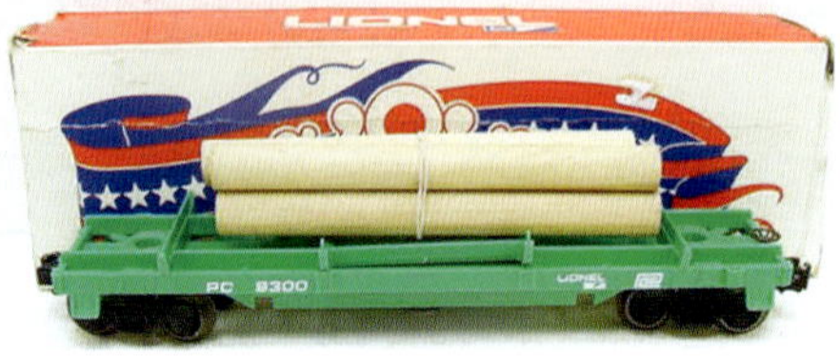

9300 PENN CENTRAL (Type II): Other cars came with wooden dowel "logs."

EX-C7	LN-C8	Scarcity
8	14	3

9302 LOUISVILLE & NASHVILLE: Uncataloged in 1972, cataloged from 1973-78, searchlight car.

EX-C7	LN-C8	Scarcity
10	15	3

9303 UNION PACIFIC: Uncataloged from 1974-78, cataloged in 1980, log dump car.

EX-C7	LN-C8	Scarcity
8	12	2

9306 SANTA FE: 1980-82, with horses.

EX-C7	LN-C8	Scarcity
8	12	3

9310 SANTA FE: Uncataloged in 1978, cataloged from 1979-83, log dump car.

EX-C7	LN-C8	Scarcity
7	13	2

9312 CONRAIL: Uncataloged in 1978, cataloged from 1979-83, searchlight car.

9312 CONRAIL (Type I): About half of the cars appear to have been produced with a gray superstructure mounted on the blue chassis.

EX-C7	LN-C8	Scarcity
7	13	4

9312 CONRAIL (Type II): The half of the cars had an orange superstructure mounted on the blue chassis.

EX-C7	LN-C8	Scarcity
7	13	4

9325 NORFOLK AND WESTERN: 1979-81, uncataloged with fences.

EX-C7	LN-C8	Scarcity
3	8	2

9333 SOUTHERN PACIFIC: 1979-80, with trailers.

EX-C7	LN-C8	Scarcity
15	20	4

9335 BALTIMORE AND OHIO: 1986, log dump car.

EX-C7	LN-C8	Scarcity
8	12	2

9345 READING: 1984-85, searchlight car.

EX-C7	LN-C8	Scarcity
15	20	4

9351 PENNSYLVANIA: 1980, tri-level auto carrier.

EX-C7	LN-C8	Scarcity
15	20	4

9352TRAILERTRAIN: 1980, with Chicago & Northwestern trailers.

EX-C7	LN-C8	Scarcity
25	35	4

[9363] NORFOLK AND WESTERN: 1979, with dump bin numbered "9325" in the traditional 027/Scout size.

EX-C7	LN-C8	Scarcity
3	5	1

[9364] NORFOLK AND WESTERN: 1979, with crane numbered "9325" in the traditional 027/Scout size.

EX-C7	LN-C8	Scarcity
3	5	1

9375 UNION PACIFIC: 1980, with fences in the traditional 027/Scout size.

EX-C7	LN-C8	Scarcity
Cataloged, but not produced.		

9378 LIONEL: 1980-82, derrick car.

EX-C7	LN-C8	Scarcity
10	15	3

9383 UNION PACIFIC: 1980, uncataloged with trailers, Famous American Railroads number two.

EX-C7	LN-C8	Scarcity
20	25	5

9389 LIONEL: 1981-82, radioactive waste car.

EX-C7	LN-C8	Scarcity
40	50	4

9553 W. & A.R.R.: Uncataloged in 1977, cataloged from 1978-80, with horses.

EX-C7	LN-C8	Scarcity
20	25	4

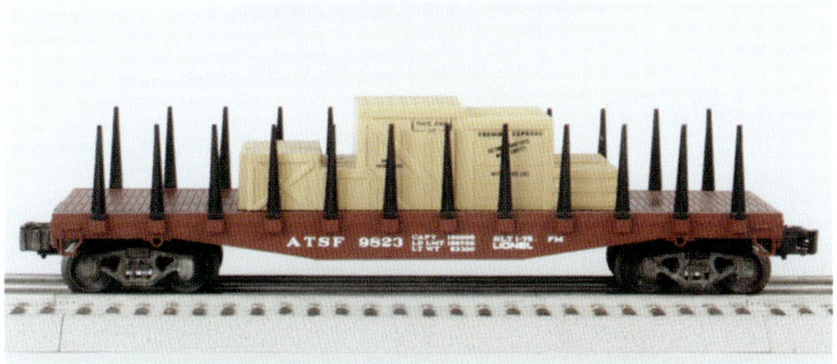

9823 SANTA FE: 1975-76, with crates with 1/48-scale proportions.

EX-C7	LN-C8	Scarcity
40	50	5

[16173] HAROLD THE HELICOPTER: 1998.

EX-C7	LN-C8	Scarcity
30	40	4

16208 PENNSYLVANIA: 1989, tri-level auto carrier with auto load. Load consists of three HO-sized Corvettes and Buick LeSabres.

EX-C7	LN-C8	Scarcity
25	30	4

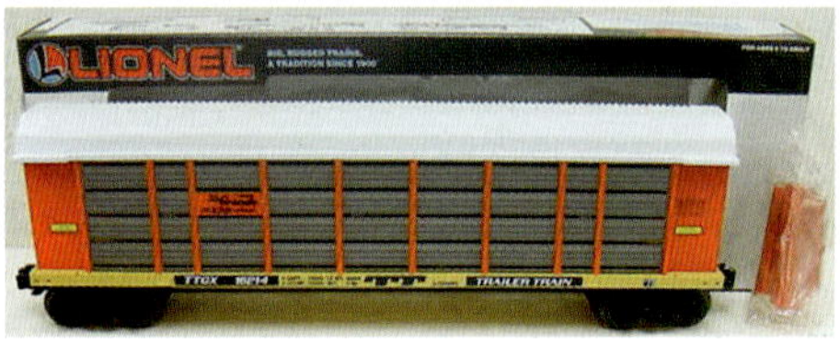

16214 DENVER & RIO GRANDE WESTERN: 1990, bi-level enclosed auto carrier.

EX-C7	LN-C8	Scarcity
20	25	4

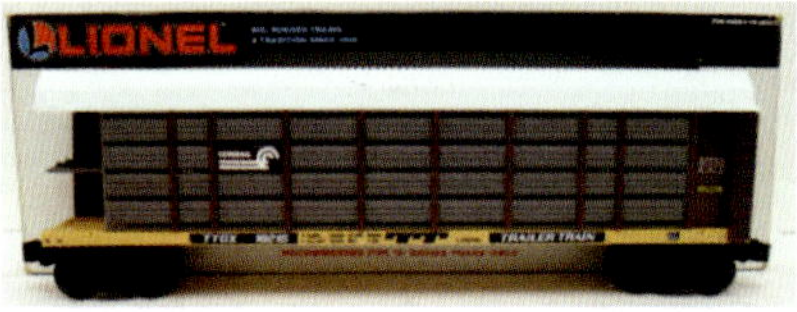

16215 CONRAIL: 1990, bi-level enclosed auto carrier.

EX-C7	LN-C8	Scarcity
20	25	4

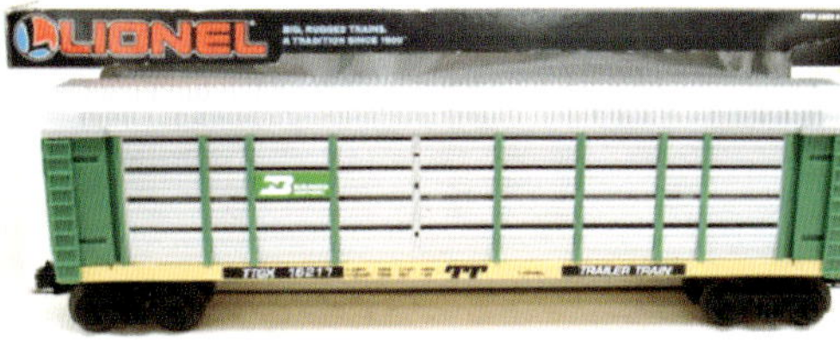

16217 BURLINGTON NORTHERN: 1992, bi-level enclosed auto carrier.

EX-C7	LN-C8	Scarcity
20	25	4

16228 UNION PACIFIC: 1992, bi-level enclosed auto carrier.

EX-C7	LN-C8	Scarcity
15	20	4

16229 ERIE-LACKAWANNA: 1991, uncataloged bi-level enclosed auto carrier.

EX-C7	LN-C8	Scarcity
20	25	4

16242 GRAND TRUNK WESTERN: 1993, bi-level enclosed auto carrier.

EX-C7	LN-C8	Scarcity
15	20	3

16253 SANTA FE: 1994, bi-level enclosed auto carrier.

EX-C7	LN-C8	Scarcity
20	25	4

16260 CHRYSLER: 1996, uncataloged bi-level enclosed auto carrier.

EX-C7	LN-C8	Scarcity
35	40	6

16300 ROCK ISLAND: 1987-88, with fences in the traditional 027/Scout size.

EX-C7	LN-C8	Scarcity
5	8	3

16301 LIONEL: 1987, barrel ramp car.

EX-C7	LN-C8	Scarcity
10	15	3

16303 PENNSYLVANIA: 1987, with trailers.

EX-C7	LN-C8	Scarcity
20	25	3

16306 SANTA FE: 1988, barrel ramp car.

EX-C7	LN-C8	Scarcity
5	8	3

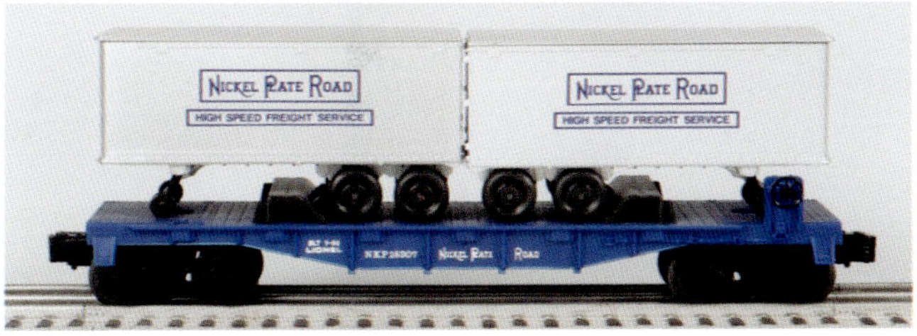

16307 NICKEL PLATE ROAD: 1988, with trailers.

EX-C7	LN-C8	Scarcity
20	25	4

16308 BURLINGTON NORTHERN: 1988-89, with trailer.

EX-C7	LN-C8	Scarcity
20	25	4

[16311] MOPAR EXPRESS: 1987-88, uncataloged with trailers numbered "1987."

EX-C7	LN-C8	Scarcity
80	100	5

16314 WABASH: 1989, with trailers.

EX-C7	LN-C8	Scarcity
15	20	3

16315 PENNSYLVANIA: Uncataloged in 1988, cataloged 1989, with fences in the traditional 027/Scout size.

EX-C7	LN-C8	Scarcity
5	8	2

16317 PENNSYLVANIA: 1989, barrel ramp car.

EX-C7	LN-C8	Scarcity
10	15	3

16318 LIONEL LINES: 1989, depressed center with cable reels.

EX-C7	LN-C8	Scarcity
15	20	4

16320 GREAT NORTHERN: 1990, barrel ramp car.

EX-C7	LN-C8	Scarcity
10	15	3

16321/16322 SEALAND TTUX: 1990, with trailers.

EX-C7	LN-C8	Scarcity
60	70	4

16323 LIONEL LINES: 1990, with trailers.

EX-C7	LN-C8	Scarcity
15	20	4

16324 PENNSYLVANIA: 1990, depressed center with cable reels.

EX-C7	LN-C8	Scarcity
10	15	4

16325 MICRORACERS EXHIBITION: 1989, uncataloged ramp car.

EX-C7	LN-C8	Scarcity
15	20	5

16326 SANTA FE: 1991, depressed center with cable reels.

EX-C7	LN-C8	Scarcity
10	15	4

16329 SOUTHERN PACIFIC: 1990-91, with horses in the traditional 027/Scout size.

EX-C7	LN-C8	Scarcity
10	15	4

16330 MISSOURI-KANSAS-TEXAS: 1991, with trailers.

EX-C7	LN-C8	Scarcity
20	25	4

16331 SOUTHERN: 1991, barrel ramp car.

EX-C7	LN-C8	Scarcity
Cataloged, but not produced.		

16332 LIONEL LINES: 1991, depressed center with transformer.

EX-C7	LN-C8	Scarcity
20	25	4

16333 FRISCO: 1991, bulkhead with wood load.

EX-C7	LN-C8	Scarcity
15	20	4

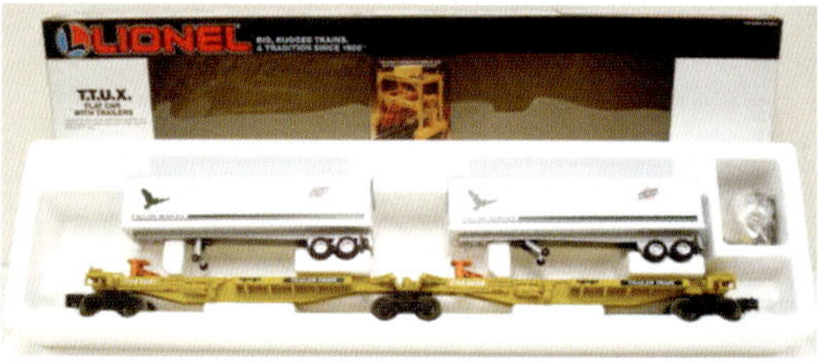

[16334] CHICAGO & NORTHWESTERN: 1991, TTUX set with trailers numbered "16337" and "16338."

EX-C7	LN-C8	Scarcity
30	40	5

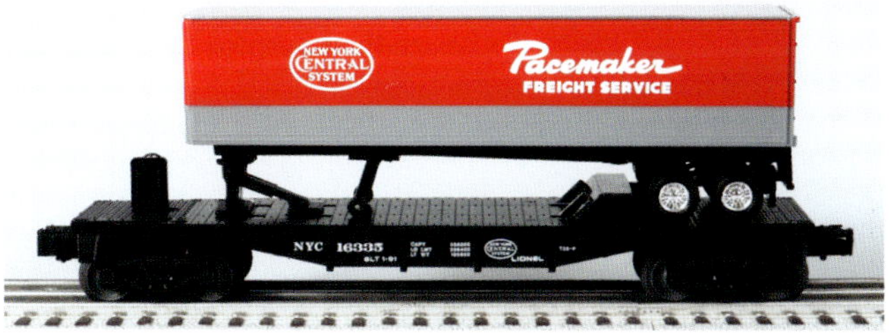

16335 NEW YORK CENTRAL: 1991, "Pacemaker" with trailer, Service Station Special item.

EX-C7	LN-C8	Scarcity
30	40	5

16337/16338 CHICAGO & NORTHWESTERN: TTUX with trailers (see 16334).

16340 AMTRAK: 1991, with stakes.

EX-C7	LN-C8	Scarcity
Cataloged, but not produced.		

16341 NEW YORK CENTRAL: 1992, depressed center with transformer.

EX-C7	LN-C8	Scarcity
15	20	4

16345/16346 SOUTHERN PACIFIC: 1992, TTUX set with trailers.

EX-C7	LN-C8	Scarcity
30	40	5

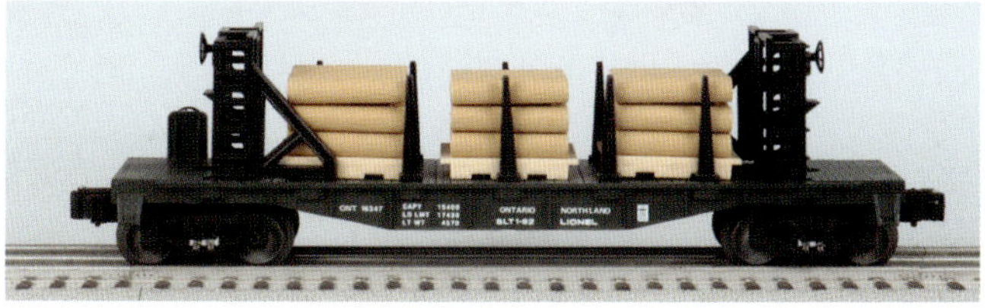

16347 ONTARIO NORTHLAND: 1992, bulkhead with pulp load.

EX-C7	LN-C8	Scarcity
20	25	4

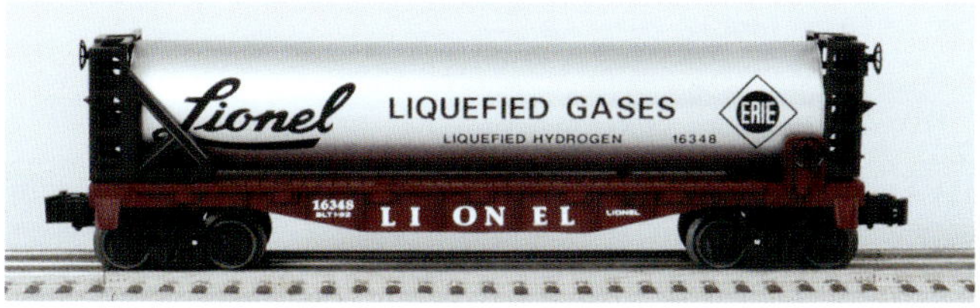

16348 LIONEL-ERIE: 1992, Liquefied Gas car.

EX-C7	LN-C8	Scarcity
20	25	4

16349 ALLIS CHALMERS: 1992, heat exchanger car.

EX-C7	LN-C8	Scarcity
20	25	4

16350 CP RAIL: 1991, uncataloged bulkhead with wood load.

EX-C7	LN-C8	Scarcity
15	20	4

16351 LIONEL: 1992, with U.S.N. submarine.

EX-C7	LN-C8	Scarcity
30	40	4

16352: 1992, with cruise missile.

EX-C7	LN-C8	Scarcity
25	30	4

16356 MISSOURI-KANSAS-TEXAS: 1992, depressed center with cable reels.

EX-C7	LN-C8	Scarcity
10	15	3

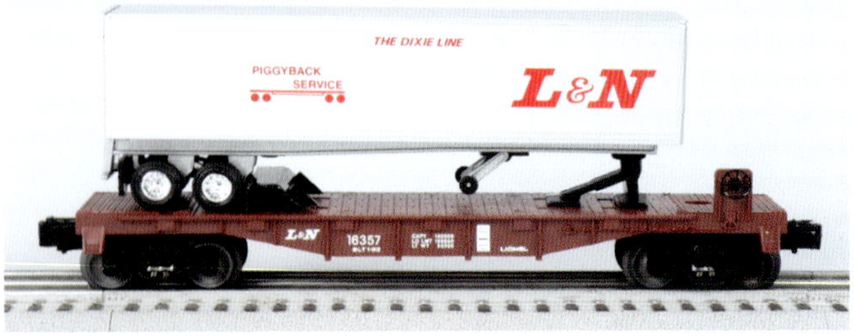

16357 LOUISVILLE AND NASHVILLE: 1992, with trailer.

EX-C7	LN-C8	Scarcity
20	25	3

[16360] NORFOLK AND WESTERN: 1993, Maxi-Stack set with containers numbered "16361" and "16362."

EX-C7	LN-C8	Scarcity
35	40	4

16361/16362 NORFOLK AND WESTERN: Maxi-Stack with containers (see 16360).

[16363] SOUTHERN TTUX: 1993, with trailers numbered "16364" and "16365."

EX-C7	LN-C8	Scarcity
35	40	4

16364/16365 SOUTHERN: TTUX with trailers (see 16363).

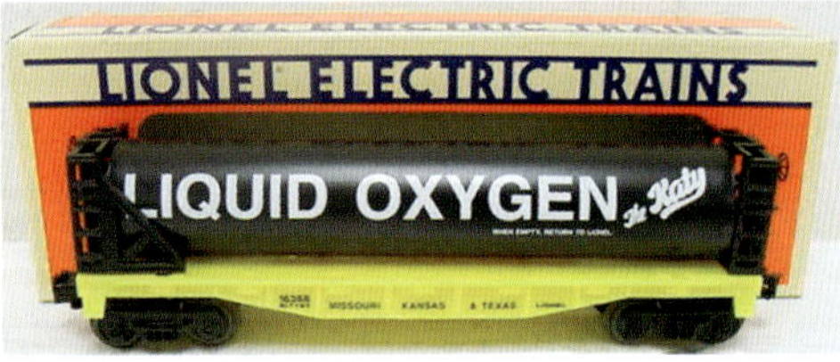

16368 MISSOURI-KANSAS-TEXAS: 1993, Liquid Oxygen car.

EX-C7	LN-C8	Scarcity
15	20	4

16369 AMTRAK: 1992, uncataloged with wheel load.

EX-C7	LN-C8	Scarcity
15	20	4

16370 AMTRAK: 1992, uncataloged with rail load.

EX-C7	LN-C8	Scarcity
15	20	4

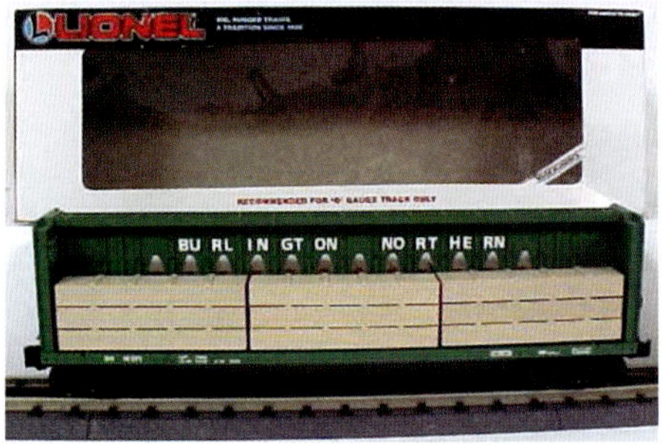

16371 BURLINGTON NORTHERN: 1992, uncataloged center beam with load.

EX-C7	LN-C8	Scarcity
20	25	4

16372 SOUTHERN: 1992, uncataloged center beam with load.

EX-C7	LN-C8	Scarcity
15	20	4

16373 ERIE-LACKAWANNA: 1993, with stakes.

EX-C7	LN-C8	Scarcity
15	20	4

16374 DENVER & RIO GRANDE WESTERN: 1993, with trailer.

EX-C7	LN-C8	Scarcity
20	25	4

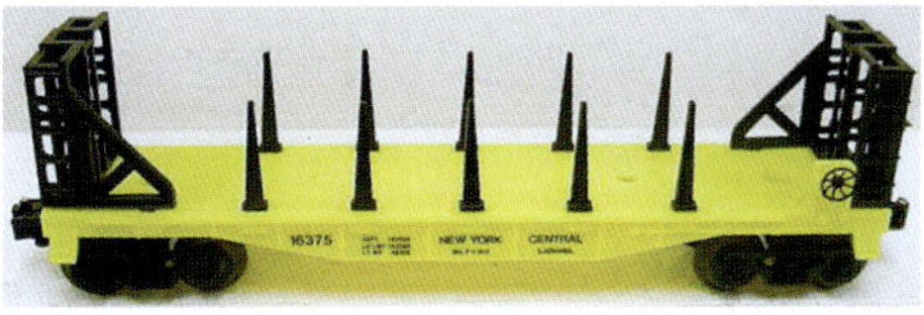

16375 NEW YORK CENTRAL: 1993-95, bulkhead.

EX-C7	LN-C8	Scarcity
15	20	4

16376 UNION PACIFIC: 1993-95, with trailer.

EX-C7	LN-C8	Scarcity
20	25	4

16378 TOYS "R" US: 1992-93, uncataloged with trailer.

EX-C7	LN-C8	Scarcity
60	80	6

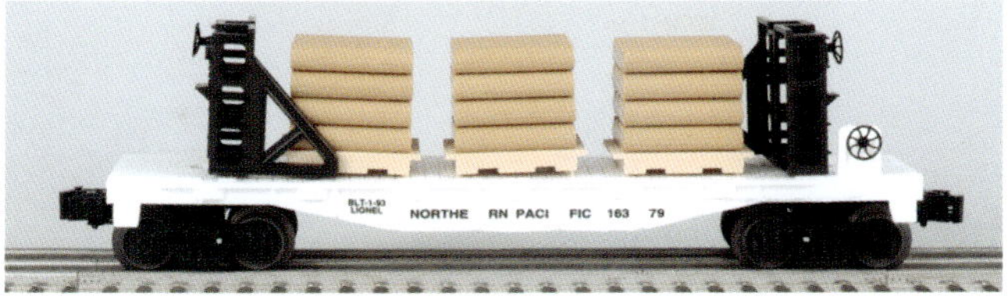

16379 NORTHERN PACIFIC: 1993, bulkhead with pulp load.

EX-C7	LN-C8	Scarcity
15	20	4

16380 UNION PACIFIC: 1993, center beam with load.

EX-C7	LN-C8	Scarcity
20	25	4

16381 CSX: 1993, center beam with load.

EX-C7	LN-C8	Scarcity
15	20	4

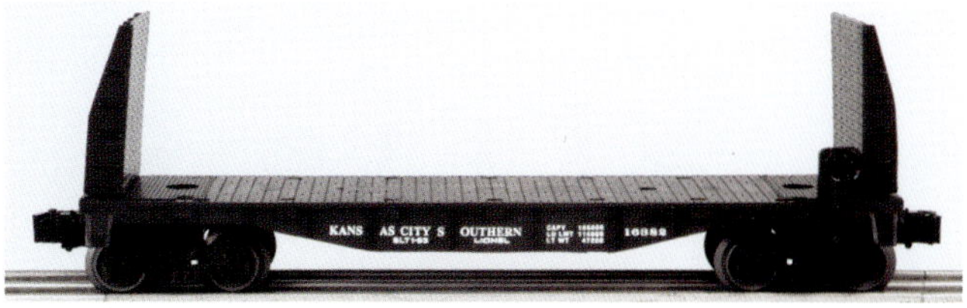

16382 KANSAS CITY SOUTHERN: 1993, bulkhead.

EX-C7	LN-C8	Scarcity
10	15	4

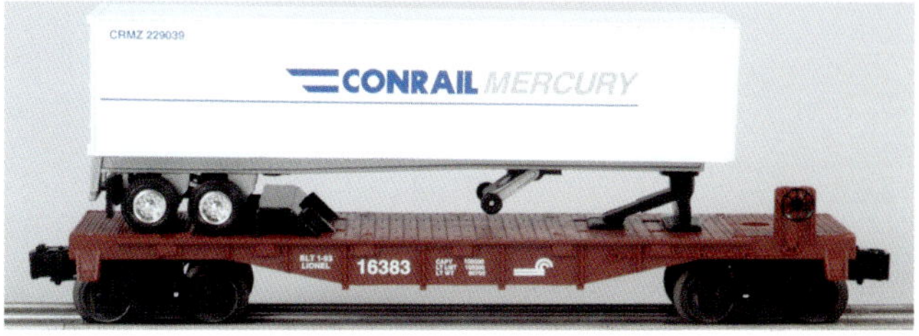

16383 CONRAIL: 1993, with trailer.

EX-C7	LN-C8	Scarcity
35	40	4

16386 SOUTHERN PACIFIC: 1994, with wood load.

EX-C7	LN-C8	Scarcity
10	15	4

16389 PENNSYLVANIA: 1994, with wheel load.

EX-C7	LN-C8	Scarcity
15	20	4

16390 LIONEL: 1994, with water tank.

EX-C7	LN-C8	Scarcity
15	20	4

16393 WISCONSIN CENTRAL: 1994, bulkhead.

EX-C7	LN-C8	Scarcity
5	10	3

16394 CENTRAL VERMONT: 1994 bulkhead.

EX-C7	LN-C8	Scarcity
15	20	4

16395 CANADIAN PACIFIC: 1994, with rail load.

EX-C7	LN-C8	Scarcity
10	15	4

16396 ALASKA RAILROAD: 1994, bulkhead.

EX-C7	LN-C8	Scarcity
10	15	4

16397 MILWAUKEE ROAD: 1994, center beam with load.

EX-C7	LN-C8	Scarcity
25	30	4

16398 CHESAPEAKE & OHIO: 1994, with trailer.

EX-C7	LN-C8	Scarcity
30	35	4

16399 WESTERN PACIFIC: 1994, center beam with load.

EX-C7	LN-C8	Scarcity
20	25	4

16601 CANADIAN NATIONAL: 1988, searchlight car.

EX-C7	LN-C8	Scarcity
10	15	4

16604 NEW YORK CENTRAL: 1987, log dump car.

EX-C7	LN-C8	Scarcity
15	20	4

16606 SOUTHERN: 1987, searchlight car.

16606 SOUTHERN (Type I): As described above.

EX-C7	LN-C8	Scarcity
10	15	3

16606 SOUTHERN (Type II): 1988, uncataloged Southern Division TCA searchlight car.

EX-C7	LN-C8	Scarcity
12	18	6

16608 LEHIGH VALLEY: 1987, searchlight car.

EX-C7	LN-C8	Scarcity
20	25	4

16609 LEHIGH VALLEY: 1987, derrick car.

EX-C7	LN-C8	Scarcity
20	25	4

16610 LIONEL TRACK: 1987-88, maintenance car.

EX-C7	LN-C8	Scarcity
15	20	4

16611 SANTA FE: 1988, log dump car.

EX-C7	LN-C8	Scarcity
15	20	4

16612 SOO LINE: 1989, log dump car.

EX-C7	LN-C8	Scarcity
15	20	4

16615 LIONEL LINES: 1989, extension searchlight car.

EX-C7	LN-C8	Scarcity
20	25	4

16616 DENVER & RIO GRANDE WESTERN: 1989, searchlight car, Service Station Special item.

EX-C7	LN-C8	Scarcity
20	25	4

16618 SANTA FE: 1989, Track Maintenance car.

EX-C7	LN-C8	Scarcity
10	15	4

16620 CHESAPEAKE AND OHIO: 1990-91, Track Maintenance car.

EX-C7	LN-C8	Scarcity
10	15	4

16621 ALASKA RAILROAD: 1990, log dump car.

EX-C7	LN-C8	Scarcity
10	15	4

16625 NEW YORK CENTRAL: 1990, extension searchlight car.

EX-C7	LN-C8	Scarcity
15	20	4

16626 CSX: 1990, searchlight car.

EX-C7	LN-C8	Scarcity
15	20	4

16627 CSX: 1990, log dump car.

EX-C7	LN-C8	Scarcity
15	20	4

16635 CP RAIL: 1991, Track Maintenance car.

EX-C7	LN-C8	Scarcity
Cataloged, but not produced.		

16636 DENVER & RIO GRANDE WESTERN: 1991, log dump car.

EX-C7	LN-C8	Scarcity
10	15	4

16637 WESTERN PACIFIC: 1991, extension searchlight car.

EX-C7	LN-C8	Scarcity
15	20	4

16652 LIONEL: 1992, rotating radar car.

EX-C7	LN-C8	Scarcity
20	25	4

16656 BURLINGTON NORTHERN: 1992, uncataloged log dump car.

EX-C7	LN-C8	Scarcity
15	20	4

16659 UNION PACIFIC: 1993-95, searchlight car.

EX-C7	LN-C8	Scarcity
10	15	4

16660 LIONEL: 1993-94, fire car with ladders.

EX-C7	LN-C8	Scarcity
20	25	4

16661 LIONEL: 1993, with boat.

EX-C7	LN-C8	Scarcity
10	15	4

16663 MISSOURI PACIFIC: 1993, searchlight car.

EX-C7	LN-C8	Scarcity
10	15	4

16665 MAINE CENTRAL: 1993, log dump car.

EX-C7	LN-C8	Scarcity
10	15	4

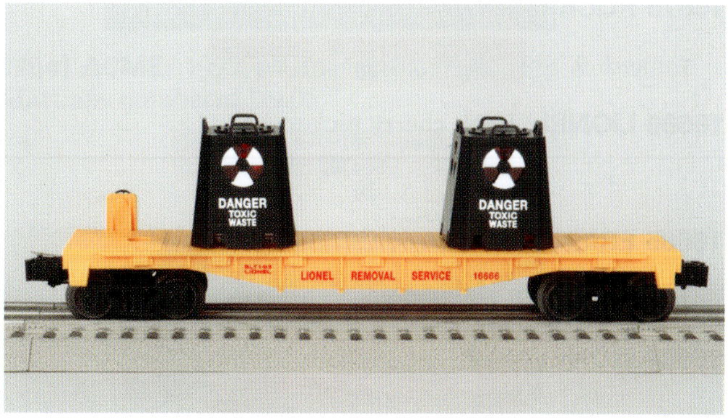

16666 LIONEL: 1993-94, toxic waste car.

EX-C7	LN-C8	Scarcity
20	25	4

16667 CONRAIL: 1993, searchlight car.

EX-C7	LN-C8	Scarcity
15	20	4

16668 ONTARIO NORTHLAND: 1993, log dump car.

EX-C7	LN-C8	Scarcity
10	15	4

16669 SOO LINE: 1993, searchlight car.

EX-C7	LN-C8	Scarcity
10	15	4

16670 LIONEL: 1993-94, TV car.

EX-C7	LN-C8	Scarcity
15	20	4

16675 GREAT NORTHERN: 1994, log dump car.

EX-C7	LN-C8	Scarcity
15	20	4

16933 LIONEL LINES: 1995, with automobiles.

EX-C7	LN-C8	Scarcity
10	15	4

16934 PENNSYLVANIA: 1995, with Ertl road grader.

EX-C7	LN-C8	Scarcity
20	25	4

16935 UNION PACIFIC: 1995, depressed center with Ertl bulldozer.

EX-C7	LN-C8	Scarcity
25	30	4

[16936] SEALAND MAXI-STACK: 1995, with containers numbered "16937" and "16938."

EX-C7	LN-C8	Scarcity
45	60	4

16937/16938 SEALAND MAXI-STACK: With containers (see 16936).

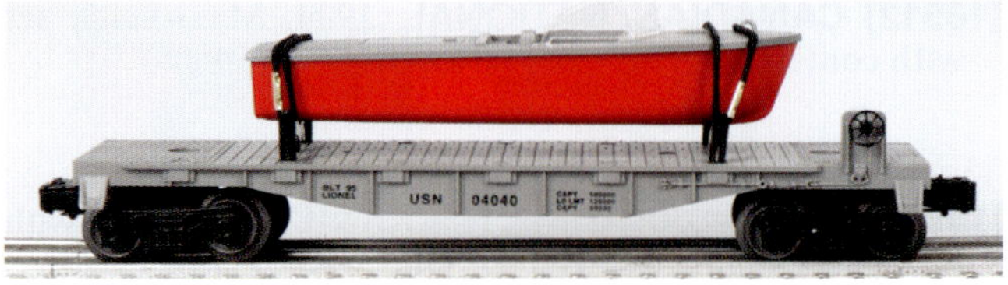

[16939] U.S. NAVY: 1995, with boat numbered "04040."

EX-C7	LN-C8	Scarcity
20	25	4

[16940] SANTA FE: 1996-99, with trailer.

EX-C7	LN-C8	Scarcity
25	30	4

[16941] SANTA FE: 1996-99, with autos.

EX-C7	LN-C8	Scarcity
15	20	4

[16944] GEORGIA POWER: 1995, uncataloged depressed center with transformer numbered "31438."

EX-C7	LN-C8	Scarcity
30	40	5

[16945] GEORGIA POWER: 1995, uncataloged depressed center with cable reels numbered "31950."

EX-C7	LN-C8	Scarcity
30	40	5

[16946] CHESAPEAKE AND OHIO: 1996, F9 Well Car numbered "3840."

EX-C7	LN-C8	Scarcity
20	25	4

[16951] SOUTHERN: 1997, center beam with load numbered "9823."

EX-C7	LN-C8	Scarcity
20	25	4

16952 U.S. NAVY: 1996, with Ertl helicopter.

EX-C7	LN-C8	Scarcity
20	25	4

[16953] NEW YORK CENTRAL: 1995, uncataloged with Red Wing Shoes trailer numbered "1905-95."

EX-C7	LN-C8	Scarcity
30	35	4

[16954] NEW YORK CENTRAL: 1996, with Ertl scraper numbered "6424."

EX-C7	LN-C8	Scarcity
20	25	4

[16955] SANTA FE: 1996, with Ertl Challenger.

EX-C7	LN-C8	Scarcity
20	25	4

[16956] ZENITH: 1995, uncataloged with trailer.

EX-C7	LN-C8	Scarcity
80	100	6

[16957] LIONEL: 1996, depressed center with Ertl Case 4WD tractor numbered "6461."

EX-C7	LN-C8	Scarcity
20	25	4

[16958] LIONEL: 1996, with Ertl New Holland loader.

EX-C7	LN-C8	Scarcity
20	25	4

[16960] U.S.C.G: 1996, with boat.

EX-C7	LN-C8	Scarcity
25	30	4

[16961] GM/AC DELCO: 1995, with trailer.

EX-C7	LN-C8	Scarcity
40	50	6

[16963] LIONEL CORPORATION: 1996-97, numbered "6411."

EX-C7	LN-C8	Scarcity
20	25	4

[16965] LIONEL SCOUT: 1996-97, with stakes numbered "6424."

EX-C7	LN-C8	Scarcity
10	15	3

[16967] LIONEL: 1996, depressed center with transformer numbered "6461."

EX-C7	LN-C8	Scarcity
15	20	4

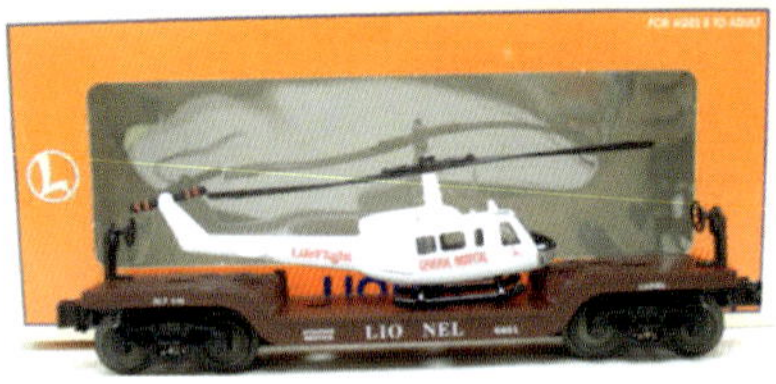

[16968] LIONEL: 1996, aviation depressed center with General Hospital LifeFlight Ertl helicopter numbered "6461."

EX-C7	LN-C8	Scarcity
15	20	4

[16969] LIONEL: 1996, with Beechcraft Bonanza numbered "6411."

EX-C7	LN-C8	Scarcity
15	20	4

[16970] L.A. COUNTY: 1996, with motorized L.A. County Lifeguard powerboat numbered "6424."

EX-C7	LN-C8	Scarcity
10	15	4

[16971] PORT OF LIONEL CITY: 1997, with boat.

EX-C7	LN-C8	Scarcity
15	20	5

[16975] LIONEL: 1997, doublestack set numbered "6480," two Well Cars.

EX-C7	LN-C8	Scarcity
50	60	4

[16978] MILWAUKEE ROAD: 1997, numbered "6424" with P & H shovel kit.

EX-C7	LN-C8	Scarcity
30	35	4

[16980] ACME: 1997, with Warner Bros. Speedy Gonzales missile numbered "6823."

EX-C7	LN-C8	Scarcity
25	30	4

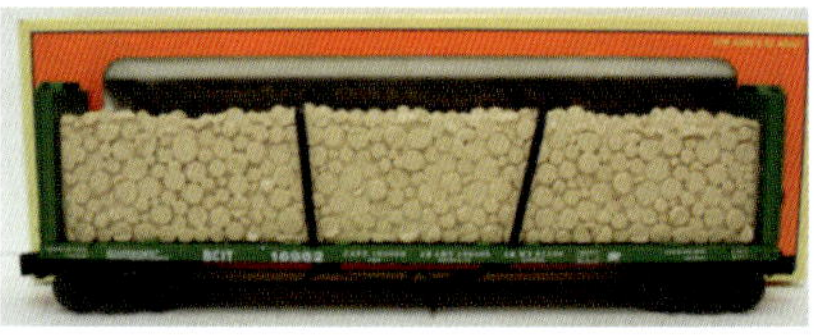

[16982] BC RAIL: 1997, bulkhead with wood load numbered "9823."

EX-C7	LN-C8	Scarcity
20	25	4

[16983] PENNSYLVANIA: 1997, F9 Well Car with cable reels numbered "6983."

EX-C7	LN-C8	Scarcity
20	25	4

[16985] EASTWOOD: 1997, uncataloged Ford with vans.

EX-C7	LN-C8	Scarcity
35	45	6

[16986] SEARS ZENITH: 1996, uncataloged with bulkheads.

EX-C7	LN-C8	Scarcity
25	30	5

[16987] MUSCO LIGHTING: 1997, uncataloged with bulkheads.

EX-C7	LN-C8	Scarcity
20	25	4

17500 CANADIAN PACIFIC: 1989, with logs and 1/48-scale proportions.

EX-C7	LN-C8	Scarcity
20	25	4

17501 CONRAIL: 1987, with stakes and 1/48-scale proportions.

EX-C7	LN-C8	Scarcity
30	35	4

17502 SANTA FE: 1990, with trailer and 1/48-scale proportions.

EX-C7	LN-C8	Scarcity
45	55	5

17503 NORFOLK SOUTHERN: 1992, with trailer and 1/48-scale proportions.

EX-C7	LN-C8	Scarcity
35	45	4

17504 NORFOLK SOUTHERN: 1992, with trailer and 1/48-scale proportions.

EX-C7	LN-C8	Scarcity
35	45	4

17505 NORFOLK SOUTHERN: 1992, with trailer and 1/48-scale proportions.

EX-C7	LN-C8	Scarcity
35	45	4

17506 NORFOLK SOUTHERN: 1992, with trailer and 1/48-scale proportions.

EX-C7	LN-C8	Scarcity
35	45	4

17507 NORFOLK SOUTHERN: 1992, with trailer and 1/48-scale proportions.

EX-C7	LN-C8	Scarcity
35	45	4

17508 BURLINGTON NORTHERN: 1992, center beam with load.

EX-C7	LN-C8	Scarcity
Cataloged, but not produced.		

17509 SOUTHERN: 1992, with load and 1/48-scale proportions.

EX-C7	LN-C8	Scarcity
Cataloged, but not produced.		

[17510] NORTHERN PACIFIC: 1994, with logs numbered "61200" and 1/48-scale proportions.

EX-C7	LN-C8	Scarcity
25	30	5

[17511] WESTERN MARYLAND: 1995, with logs, set of three, with 1/48-scale proportions.

EX-C7	LN-C8	Scarcity
100	125	5

17512 WESTERN MARYLAND: 1995, with logs and 1/48-scale proportions.

EX-C7	LN-C8	Scarcity
25	30	5

17513 WESTERN MARYLAND: 1995, with logs and 1/48-scale proportions.

EX-C7	LN-C8	Scarcity
25	30	5

17514 WESTERN MARYLAND: 1995, with logs and 1/48-scale proportions.

EX-C7	LN-C8	Scarcity
25	30	5

17515 NORFOLK SOUTHERN: 1995, with tractor and 1/48-scale proportions.

EX-C7	LN-C8	Scarcity
25	30	4

[17516] TEXAS & PACIFIC: 1997, with two Beechcraft Bonanzas numbered "9823" and 1/48-scale proportions.

EX-C7	LN-C8	Scarcity
25	30	4

[17517] WESTERN PACIFIC: 1997, with Ertl Caterpillar front-end loader numbered "9823" and 1/48-scale proportions.

EX-C7	LN-C8	Scarcity
25	30	4

[17518] PENNSYLVANIA: 1997, with two Corgi Mack trucks numbered "9823" and 1/48-scale proportions.

EX-C7	LN-C8	Scarcity
60	65	4

[17522] "PROWLER TRANSPORT": 1998, with Plymouth Prowler.

EX-C7	LN-C8	Scarcity
25	30	4

[17527]: 1998, with a pair of Dodge Vipers.

EX-C7	LN-C8	Scarcity
25	30	4

[17529] SANTA FE: 1999, with a Ford milk truck numbered "90010."

EX-C7	LN-C8	Scarcity
25	30	4

[17533] FORD: 1999, with auto frames.

EX-C7	LN-C8	Scarcity
25	30	4

[17534] DIAMOND T: 1999, with trucks numbered "9823."

EX-C7	LN-C8	Scarcity
65	75	4

[17536] ROUTE 66: 1999, with two coupes numbered "9823-3."

EX-C7	LN-C8	Scarcity
25	30	4

[17537] ROUTE 66: 1999, with two touring coupes numbered "9823-4."

EX-C7	LN-C8	Scarcity
25	30	4

[17538] NEW YORK CENTRAL: 1999, with a Ford tow truck.

EX-C7	LN-C8	Scarcity
25	30	4

[17539]: 1999, with two Corvettes numbered "9823" with 1/48-scale proportions.

EX-C7	LN-C8	Scarcity
40	50	4

[17540]: 1999, with two Corvettes numbered "9823" with 1/48-scale proportions.

EX-C7	LN-C8	Scarcity
40	50	4

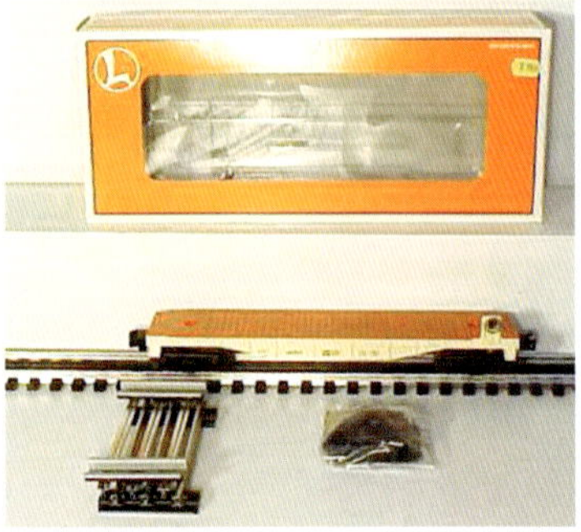

[17546] LIONEL LINES: 1999, Recovery with rails numbered "6424."

EX-C7	LN-C8	Scarcity
25	30	4

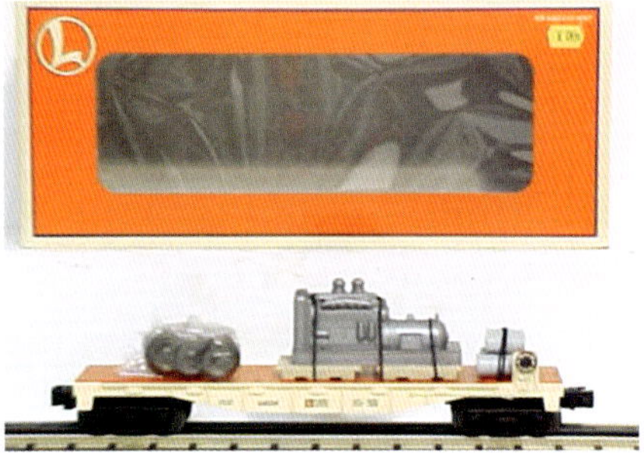

[17547] LIONEL LINES: 1999, Recovery with machinery numbered "6429."

EX-C7	LN-C8	Scarcity
25	30	4

[17548] ROUTE 66: 1999, with two station wagons numbered "9823-6."

EX-C7	LN-C8	Scarcity
25	30	4

[17549] ROUTE 66: 1999, with woodie and trailer numbered "9823-5."

EX-C7	LN-C8	Scarcity
25	30	4

[17550] BURLINGTON NORTHERN: 1999, center beam with lumber load numbered "6216" and 1/48-scale proportions.

EX-C7	LN-C8	Scarcity
25	30	4

[17551] NEW YORK CENTRAL: 1999, with New York Central pickups numbered "499."

EX-C7	LN-C8	Scarcity
30	35	4

[17553] TRAILER TRAIN: 1999, numbered "98102" with combine and 1/48-scale proportions.

EX-C7	LN-C8	Scarcity
75	100	5

[17554] GREAT NORTHERN: 2000, numbered "61042" with logs.

EX-C7	LN-C8	Scarcity
25	30	4

[17557] ROUTE 66: 1999-2000, numbered "9823-7" with black sedans.

EX-C7	LN-C8	Scarcity
25	30	4

[17558] ROUTE 66: 1999, numbered "9823-8" with brown sedans.

EX-C7	LN-C8	Scarcity
25	30	4

[17871] NEW YORK CENTRAL: 1987, uncataloged TTOS with Kodak and Xerox trailers numbered "81487."

EX-C7	LN-C8	Scarcity
275	300	6

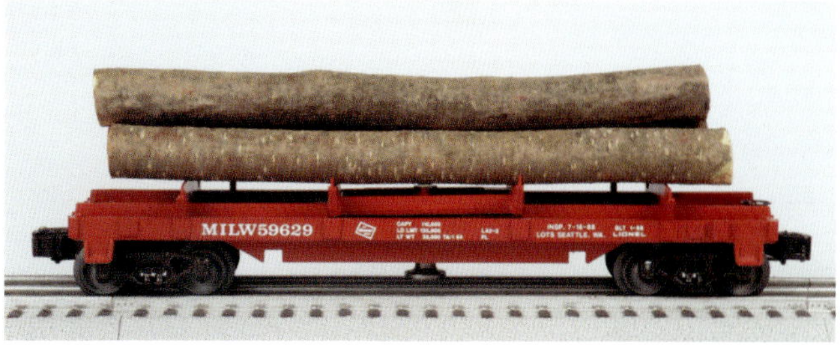

[17874] MILWAUKEE ROAD: 1988, uncataloged LOTS log dump car numbered "59629."

EX-C7	LN-C8	Scarcity
100	125	6

17887 CONRAIL: 1991, uncataloged LCCA with Armstrong Tile trailer with 1/48-scale proportions.

EX-C7	LN-C8	Scarcity
40	60	6

17888 CONRAIL: 1991, uncataloged LCCA with a Ford New Holland trailer with 1/48-scale proportions.

EX-C7	LN-C8	Scarcity
40	60	6

[17889] SOUTHERN PACIFIC: 1991, uncataloged TTOS with trailer numbered "15791" with 1/48-scale proportions.

EX-C7	LN-C8	Scarcity
40	50	6

FLATCARS AND INTERMODAL CARS

[17890] CSX: 1991, uncataloged LOTS bi-level enclosed auto carrier numbered "151161."

EX-C7	LN-C8	Scarcity
60	70	6

[17892] CONRAIL: 1991, LCCA with trailers with 1/48-scale proportions. (See 17887, 17888.)

19404 TRAILER TRAIN: 1989, with Western Maryland trailers, Fallen Flags number four.

EX-C7	LN-C8	Scarcity
25	30	5

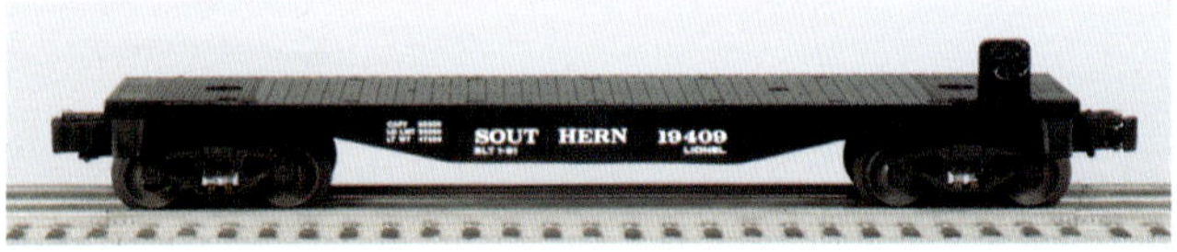

19409 SOUTHERN: 1991, with stakes.

EX-C7	LN-C8	Scarcity
15	20	4

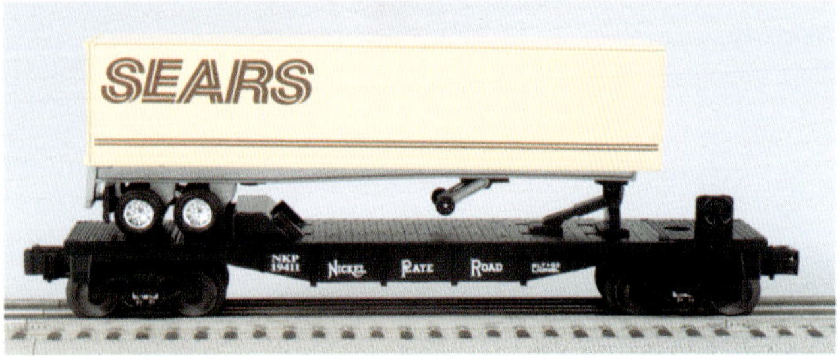

19411 NICKEL PLATE ROAD: 1992, with Sears trailer, Fallen Flags number six.

EX-C7	LN-C8	Scarcity
40	45	5

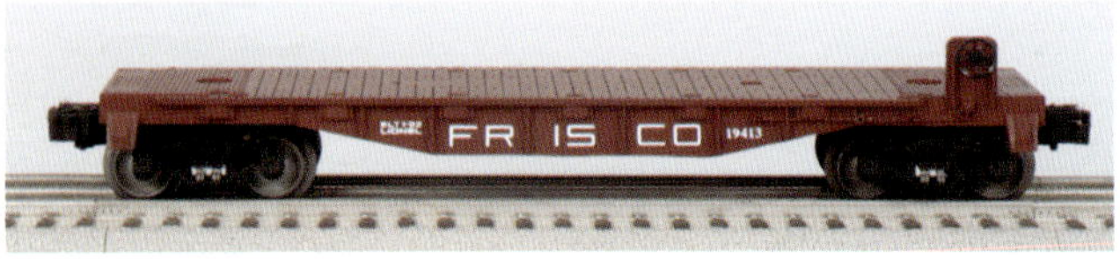

19413 FRISCO: 1992, with stakes.

EX-C7	LN-C8	Scarcity
15	20	4

19414 UNION PACIFIC: 1992, with stakes, Service Station Special item.

EX-C7	LN-C8	Scarcity
15	20	4

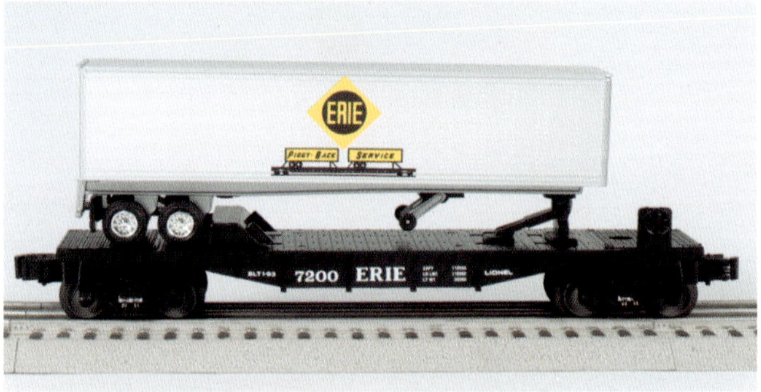

[19415] ERIE: 1993, with trailer numbered "7200," Fallen Flags number seven.

EX-C7	LN-C8	Scarcity
20	25	5

[19416] ILLINOIS CENTRAL GULF: 1993, TTUX set with trailers numbered "19417" and "19418," Service Station Special item.

EX-C7	LN-C8	Scarcity
60	70	6

19417/19418 ILLINOIS CENTRAL GULF: TTUX with trailers (see 19416).

[19423] CIRCLE-L RACING: 1996, with stock cars numbered "6424."

EX-C7	LN-C8	Scarcity
20	25	4

[19424] EDISON ELECTRIC: 1997, depressed center with transformer numbered "6461."

EX-C7	LN-C8	Scarcity
25	30	4

[19425] CSX: 1996, uncataloged Artrain with trailer.

EX-C7	LN-C8	Scarcity
65	75	6

[19427] EVANS: 1999, Auto Loader numbered "6414."

EX-C7	LN-C8	Scarcity
40	50	4

[19428] EVANS: 1999, Boat Loader numbered "6414."

EX-C7	LN-C8	Scarcity
40	50	4

[19430] SANTA FE: 1998, with Beechcraft Bonanza numbered "6411."

EX-C7	LN-C8	Scarcity
25	30	4

[19437] LIONEL RAILROADER CLUB: 1997, uncataloged with trailer.

EX-C7	LN-C8	Scarcity
35	40	4

[19439]: 1998, with Safes.

EX-C7	LN-C8	Scarcity
20	25	4

[19440]: 1998, with FedEx trailer.

EX-C7	LN-C8	Scarcity
20	25	4

[19442] LIONEL CORPORATION: 1998, Water Supply with tank, Service Station Special item.

EX-C7	LN-C8	Scarcity
20	25	5

[19444]: 1998, with Volkswagen beetle.

EX-C7	LN-C8	Scarcity
25	30	4

[19449]: 1999, Liquefied Gas tank car numbered "6469."

EX-C7	LN-C8	Scarcity
20	25	4

[19450]: 1999, barrel ramp car numbered "6343."

EX-C7	LN-C8	Scarcity
20	25	4

[19451]: 1999, wheel car numbered "6262."

EX-C7	LN-C8	Scarcity
20	25	4

[19455] LIONEL LINES: 1999, with Cooper-Jarrett trailers numbered "6430."

EX-C7	LN-C8	Scarcity
30	40	5

[19456] LIONEL LINES: 1999, postwar with stakes and pipes.

EX-C7	LN-C8	Scarcity
30	40	5

[19457] LIONEL LINES: 1999, extension searchlight car.

EX-C7	LN-C8	Scarcity
25	30	4

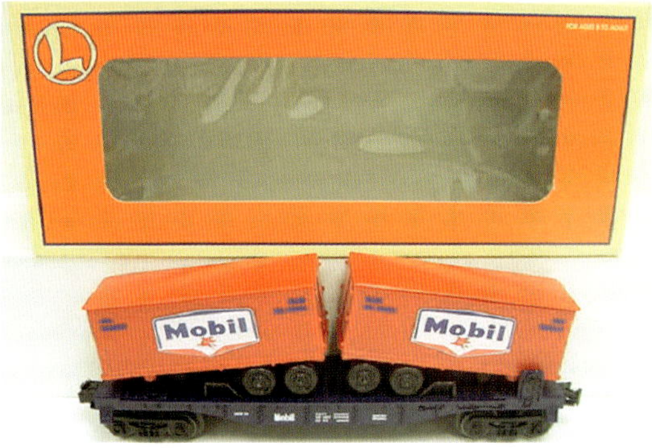

[19471] MOBIL: 2000, uncataloged with two trailers.

EX-C7	LN-C8	Scarcity
60	70	4

[19472] MOBIL: 2000, uncataloged bulkhead with tank.

EX-C7	LN-C8	Scarcity
35	45	4

[19473] LIONEL RAILROADER CLUB: 1999, uncataloged log dump car.

EX-C7	LN-C8	Scarcity
20	25	4

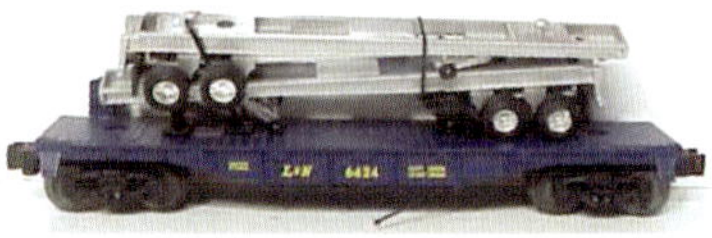

[19474] LOUISVILLE AND NASHVILLE: 1999, with die-cast trailer frames numbered "6424."

EX-C7	LN-C8	Scarcity
20	25	4

[19479] BORDEN'S MILK: 2000, car numbered "521."

EX-C7	LN-C8	Scarcity
25	30	4

[19482] NEW YORK CENTRAL: 2000, with two trailers numbered "6424."

EX-C7	LN-C8	Scarcity
40	50	4

[19483] VOLKSWAGEN: 2000, Beetle numbered "2000."

EX-C7	LN-C8	Scarcity
35	40	4

[19484] LIONEL: 2000, with timbers numbered "6264."

EX-C7	LN-C8	Scarcity
15	20	4

[19487] LIONEL: 2000, with airplane numbered "6800."

EX-C7	LN-C8	Scarcity
20	25	4

19489 EVANS: 2000, Auto Loader numbered "500085."

EX-C7	LN-C8	Scarcity
30	35	4

[19773] LIONEL KIDS CLUB: 1996, uncataloged barrel ramp car numbered "6343."

EX-C7	LN-C8	Scarcity
25	30	5

[19858] LIONELVILLE: 1999, operating searchlight car numbered "19854."

EX-C7	LN-C8	Scarcity
25	30	4

[19878]: 1999, operating helium tank numbered "3362."

EX-C7	LN-C8	Scarcity
15	20	4

19880 LIONEL LINES: 2000, extension searchlight car.

EX-C7	LN-C8	Scarcity
25	30	4

[19948] VISITORS CENTER: 1996, uncataloged with trailer.

EX-C7	LN-C8	Scarcity
35	40	5

[21934] CUSTOM SERIES: 1999, Consist II three-pack numbered "6424."

EX-C7	LN-C8	Scarcity
100	125	4

[26000] MONOPOLY: 2000, uncataloged with airplane.

EX-C7	LN-C8	Scarcity
Too rarely traded to establish accurate pricing.		

[26707] LIONEL STEEL: 2000, operating welding numbered "1108."

EX-C7	LN-C8	Scarcity
60	70	4

[26709]: 1999, with Psychedelic Psubmarine numbered "6511."

EX-C7	LN-C8	Scarcity
20	25	4

[26713] WESTSIDE LUMBER: 1999, log car three-pack numbered "9823."

EX-C7	LN-C8	Scarcity
80	100	5

[26714] WESTSIDE LUMBER: 1999, with 1/48-scale proportions with logs.

EX-C7	LN-C8	Scarcity
30	35	5

[26715] WESTSIDE LUMBER: 1999, with 1/48-scale proportions with logs.

EX-C7	LN-C8	Scarcity
30	35	5

[26716] WESTSIDE LUMBER: 1999, with 1/48-scale proportions with logs.

EX-C7	LN-C8	Scarcity
30	35	5

[26722] LIONEL LINES: 2000, log dump car numbered "3351."

EX-C7	LN-C8	Scarcity
15	20	3

26775 U.S. ARMY: 2000, searchlight car.

EX-C7	LN-C8	Scarcity
30	35	4

[26906] SOUTHERN PACIFIC: 1998, with Corgi 1957 Chevrolet police car numbered "9823."

EX-C7	LN-C8	Scarcity
25	30	4

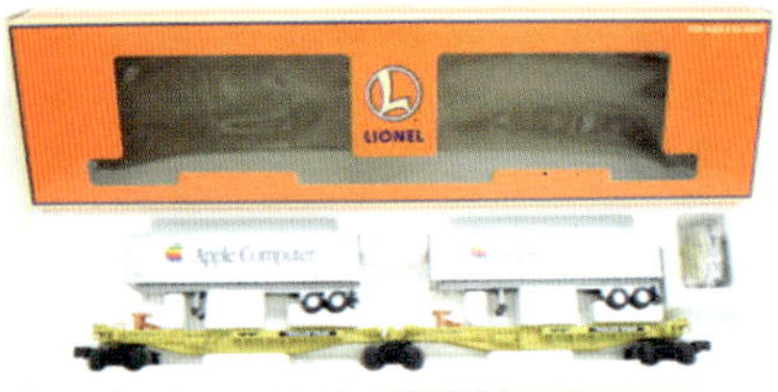

[26908] T.T.U.X.: 1998, with Apple trailers numbered "6300."

EX-C7	LN-C8	Scarcity
50	60	4

[26949] NORTHERN PACIFIC: 1998, with trailer numbered "6424-2017."

EX-C7	LN-C8	Scarcity
30	35	4

[26950] NORTHERN PACIFIC: 1998, with trailer numbered "6424-2016."

EX-C7	LN-C8	Scarcity
30	35	4

[26951] TRAILER TRAIN: 1998, with Pennsylvania trailer numbered "475185."

EX-C7	LN-C8	Scarcity
40	45	4

[26952] TRAILER TRAIN: 1998, with J.B. Hunt trailer.

EX-C7	LN-C8	Scarcity
25	30	4

[26953] TRAILER TRAIN: 1998, with J.B. Hunt trailer.

EX-C7	LN-C8	Scarcity
25	30	4

[26954] TRAILER TRAIN: 1998, with J.B. Hunt trailer.

EX-C7	LN-C8	Scarcity
25	30	4

[26955] TRAILER TRAIN: 1998, with J.B. Hunt trailer.

EX-C7	LN-C8	Scarcity
25	30	4

[26957] DELAWARE AND HUDSON: 1998, with stakes.

EX-C7	LN-C8	Scarcity
10	15	3

[26961] LIONELVILLE FIRE CO.: 1998, with ladder, Service Station Special item load numbered "6418-1."

EX-C7	LN-C8	Scarcity
35	40	5

[26971] LIONEL STEEL: 1998, 16-wheel depressed center.

EX-C7	LN-C8	Scarcity
100	125	4

[26991] LIONELVILLE: 1999, Firecar with ladders, Dept. #2.

EX-C7	LN-C8	Scarcity
35	40	4

29108: 2000, searchlight car.

EX-C7	LN-C8	Scarcity
15	20	4

[36000] ROUTE 66: 1998, with two red Sedans.

EX-C7	LN-C8	Scarcity
30	35	4

[36001] ROUTE 66: 1998, with two wagons.

EX-C7	LN-C8	Scarcity
30	35	4

[36006] URANIUM TRANSPORT: 1999, numbered "6508."

EX-C7	LN-C8	Scarcity
35	45	4

[36016] LIONEL NAVAL SUPPORT: 1998, with propellers.

EX-C7	LN-C8	Scarcity
30	40	4

[36020] TRAILER TRAIN: 1999, numbered "TT-6424" with auto frames.

EX-C7	LN-C8	Scarcity
25	30	4

[36021] ALASKA RAILROAD: 1999, with airplane numbered "6424."

EX-C7	LN-C8	Scarcity
25	30	4

[36024] TRAILER TRAIN: 1999, flatcar with J.B. Hunt trailer numbered "64245."

EX-C7	LN-C8	Scarcity
25	30	4

[36025] TRAILER TRAIN: 1999, with J.B. Hunt trailer numbered "64246."

EX-C7	LN-C8	Scarcity
25	30	4

[36026] TRAILER TRAIN: 1999, with J.B. Hunt trailers, two-pack.

EX-C7	LN-C8	Scarcity
50	60	4

[36027] TREDEGAR IRON WORKS: 1999, with cannon.

EX-C7	LN-C8	Scarcity
25	30	4

[36028] HEAVY ARTILLERY: 1999, with cannon.

EX-C7	LN-C8	Scarcity
25	30	4

[36029] SOUTHERN PACIFIC: 1999, enclosed auto rack numbered "516712."

EX-C7	LN-C8	Scarcity
25	30	4

[36040] BETHLEHEM: 1999, with block, Service Station Special item.

EX-C7	LN-C8	Scarcity
50	60	5

[36043] CUSTOM CONSIST: 1999, with pickup truck.

EX-C7	LN-C8	Scarcity
25	30	4

[36044] CUSTOM CONSIST: 1999, with dragster.

EX-C7	LN-C8	Scarcity
25	30	4

[36064] BILLBOARD: 2000, numbered "6424."

EX-C7	LN-C8	Scarcity
25	30	4

[36065] WABASH: 2000, numbered "25536" with trailer.

EX-C7	LN-C8	Scarcity
20	25	4

[36067] KING AUTO SALES: 2000, with pink Cadillac numbered "6424."

EX-C7	LN-C8	Scarcity
30	35	4

[36079] SERVICE STATION LIMITED: 2000, with trailer.

EX-C7	LN-C8	Scarcity
30	35	5

[36082] WHIRLPOOL: 2000, uncataloged with trailer.

EX-C7	LN-C8	Scarcity
Too rarely traded to establish accurate pricing.		

[36088] ALLIS CHALMERS: 2000, condenser car numbered "6519."

EX-C7	LN-C8	Scarcity
30	35	4

36089 FRISCO: 2000, with airplane.

EX-C7	LN-C8	Scarcity
25	30	4

36091 MAERSK: 2000, with die-cast tractors numbered "250129."

EX-C7	LN-C8	Scarcity
35	40	4

36092 MAERSK: 2000, with die-cast tractors numbered "250130."

EX-C7	LN-C8	Scarcity
35	40	4

36093 SOO LINE TRAILER TRAIN: 2000, bi-level enclosed auto carrier numbered "906760."

EX-C7	LN-C8	Scarcity
35	40	4

[36900]: 1999, depressed center with backshop load.

EX-C7	LN-C8	Scarcity
80	90	4

[36935] MAERSK MAXI-STACK: 2000, two-pack numbered "250131" and "250132."

EX-C7	LN-C8	Scarcity
70	85	4

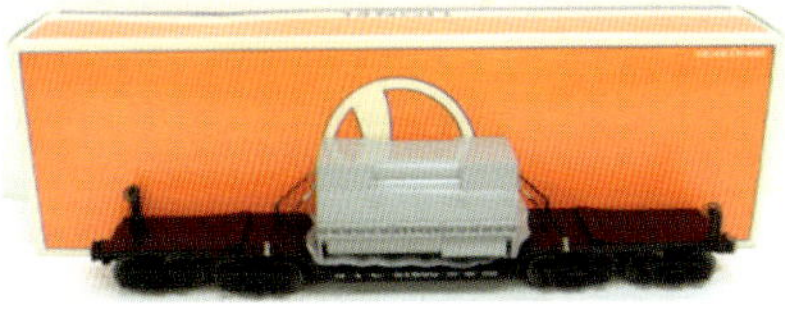

[51600] NEW YORK CENTRAL: 1996, depressed center with transformer numbered "6418."

EX-C7	LN-C8	Scarcity
80	100	4

[51800] LIONEL LINES: 1989, searchlight car numbered "8820."

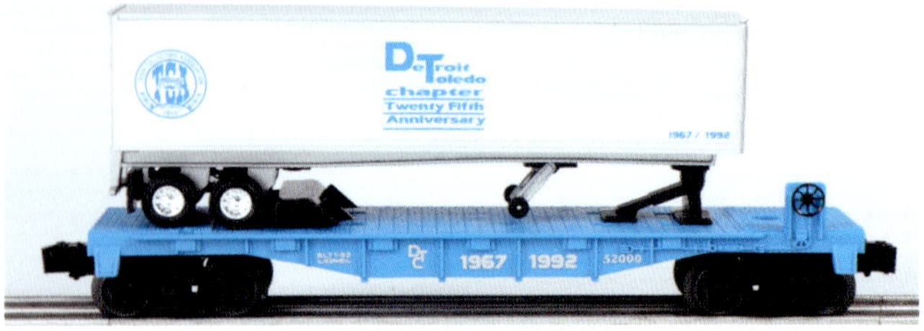

52000 DETROIT-TOLEDO TCA: 1992, uncataloged with trailer.

EX-C7	LN-C8	Scarcity
65	75	6

52003 OZARK TCA: 1992, uncataloged, "Meet Me in St. Louis," with trailer.

EX-C7	LN-C8	Scarcity
300	350	6

52013 NORFOLK SOUTHERN: 1992, uncataloged Artrain with trailer with 1/48-scale proportions.

EX-C7	LN-C8	Scarcity
200	250	6

[52014] BURLINGTON NORTHERN TTUX: 1993, uncataloged LOTS set with Norfolk and Western trailers numbered "637500A" and "637500B."

EX-C7	LN-C8	Scarcity
125	150	6

52024 CONRAIL: 1993, uncataloged Artrain bi-level enclosed auto carrier.

EX-C7	LN-C8	Scarcity
80	100	6

[52026] LONG ISLAND NLOE: 1994, uncataloged with Grumman trailer numbered "8394."

EX-C7	LN-C8	Scarcity
275	325	6

[52034] GRAND TRUNK WESTERN: See 52040.

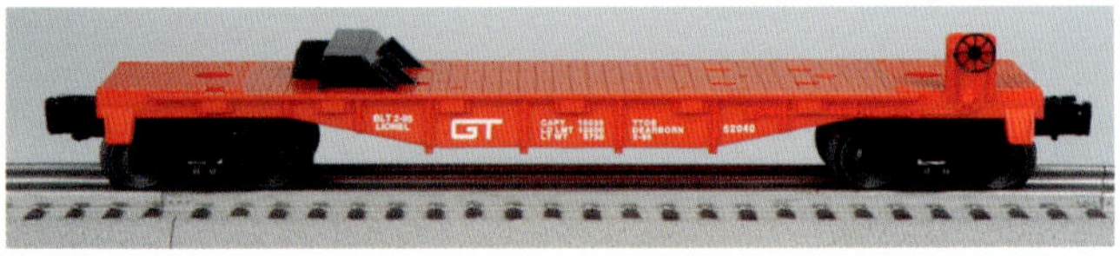

52040 GRAND TRUNK WESTERN: 1994, uncataloged Wolverine TTOS with Lionel Lines tractor and trailer.

EX-C7	LN-C8	Scarcity
40	50	6

[52041] BURLINGTON NORTHERN TTUX: 1994, uncataloged LOTS set with Conrail trailers numbered "637500d" and "637500E."

EX-C7	LN-C8	Scarcity
65	85	6

[52042] BURLINGTON NORTHERN TTUX: 1994, uncataloged LOTS with Canadian National trailer numbered "637500C."

EX-C7	LN-C8	Scarcity
40	50	6

[52080] BOSTON AND MAINE: 1995, uncataloged New England Division of Train Collectors Association with trailer numbered "91095."

EX-C7	LN-C8	Scarcity
175	200	6

[52083] EASTWOOD CHEMICALS: 1995, uncataloged with tanker numbered "16380."

EX-C7	LN-C8	Scarcity
35	40	6

[52084] UNION PACIFIC: 1995, uncataloged TTOS center beam with load numbered "16380."

EX-C7	LN-C8	Scarcity
125	150	6

[52099] MISSOURI PACIFIC: 1996, uncataloged TOFC.

EX-C7	LN-C8	Scarcity
55	65	6

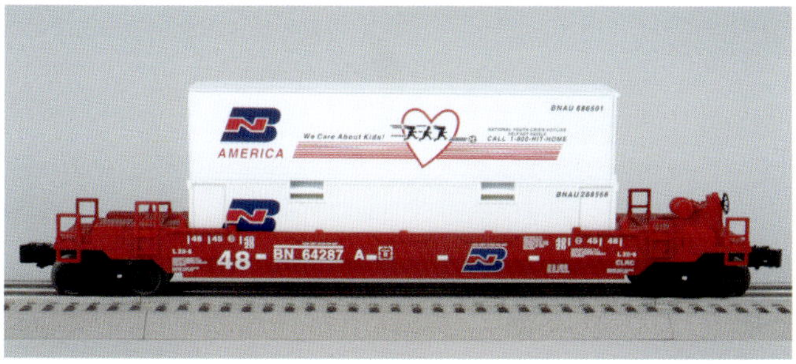

[52101] MAXISTACK: 1997, uncataloged Chicagoland RR Club numbered "64287."

EX-C7	LN-C8	Scarcity
55	65	6

52111 BEN & JERRY'S: 1994, New England Division of Train Collectors Association with tractor-trailer.

EX-C7	LN-C8	Scarcity
300	375	6

[52114] NEW YORK CENTRAL: 1997, uncataloged with trailer.

EX-C7	LN-C8	Scarcity
45	50	5

[52115] WABASH: 1998, uncataloged Lionel Collectors Association of Canada auto carrier numbered "9519."

EX-C7	LN-C8	Scarcity
60	75	6

[52116] MILWAUKEE ROAD: 1997, uncataloged with tractor and trailer numbered "194797."

EX-C7	LN-C8	Scarcity
45	50	5

[52117] WABUSH: 1997, uncataloged St. Louis Lionel Railroader Club with trailer.

EX-C7	LN-C8	Scarcity
45	50	5

[52130] HOT WHEELS: 1997, uncataloged TOFC numbered "21697."

EX-C7	LN-C8	Scarcity
45	50	5

52142 MASS CENTRAL: 1998, uncataloged Maxi-Stack.

EX-C7	LN-C8	Scarcity
80	100	6

[52144] LIRR/GRUMMAN: 1998, uncataloged NLOE TOFC numbered "8398."

EX-C7	LN-C8	Scarcity
80	100	6

FLATCARS AND INTERMODAL CARS

[52147] FRISCO: 1998, uncataloged Campbell 66 TOFC.

EX-C7	LN-C8	Scarcity
50	65	5

[52149] CONRAIL: 1998, uncataloged TTOS with shovel.

EX-C7	LN-C8	Scarcity
35	40	6

[52150] FRISCO: 1998, uncataloged with Campbell 66 trailer.

EX-C7	LN-C8	Scarcity
100	125	6

[52159] MONOPOLY: 1998, depressed center with transformer.

EX-C7	LN-C8	Scarcity
80	100	6

[52166] LIRR/NORTHROP: 1999, uncataloged NLOE TOFC numbered "8399."

EX-C7	LN-C8	Scarcity
80	100	6

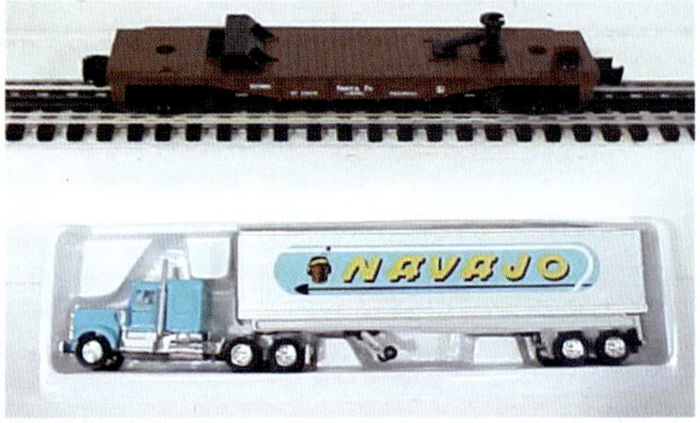

[52167] SANTA FE: 1999, uncataloged with Navajo trailer numbered "83199."

EX-C7	LN-C8	Scarcity
50	60	6

[52168] CARAIL: 1999, uncataloged with trailer numbered "17455."

EX-C7	LN-C8	Scarcity
60	65	6

[52169] ZEP MANUFACTURING CO.: 1999, uncataloged with trailer numbered "62734."

EX-C7	LN-C8	Scarcity
Too rarely traded to establish accurate pricing.		

[52180] MILWAUKEE ROAD: 1999, uncataloged with trailer numbered "194799."

EX-C7	LN-C8	Scarcity
45	55	6

[52184] MONOPOLY FREE PARKING: 1999, with two autos.

EX-C7	LN-C8	Scarcity
60	75	6

[52187] MADISON HARDWARE: 1999, with trailers numbered "1909-1999."

EX-C7	LN-C8	Scarcity
60	75	6

[52190] ILLINOIS CENTRAL: 2000, uncataloged St. Louis LRC TOFC.

EX-C7	LN-C8	Scarcity
60	75	6

[52195] CANADIAN PACIFIC: 2000, uncataloged LCCA Maxistack numbered "200030."

EX-C7	LN-C8	Scarcity
70	80	6

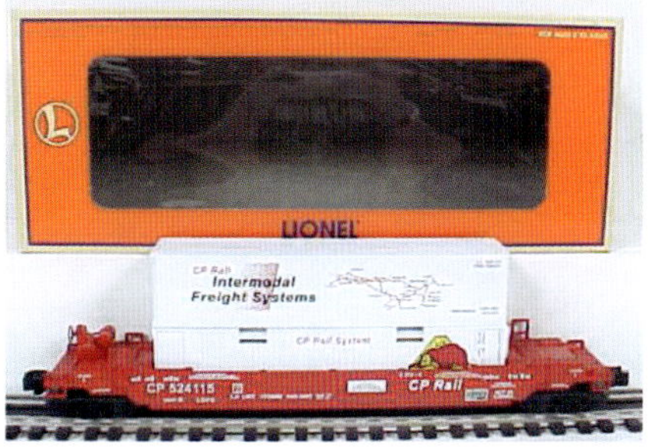

[52196] CANADIAN PACIFIC: 2000, uncataloged LOTS Maxistack numbered "524115."

EX-C7	LN-C8	Scarcity
65	75	6

[99006] KEEBLER: 1999, uncataloged with bulkheads.

EX-C7	LN-C8	Scarcity
Too rarely traded to establish accurate pricing.		

[900013] CANADIAN NATIONAL: 1990, uncataloged Lionel Collectors Association of Canada with trailers.

EX-C7	LN-C8	Scarcity
150	175	6

UNNUMBERED LIONEL CONSTRUCTION: 1995, depressed center with Ertl Uniloader numbered "6461."

EX-C7	LN-C8	Scarcity
Too rarely traded to establish accurate pricing.		

Chapter 9

GONDOLA AND COAL DUMP CARS

Gondola cars have been a mainstay of introductory level train sets for as long as Lionel has been making trains. Lionel's first electric train was a motorized gondola. Gondolas represent excellent play value, allowing a youth's imagination to be involved. Rocks, coins, plastic dinosaurs, Lincoln Logs, and a host of other items make excellent cargo for gondola cars circling the Christmas tree. The longer the starter set holds a child's imagination and interest, the more likely the child is to want to expand the miniature railroad "empire." Gondola cars are also cheap and easy to manufacture—and the combination of low cost and enormous utility was irresistible for Lionel, who included a gondola in almost every set. Perhaps because the body type is so common, and its decoration often so plain, there is little collector interest in gondolas as a whole.

From 1970 onward Lionel has produced cars based on both the postwar 6462 and 1002 cars. The latter tend to be found only in introductory sets, while the former is found not just in starter sets, but also advanced sets aimed at the collector market as well as separate sale items.

In 1973, these car styles were joined by the larger "Standard 0" cars that were produced from molds Lionel bought from Pola, an Austrian firm, and modified slightly. These cars were proportioned to nearly true 1/48-scale, making them look "odd" to conventional Lionel fans. Sales of such cars were slow throughout the first 20 years of the modern era, leading to the "Standard 0" cars being dropped for a period of time. However, interest in scale-like locomotives and rolling stock began to increase from 1987 onward, leading to the revival of the "Standard 0" cars—and subsequently the flourishing of the type.

For added interest in both the 1/48-scale and 6462-sized gondolas, Lionel has created removable molded plastic covers for a certain number of the cars. These cars simulate the covers placed on cars hauling rolled steel coils, protecting the new raw steel from the weather.

Two types of operating gondolas based on cars from the postwar period have also been produced in the modern era. The "cop and hobo" gondola was reintroduced in 1979, initially as a faithful reproduction of the postwar item including its vibrator-powered belt. Later versions however used a belt driven mechanically from an axle, meaning the speed of the animation varied with that of the train—and stopped when the train did.

In 1983, the animated barrel car returned to the Lionel catalog. Based on the postwar 3562, these cars feature a rubber workman "shoving" wooden barrels off the cars' integral metal conveyor.

Similar in appearance to gondolas, Lionel has also produced a number of operating side dump cars. Introduced in 1974, these cars were based on Lionel's operating log dump car with the addition of a dumping bin. The cars are not particularly handsome, nor do they work especially well, resulting in there being little collector interest in the type, despite the fragility of the cars which will result in them ultimately being scarcer then many other types.

6200 FLORIDA EAST COAST: 1981-82, with canisters.

EX-C7	LN-C8	Scarcity
10	15	3

6201 UNION PACIFIC: 1982-83, animated.

EX-C7	LN-C8	Scarcity
15	20	4

6202 WESTERN MARYLAND: 1982, with coal load.

EX-C7	LN-C8	Scarcity
15	20	4

[6203] BLACK CAVE GONDOLA: 1982, in the traditional 027/Scout size.

EX-C7	LN-C8	Scarcity
2	3	2

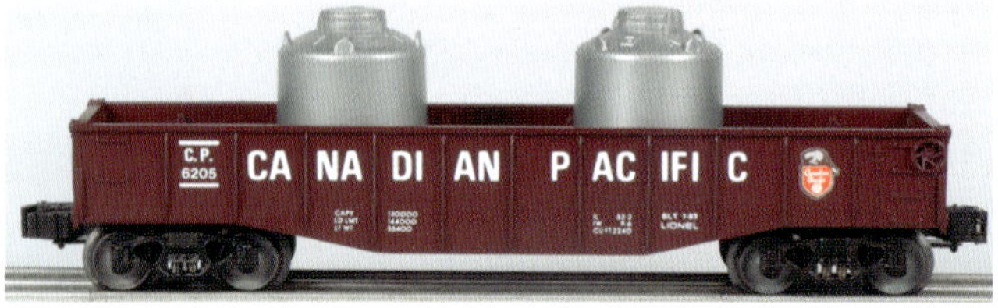

6205 CANADIAN PACIFIC: 1983, with canisters.

EX-C7	LN-C8	Scarcity
15	20	4

6206 CHICAGO & ILLINOIS MIDLAND: 1983-85, with canisters.

EX-C7	LN-C8	Scarcity
15	20	4

6207 SOUTHERN: 1983-85, with canisters in the traditional 027/Scout size.

EX-C7	LN-C8	Scarcity
3	5	3

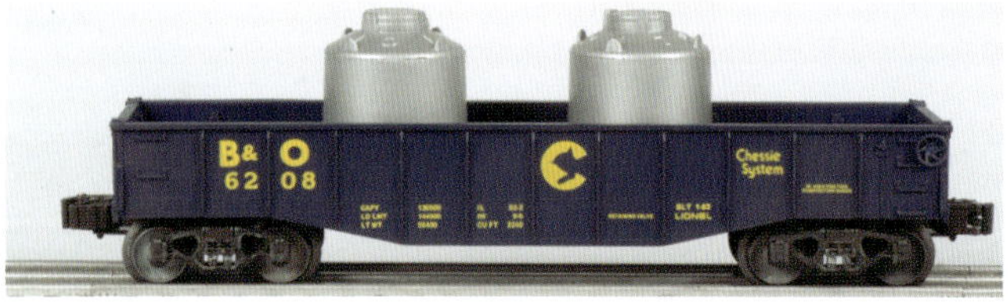

6208 CHESSIE SYSTEM: 1983, uncataloged with canisters.

EX-C7	LN-C8	Scarcity
15	20	4

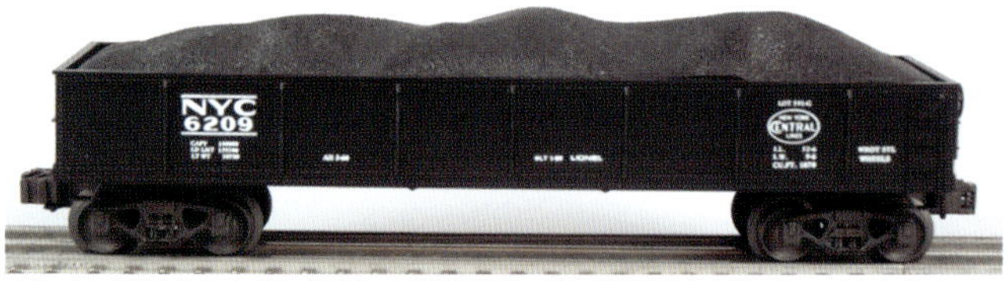

6209 NEW YORK CENTRAL: 1984-85, coal load with 1/48-scale proportions.

EX-C7	LN-C8	Scarcity
20	30	5

6210 ERIE-LACKAWANNA: 1984, with canisters.

EX-C7	LN-C8	Scarcity
15	20	4

6211 CHESAPEAKE AND OHIO: 1984-85, black with canisters.

6211 CHESAPEAKE AND OHIO (Type I): As described above.

EX-C7	LN-C8	Scarcity
3	5	3

6211 CHESAPEAKE AND OHIO (Type II): In 1986, some cars were overstamped to make this uncataloged car for LOTS.

EX-C7	LN-C8	Scarcity
30	40	4

6214 LIONEL LINES: 1984, uncataloged with canisters.

EX-C7	LN-C8	Scarcity
20	30	3

6231 RAILGON: 1986, uncataloged with coal load with 1/48-scale proportions.

EX-C7	LN-C8	Scarcity
40	50	5

6251 NEW YORK CENTRAL: 1985, coal dump car.

EX-C7	LN-C8	Scarcity
10	15	3

6254 NICKEL PLATE ROAD: 1986-91, with canisters.

EX-C7	LN-C8	Scarcity
5	10	3

6258 SANTA FE: 1985-86, 1992, uncataloged with canisters in the traditional 027/Scout size.

EX-C7	LN-C8	Scarcity
1	3	1

X6260 NEW YORK CENTRAL: 1985-86, with canisters.

EX-C7	LN-C8	Scarcity
5	10	3

6272 SANTA FE: 1986, with cable reels Service Station Special item.

EX-C7	LN-C8	Scarcity
15	20	5

[6573] REDWOOD VALLEY EXPRESS: 1984-85, flatcar with dump bin in the traditional 027/Scout size.

EX-C7	LN-C8	Scarcity
5	10	2

9017 WABASH: 1978-82, with canister load in the traditional 027/Scout size.

EX-C7	LN-C8	Scarcity
3	5	1

[9030] KICKAPOO VALLEY: 1972, 1979, in the traditional 027/Scout size.

[9030] KICKAPOO VALLEY (Type I): Red.

EX-C7	LN-C8	Scarcity
3	5	2

[9030] KICKAPOO VALLEY (Type II): Green.

EX-C7	LN-C8	Scarcity
3	5	2

[9030] KICKAPOO VALLEY (Type III): Yellow.

EX-C7	LN-C8	Scarcity
3	5	2

9031 NICKEL PLATE ROAD: 1973-75, 1982-83, uncataloged from 1984-91, with canisters in the traditional 027/Scout size.

9031 NICKEL PLATE ROAD (Type I): Features large molded-in brakewheels.

EX-C7	LN-C8	Scarcity
3	5	1

9031 NICKEL PLATE ROAD (Type II): Features small molded-in brakewheels.

EX-C7	LN-C8	Scarcity
3	5	1

9032 SOUTHERN PACIFIC: 1975-78, with canisters in the traditional 027/Scout size.

9032 SOUTHERN PACIFIC (Type I): Features large molded-in brakewheels.

EX-C7	LN-C8	Scarcity
2	4	1

9032 SOUTHERN PACIFIC (Type II): Features small molded-in brakewheels.

EX-C7	LN-C8	Scarcity
2	4	1

9033 PENN CENTRAL: Cataloged from 1976-78, 1982, uncataloged in 1986, 1987-90, uncataloged in 1992, with canisters in the traditional 027/Scout size.

EX-C7	LN-C8	Scarcity
2	4	1

9055 REPUBLIC STEEL: 1978, uncataloged with canisters.

EX-C7	LN-C8	Scarcity
5	10	4

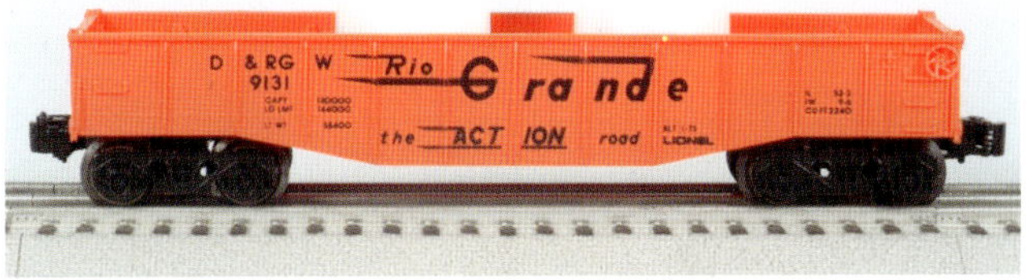

9131 DENVER & RIO GRANDE WESTERN: 1973-77, with canisters.

EX-C7	LN-C8	Scarcity
3	5	3

9136 REPUBLIC STEEL: 1972-76, 1979, with canister load.

EX-C7	LN-C8	Scarcity
5	8	2

9140 BURLINGTON: 1970, 1973-82, 1987-89, with canisters.

9140 BURLINGTON (Type I): Initially, AAR trucks were used on this car.

EX-C7	LN-C8	Scarcity
5	8	2

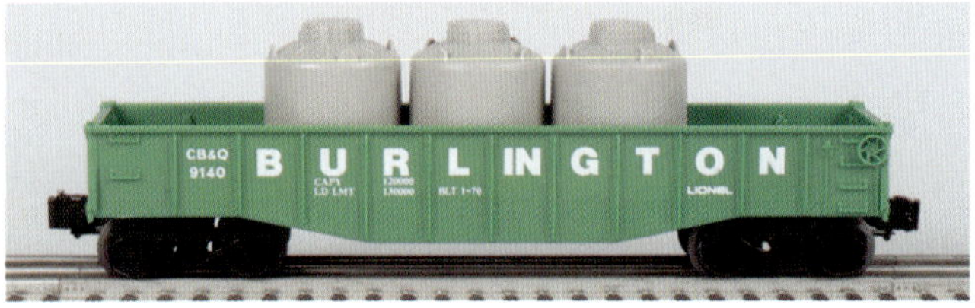

9140 BURLINGTON (Type II): Later production cars used Symington-Wayne trucks.

EX-C7	LN-C8	Scarcity
5	8	2

9141 BURLINGTON NORTHERN: 1970-72, with canisters.

9141 BURLINGTON NORTHERN (Type I): Most of these cars were molded in green plastic of various shades.

EX-C7	LN-C8	Scarcity
5	8	2

9141 BURLINGTON NORTHERN (Type II): However, some cars destined for the Canadian market had molded Tuscan bodies.

EX-C7	LN-C8	Scarcity
80	100	6

9142 REPUBLIC STEEL: 1971, green with canisters.

9142 REPUBLIC STEEL (Type I): As described above.

EX-C7	LN-C8	Scarcity
5	8	2

9142 REPUBLIC STEEL (Type II): From 1977-78, some cars were overstamped to create this uncataloged LCCA gondola with canisters.

EX-C7	LN-C8	Scarcity
10	15	6

9143 CANADIAN NATIONAL: 1971-73, uncataloged with canisters.

EX-C7	LN-C8	Scarcity
20	25	5

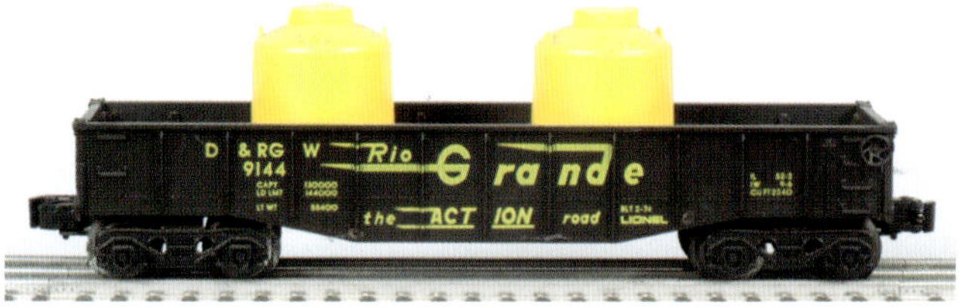

9144 DENVER & RIO GRANDE WESTERN: 1974-76, with canisters, Service Station Special item.

EX-C7	LN-C8	Scarcity
8	12	6

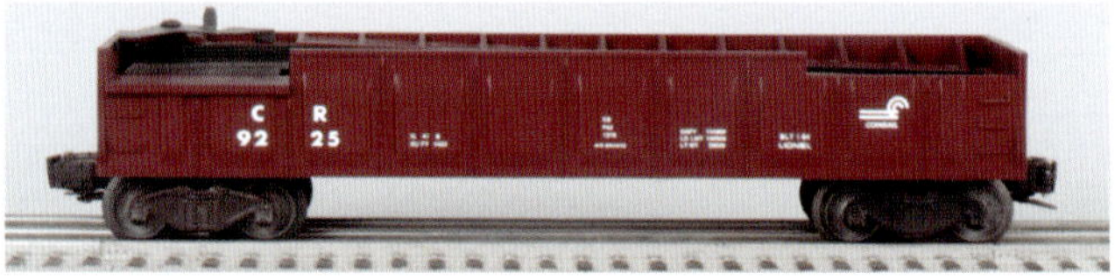

9225 CONRAIL: 1984, operating barrel car.

EX-C7	LN-C8	Scarcity
40	65	5

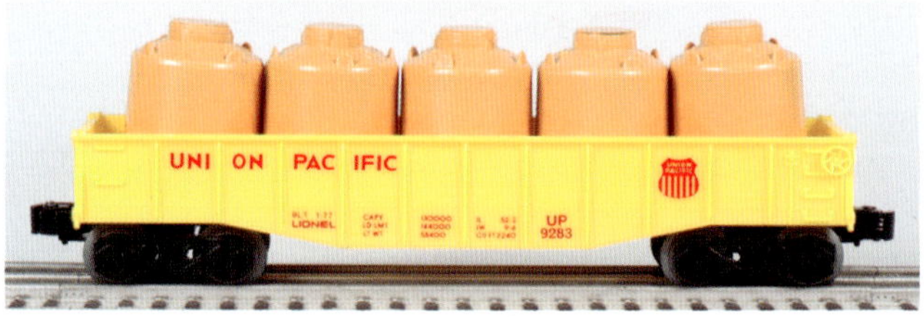

9283 UNION PACIFIC: 1977, with canisters.

EX-C7	LN-C8	Scarcity
10	15	4

9284 SANTA FE: 1977, with canisters.

EX-C7	LN-C8	Scarcity
10	15	4

9290 UNION PACIFIC: 1983, operating barrel car.

EX-C7	LN-C8	Scarcity
40	50	5

9304 CHESAPEAKE & OHIO: 1974-78, coal dump car.

EX-C7	LN-C8	Scarcity
5	10	2

9307 ERIE: 1980-84, animated.

EX-C7	LN-C8	Scarcity
30	40	5

9311 UNION PACIFIC: Uncataloged in 1978, cataloged from 1979-82, coal dump car.

EX-C7	LN-C8	Scarcity
7	13	2

9315 SOUTHERN PACIFIC: 1979, uncataloged with canisters.

9315 SOUTHERN PACIFIC (Type I): Some cars were equipped with Symington-Wayne trucks.

EX-C7	LN-C8	Scarcity
15	20	4

9315 SOUTHERN PACIFIC (Type II): Other cars were equipped with Standard 0 trucks.

EX-C7	LN-C8	Scarcity
15	20	4

[9330] KICKAPOO VALLEY: 1972, 1979, four-wheel dump car.

[9330] KICKAPOO VALLEY (Type I): Red.

EX-C7	LN-C8	Scarcity
2	5	1

[9330] KICKAPOO VALLEY (Type II): Green.

EX-C7	LN-C8	Scarcity
2	5	1

[9330] KICKAPOO VALLEY (Type III): Yellow.

EX-C7	LN-C8	Scarcity
2	5	1

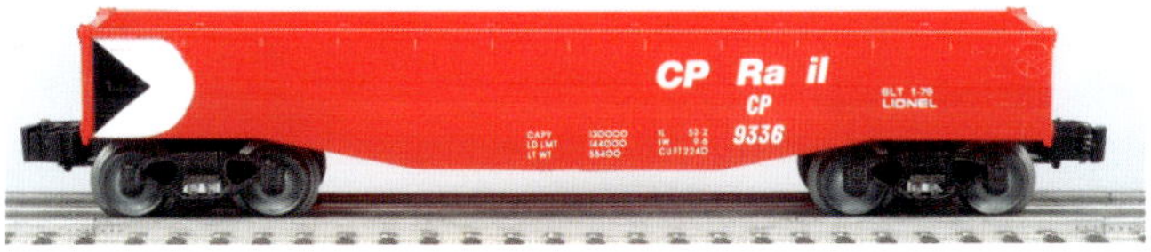

9336 CP RAIL: 1979, with canisters.

EX-C7	LN-C8	Scarcity
10	15	3

9340 ILLINOIS CENTRAL: Cataloged from 1979-81, uncataloged in 1982, cataloged again in 1983, with canisters in the traditional 027/Scout size.

EX-C7	LN-C8	Scarcity
3	5	2

[9363] NORFOLK AND WESTERN: 1979, flatcar with dump bin "9325" in the traditional 027/Scout size.

EX-C7	LN-C8	Scarcity
3	5	1

9370 SEABOARD: 1980, with canisters.

EX-C7	LN-C8	Scarcity
15	20	4

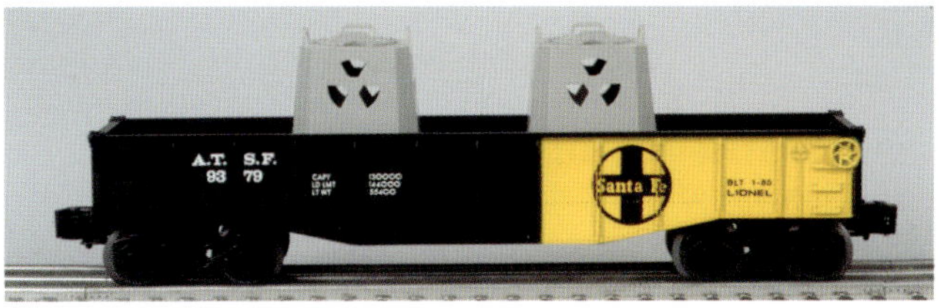

9379 SANTA FE: 1980-81, 1983, uncataloged with canisters.

EX-C7	LN-C8	Scarcity
10	15	2

9385 ALASKA RAILROAD: 1981, with canisters.

EX-C7	LN-C8	Scarcity
15	20	4

9398 PENNSYLVANIA: 1983-84, coal dump car.

EX-C7	LN-C8	Scarcity
10	15	2

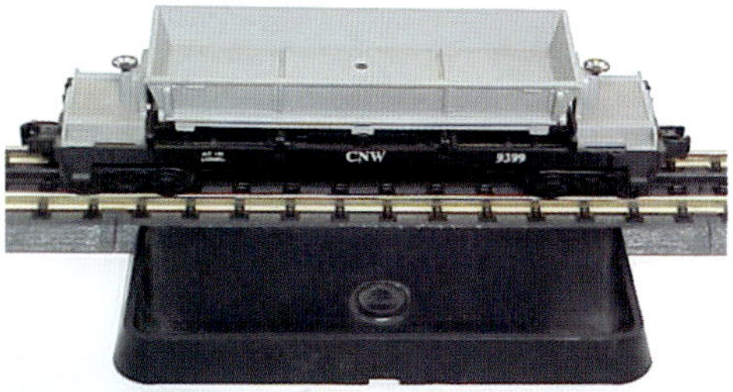

9399 CHICAGO & NORTHWESTERN: 1983-85, coal dump car.

EX-C7	LN-C8	Scarcity
10	15	2

9820 WABASH: 1973-74, coal load with 1/48-scale proportions.

EX-C7	LN-C8	Scarcity
20	25	4

9821 SOUTHERN PACIFIC: 1973-75, with coal load and 1/48-scale proportions.

9821 SOUTHERN PACIFIC (Type I): Most of these cars had brown bodies.

EX-C7	LN-C8	Scarcity
25	30	5

9821 SOUTHERN PACIFIC (Type II): A few of these cars had black bodies.

EX-C7	LN-C8	Scarcity
150	200	7

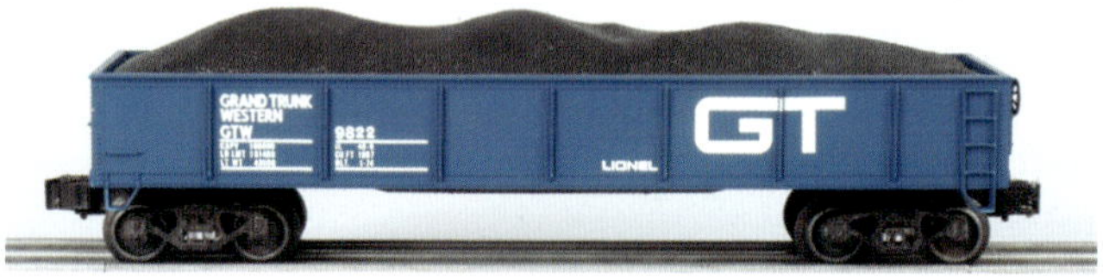

9822 GRAND TRUNK WESTERN: 1974-75, coal load with 1/48-scale proportions.

EX-C7	LN-C8	Scarcity
20	25	5

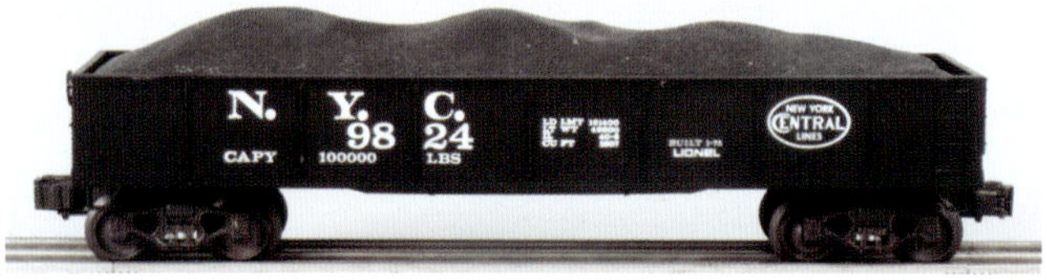

9824 NEW YORK CENTRAL: 1975-76, coal load with 1/48-scale proportions.

EX-C7	LN-C8	Scarcity
35	40	5

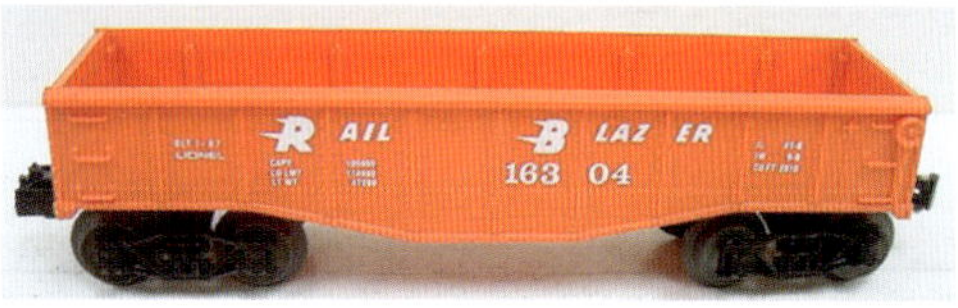

16304 ROCK ISLAND: 1987-88, with cable reel in the traditional 027/Scout size.

EX-C7	LN-C8	Scarcity
5	8	3

16309 WABASH: 1988-91, with canisters.

EX-C7	LN-C8	Scarcity
5	8	2

[16310] MOPAR EXPRESS: 1987-88, uncataloged with canisters, numbered "1987."

EX-C7	LN-C8	Scarcity
20	25	5

16313 PENNSYLVANIA: Uncataloged in 1988, cataloged in 1989, with cable reels in the traditional 027/Scout size.

EX-C7	LN-C8	Scarcity
5	8	2

[16327] "THE BIG TOP" CIRCUS: 1989, uncataloged with canisters.

EX-C7	LN-C8	Scarcity
10	15	4

16328 NICKEL PLATE ROAD: 1990-91, with cable reels.

16328 NICKEL PLATE ROAD (Type I): Some of the cars had the "NKP 16328" stamped in the third panel from the end.

EX-C7	LN-C8	Scarcity
10	15	4

16328 NICKEL PLATE ROAD (Type II): Other cars had the "NKP 16328" stamped in the fourth panel from the end.

EX-C7	LN-C8	Scarcity
10	15	4

[16336] UNION PACIFIC: 1990-91, uncataloged with canisters, numbered "6336."

EX-C7	LN-C8	Scarcity
10	15	3

16339 MICKEY'S WORLD TOUR: 1991, 1992, uncataloged with canisters in the traditional 027/Scout size.

EX-C7	LN-C8	Scarcity
10	15	4

16342 CSX: 1992, with coil covers.

EX-C7	LN-C8	Scarcity
10	15	3

16343 BURLINGTON: 1992, with coil covers.

EX-C7	LN-C8	Scarcity
10	15	3

16353 BOSTON AND MAINE: 1991, uncataloged with coil covers.

EX-C7	LN-C8	Scarcity
25	30	4

16355 BURLINGTON: Cataloged in 1992, uncataloged in 1993, cataloged again from 1994-95, red gondola.

EX-C7	LN-C8	Scarcity
5	10	2

16358 LOUISVILLE AND NASHVILLE: 1992, with coil covers.

EX-C7	LN-C8	Scarcity
10	15	3

16359 PACIFIC COAST: 1992, with coil cover, Service Station Special item.

EX-C7	LN-C8	Scarcity
25	30	5

16367 CLINCHFIELD: 1993, with coil covers.

EX-C7	LN-C8	Scarcity
10	15	4

16384 SOO LINE: 1993, with cable reels.

EX-C7	LN-C8	Scarcity
10	15	4

16387 KANSAS CITY SOUTHERN: 1994, with coil covers.

EX-C7	LN-C8	Scarcity
10	15	4

16388 LEHIGH VALLEY: 1994, with canisters.

EX-C7	LN-C8	Scarcity
10	15	4

16391 LIONEL LINES: 1993, uncataloged.

EX-C7	LN-C8	Scarcity
5	10	3

16392 WABASH: Uncataloged in 1993, cataloged in 1994, gondola with canisters in the traditional 027/Scout size.

EX-C7	LN-C8	Scarcity
4	8	5

[16442] BETHLEHEM: 1999, Service Station Special item, numbered "6462."

EX-C7	LN-C8	Scarcity
25	30	5

16600 ILLINOIS CENTRAL: 1988, coal dump car.

EX-C7	LN-C8	Scarcity
10	15	4

16602 ERIE-LACKAWANNA: 1987, coal dump car.

EX-C7	LN-C8	Scarcity
10	15	4

[16607] SOUTHERN: 1987, coal dump car numbered "16707," Service Station Special item.

EX-C7	LN-C8	Scarcity
15	20	5

16613 MISSOURI-KANSAS-TEXAS: 1989, coal dump car.

EX-C7	LN-C8	Scarcity
15	20	4

16619 WABASH: 1990, coal dump car.

EX-C7	LN-C8	Scarcity
10	15	4

16628 "LAUGHTER" CIRCUS: 1990-91, animated.

EX-C7	LN-C8	Scarcity
30	35	5

16634 WESTERN MARYLAND: 1991, coal dump car.

EX-C7	LN-C8	Scarcity
20	25	4

16643 AMTRAK: 1991, coal dump car.

EX-C7	LN-C8	Scarcity
Cataloged, but not produced.		

16657 LEHIGH VALLEY: 1992, uncataloged coal dump car.

EX-C7	LN-C8	Scarcity
15	20	4

16664 LOUISVILLE AND NASHVILLE: 1993, coal dump car.

EX-C7	LN-C8	Scarcity
10	15	4

16674 PINKERTON: 1994, animated.

EX-C7	LN-C8	Scarcity
20	25	4

16676 BURLINGTON NORTHERN: 1994, coal dump car.

EX-C7	LN-C8	Scarcity
15	20	4

16712 PINKERTON: 1995, animated.

EX-C7	LN-C8	Scarcity
20	25	4

16714 BURLINGTON NORTHERN: 1995, coal dump car.

EX-C7	LN-C8	Scarcity
Cataloged, but not produced.		

[16737] ACME: 1996, Runner & Wile E. Coyote numbered "3444."

EX-C7	LN-C8	Scarcity
25	30	4

[16749] MIDGET MINES: 1997, ore dump car.

EX-C7	LN-C8	Scarcity
15	20	4

[16760] PLUTO AND CATS: 1997, animated, numbered "3444."

EX-C7	LN-C8	Scarcity
35	40	4

[16766] BUREAU OF LAND MANAGEMENT: 1998, ore dump car numbered "3479."

EX-C7	LN-C8	Scarcity
20	25	4

[16782] BETHLEHEM: 1999, ore dump car numbered "3479."

EX-C7	LN-C8	Scarcity
65	85	4

[16784] PRATT'S HOLLOW SEED: 1999, dump car numbered "3479."

EX-C7	LN-C8	Scarcity
30	35	4

[16795] ELF CHASING RUDOLPH: 1999, numbered "6462."

EX-C7	LN-C8	Scarcity
35	45	4

[16909] U.S. NAVY: 1994-95, with canisters numbered "16556."

EX-C7	LN-C8	Scarcity
12	18	4

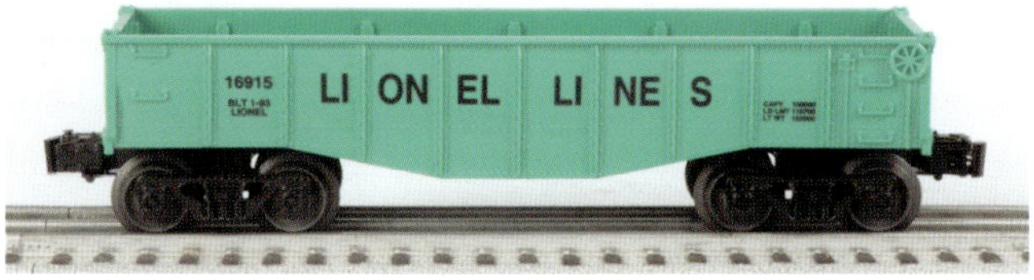

16915 LIONEL LINES: 1993-94, uncataloged in the traditional 027/Scout size.

EX-C7	LN-C8	Scarcity
4	7	2

[16917] CRAYOLA: Uncataloged in 1994, cataloged in 1995, with crayons.

EX-C7	LN-C8	Scarcity
4	7	2

[16919] CHRYSLER: 1994-96, Mopar with coil covers.

EX-C7	LN-C8	Scarcity
25	30	5

16927 NEW YORK CENTRAL: 1995, flatcar with gondola.

EX-C7	LN-C8	Scarcity
10	15	4

16928 SOO LINE: 1995, flatcar with dump bin in the traditional 027/Scout size.

EX-C7	LN-C8	Scarcity
10	15	4

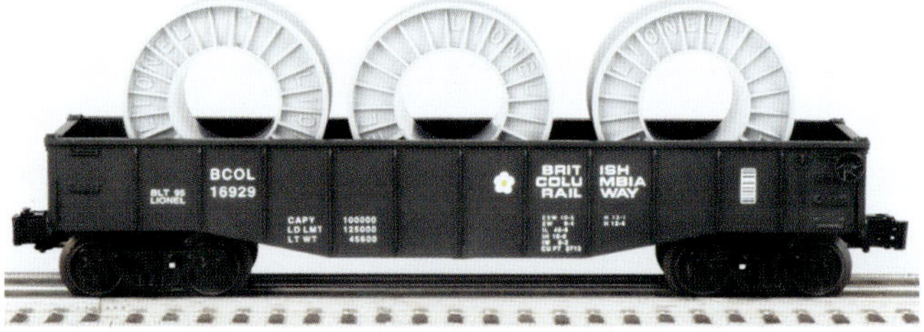

16929 BC RAIL: 1995, with cable reels.

EX-C7	LN-C8	Scarcity
10	15	4

16943 JERSEY CENTRAL: 1996.

EX-C7	LN-C8	Scarcity
10	15	4

[16964] LIONEL CORPORATION: 1997, numbered "6462."

EX-C7	LN-C8	Scarcity
10	15	3

[16972] P & LE: 1997, numbered "6462."

[17143]: 1999, gondola with parts load, Service Station Special item, 2000 (six-pack).

EX-C7	LN-C8	Scarcity
100	125	6

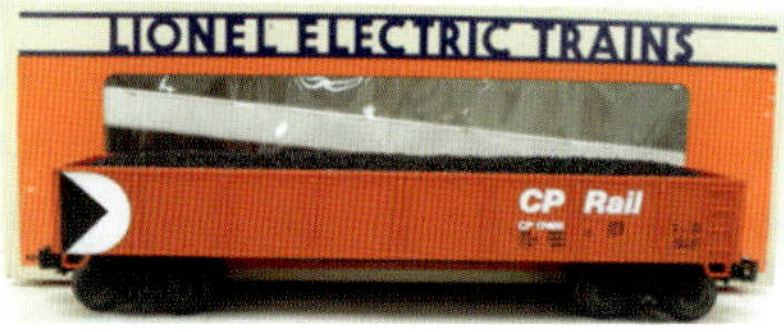

17400 CP RAIL: 1989, gondola with 1/48-scale proportions and coal load.

EX-C7	LN-C8	Scarcity
25	30	4

17401 CONRAIL: 1987, gondola with 1/48-scale proportions and coal load.

EX-C7	LN-C8	Scarcity
25	30	4

17402 SANTA FE: 1990, gondola with 1/48-scale proportions and coal load.

EX-C7	LN-C8	Scarcity
20	25	4

[17403] CHESSIE SYSTEM: 1993, numbered "371629" with coil covers and 1/48-scale proportions.

EX-C7	LN-C8	Scarcity
20	25	4

[17404] ILLINOIS CENTRAL GULF: 1993, with coil covers numbered "245998," with 1/48-scale proportions.

EX-C7	LN-C8	Scarcity
25	30	4

GONDOLA AND COAL DUMP CARS

[17405] READING: 1994, with coil covers numbered "24876," with 1/48-scale proportions.

EX-C7	LN-C8	Scarcity
20	25	4

[17406] PENNSYLVANIA: 1995, with coil covers numbered "385405," with 1/48-scale proportions.

EX-C7	LN-C8	Scarcity
25	30	4

[17407] NICKEL PLATE ROAD: 1996, with scrap load and 1/48-scale proportions.

EX-C7	LN-C8	Scarcity
20	25	4

[17408] COTTON BELT: 1997, with scrap load numbered "9820," with 1/48-scale proportions.

EX-C7	LN-C8	Scarcity
20	25	4

[17410] UNION PACIFIC: 1999, with scrap numbered "903004," with 1/48-scale proportions.

EX-C7	LN-C8	Scarcity
20	25	4

[17413] SERVICE CENTER: 2000, with parts load, Service Station Special item.

EX-C7	LN-C8	Scarcity
15	20	5

19400 MILWAUKEE ROAD: 1987, with cable reels, Fallen Flags number two.

EX-C7	LN-C8	Scarcity
20	25	5

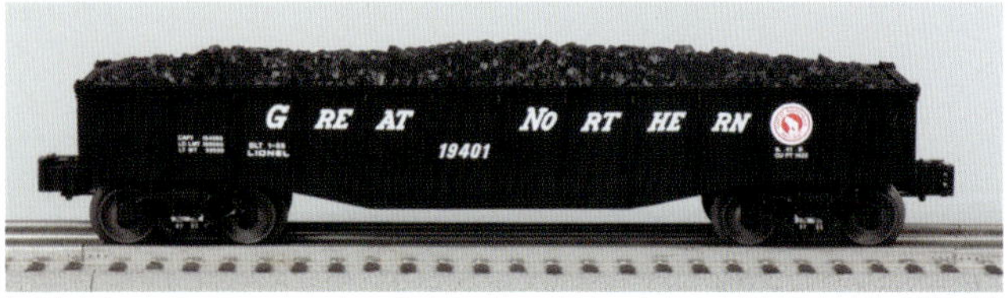

19401 GREAT NORTHERN: 1988, with coal load, Fallen Flags number three.

EX-C7	LN-C8	Scarcity
20	25	5

19403 WESTERN MARYLAND: 1989, with coal load, Fallen Flags number four.

EX-C7	LN-C8	Scarcity
15	20	5

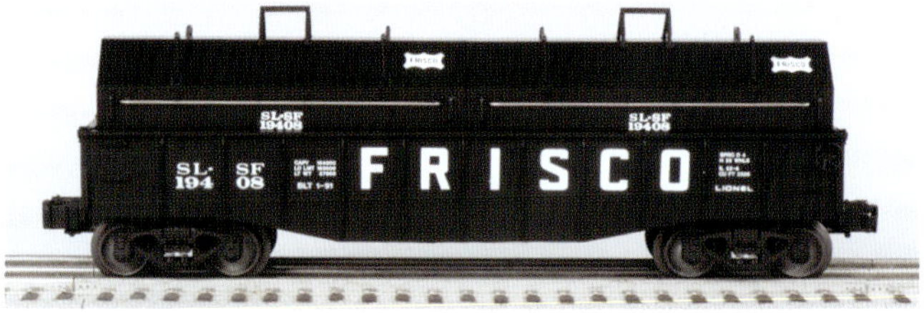

19408 FRISCO: 1991, with coil covers, Fallen Flags number five.

EX-C7	LN-C8	Scarcity
25	30	5

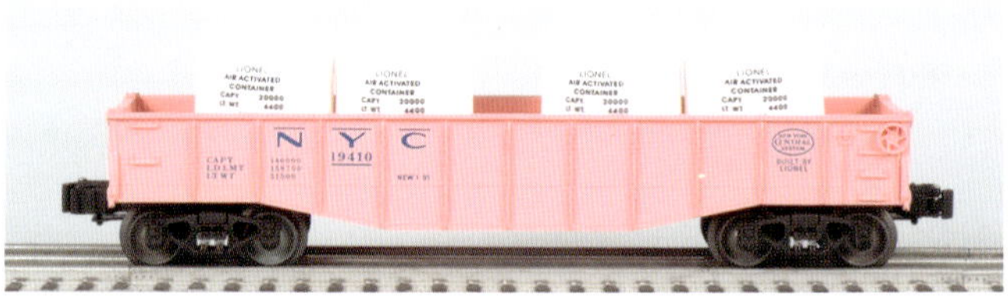

19410 NEW YORK CENTRAL: 1991, with canisters.

EX-C7	LN-C8	Scarcity
35	40	4

[19429] NEW YORK CENTRAL: 1998-99, numbered "6362" with culvert load.

EX-C7	LN-C8	Scarcity
30	35	4

[19438] STANDARD 0 CHRISTMAS: 1998.

EX-C7	LN-C8	Scarcity
25	30	4

[19448]: 1999, Easter gondola with candy, numbered "6462."

EX-C7	LN-C8	Scarcity
20	25	4

[19454] PENNSYLVANIA: 1999, flatcar with gondola cargo.

EX-C7	LN-C8	Scarcity
15	20	4

[19459] VALENTINE: 1999, with candy.

EX-C7	LN-C8	Scarcity
30	35	4

[19476] LIONEL ZOO: 1999-2000, with animals.

EX-C7	LN-C8	Scarcity
20	25	4

[19478] NEW YORK CENTRAL: 1999, green culvert gondola numbered "6342."

EX-C7	LN-C8	Scarcity
25	30	4

[19877] SANTA FE: 1999, operating barrel car numbered "356225," gray with red lettering.

EX-C7	LN-C8	Scarcity
25	30	4

[19955] LIONEL VISITOR'S CENTER: 1998, uncataloged with coil covers.

EX-C7	LN-C8	Scarcity
25	30	5

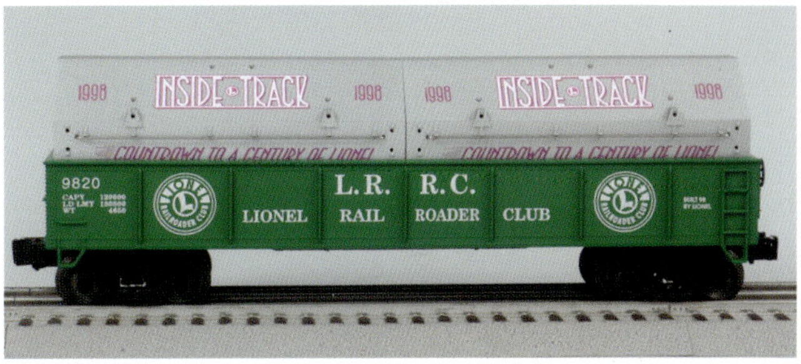

[19966] LIONEL RAILROADER CLUB: 1998, uncataloged, numbered "9820" with 1/48-scale proportions.

EX-C7	LN-C8	Scarcity
15	20	5

[19967] KIDS CLUB: 1998, uncataloged animated gondola.

EX-C7	LN-C8	Scarcity
25	30	5

[26721] LIONEL LINES: 2000, coal dump car "3379."

EX-C7	LN-C8	Scarcity
15	20	3

[26723]: 2000, lion-chasing-trainer gondola numbered "3444."

EX-C7	LN-C8	Scarcity
35	40	4

[26737] CHASING SANTA: 2000, uncataloged operating gondola.

EX-C7	LN-C8	Scarcity
35	40	5

[26738] LIONEL MINES: 2000, uncataloged.

EX-C7	LN-C8	Scarcity
Too rarely traded to establish accurate pricing.		

[26757] SANTA FE: 2000, operating black barrel car numbered "35621."

EX-C7	LN-C8	Scarcity
30	35	4

[26905] BETHLEHEM STEEL: 1998, with canisters.

EX-C7	LN-C8	Scarcity
20	25	4

[26913] E. ST. LOUIS: 1998.

EX-C7	LN-C8	Scarcity
15	20	4

[26956] CHESAPEAKE AND OHIO: 1998-99, in the traditional 027/Scout size.

EX-C7	LN-C8	Scarcity
10	15	3

[26972] PONY EXPRESS: 1998, animated.

EX-C7	LN-C8	Scarcity
20	25	3

[36030] TROUBLESOME TRUCK: 1999, numbered "1," goes with "Thomas the Tank Engine."

EX-C7	LN-C8	Scarcity
20	25	4

[36031] TROUBLESOME TRUCK: 1999, numbered "2," goes with "Thomas the Tank Engine."

EX-C7	LN-C8	Scarcity
20	25	4

[36032] CHRISTMAS: 1999, with gifts.

EX-C7	LN-C8	Scarcity
30	35	4

[36036] CHESAPEAKE AND OHIO: 1999.

EX-C7	LN-C8	Scarcity
15	20	4

[36038] CONSTRUCTION ZONE: 1999, uncataloged.

EX-C7	LN-C8	Scarcity
Too rarely traded to establish accurate pricing.		

[36047] CONSTRUCTION ZONE: 1999, uncataloged.

EX-C7	LN-C8	Scarcity
Too rarely traded to establish accurate pricing.		

[36048] CONSTRUCTION ZONE: 1999, uncataloged.

EX-C7	LN-C8	Scarcity
Too rarely traded to establish accurate pricing.		

[36054] ARCHAELOGICAL EXP: 2000, uncataloged with eggs.

EX-C7	LN-C8	Scarcity
40	45	4

[36059] SEASON'S GREETINGS: 1999, uncataloged.

EX-C7	LN-C8	Scarcity
35	40	4

[36062] NEW YORK CENTRAL: 1999-2000, numbered "6462."

EX-C7	LN-C8	Scarcity
10	15	3

[36063] CONRAIL: 1999-2000, numbered "604768."

EX-C7	LN-C8	Scarcity
10	15	3

[36066] CHRISTMAS: 2000, with gifts load.

EX-C7	LN-C8	Scarcity
20	25	4

[36068] PINE PEAK: 2000, tree transport.

EX-C7	LN-C8	Scarcity
Too rarely traded to establish accurate pricing.		

36084 GRAND TRUNK WESTERN: 2000, with coil covers.

EX-C7	LN-C8	Scarcity
25	30	4

36085 FLORIDA EAST COAST: 2000, with coil covers.

EX-C7	LN-C8	Scarcity
25	30	4

[52004] ALGOMA CENTRAL: 1992, uncataloged Lionel Collectors Association of Canada with coil covers, numbered "9215."

EX-C7	LN-C8	Scarcity
65	75	6

52016 BOSTON AND MAINE: 1993, uncataloged New England Division of Train Collectors Association with coil covers.

EX-C7	LN-C8	Scarcity
45	55	6

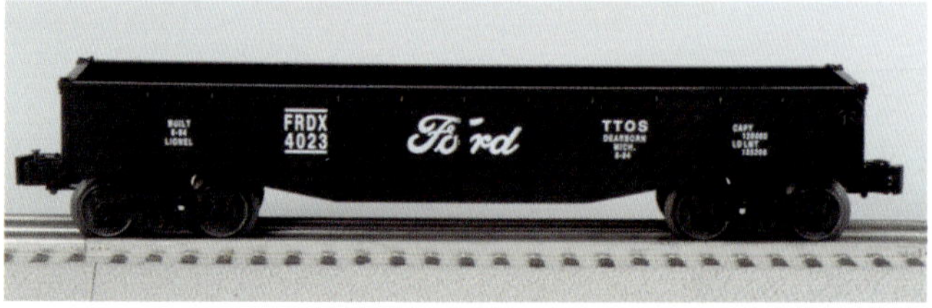

[52030] FORD: 1994, uncataloged TTOS numbered "4023."

EX-C7	LN-C8	Scarcity
25	30	6

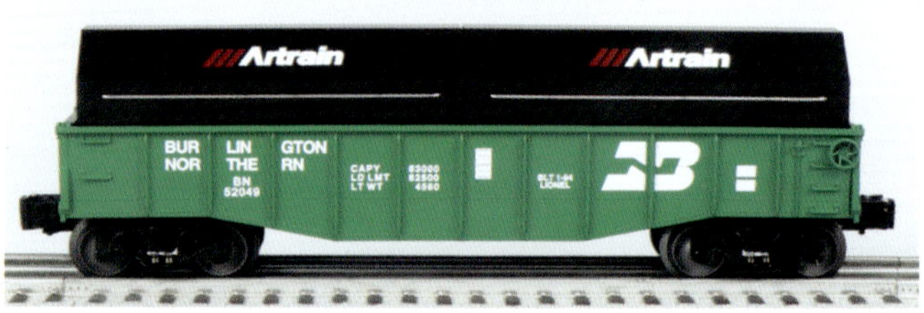

52049 BURLINGTON NORTHERN: 1994, uncataloged Artrain with coil covers.

EX-C7	LN-C8	Scarcity
50	60	6

[52105] SUPERSTITION MOUNTAIN: 1997, uncataloged operating gondola numbered "61997."

EX-C7	LN-C8	Scarcity
55	65	6

[52185] MONOPOLY CHANCE: 1999, numbered "M-0893."

EX-C7	LN-C8	Scarcity
45	55	6

[52192] SOUTHERN PACIFIC: 2000, uncataloged TTOS crane and gondola two-pack.

EX-C7	LN-C8	Scarcity
60	75	6

[52194] SOUTHERN PACIFIC: 2000, uncataloged TTOS gondola.

EX-C7	LN-C8	Scarcity
20	25	6

[99014] CASE CUTLERY: 2000, uncataloged gondola numbered "1889."

EX-C7	LN-C8	Scarcity
Too rarely traded to establish accurate pricing.		

[19454] PENNSYLVANIA: 1999, flatcar with gondola cargo.

EX-C7	LN-C8	Scarcity
15	20	4

Chapter 10

HOPPER AND ORE CARS

Real railroads use hopper cars to transport bulk dry commodities from grains to coal to cement. For products that are weather-sensitive, such as grains and cement powder, totally enclosed cars are used for transport. For material that is largely impervious to weather, such as coal and rock, open top hopper cars are used.

The latter-type is also a favorite of children, allowing them to transport aquarium gravel, Lego blocks, and a host of other items found in the toy box. It is not surprising then that open-top hopper cars, based on the postwar 2456 design, have been included in many introductory train sets. The further advantage for Lionel is the relatively low manufacturing cost of this type car, which is essentially a single piece of molded plastic with trucks attached.

In 1981, this car was modified to create an operating bottom-dump hopper car, just as had been done in the postwar era to create the 3456.

Like the 2456-style, the 6446-style hopper was also revived in 1970. These large cars, known among collectors as "quad" hoppers, were available in both open and covered versions. In the closed form, these cars replicated those used to transport grain, cement and other weather-sensitive materials. In open form the car was a larger version of the 6456-type open hopper. Lionel even introduced a molded "coal load" which was found in some cars. In addition to adding interest, these loads also served to reinforce the large car body, which was rather flimsy without the cover, especially if Lionel did not install the steel-reinforcing rod designed for this purpose decades earlier.

In 1984, Lionel introduced a molded plastic "ore car." These short cars resemble small hoppers. In actual railroad use, these cars are much more substantially built than normal hopper cars, and are used to transport unusually dense, bulk ores. Ultimately, a molded plastic "load" insert for some of these cars was made.

In 1996, a new variation of the ore car was introduced, the die-cast car, initiated by the 51503 and 51504 that came in the 11912 Service Station Special set. Not only do these cars have die-cast bodies, they are also 9/32 of an inch wider than their plastic predecessors. Since 1996, both plastic and die-cast ore cars have been produced.

The die-cast ore car was not the first new hopper introduced in the modern era. In 1986, the company had introduced a 1/48-scale-proportioned detailed replica of the American Car and Foundry (ACF) two-bay center-flow hopper. In 1988, a longer, three-bay version joined the line. Both the two- and three-bay versions ride on the die-cast sprung "Standard 0" trucks. Bright colorful decorations are hallmarks of these series.

In 1991, a larger, equally detailed car was introduced. Representing a modern 48-foot hopper car, the new model was also in 1/48-scale proportions, and rode on "Standard 0" trucks. These cars came with user-installed operating bottom hatches, somewhat ironic in that Lionel included a molded solid load representation in the car. In 1995, a cover was created for this car body, and since then both covered and open but "loaded" versions of the car have been made.

Also in 1991, returning after a long absence was a hopper replicating Lionel's 1940 die-cast scale hopper car. Like its prewar brother, this car wore B & O markings, and the 1991 issue was the sole example of this car body until 1998 when the car returned yet again, now in an array of road names.

0784 LIONEL RAILROADER CLUB: 1984, uncataloged covered quad hopper car.

EX-C7	LN-C8	Scarcity
25	40	5

[1981] IETCA: 1981, uncataloged quad hopper car.

EX-C7	LN-C8	Scarcity
5	15	6

[1985] TTOS SNOWBIRD: 1985, uncataloged covered quad hopper car.

EX-C7	LN-C8	Scarcity
20	40	6

6076 LEHIGH VALLEY: 1970, uncataloged hopper car in the traditional 027/Scout size.

EX-C7	LN-C8	Scarcity
10	15	6

6076 TTOS SANTA FE: 1970, uncataloged hopper car in the traditional 027/Scout size.

EX-C7	LN-C8	Scarcity
30	45	6

6100 ONTARIO NORTHLAND: 1981-82, blue-covered quad hopper car.

6100 ONTARIO NORTHLAND (Type I): As described above.

EX-C7	LN-C8	Scarcity
15	20	3

6100 ONTARIO NORTHLAND (Type II): 1982, uncataloged Lionel Collectors Association of Canada covered quad hopper car.

EX-C7	LN-C8	Scarcity
125	175	6

6101 BURLINGTON NORTHERN: 1981-82, green-covered quad hopper car.

6101 BURLINGTON NORTHERN (Type I): As described above.

EX-C7	LN-C8	Scarcity
10	20	4

6101 BURLINGTON NORTHERN (Type II): 1982, uncataloged overstamped car for Atlantic Division of TCA.

EX-C7	LN-C8	Scarcity
15	25	6

6102 GREAT NORTHERN: 1981, covered quad hopper car, Famous American Railroads number three.

EX-C7	LN-C8	Scarcity
15	25	5

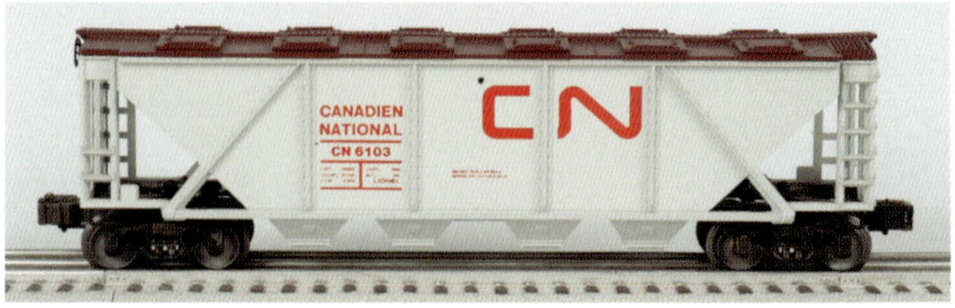

6103 CANADIAN NATIONAL: 1981, covered quad hopper car.

EX-C7	LN-C8	Scarcity
15	25	5

6104 SOUTHERN: 1983, quad hopper car with coal load, Famous American Railroads number four.

EX-C7	LN-C8	Scarcity
30	40	5

6105 READING: 1982, operating hopper car.

EX-C7	LN-C8	Scarcity
20	25	4

6106 NORFOLK AND WESTERN: 1982, covered quad hopper car.

EX-C7	LN-C8	Scarcity
15	20	4

6107 SHELL: 1982, covered quad hopper car.

EX-C7	LN-C8	Scarcity
15	20	4

6109 CHESAPEAKE & OHIO: 1983, operating hopper car.

EX-C7	LN-C8	Scarcity
15	20	4

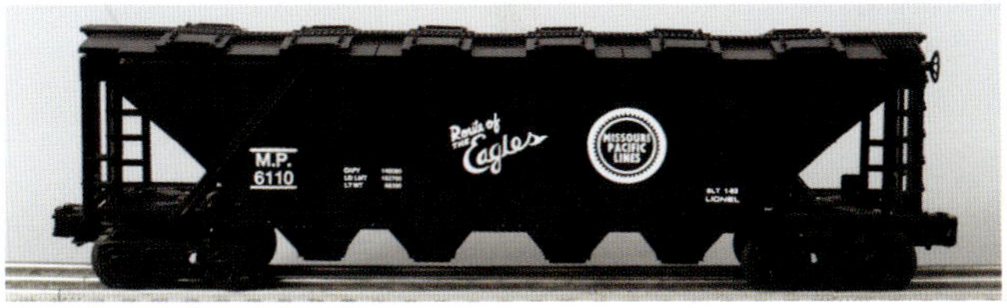

6110 MISSOURI PACIFIC: 1983-84, covered quad hopper car.

EX-C7	LN-C8	Scarcity
10	15	4

6111 LOUISVILLE & NASHVILLE: 1983-84, gray covered quad hopper car.

6111 LOUISVILLE & NASHVILLE (Type I): As described above.

EX-C7	LN-C8	Scarcity
10	15	4

6111 LOUISVILLE & NASHVILLE (Type II): 1983, uncataloged overstamped for Southern Division of TCA.

EX-C7	LN-C8	Scarcity
15	20	5

6111 LOUISVILLE & NASHVILLE (Type III): 1983, uncataloged overstamped for LOTS.

EX-C7	LN-C8	Scarcity
20	25	5

6112 COMMONWEALTH EDISON: 1983, uncataloged car made for the LCCA comes with coal load.

EX-C7	LN-C8	Scarcity
25	35	6

6113 ILLINOIS CENTRAL: 1983-85, hopper car in the traditional 027/Scout size.

EX-C7	LN-C8	Scarcity
10	15	4

6114 CHICAGO & NORTHWESTERN: 1983, covered quad hopper car.

EX-C7	LN-C8	Scarcity
25	35	6

6115 SOUTHERN: 1983-86, hopper car in the traditional 027/Scout size.

EX-C7	LN-C8	Scarcity
10	15	4

6116 SOO LINE: 1984, ore car.

EX-C7	LN-C8	Scarcity
20	25	4

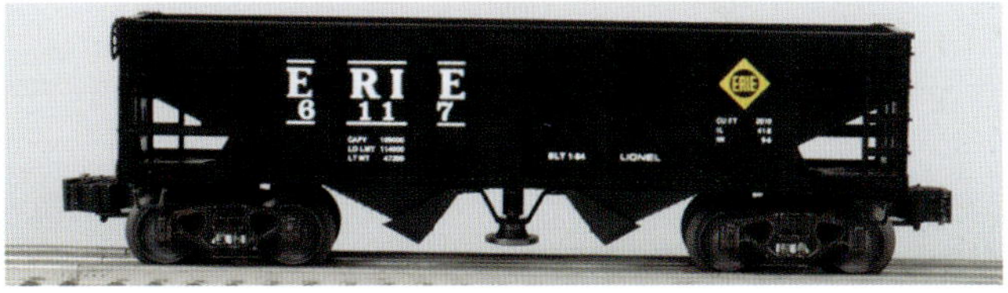

6117 ERIE: 1984, operating hopper car.

EX-C7	LN-C8	Scarcity
20	25	4

6118 ERIE: 1984, covered quad hopper car.

EX-C7	LN-C8	Scarcity
20	25	4

6122 PENN CENTRAL: 1984, ore car.

EX-C7	LN-C8	Scarcity
20	25	4

6123 PENNSYLVANIA: 1984-85, covered quad hopper car, Famous American Railroads number five.

EX-C7	LN-C8	Scarcity
25	50	5

6124 DELAWARE & HUDSON: 1984, red-covered quad hopper car.

6124 DELAWARE & HUDSON (Type I): As described above.

EX-C7	LN-C8	Scarcity
15	20	4

6124 DELAWARE & HUDSON (Type II): 1984, uncataloged overstamped for the New England Division of Train Collectors Association.

EX-C7	LN-C8	Scarcity
18	25	5

6126 CANADIAN NATIONAL: 1986, ore car.

EX-C7	LN-C8	Scarcity
20	25	4

6127 NORTHERN PACIFIC: 1986, ore car.

EX-C7	LN-C8	Scarcity
15	20	4

6131 ILLINOIS TERMINAL: 1985-86, covered quad hopper car.

EX-C7	LN-C8	Scarcity
10	15	4

6134 BURLINGTON NORTHERN: 1986, uncataloged two-bay ACF hopper car with 1/48-scale proportions.

EX-C7	LN-C8	Scarcity
55	75	6

6135 CHICAGO & NORTHWESTERN: 1986, uncataloged two-bay ACF hopper car with 1/48-scale proportions.

EX-C7	LN-C8	Scarcity
55	75	6

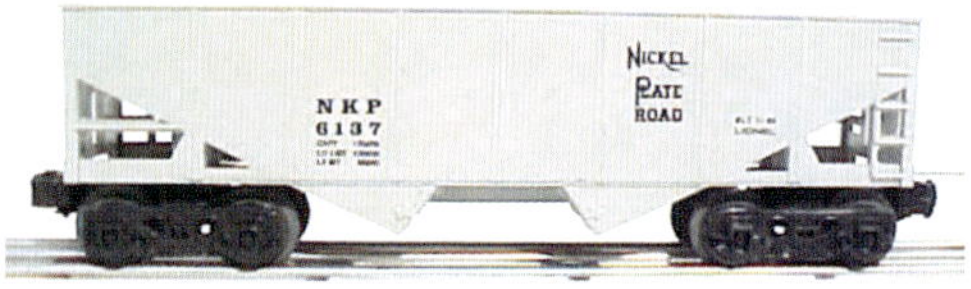

6137 NICKEL PLATE ROAD: 1986-91, hopper car in the traditional 027/Scout size.

EX-C7	LN-C8	Scarcity
10	15	4

6138 BALTIMORE & OHIO: 1986, quad hopper car with coal load.

EX-C7	LN-C8	Scarcity
10	15	3

6150 SANTA FE: 1985-86, 1992, uncataloged hopper car in the traditional 027/Scout size.

EX-C7	LN-C8	Scarcity
10	15	3

6177 READING: 1986-90, hopper car in the traditional 027/Scout size.

EX-C7	LN-C8	Scarcity
10	15	3

6446-25 NORFOLK & WESTERN: 1970, uncataloged covered quad hopper car.

EX-C7	LN-C8	Scarcity
75	150	7

[6476-135] LEHIGH VALLEY: 1970-71, uncataloged hopper car numbered "25000" in the traditional 027/Scout size.

EX-C7	LN-C8	Scarcity
5	10	5

7504 LIONEL 75TH ANNIVERSARY: 1975-77, covered quad hopper car.

EX-C7	LN-C8	Scarcity
15	20	4

[7682]VIRGINIATRAIN COLLECTORS: 1982, uncataloged covered quad hopper car.

EX-C7	LN-C8	Scarcity
15	20	5

[8390] LONG ISLAND: 1990, uncataloged NLOE covered quad hopper car.

EX-C7	LN-C8	Scarcity
35	50	6

[8912] CANADA SOUTHERN: 1989, uncataloged, Lionel Collectors Association of Canada operating hopper car.

EX-C7	LN-C8	Scarcity
50	75	6

9010 GREAT NORTHERN: 1970-71, hopper car molded with a big sky blue plastic body. In the traditional 027/Scout size.

9010 GREAT NORTHERN (Type I): This light blue car rode on AAR trucks and the markings include the date "1-70."

EX-C7	LN-C8	Scarcity
3	5	2

9010 GREAT NORTHERN (Type II): This medium blue car rode on AAR trucks and the markings include the date "1-70."

EX-C7	LN-C8	Scarcity
3	5	2

9010 GREAT NORTHERN (Type III): Some of the blue cars were equipped with Symington-Wayne trucks, yet the markings still include the date "1-70."

EX-C7	LN-C8	Scarcity
3	5	2

9010 GREAT NORTHERN (Type IV): Some of the medium blue cars riding on AAR trucks were marked with the date "7-70."

EX-C7	LN-C8	Scarcity
3	5	2

9011 GREAT NORTHERN: Uncataloged in 1970, 1975-76, 1978-83, hopper car in the traditional 027/Scout size.

9011 GREAT NORTHERN (Type I): The early cars had separately installed brakewheels, and the decoration included the MPC logo. These cars rode on AAR trucks.

EX-C7	LN-C8	Scarcity
5	10	1

9011 GREAT NORTHERN (Type II): Later cars rode on Symington-Wayne trucks and had separately installed brakewheels, and the decoration included the MPC logo.

EX-C7	LN-C8	Scarcity
5	10	1

9011 GREAT NORTHERN (TYPE III): Later cars had molded-in brakewheels, and the decoration continued to include the MPC logo. These cars also rode on Symington-Wayne trucks.

EX-C7	LN-C8	Scarcity
5	10	1

9011 GREAT NORTHERN (Type IV): Later cars had molded-in brakewheels, but the decoration lacked the MPC logo. These cars also rode on Symington-Wayne trucks.

EX-C7	LN-C8	Scarcity
5	10	1

9011 GREAT NORTHERN (TypeV): A handful of cars were produced which were molded from a deep royal blue.

EX-C7	LN-C8	Scarcity
80	100	6

9012 T.A. & G.: 1971-72, hopper car in the traditional 027/Scout size.

9012 T. A. & G. (Type I): Navy blue body molding.

EX-C7	LN-C8	Scarcity
5	10	2

9012 T. A .& G. (Type II): Bright royal blue body molding.

EX-C7	LN-C8	Scarcity
25	35	5

9013 CANADIAN NATIONAL: 1972-76, hopper car in the traditional 027/Scout size.

9013 CANADIAN NATIONAL (Type I): Light red body molding.

EX-C7	LN-C8	Scarcity
5	10	2

9013 CANADIAN NATIONAL (Type II): Medium red body molding.

EX-C7	LN-C8	Scarcity
5	10	2

9013 CANADIAN NATIONAL (Type III): Dark red body molding.

EX-C7	LN-C8	Scarcity
5	10	2

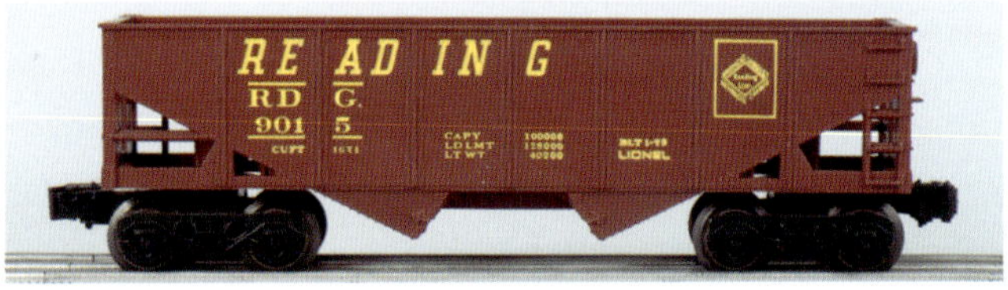

9015 READING: 1973-75, hopper car in the traditional 027/Scout size.

EX-C7	LN-C8	Scarcity
10	15	1

9016 CHESSIE SYSTEM: 1975-79, 1987-88, uncataloged in 1989, hopper car in the traditional 027/Scout size.

9016 CHESSIE SYSTEM (Type I): Light yellow body molding.

EX-C7	LN-C8	Scarcity
3	5	1

9016 CHESSIE SYSTEM (Type II): Medium yellow body molding.

EX-C7	LN-C8	Scarcity
3	5	1

9016 CHESSIE SYSTEM (Type III): Uncataloged hopper car with overstamped lettering reading "LCCA 1980-81 MEET CAR."

EX-C7	LN-C8	Scarcity
5	15	2

9018 DT & I: 1978-79, 1981-82, hopper car in the traditional 027/Scout size.

EX-C7	LN-C8	Scarcity
3	5	1

9034 LIONEL LEISURE: 1977, uncataloged hopper car in the traditional 027/Scout size.

EX-C7	LN-C8	Scarcity
20	30	6

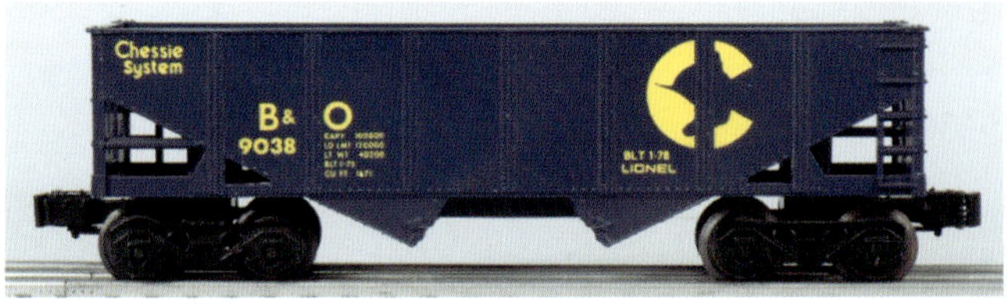

9038 CHESSIE SYSTEM: Uncataloged in 1978, cataloged in 1980, hopper car in the traditional 027/Scout size.

EX-C7	LN-C8	Scarcity
10	15	1

9079 GRAND TRUNK WESTERN: 1977, hopper car in the traditional 027/Scout size.

EX-C7	LN-C8	Scarcity
15	20	5

9110 BALTIMORE & OHIO: 1971, black quad hopper car.

9110 BALTIMORE & OHIO (Type I): Gray lettering on car.

EX-C7	LN-C8	Scarcity
40	50	6

9110 BALTIMORE & OHIO (Type II): White lettering on car.

EX-C7	LN-C8	Scarcity
20	25	4

9111 NORFOLK & WESTERN: 1972-75, brown quad hopper car. The early quad hoppers came with these cardboard packaging inserts which are often missing today.

9111 NORFOLK & WESTERN (Type I): Unpainted body.

EX-C7	LN-C8	Scarcity
12	18	4

9111 NORFOLK & WESTERN (Type II): Body painted Tuscan.

EX-C7	LN-C8	Scarcity
20	25	4

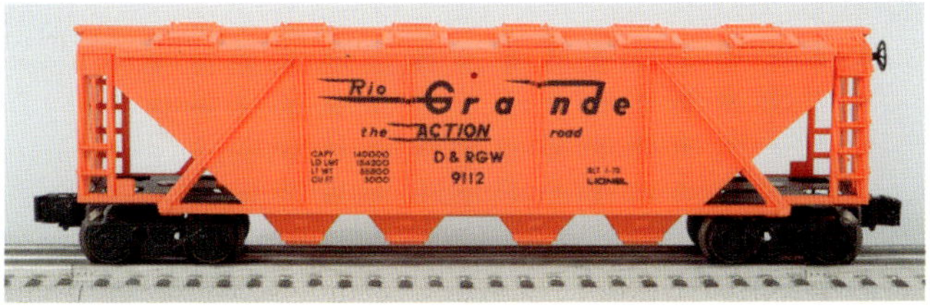

9112 DENVER & RIO GRANDE WESTERN: 1973-75, covered quad hopper car.

9112 DENVER & RIO GRANDE WESTERN (Type I): Light orange body molding.

EX-C7	LN-C8	Scarcity
12	18	4

9112 DENVER & RIO GRANDE WESTERN (Type II): Dark orange body molding.

EX-C7	LN-C8	Scarcity
12	18	4

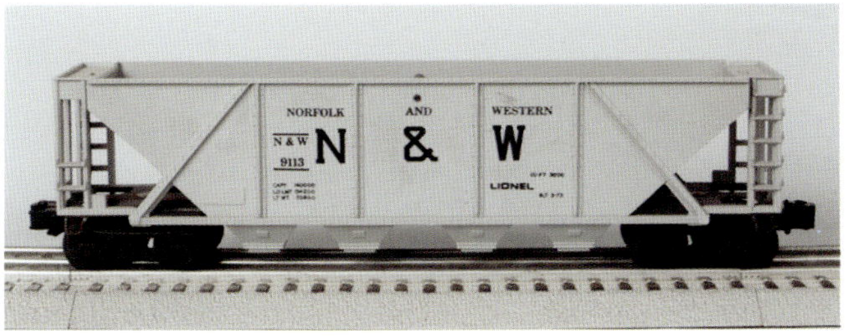

9113 NORFOLK & WESTERN (Type I): 1973, quad hopper car Service Station Special item.

EX-C7	LN-C8	Scarcity
15	20	5

9113 NORFOLK & WESTERN (Type II): 1976, uncataloged Three Rivers TCA quad hopper car.

EX-C7	LN-C8	Scarcity
20	25	6

9114 MORTON SALT: 1974-76, covered quad hopper car.

EX-C7	LN-C8	Scarcity
15	20	4

9115 PLANTER'S: 1974-76, covered quad hopper car.

EX-C7	LN-C8	Scarcity
15	20	4

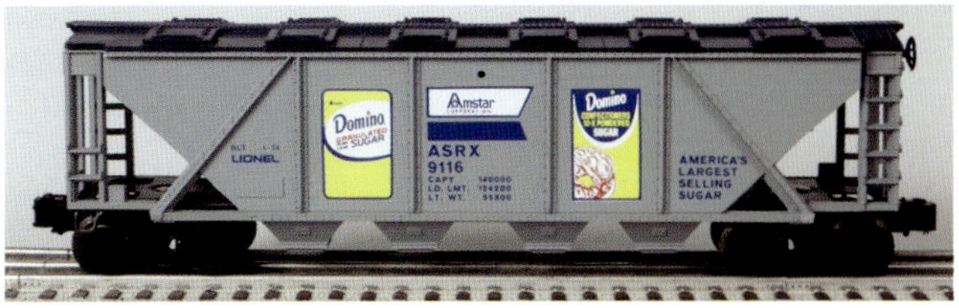

9116 DOMINO SUGAR: 1974-76, covered quad hopper car.

EX-C7	LN-C8	Scarcity
15	20	4

9117 ALASKA RAILROAD: 1974-76, covered quad hopper car Service Station Special item.

9117 ALASKA RAILROAD (Type I): Body molding includes simulated builder's plate.

EX-C7	LN-C8	Scarcity
20	25	5

9117 ALASKA RAILROAD (Type II): Body molding lacks simulated builder's plate.

EX-C7	LN-C8	Scarcity
20	25	5

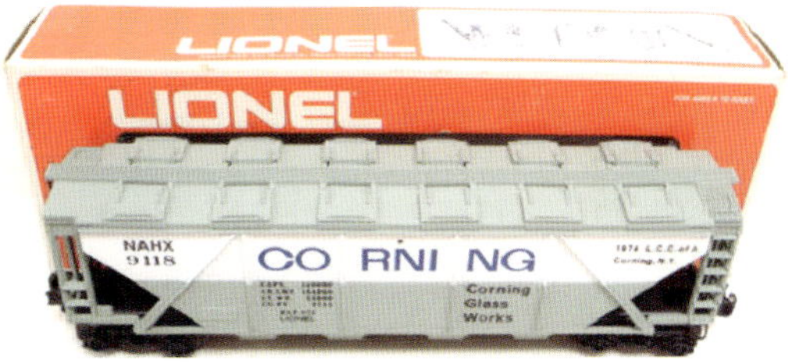

9118 CORNING: 1974, uncataloged LCCA covered quad hopper car.

EX-C7	LN-C8	Scarcity
40	55	6

9119 DETROIT & MACKINAC: 1975, red covered quad hopper car; Service Station Special item.

9119 DETROIT & MACKINAC (Type I): As described above.

EX-C7	LN-C8	Scarcity
15	20	4

9119 DETROIT & MACKINAC (Type II): 1977, uncataloged covered quad hopper car overstamped "Season's Greetings – made for the Detroit-Toledo chapter of the TCA."

EX-C7	LN-C8	Scarcity
18	24	6

9119 DETROIT & MACKINAC (Type III): 1978, uncataloged North Texas TCA covered quad hopper car.

EX-C7	LN-C8	Scarcity
20	25	6

9130 BALTIMORE & OHIO: 1970, quad hopper car.

9130 BALTIMORE & OHIO (Type I): The early production cars featured metal truck mounting plates.

EX-C7	LN-C8	Scarcity
15	20	4

9130 BALTIMORE & OHIO (Type II): Later cars featured molded plastic truck mounting plates.

EX-C7	LN-C8	Scarcity
15	20	4

9134 VIRGINIAN: 1976-77, covered quad hopper car.

9134 VIRGINIAN (Type I): Body molding includes a simulated builder's plate.

EX-C7	LN-C8	Scarcity
20	25	4

9134 VIRGINIAN (Type II): Body molding lacks simulated builder's plate.

EX-C7	LN-C8	Scarcity
20	25	4

9135 NORFOLK & WESTERN: Uncataloged in 1970, cataloged in 1971, 1975, covered quad hopper car.

9135 NORFOLK & WESTERN (Type I): Features a light sky blue body molding including simulated builder's plate. Rides on AAR trucks.

EX-C7	LN-C8	Scarcity
15	20	4

9135 NORFOLK & WESTERN (Type II): Features a royal blue body molding including simulated builder's plate. Rides on Symington-Wayne trucks.

EX-C7	LN-C8	Scarcity
15	20	4

9135 NORFOLK & WESTERN (Type III): Features a royal blue body molding that lacks simulated builder's plate. Rides on Symington-Wayne trucks.

EX-C7	LN-C8	Scarcity
15	20	4

9135 NORFOLK & WESTERN (Type IV): Features a purple body molding that includes a simulated builder's plate. Rides on Symington-Wayne trucks.

EX-C7	LN-C8	Scarcity
20	25	5

9213 MINNEAPOLIS AND ST. LOUIS: 1978, covered quad hopper car, Service Station Special item.

EX-C7	LN-C8	Scarcity
15	25	5

9240 NEW YORK CENTRAL: 1986, operating hopper car.

EX-C7	LN-C8	Scarcity
20	25	4

9240 NEW YORK CENTRAL: 1987, uncataloged hopper car in the traditional 027/Scout size.

EX-C7	LN-C8	Scarcity
12	18	4

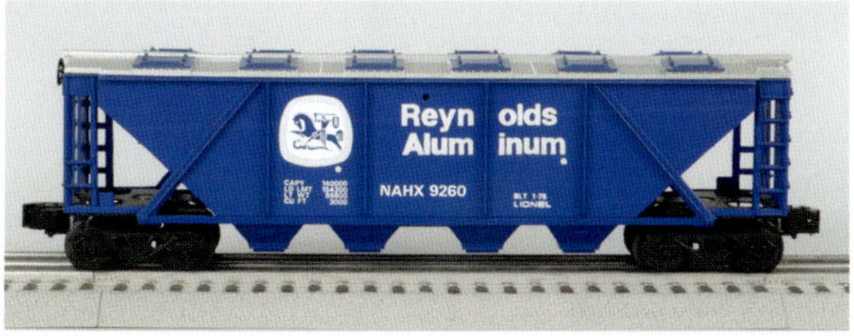

9260 REYNOLDS ALUMINUM: 1975-76, covered quad hopper car.

9260 REYNOLDS ALUMINUM (Type I): Body molding includes a simulated builder's plate.

EX-C7	LN-C8	Scarcity
15	20	4

9260 REYNOLDS ALUMINUM (Type II): Body molding lacks simulated builder's plate.

EX-C7	LN-C8	Scarcity
15	20	4

9261 SUN-MAID RAISINS: Uncataloged in 1975, cataloged in 1976, covered quad hopper car.

EX-C7	LN-C8	Scarcity
15	20	4

9262 RALSTON PURINA: Uncataloged in 1975, cataloged in 1976, covered quad hopper car.

EX-C7	LN-C8	Scarcity
25	30	4

9263 PENNSYLVANIA: Uncataloged in 1975, cataloged from 1976-77, covered quad hopper car.

9263 PENNSYLVANIA (Type I): The early production cars featured metal truck mounting plates.

EX-C7	LN-C8	Scarcity
15	20	4

9263 PENNSYLVANIA (Type II): Later cars featured molded plastic truck mounting plates.

EX-C7	LN-C8	Scarcity
15	20	4

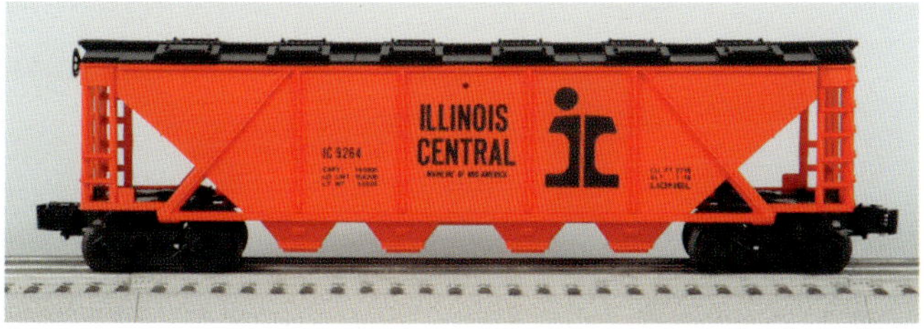

9264 ILLINOIS CENTRAL: Uncataloged in 1975, cataloged from 1976-77, covered quad hopper car.

9264 ILLINOIS CENTRAL (Type I): Some of the cars were built with metal truck mounting plates and body moldings, which included simulated builder's plates.

EX-C7	LN-C8	Scarcity
15	20	4

9264 ILLINOIS CENTRAL (Type II): Other cars were built with metal truck mounting plates and body moldings, which lacked simulated builder's plates.

EX-C7	LN-C8	Scarcity
15	20	4

9264 ILLINOIS CENTRAL (Type III): Some of the cars had plastic truck mounting plates and body moldings, which included simulated builder's plates.

EX-C7	LN-C8	Scarcity
15	20	4

9264 ILLINOIS CENTRAL (Type IV): Some of the cars had plastic truck mounting plates and body moldings that lacked simulated builder's plates.

EX-C7	LN-C8	Scarcity
15	20	4

9264 ILLINOIS CENTRAL (Type V): In 1978, some cars were overstamped "TCA Museum Express" for the Midwest Division creating this uncataloged covered quad hopper car.

EX-C7	LN-C8	Scarcity
18	24	6

9265 WESTERN MARYLAND/CHESSIE SYSTEM: Uncataloged in 1975, cataloged from 1976-77, covered quad hopper car.

9265 WESTERN MARYLAND/CHESSIE SYSTEM: (Type I): The early production cars featured metal truck mounting plates.

EX-C7	LN-C8	Scarcity
15	20	4

9265 WESTERN MARYLAND/CHESSIE SYSTEM: (Type II): Later cars featured molded plastic truck mounting plates.

EX-C7	LN-C8	Scarcity
15	20	4

9266 SOUTHERN: 1976, "Big John" covered quad hopper car.

9266 SOUTHERN (Type I): Body molding includes a simulated builder's plate.

EX-C7	LN-C8	Scarcity
25	30	5

9266 SOUTHERN (Type II): Body molding lacks simulated builder's plate.

EX-C7	LN-C8	Scarcity
25	30	5

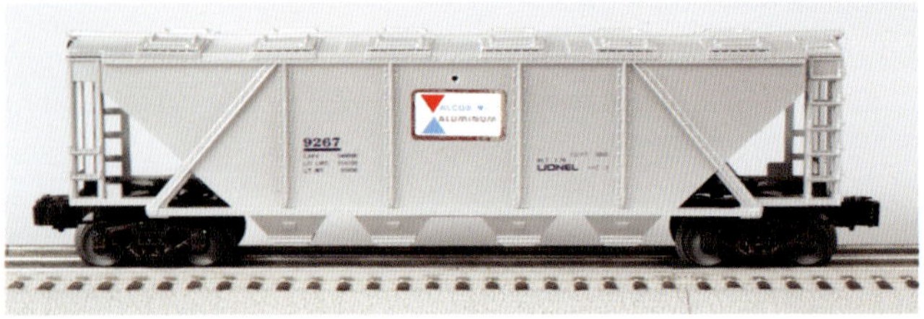

9267 ALCOA: 1976, covered quad hopper car, Service Station Special item.

EX-C7	LN-C8	Scarcity
20	25	6

9276 PEABODY: 1978, quad hopper car.

EX-C7	LN-C8	Scarcity
15	20	4

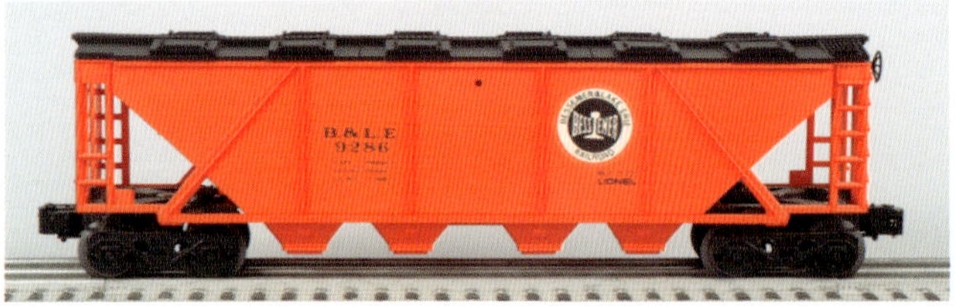

9286 B. & L. E.: 1977, covered quad hopper car.

EX-C7	LN-C8	Scarcity
10	15	4

9322 SANTA FE: 1979, covered quad hopper car, Famous American Railroads number one.

EX-C7	LN-C8	Scarcity
25	30	5

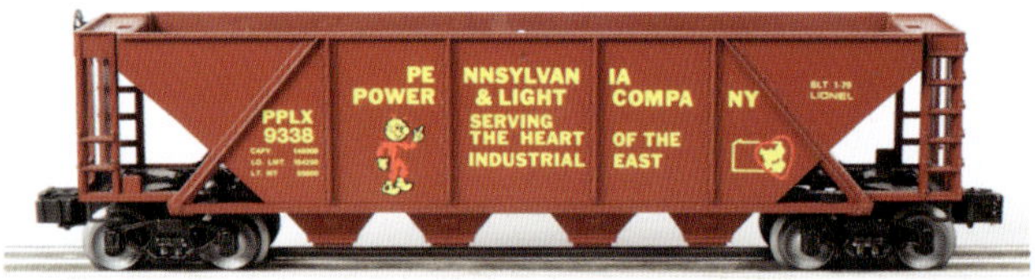

9338 PENN POWER: 1979, quad hopper car.

EX-C7	LN-C8	Scarcity
40	50	5

9358 SANDS OF IOWA: 1980, uncataloged LCCA covered quad hopper car.

EX-C7	LN-C8	Scarcity
15	20	5

9366 UNION PACIFIC: 1980, covered quad hopper car, Famous American Railroads number two.

EX-C7	LN-C8	Scarcity
15	20	4

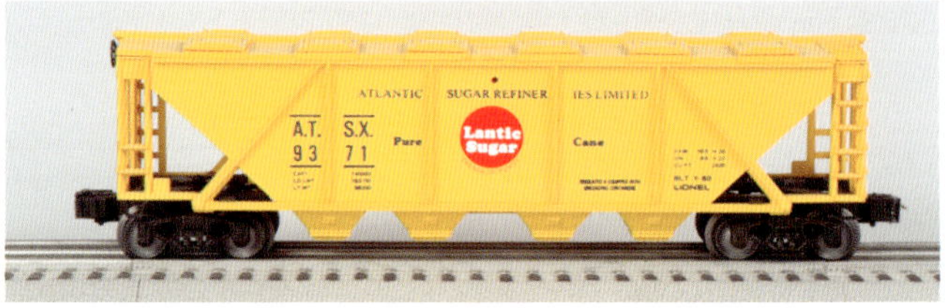

9371 ATLANTIC SUGAR: 1980, covered quad hopper car.

EX-C7	LN-C8	Scarcity
15	20	4

9374 READING: 1980-81, uncataloged in 1983, covered quad hopper car.

EX-C7	LN-C8	Scarcity
20	25	4

9384 GREAT NORTHERN: 1981, operating hopper car.

EX-C7	LN-C8	Scarcity
30	35	5

[11844] UNION PACIFIC: 1998, die-cast ore cars, four-pack.

EX-C7	LN-C8	Scarcity
150	175	4

11982 NEW JERSEY TRANSIT: 1998, ore car set.

EX-C7	LN-C8	Scarcity
175	200	4

[16175] NEW JERSEY TRANSIT: 1998, ore car numbered "9125," Port Morris.

EX-C7	LN-C8	Scarcity
30	40	4

[16176] NEW JERSEY TRANSIT: 1998, uncataloged ore car numbered "9126," Raritan Yard.

EX-C7	LN-C8	Scarcity
30	40	5

[16177] NEW JERSEY TRANSIT: 1998, uncataloged ore car numbered "9127," Gladstone Yard.

EX-C7	LN-C8	Scarcity
30	40	5

[16178] NEW JERSEY TRANSIT: 1998, uncataloged ore car numbered "9128," Bay Head Yard.

EX-C7	LN-C8	Scarcity
30	40	5

[16179] NEW JERSEY TRANSIT: 1998, uncataloged ore car numbered "9129," Dover Yard.

EX-C7	LN-C8	Scarcity
30	40	5

16305 LEHIGH VALLEY: 1987, ore car.

EX-C7	LN-C8	Scarcity
60	80	6

16385 SOO LINE: 1993, ore car.

EX-C7	LN-C8	Scarcity
35	40	4

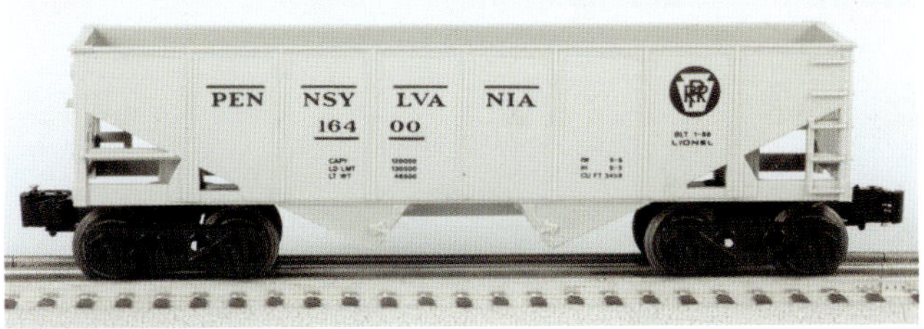

16400 PENNSYLVANIA: Uncataloged in 1988, cataloged in 1989, hopper car in the traditional 027/Scout size.

EX-C7	LN-C8	Scarcity
10	15	3

16402 SOUTHERN: 1987, quad hopper car with coal load, Service Station Special item.

EX-C7	LN-C8	Scarcity
20	25	5

16406 CSX: 1990, quad hopper car with coal load.

EX-C7	LN-C8	Scarcity
20	25	4

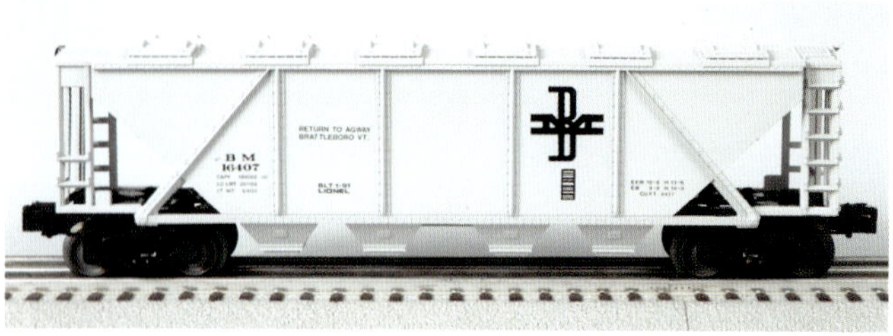

16407 BOSTON AND MAINE: 1991, covered quad hopper car, Service Station Special item.

EX-C7	LN-C8	Scarcity
20	25	5

[16408] UNION PACIFIC: 1990-91, uncataloged hopper car numbered "6408" in the traditional 027/Scout size.

EX-C7	LN-C8	Scarcity
10	15	3

16410 MISSOURI-KANSAS-TEXAS: Cataloged in 1992, uncataloged in 1993, hopper car in the traditional 027/Scout size.

EX-C7	LN-C8	Scarcity
10	15	3

16411 LOUISVILLE & NASHVILLE: 1992, quad hopper car with coal load.

EX-C7	LN-C8	Scarcity
20	25	4

16412 CHICAGO AND NORTHWESTERN: 1994, covered quad hopper car.

EX-C7	LN-C8	Scarcity
10	15	4

16413 CLINCHFIELD: 1994, quad hopper car with coal load.

EX-C7	LN-C8	Scarcity
10	15	4

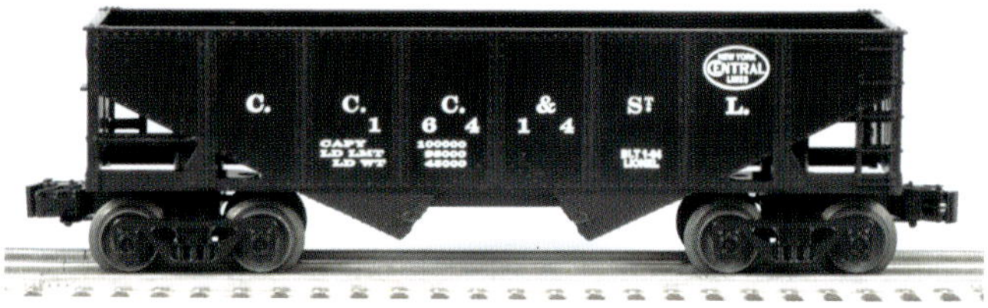

16414 C.C.C. & ST. L: 1994, hopper car in the traditional 027/Scout size.

EX-C7	LN-C8	Scarcity
10	15	4

16416 DENVER & RIO GRANDE WESTERN: 1995, covered quad hopper car.

EX-C7	LN-C8	Scarcity
10	15	4

16417 WABASH: 1995, quad hopper car with coal load.

EX-C7	LN-C8	Scarcity
10	15	4

16418 CHICAGO & NORTHWESTERN: 1995, hopper car with coal load in the traditional 027/Scout size.

EX-C7	LN-C8	Scarcity
10	15	4

[16419] TENNESSEE CENTRAL: 1996, hopper car.

EX-C7	LN-C8	Scarcity
8	12	4

16420 WESTERN MARYLAND: 1995, quad hopper car with coal load, Service Station Special item.

EX-C7	LN-C8	Scarcity
15	20	5

16421 WESTERN MARYLAND: 1995, quad hopper car with coal load, Service Station Special item.

EX-C7	LN-C8	Scarcity
15	20	5

16422 WESTERN MARYLAND: 1995, quad hopper car with coal load, Service Station Special item.

EX-C7	LN-C8	Scarcity
15	20	5

16423 WESTERN MARYLAND: 1995, quad hopper car with coal load, Service Station Special item.

EX-C7	LN-C8	Scarcity
15	20	5

16424 WESTERN MARYLAND: 1995, covered quad hopper car, Service Station Special item.

EX-C7	LN-C8	Scarcity
15	20	5

16425 WESTERN MARYLAND: 1995, covered quad hopper car, Service Station Special item.

EX-C7	LN-C8	Scarcity
15	20	5

16426 WESTERN MARYLAND: 1995, covered quad hopper car, Service Station Special item.

EX-C7	LN-C8	Scarcity
15	20	5

16427 WESTERN MARYLAND: 1995, covered quad hopper car, Service Station Special item.

EX-C7	LN-C8	Scarcity
15	20	5

[16429] WESTERN MARYLAND: Pair of quad hopper cars with coal loads.

EX-C7	LN-C8	Scarcity
50	60	5

[16430] GEORGIA POWER: 1995, uncataloged quad hopper car with coal load "82947."

EX-C7	LN-C8	Scarcity
75	90	5

[16431] LIONEL CORPORATION: 1996, two-bay hopper car numbered "6456-1."

EX-C7	LN-C8	Scarcity
10	15	4

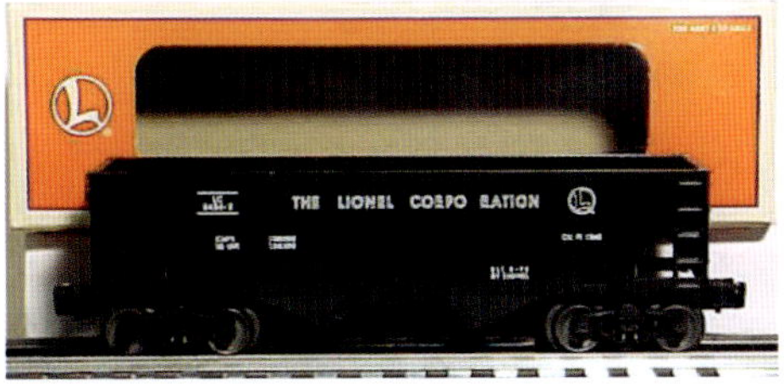

[16432] LIONEL CORPORATION: 1996, two-bay hopper car numbered "6456-2."

EX-C7	LN-C8	Scarcity
10	15	4

[16433] LIONEL CORPORATION: 1996, two-bay hopper car numbered "6456-3."

EX-C7	LN-C8	Scarcity
10	15	4

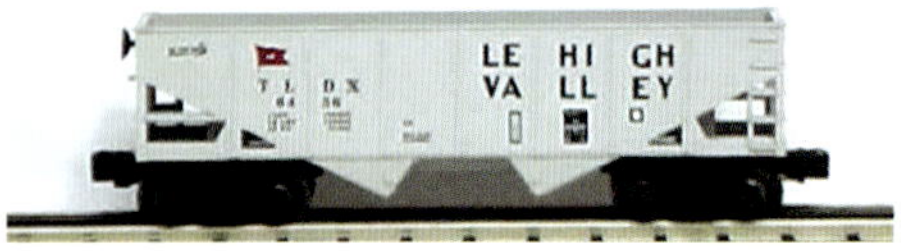

[16434] LEHIGH VALLEY: 1997, two-bay hopper car numbered "6456," "TLDX."

EX-C7	LN-C8	Scarcity
10	15	4

[16435] VIRGINIAN: 1997, two-bay hopper car numbered "6456-1."

EX-C7	LN-C8	Scarcity
15	20	4

[16436] NORFOLK AND WESTERN: 1997, two-bay hopper car numbered "6456-2."

EX-C7	LN-C8	Scarcity
15	20	4

[16437] CHESAPEAKE & OHIO: 1997, two-bay hopper car numbered "6456-3."

EX-C7	LN-C8	Scarcity
15	20	4

[16438] FRISCO: 1998, four-bay covered hopper car numbered "87538."

EX-C7	LN-C8	Scarcity
15	20	4

[16439] SOUTHERN: 1998, four-bay covered hopper car numbered "87538."

EX-C7	LN-C8	Scarcity
15	20	4

[16440] ALASKA RAILROAD: 1998-99, two-bay hopper car numbered "7100."

EX-C7	LN-C8	Scarcity
20	25	4

[16441] NEW YORK CENTRAL: 1999, four-bay hopper car numbered "6446" and "886888."

EX-C7	LN-C8	Scarcity
15	20	4

[16443] GREAT NORTHERN: 1999-2000, two-bay hopper car numbered "172364."

EX-C7	LN-C8	Scarcity
10	15	4

[16444] JERSEY CENTRAL: 2000, two-bay hopper car numbered "643."

EX-C7	LN-C8	Scarcity
10	15	4

[16445] FRISCO: 2000, two-bay hopper car numbered "93108."

EX-C7	LN-C8	Scarcity
10	15	4

[16446] BURLINGTON NORTHERN: 2000, two-bay hopper car.

EX-C7	LN-C8	Scarcity
10	15	4

[16447] PENNSYLVANIA: 2000, uncataloged Tuscan two-bay hopper car.

EX-C7	LN-C8	Scarcity
15	20	4

[16448] PENNSYLVANIA: 2000, uncataloged gray two-bay hopper car.

EX-C7	LN-C8	Scarcity
15	20	4

[16449] PENNSYLVANIA: 2000, uncataloged black two-bay hopper car.

EX-C7	LN-C8	Scarcity
15	20	4

[16450] PENNSYLVANIA: 2000, uncataloged green two-bay hopper car.

EX-C7	LN-C8	Scarcity
15	20	4

[16451] LIONEL MINES: 2000, uncataloged two-bay hopper car.

EX-C7	LN-C8	Scarcity
30	40	4

[16455] PIONEER SEED: 2000, uncataloged two-bay hopper car.

EX-C7	LN-C8	Scarcity
30	40	4

16800 LIONEL RAILROADER CLUB: 1986, uncataloged ore car.

EX-C7	LN-C8	Scarcity
45	55	6

[16812] GRAND TRUNK WESTERN: 1996, uncataloged LOTS two-bay hopper car.

EX-C7	LN-C8	Scarcity
35	45	6

[16813] PENNSYLVANIA POWER & LIGHT: 1997, uncataloged LOTS hopper car with 1/48-scale proportions.

EX-C7	LN-C8	Scarcity
60	70	6

17002 CONRAIL: 1987, two-bay ACF hopper car with 1/48-scale proportions.

EX-C7	LN-C8	Scarcity
40	45	4

17003 DU PONT: 1990, two-bay ACF hopper car with 1/48-scale proportions.

EX-C7	LN-C8	Scarcity
40	45	4

17004 MISSOURI-KANSAS-TEXAS: 1991, two-bay ACF hopper car with 1/48-scale proportions.

EX-C7	LN-C8	Scarcity
20	25	4

17005 CARGILL: 1992, two-bay ACF hopper car with 1/48-scale proportions.

EX-C7	LN-C8	Scarcity
20	25	4

17006 SOO LINE: 1993, two-bay ACF hopper car with 1/48-scale proportions, Service Station Special item.

EX-C7	LN-C8	Scarcity
35	40	5

[17007] GREAT NORTHERN: 1994, two-bay ACF hopper car numbered "173872" with 1/48-scale proportions.

EX-C7	LN-C8	Scarcity
20	25	4

[17008] DENVER & RIO GRANDE WESTERN: 1995, two-bay ACF hopper car numbered "10009" with 1/48-scale proportions.

EX-C7	LN-C8	Scarcity
20	25	4

[17009] NEW YORK CENTRAL: 1996, two-bay ACF hopper car.

EX-C7	LN-C8	Scarcity
20	25	4

[17010] GOVERNMENT DU CANADA: 1998, ACF two-bay covered hopper car "7000."

EX-C7	LN-C8	Scarcity
20	25	4

[17011] NORTHERN PACIFIC: 1998, ACF two-bay covered hopper car numbered "75052."

EX-C7	LN-C8	Scarcity
30	35	4

[17012] GOVERNMENT DU CANADA: 1998, ACF two-bay covered hopper car numbered "7001."

EX-C7	LN-C8	Scarcity
30	35	4

[17013] NEW YORK CENTRAL: 1999, graffiti two-bay covered hopper car numbered "7000."

EX-C7	LN-C8	Scarcity
30	35	4

[17014] GOLDEN WEST: 1999, graffiti two-bay covered hopper car numbered "7000" with 1/48-scale proportions.

EX-C7	LN-C8	Scarcity
30	35	4

17100 CHESSIE SYSTEM: 1988, three-bay ACF hopper car with 1/48-scale proportions.

EX-C7	LN-C8	Scarcity
30	40	4

17101 CHESSIE SYSTEM: 1988, three-bay ACF hopper car with 1/48-scale proportions.

EX-C7	LN-C8	Scarcity
30	40	4

17102 CHESSIE SYSTEM: 1988, three-bay ACF hopper car with 1/48-scale proportions.

EX-C7	LN-C8	Scarcity
30	40	4

17103 CHESSIE SYSTEM: 1988, three-bay ACF hopper car with 1/48-scale proportions.

EX-C7	LN-C8	Scarcity
30	40	4

17104 CHESSIE SYSTEM: 1988, three-bay ACF hopper car with 1/48-scale proportions.

EX-C7	LN-C8	Scarcity
30	40	4

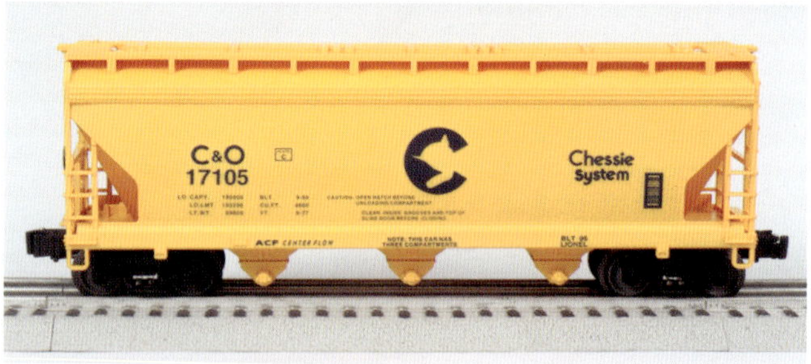

17105 CHESSIE SYSTEM: 1995, three-bay ACF hopper car with 1/48-scale proportions.

EX-C7	LN-C8	Scarcity
30	40	4

17107 SCLAIR: 1989, three-bay ACF hopper car with 1/48-scale proportions.

EX-C7	LN-C8	Scarcity
50	60	5

17108 SANTA FE: 1990, three-bay ACF hopper car with 1/48-scale proportions.

EX-C7	LN-C8	Scarcity
40	50	4

17109 NORFOLK AND WESTERN: 1991, three-bay ACF hopper car with 1/48-scale proportions.

EX-C7	LN-C8	Scarcity
20	25	4

17110 UNION PACIFIC: 1991, hopper car with coal load with 1/48-scale proportions.

EX-C7	LN-C8	Scarcity
20	25	4

17111 READING: 1991, hopper car with coal load with 1/48-scale proportions.

EX-C7	LN-C8	Scarcity
20	25	4

17112 ERIE-LACKAWANNA: 1992, three-bay ACF hopper car with 1/48-scale proportions.

EX-C7	LN-C8	Scarcity
20	25	4

17113 LEHIGH VALLEY: 1992-93, hopper car with coal load with 1/48-scale proportions.

EX-C7	LN-C8	Scarcity
20	25	4

17114 PEABODY: 1992-93, hopper car with coal load with 1/48-scale proportions.

EX-C7	LN-C8	Scarcity
25	30	5

[17118] ARCHER DANIELS MIDLAND: 1993, three-bay ACF hopper car numbered "60029" with 1/48-scale proportions.

EX-C7	LN-C8	Scarcity
25	30	5

[17120] CSX: 1994, hopper car with coal load numbered "295110" with 1/48-scale proportions.

EX-C7	LN-C8	Scarcity
25	30	5

[17121] ILLINOIS CENTRAL GULF: 1994, hopper car with coal load numbered "72867" with 1/48-scale proportions.

EX-C7	LN-C8	Scarcity
25	30	5

[17122] ROCK ISLAND: 1994, three-bay ACF hopper car numbered "800200" with 1/48-scale proportions.

EX-C7	LN-C8	Scarcity
25	30	5

[17123] CARGILL: 1995, covered grain hopper car numbered "844304" with 1/48-scale proportions.

EX-C7	LN-C8	Scarcity
25	30	5

[17124] ARCHER DANIELS MIDLAND: 1995, three-bay ACF hopper car numbered "50224" with 1/48-scale proportions.

EX-C7	LN-C8	Scarcity
25	30	5

[17125] GOODYEAR: 1995, three-bay ACF hopper car with 1/48-scale proportions.

EX-C7	LN-C8	Scarcity
Cataloged, but not produced.		

[17127] DELAWARE & HUDSON: 1996, three-bay hopper car with 1/48-scale proportions.

EX-C7	LN-C8	Scarcity
25	30	5

[17128] CHESAPEAKE AND OHIO: 1996, three-bay hopper car with 1/48-scale proportions.

EX-C7	LN-C8	Scarcity
25	30	5

[17129] WESTERN MARYLAND: 1997, three-bay hopper car with coal load numbered "9300" with 1/48-scale proportions.

EX-C7	LN-C8	Scarcity
25	30	5

[17132] PENNSYLVANIA: 1998, three-bay ACF hopper car numbered "260815" with 1/48-scale proportions.

EX-C7	LN-C8	Scarcity
30	35	5

[17133] BNSF ACF: 1998, three-bay covered hopper car numbered "403697" with 1/48-scale proportions.

EX-C7	LN-C8	Scarcity
25	30	4

[17134] BNSF ACF: 1998, three-bay covered hopper car numbered "403698" with 1/48-scale proportions.

EX-C7	LN-C8	Scarcity
25	30	4

[17135] BNSF ACF: 1998, three-bay covered hopper car with end of train device (ETD) with 1/48-scale proportions.

EX-C7	LN-C8	Scarcity
25	30	4

[17137] CARGILL: 1999, three-bay covered hopper car numbered "1219" with 1/48-scale proportions.

EX-C7	LN-C8	Scarcity
30	35	4

[17138] FARMERS ELEVATOR: 1999, three-bay covered hopper car with 1/48-scale proportions.

EX-C7	LN-C8	Scarcity
30	35	4

[17139] GRAIN TRAIN: 1999-2000, three-bay hopper car numbered "BLMR 1025" with 1/48-scale proportions.

EX-C7	LN-C8	Scarcity
30	35	4

[17140] VIRGINIAN: 1999, three-bay hopper car with 1/48-scale proportions numbered "5260-5265" (six-pack).

EX-C7	LN-C8	Scarcity
150	175	4

[17147] CHESAPEAKE AND OHIO: 1999, three-bay hopper car with 1/48-scale proportions numbered "156330-156335" (six-pack).

EX-C7	LN-C8	Scarcity
150	175	4

[17170] GENERAL MILLS: 2000, uncataloged three-bay covered hopper car with 1/48-scale proportions.

EX-C7	LN-C8	Scarcity
45	55	5

17198 CANADIAN PACIFIC: 1989, four-bay covered hopper car with 1/48-scale proportions.

EX-C7	LN-C8	Scarcity
25	30	4

17199 CONRAIL: 1987, four-bay covered hopper car with 1/48-scale proportions.

EX-C7	LN-C8	Scarcity
30	35	4

[17800] ONTARIO NORTHLAND: 2000, ore car numbered "6126/6021."

EX-C7	LN-C8	Scarcity
20	25	4

[17801] CANADIAN NATIONAL: 2000, ore car numbered "6126/345165."

EX-C7	LN-C8	Scarcity
20	25	4

[17802] CANADIAN PACIFIC: 2000, ore car numbered "377249."

EX-C7	LN-C8	Scarcity
15	20	4

[17803] DMIR: 2000, ore car numbered "51456."

EX-C7	LN-C8	Scarcity
15	20	4

[17872] ANACONDA: 1988, uncataloged TTOS ore car numbered "81988."

EX-C7	LN-C8	Scarcity
60	70	6

17878 MAGMA: 1989, uncataloged Gadsden Pacific ore car with load.

EX-C7	LN-C8	Scarcity
70	80	6

17881 PHELPS-DODGE: 1990, uncataloged Gadsden Pacific ore car with load.

EX-C7	LN-C8	Scarcity
30	40	6

17886 CYPRUS: 1991, uncataloged Gadsden Pacific ore car with load.

EX-C7	LN-C8	Scarcity
30	40	6

19300 PENNSYLVANIA: 1987, ore car.

EX-C7	LN-C8	Scarcity
15	20	4

19301 MILWAUKEE ROAD: 1987, ore car.

EX-C7	LN-C8	Scarcity
20	25	4

19302 MILWAUKEE ROAD: 1987, quad hopper car with coal load, Fallen Flags number two.

EX-C7	LN-C8	Scarcity
20	25	5

19303 LIONEL LINES: 1987, uncataloged quad hopper car with coal load.

EX-C7	LN-C8	Scarcity
20	25	4

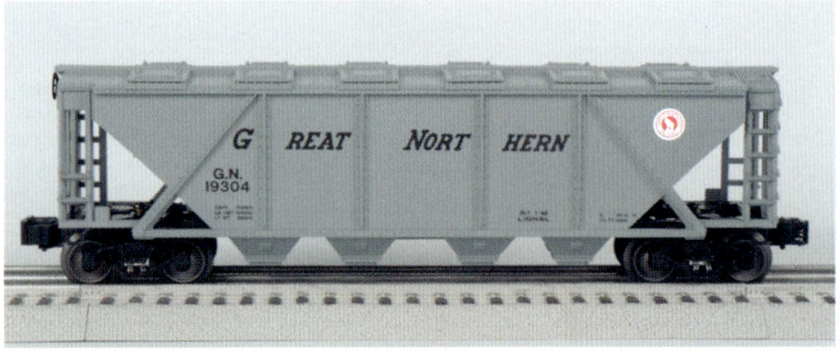

19304 GREAT NORTHERN: 1988, covered quad hopper car, Fallen Flags number three.

EX-C7	LN-C8	Scarcity
20	25	4

19305 CHESSIE SYSTEM: 1988, ore car.

EX-C7	LN-C8	Scarcity
15	20	4

19307 B. & L. E.: 1989, ore car with load.

EX-C7	LN-C8	Scarcity
15	20	4

19308 GREAT NORTHERN: 1989, ore car with load.

EX-C7	LN-C8	Scarcity
15	20	4

19309 SEABOARD: 1989, covered quad hopper car.

EX-C7	LN-C8	Scarcity
15	20	4

19310 LANCASTER AND CHESTER: 1989, quad hopper car with coal load.

EX-C7	LN-C8	Scarcity
20	25	4

19311 SOUTHERN PACIFIC: 1990, covered quad hopper car.

EX-C7	LN-C8	Scarcity
15	20	4

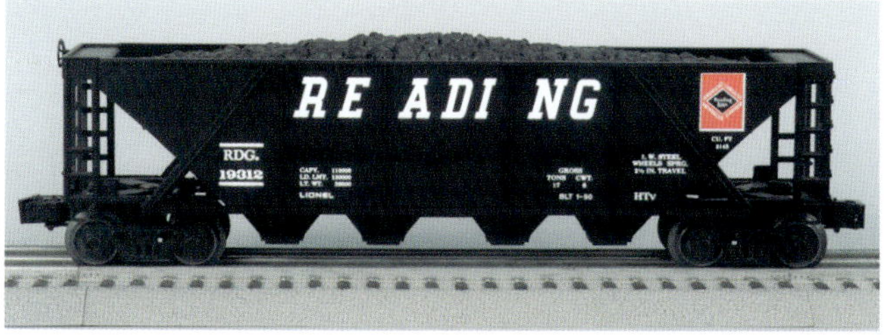

19312 READING: 1990, quad hopper car with coal load.

EX-C7	LN-C8	Scarcity
20	25	4

19313 BALTIMORE & OHIO: 1990-91, ore car with load.

EX-C7	LN-C8	Scarcity
20	25	4

19315 AMTRAK: 1991, ore car with load.

EX-C7	LN-C8	Scarcity
25	30	4

19316 WABASH: 1991, covered quad hopper car.

EX-C7	LN-C8	Scarcity
20	25	4

19317 LEHIGH VALLEY: 1991, quad hopper car with coal load.

EX-C7	LN-C8	Scarcity
35	40	5

19318 NICKEL PLATE ROAD: 1992, quad hopper car with coal load, Fallen Flags number six.

EX-C7	LN-C8	Scarcity
20	25	4

19319 UNION PACIFIC: 1992, covered quad hopper car.

EX-C7	LN-C8	Scarcity
15	20	4

19320 PENNSYLVANIA: 1992, ore car with load.

EX-C7	LN-C8	Scarcity
20	25	4

19321 B. & L. E.: 1992, ore car with load.

EX-C7	LN-C8	Scarcity
20	25	4

19322 CHICAGO & NORTHWESTERN: 1993, ore car with load.

EX-C7	LN-C8	Scarcity
20	25	4

19323 DETROIT & MACKINAC: 1993, ore car with load.

EX-C7	LN-C8	Scarcity
20	25	4

19324 ERIE: 1993, quad hopper car with coal load Fallen Flags number seven.

EX-C7	LN-C8	Scarcity
20	25	5

[19325] NORFOLK & WESTERN: 1996, four-bay hopper car with coal numbered "6446-1."

EX-C7	LN-C8	Scarcity
40	45	4

[19326] NORFOLK & WESTERN: 1996, four-bay hopper car with coal numbered "6446-2."

EX-C7	LN-C8	Scarcity
40	45	4

[19327] NORFOLK & WESTERN: 1996, four-bay hopper car with coal numbered "6446-3."

EX-C7	LN-C8	Scarcity
40	45	4

[19328] NORFOLK & WESTERN: 1996, four-bay hopper car with coal numbered "6446-4."

EX-C7	LN-C8	Scarcity
40	45	4

[19329] NORFOLK & WESTERN: 1997, four-bay hopper car with coal numbered "6436."

EX-C7	LN-C8	Scarcity
40	45	4

[19330] COTTON BELT: 1998, four-bay hopper car with coal numbered "64661."

EX-C7	LN-C8	Scarcity
30	35	4

[19331] COTTON BELT: 1998, four-bay hopper car with coal numbered "64662."

EX-C7	LN-C8	Scarcity
30	35	4

[19332] COTTON BELT: 1998, four-bay hopper car with coal numbered "64663."

EX-C7	LN-C8	Scarcity
30	35	4

[19333] COTTON BELT: 1998, four-bay hopper car with coal numbered "64664."

EX-C7	LN-C8	Scarcity
30	35	4

[19338] COTTON BELT: 1999, four-bay hopper car, two-pack.

EX-C7	LN-C8	Scarcity
55	65	4

[19339] COTTON BELT: 1999, four-bay hopper car numbered "64469."

EX-C7	LN-C8	Scarcity
30	35	4

[19340] COTTON BELT: 1999, four-bay hopper car numbered "64470."

EX-C7	LN-C8	Scarcity
30	35	4

[19341] LEHIGH VALLEY: 1999, two-bay hopper car numbered "6456."

EX-C7	LN-C8	Scarcity
20	25	4

[19344] DENVER & RIO GRANDE WESTERN: 1999-2000, three-bay cylindrical hopper car numbered "15990."

EX-C7	LN-C8	Scarcity
35	40	4

[19345] CANADIAN NATIONAL: 1999-2000, three-bay cylindrical hopper car numbered "370708."

EX-C7	LN-C8	Scarcity
50	65	5

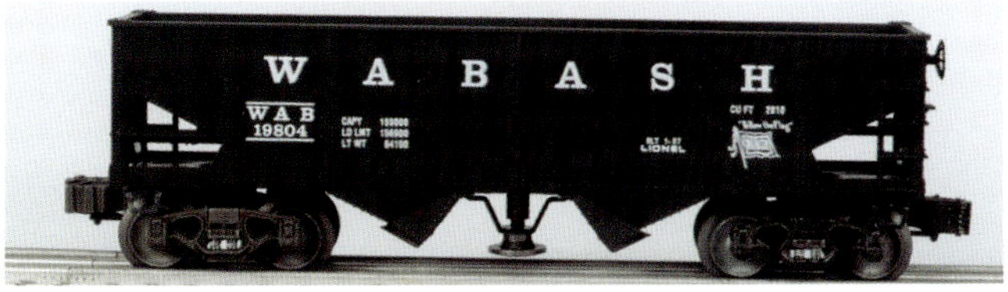

19804 WABASH: 1987, operating hopper car.

EX-C7	LN-C8	Scarcity
15	20	4

19806 PENNSYLVANIA: 1988, operating hopper car.

EX-C7	LN-C8	Scarcity
15	20	4

[19885] NORFOLK AND WESTERN: 2000, operating hopper car numbered "22000."

EX-C7	LN-C8	Scarcity
20	25	4

19930 LIONEL RAILROADER CLUB: 1994, uncataloged quad hopper car with coal load.

EX-C7	LN-C8	Scarcity
20	25	5

19961 INSPIRATION CONSOLIDATED COPPER COMPANY: 1992, uncataloged Gadsden Pacific ore car with load.

EX-C7	LN-C8	Scarcity
30	35	5

[19962] SOUTHERN PACIFIC: 1992, uncataloged TTOS Southwest three-bay ACF hopper car numbered "496035" with 1/48-scale proportions.

EX-C7	LN-C8	Scarcity
40	50	5

[19963] UNION EQUITY: 1992, uncataloged TTOS three-bay ACF hopper car numbered "86892" with 1/48-scale proportions.

EX-C7	LN-C8	Scarcity
25	30	5

[21754] BNSF: 1998, three-bay covered hopper car two-pack with 1/48-scale proportions.

EX-C7	LN-C8	Scarcity
40	50	4

[21755]: 1998, four-bay covered hopper cars two-pack.

EX-C7	LN-C8	Scarcity
40	50	4

[26920] UNION PACIFIC: 1997, die-cast ore car numbered "64861."

EX-C7	LN-C8	Scarcity
40	45	4

[26921] UNION PACIFIC: 1997, die-cast ore car numbered "64862."

EX-C7	LN-C8	Scarcity
40	45	4

[26922] UNION PACIFIC: 1997, die-cast ore car numbered "64863."

EX-C7	LN-C8	Scarcity
40	45	4

[26923] UNION PACIFIC: 1997, die-cast ore car numbered "64864."

EX-C7	LN-C8	Scarcity
40	45	4

[26924] UNION PACIFIC: 1997, die-cast ore car numbered "64865."

EX-C7	LN-C8	Scarcity
40	45	4

[26925] UNION PACIFIC: 1997, die-cast ore car numbered "64866."

EX-C7	LN-C8	Scarcity
40	45	4

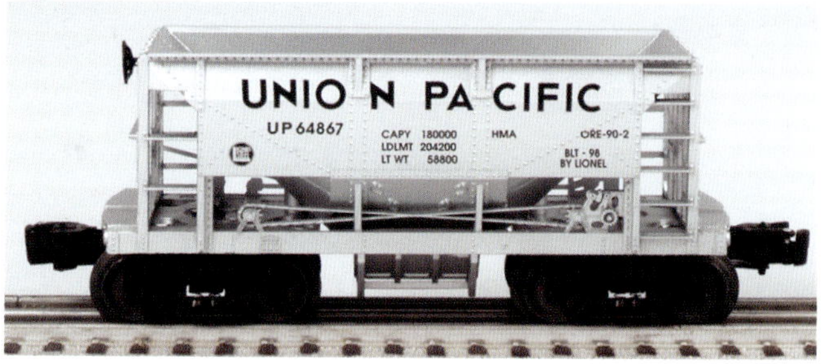

[26926] UNION PACIFIC: 1998, die-cast ore car.

EX-C7	LN-C8	Scarcity
40	45	4

[26927] UNION PACIFIC: 1998, die-cast ore car.

EX-C7	LN-C8	Scarcity
40	45	4

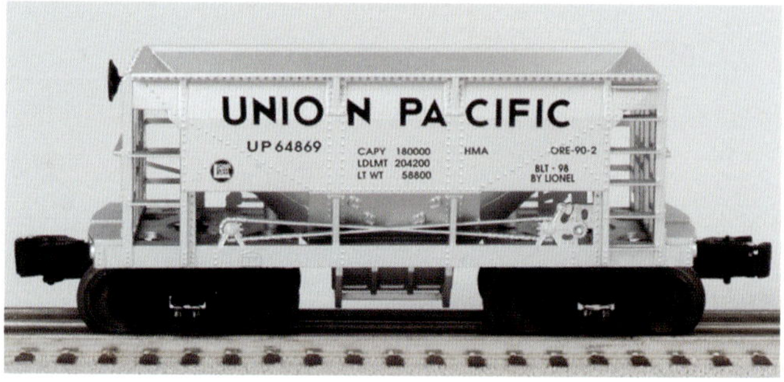

[26928] UNION PACIFIC: 1998, die-cast ore car.

EX-C7	LN-C8	Scarcity
40	45	4

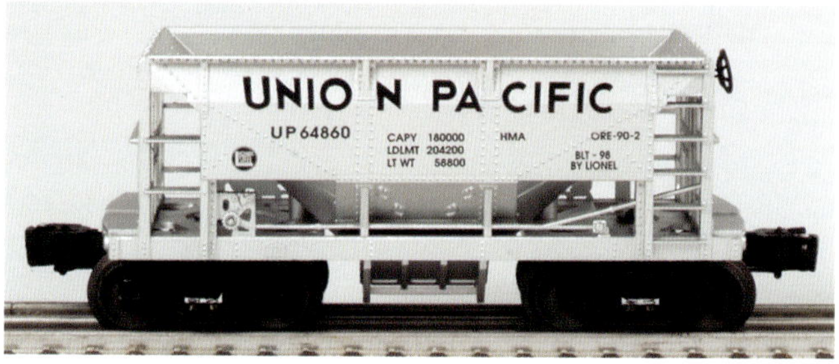

[26929] UNION PACIFIC: 1998, die-cast ore car.

EX-C7	LN-C8	Scarcity
40	45	4

[26937]: 1998, die-cast hopper car four-pack.

EX-C7	LN-C8	Scarcity
300	325	4

[26946] DELAWARE AND HUDSON: Semi-scale hopper car numbered "9642."

EX-C7	LN-C8	Scarcity
70	80	4

[26948] P & LE: 1998, die-cast hopper car.

EX-C7	LN-C8	Scarcity
60	65	4

[26985] BALTIMORE AND OHIO: 1999, die-cast hopper car two-pack numbered "235154."

EX-C7	LN-C8	Scarcity
125	150	4

[26987] CHESSIE SYSTEM: 1999, die-cast four-bay hopper car numbered "235154."

EX-C7	LN-C8	Scarcity
65	80	4

[36041] BETHLEHEM: 1999, ore car, Service Station Special item.

EX-C7	LN-C8	Scarcity
30	35	5

[51500] LIONEL LINES: 1989, hopper car numbered "8816."

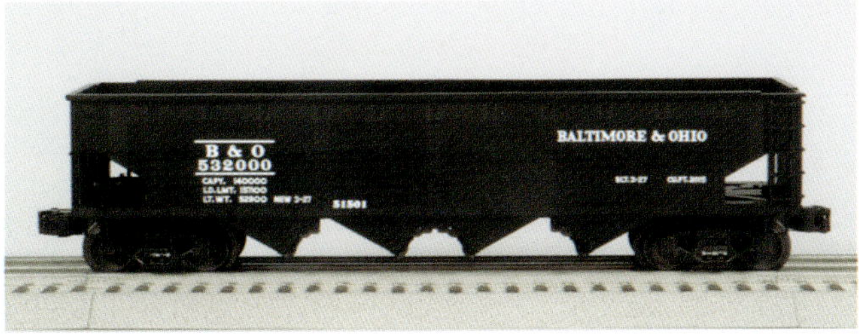

51501 BALTIMORE & OHIO: 1991, semi-scale hopper car numbered "532000."

EX-C7	LN-C8	Scarcity
85	100	4

[51502] LIONEL STEEL: 1996, die-cast ore car numbered "6486-3" Service Station Special item.

EX-C7	LN-C8	Scarcity
50	60	5

[51503] LIONEL STEEL: 1996, die-cast ore car numbered "6486-1" Service Station Special item.

EX-C7	LN-C8	Scarcity
50	60	5

[51504] LIONEL STEEL: 1996, steel die-cast ore car numbered "6486-2" Service Station Special item.

EX-C7	LN-C8	Scarcity
50	60	5

52001 BOSTON AND MAINE: 1992, uncataloged New England Division of Train Collectors Association quad hopper car with coal load.

EX-C7	LN-C8	Scarcity
40	50	6

52011 TUCSON, CORNELIA AND GILA BEND: 1993, uncataloged Gadsden Pacific ore car with load.

EX-C7	LN-C8	Scarcity
30	35	6

[52023] D&TS: 1993, uncataloged LCCA two-bay ACF hopper car numbered "2601" with 1/48-scale proportions.

EX-C7	LN-C8	Scarcity
30	35	6

52027 PINTO VALLEY MINE: 1994, uncataloged Gadsden Pacific ore car with load.

EX-C7	LN-C8	Scarcity
25	30	6

[52031] FORD: 1994, uncataloged TTOS hopper car numbered "1458" in the traditional 027/Scout size.

EX-C7	LN-C8	Scarcity
25	30	6

[52038] SOUTHERN: 1994, uncataloged LCCA hopper car with coal load numbered "360794" with 1/48-scale proportions.

EX-C7	LN-C8	Scarcity
30	35	6

[52059] CLINCHFIELD: 1994, uncataloged Eastern Division TCA quad hopper car with coal load numbered "16413."

EX-C7	LN-C8	Scarcity
70	80	6

52071 COPPER BASIN RAILWAY GADSDEN PACIFIC: 1995, uncataloged ore car with load.

EX-C7	LN-C8	Scarcity
25	30	6

52089 SMARRCO: 1996, uncataloged Gadsden Pacific ore car with load.

EX-C7	LN-C8	Scarcity
25	30	6

[52113] NDG & W: 1997, uncataloged three-bay hopper car.

EX-C7	LN-C8	Scarcity
35	45	6

[52124] EL PASO & SOUTHWESTERN: 1997, uncataloged ore car with load.

EX-C7	LN-C8	Scarcity
30	35	6

[52127] SOUTHERN: 1998, uncataloged TCA hopper car with 1/48-scale proportions "360997."

EX-C7	LN-C8	Scarcity
55	60	6

[52164] SOUTHERN PACIFIC: 1998, uncataloged ore car with load.

EX-C7	LN-C8	Scarcity
30	35	6

[52177] ARIZONA SOUTHERN RR: 1999, uncataloged ore car with load.

EX-C7	LN-C8	Scarcity
35	40	6

52199 REAL PLASTIC SNOW: 2000, four-bay hopper car numbered "6756."

EX-C7	LN-C8	Scarcity
Too rarely traded to establish accurate pricing.		

[52213] BHP COPPER: 2000, uncataloged ore car.

EX-C7	LN-C8	Scarcity
30	35	6

[840006] CANADIAN WHEAT BOARD: 1984, uncataloged Lionel Collectors Association of Canada covered quad hopper car.

EX-C7	LN-C8	Scarcity
75	125	6

Chapter 11
HOUSE CARS

While railroad enthusiasts born in the 1980s and later think of seeming-unending trains of containers or highway trailers on flatcars, older buffs have a different memory—unending streams of boxcars and refrigerator cars. During the first half of the 20th Century, most goods shipped in the United States traveled in what railroads termed "house cars." To describe enclosed freight cars such as box, stock, refrigerator, and poultry, rail car builders used this term. These cars are used for loads requiring protection from weather. All of these cars are built much like a house, with permanently installed roof and sides, and side or end doors. They vaguely resemble a house as well.

To assist the layman in locating a specific car, the item listings in this book group all house cars together in numeric order, rather than separating them into specific categories such as stock, box, refrigerator, etc., although a brief overview of the three main types is given.

Boxcars were the dominant means of shipping goods that needed protection. Everything from clothing and appliances to automobiles was shipped inside boxcars. During the modern era, Lionel produced several body styles of boxcars, and some body styles, notably the 10-5/8-inch cars, were produced in multiple number series.

Regardless of number or body molding, the modern-era house cars can quickly be distinguished from their postwar predecessor by their brilliant colors and elaborate decoration. When compared to the postwar era, the shear number of these cars is staggering. While many postwar collectors have "complete" collections of house cars, to do the same in the modern era would literally fill a house!

The primary types of boxcars described in this volume include what we refer to here as the Scout-type boxcar. These cars evolved from 8-1/2-inch-long double-door cars introduced in 1948, with doors molded integral with the body.

The injection-molded 9-1/4-inch boxcar also returned during the modern era, this size having last been produced by Lionel in the 1960s. However, although similar-looking, the new version was made from all-new tooling, it's styling more a tribute to its predecessor than a duplication of it. These cars were provided with a realistic opening door on each side, and a brakewheel on one end.

The 10-5/8-inch-long car traces its heritage to the famed 6464 series boxcars of the postwar era. Initially offered as part of the 9200 series cars, these cars also formed the 9400 and 9700 series. The bright paint schemes and large flat sides lending themselves to elaborate graphics, as well as the well-balanced proportions of the car, have helped make these cars one of the most-collected series of Lionel rolling stock.

New styles of boxcars also debuted in the modern era. The Hi-Cube boxcar, the standard 0 boxcar, and the wood-side boxcar were all new. The Hi-Cube, added to the line in 1976, was an attempt by Lionel to update the look of their trains by replicating the taller cars that had come into use by railroads. These cars typically transport relatively light but bulky items such as household appliances. The standard 0 boxcar was part of a series of 1/48-scale proportioned cars—the tooling for which Lionel purchased from Rivarossi in Italy. Though attractive, these cars were literally ahead of their time when introduced in 1973, it would be almost 25 years before these scale-sized cars became popular—so popular in fact as to overtake the more traditionally proportioned cars in popularity. The wood-side boxcar was Lionel's effort to mimic turn of the 20th Century freight car styling.

Another popular type of house car was the refrigerator car—also known as "reefers." They were found in two major varieties in real rail yards. The earliest cars were chilled with ice. Compartments, known as bunkers, were built into each end of the car. Massive blocks of ice were loaded into these bunkers through rooftop hatches. The air inside was circulated to maintain an even temperature throughout the cargo, and thick insulation was provided to prolong the cooling.

The necessity of maintaining extensive ice plants and docks, and the large workforce required to keep these cars serviced, was a considerable expense for railroads. The advent of the second type of reefer, the mechanical refrigerator car, dispensed with much of this expense. Mechanical refrigerator cars work much like your home refrigerator or air conditioner, with the power to drive them supplied in most cases by a diesel engine.

During the modern era Lionel has offered cars replicating both ice-bunker type cars, as the roof top hatch details reveal, and mechanical refrigerator cars. Strangely,

5709 REA: 1982-83, refrigerator car.

EX-C7	LN-C8	Scarcity
15	20	4

5710 CANADIAN PACIFIC: 1982-83, refrigerator car.

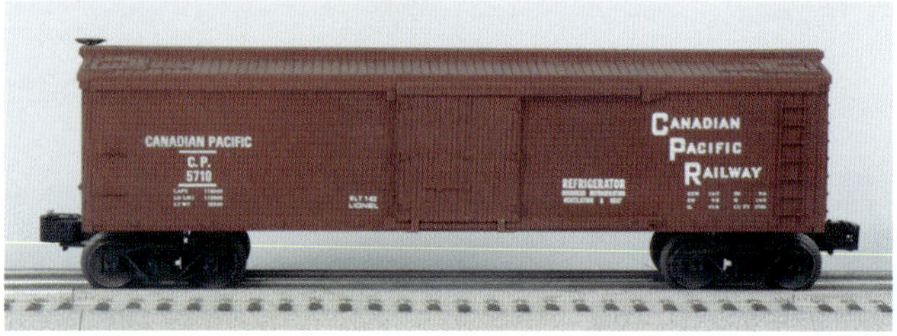

5710 CANADIAN PACIFIC (Type I): As cataloged.

EX-C7	LN-C8	Scarcity
10	15	3

5710 CANADIAN PACIFIC (Type II): 1982, uncataloged New England Division of Train Collectors Association refrigerator car.

EX-C7	LN-C8	Scarcity
15	25	6

5710 CANADIAN PACIFIC (Type III): 1983, uncataloged Lionel Collectors Association of Canada refrigerator car.

EX-C7	LN-C8	Scarcity
100	175	6

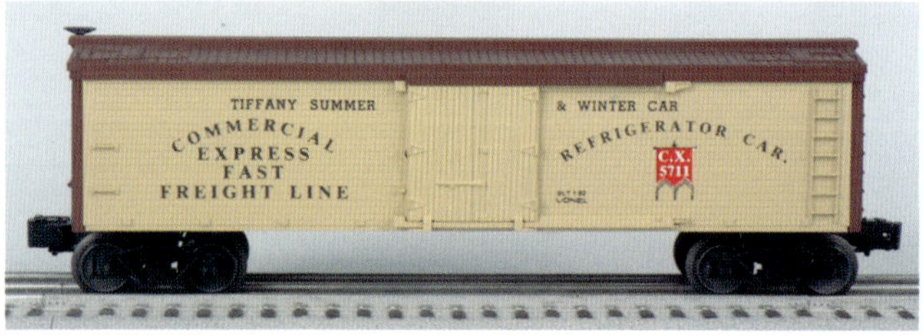

5711 COMMERCIAL EXPRESS: 1982-83, refrigerator car.

EX-C7	LN-C8	Scarcity
10	15	3

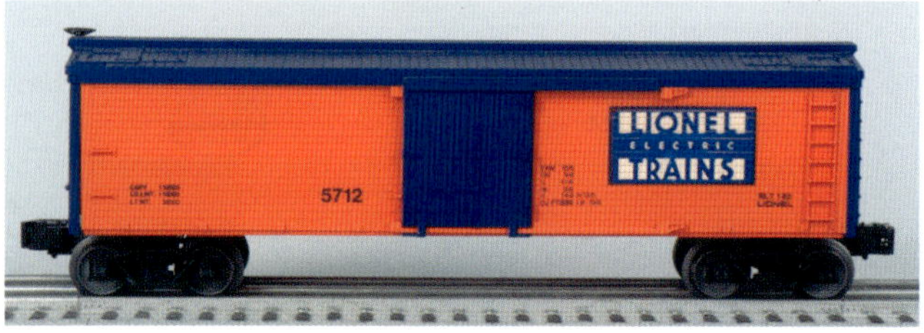

5712 LIONEL LINES: 1982, uncataloged refrigerator car.

EX-C7	LN-C8	Scarcity
75	150	6

5713 COTTON BELT: 1983-84, refrigerator car.

EX-C7	LN-C8	Scarcity
10	15	3

5714 MICHIGAN CENTRAL: 1983-84, refrigerator car.

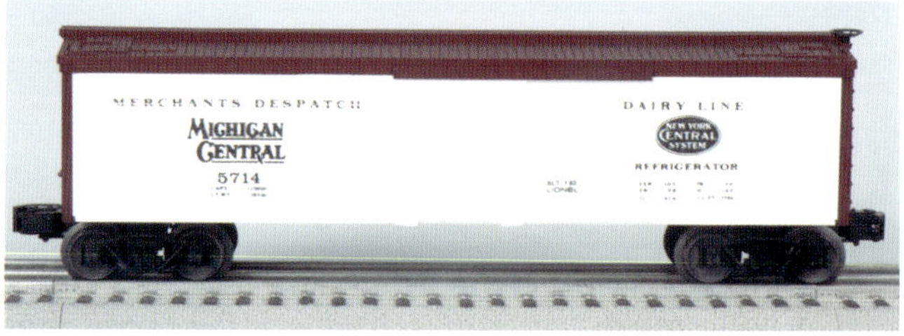

5714 MICHIGAN CENTRAL (Type I): As cataloged.

EX-C7	LN-C8	Scarcity
10	15	3

5714 MICHIGAN CENTRAL (Type II): 1985, uncataloged Lionel Collectors Association of Canada refrigerator car.

EX-C7	LN-C8	Scarcity
80	120	5

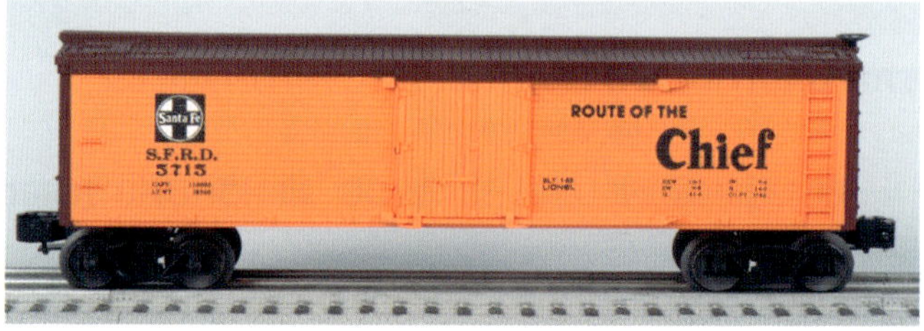

5715 SANTA FE: 1983-84, refrigerator car.

EX-C7	LN-C8	Scarcity
10	20	3

5716 CENTRAL VERMONT: 1983-84, refrigerator car.

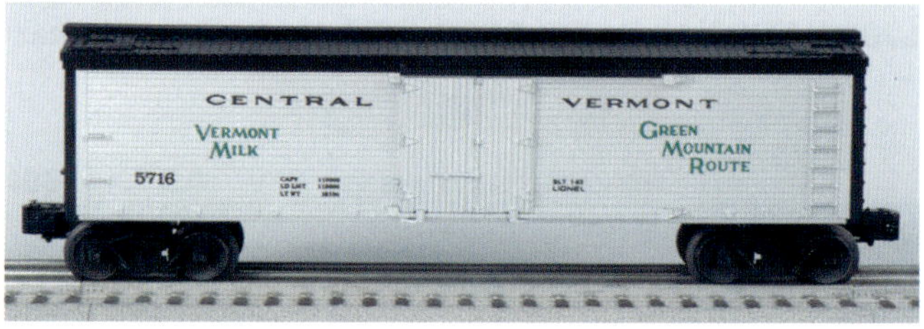

5716 CENTRAL VERMONT (Type I): As cataloged.

EX-C7	LN-C8	Scarcity
10	20	3

5716 CENTRAL VERMONT (Type II): 1983, uncataloged New England Division of Train Collectors Association refrigerator car.

EX-C7	LN-C8	Scarcity
15	25	5

5717 SANTA FE: 1983, bunk car.

EX-C7	LN-C8	Scarcity
10	20	3

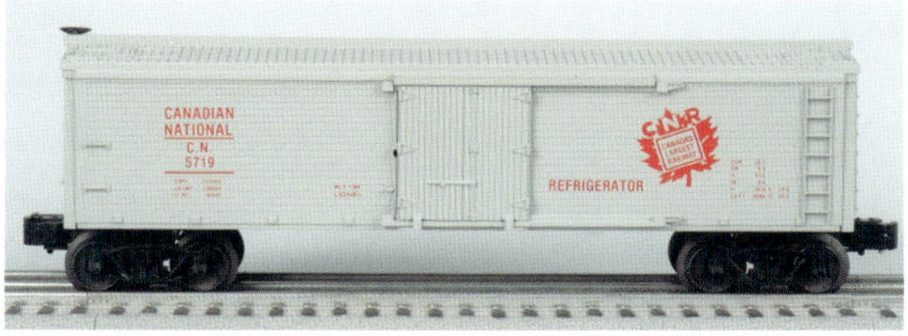

5719 CANADIAN NATIONAL: 1984, refrigerator car.

EX-C7	LN-C8	Scarcity
10	15	3

5720 GREAT NORTHERN: 1984, refrigerator car.

EX-C7	LN-C8	Scarcity
25	50	5

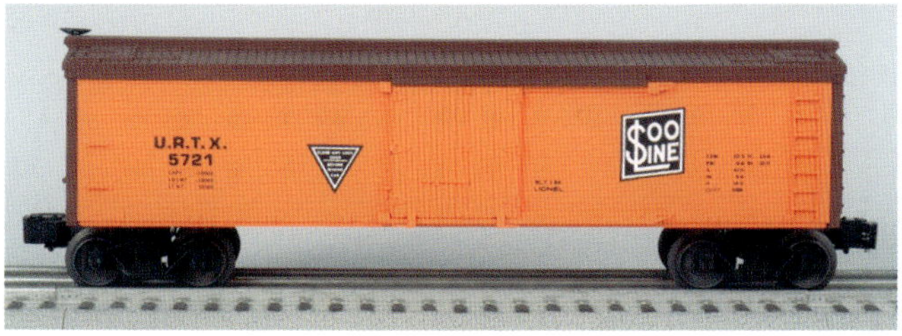

5721 SOO LINE: 1984, refrigerator car.

EX-C7	LN-C8	Scarcity
10	15	3

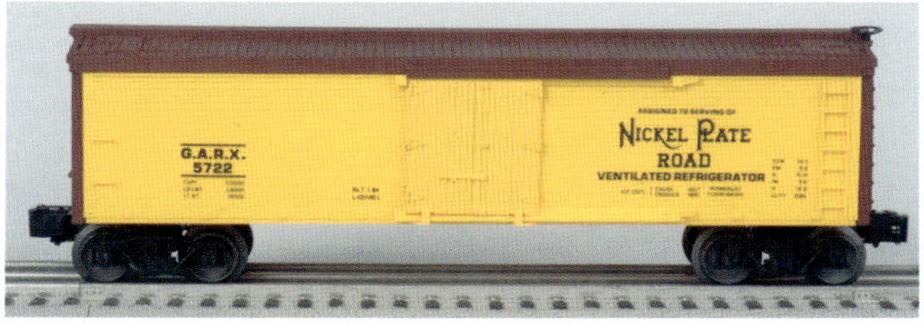

5722 NICKEL PLATE: 1984, refrigerator car.

EX-C7	LN-C8	Scarcity
10	15	3

5724 PENNSYLVANIA: 1984, bunk car.

5724 PENNSYLVANIA (Type I): As cataloged.

EX-C7	LN-C8	Scarcity
15	25	4

5724 PENNSYLVANIA (Type II): 1984, uncataloged LCOL bunk car.

EX-C7	LN-C8	Scarcity
15	25	4

5726 SOUTHERN: 1984, uncataloged bunk car.

EX-C7	LN-C8	Scarcity
15	20	4

5727 U.S. MARINES: 1984-85, bunk car.

EX-C7	LN-C8	Scarcity
15	20	4

5728 CANADIAN PACIFIC: 1986, bunk car.

EX-C7	LN-C8	Scarcity
15	20	4

5730 STRASBURG RR: 1985-86, refrigerator car.

EX-C7	LN-C8	Scarcity
15	20	4

5731 LOUISVILLE & NASHVILLE: 1985-86, refrigerator car.

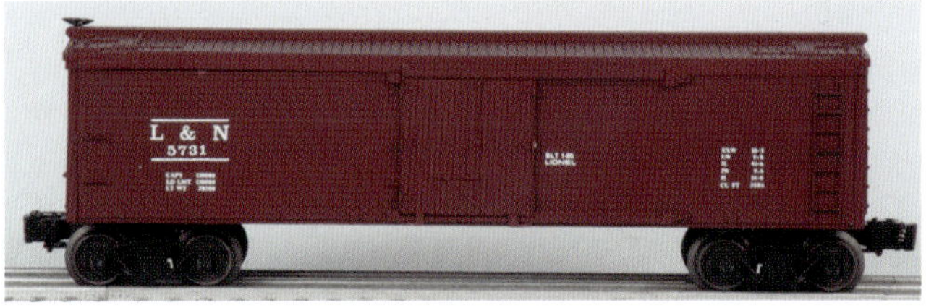

5731 LOUISVILLE & NASHVILLE (Type I): As cataloged.

EX-C7	LN-C8	Scarcity
10	15	3

5731 LOUISVILLE & NASHVILLE (Type II): 1990, uncataloged TCA Museum refrigerator car.

EX-C7	LN-C8	Scarcity
30	60	5

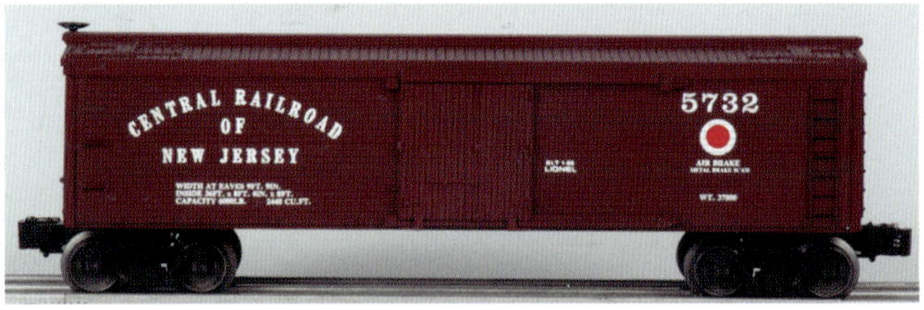

5732 JERSEY CENTRAL: 1985-86, refrigerator car.

EX-C7	LN-C8	Scarcity
10	15	3

5733 LIONEL LINES: 1986, uncataloged bunk car.

EX-C7	LN-C8	Scarcity
15	20	4

5734 TCA REA: 1985, uncataloged refrigerator car.

EX-C7	LN-C8	Scarcity
30	60	5

5735 NEW YORK CENTRAL: 1985-86, bunk car.

EX-C7	LN-C8	Scarcity
15	20	4

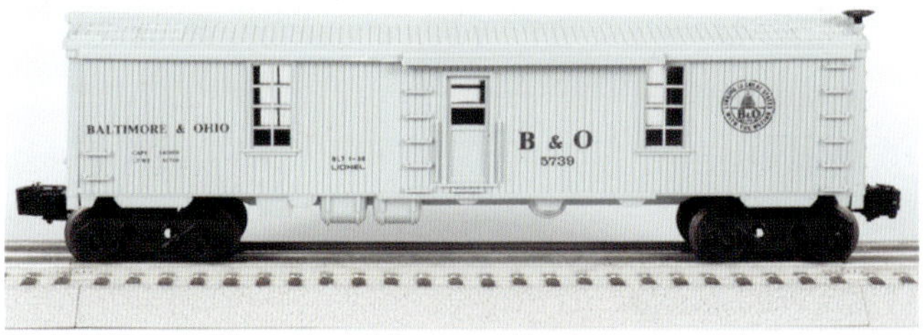

5739 BALTIMORE & OHIO: 1986, tool car.

EX-C7	LN-C8	Scarcity
15	20	4

5745 SANTA FE: 1986, bunk car, Service Station Special item.

EX-C7	LN-C8	Scarcity
15	25	5

5760 SANTA FE: 1986, tool car, Service Station Special item.

EX-C7	LN-C8	Scarcity
15	25	5

[6014-900] FRISCO: 1975-76, uncataloged LCCA boxcar in the traditional 027/Scout size.

EX-C7	LN-C8	Scarcity
10	20	5

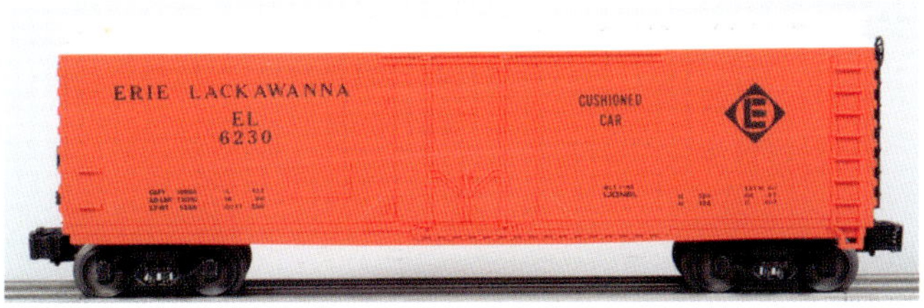

6230 ERIE-LACKAWANNA: 1986, uncataloged refrigerator car with 1/48-scale proportions.

EX-C7	LN-C8	Scarcity
50	75	5

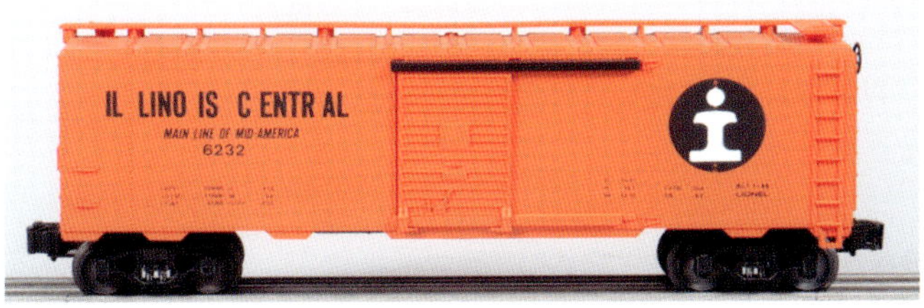

6232 ILLINOIS CENTRAL: 1986, uncataloged boxcar with 1/48-scale proportions.

EX-C7	LN-C8	Scarcity
50	75	5

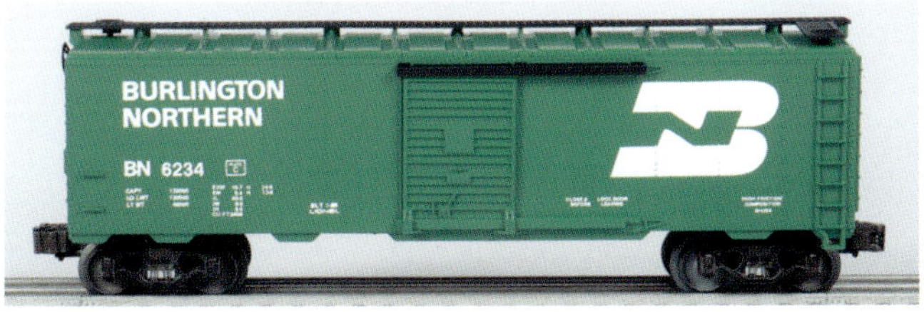

6234 BURLINGTON NORTHERN: 1985, boxcar with 1/48-scale proportions.

EX-C7	LN-C8	Scarcity
50	60	5

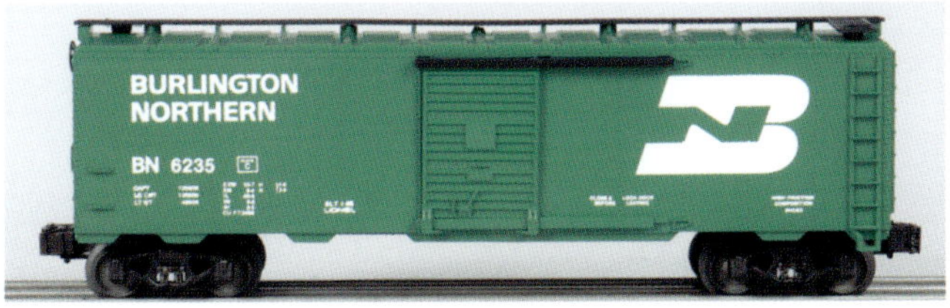

6235 BURLINGTON NORTHERN: 1985, boxcar with 1/48-scale proportions.

EX-C7	LN-C8	Scarcity
20	30	4

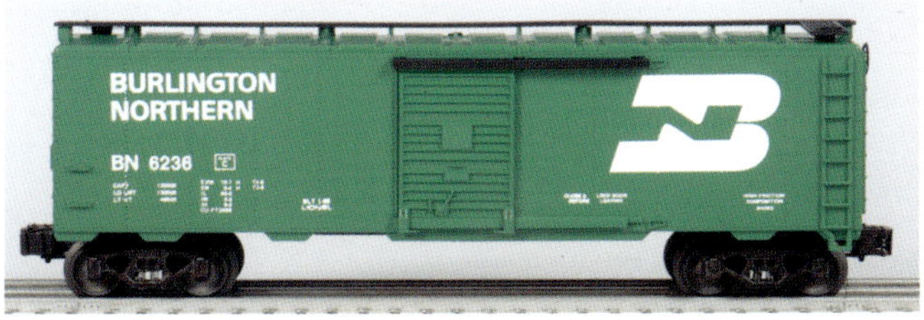

6236 BURLINGTON NORTHERN: 1985, boxcar with 1/48-scale proportions.

EX-C7	LN-C8	Scarcity
20	30	4

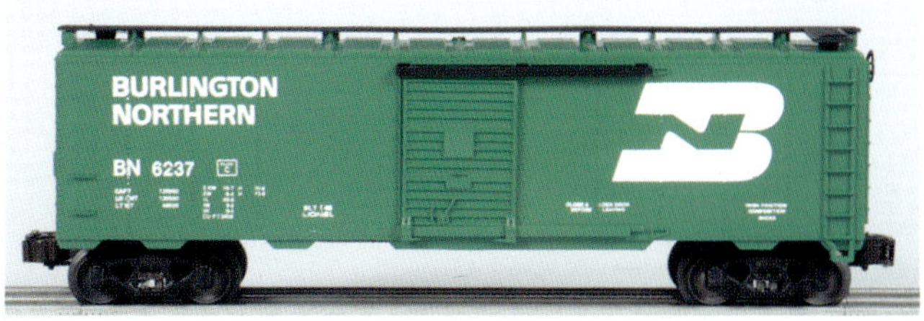

6237 BURLINGTON NORTHERN: 1985, boxcar with 1/48-scale proportions.

EX-C7	LN-C8	Scarcity
20	30	4

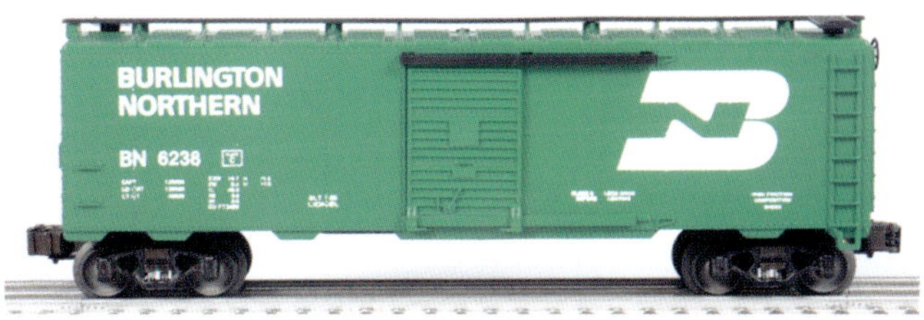

6238 BURLINGTON NORTHERN: 1985, boxcar with 1/48-scale proportions.

EX-C7	LN-C8	Scarcity
20	30	4

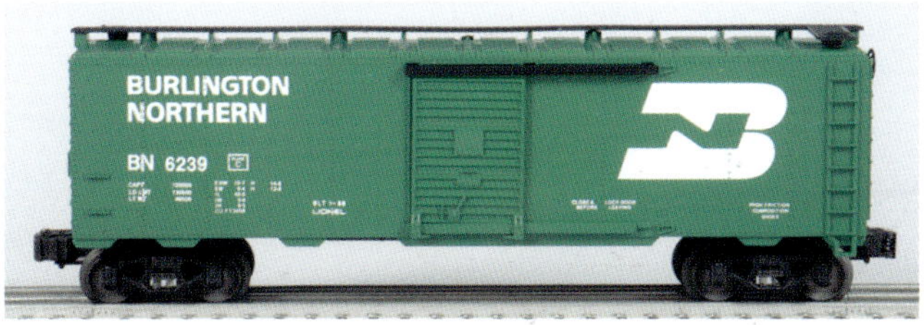

6239 BURLINGTON NORTHERN: 1986, uncataloged boxcar with 1/48-scale proportions.

EX-C7	LN-C8	Scarcity
25	40	5

6464-500 TIMKEN: 1970, uncataloged boxcar.

EX-C7	LN-C8	Scarcity
100	150	7

6464-1970 TCA CHICAGO: 1970, uncataloged boxcar.

6464-1970 TCA CHICAGO (Type I): Door painted red.

EX-C7	LN-C8	Scarcity
75	125	6

6464-1970 TCA CHICAGO (Type II): Door unpainted, red plastic instead.

EX-C7	LN-C8	Scarcity
75	125	6

6464-1971 TCA DISNEYLAND: 1971, uncataloged boxcar.

EX-C7	LN-C8	Scarcity
175	225	7

6700 PACIFIC FRUIT EXPRESS: 1982-83, ice car, came with 2306 icing station.

EX-C7	LN-C8	Scarcity
30	60	5

7301 NORFOLK AND WESTERN: 1982, stock car.

EX-C7	LN-C8	Scarcity
20	25	4

7302 TEXAS & PACIFIC: 1983-84, stock car in the traditional 027/Scout size.

EX-C7	LN-C8	Scarcity
5	10	2

7303 ERIE: 1984, stock car.

EX-C7	LN-C8	Scarcity
20	30	5

7304 SOUTHERN: 1983, uncataloged stock car, Famous American Railroads number four.

EX-C7	LN-C8	Scarcity
20	30	5

7309 SOUTHERN: 1985-86, stock car in the traditional 027/Scout size.

EX-C7	LN-C8	Scarcity
5	10	2

7312 W & ARR: 1986, uncataloged stock car in the traditional 027/Scout size.

EX-C7	LN-C8	Scarcity
15	20	5

7401 CHESSIE SYSTEM: 1984-85, stock car in the traditional 027/Scout size.

EX-C7	LN-C8	Scarcity
5	10	2

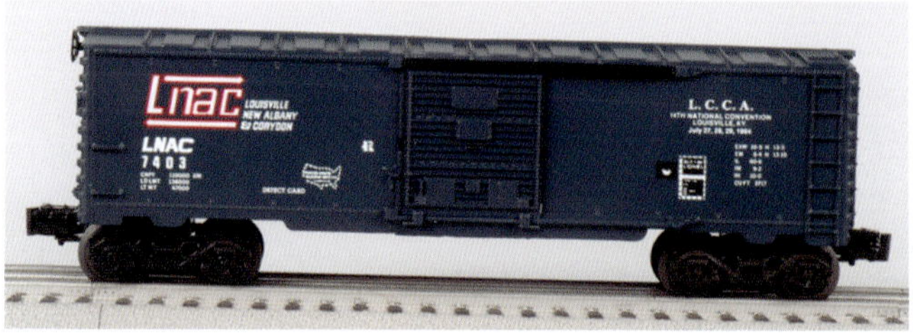

7403 LNAC: 1984, uncataloged LCCA boxcar.

EX-C7	LN-C8	Scarcity
10	15	5

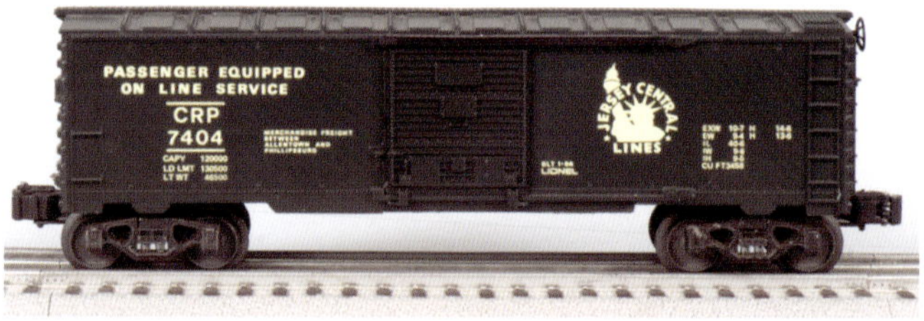

7404 JERSEY CENTRAL: 1986, boxcar.

EX-C7	LN-C8	Scarcity
15	25	4

7501 LIONEL 75TH ANNIVERSARY: 1975-77, boxcar.

EX-C7	LN-C8	Scarcity
15	20	4

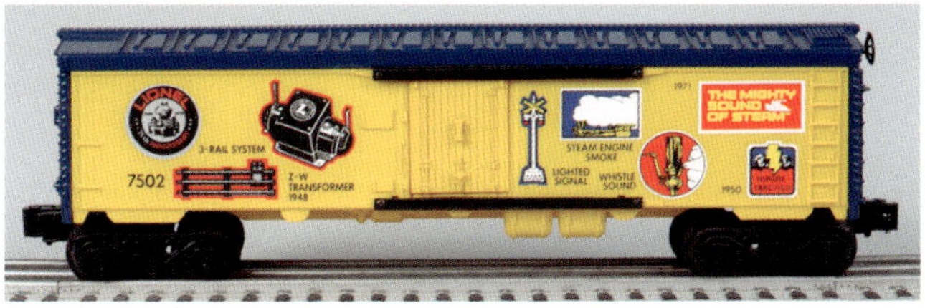

7502 LIONEL 75TH ANNIVERSARY: 1975-77, refrigerator car.

EX-C7	LN-C8	Scarcity
15	20	4

7503 LIONEL 75TH ANNIVERSARY: 1975-77, refrigerator car.

EX-C7	LN-C8	Scarcity
15	20	4

7505 LIONEL 75TH ANNIVERSARY: 1975-77, boxcar.

EX-C7	LN-C8	Scarcity
15	20	4

7506 LIONEL 75TH ANNIVERSARY: 1975-77, boxcar.

EX-C7	LN-C8	Scarcity
15	20	4

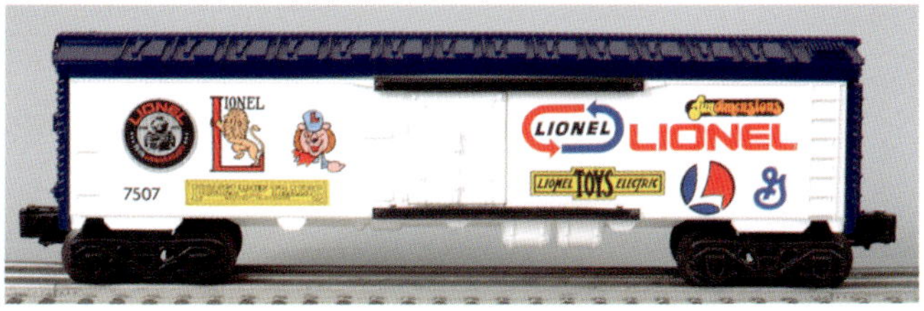

7507 LIONEL 75TH ANNIVERSARY: 1975-77, refrigerator car.

EX-C7	LN-C8	Scarcity
15	20	4

7509 KENTUCKY FRIED CHICKEN: 1981-82, refrigerator car.

EX-C7	LN-C8	Scarcity
12	20	4

7510 RED LOBSTER: 1981-82, refrigerator car.

EX-C7	LN-C8	Scarcity
12	20	4

7511 PIZZA HUT: 1981-82, refrigerator car.

EX-C7	LN-C8	Scarcity
12	20	4

7512 ARTHUR TREACHER'S: 1982, refrigerator car.

EX-C7	LN-C8	Scarcity
12	20	4

7513 BONANZA: 1982, refrigerator car.

EX-C7	LN-C8	Scarcity
12	20	4

7514 TACO BELL: 1982, refrigerator car.

EX-C7	LN-C8	Scarcity
20	30	5

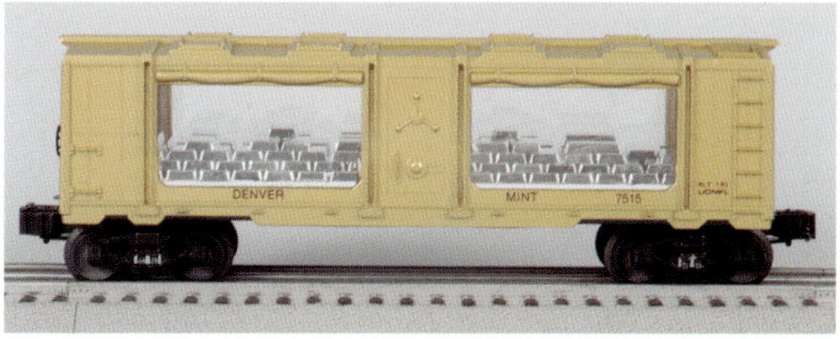

7515 DENVER MINT: 1981, mint car.

EX-C7	LN-C8	Scarcity
30	40	4

7517 PHILADELPHIA MINT: 1982, mint car.

EX-C7	LN-C8	Scarcity
20	30	3

7518 CARSON CITY MINT: 1983, black mint car.

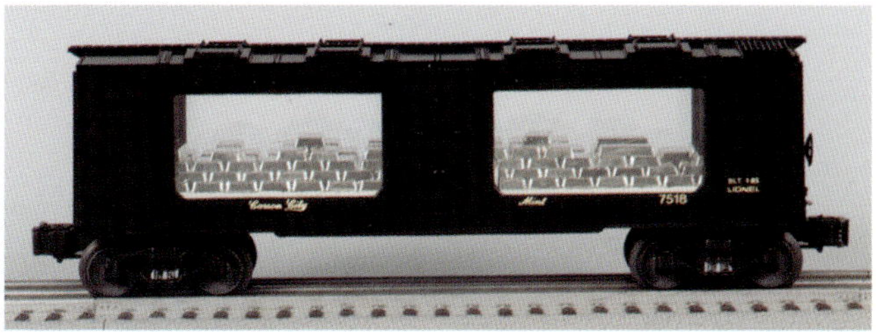

7518 CARSON CITY MINT (Type I): As described above.

EX-C7	LN-C8	Scarcity
20	30	3

7518 CARSON CITY MINT (Type II): 1984, uncataloged car overstamped IETCA.

EX-C7	LN-C8	Scarcity
25	35	6

7519 TOY FAIR: 1982, uncataloged refrigerator car.

EX-C7	LN-C8	Scarcity
40	50	7

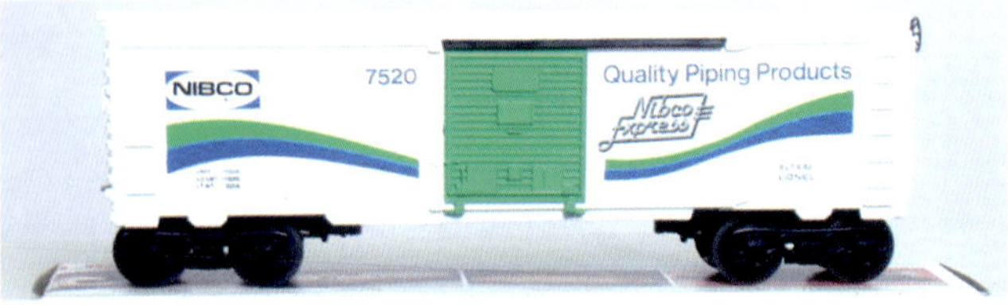

7520 NIBCO EXPRESS: 1982, uncataloged boxcar.

EX-C7	LN-C8	Scarcity
150	275	7

7521 TOY FAIR: 1983, uncataloged refrigerator car.

EX-C7	LN-C8	Scarcity
40	50	7

7522 NEW ORLEANS MINT: 1984, blue mint car.

7522 NEW ORLEANS MINT (Type I): As described above.

EX-C7	LN-C8	Scarcity
20	25	5

7522 NEW ORLEANS MINT (Type II): 1986, uncataloged overstamped Lone Star TCA car with coin.

EX-C7	LN-C8	Scarcity
185	250	6

7523 TOY FAIR: 1984, uncataloged refrigerator car.

EX-C7	LN-C8	Scarcity
40	50	7

7524 TOY FAIR: 1985, uncataloged refrigerator car.

EX-C7	LN-C8	Scarcity
50	75	7

7525 TOY FAIR: 1986, uncataloged boxcar.

EX-C7	LN-C8	Scarcity
50	75	7

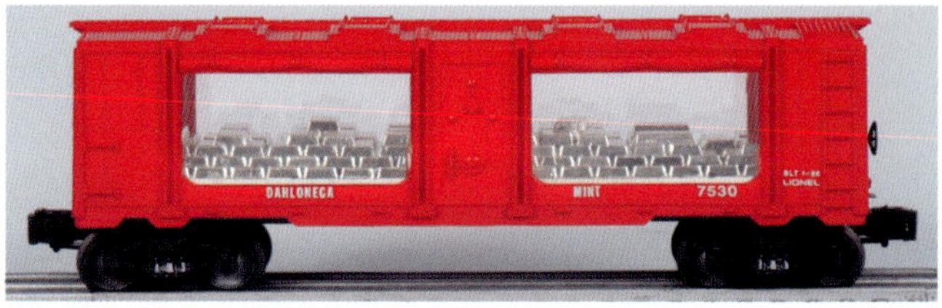

7530 DAHLONEGA MINT: 1986, uncataloged mint car.

EX-C7	LN-C8	Scarcity
25	35	4

7601 DELAWARE: 1974-76, boxcar.

EX-C7	LN-C8	Scarcity
15	20	3

7602 PENNSYLVANIA: 1974-76, boxcar.

7602 PENNSYLVANIA (Type I): Doors molded in blue, then painted blue.

EX-C7	LN-C8	Scarcity
20	25	3

7602 PENNSYLVANIA (Type II): Unpainted blue plastic doors.

EX-C7	LN-C8	Scarcity
20	25	3

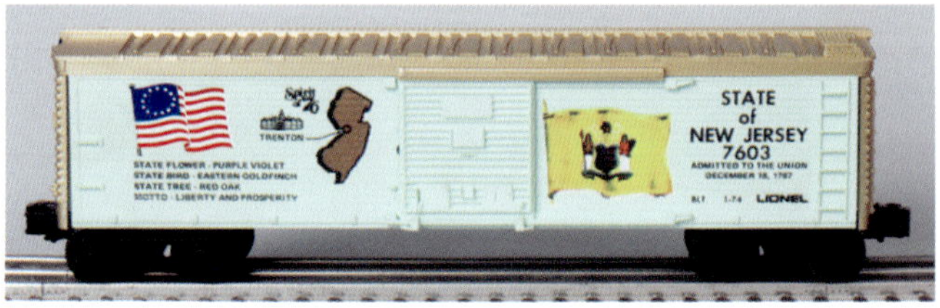

7603 NEW JERSEY: 1974-76, boxcar.

EX-C7	LN-C8	Scarcity
20	25	3

7604 GEORGIA: Uncataloged in 1974, cataloged from 1975-76, boxcar.

7604 GEORGIA (Type I): With a molded white roof painted red.

EX-C7	LN-C8	Scarcity
15	20	3

7604 GEORGIA (Type II): With a molded red roof painted red.

EX-C7	LN-C8	Scarcity
15	20	3

7605 CONNECTICUT: Uncataloged in 1974, cataloged from 1975-76, boxcar.

7605 CONNECTICUT (Type I): White molded body painted blue.

EX-C7	LN-C8	Scarcity
15	20	3

7605 CONNECTICUT (Type II): Blue molded body painted blue.

EX-C7	LN-C8	Scarcity
15	20	3

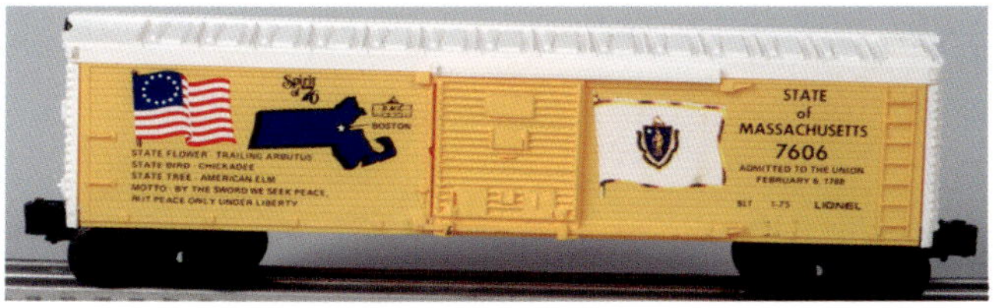

7606 MASSACHUSETTS: Uncataloged in 1974, cataloged from 1975-76, boxcar.

EX-C7	LN-C8	Scarcity
15	20	3

7607 MARYLAND: Uncataloged in 1974, cataloged from 1975-76, boxcar.

7607 MARYLAND (Type I): White molded body painted light yellow.

EX-C7	LN-C8	Scarcity
20	25	3

7607 MARYLAND (Type II): White molded body painted mustard yellow.

EX-C7	LN-C8	Scarcity
20	25	3

7607 MARYLAND (Type III): Yellow molded body painted light yellow.

EX-C7	LN-C8	Scarcity
20	25	3

7608 SOUTH CAROLINA: Uncataloged in 1975, cataloged in 1976, boxcar.

EX-C7	LN-C8	Scarcity
25	30	4

7609 NEW HAMPSHIRE: Uncataloged in 1975, cataloged in 1976, boxcar.

EX-C7	LN-C8	Scarcity
30	35	4

7610 VIRGINIA: Uncataloged in 1975, cataloged in 1976, boxcar.

7610 VIRGINIA (Type I): White molded body painted orange.

EX-C7	LN-C8	Scarcity
100	160	5

7610 VIRGINIA (Type II): Orange molded body painted orange.

EX-C7	LN-C8	Scarcity
100	160	5

7611 NEW YORK: Uncataloged in 1975, cataloged in 1976, boxcar.

EX-C7	LN-C8	Scarcity
30	35	4

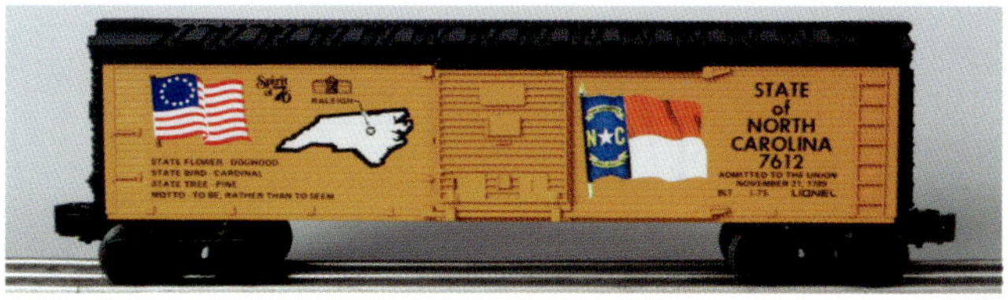

7612 NORTH CAROLINA: Uncataloged in 1975, cataloged in 1976, boxcar.

EX-C7	LN-C8	Scarcity
20	25	4

7613 RHODE ISLAND: Uncataloged in 1975, cataloged in 1976, boxcar.

EX-C7	LN-C8	Scarcity
20	25	4

[7679] VIRGINIA TRAIN COLLECTORS: 1979, uncataloged boxcar.

EX-C7	LN-C8	Scarcity
5	10	5

[7683] VIRGINIA FRUIT EXPRESS: 1983, uncataloged Virginia Train Collectors refrigerator car.

EX-C7	LN-C8	Scarcity
15	20	5

[7685] VIRGINIA TRAIN COLLECTORS: 1985, uncataloged boxcar.

EX-C7	LN-C8	Scarcity
15	20	5

7700 UNCLE SAM: 1975, uncataloged boxcar.

EX-C7	LN-C8	Scarcity
25	35	5

7701 CAMEL: 1976-77, boxcar.

EX-C7	LN-C8	Scarcity
20	25	3

7702 PRINCE ALBERT: 1976-77, boxcar.

EX-C7	LN-C8	Scarcity
20	25	3

7703 BEECH-NUT: 1976-77, boxcar.

EX-C7	LN-C8	Scarcity
15	20	3

7704 TOY FAIR: 1976, uncataloged boxcar.

EX-C7	LN-C8	Scarcity
75	100	7

7705 CANADIAN TOY FAIR: 1976, uncataloged boxcar.

EX-C7	LN-C8	Scarcity
100	125	7

7706 SIR WALTER RALEIGH: 1977-78, boxcar.

EX-C7	LN-C8	Scarcity
20	25	3

7707 WHITE OWL: 1977-78, boxcar.

EX-C7	LN-C8	Scarcity
20	25	3

7708 WINSTON: 1977-78, boxcar.

EX-C7	LN-C8	Scarcity
20	25	3

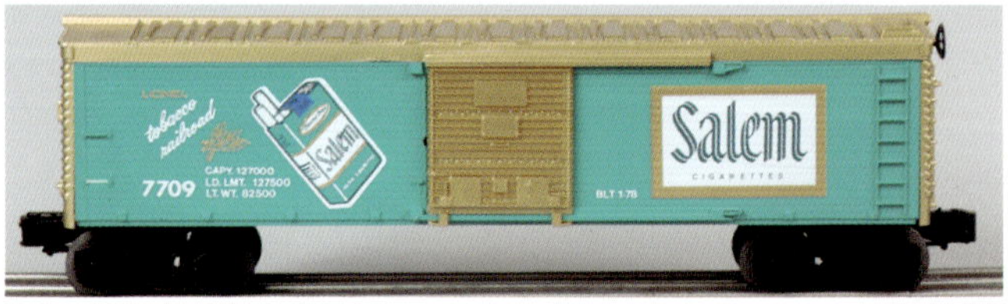

7709 SALEM: 1978, boxcar.

EX-C7	LN-C8	Scarcity
20	25	3

7710 MAIL POUCH: 1978, boxcar.

EX-C7	LN-C8	Scarcity
25	30	3

7711 EL PRODUCTO: 1978, boxcar.

EX-C7	LN-C8	Scarcity
25	30	3

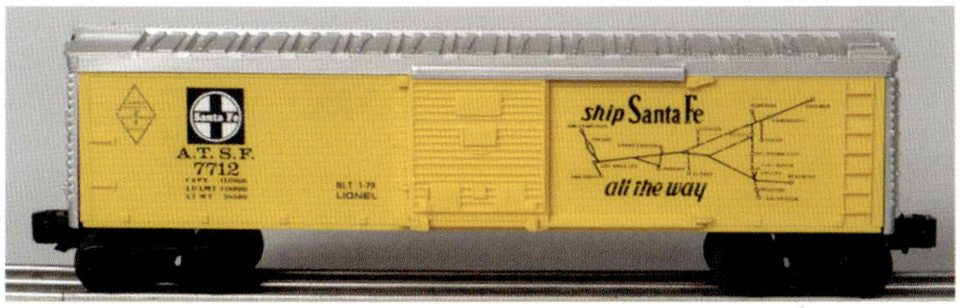

7712 SANTA FE: 1979 boxcar, Famous American Railroads number one.

EX-C7	LN-C8	Scarcity
20	25	3

[7780] TCA MUSEUM: 1980, uncataloged boxcar.

EX-C7	LN-C8	Scarcity
15	20	6

[7781] TCA HAFNER: 1981, uncataloged boxcar.

EX-C7	LN-C8	Scarcity
15	20	6

[7782] TCA CARLISLE & FINCH: 1982, uncataloged boxcar.

EX-C7	LN-C8	Scarcity
15	20	6

[7783] TCA IVES: 1983, uncataloged boxcar.

EX-C7	LN-C8	Scarcity
15	20	6

[7784] TCA VOLTAMP: 1984, uncataloged boxcar.

EX-C7	LN-C8	Scarcity
15	20	6

[7785] TCA HOGE: 1985, uncataloged boxcar.

EX-C7	LN-C8	Scarcity
15	20	6

7800 PEPSI: Uncataloged in 1976, cataloged in 1977, boxcar.

EX-C7	LN-C8	Scarcity
20	35	5

7801 A & W: Uncataloged in 1976, cataloged in 1977, boxcar.

EX-C7	LN-C8	Scarcity
20	25	4

7802 CANADA DRY: Uncataloged in 1976, cataloged in 1977, boxcar.

EX-C7	LN-C8	Scarcity
20	25	4

7803 TRAINS N' TRUCKIN': 1977, uncataloged boxcar.

EX-C7	LN-C8	Scarcity
15	25	4

7806 SEASONS GREETINGS: 1976, uncataloged boxcar.

EX-C7	LN-C8	Scarcity
60	80	7

7807 TOY FAIR: 1977, uncataloged boxcar.

EX-C7	LN-C8	Scarcity
65	100	7

7808 NORTHERN PACIFIC: 1977, stock car.

EX-C7	LN-C8	Scarcity
25	30	5

7809 VERNORS: Uncataloged in 1977, cataloged in 1978, boxcar.

EX-C7	LN-C8	Scarcity
20	25	4

7810 ORANGE CRUSH: Uncataloged in 1977, cataloged in 1978, boxcar.

EX-C7	LN-C8	Scarcity
20	25	4

7811 DR PEPPER: Uncataloged in 1975, cataloged in 1978, boxcar.

EX-C7	LN-C8	Scarcity
20	25	4

7812 TCA HOUSTON: 1977, uncataloged stock car.

EX-C7	LN-C8	Scarcity
15	20	6

7813 SEASONS GREETINGS: 1977, uncataloged boxcar.

EX-C7	LN-C8	Scarcity
60	80	7

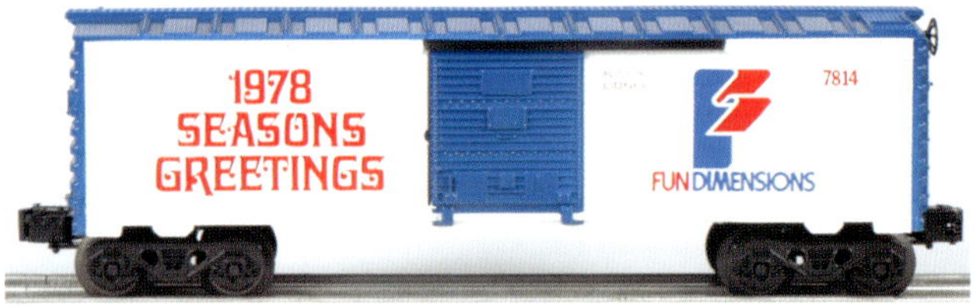

7814 SEASONS GREETINGS: 1978, uncataloged boxcar.

EX-C7	LN-C8	Scarcity
55	80	7

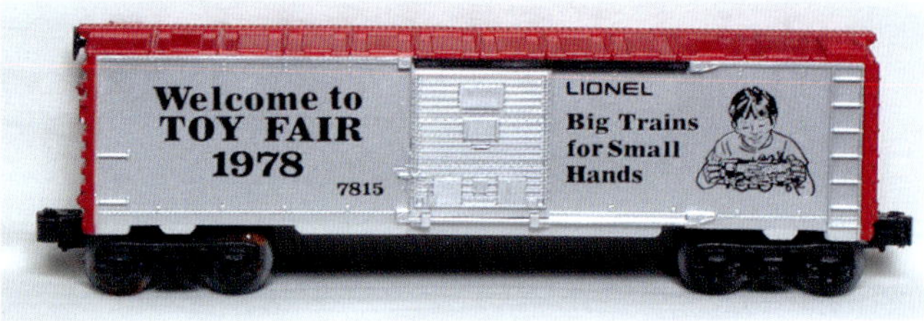

7815 TOY FAIR: 1978, uncataloged boxcar.

EX-C7	LN-C8	Scarcity
60	90	7

7816 TOY FAIR: 1979, uncataloged boxcar.

EX-C7	LN-C8	Scarcity
65	100	7

7817 TOY FAIR: 1980, uncataloged boxcar.

EX-C7	LN-C8	Scarcity
80	110	7

7900 DENVER & RIO GRANDE WESTERN: 1982-83, operating cowboy car in the traditional 027/Scout size.

EX-C7	LN-C8	Scarcity
10	20	3

7901 LIONEL LINES: 1982-83, cop and hobo car in the traditional 027/Scout size.

EX-C7	LN-C8	Scarcity
15	20	3

7902 SANTA FE: 1982-85, boxcar in the traditional 027/Scout size.

EX-C7	LN-C8	Scarcity
3	5	3

7903 ROCK ISLAND: 1983, boxcar in the traditional 027/Scout size.

EX-C7	LN-C8	Scarcity
3	7	2

7904 SAN DIEGO ZOO: 1983-84, giraffe car in the traditional 027/Scout size.

EX-C7	LN-C8	Scarcity
20	30	4

[7905] BLACK CAVE: 1982, boxcar in the traditional 027/Scout size.

EX-C7	LN-C8	Scarcity
3	5	2

7908 TAPPAN: 1982, uncataloged boxcar in the traditional 027/Scout size.

EX-C7	LN-C8	Scarcity
35	50	7

7909 LOUISVILLE AND NASHVILLE: 1983-84, boxcar in the traditional 027/Scout size.

EX-C7	LN-C8	Scarcity
35	50	7

7910 CHESSIE SYSTEM: 1984-85, boxcar in the traditional 027/Scout size.

EX-C7	LN-C8	Scarcity
10	15	3

7912 TOYS "R" US: 1982-84, uncataloged giraffe car in the traditional 027/Scout size.

EX-C7	LN-C8	Scarcity
30	50	6

7913 TURTLEBACK ZOO: 1985-86, giraffe car in the traditional 027/Scout size.

EX-C7	LN-C8	Scarcity
20	30	4

7914 TOYS "R" US: 1985-89, uncataloged giraffe car in the traditional 027/Scout size.

EX-C7	LN-C8	Scarcity
35	60	6

7920 SEARS: 1985-86, uncataloged Centennial boxcar in the traditional 027/Scout size.

EX-C7	LN-C8	Scarcity
25	35	6

7925 ERIE-LACKAWANNA: 1986-90, boxcar in the traditional 027/Scout size.

EX-C7	LN-C8	Scarcity
5	10	3

7926 NICKEL PLATE ROAD: 1986-91, boxcar in the traditional 027/Scout size.

EX-C7	LN-C8	Scarcity
2	5	2

7930 TRUE VALUE: 1986-87, uncataloged boxcar in the traditional 027/Scout size.

EX-C7	LN-C8	Scarcity
20	30	6

7931 TOWN HOUSE TV AND APPLIANCES: 1986, uncataloged boxcar in the traditional 027/Scout size.

EX-C7	LN-C8	Scarcity
25	35	6

7932 KAY BEE TOYS: 1985-87, uncataloged boxcar in the traditional 027/Scout size.

EX-C7	LN-C8	Scarcity
35	50	7

[8051] HOOD'S MILK: 1986, uncataloged New England Division of Train Collectors Association boxcar.

EX-C7	LN-C8	Scarcity
35	50	6

[8103] TORONTO, HAMILTON & BUFFALO: 1981, uncataloged Lionel Collectors Association of Canada boxcar.

EX-C7	LN-C8	Scarcity
40	75	6

[8204] ALGOMA CENTRAL: 1982, uncataloged Lionel Collectors Association of Canada boxcar.

EX-C7	LN-C8	Scarcity
40	75	6

[8389] LONG ISLAND: 1989, NLOE uncataloged boxcar.

EX-C7	LN-C8	Scarcity
35	50	6

[8391A] LONG ISLAND: 1991, uncataloged NLOE bunk car.

EX-C7	LN-C8	Scarcity
30	45	6

[8391B] LONG ISLAND: 1997, uncataloged NLOE tool car.

EX-C7	LN-C8	Scarcity
30	45	6

8999 LONE STAR: 1999, aquarium car.

EX-C7	LN-C8	Scarcity
Too rarely traded to establish accurate pricing.		

9001 CONRAIL: Uncataloged from 1986-87, cataloged from 1988-90, boxcar in the traditional 027/Scout size.

EX-C7	LN-C8	Scarcity
5	10	2

9035 CONRAIL: 1978-82, boxcar in the traditional 027/Scout size.

EX-C7	LN-C8	Scarcity
5	10	2

9037 CONRAIL: Uncataloged in 1978, cataloged in 1980, boxcar in the traditional 027/Scout size.

EX-C7	LN-C8	Scarcity
5	10	2

9040 WHEATIES: 1970-72, General Mills boxcar in the traditional 027/Scout size.

9040 WHEATIES (Type I): The earliest cars rode on AAR trucks.

EX-C7	LN-C8	Scarcity
10	15	1

9040 WHEATIES (Type II): Later cars rode on Symington-Wayne trucks.

EX-C7	LN-C8	Scarcity
10	15	1

9041 HERSHEY'S: 1970-71 and 1973-76, boxcar in the traditional 027/Scout size.

EX-C7	LN-C8	Scarcity
12	18	2

9042 FORD-AUTOLITE: Uncataloged in 1971, cataloged in 1972 and 1974-76, boxcar in the traditional 027/Scout size.

EX-C7	LN-C8	Scarcity
12	18	2

9043 ERIE-LACKAWANNA: 1973-75, boxcar in the traditional 027/Scout size.

EX-C7	LN-C8	Scarcity
12	18	2

9044 DENVER & RIO GRANDE WESTERN: 1975-76, boxcar in the traditional 027/Scout size.

EX-C7	LN-C8	Scarcity
5	10	2

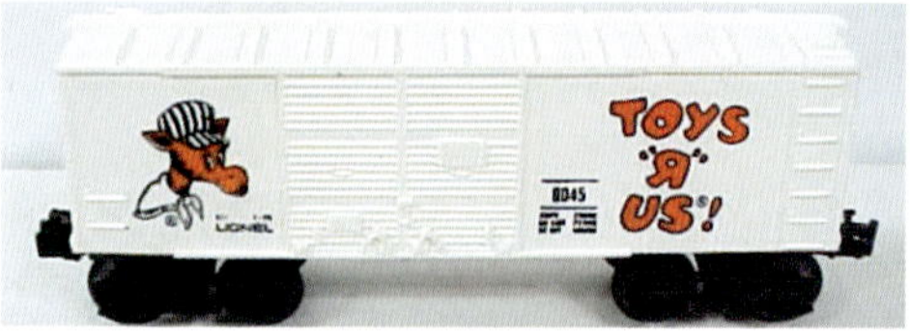

9045 TOYS "R" US: 1975, uncataloged boxcar in the traditional 027/Scout size.

EX-C7	LN-C8	Scarcity
25	35	6

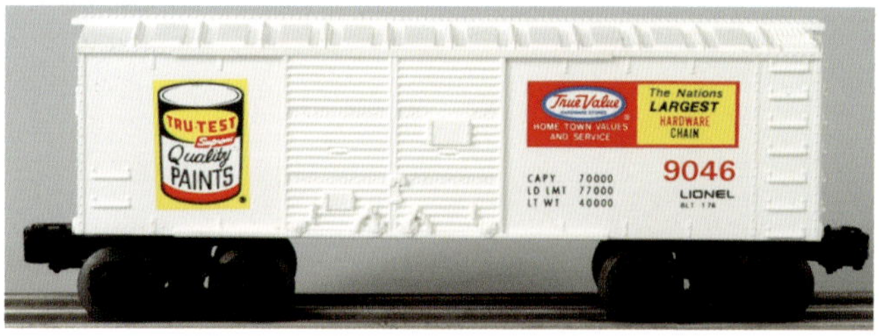

9046 TRUE VALUE: 1976, uncataloged boxcar in the traditional 027/Scout size.

EX-C7	LN-C8	Scarcity
25	35	6

9047 TOYS "R" US: 1976, uncataloged boxcar in the traditional 027/Scout size.

EX-C7	LN-C8	Scarcity
30	40	6

9048 TOYS "R" US: 1976, uncataloged boxcar in the traditional 027/Scout size.

EX-C7	LN-C8	Scarcity
30	40	6

[9049] TOYS "R" US: 1978, uncataloged boxcar in the traditional 027/Scout size.

EX-C7	LN-C8	Scarcity
Too rarely traded to establish accurate pricing.		

9052 TOYS "R" US: 1977, uncataloged boxcar in the traditional 027/Scout size.

EX-C7	LN-C8	Scarcity
25	35	6

9053 TRUE VALUE: 1977, uncataloged boxcar in the traditional 027/Scout size.

EX-C7	LN-C8	Scarcity
25	35	6

9054 JCPENNEY: 1977, uncataloged boxcar in the traditional 027/Scout size.

EX-C7	LN-C8	Scarcity
15	20	6

9090 GENERAL MILLS: 1971, Mini-Max car.

EX-C7	LN-C8	Scarcity
15	20	4

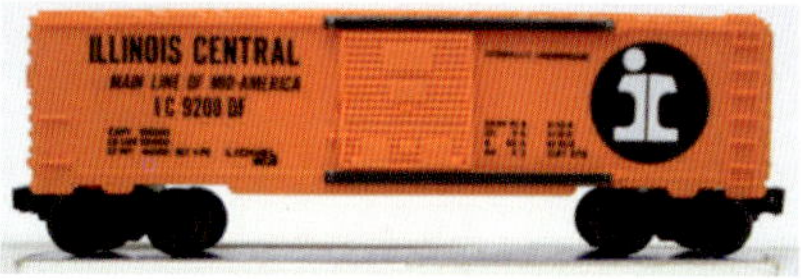

9200 ILLINOIS CENTRAL: 1970-71, orange boxcar.

9200 ILLINOIS CENTRAL (Type I): The early cars used AAR trucks and metal door guides. The "IC" in the logo is very closely spaced together.

EX-C7	LN-C8	Scarcity
10	20	4

9200 ILLINOIS CENTRAL (Type II): Some of the cars with AAR trucks and metal door guides had widely spaced "IC" lettering in the logo.

EX-C7	LN-C8	Scarcity
10	20	4

9200 ILLINOIS CENTRAL (Type III): Some of the cars with metal door guides and widely spaced "IC" lettering in the logo rode on Symington-Wayne trucks.

EX-C7	LN-C8	Scarcity
10	20	4

9200 ILLINOIS CENTRAL (Type IV): Later production cars came with two plastic guides retaining each door and widely spaced "IC" lettering in the logo and rode on Symington-Wayne trucks.

EX-C7	LN-C8	Scarcity
10	20	4

9201 PENN CENTRAL: 1970, boxcar.

EX-C7	LN-C8	Scarcity
10	20	4

9202 SANTA FE: 1970, boxcar.

EX-C7	LN-C8	Scarcity
15	25	4

9203 UNION PACIFIC: 1970, boxcar.

EX-C7	LN-C8	Scarcity
10	20	4

9204 NORTHERN PACIFIC: 1970, boxcar.

9204 NORTHERN PACIFIC (Type I): The early cars used AAR trucks and metal door guides.

EX-C7	LN-C8	Scarcity
10	20	4

9204 NORTHERN PACIFIC (Type II): Later production cars came with plastic guides and rode on Symington-Wayne trucks.

EX-C7	LN-C8	Scarcity
10	20	4

9205 NORFOLK AND WESTERN: 1970, boxcar.

9205 NORFOLK AND WESTERN (Type I): The early cars used AAR trucks and metal door guides.

EX-C7	LN-C8	Scarcity
15	25	4

9205 NORFOLK AND WESTERN (Type II): Later production cars came with Symington-Wayne trucks.

EX-C7	LN-C8	Scarcity
15	25	4

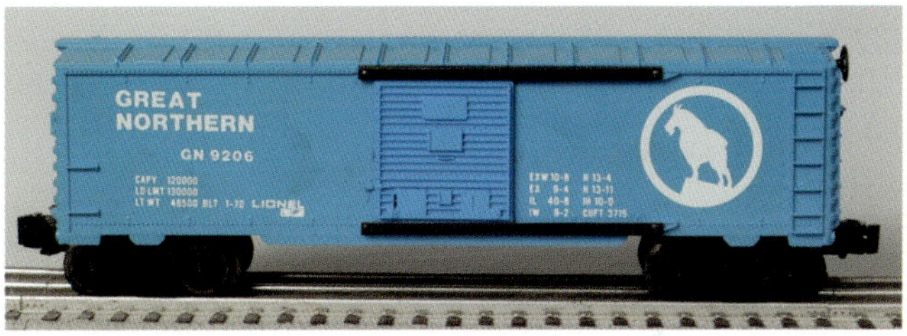

9206 GREAT NORTHERN: 1970-71, boxcar.

9206 GREAT NORTHERN (Type I): The early cars used AAR trucks and metal door guides.

EX-C7	LN-C8	Scarcity
10	20	4

9206 GREAT NORTHERN (Type II): Later production cars came with Symington-Wayne trucks.

EX-C7	LN-C8	Scarcity
10	20	4

9207 SOO LINE: 1971, boxcar.

9207 SOO LINE (Type I): The early cars used AAR trucks and metal door guides.

EX-C7	LN-C8	Scarcity
10	20	4

9207 SOO LINE (Type II): Later production cars came with metal door guides and rode on Symington-Wayne trucks.

EX-C7	LN-C8	Scarcity
10	20	4

9207 SOO LINE (Type III): The final production cars came with plastic guides and rode on Symington-Wayne trucks.

EX-C7	LN-C8	Scarcity
10	20	4

9208 CP RAIL: 1971, boxcar.

9208 CP RAIL (Type I): Some cars used Symington-Wayne trucks and metal door guides.

EX-C7	LN-C8	Scarcity
10	20	4

9208 CP RAIL (Type II): Other cars came with plastic door guides and rode on Symington-Wayne trucks.

EX-C7	LN-C8	Scarcity
10	20	4

9209 BURLINGTON NORTHERN: 1971-72, boxcar.

9209 BURLINGTON NORTHERN (Type I): The early cars used AAR trucks and metal door guides. The bodies were painted bright green, and the doors were slightly darker.

EX-C7	LN-C8	Scarcity
10	20	4

9209 BURLINGTON NORTHERN (Type II): Later production cars came with metal door guides and rode on Symington-Wayne trucks. Both the bodies and the doors were dark green.

EX-C7	LN-C8	Scarcity
10	20	4

9209 BURLINGTON NORTHERN (Type III): The final production cars came with plastic guides and rode on Symington-Wayne trucks.

EX-C7	LN-C8	Scarcity
10	20	4

9210 BALTIMORE & OHIO: 1971, double-door automobile boxcar riding on AAR trucks. Note: numerous variations of this car exist with regard to door color. However, only black doors were factory installed.

EX-C7	LN-C8	Scarcity
10	20	4

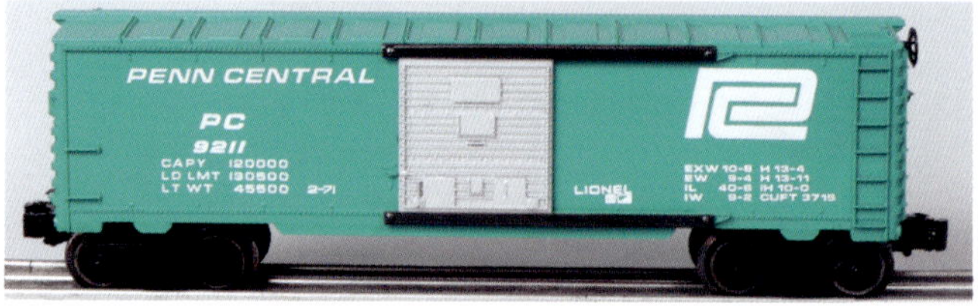

9211 PENN CENTRAL: 1971, boxcar.

9211 PENN CENTRAL (Type I): The early cars used AAR trucks and metal door guides. The bodies were painted jade green.

EX-C7	LN-C8	Scarcity
20	30	5

9211 PENN CENTRAL (Type II): Later production cars were painted a pale green, but still came with metal door guides and rode on AAR trucks.

EX-C7	LN-C8	Scarcity
15	25	4

9211 PENN CENTRAL (Type III): Some cars were painted medium green, yet still came with metal door guides and rode on AAR trucks.

EX-C7	LN-C8	Scarcity
15	25	4

9211 PENN CENTRAL (Type IV): Some of the medium green cars came with metal door guides but rode on Symington-Wayne trucks.

EX-C7	LN-C8	Scarcity
15	25	4

9211 PENN CENTRAL (Type V): The final production cars were dark green and came with plastic guides and rode on Symington-Wayne trucks.

EX-C7	LN-C8	Scarcity
15	25	4

9214 NORTHERN PACIFIC: 1971-72, boxcar.

9214 NORTHERN PACIFIC (Type I): Some cars were painted red oxide and used AAR trucks and metal door guides.

EX-C7	LN-C8	Scarcity
10	20	4

9214 NORTHERN PACIFIC (Type II): Other red oxide cars using metal door guides rode on Symington-Wayne trucks.

EX-C7	LN-C8	Scarcity
10	20	4

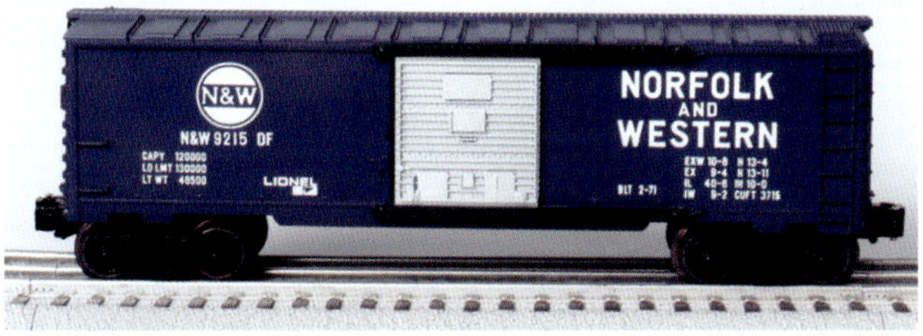

9215 NORFOLK AND WESTERN: 1971, boxcar.

9215 NORFOLK AND WESTERN (Type I): The earliest cars used AAR trucks and plastic door guides. The bodies were painted royal blue.

EX-C7	LN-C8	Scarcity
10	20	4

9215 NORFOLK AND WESTERN (Type II): Other cars used AAR trucks and plastic door guides, the bodies were painted dark blue.

EX-C7	LN-C8	Scarcity
10	20	4

9215 NORFOLK AND WESTERN (Type III): Dark blue bodies were also used on some cars with Symington-Wayne trucks and plastic door guides.

EX-C7	LN-C8	Scarcity
10	20	4

9215 NORFOLK AND WESTERN (Type IV): AAR trucks were used on some of the dark blue cars with plastic door guides.

EX-C7	LN-C8	Scarcity
10	20	4

9217 SOO LINE: 1982-84, operating boxcar.

EX-C7	LN-C8	Scarcity
10	20	4

9218 MONON: 1981, operating boxcar.

EX-C7	LN-C8	Scarcity
20	25	4

9219 MISSOURI PACIFIC: 1983, operating boxcar.

EX-C7	LN-C8	Scarcity
20	25	4

9220 BORDEN MILK CAR: 1983-86.

EX-C7	LN-C8	Scarcity
75	100	5

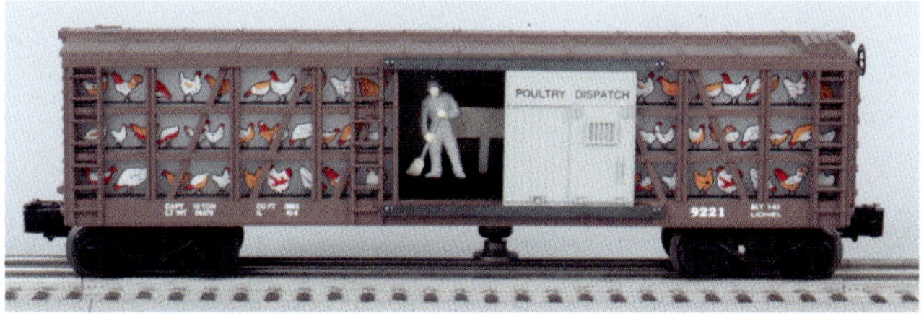

9221 POULTRY DISPATCH: 1983-85, operating chicken car.

EX-C7	LN-C8	Scarcity
25	30	4

9223 READING: 1984, operating boxcar.

EX-C7	LN-C8	Scarcity
20	25	4

9224 CHURCHILL DOWNS: 1984-86, operating horse car.

EX-C7	LN-C8	Scarcity
65	90	5

9228 CANADIAN PACIFIC: 1986, operating boxcar.

EX-C7	LN-C8	Scarcity
15	20	4

9229 EXPRESS MAIL: 1985-86, operating boxcar.

EX-C7	LN-C8	Scarcity
20	25	4

9230 MONON: Cataloged in 1971, available but uncataloged in 1972, a boxcar with Symington-Wayne trucks. Service Station Special item.

9230 MONON (Type I): The early cars used metal door guides.

EX-C7	LN-C8	Scarcity
10	20	4

9230 MONON (Type II): Later production cars came with plastic guides.

EX-C7	LN-C8	Scarcity
15	20	5

9237 UNION PACIFIC: 1984, operating boxcar.

EX-C7	LN-C8	Scarcity
Cataloged, but not produced.		

9280 SANTA FE: 1977-81, operating stock car in the traditional 027/Scout size.

EX-C7	LN-C8	Scarcity
15	20	4

9301 U.S. MAIL: 1973-84, operating red, white and blue boxcar with mail sack.

9301 U.S. MAIL (Type I): On some of the cars the blue is very dark.

EX-C7	LN-C8	Scarcity
15	20	4

9301 U.S. MAIL (Type II): On other cars the blue is light.

EX-C7	LN-C8	Scarcity
15	20	4

9301 U.S. MAIL (Type III): On other cars the blue is more medium.

EX-C7	LN-C8	Scarcity
15	20	4

9301 U.S. MAIL (Type IV): In 1976, some of these cars were overstamped to make an uncataloged Sacramento-Sierra TCA car.

EX-C7	LN-C8	Scarcity
15	20	6

9305 SANTA FE: 1980-82, operating Cowboy car in the traditional 027/Scout size.

EX-C7	LN-C8	Scarcity
8	12	3

9308 LIONEL: 1981-84, aquarium car.

EX-C7	LN-C8	Scarcity
125	150	5

9319 TCA SILVER JUBILEE: 1979, uncataloged mint car.

9319 TCA SILVER JUBILEE (Type I): Basic car.

EX-C7	LN-C8	Scarcity
100	150	6

9319 TCA SILVER JUBILEE (Type II): In addition to the basic car, convention attendees got a "coin" which sits in the roof top slot.

EX-C7	LN-C8	Scarcity
110	165	6

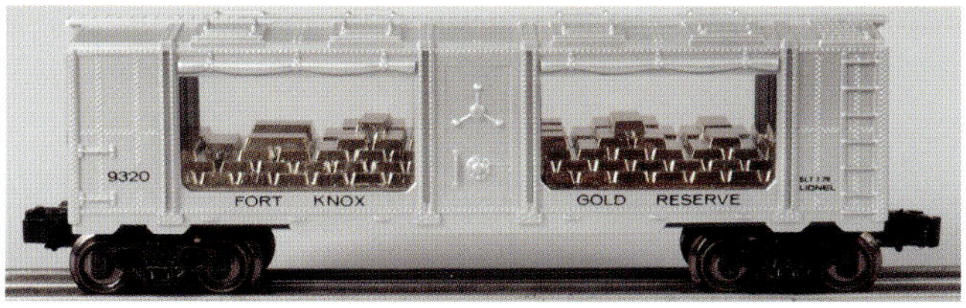

9320 FORT KNOX: 1979, uncataloged mint car.

EX-C7	LN-C8	Scarcity
125	175	5

9339 GREAT NORTHERN: Cataloged from 1979-83, uncataloged in 1985, cataloged again in 1986, a boxcar in the traditional 027/Scout size riding on Symington-Wayne trucks.

9339 GREAT NORTHERN (Type I): One operating and one non-operating coupler.

EX-C7	LN-C8	Scarcity
3	5	2

9339 GREAT NORTHERN (Type II): Two operating couplers.

EX-C7	LN-C8	Scarcity
3	5	2

9349 SAN FRANCISCO: 1980, Mint car.

EX-C7	LN-C8	Scarcity
50	75	5

9359 NATIONAL BASKETBALL ASSOCIATION: 1979-80, uncataloged boxcar in the traditional 027/Scout size.

EX-C7	LN-C8	Scarcity
15	20	3

9360 NATIONAL HOCKEY LEAGUE: 1979-80, uncataloged boxcar in the traditional 027/Scout size.

EX-C7	LN-C8	Scarcity
15	20	3

9362 MAJOR LEAGUE BASEBALL: 1979-80, uncataloged boxcar in the traditional 027/Scout size.

EX-C7	LN-C8	Scarcity
15	20	3

9365 TOYS "R" US: 1979, uncataloged boxcar in the traditional 027/Scout size.

EX-C7	LN-C8	Scarcity
20	25	5

9376 SOO LINE: 1981, uncataloged boxcar in the traditional 027/Scout size.

EX-C7	LN-C8	Scarcity
20	25	4

9377 MISSOURI PACIFIC: 1980, boxcar in the traditional 027/Scout size.

EX-C7	LN-C8	Scarcity
Cataloged, but not produced.		

9388 TOYS "R" US: 1981, uncataloged boxcar in the traditional 027/Scout size.

EX-C7	LN-C8	Scarcity
25	30	6

9400 CONRAIL: 1978, boxcar.

9400 CONRAIL (Type I): As cataloged.

EX-C7	LN-C8	Scarcity
10	15	2

[9400] CONRAIL (Type II): This uncataloged New England Division of Train Collectors Association overstamped boxcar was also produced in 1978.

EX-C7	LN-C8	Scarcity
12	18	6

9401 GREAT NORTHERN: 1978, boxcar.

9401 GREAT NORTHERN (Type I): As cataloged.

EX-C7	LN-C8	Scarcity
10	15	4

9401 GREAT NORTHERN (Type II): 1978, uncataloged Detroit-Toledo TCA boxcar.

EX-C7	LN-C8	Scarcity
12	18	6

9402 SUSQUEHANNA: 1978, boxcar.

EX-C7	LN-C8	Scarcity
10	15	4

9403 SEABOARD COAST LINE: 1978, boxcar.

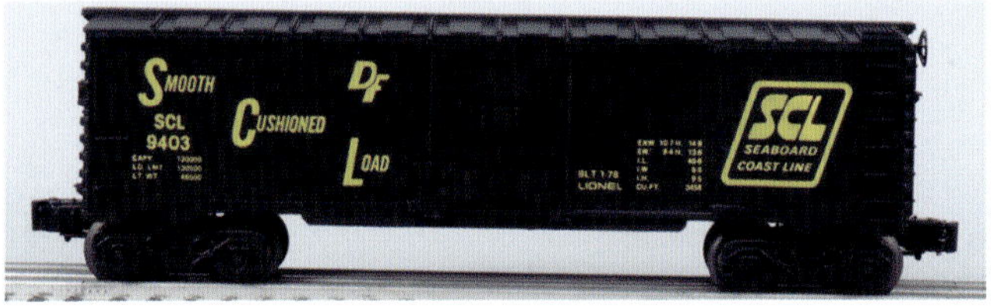

9403 SEABOARD COAST LINE (Type I): As cataloged.

EX-C7	LN-C8	Scarcity
10	15	4

9403 SEABOARD COAST LINE (Type II): 1978, uncataloged Southern Division TCA boxcar.

EX-C7	LN-C8	Scarcity
10	15	6

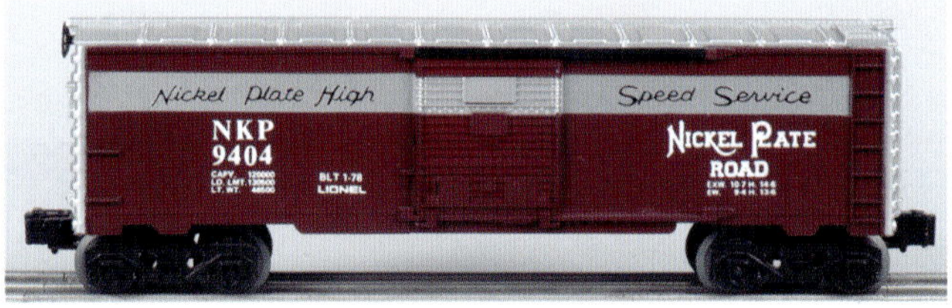

9404 NICKEL PLATE ROAD: 1978, boxcar.

EX-C7	LN-C8	Scarcity
10	15	4

9405 CHATTAHOOCHEE: 1978, boxcar.

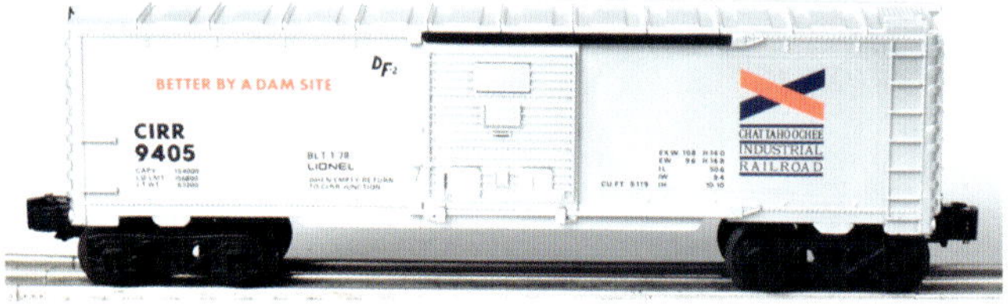

9405 CHATTAHOOCHEE (Type I): As cataloged.

EX-C7	LN-C8	Scarcity
10	15	4

9405 CHATTAHOOCHEE (Type II): 1979, uncataloged Southern Division TCA boxcar.

EX-C7	LN-C8	Scarcity
10	15	6

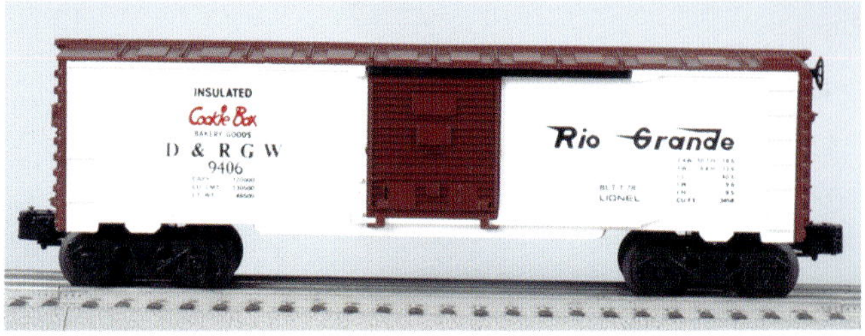

9406 DENVER & RIO GRANDE WESTERN: 1978-79, boxcar.

EX-C7	LN-C8	Scarcity
10	15	4

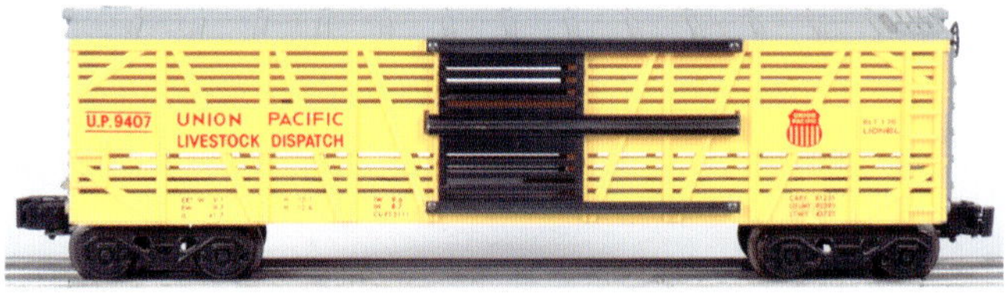

9407 UNION PACIFIC: 1978, stock car.

EX-C7	LN-C8	Scarcity
15	20	4

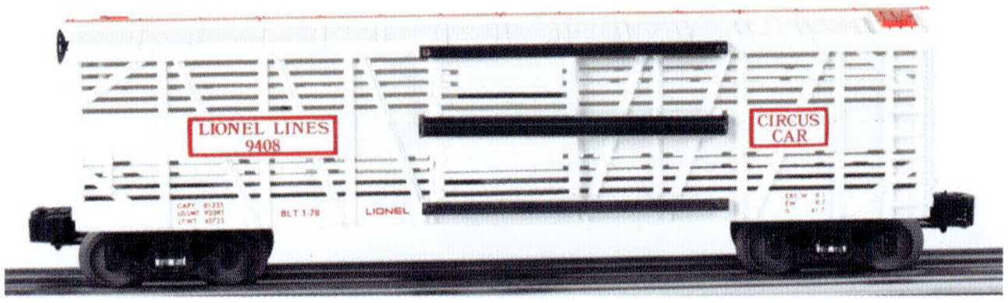

9408 LIONEL LINES: 1978, Circus stock car, Service Station Special item.

EX-C7	LN-C8	Scarcity
15	20	4

9411 LACKAWANNA: 1978, "Phoebe Snow" boxcar.

EX-C7	LN-C8	Scarcity
20	25	5

9412 RF & P: 1979, boxcar.

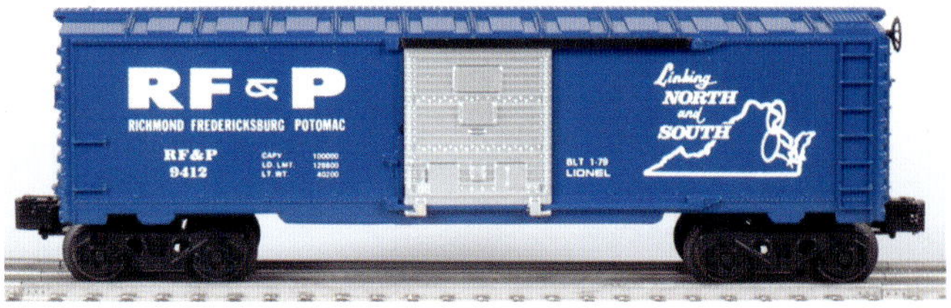

9412 RF & P (Type I): As cataloged.

EX-C7	LN-C8	Scarcity
15	20	4

9412 RF & P (Type II): 1979, uncataloged WBA TCA overstamped boxcar.

EX-C7	LN-C8	Scarcity
10	15	4

9413 NAPIERVILLE JUNCTION: 1979, boxcar.

9413 NAPIERVILLE JUNCTION (Type I): As cataloged.

EX-C7	LN-C8	Scarcity
10	15	4

9413 NAPIERVILLE JUNCTION (Type II): 1980, uncataloged overstamped Lionel Collectors Association of Canada boxcar.

EX-C7	LN-C8	Scarcity
Too rarely traded to establish accurate pricing.		

9414 COTTON BELT: 1979, boxcar.

9414 COTTON BELT (Type I): As cataloged.

EX-C7	LN-C8	Scarcity
10	15	4

9414 COTTON BELT (Type II): 1980, uncataloged Sacramento-Sierra TCA boxcar.

EX-C7	LN-C8	Scarcity
15	20	6

9414 COTTON BELT (Type III): 1980, uncataloged LOTS boxcar.

EX-C7	LN-C8	Scarcity
20	25	6

9415 PROVIDENCE & WORCESTER: 1979, boxcar.

9415 PROVIDENCE & WORCESTER (Type I): As cataloged.

EX-C7	LN-C8	Scarcity
10	15	4

9415 PROVIDENCE & WORCESTER (Type II): 1979, New England Division of Train Collectors Association boxcar.

EX-C7	LN-C8	Scarcity
15	20	6

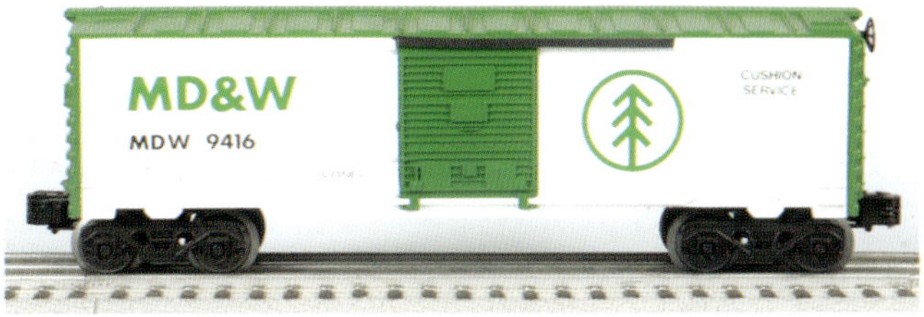

9416 MD & W: 1979 and 1981, boxcar.

EX-C7	LN-C8	Scarcity
10	15	4

9417 CP RAIL: 1979, boxcar.

EX-C7	LN-C8	Scarcity
20	25	5

9418 FAMOUS AMERICAN RAILROADS: This 1979 boxcar was used to promote the introduction of the Famous American Railroad series.

EX-C7	LN-C8	Scarcity
40	50	6

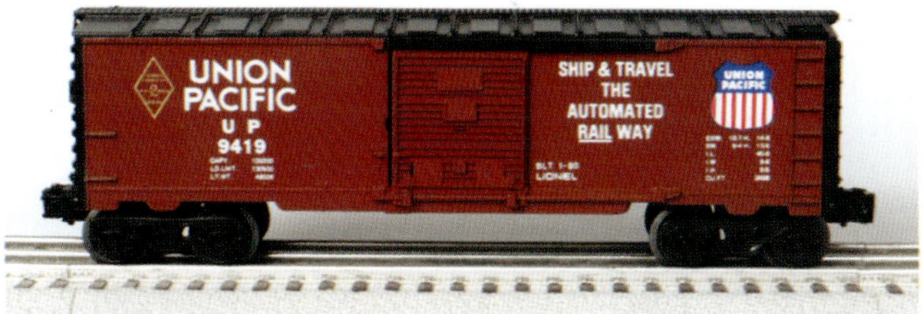

9419 UNION PACIFIC: 1980, boxcar, Famous American Railroads number two.

EX-C7	LN-C8	Scarcity
20	25	4

9420 BALTIMORE & OHIO: 1980, "Sentinel" boxcar.

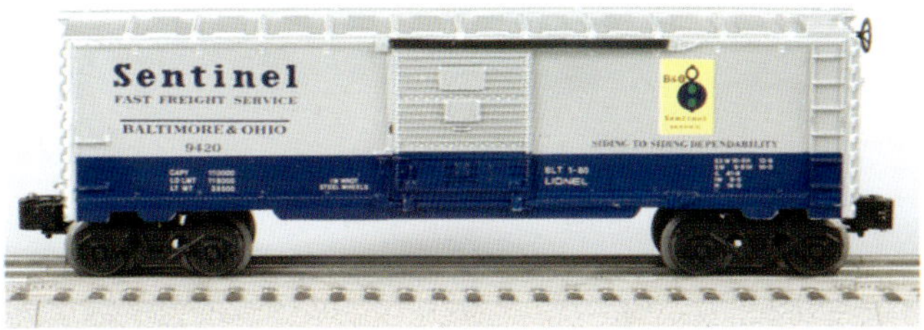

9420 BALTIMORE & OHIO (Type I): As cataloged.

EX-C7	LN-C8	Scarcity
30	35	4

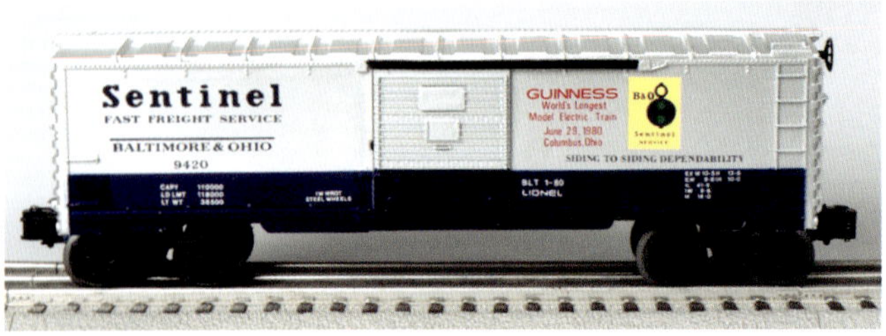

9420 BALTIMORE & OHIO (Type II): 1980, "Sentinel" boxcar, overstamped with "World's longest train" markings, uncataloged.

EX-C7	LN-C8	Scarcity
100	125	6

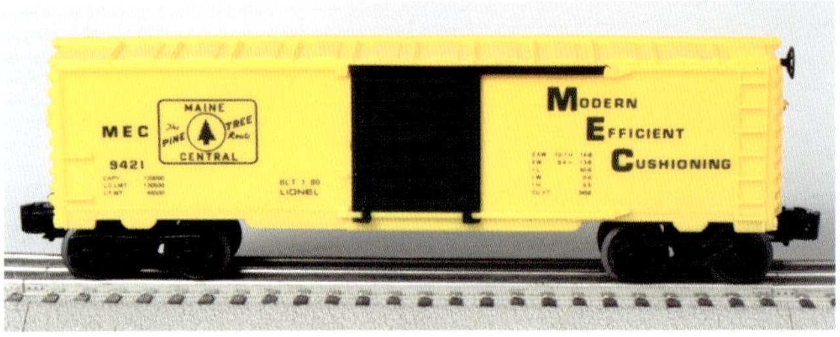

9421 MAINE CENTRAL: 1980, boxcar.

EX-C7	LN-C8	Scarcity
15	20	4

9422 EJ & E: 1980, boxcar.

EX-C7	LN-C8	Scarcity
15	20	4

9423 NYNH & H: 1980, boxcar.

9423 NYNH & H (Type I): As cataloged.

EX-C7	LN-C8	Scarcity
15	20	4

9423 NYNH & H (Type II): 1980, uncataloged New England Division of Train Collectors Association boxcar.

EX-C7	LN-C8	Scarcity
25	30	4

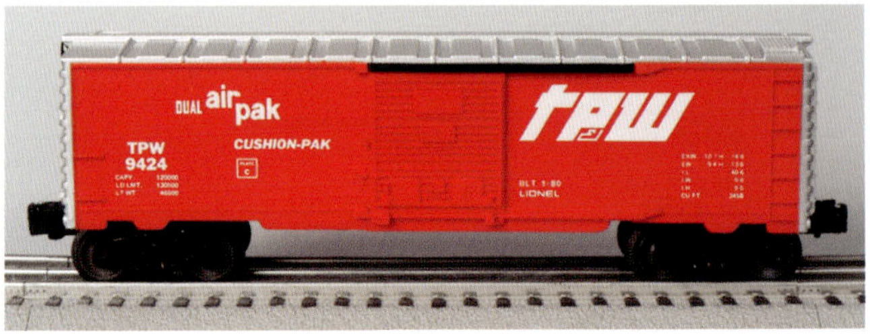

9424 TP & W: 1980, boxcar.

EX-C7	LN-C8	Scarcity
20	25	4

9425 BRITISH COLUMBIA: 1980, double-door boxcar.

EX-C7	LN-C8	Scarcity
25	30	4

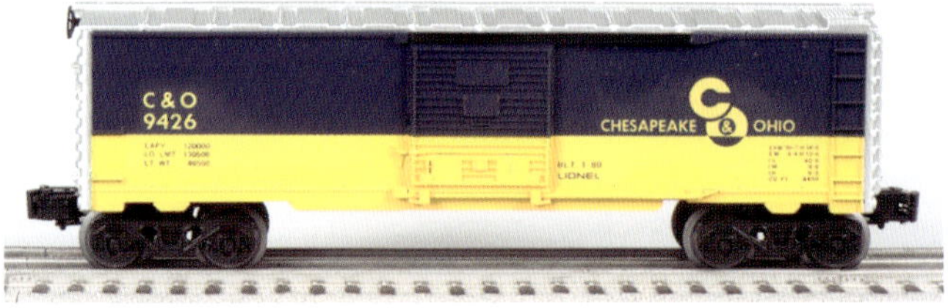

9426 CHESAPEAKE & OHIO: 1980, boxcar.

EX-C7	LN-C8	Scarcity
20	30	4

9427 BAY LINE: 1980-81, boxcar.

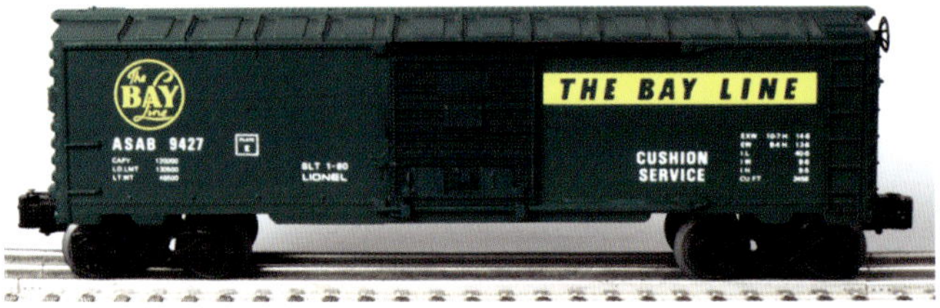

9427 BAY LINE (Type I): As cataloged.

EX-C7	LN-C8	Scarcity
15	20	4

9427 BAY LINE (Type II): 1981, uncataloged overstamped Sacramento-Sierra TCA boxcar.

EX-C7	LN-C8	Scarcity
25	30	6

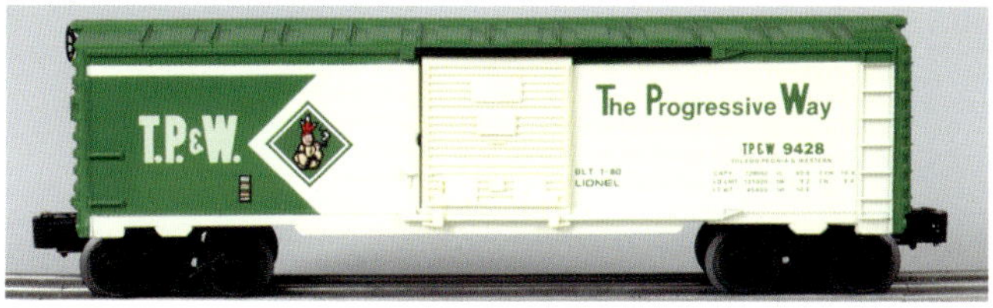

9428 T.P. & W.: Cataloged from 1980-81, uncataloged in 1983, boxcar.

EX-C7	LN-C8	Scarcity
20	25	4

9429 "THE EARLY YEARS": 1980, boxcar.

EX-C7	LN-C8	Scarcity
25	35	5

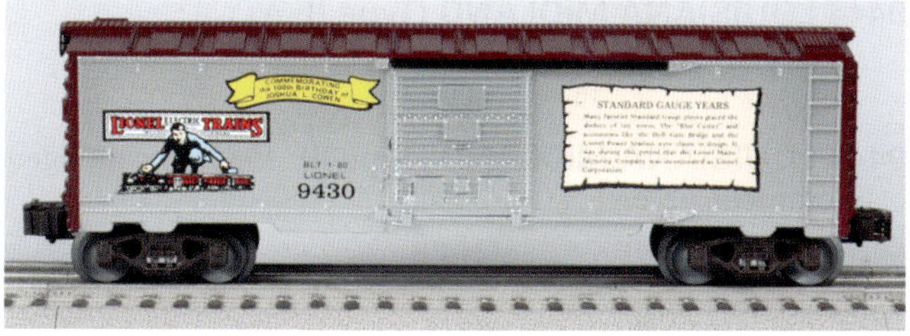

9430 "THE STANDARD GAUGE YEARS": 1980, boxcar.

EX-C7	LN-C8	Scarcity
20	25	5

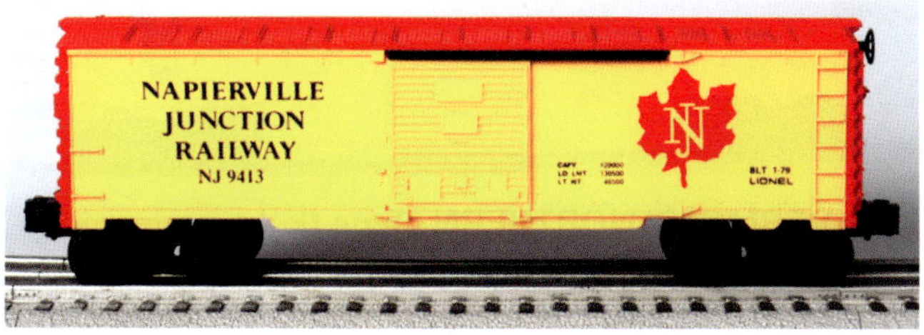

9431 "THE PREWAR YEARS": 1980, boxcar.

EX-C7	LN-C8	Scarcity
20	25	5

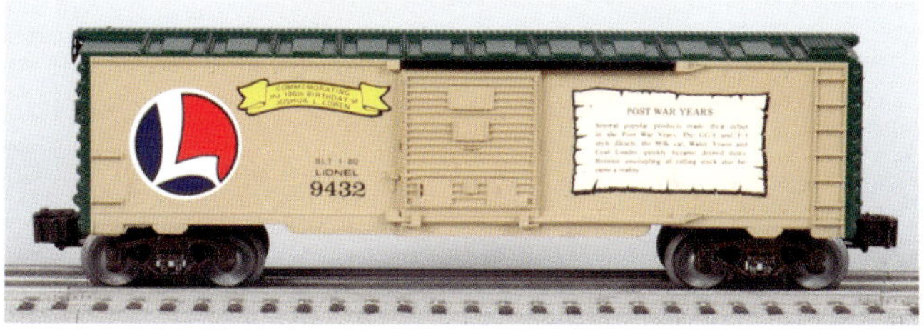

9432 "THE POSTWAR YEARS": 1980, boxcar.

EX-C7	LN-C8	Scarcity
60	70	6

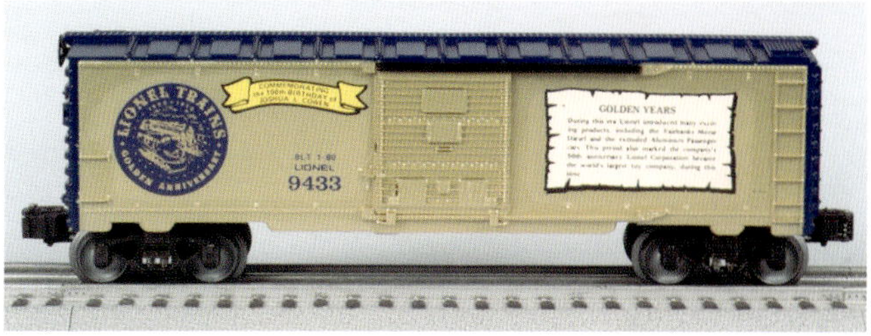

9433 "THE GOLDEN YEARS": 1980, boxcar.

EX-C7	LN-C8	Scarcity
60	70	6

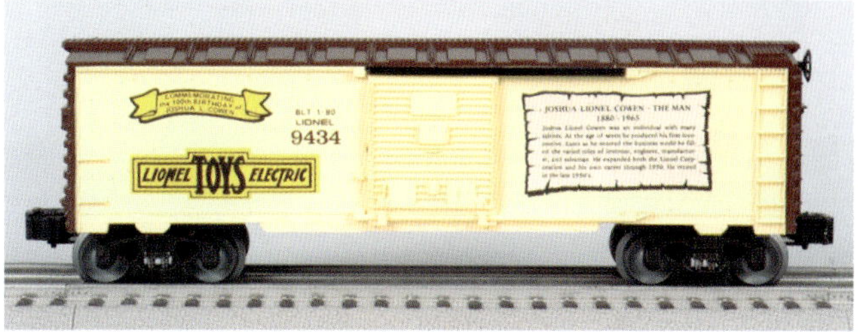

9434 JOSHUA LIONEL COWEN "THE MAN": 1980, uncataloged boxcar.

EX-C7	LN-C8	Scarcity
30	40	5

9435 CENTRAL OF GEORGIA: 1981, uncataloged LCCA boxcar.

EX-C7	LN-C8	Scarcity
25	30	6

9436 BURLINGTON: 1981, boxcar.

EX-C7	LN-C8	Scarcity
35	40	4

9437 NORTHERN PACIFIC: 1981, stock car.

EX-C7	LN-C8	Scarcity
20	35	4

9438 ONTARIO NORTHLAND: 1981, boxcar.

EX-C7	LN-C8	Scarcity
30	45	4

9439 ASHLEY, DREW & NORTHERN: 1981, boxcar.

EX-C7	LN-C8	Scarcity
15	20	4

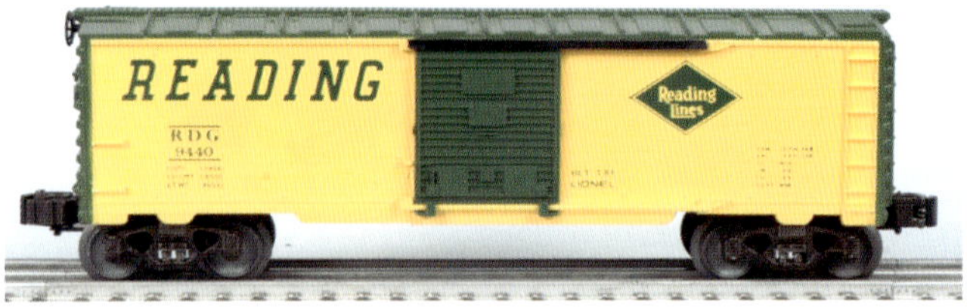

9440 READING: 1981, boxcar.

EX-C7	LN-C8	Scarcity
45	60	5

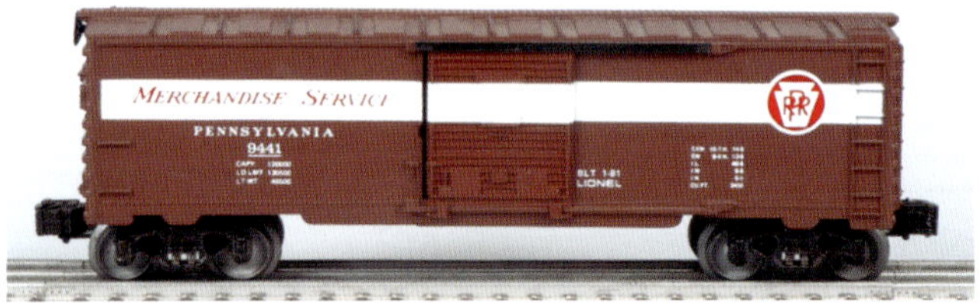

9441 PENNSYLVANIA: 1981, boxcar.

EX-C7	LN-C8	Scarcity
40	50	5

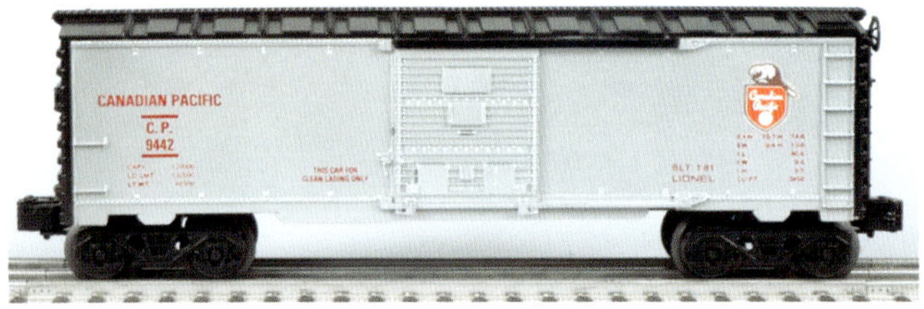

9442 CANADIAN PACIFIC: 1981, boxcar.

EX-C7	LN-C8	Scarcity
15	25	4

9443 FLORIDA EAST COAST: 1981, boxcar.

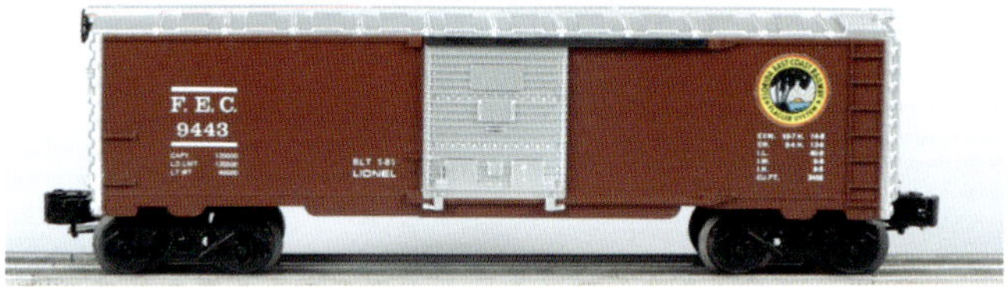

9443 FLORIDA EAST COAST (Type I): As cataloged.

EX-C7	LN-C8	Scarcity
15	20	4

9443 FLORIDA EAST COAST (Type II): 1981, uncataloged Southern Division TCA overstamped boxcar.

EX-C7	LN-C8	Scarcity
20	25	6

9444 LOUISIANA MIDLAND: 1981, boxcar.

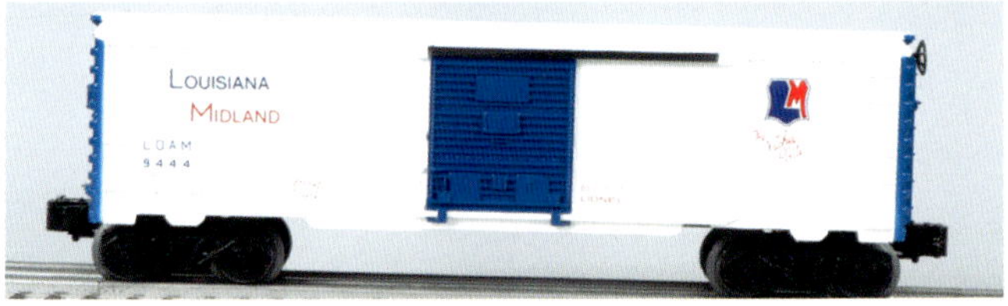

9444 LOUISIANA MIDLAND (Type I): As cataloged.

EX-C7	LN-C8	Scarcity
15	20	4

9444 LOUISIANA MIDLAND (Type II): 1982, uncataloged Sacramento-Sierra TCA boxcar.

EX-C7	LN-C8	Scarcity
25	35	6

9445 VERMONT NORTHERN: 1981, boxcar.

9445 VERMONT NORTHERN (Type I): As cataloged.

EX-C7	LN-C8	Scarcity
15	20	4

9445 VERMONT NORTHERN (Type II): 1981, uncataloged New England Division of Train Collectors Association boxcar.

EX-C7	LN-C8	Scarcity
30	35	6

9446 SABINE RIVER & NORTHERN: 1981, boxcar.

EX-C7	LN-C8	Scarcity
15	20	4

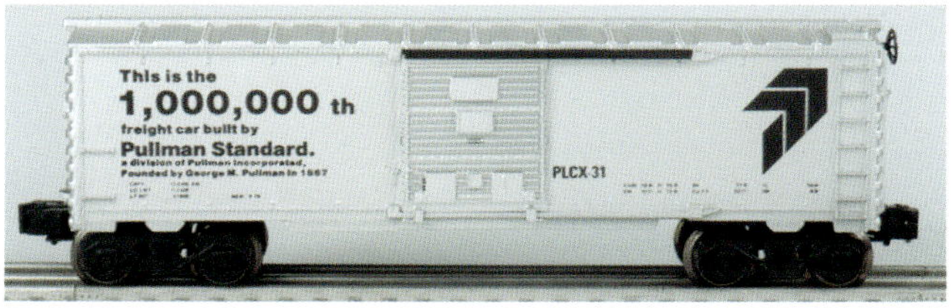

9447 PULLMAN STANDARD: 1981, boxcar.

EX-C7	LN-C8	Scarcity
15	20	4

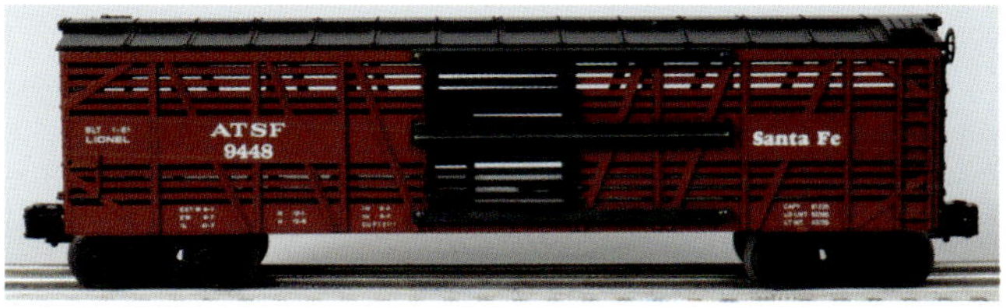

9448 SANTA FE: 1981-82, stock car.

EX-C7	LN-C8	Scarcity
35	40	4

9449 GREAT NORTHERN: 1981, boxcar, Famous American Railroads number three.

EX-C7	LN-C8	Scarcity
30	40	5

9450 GREAT NORTHERN: 1981, stock car, Famous American Railroads number three, uncataloged.

EX-C7	LN-C8	Scarcity
55	60	5

9451 SOUTHERN: 1983, boxcar, Famous American Railroads number four.

EX-C7	LN-C8	Scarcity
35	40	5

9452 WESTERN PACIFIC: 1982-83, boxcar.

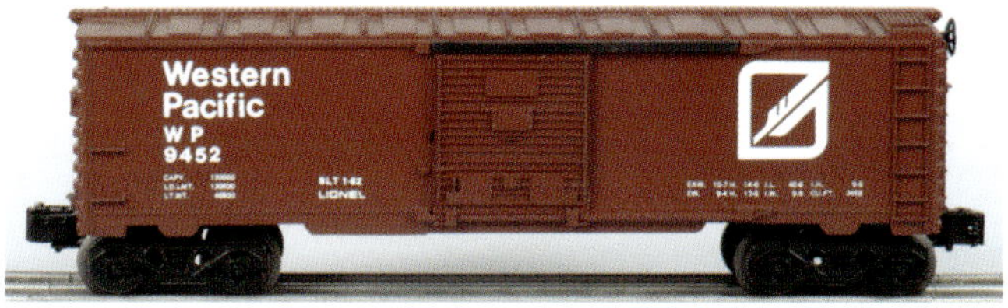

9452 WESTERN PACIFIC (Type I): As cataloged.

EX-C7	LN-C8	Scarcity
15	20	4

9452 WESTERN PACIFIC (Type II): 1983, uncataloged Sacramento-Sierra TCA boxcar.

EX-C7	LN-C8	Scarcity
30	35	6

9453 MISSOURI PACIFIC: 1982-83, boxcar.

EX-C7	LN-C8	Scarcity
15	20	4

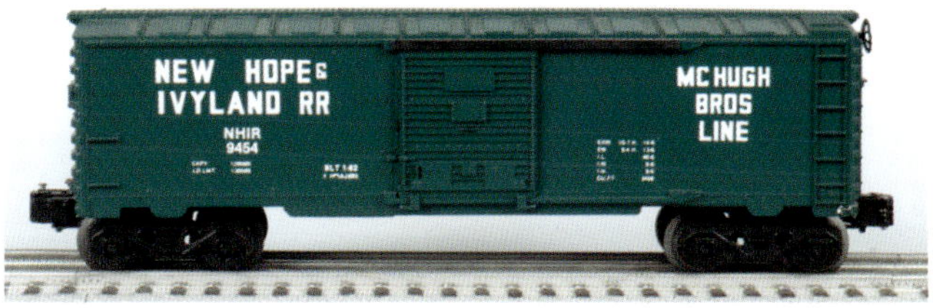

9454 NEW HOPE & IVYLAND: 1982-83, boxcar.

EX-C7	LN-C8	Scarcity
20	30	4

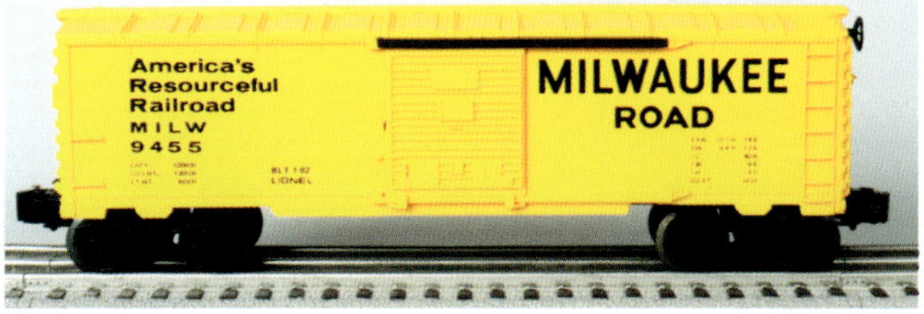

9455 MILWAUKEE ROAD: 1982-83, boxcar.

EX-C7	LN-C8	Scarcity
15	20	4

9456 PENNSYLVANIA: 1984-85, double-door boxcar, Famous American Railroads number five.

EX-C7	LN-C8	Scarcity
30	35	5

9460 D & TS: 1982, uncataloged LCCA double-door boxcar.

EX-C7	LN-C8	Scarcity
25	35	4

9461 NORFOLK & SOUTHERN: 1982, boxcar.

EX-C7	LN-C8	Scarcity
35	45	4

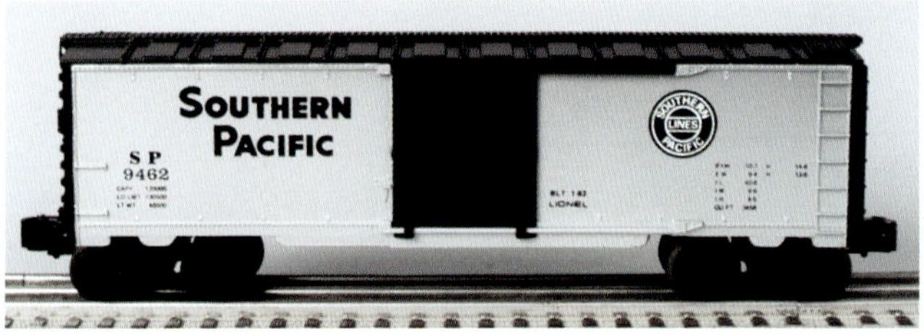

9462 SOUTHERN PACIFIC: 1983-84, boxcar.

EX-C7	LN-C8	Scarcity
20	25	4

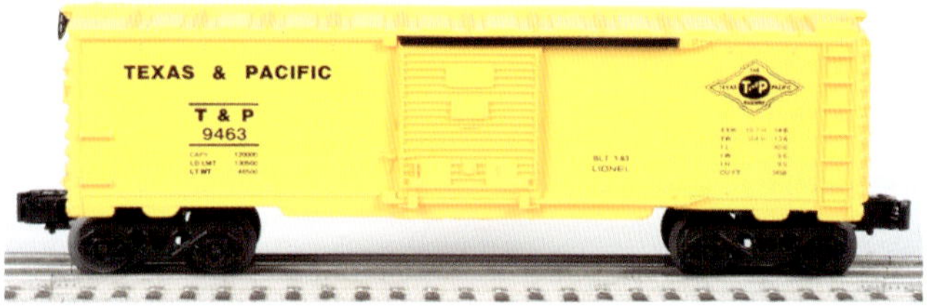

9463 TEXAS & PACIFIC: 1983-84, boxcar.

EX-C7	LN-C8	Scarcity
15	20	4

9464 NC & ST. L: 1983-84, boxcar.

EX-C7	LN-C8	Scarcity
15	25	4

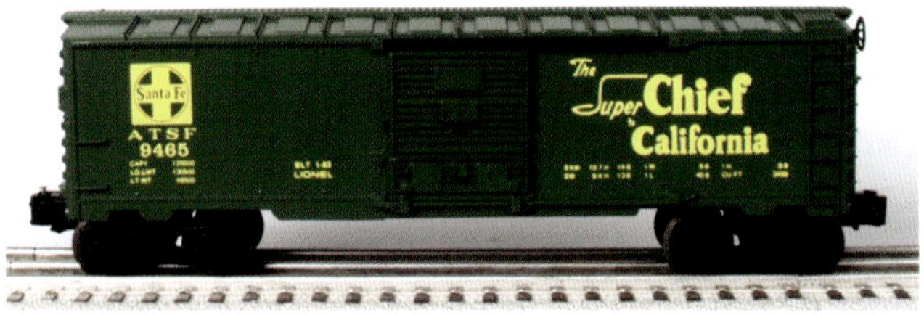

9465 SANTA FE: 1983-84, boxcar.

EX-C7	LN-C8	Scarcity
15	20	4

9466 WANAMAKER: 1982, uncataloged boxcar.

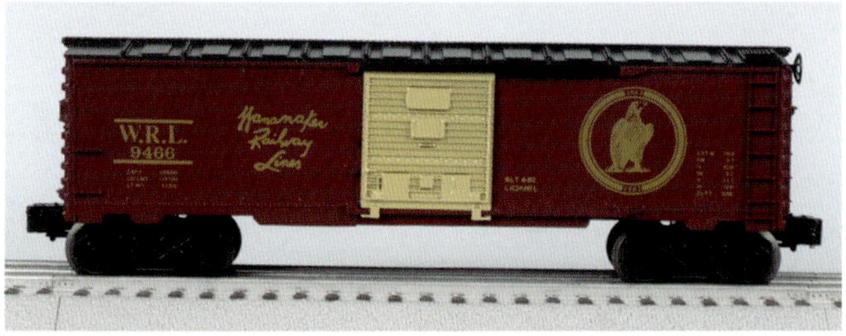

9466 WANAMAKER (Type I): 1982, standard production.

EX-C7	LN-C8	Scarcity
60	75	6

9466 WANAMAKER (Type II): 1983, uncataloged boxcar overstamped for Atlantic Division TCA.

EX-C7	LN-C8	Scarcity
100	125	6

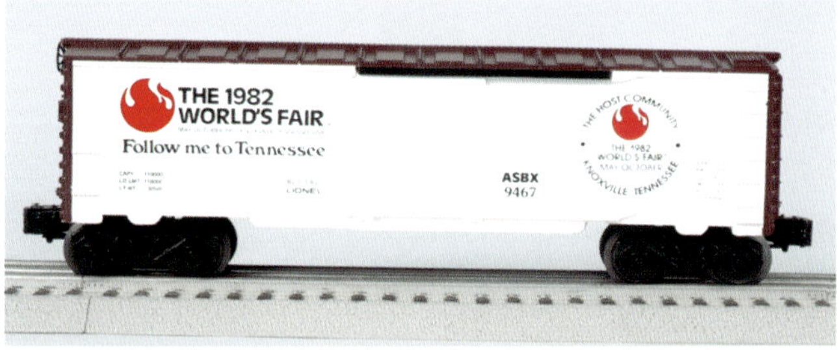

9467 TENNESSEE WORLD'S FAIR: 1982, uncataloged boxcar.

EX-C7	LN-C8	Scarcity
30	40	5

9468 UNION PACIFIC: 1983, double-door boxcar.

EX-C7	LN-C8	Scarcity
35	40	4

9469 NEW YORK CENTRAL: 1984-85, "Pacemaker" boxcar with 1/48-scale proportions.

EX-C7	LN-C8	Scarcity
45	55	4

9470 CHICAGO BELTLINE: 1984, boxcar.

EX-C7	LN-C8	Scarcity
15	20	4

9471 ATLANTIC COAST LINE: 1984, boxcar.

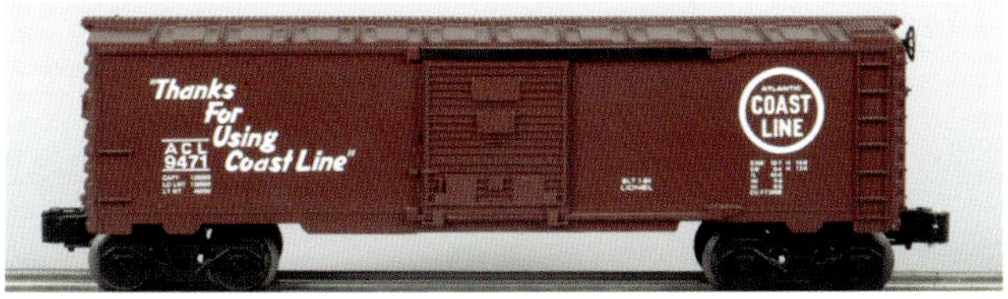

9471 ATLANTIC COAST LINE (Type I): As cataloged.

EX-C7	LN-C8	Scarcity
15	20	4

9471 ATLANTIC COAST LINE (Type II): 1984, Southern Division TCA overstamped uncataloged boxcar.

EX-C7	LN-C8	Scarcity
15	20	6

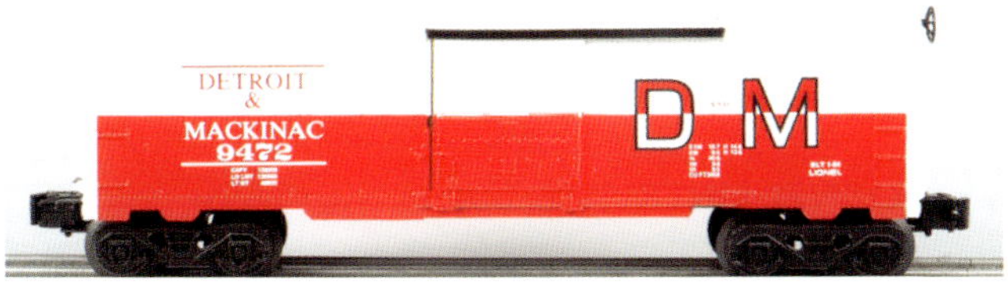

9472 DETROIT & MACKINAC: 1984, boxcar.

EX-C7	LN-C8	Scarcity
25	30	4

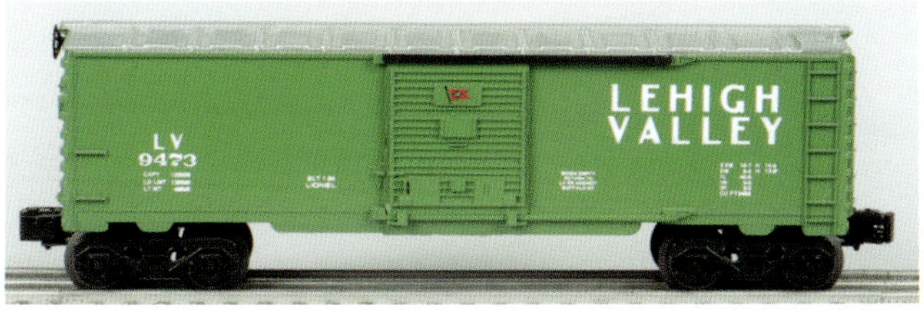

9473 LEHIGH VALLEY: 1984, boxcar.

EX-C7	LN-C8	Scarcity
25	30	4

9474 ERIE-LACKAWANNA: 1984, boxcar.

EX-C7	LN-C8	Scarcity
35	40	4

9475 DELAWARE AND HUDSON: 1984, "I Love NY" boxcar.

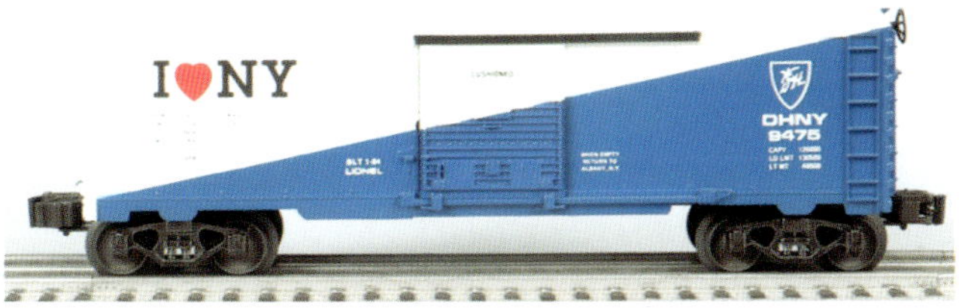

9475 DELAWARE AND HUDSON (Type I): As cataloged.

EX-C7	LN-C8	Scarcity
30	40	4

9475 DELAWARE AND HUDSON (Type II): 1985, uncataloged LCOL overstamped boxcar.

EX-C7	LN-C8	Scarcity
30	35	6

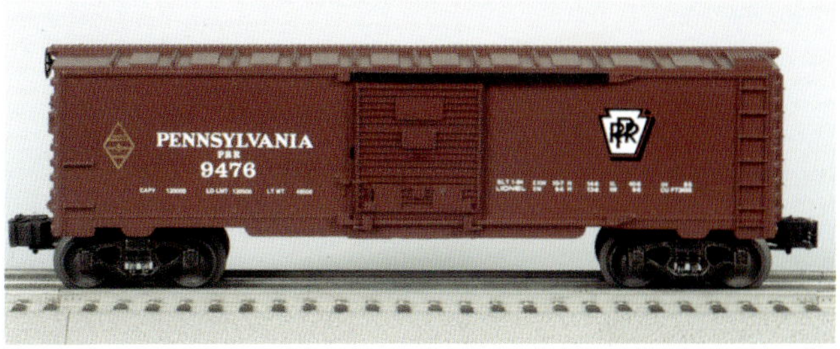

9476 PENNSYLVANIA: 1984-85, boxcar, Famous American Railroads number five.

EX-C7	LN-C8	Scarcity
35	40	5

9480 MN & S: 1985-86, boxcar.

EX-C7	LN-C8	Scarcity
15	20	4

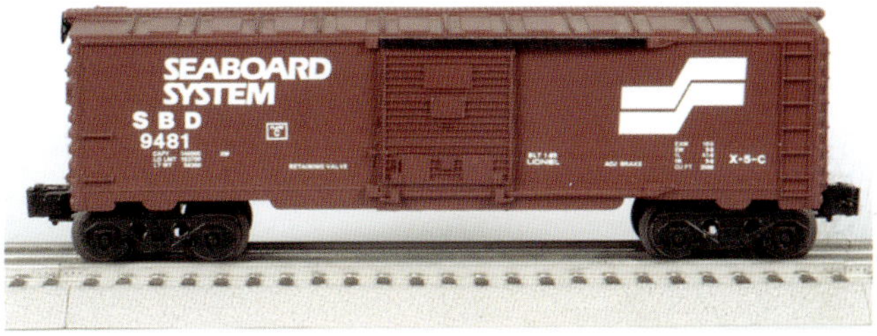

9481 SEABOARD SYSTEM: 1985-86, boxcar.

EX-C7	LN-C8	Scarcity
15	20	4

9482 NORFOLK & SOUTHERN: 1985-86, boxcar.

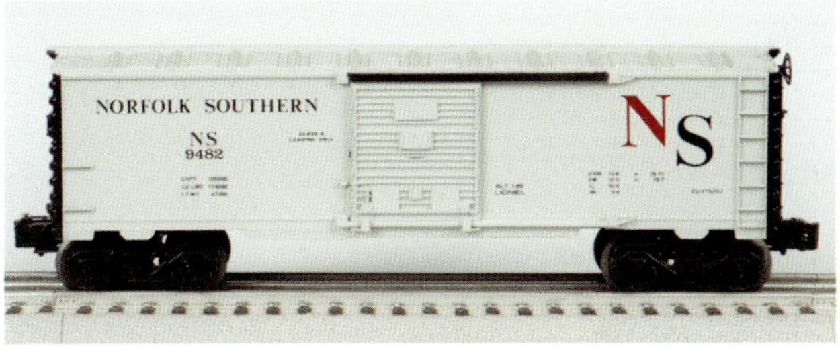

9482 NORFOLK & SOUTHERN (Type I): As cataloged.

EX-C7	LN-C8	Scarcity
15	20	4

9482 NORFOLK & SOUTHERN (Type II): 1985, uncataloged overstamped boxcar for the Southern Division TCA.

EX-C7	LN-C8	Scarcity
20	25	6

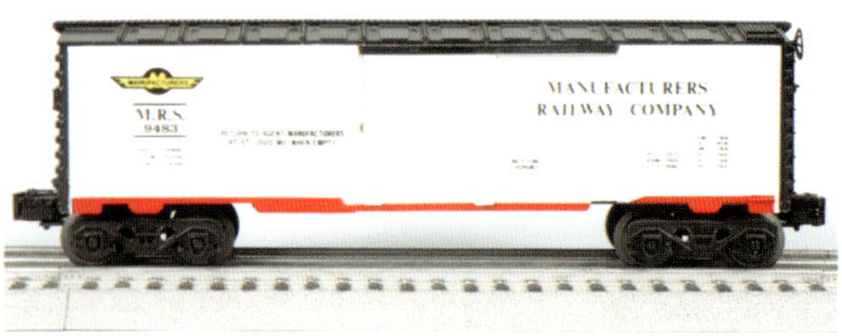

9483 MANUFACTURERS RAILWAY: 1985-86, boxcar.

EX-C7	LN-C8	Scarcity
20	25	4

9484 LIONEL 85TH ANNIVERSARY: 1985, boxcar.

EX-C7	LN-C8	Scarcity
20	25	4

9486 GRAND TRUNK WESTERN: 1986, "I Love Michigan" boxcar.

9486 GRAND TRUNK WESTERN (Type I): As cataloged.

EX-C7	LN-C8	Scarcity
25	30	4

9486 GRAND TRUNK WESTERN (Type II): 1987, uncataloged overstamped Artrain boxcar.

EX-C7	LN-C8	Scarcity
200	250	7

9490 CHRISTMAS: 1985, boxcar for Lionel employees, uncataloged.

EX-C7	LN-C8	Scarcity
1,500	1,800	7

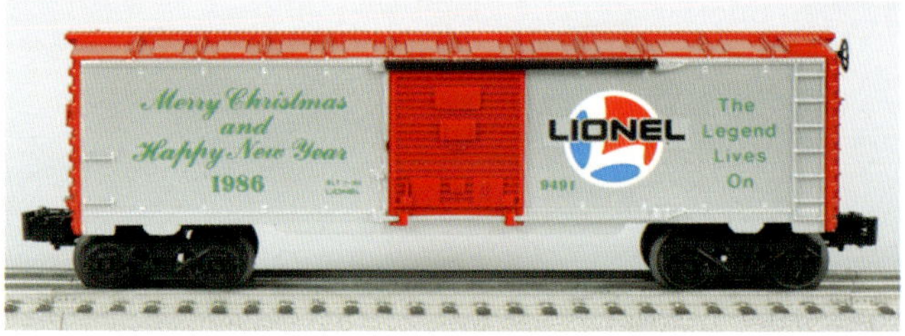

9491 CHRISTMAS: 1986, boxcar, uncataloged.

EX-C7	LN-C8	Scarcity
35	50	5

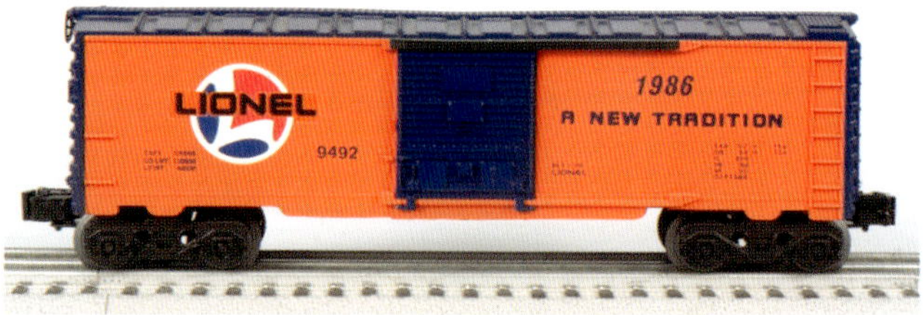

9492 LIONEL LINES: 1986, boxcar.

EX-C7	LN-C8	Scarcity
25	30	4

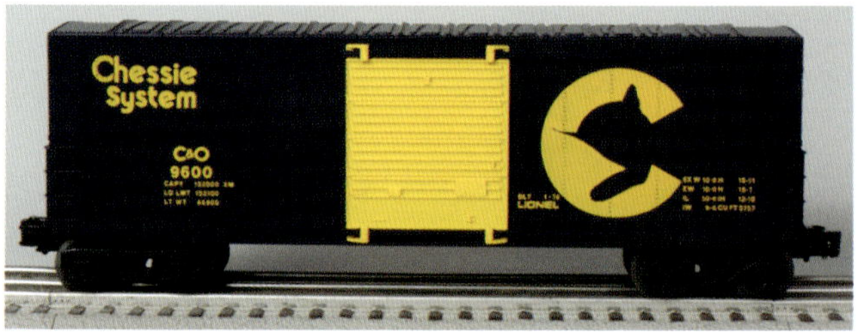

9600 CHESSIE SYSTEM: Uncataloged in 1975, cataloged from 1976-77, High-Cube boxcar.

EX-C7	LN-C8	Scarcity
12	15	4

9601 ILLINOIS CENTRAL GULF: Uncataloged in 1975, cataloged from 1976-77, High-Cube boxcar.

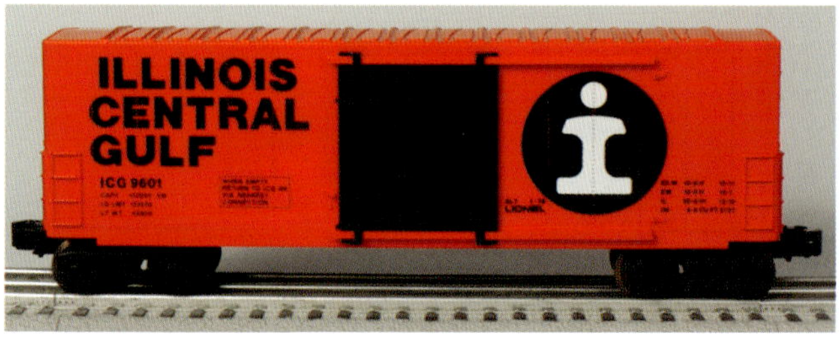

9601 ILLINOIS CENTRAL GULF (Type I): As cataloged.

EX-C7	LN-C8	Scarcity
12	15	4

9601 ILLINOIS CENTRAL GULF (Type II): 1977, uncataloged overstamped Gateway Chapter TCA High-Cube boxcar.

EX-C7	LN-C8	Scarcity
12	15	6

9602 SANTA FE: Uncataloged in 1975, cataloged from 1976-77, High-Cube boxcar.

EX-C7	LN-C8	Scarcity
12	15	4

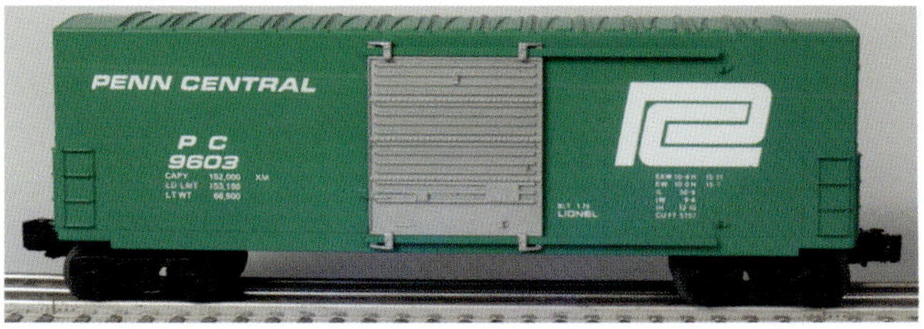

9603 PENN CENTRAL: 1976-77, High-Cube boxcar.

EX-C7	LN-C8	Scarcity
12	15	4

9604 NORFOLK AND WESTERN: 1976-77, High-Cube boxcar.

EX-C7	LN-C8	Scarcity
12	15	4

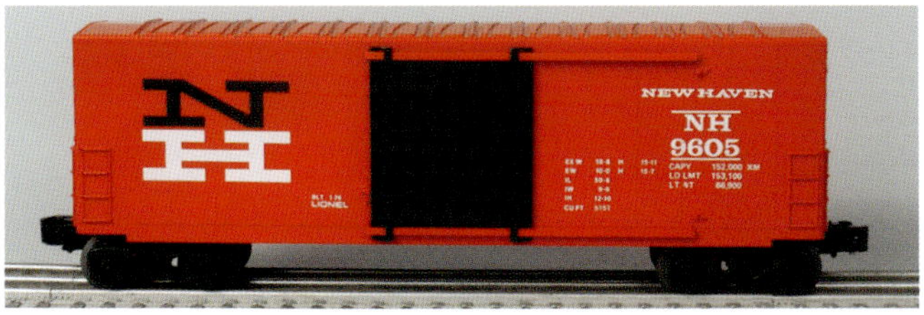

9605 NEW HAVEN: 1976-77, High-Cube boxcar.

EX-C7	LN-C8	Scarcity
12	15	4

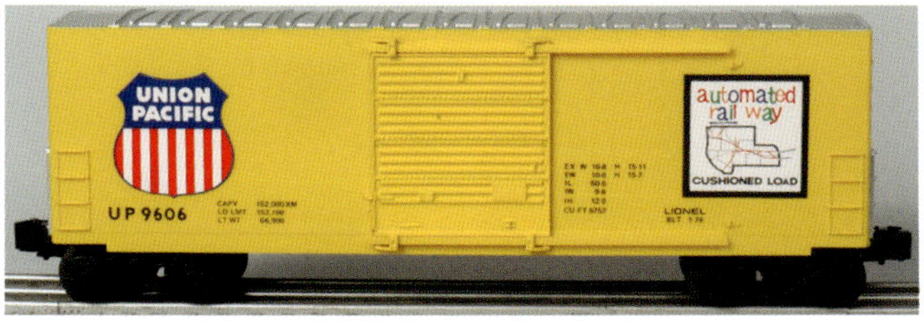

9606 UNION PACIFIC: Uncataloged in 1976, cataloged in 1977, High-Cube boxcar.

EX-C7	LN-C8	Scarcity
12	15	4

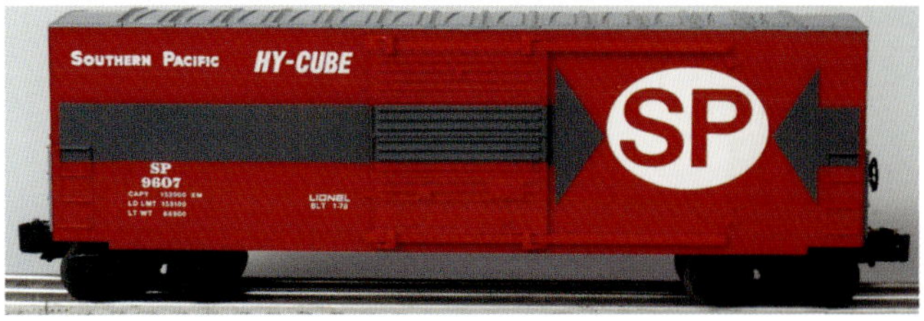

9607 SOUTHERN PACIFIC: Uncataloged in 1976, cataloged in 1977, High-Cube boxcar.

EX-C7	LN-C8	Scarcity
12	15	4

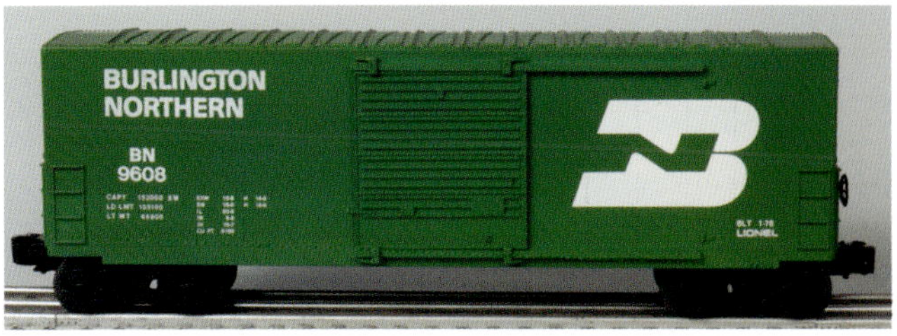

9608 BURLINGTON NORTHERN: Uncataloged in 1976, cataloged in 1977, High-Cube boxcar.

EX-C7	LN-C8	Scarcity
12	15	4

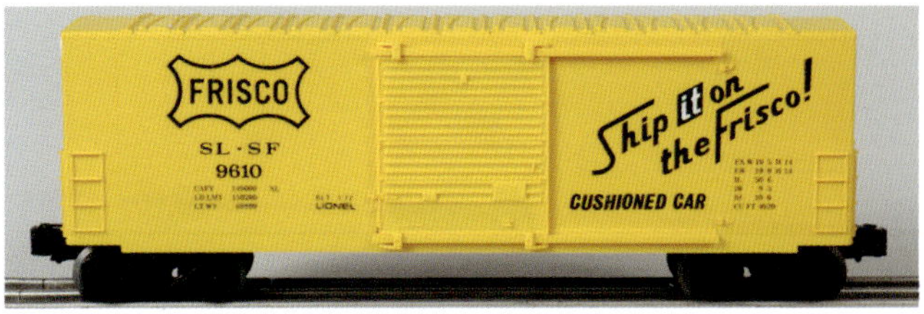

9610 FRISCO: 1977, High-Cube boxcar.

EX-C7	LN-C8	Scarcity
15	20	4

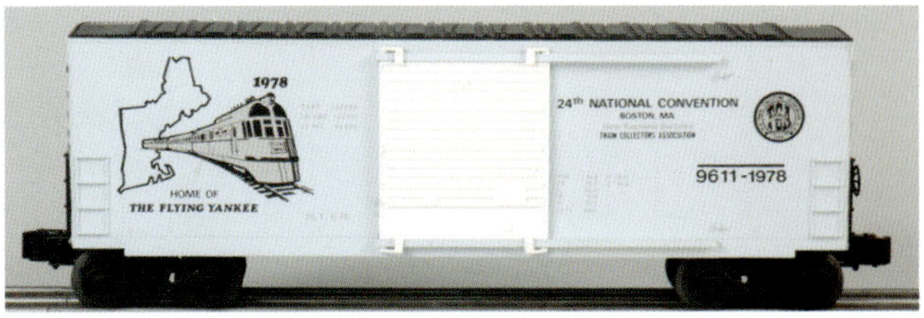

9611 TCA BOSTON HIGH-CUBE: 1978, uncataloged boxcar.

EX-C7	LN-C8	Scarcity
15	20	6

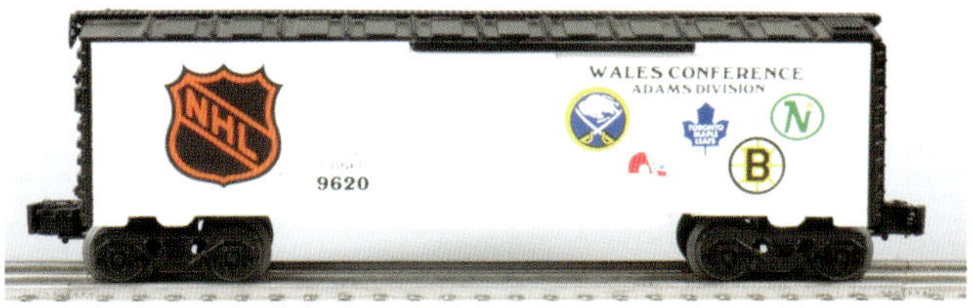

9620 NHL WALES: 1980, boxcar.

EX-C7	LN-C8	Scarcity
12	15	4

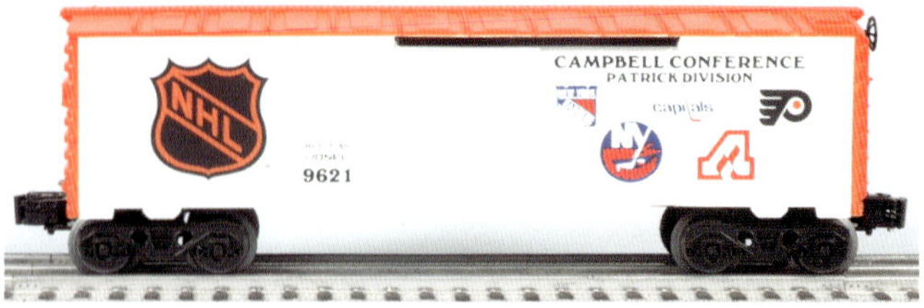

9621 NHL CAMPBELL: 1980, boxcar.

EX-C7	LN-C8	Scarcity
12	15	4

9622 NBA WESTERN: 1980, boxcar.

EX-C7	LN-C8	Scarcity
12	15	4

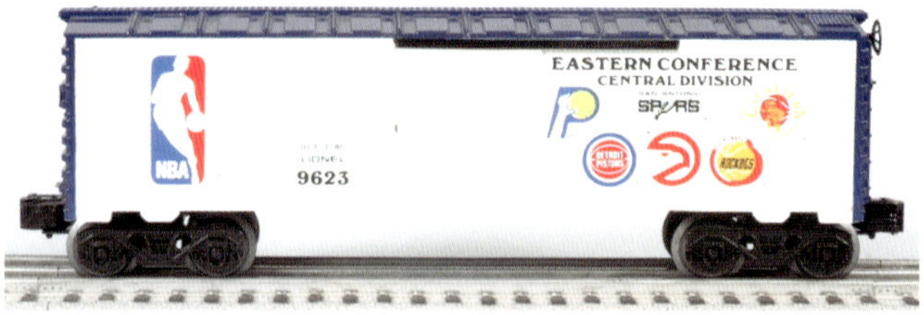

9623 NBA EASTERN: 1980, boxcar.

EX-C7	LN-C8	Scarcity
12	15	4

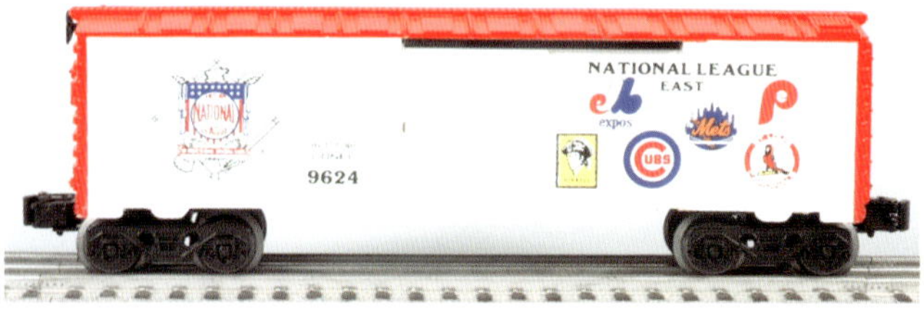

9624 NATIONAL LEAGUE BASEBALL: 1980, boxcar.

EX-C7	LN-C8	Scarcity
12	15	4

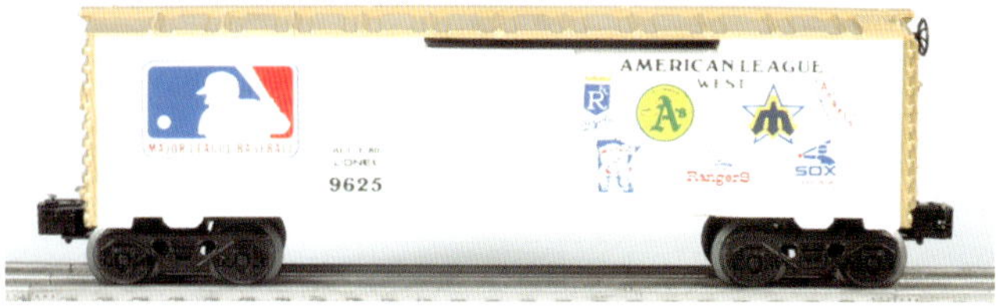

9625 AMERICAN LEAGUE BASEBALL: 1980, boxcar.

EX-C7	LN-C8	Scarcity
12	15	4

9626 SANTA FE: 1982-84, High-Cube boxcar.

EX-C7	LN-C8	Scarcity
10	15	3

9627 UNION PACIFIC: 1982-83, High-Cube boxcar.

EX-C7	LN-C8	Scarcity
12	15	4

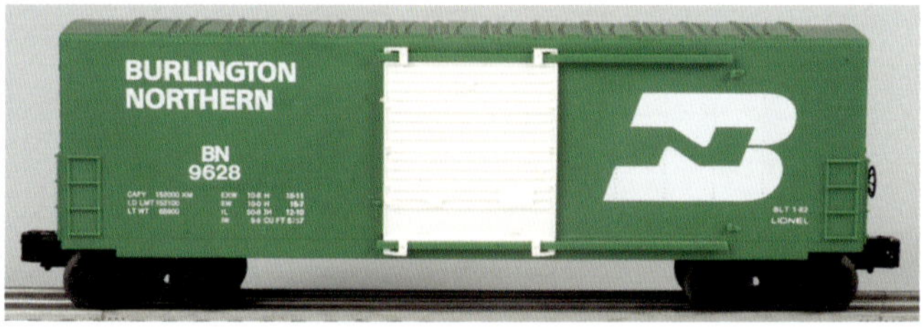

9628 BURLINGTON NORTHERN: 1982-84, High-Cube boxcar.

EX-C7	LN-C8	Scarcity
10	15	3

9629 CHESSIE SYSTEM: 1983-84, High-Cube boxcar.

EX-C7	LN-C8	Scarcity
12	15	4

9660 MICKEY MOUSE: 1977-78, High-Cube boxcar.

EX-C7	LN-C8	Scarcity
30	40	5

9661 GOOFY: 1977-78, High-Cube boxcar.

EX-C7	LN-C8	Scarcity
30	40	5

9662 DONALD DUCK: 1977-78, High-Cube boxcar.

EX-C7	LN-C8	Scarcity
30	40	5

9663 DUMBO: Uncataloged in 1977, cataloged in 1978, High-Cube boxcar.

EX-C7	LN-C8	Scarcity
35	45	5

9664 CINDERELLA: Uncataloged in 1977, cataloged in 1978, High-Cube boxcar.

EX-C7	LN-C8	Scarcity
40	50	5

9665 PETER PAN: Uncataloged in 1977, cataloged in 1978, High-Cube boxcar.

EX-C7	LN-C8	Scarcity
40	50	5

9666 PINOCCHIO: 1978, High-Cube boxcar.

EX-C7	LN-C8	Scarcity
100	140	6

9667 SNOW WHITE: 1978, High-Cube boxcar.

EX-C7	LN-C8	Scarcity
300	375	6

9668 PLUTO: 1978, High-Cube boxcar.

EX-C7	LN-C8	Scarcity
100	140	6

9669 BAMBI: 1978, uncataloged High-Cube boxcar.

EX-C7	LN-C8	Scarcity
40	65	5

9670 ALICE IN WONDERLAND: 1978, uncataloged High-Cube boxcar.

EX-C7	LN-C8	Scarcity
40	65	5

9671 FANTASIA: 1978, uncataloged High-Cube boxcar.

EX-C7	LN-C8	Scarcity
40	65	5

9672 MICKEY MOUSE 50TH ANNIVERSARY: 1978, uncataloged High-Cube boxcar.

EX-C7	LN-C8	Scarcity
300	375	6

9678 TTOS HOLLYWOOD: 1978, uncataloged High-Cube boxcar.

EX-C7	LN-C8	Scarcity
15	20	5

9700 SOUTHERN: 1972-73, boxcar.

EX-C7	LN-C8	Scarcity
15	20	4

9701 BALTIMORE & OHIO: 1972, double-door automobile boxcar.

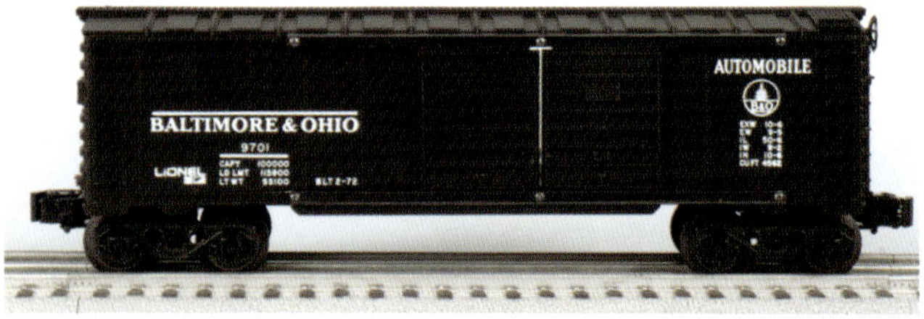

9701 BALTIMORE & OHIO (Type I): Some (reportedly 900) of these cars were painted gloss black with white lettering.

EX-C7	LN-C8	Scarcity
80	100	6

9701 BALTIMORE & OHIO (Type II): The regular production cars were painted silver with black doors.

EX-C7	LN-C8	Scarcity
40	50	6

9701 BALTIMORE & OHIO (Type III): Some of the black cars had their underframes rubber stamped "LCCA CONVENTION CAR" in white.

EX-C7	LN-C8	Scarcity
125	150	6

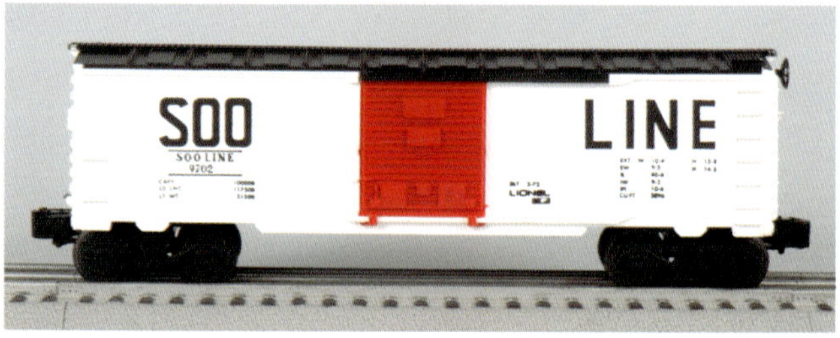

9702 SOO LINE: 1972-73, boxcar.

EX-C7	LN-C8	Scarcity
12	18	4

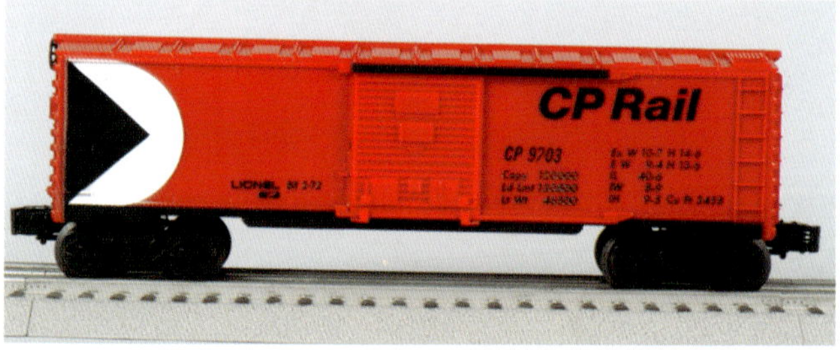

9703 CP RAIL: 1972, boxcar.

EX-C7	LN-C8	Scarcity
18	25	4

9704 NORFOLK AND WESTERN: 1972, boxcar.

EX-C7	LN-C8	Scarcity
12	18	4

9705 DENVER & RIO GRANDE WESTERN: 1972, boxcar.

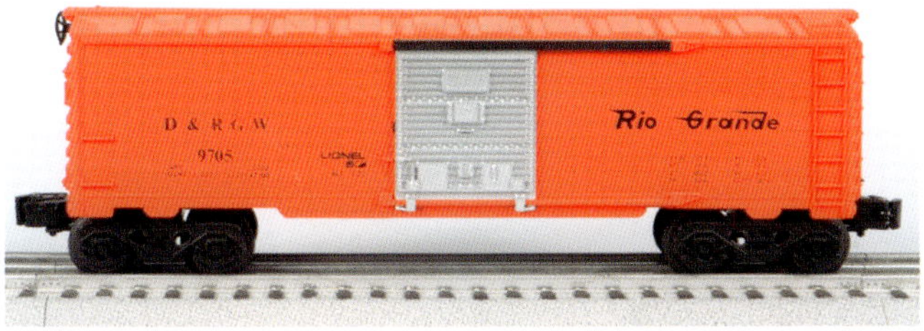

9705 DENVER & RIO GRANDE WESTERN (Type I): As cataloged.

EX-C7	LN-C8	Scarcity
12	18	4

9705 DENVER & RIO GRANDE WESTERN (Type II): 1975, uncataloged Sacramento-Sierra TCA boxcar.

EX-C7	LN-C8	Scarcity
18	25	6

9706 CHESAPEAKE & OHIO: 1972, boxcar.

EX-C7	LN-C8	Scarcity
12	18	4

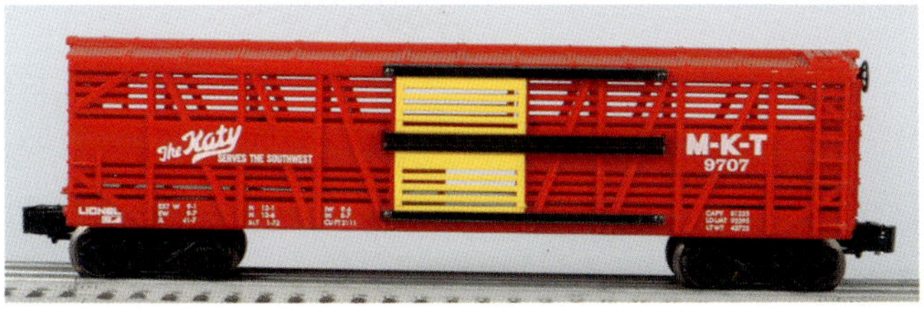

9707 MISSOURI-KANSAS-TEXAS: 1972-75, stock car.

EX-C7	LN-C8	Scarcity
12	18	4

9708 U.S. MAIL: 1972-75, red, white and blue boxcar.

9708 U.S. MAIL (Type I): Some of the cars had red doors.

EX-C7	LN-C8	Scarcity
60	75	6

9708 U.S. MAIL (Type II): Most of the cars had red, white and blue doors.

EX-C7	LN-C8	Scarcity
12	18	4

9708 U.S. MAIL (Type III): In 1973, an uncataloged version was made with "Toy Fair" overstamping.

EX-C7	LN-C8	Scarcity
60	75	6

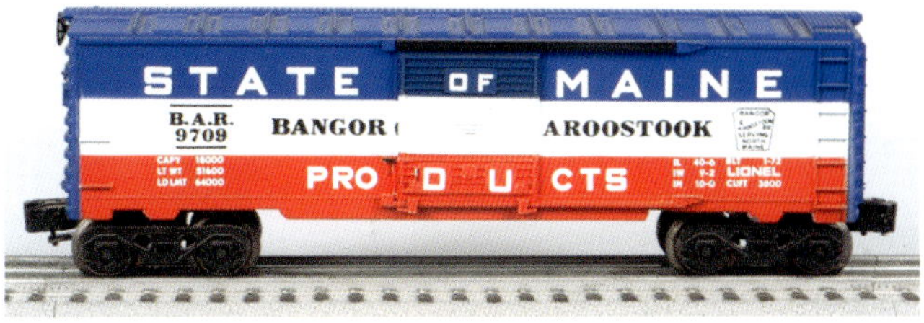

9709 BANGOR AND AROOSTOOK: 1972-74, "State of Maine" boxcar, a Service Station Special item.

EX-C7	LN-C8	Scarcity
20	25	4

9710 RUTLAND: 1972-74, boxcar, a Service Station Special item.

EX-C7	LN-C8	Scarcity
12	18	4

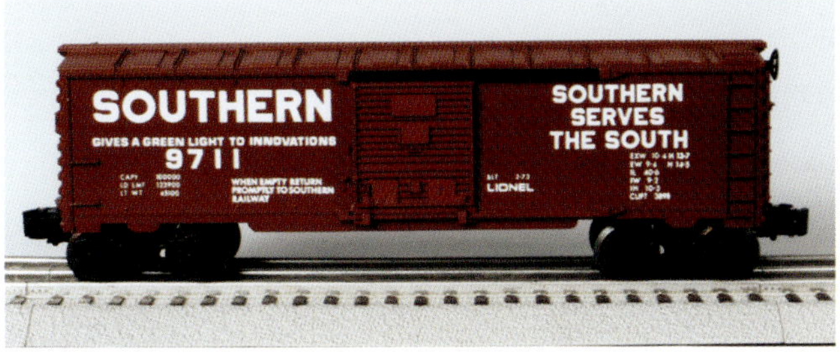

9711 SOUTHERN: 1974-75, boxcar.

EX-C7	LN-C8	Scarcity
12	18	4

9712 BALTIMORE & OHIO: 1973-74, double-door automobile boxcar.

EX-C7	LN-C8	Scarcity
15	20	4

9713 CP RAIL: 1973-74, green boxcar.

9713 CP RAIL (Type I): As described above.

EX-C7	LN-C8	Scarcity
15	20	4

9713 CP RAIL (Type II): 1974, uncataloged version with "Season's Greetings" overstamping.

EX-C7	LN-C8	Scarcity
90	100	6

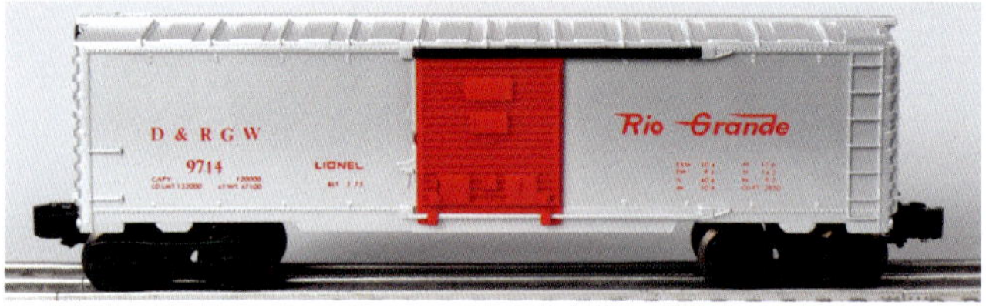

9714 DENVER & RIO GRANDE WESTERN: 1973-74, boxcar.

EX-C7	LN-C8	Scarcity
15	20	4

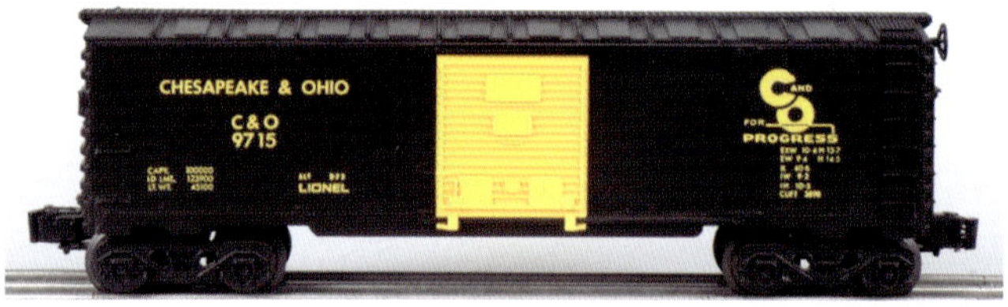

9715 CHESAPEAKE & OHIO: 1973-74, boxcar.

EX-C7	LN-C8	Scarcity
15	20	4

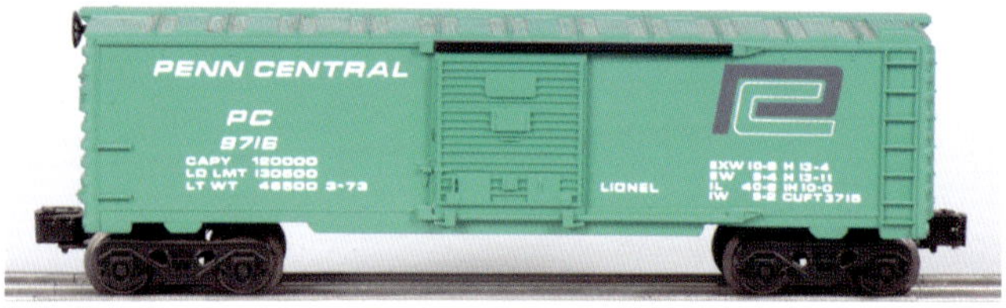

9716 PENN CENTRAL: 1973-74, boxcar.

EX-C7	LN-C8	Scarcity
15	20	4

9717 UNION PACIFIC: 1973-74, boxcar.

EX-C7	LN-C8	Scarcity
20	25	4

9718 CANADIAN NATIONAL: 1973-74, Tuscan boxcar.

9718 CANADIAN NATIONAL (Type I): As described above.

EX-C7	LN-C8	Scarcity
15	20	4

9718 CANADIAN NATIONAL (Type II): 1979, uncataloged Lionel Collectors Association of Canada boxcar.

EX-C7	LN-C8	Scarcity
Too rarely traded to establish accurate pricing.		

9719 NEW HAVEN: 1973, uncataloged double-door automobile boxcar that was part of a Lionel box coupon promotion.

EX-C7	LN-C8	Scarcity
20	25	4

9723 WESTERN PACIFIC: 1973-74, orange boxcar.

9723 WESTERN PACIFIC (Type I): As described above, Service Station Special item.

EX-C7	LN-C8	Scarcity
20	25	4

9723 WESTERN PACIFIC (Type II): In 1974, some of these cars were overstamped "Toy Fair" in gold to create this uncataloged boxcar.

EX-C7	LN-C8	Scarcity
65	75	6

9723 WESTERN PACIFIC (Type III): 1973, uncataloged Sacramento-Sierra TCA boxcar.

EX-C7	LN-C8	Scarcity
20	25	6

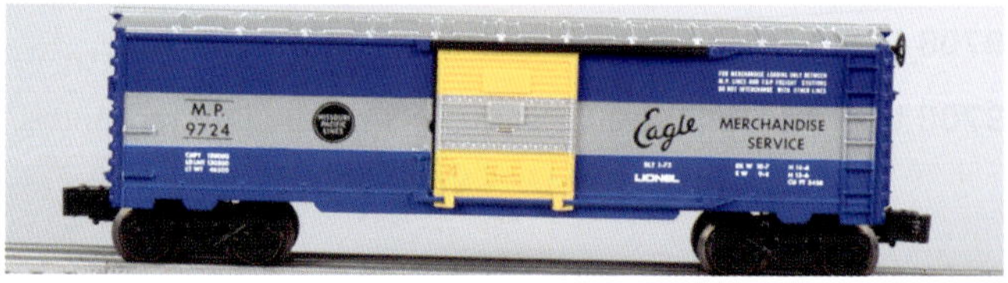

9724 MISSOURI PACIFIC: 1973-74, boxcar, a Service Station Special item.

EX-C7	LN-C8	Scarcity
20	25	4

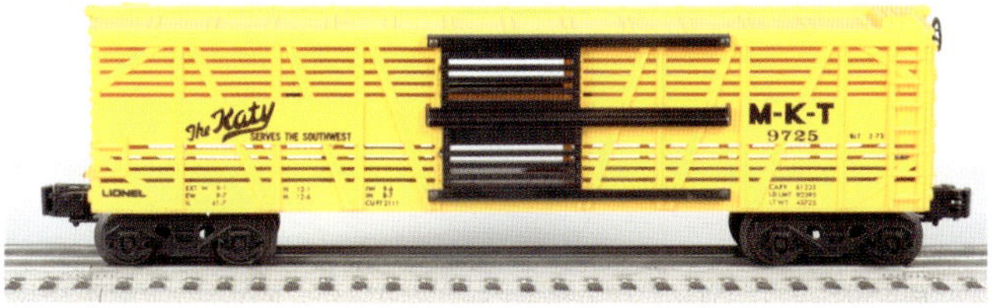

9725 MISSOURI-KANSAS-TEXAS: 1973-75, "Katy" stock car, Service Station Special item.

EX-C7	LN-C8	Scarcity
15	20	4

9726 ERIE-LACKAWANNA (Type I): 1978, boxcar, a Service Station Special item.

EX-C7	LN-C8	Scarcity
15	20	4

9726 ERIE-LACKAWANNA (Type II): 1979, uncataloged Sacramento-Sierra TCA boxcar.

EX-C7	LN-C8	Scarcity
15	20	6

9727 TA & G: 1973, uncataloged LCCA boxcar.

EX-C7	LN-C8	Scarcity
100	110	6

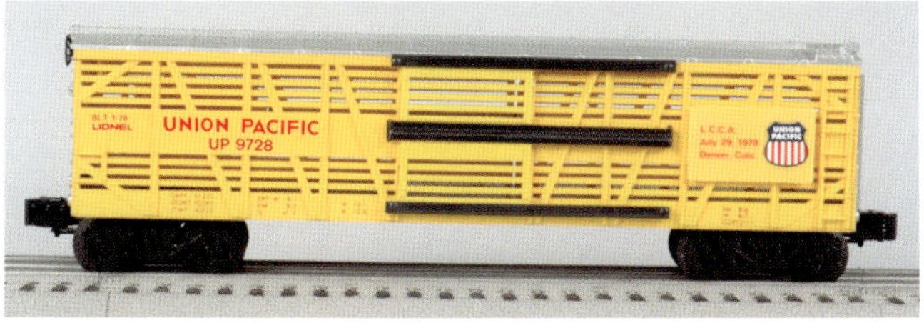

9728 UNION PACIFIC: 1978, uncataloged LCCA stock car.

EX-C7	LN-C8	Scarcity
15	20	5

9729 CP RAIL: 1978, boxcar.

EX-C7	LN-C8	Scarcity
15	20	4

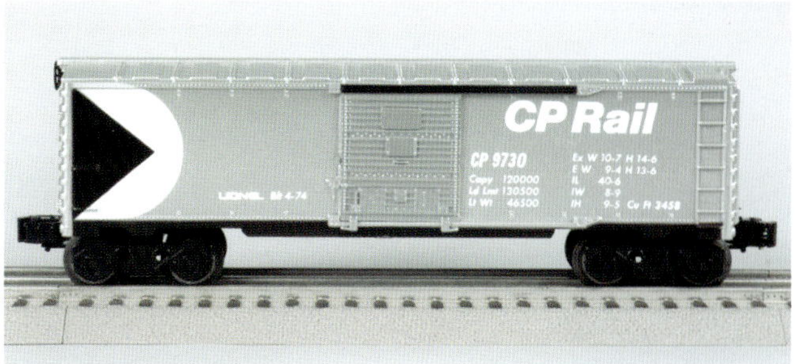

9730 CP RAIL (Type I): 1974-75, silver boxcar.

9730 CP RAIL (Type II): The lettering on some cars was primarily white.

EX-C7	LN-C8	Scarcity
20	25	5

9730 CP RAIL (Type III): Slightly more common are cars with black lettering.

EX-C7	LN-C8	Scarcity
15	20	4

9730 CP RAIL (Type IV): 1976, uncataloged Detroit-Toledo Chapter TCA overstamped boxcar.

EX-C7	LN-C8	Scarcity
18	22	6

9730 CP RAIL (Type V): 1977, uncataloged Sacramento-Sierra TCA overstamped boxcar.

EX-C7	LN-C8	Scarcity
20	25	6

9730 CP RAIL (Type VI): 1974, uncataloged Western Michigan TCA overstamped boxcar.

EX-C7	LN-C8	Scarcity
18	22	6

9731 MILWAUKEE ROAD: 1974-75, boxcar.

EX-C7	LN-C8	Scarcity
10	15	4

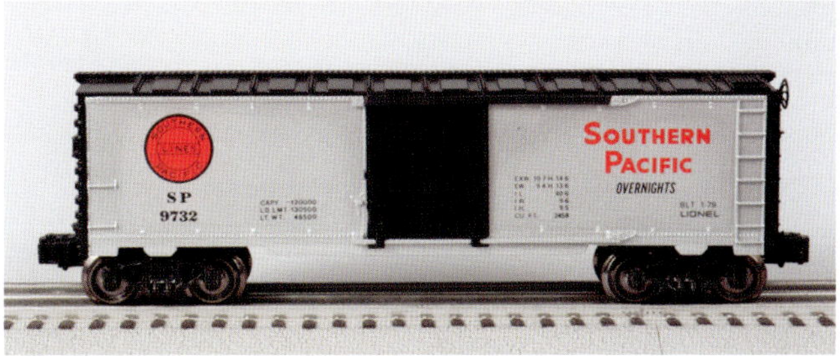

9732 SOUTHERN PACIFIC: 1979, uncataloged boxcar.

EX-C7	LN-C8	Scarcity
15	20	5

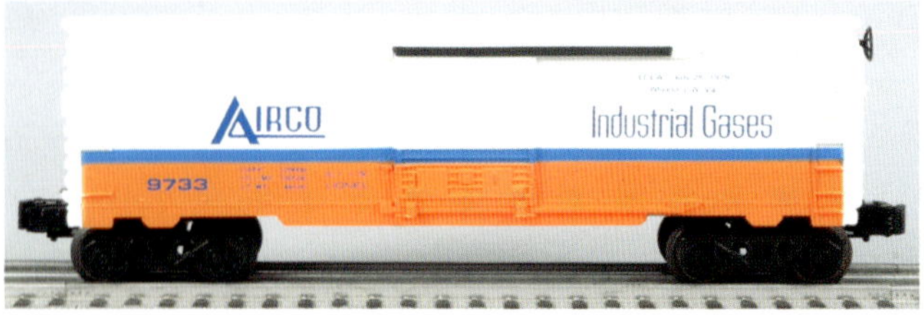

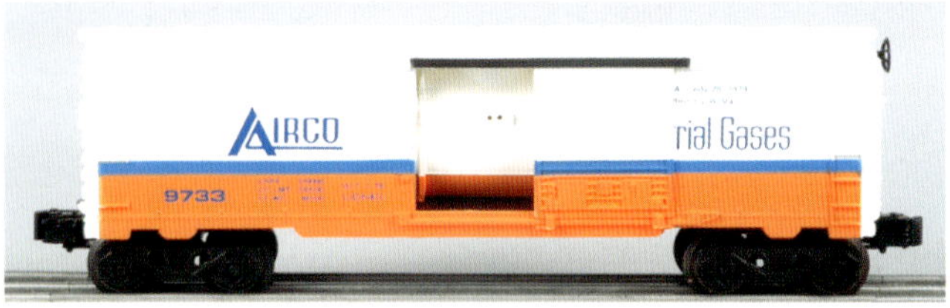

9733 AIRCO: 1979, uncataloged LCCA boxcar with tank.

EX-C7	LN-C8	Scarcity
35	45	6

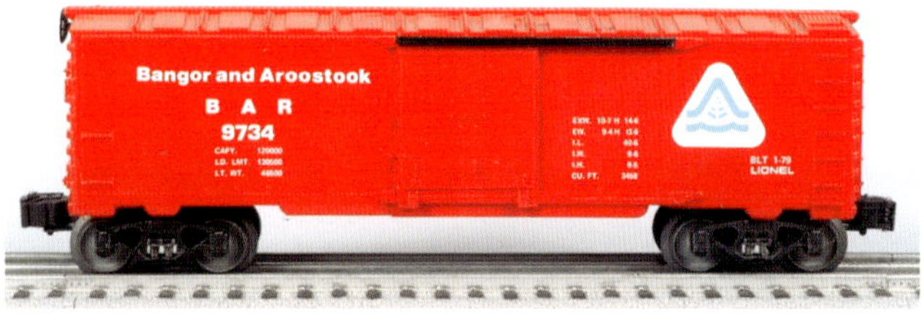

9734 BANGOR AND AROOSTOOK: 1979, boxcar.

EX-C7	LN-C8	Scarcity
15	20	4

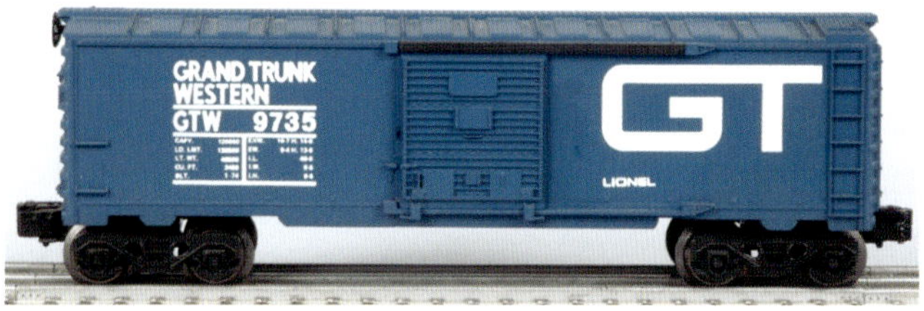

9735 GRAND TRUNK WESTERN: 1974-75, boxcar.

EX-C7	LN-C8	Scarcity
10	15	4

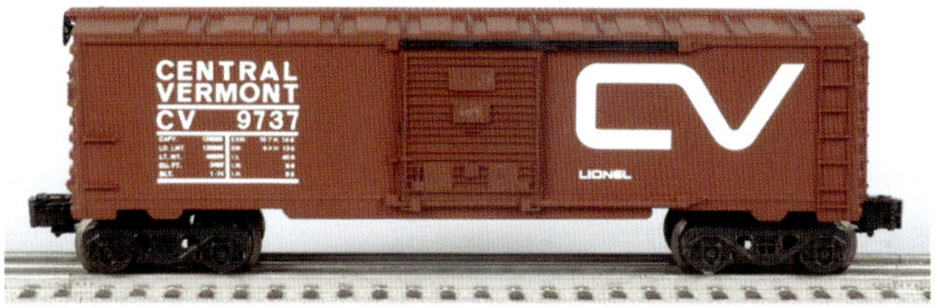

9737 CENTRAL VERMONT: 1974-76, boxcar.

EX-C7	LN-C8	Scarcity
10	15	4

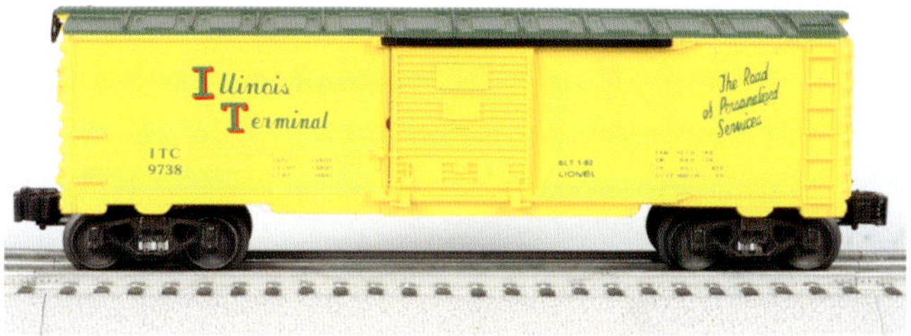

9738 ILLINOIS TERMINAL: 1982, boxcar.

EX-C7	LN-C8	Scarcity
25	30	5

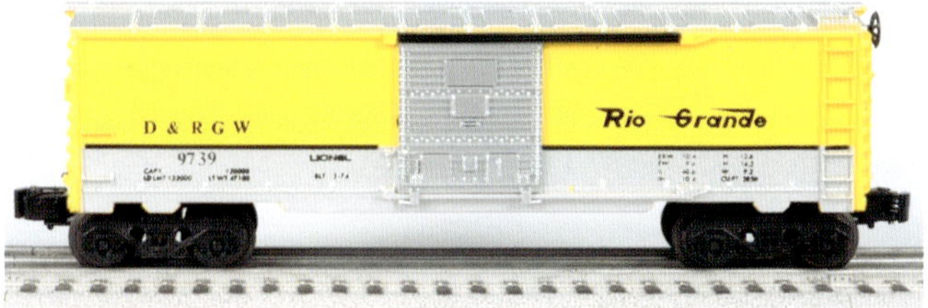

9739 DENVER & RIO GRANDE WESTERN: 1974-76, yellow, silver and black boxcar, some were included in Service Station Special sets.

9739 DENVER & RIO GRANDE WESTERN (Type I): Car as described above with thin black stripe separating the yellow from the silver.

EX-C7	LN-C8	Scarcity
10	15	4

9739 DENVER & RIO GRANDE WESTERN (Type II): The black stripe was inadvertently omitted from a number of these cars. There are enough cars to make a legitimate collectible variation, but not enough to warrant a premium.

EX-C7	LN-C8	Scarcity
100	125	6

9739 DENVER & RIO GRANDE WESTERN (Type III): 1978, uncataloged LCCA overstamped boxcar.

EX-C7	LN-C8	Scarcity
100	125	6

9739 DENVER & RIO GRANDE WESTERN (Type IV): 1976, uncataloged North Texas TCA overstamped boxcar.

EX-C7	LN-C8	Scarcity
10	15	6

9740 CHESSIE SYSTEM: 1974-75, yellow boxcar.

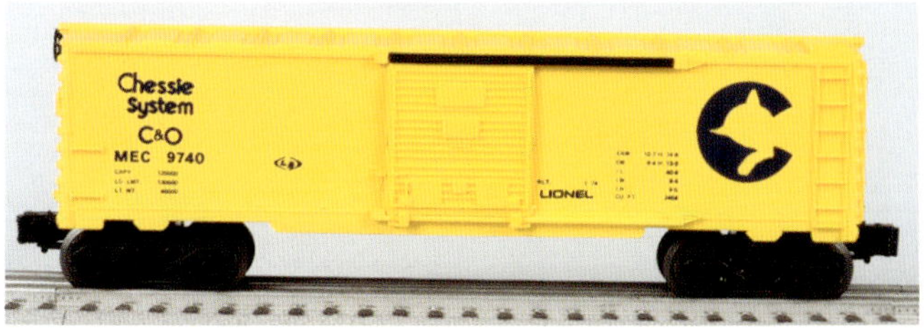

9740 CHESSIE SYSTEM (Type I): As described above.

EX-C7	LN-C8	Scarcity
10	15	4

9740 CHESSIE SYSTEM (Type II): In 1976, some cars were overstamped to create an uncataloged Great Lakes TCA boxcar.

EX-C7	LN-C8	Scarcity
15	20	6

9740 CHESSIE SYSTEM (Type III): In 1976, some cars were overstamped to create an uncataloged WBA TCA boxcar.

EX-C7	LN-C8	Scarcity
15	20	6

9742 MINNEAPOLIS & ST. LOUIS: 1973, uncataloged green boxcar that was part of a Lionel box coupon promotion.

9742 MINNEAPOLIS & ST. LOUIS (Type I): As described above.

EX-C7	LN-C8	Scarcity
15	20	5

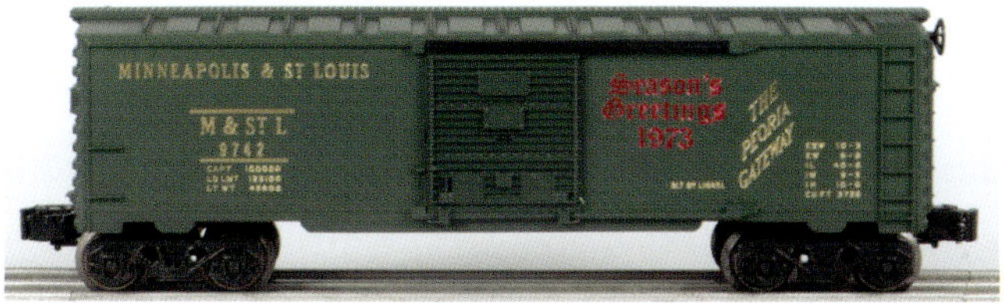

9742 MINNEAPOLIS & ST. LOUIS (Type II): 1973, uncataloged boxcar, overstamped "Season's Greetings."

EX-C7	LN-C8	Scarcity
80	100	6

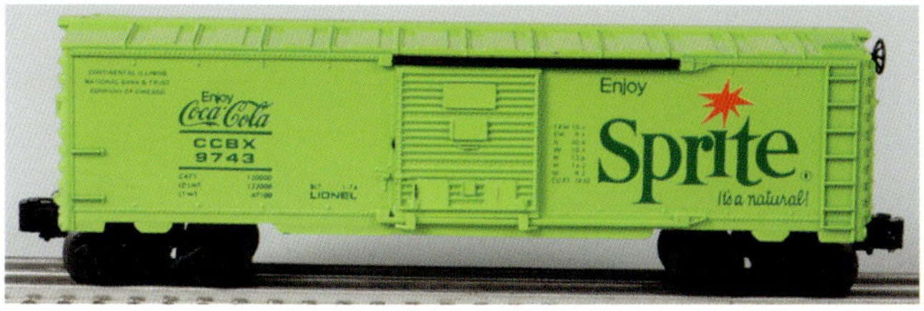

9743 SPRITE: Uncataloged in 1974, cataloged in 1975, boxcar.

EX-C7	LN-C8	Scarcity
10	15	3

9744 TAB: Uncataloged in 1974, cataloged in 1975, boxcar.

EX-C7	LN-C8	Scarcity
10	15	3

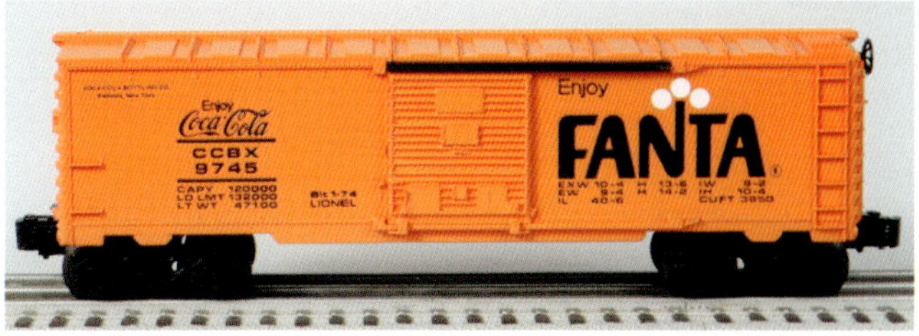

9745 FANTA: Uncataloged in 1974, cataloged in 1975, boxcar.

EX-C7	LN-C8	Scarcity
10	15	3

9747 CHESSIE SYSTEM: 1975-76, double-door boxcar.

EX-C7	LN-C8	Scarcity
15	20	4

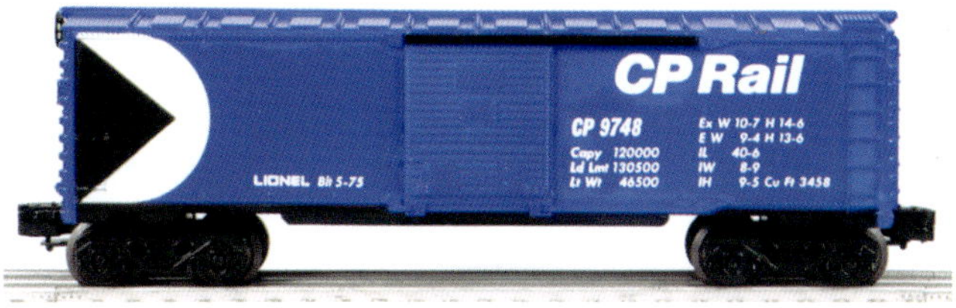

9748 CP RAIL: 1975-76, boxcar.

EX-C7	LN-C8	Scarcity
10	15	4

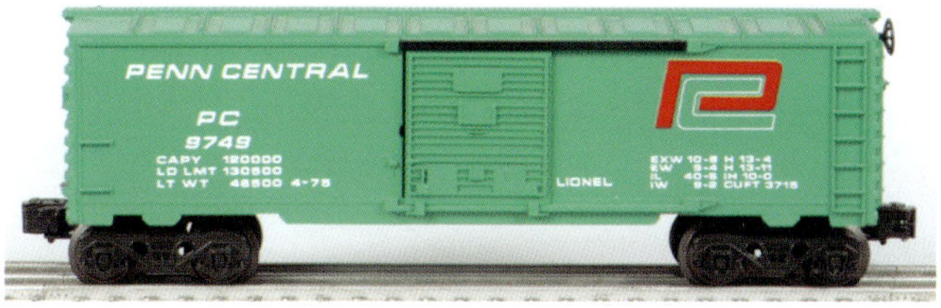

9749 PENN CENTRAL: 1975-76, boxcar.

EX-C7	LN-C8	Scarcity
10	15	4

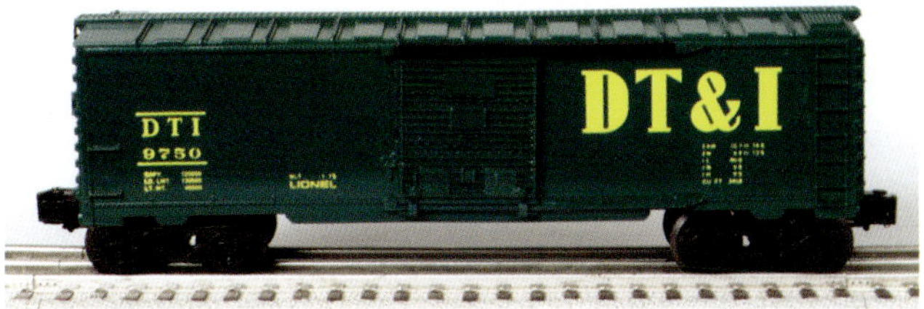

9750 DT & I: 1975-76, boxcar.

EX-C7	LN-C8	Scarcity
10	15	4

9751 FRISCO: 1975-76, red boxcar.

EX-C7	LN-C8	Scarcity
10	15	4

9752 LOUISVILLE & NASHVILLE: 1975-76, blue boxcar.

EX-C7	LN-C8	Scarcity
10	15	4

9753 MAINE CENTRAL: 1975-76, yellow boxcar.

9753 MAINE CENTRAL (Type I): As described above.

EX-C7	LN-C8	Scarcity
10	15	4

9753 MAINE CENTRAL (Type II): In 1975, some cars were overstamped to create this uncataloged New England Division of Train Collectors Association boxcar.

EX-C7	LN-C8	Scarcity
20	25	6

9754 NEW YORK CENTRAL: 1975-77, "Pacemaker" boxcar, Service Station Special item.

9754 NEW YORK CENTRAL (Type I): Normal production.

EX-C7	LN-C8	Scarcity
18	24	4

9754 NEW YORK CENTRAL (Type II): 1976, uncataloged Metropolitan Division of Train Collectors Association overstamped car.

EX-C7	LN-C8	Scarcity
20	25	6

9755 UNION PACIFIC: 1975-76, boxcar.

EX-C7	LN-C8	Scarcity
15	20	4

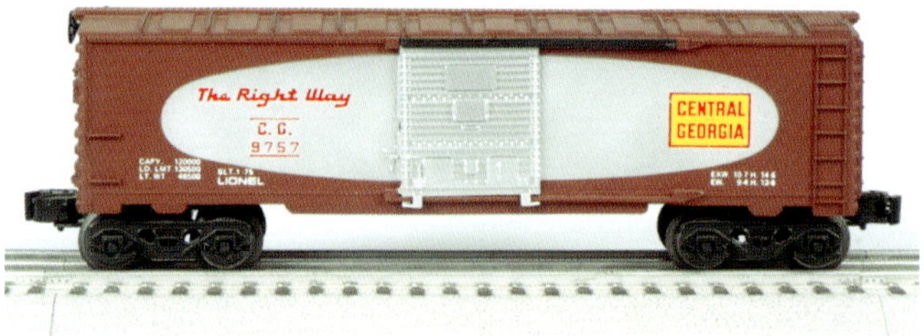

9757 CENTRAL OF GEORGIA: 1974, uncataloged boxcar.

EX-C7	LN-C8	Scarcity
15	20	4

9758 ALASKA RAILROAD: 1975-77, boxcar, Service Station Special item.

EX-C7	LN-C8	Scarcity
20	25	5

9759 PAUL REVERE: 1975, uncataloged boxcar.

EX-C7	LN-C8	Scarcity
20	25	5

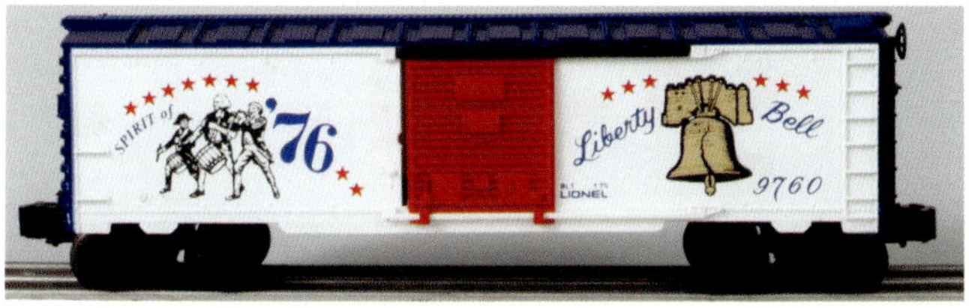

9760 LIBERTY BELL: 1975, uncataloged boxcar.

EX-C7	LN-C8	Scarcity
20	25	5

9761 GEORGE WASHINGTON: 1975, uncataloged boxcar.

EX-C7	LN-C8	Scarcity
20	25	5

[9762] TOY FAIR: 1975, uncataloged boxcar.

EX-C7	LN-C8	Scarcity
125	150	6

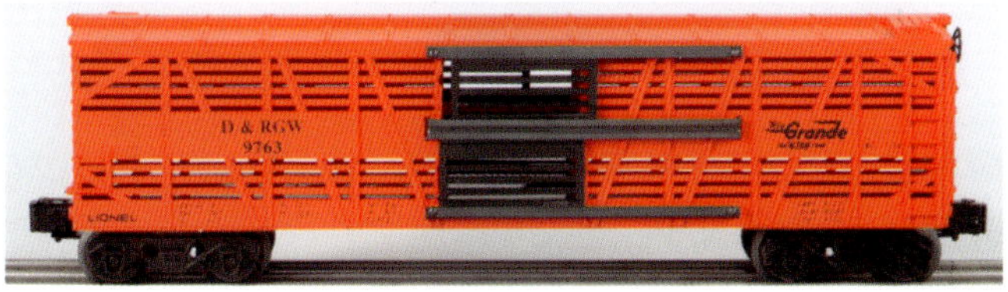

9763 DENVER & RIO GRANDE WESTERN: 1976-77, stock car.

EX-C7	LN-C8	Scarcity
15	20	4

9764 GRAND TRUNK WESTERN: 1976-77 and 1990, double-door automoblle boxcar.

9764 GRAND TRUNK WESTERN (Type I): The initial production cars are dated "1-76" and came in red boxes.

EX-C7	LN-C8	Scarcity
20	25	4

9764 GRAND TRUNK WESTERN (Type II): The 1990 production cars are dated "9-90" and came in black and white boxes.

EX-C7	LN-C8	Scarcity
Too rarely traded to establish accurate pricing.		

9767 RAILBOX: 1976-77, yellow boxcar.

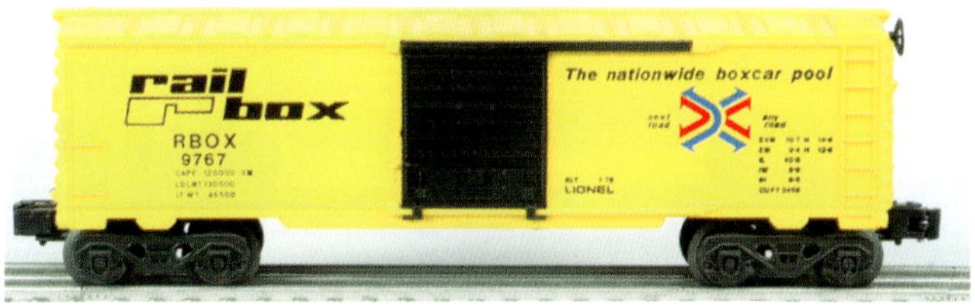

9767 RAILBOX (Type I): as described above.

EX-C7	LN-C8	Scarcity
15	20	4

9767 RAILBOX (Type II): 1978, uncataloged overstamped Gateway Chapter TCA boxcar.

EX-C7	LN-C8	Scarcity
15	20	6

9768 BOSTON AND MAINE: 1976-77, blue boxcar.

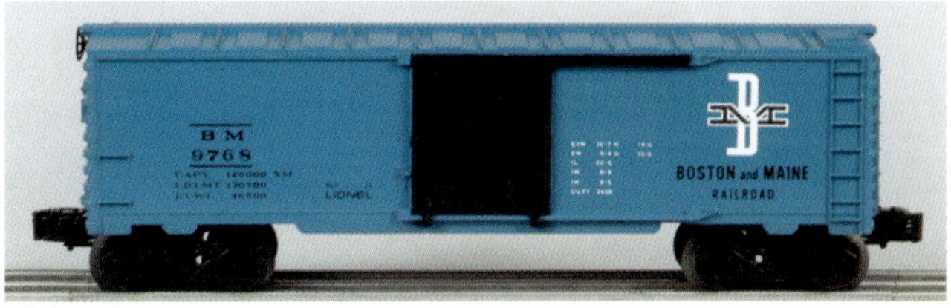

9768 BOSTON AND MAINE (Type I): As described above.

EX-C7	LN-C8	Scarcity
20	25	4

9768 BOSTON AND MAINE (Type II): 1976, uncataloged overstamped New England Division of Train Collectors Association boxcar.

EX-C7	LN-C8	Scarcity
20	25	6

9769 B. & L.E: 1976-77, boxcar.

EX-C7	LN-C8	Scarcity
15	20	4

9788 LEHIGH VALLEY: 1977-79, cream-colored boxcar.

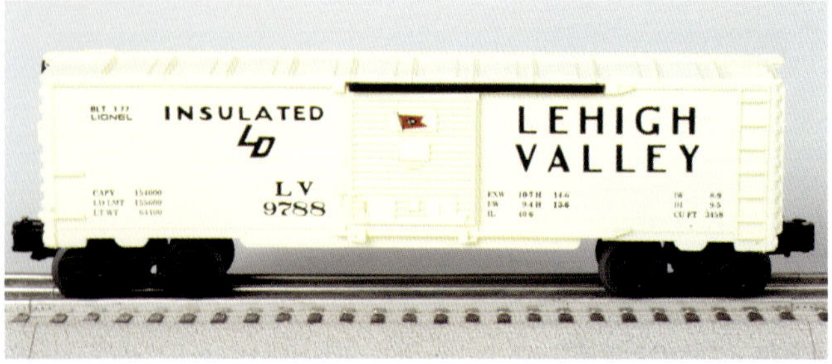

9788 LEHIGH VALLEY (Type I): As described above.

EX-C7	LN-C8	Scarcity
15	20	4

9788 LEHIGH VALLEY (Type II): 1978, uncataloged overstamped Atlantic Division TCA boxcar.

EX-C7	LN-C8	Scarcity
15	20	6

9789 PICKENS: 1977, boxcar.

EX-C7	LN-C8	Scarcity
20	25	4

9801 BALTIMORE & OHIO: 1973-75, "Sentinel" boxcar with 1/48-scale proportions.

EX-C7	LN-C8	Scarcity
25	30	4

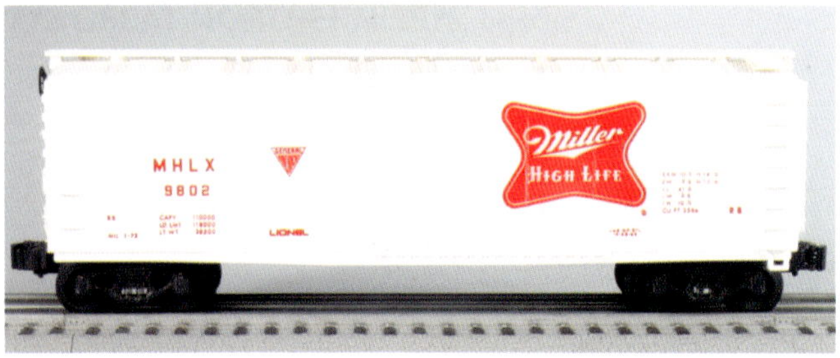

9802 MILLER HIGH LIFE: 1973-75, refrigerator car with 1/48-scale proportions.

EX-C7	LN-C8	Scarcity
25	30	4

9803 JOHNSON WAX: 1973-75, boxcar with 1/48-scale proportions.

EX-C7	LN-C8	Scarcity
25	30	4

9805 GRAND TRUNK: 1973-75, refrigerator car with 1/48-scale proportions.

EX-C7	LN-C8	Scarcity
20	25	4

9806 ROCK ISLAND: 1974-75, boxcar with 1/48-scale proportions.

EX-C7	LN-C8	Scarcity
30	35	4

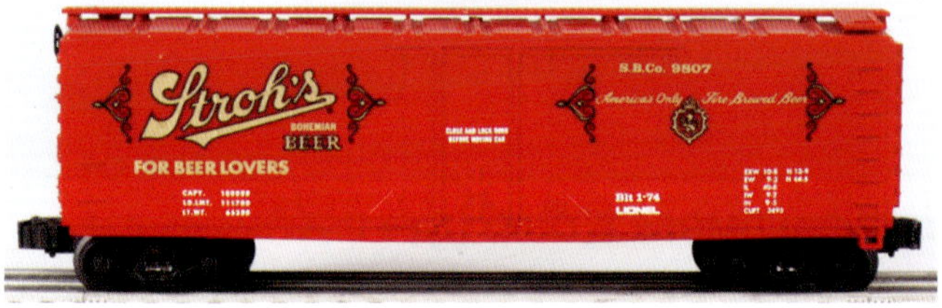

9807 STROH'S BEER: 1974-76, refrigerator car with 1/48-scale proportions.

EX-C7	LN-C8	Scarcity
40	50	5

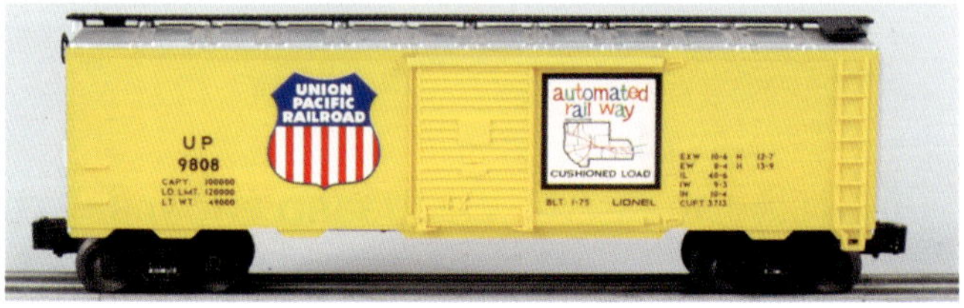

9808 UNION PACIFIC: 1975-76, boxcar with 1/48-scale proportions.

EX-C7	LN-C8	Scarcity
40	50	5

9809 CLARK: 1975-76, refrigerator car with 1/48-scale proportions.

EX-C7	LN-C8	Scarcity
30	35	4

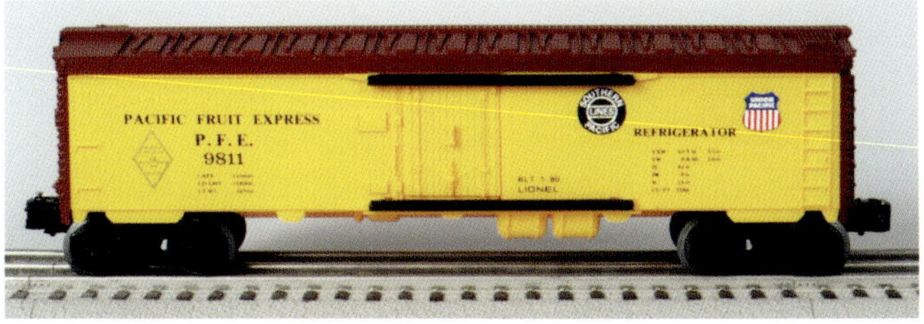

9811 PACIFIC FRUIT EXPRESS: 1980, refrigerator car, Famous American Railroads number two.

EX-C7	LN-C8	Scarcity
20	25	4

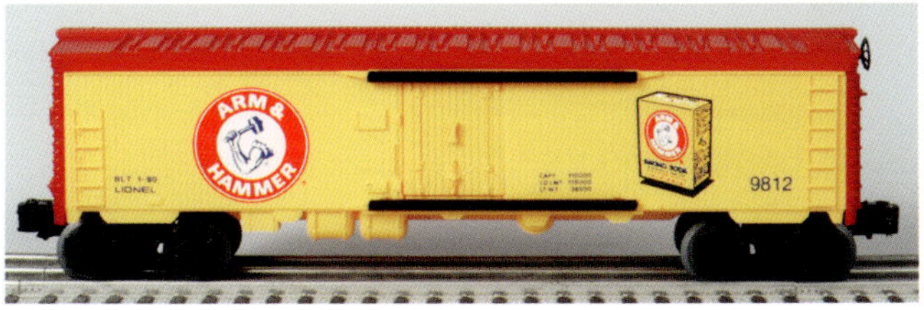

9812 ARM & HAMMER: 1980, refrigerator car.

EX-C7	LN-C8	Scarcity
15	20	4

9813 RUFFLES: 1980, refrigerator car.

EX-C7	LN-C8	Scarcity
15	20	4

9814 PERRIER: 1980, refrigerator car.

EX-C7	LN-C8	Scarcity
20	25	4

9815 NEW YORK CENTRAL: 1984-85, "Early Bird" refrigerator car with 1/48-scale proportions.

EX-C7	LN-C8	Scarcity
30	40	5

9816 BRACH'S CANDY: 1980, refrigerator car.

EX-C7	LN-C8	Scarcity
15	20	4

9817 BAZOOKA GUM: 1980, refrigerator car.

EX-C7	LN-C8	Scarcity
15	20	4

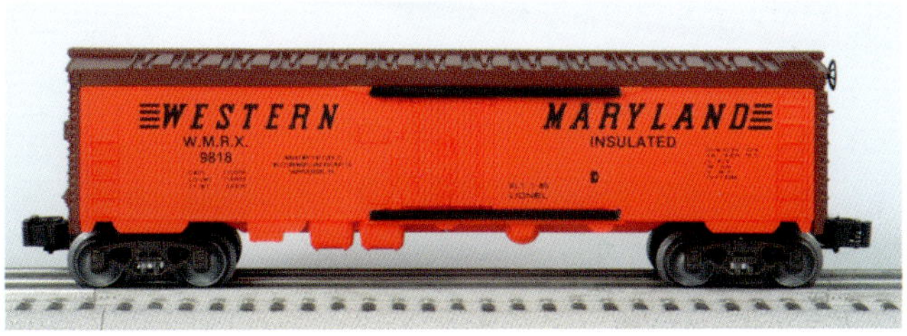

9818 WESTERN MARYLAND: 1980, refrigerator car.

EX-C7	LN-C8	Scarcity
20	25	4

9819 WESTERN FRUIT EXPRESS: 1981, refrigerator car, Famous American Railroads number three.

EX-C7	LN-C8	Scarcity
25	30	5

9825 SCHAEFER: 1976-77, refrigerator car with 1/48-scale proportions.

EX-C7	LN-C8	Scarcity
40	50	5

9826 P & LE: 1976-77, boxcar with 1/48-scale proportions.

9826 P & LE (Type I): Flat green-painted body and doors.

EX-C7	LN-C8	Scarcity
50	65	6

9826 P & LE (Type II): Glossy green-painted body and doors.

EX-C7	LN-C8	Scarcity
40	50	5

9827 CUTTY SARK: 1984, refrigerator car.

EX-C7	LN-C8	Scarcity
15	20	4

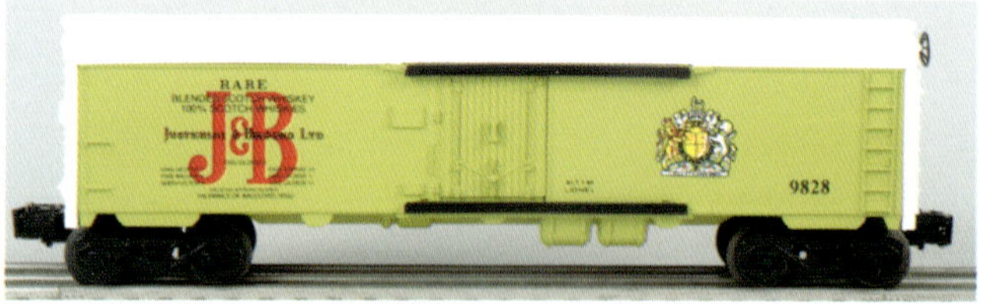

9828 J & B: 1984, refrigerator car.

EX-C7	LN-C8	Scarcity
20	25	4

9829 DEWAR'S WHITE LABEL: 1984, refrigerator car.

EX-C7	LN-C8	Scarcity
15	20	4

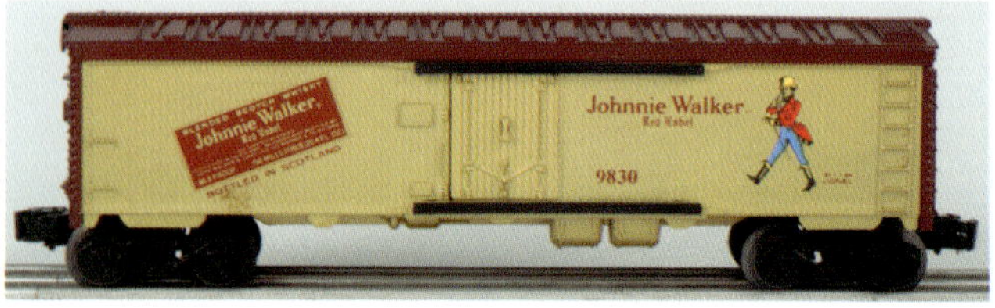

9830 JOHNNIE WALKER RED LABEL: 1984, refrigerator car.

EX-C7	LN-C8	Scarcity
15	20	4

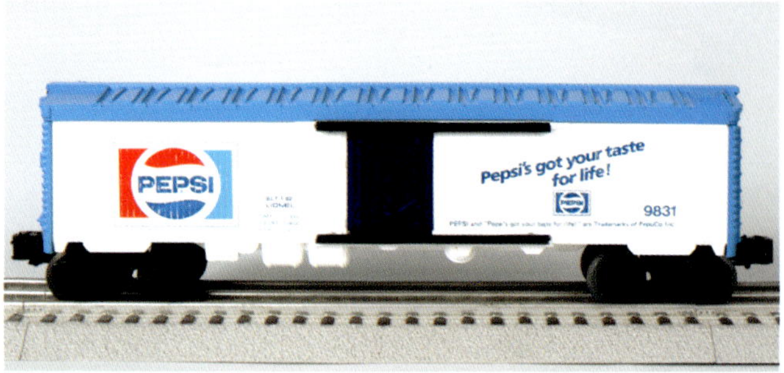

9831 PEPSI COLA: 1982, refrigerator car.

EX-C7	LN-C8	Scarcity
35	45	5

9832 CHEERIOS: 1982, refrigerator car.

EX-C7	LN-C8	Scarcity
70	100	5

9833 VLASIC PICKLES: 1982, refrigerator car.

EX-C7	LN-C8	Scarcity
15	20	4

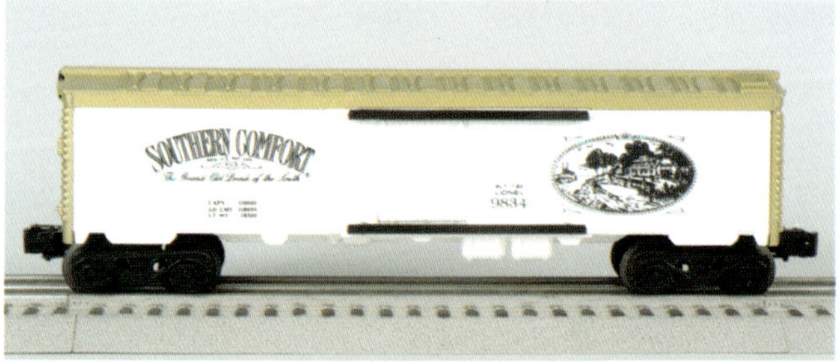

9834 SOUTHERN COMFORT: 1983-84, refrigerator car.

EX-C7	LN-C8	Scarcity
20	25	4

9835 JIM BEAM: 1983-84, refrigerator car.

EX-C7	LN-C8	Scarcity
15	20	4

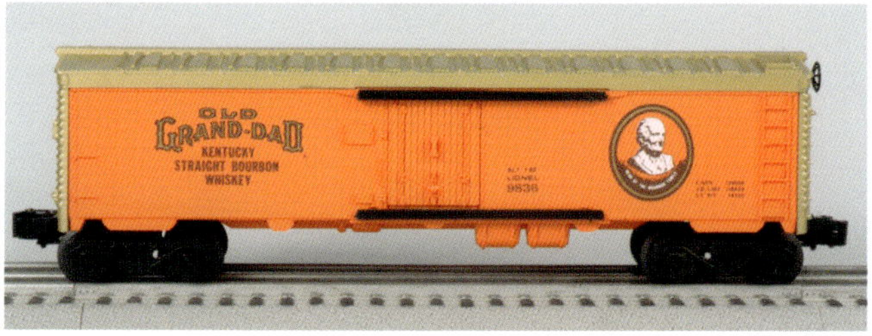

9836 OLD GRAND-DAD: 1983-84, refrigerator car.

EX-C7	LN-C8	Scarcity
15	20	4

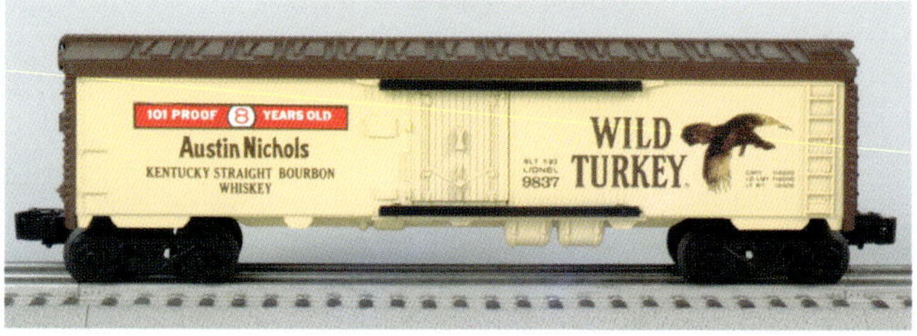

9837 WILD TURKEY: 1983-84, refrigerator car.

EX-C7	LN-C8	Scarcity
30	40	5

9840 FLEISCHMANN'S GIN: 1985, refrigerator car.

EX-C7	LN-C8	Scarcity
15	20	4

9841 CALVERT GIN: 1985, refrigerator car.

EX-C7	LN-C8	Scarcity
15	20	4

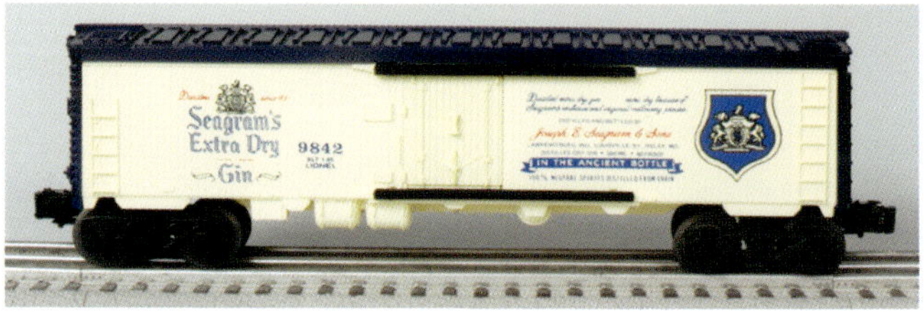

9842 SEAGRAM'S GIN: 1985, refrigerator car.

EX-C7	LN-C8	Scarcity
15	20	4

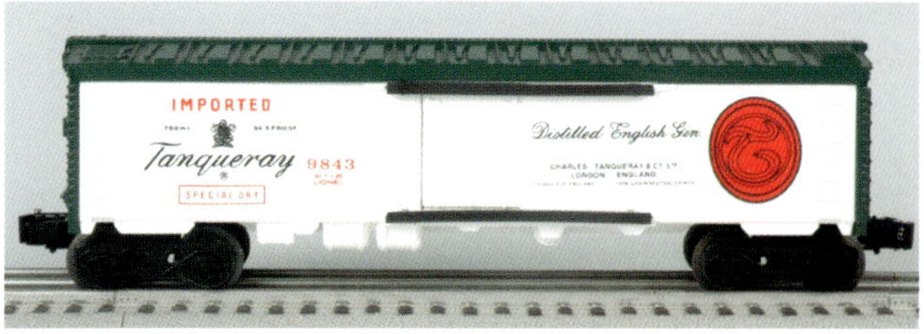

9843 TANQUERAY GIN: 1985, refrigerator car.

EX-C7	LN-C8	Scarcity
15	20	4

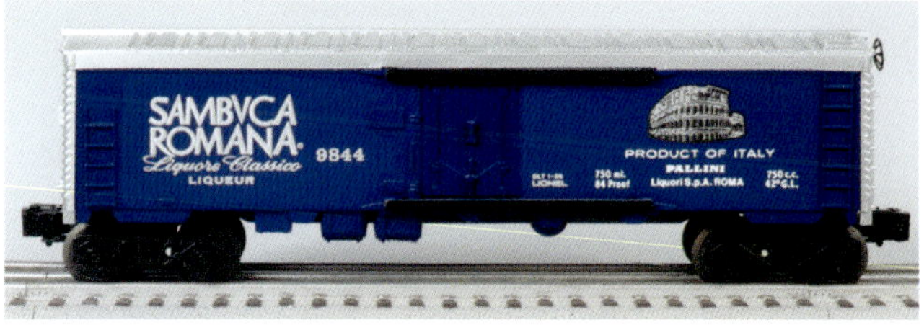

9844 SAMBUCA: 1986, refrigerator car.

EX-C7	LN-C8	Scarcity
15	20	4

9845 BAILEYS IRISH CREAM: 1986, refrigerator car.

EX-C7	LN-C8	Scarcity
30	40	5

9846 SEAGRAM'S VODKA: 1986, refrigerator car.

EX-C7	LN-C8	Scarcity
20	25	4

9847 WOLFSCHMIDT VODKA: 1986, refrigerator car.

EX-C7	LN-C8	Scarcity
20	25	4

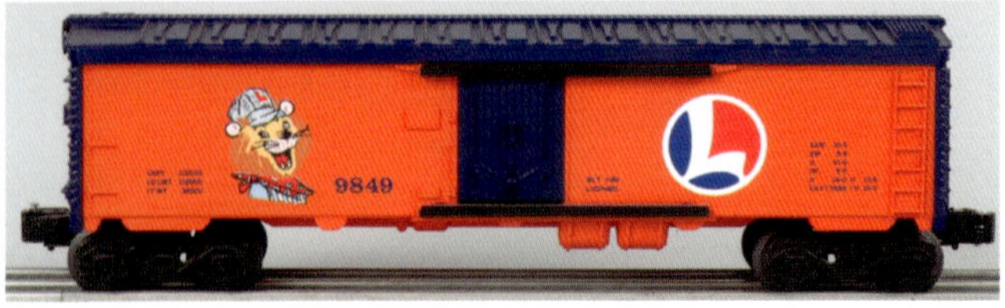

9849 LIONEL LINES: 1983, uncataloged refrigerator car.

EX-C7	LN-C8	Scarcity
50	60	6

9850 BUDWEISER: Uncataloged in 1972, cataloged from 1973-75, refrigerator car.

EX-C7	LN-C8	Scarcity
25	30	4

9851 SCHLITZ: Uncataloged in 1972, cataloged from 1973-75, refrigerator car.

EX-C7	LN-C8	Scarcity
20	25	4

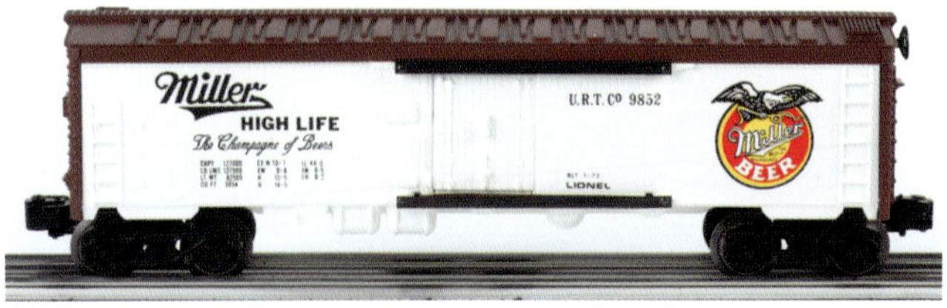

9852 MILLER: Uncataloged in 1972, cataloged from 1973-77, refrigerator car.

EX-C7	LN-C8	Scarcity
20	25	4

9853 CRACKER JACK: 1972-75, refrigerator car.

9853 CRACKER JACK (Type I): Uncataloged in 1972, refrigerator car with a caramel color body.

EX-C7	LN-C8	Scarcity
20	25	4

9853 CRACKER JACK (Type II): 1973-75, refrigerator car with a white body, black logo border.

EX-C7	LN-C8	Scarcity
20	25	4

9854 BABY RUTH: Uncataloged in 1972, cataloged from 1973-76, refrigerator car.

EX-C7	LN-C8	Scarcity
15	20	4

9855 SWIFT: Uncataloged in 1972, cataloged from 1973-77, refrigerator car.

EX-C7	LN-C8	Scarcity
20	25	4

9856 OLD MILWAUKEE: 1975-76, refrigerator car.

EX-C7	LN-C8	Scarcity
20	25	4

9858 BUTTERFINGER: Uncataloged in 1973, cataloged from 1974-76, refrigerator car.

EX-C7	LN-C8	Scarcity
20	25	4

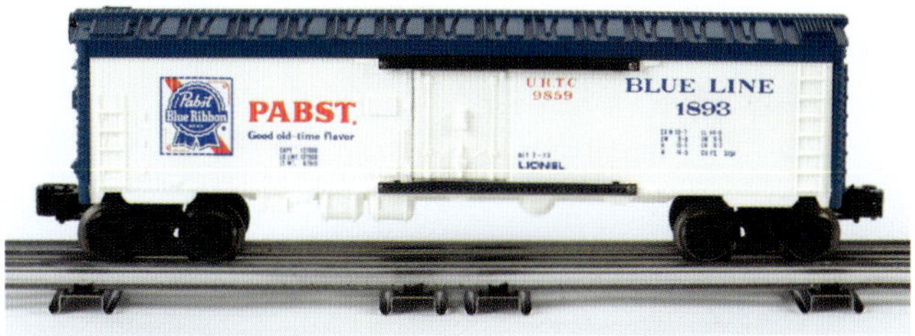

9859 PABST: Uncataloged in 1973, cataloged from 1974-75, refrigerator car.

EX-C7	LN-C8	Scarcity
20	25	4

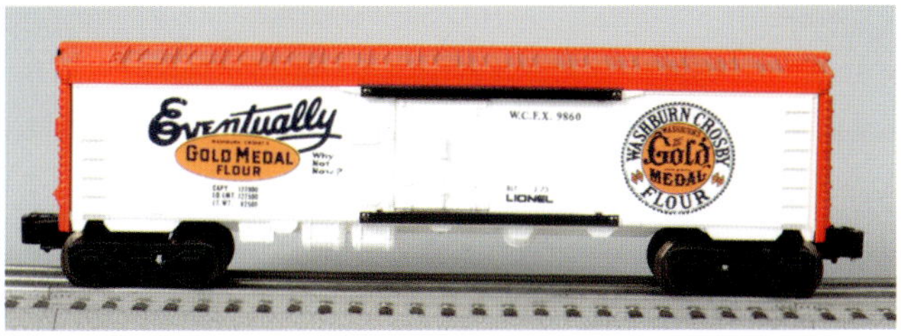

9860 GOLD MEDAL: Uncataloged in 1973, cataloged from 1974-76, refrigerator car.

9860 GOLD MEDAL (Type I): Car with dark orange roof.

EX-C7	LN-C8	Scarcity
15	20	4

9860 GOLD MEDAL (Type II): Car with bright orange roof.

EX-C7	LN-C8	Scarcity
15	20	4

9861 TROPICANA: 1975-77, refrigerator car.

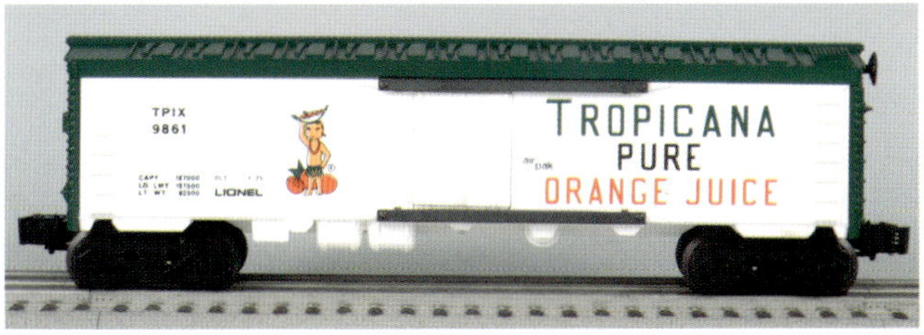

9861 TROPICANA (Type I): Some of the cars had flat green roofs and metal door guides.

EX-C7	LN-C8	Scarcity
20	25	4

9861 TROPICANA (Type II): Other cars had shiny green roofs and plastic door guides.

EX-C7	LN-C8	Scarcity
20	25	4

9862 HAMM'S: 1975-76, refrigerator car.

EX-C7	LN-C8	Scarcity
20	25	4

9863 REA: 1974-76, refrigerator car, a Service Station Special item.

EX-C7	LN-C8	Scarcity
20	25	4

9864 TCA SEATTLE: 1974, uncataloged refrigerator car.

EX-C7	LN-C8	Scarcity
20	25	6

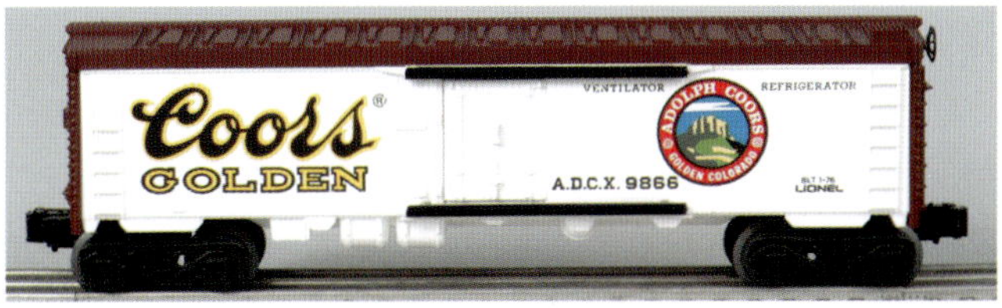

9866 COORS: 1976-77, refrigerator car.

EX-C7	LN-C8	Scarcity
25	30	5

9867 HERSHEY'S: 1976-77, refrigerator car.

EX-C7	LN-C8	Scarcity
25	30	5

9868 TTOS OKLAHOMA CITY: 1980, uncataloged refrigerator car.

EX-C7	LN-C8	Scarcity
20	25	6

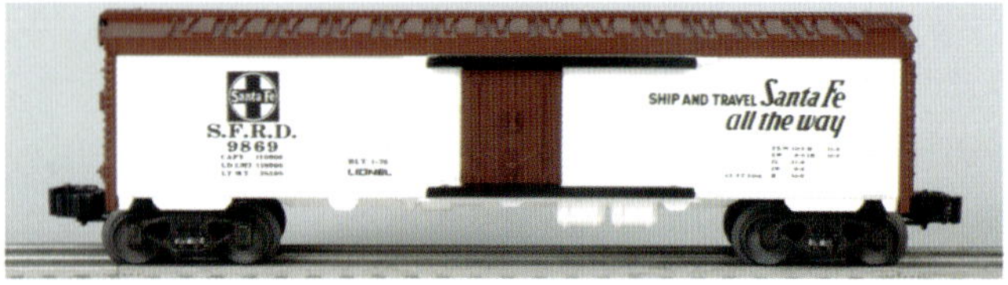

9869 SANTA FE: 1976, refrigerator car, a Service Station Special item.

EX-C7	LN-C8	Scarcity
20	25	4

9870 OLD DUTCH CLEANSER: 1977-78 and 1980, refrigerator car.

EX-C7	LN-C8	Scarcity
15	20	4

9871 CARLING BLACK LABEL: 1977-78 and 1980, refrigerator car.

EX-C7	LN-C8	Scarcity
20	25	4

9872 PACIFIC FRUIT EXPRESS: 1977-79, refrigerator car.

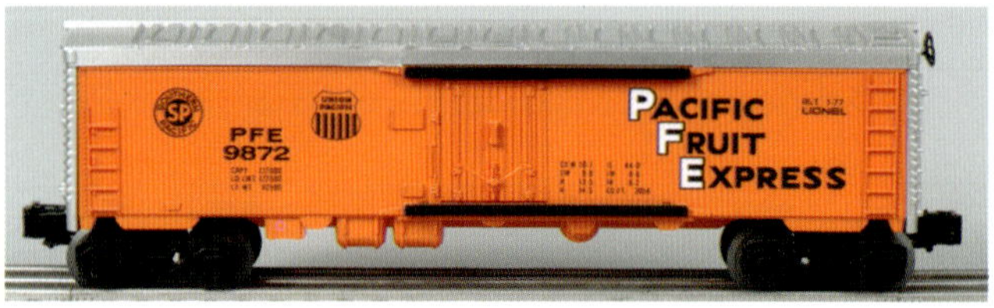

9872 PACIFIC FRUIT EXPRESS (Type I): As cataloged.

EX-C7	LN-C8	Scarcity
15	20	4

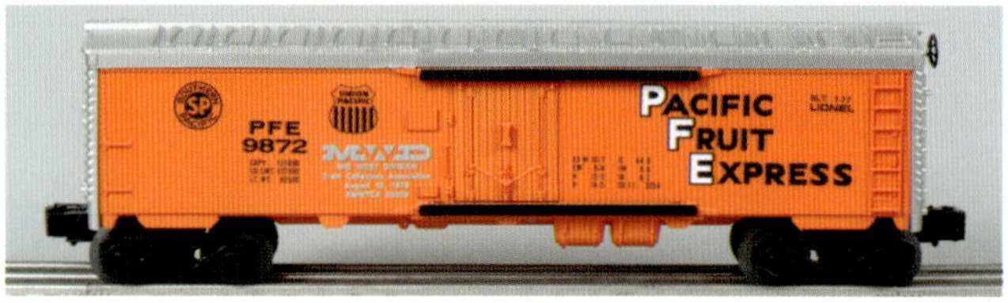

9872 PACIFIC FRUIT EXPRESS (Type II): 1979, uncataloged Midwest TCA refrigerator car.

EX-C7	LN-C8	Scarcity
20	25	6

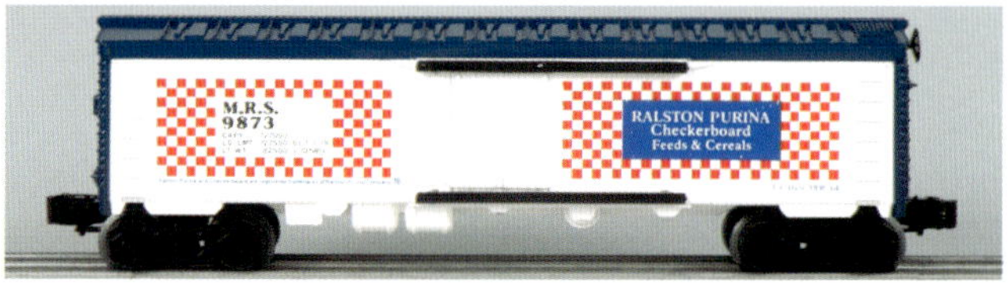

9873 RALSTON PURINA: 1978, refrigerator car.

EX-C7	LN-C8	Scarcity
20	25	4

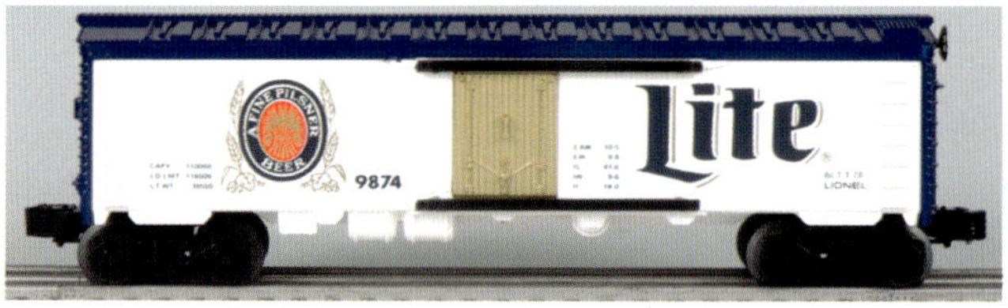

9874 MILLER LITE BEER: 1978-79, refrigerator car.

EX-C7	LN-C8	Scarcity
30	40	4

9875 A & P: 1978-79, refrigerator car.

EX-C7	LN-C8	Scarcity
15	20	4

9876 CENTRAL VERMONT: 1978, refrigerator car.

EX-C7	LN-C8	Scarcity
15	20	4

9877 GERBER: 1979-80, refrigerator car.

EX-C7	LN-C8	Scarcity
50	60	5

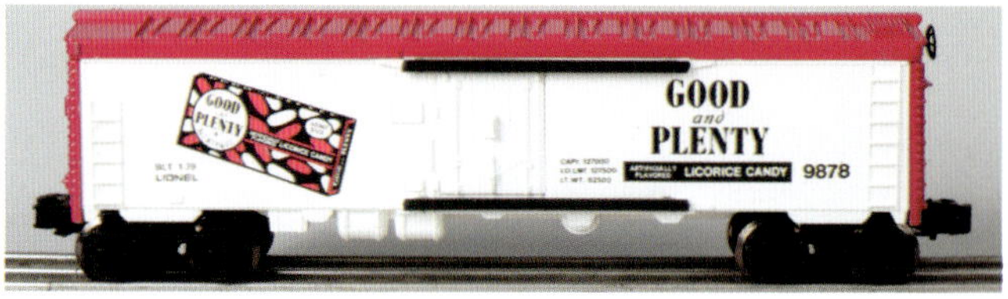

9878 GOOD AND PLENTY: 1979, refrigerator car.

EX-C7	LN-C8	Scarcity
15	20	4

9879 HILLS BROS: 1979-80, refrigerator car.

EX-C7	LN-C8	Scarcity
15	20	4

9879 KRAFT: 1979, refrigerator car.

EX-C7	LN-C8	Scarcity
Shown in advance catalog, but not produced.		

9880 SANTA FE: 1979, refrigerator car, Famous American Railroads number one.

EX-C7	LN-C8	Scarcity
20	25	5

9881 RATH PACKING: 1979, uncataloged refrigerator car.

EX-C7	LN-C8	Scarcity
25	30	5

9882 NEW YORK CENTRAL: 1979, "Early Bird" refrigerator car.

EX-C7	LN-C8	Scarcity
20	25	4

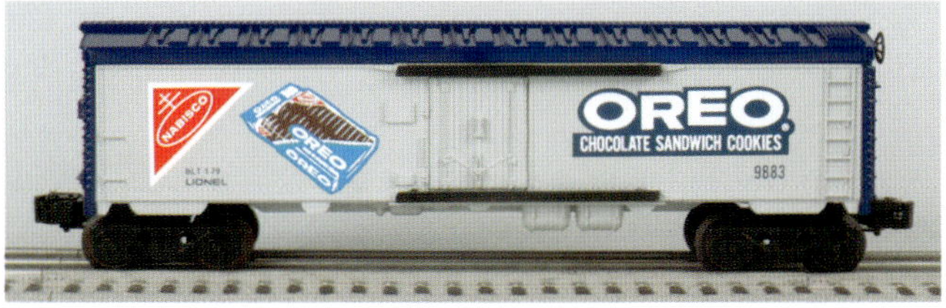

9883 NABISCO OREO: 1979, refrigerator car.

EX-C7	LN-C8	Scarcity
50	60	5

[9883] TTOS PHOENIX: 1983, uncataloged refrigerator car.

EX-C7	LN-C8	Scarcity
30	40	6

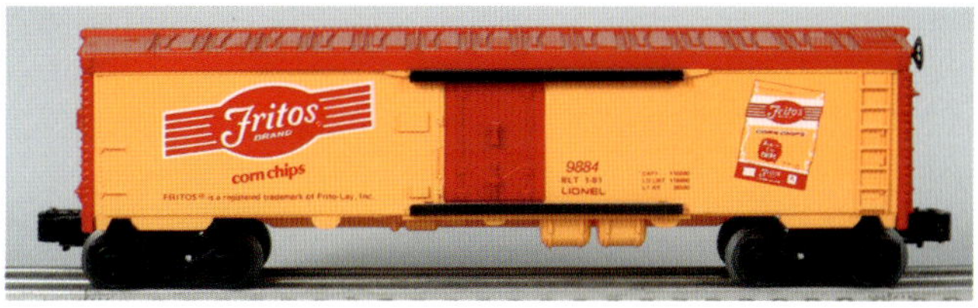

9884 FRITOS: 1981-82, refrigerator car.

EX-C7	LN-C8	Scarcity
15	20	4

9885 LIPTON TEA: 1981-82, refrigerator car.

EX-C7	LN-C8	Scarcity
15	20	4

9886 MOUNDS: 1981-82, refrigerator car.

EX-C7	LN-C8	Scarcity
15	20	4

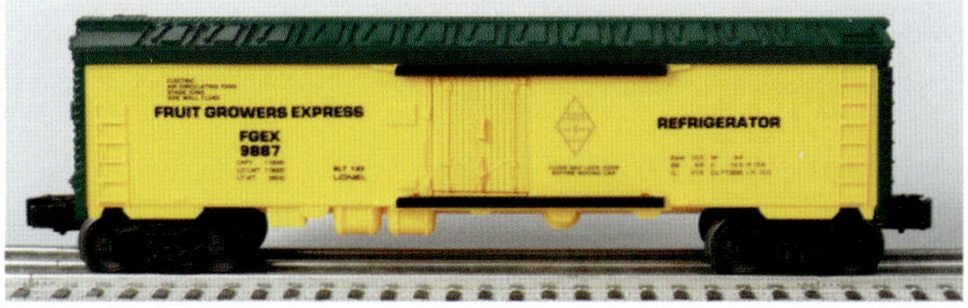

9887 FRUIT GROWERS EXPRESS: 1983, refrigerator car, Famous American Railroads number four.

EX-C7	LN-C8	Scarcity
20	25	4

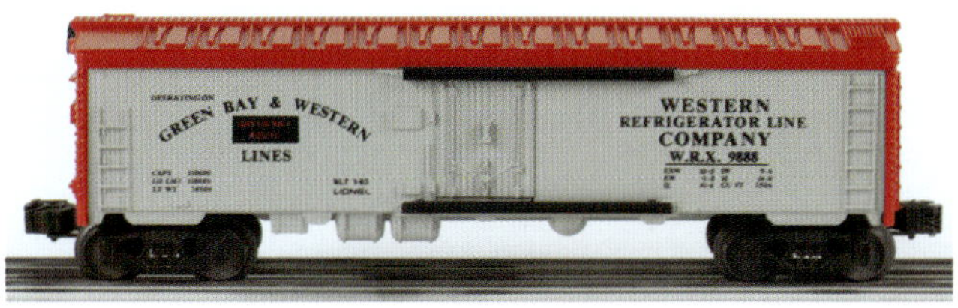

9888 GREEN BAY & WESTERN: 1983, refrigerator car.

EX-C7	LN-C8	Scarcity
35	45	5

HOUSE CARS

[11849] 1998 LIONEL CENTENNIAL SERIES: 1998, refrigerator car, four-pack.

EX-C7	LN-C8	Scarcity
100	125	4

[11977] NORTHERN PACIFIC: 1998, four-pack freight cars.

EX-C7	LN-C8	Scarcity
125	150	4

[11988] NEW YORK CENTRAL: 1999, fire car "18444" and firefighting instruction car "19853" set.

EX-C7	LN-C8	Scarcity
100	125	4

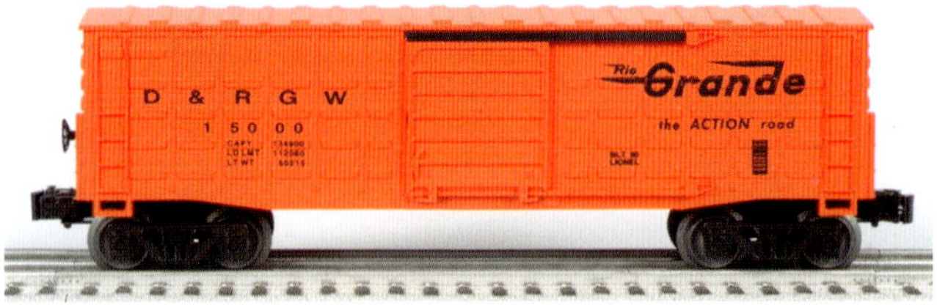

15000 DENVER & RIO GRANDE WESTERN: 1995, waffle-side boxcar.

EX-C7	LN-C8	Scarcity
10	15	4

15001 SEABOARD: 1995, waffle-side boxcar.

EX-C7	LN-C8	Scarcity
10	15	4

[15002] CHESAPEAKE AND OHIO: 1996, waffle-sided boxcar.

EX-C7	LN-C8	Scarcity
15	20	4

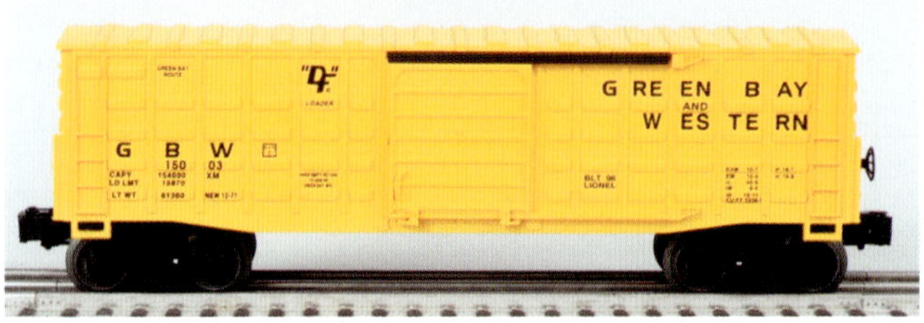

[15003] GREEN BAY AND WESTERN: 1996, waffle-side boxcar.

EX-C7	LN-C8	Scarcity
10	15	4

[15004] BLOOMINGDALES: 1997, uncataloged boxcar.

EX-C7	LN-C8	Scarcity
25	30	6

[15005] I LOVE NY: 1997, uncataloged boxcar.

EX-C7	LN-C8	Scarcity
40	50	6

15013 LOUISVILLE AND NASHVILLE: 2000, waffle-side boxcar numbered "102402."

EX-C7	LN-C8	Scarcity
15	20	4

15014 SEABOARD: 2000, waffle-side boxcar numbered "125925."

EX-C7	LN-C8	Scarcity
15	20	4

[16110] CIRCUS ANIMALS: 1989, uncataloged operating stock car numbered "1989" in the traditional 027/Scout size.

EX-C7	LN-C8	Scarcity
20	25	5

16121 CHICAGO & NORTHWESTERN: 1992, stock car, a Service Station Special item.

EX-C7	LN-C8	Scarcity
35	45	5

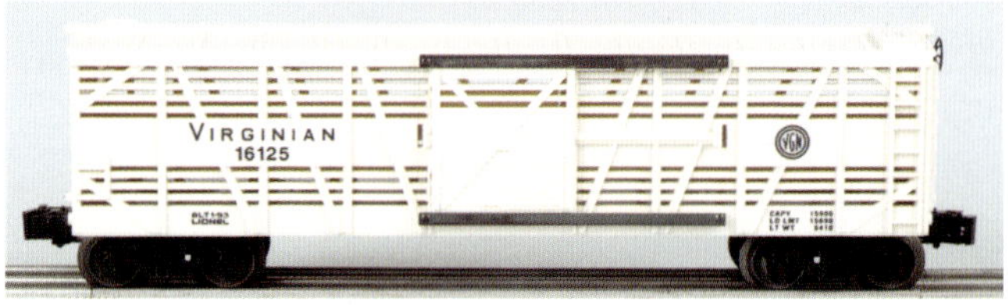

16125 VIRGINIAN: 1993, stock car.

EX-C7	LN-C8	Scarcity
10	15	4

16130 SOUTHERN PACIFIC: Uncataloged in 1993, cataloged in 1994, stock car in the traditional 027/Scout size.

EX-C7	LN-C8	Scarcity
4	8	3

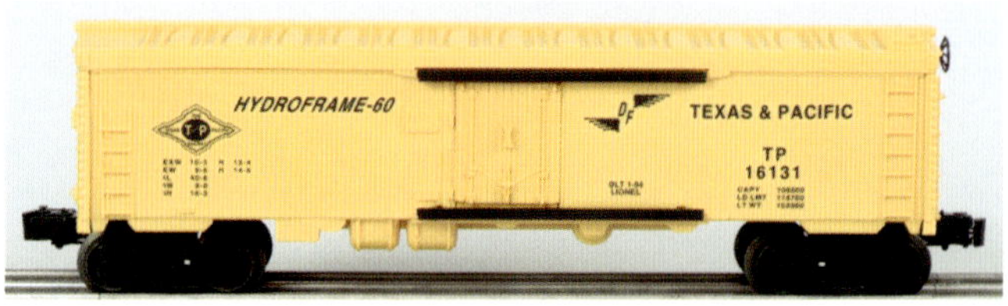

16131 TEXAS & PACIFIC: 1994, refrigerator car.

EX-C7	LN-C8	Scarcity
15	20	4

16133 SANTA FE: 1994, refrigerator car.

EX-C7	LN-C8	Scarcity
20	25	4

16134 READING: 1994, refrigerator car.

EX-C7	LN-C8	Scarcity
10	15	4

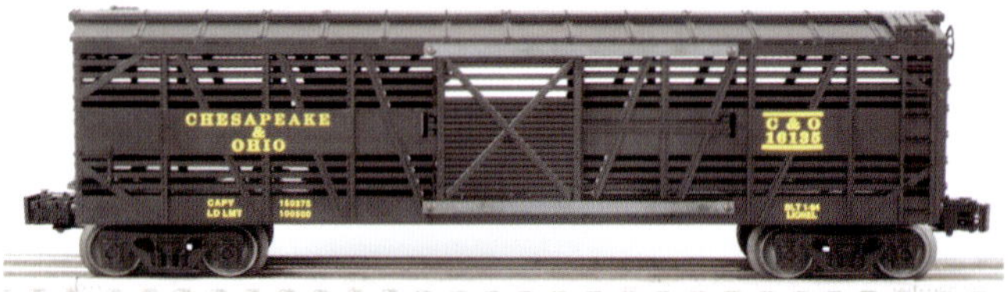

16135 CHESAPEAKE & OHIO: 1994, stock car.

EX-C7	LN-C8	Scarcity
15	20	4

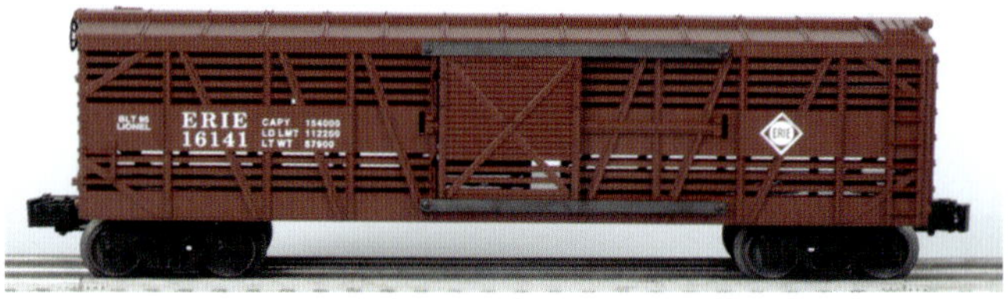

16141 ERIE: 1995, stock car.

EX-C7	LN-C8	Scarcity
15	20	4

16143 READING: 1995, refrigerator car.

EX-C7	LN-C8	Scarcity
15	20	4

16146 DAIRY DESPATCH: 1995, refrigerator car.

EX-C7	LN-C8	Scarcity
15	20	4

16200 ROCK ISLAND: 1987-88, boxcar in the traditional 027/Scout size.

EX-C7	LN-C8	Scarcity
4	8	2

16201 WABASH: 1988-91, boxcar in the traditional 027/Scout size.

EX-C7	LN-C8	Scarcity
4	8	2

16203 KEY AMERICA: 1987, uncataloged boxcar in the traditional 027/Scout size.

EX-C7	LN-C8	Scarcity
40	50	6

16204 HAWTHORNE: 1987, uncataloged boxcar in the traditional 027/Scout size.

EX-C7	LN-C8	Scarcity
60	70	6

[16205] MOPAR EXPRESS: 1987-88, uncataloged boxcar numbered "1987" in the traditional 027/Scout size.

EX-C7	LN-C8	Scarcity
35	45	6

16206 DENVER & RIO GRANDE WESTERN: 1989, boxcar, a Service Station Special item.

EX-C7	LN-C8	Scarcity
30	40	5

16207 TRUE VALUE: 1988, uncataloged boxcar in the traditional 027/Scout size.

EX-C7	LN-C8	Scarcity
30	40	6

16209 DISNEY MAGIC: 1988, uncataloged boxcar in the traditional 027/Scout size.

EX-C7	LN-C8	Scarcity
70	80	6

16211 HAWTHORNE: 1988, uncataloged boxcar in the traditional 027/Scout size.

EX-C7	LN-C8	Scarcity
40	50	6

16213 SHOPRITE: 1988, uncataloged boxcar in the traditional 027/Scout size.

EX-C7	LN-C8	Scarcity
50	65	6

16219 TRUE VALUE: 1989, uncataloged boxcar in the traditional 027/Scout size.

EX-C7	LN-C8	Scarcity
45	60	6

[16220] ACE HARDWARE: 1989, uncataloged boxcar in the traditional 027/Scout size.

EX-C7	LN-C8	Scarcity
45	60	6

[16221] MACY'S: 1989, uncataloged boxcar in the traditional 027/Scout size.

EX-C7	LN-C8	Scarcity
45	60	6

16222 GREAT NORTHERN: 1990-91, boxcar in the traditional 027/Scout size.

EX-C7	LN-C8	Scarcity
5	10	2

[16223] BUDWEISER: 1989-92, uncataloged refrigerator car.

EX-C7	LN-C8	Scarcity
25	30	5

16224 TRUE VALUE: 1990, uncataloged "Lawn Chief" boxcar in the traditional 027/Scout size.

EX-C7	LN-C8	Scarcity
40	50	6

[16226] UNION PACIFIC: 1990-91, uncataloged boxcar numbered "6226" in the traditional 027/Scout size.

EX-C7	LN-C8	Scarcity
10	15	5

16227 SANTA FE: 1991, boxcar in the traditional 027/Scout size.

EX-C7	LN-C8	Scarcity
8	12	3

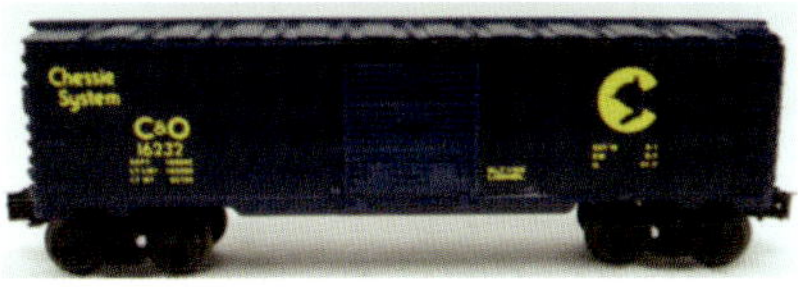

16232 CHESSIE SYSTEM: Cataloged in 1992, uncataloged in 1993, cataloged again in 1994, uncataloged again in 1995, boxcar.

EX-C7	LN-C8	Scarcity
15	20	4

16233 MISSOURI-KANSAS-TEXAS: 1992, boxcar.

EX-C7	LN-C8	Scarcity
15	20	4

16234 ACY: 1992, boxcar, Service Station Special item.

EX-C7	LN-C8	Scarcity
25	30	5

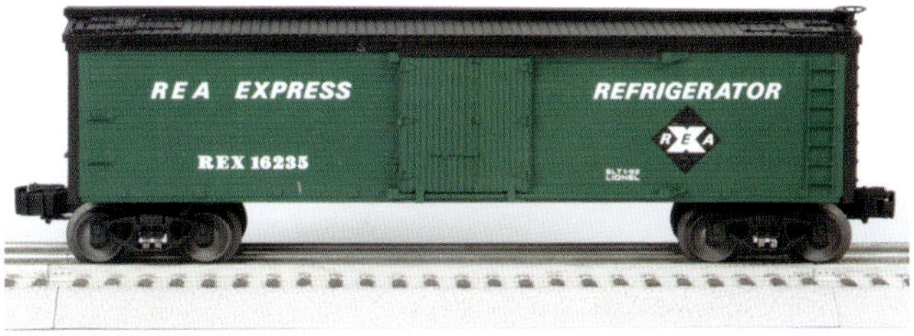

16235 RAILWAY EXPRESS AGENCY: 1992, refrigerator car.

EX-C7	LN-C8	Scarcity
20	25	4

16236 NEW YORK CENTRAL: 1992, uncataloged "Pacemaker" boxcar.

EX-C7	LN-C8	Scarcity
20	25	4

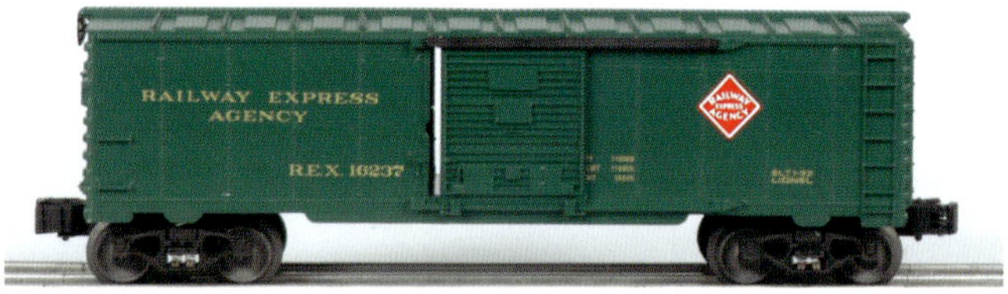

16237 RAILWAY EXPRESS AGENCY: 1992, uncataloged boxcar.

EX-C7	LN-C8	Scarcity
20	25	4

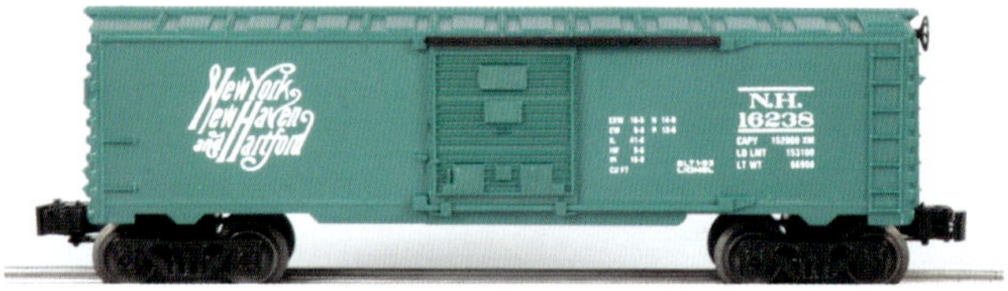

16238 NYNH & H: 1993-95, boxcar.

EX-C7	LN-C8	Scarcity
15	20	3

16239 UNION PACIFIC: 1993-95, boxcar.

EX-C7	LN-C8	Scarcity
15	20	3

16241 TOYS "R" US: 1992-93, uncataloged boxcar.

EX-C7	LN-C8	Scarcity
30	40	6

16243 CONRAIL: 1993, boxcar.

EX-C7	LN-C8	Scarcity
20	25	4

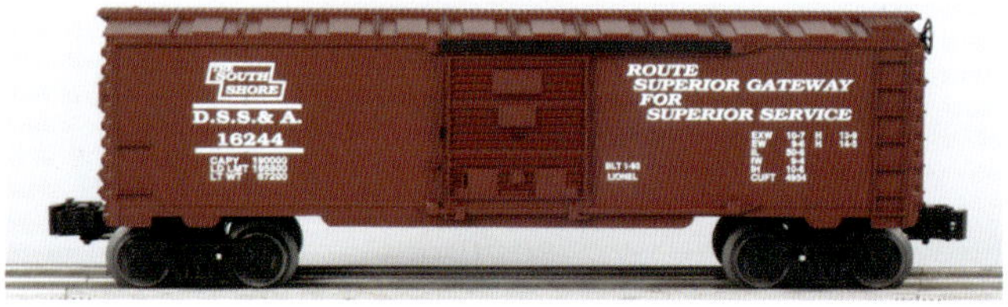

16244 DULUTH, SOUTH SHORE & ATLANTIC: 1993, boxcar.

EX-C7	LN-C8	Scarcity
15	20	3

16245 CONTADINA: 1993, boxcar.

EX-C7	LN-C8	Scarcity
15	20	3

16247 ATLANTIC COAST LINE: 1994, boxcar.

EX-C7	LN-C8	Scarcity
15	20	3

16248 BUDWEISER: 1993-94, uncataloged boxcar.

EX-C7	LN-C8	Scarcity
25	30	5

16249 UNITED AUTO WORKERS: 1993, uncataloged boxcar.

EX-C7	LN-C8	Scarcity
35	40	5

16250 SANTA FE: Uncataloged in 1993, cataloged in 1994, boxcar in the traditional 027/Scout size.

EX-C7	LN-C8	Scarcity
5	8	3

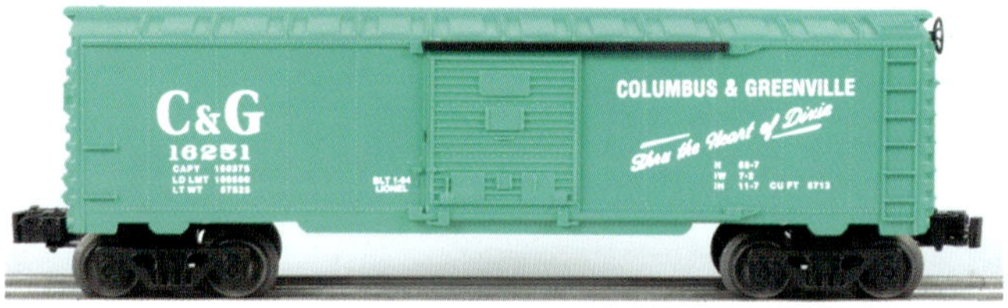

16251 COLUMBUS & GREENVILLE: 1994, boxcar.

EX-C7	LN-C8	Scarcity
5	10	3

[16252] U.S. NAVY: 1994-95, boxcar numbered "6106888."

EX-C7	LN-C8	Scarcity
15	20	4

16255 WABASH: 1995, double-door automobile boxcar.

EX-C7	LN-C8	Scarcity
15	20	4

16256 FORD: 1994, uncataloged double-door automobile boxcar.

EX-C7	LN-C8	Scarcity
20	25	6

[16257] CRAYOLA: Uncataloged in 1994, cataloged in 1995, boxcar.

EX-C7	LN-C8	Scarcity
10	15	3

16258 LEHIGH VALLEY: 1995, boxcar.

EX-C7	LN-C8	Scarcity
15	20	4

16259 CHRYSLER: 1997, uncataloged Mopar boxcar.

EX-C7	LN-C8	Scarcity
20	25	6

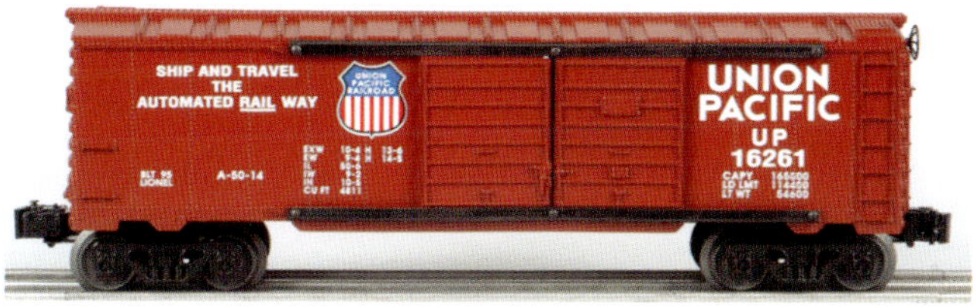

16261 UNION PACIFIC: 1995, double-door boxcar.

EX-C7	LN-C8	Scarcity
20	25	4

[16263] SANTA FE: 1996-99, boxcar.

EX-C7	LN-C8	Scarcity
15	20	4

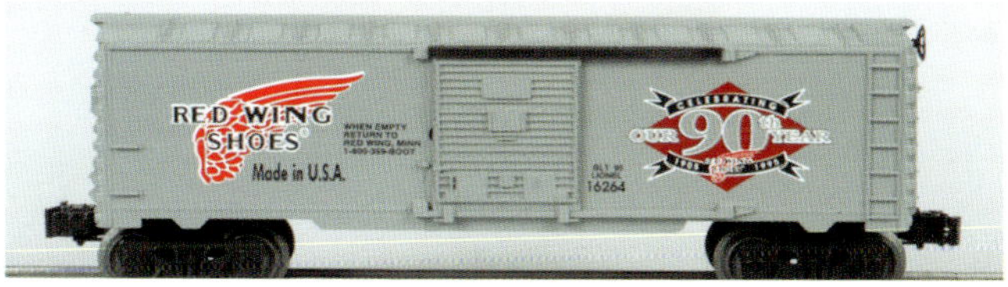

16264 RED WING SHOES: 1995, boxcar.

EX-C7	LN-C8	Scarcity
20	25	4

16265 GEORGIA POWER: 1995, uncataloged "Atlanta '96" boxcar.

EX-C7	LN-C8	Scarcity
150	175	6

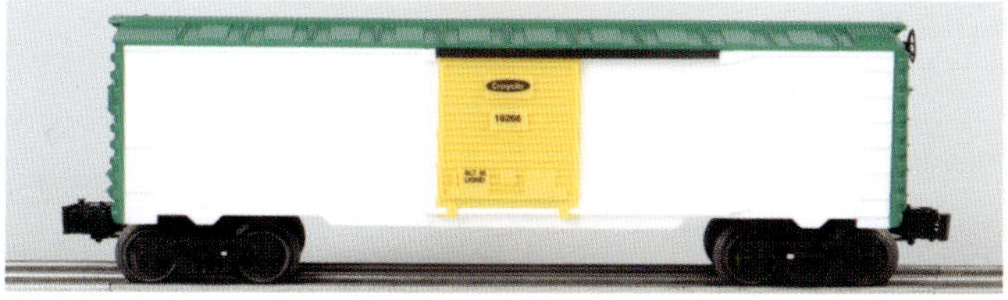

16266 CRAYOLA: 1995, boxcar.

EX-C7	LN-C8	Scarcity
15	20	4

16267 SEARS/ZENITH: 1995-96, uncataloged boxcar.

EX-C7	LN-C8	Scarcity
35	40	5

16268 GM/AC DELCO: 1995, uncataloged boxcar.

EX-C7	LN-C8	Scarcity
35	40	5

[16270] DEPT. 56: 1996, uncataloged boxcar numbered "9746."

EX-C7	LN-C8	Scarcity
45	55	5

[16272] 1997 CHRISTMAS: 1997, boxcar numbered "9700."

EX-C7	LN-C8	Scarcity
25	30	4

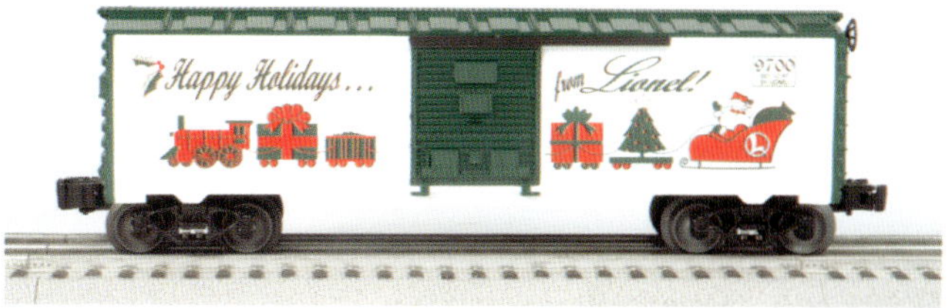

[16273] 1997 CHRISTMAS: 1997, boxcar numbered "9700."

EX-C7	LN-C8	Scarcity
25	30	4

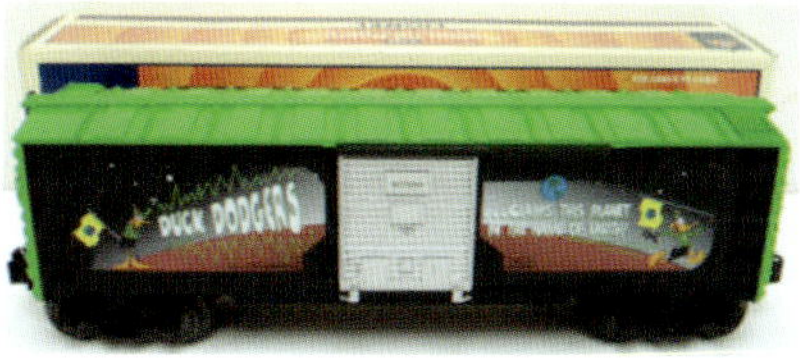

[16274] MARVIN THE MARTIAN: 1997, boxcar numbered "9700."

EX-C7	LN-C8	Scarcity
25	30	4

16275 EASTWOOD RADIO FLYER: 1996, boxcar numbered "16275."

EX-C7	LN-C8	Scarcity
Too rarely traded to establish accurate pricing.		

[16279] DODGE MOTORSPORTS: 1996, uncataloged boxcar.

EX-C7	LN-C8	Scarcity
100	125	6

[16281] MACGREGOR LITTLE LEAGUE BASEBALL: Boxcar was part of the Lionel Little League set.

EX-C7	LN-C8	Scarcity
30	60	6

[16284] GALVESTON WHARVES: 1998, boxcar numbered "9700."

EX-C7	LN-C8	Scarcity
15	20	4

[16285] SAVANNAH STATE DOCKS: 1998, boxcar numbered "9700."

EX-C7	LN-C8	Scarcity
15	20	4

[16291] 1998 CHRISTMAS: 1998, boxcar.

EX-C7	LN-C8	Scarcity
30	35	4

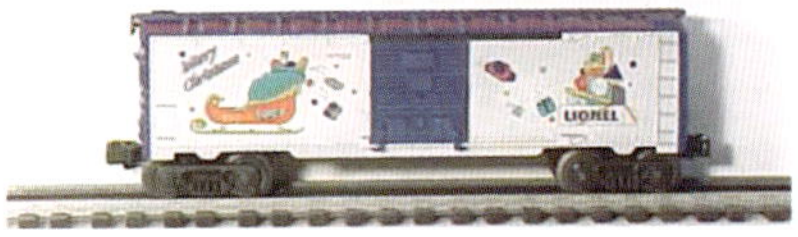

[16292] LIONEL CHRISTMAS: 1998, employee boxcar numbered "9700."

EX-C7	LN-C8	Scarcity
275	325	7

[16293] JCPENNEY: 1997, boxcar.

EX-C7	LN-C8	Scarcity
75	100	5

[16294] PEDIGREE: 1997, boxcar.

EX-C7	LN-C8	Scarcity
85	110	5

[16295] KAL KAN: 1997, boxcar.

EX-C7	LN-C8	Scarcity
85	110	5

[16296] WHISKAS: 1997, boxcar.

EX-C7	LN-C8	Scarcity
85	110	5

[16297] SHEBA: 1997, boxcar.

EX-C7	LN-C8	Scarcity
85	110	5

[16298] MOBIL: 1997, boxcar numbered "9700."

EX-C7	LN-C8	Scarcity
20	25	6

16603 DETROIT ZOO: 1987, giraffe car in the traditional 027/Scout size.

16603 DETROIT ZOO (Type I): Equipped with a single operating coupler, and a non-operating coupler.

EX-C7	LN-C8	Scarcity
30	35	4

16603 DETROIT ZOO (Type II): Equipped with two operating couplers.

EX-C7	LN-C8	Scarcity
30	35	4

16605 BRONX ZOO: 1988, giraffe car in the traditional 027/Scout size.

EX-C7	LN-C8	Scarcity
30	35	4

16614 READING: 1989, cop and hobo car in the traditional 027/Scout size.

EX-C7	LN-C8	Scarcity
20	25	4

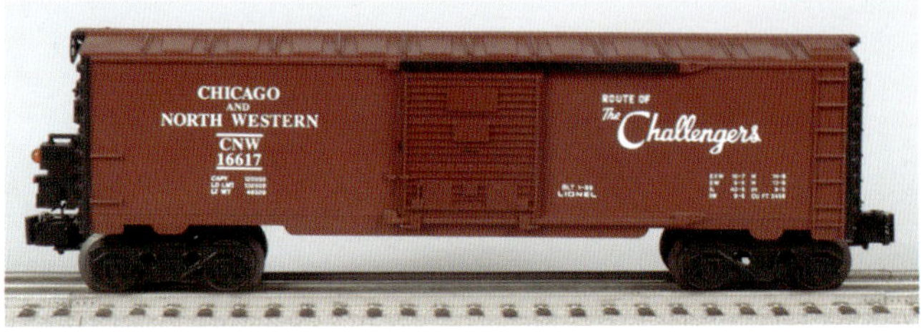

16617 CHICAGO AND NORTHWESTERN: 1989, boxcar with end of train device (ETD).

EX-C7	LN-C8	Scarcity
20	25	4

16622 CSX: 1990-91, boxcar with end of train device (ETD).

EX-C7	LN-C8	Scarcity
15	20	4

16623 MISSOURI-KANSAS-TEXAS: 1991, double-door boxcar with end of train device (ETD).

EX-C7	LN-C8	Scarcity
15	20	4

16624 NEW HAVEN: 1990-91, cop and hobo car in the traditional 027/Scout size.

EX-C7	LN-C8	Scarcity
20	25	4

16629 "ANIMAL CAR" CIRCUS: 1990-91, elephant car in the traditional 027/Scout size.

EX-C7	LN-C8	Scarcity
35	40	5

16630 SOUTHERN PACIFIC: 1990-91, operating cowboy car in the traditional 027/Scout size.

EX-C7	LN-C8	Scarcity
15	20	4

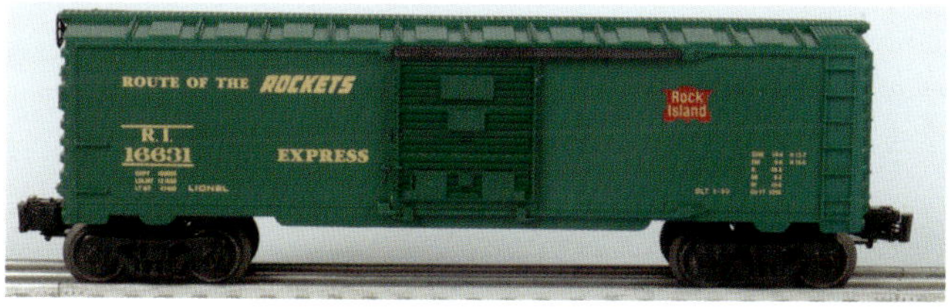

16631 ROCK ISLAND: 1990, boxcar with steam RailSounds.

EX-C7	LN-C8	Scarcity
80	100	5

16632 BURLINGTON NORTHERN: 1990, boxcar with diesel RailSounds.

EX-C7	LN-C8	Scarcity
80	100	5

16633 GREAT NORTHERN: 1991, cop and hobo car in the traditional 027/Scout size.

EX-C7	LN-C8	Scarcity
Cataloged, but not produced.		

16638 LIONELVILLE CIRCUS: 1991, operating animal car in the traditional 027/Scout size.

EX-C7	LN-C8	Scarcity
45	50	5

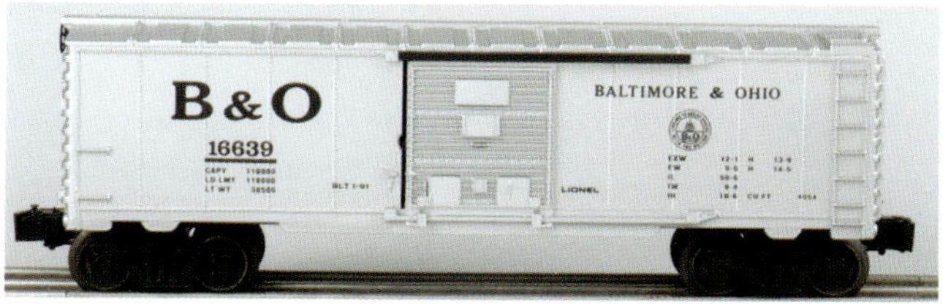

16639 BALTIMORE & OHIO: 1991, boxcar with steam RailSounds.

EX-C7	LN-C8	Scarcity
80	100	5

16640 RUTLAND: 1991, boxcar with diesel RailSounds.

EX-C7	LN-C8	Scarcity
80	100	5

16641 TOYS "R" US: 1990-91, uncataloged giraffe car in the traditional 027/Scout size.

EX-C7	LN-C8	Scarcity
40	50	6

16642 MICKEY'S WORLD TOUR GOOFY: 1991 and 1992, uncataloged car in the traditional 027/Scout size.

EX-C7	LN-C8	Scarcity
35	40	5

16646 RAILBOX: 1992, boxcar with end of train device (ETD).

EX-C7	LN-C8	Scarcity
Cataloged, but not produced.		

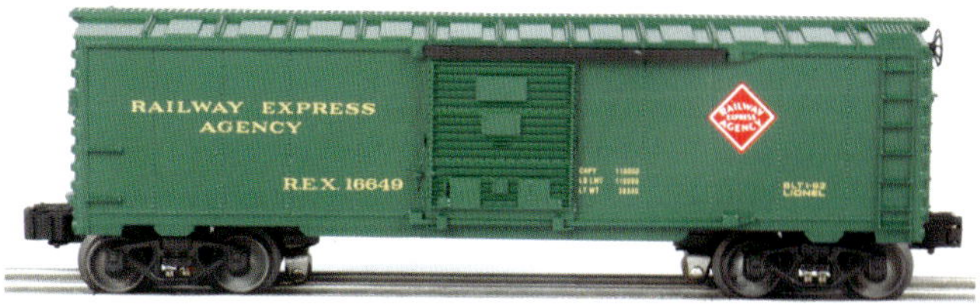

16649 RAILWAY EXPRESS AGENCY: 1992, boxcar with steam RailSounds.

EX-C7	LN-C8	Scarcity
80	110	4

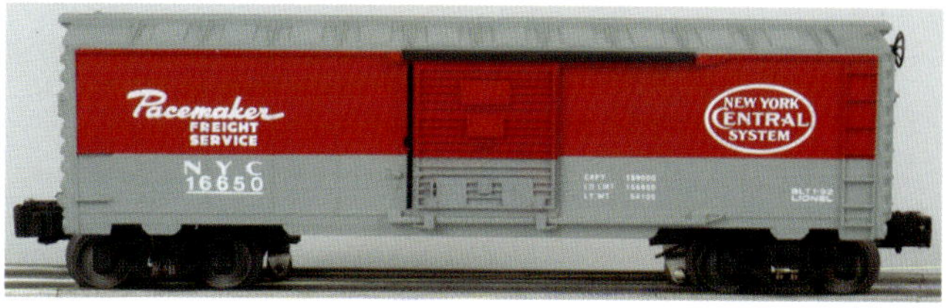

16650 NEW YORK CENTRAL: 1992, "Pacemaker" boxcar with diesel RailSounds.

EX-C7	LN-C8	Scarcity
80	110	4

16651 CIRCUS: 1992, operating clown car in the traditional 027/Scout size.

EX-C7	LN-C8	Scarcity
25	30	4

16662 LOONEY TUNES OPERATING BUGS BUNNY AND YOSEMITE SAM: 1993-94, car in the traditional 027/Scout size.

EX-C7	LN-C8	Scarcity
20	25	4

16679 U.S. MAIL: 1994, operating boxcar.

EX-C7	LN-C8	Scarcity
35	40	4

16681 AQUARIUM: 1995.

EX-C7	LN-C8	Scarcity
35	40	4

16682 LIONELVILLE FARMS: 1994, operating stock car in the traditional 027/Scout size.

EX-C7	LN-C8	Scarcity
15	20	4

16683 LOS ANGELES ZOO: 1994, elephant car in the traditional 027/Scout size.

EX-C7	LN-C8	Scarcity
15	20	4

16686 MICKEY MOUSE AND BIG BAD PETE: 1995, animated boxcar.

EX-C7	LN-C8	Scarcity
25	30	4

16687 U.S. MAIL: 1994, operating boxcar.

EX-C7	LN-C8	Scarcity
30	35	4

16690 LOONEY TUNES: 1994, operating Bugs Bunny and Yosemite Sam car in the traditional 027/Scout size.

EX-C7	LN-C8	Scarcity
25	30	4

16701 SOUTHERN: 1987, tool car, Service Station Special item.

EX-C7	LN-C8	Scarcity
35	45	4

16702 AMTRAK: 1991 and 1992, uncataloged bunk car.

EX-C7	LN-C8	Scarcity
20	25	4

16703 NEW YORK CENTRAL: 1992, tool car.

EX-C7	LN-C8	Scarcity
15	20	4

16705 CHESAPEAKE AND OHIO: 1995, cop and hobo car.

EX-C7	LN-C8	Scarcity
20	25	4

16706 ANIMAL TRANSPORT SERVICE: 1995, giraffe car.

EX-C7	LN-C8	Scarcity
20	25	4

[16719] EXPLODING: 1996, boxcar.

EX-C7	LN-C8	Scarcity
20	25	4

[16725] RHINO TRANSPORT: 1997, car.

EX-C7	LN-C8	Scarcity
15	20	4

[16738] WARNER BROS: 1996, Pepe Le Pew and Penelope boxcar numbered "3370."

EX-C7	LN-C8	Scarcity
25	30	4

[16739] WARNER BROS: 1996, Foghorn Leghorn poultry car numbered "6434."

EX-C7	LN-C8	Scarcity
30	35	4

[16740] LIONEL CORPORATION: 1996, mail car numbered "3428."

EX-C7	LN-C8	Scarcity
30	35	4

[16741] UNION PACIFIC: 1997, illuminated bunk car.

EX-C7	LN-C8	Scarcity
15	20	4

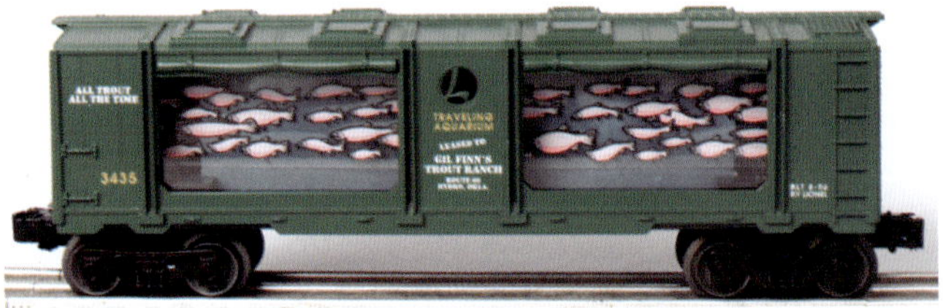

[16742] TROUT RANCH: 1996, aquarium car numbered "3435."

EX-C7	LN-C8	Scarcity
30	35	4

[16747] BREYER: 1997, animated horse car numbered "6473."

EX-C7	LN-C8	Scarcity
15	20	4

[16750] LIONEL CITY: 1997, aquarium car numbered "3436."

EX-C7	LN-C8	Scarcity
15	20	4

[16767] NEW YORK CENTRAL: 1998, Ice Docks ice car numbered "6352."

EX-C7	LN-C8	Scarcity
30	35	4

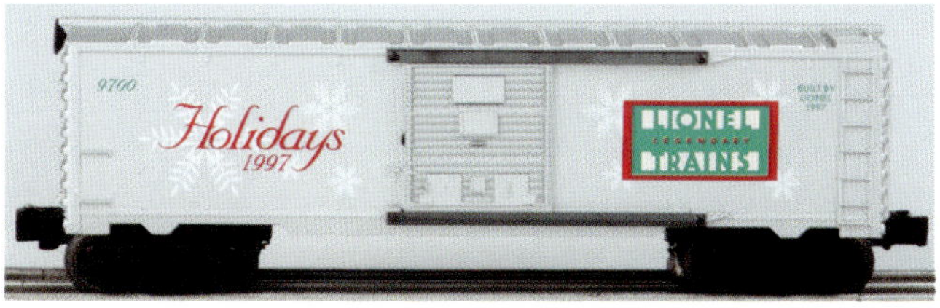

[16776] LIONEL: 1998, holiday RailSounds boxcar.

EX-C7	LN-C8	Scarcity
65	85	4

[16777] LIONEL COLA: 1998, animated car and platform.

EX-C7	LN-C8	Scarcity
65	85	4

[16785] HAPPY HOLIDAYS MUSIC: 1999, refrigerator car numbered "5700."

EX-C7	LN-C8	Scarcity
90	110	5

[16789] EASTER: 1999, operating boxcar numbered "9700."

EX-C7	LN-C8	Scarcity
25	30	4

[16790] UNION PACIFIC: 1999, cowsounds stock car numbered "3356."

EX-C7	LN-C8	Scarcity
65	85	4

[16791] NY CITY LIGHTS: 1999, boxcar numbered "9700."

EX-C7	LN-C8	Scarcity
30	35	4

[16792] CONSTELLATION: 1999, boxcar numbered "9600."

EX-C7	LN-C8	Scarcity
30	35	4

[16793] ANIMATED GLOW-IN-THE-DARK ALIEN: 1999, boxcar numbered "9700."

EX-C7	LN-C8	Scarcity
30	35	4

[16794] WICKED WITCH HALLOWEEN: 1999, boxcar numbered "9700."

EX-C7	LN-C8	Scarcity
25	30	4

[16796] SNOWMAN: 1999, loading ice car numbered "6352."

EX-C7	LN-C8	Scarcity
35	45	4

16801 LIONEL RAILROADER CLUB: 1988, uncataloged bunk car.

EX-C7	LN-C8	Scarcity
35	45	6

16802 LIONEL RAILROADER CLUB: 1989, uncataloged tool car.

EX-C7	LN-C8	Scarcity
20	25	6

[16805] BUDWEISER: 1991-92, uncataloged Malt Nutrine refrigerator car numbered "3285."

EX-C7	LN-C8	Scarcity
60	80	5

16806 TOYS "R" US: 1992, uncataloged boxcar.

EX-C7	LN-C8	Scarcity
20	25	5

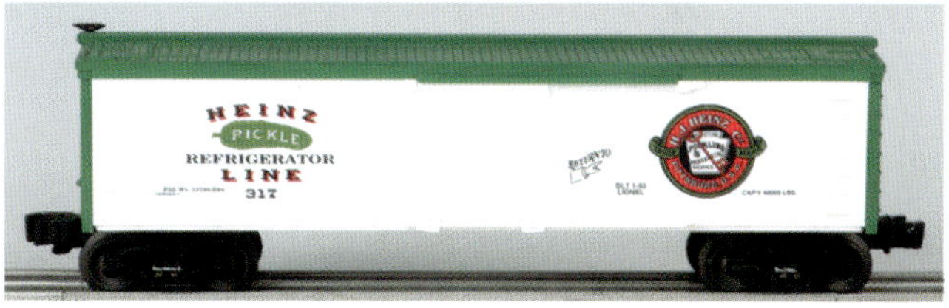

[16807] H.J. HEINZ: 1993, refrigerator car numbered "301."

EX-C7	LN-C8	Scarcity
15	20	4

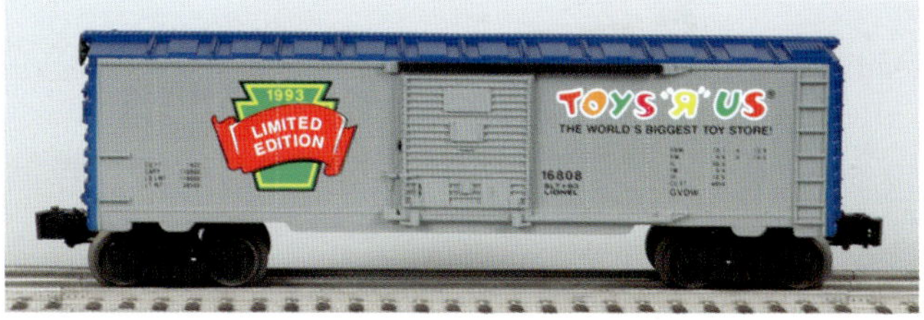

16808 TOYS "R" US: 1993, uncataloged boxcar.

EX-C7	LN-C8	Scarcity
25	30	4

16811 RUTLAND: 1996, boxcar TCA.

EX-C7	LN-C8	Scarcity
40	60	5

[16820] AMBASSADOR THANK YOU: 2000, uncataloged boxcar numbered "2000."

EX-C7	LN-C8	Scarcity
250	300	6

17200 SANTA FE: 1990, boxcar with diesel RailSounds with 1/48-scale proportions.

EX-C7	LN-C8	Scarcity
70	80	4

17203 COTTON BELT: 1991, double-door boxcar with 1/48-scale proportions.

EX-C7	LN-C8	Scarcity
25	30	4

17204 MISSOURI PACIFIC: 1991, double-door boxcar with 1/48-scale proportions.

EX-C7	LN-C8	Scarcity
25	30	4

17207 CHICAGO & ILLINOIS MIDLAND: 1992, double-door boxcar with 1/48-scale proportions.

EX-C7	LN-C8	Scarcity
25	30	4

17208 UNION PACIFIC: 1992, double-door boxcar with 1/48-scale proportions.

EX-C7	LN-C8	Scarcity
20	25	4

[17209] BALTIMORE AND OHIO: 1993, double-door boxcar numbered "296000" with 1/48-scale proportions.

EX-C7	LN-C8	Scarcity
30	35	4

[17210] CHICAGO & ILLINOIS MIDLAND: 1992, uncataloged boxcar numbered "16021" with 1/48-scale proportions.

EX-C7	LN-C8	Scarcity
30	35	4

[17211] CHICAGO & ILLINOIS MIDLAND: 1992, uncataloged boxcar numbered "16022" with 1/48-scale proportions.

EX-C7	LN-C8	Scarcity
30	35	4

[17212] CHICAGO & ILLINOIS MIDLAND: 1992, uncataloged boxcar numbered "16023" with 1/48-scale proportions.

EX-C7	LN-C8	Scarcity
20	25	4

[17213] SUSQUEHANNA: 1993, boxcar numbered "501" with 1/48-scale proportions.

EX-C7	LN-C8	Scarcity
20	25	4

17214 RAILBOX: 1993, boxcar with diesel RailSounds with 1/48-scale proportions.

EX-C7	LN-C8	Scarcity
70	80	5

[17216] PENNSYLVANIA: 1994, double-door boxcar numbered "60155" with 1/48-scale proportions.

EX-C7	LN-C8	Scarcity
30	35	4

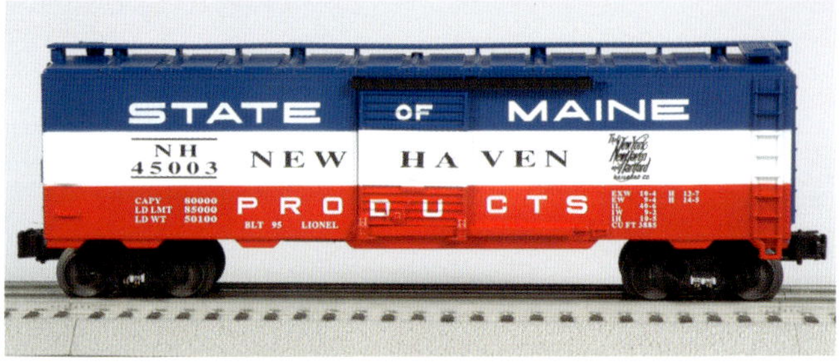

[17217] NEW HAVEN: 1995, "State of Maine" boxcar numbered "45003" with 1/48-scale proportions.

EX-C7	LN-C8	Scarcity
20	25	4

[17218] BANGOR AND AROOSTOOK: 1995, "State of Maine" boxcar numbered "2184" with 1/48-scale proportions.

EX-C7	LN-C8	Scarcity
20	25	4

17219 TAZMANIAN DEVIL 40TH BIRTHDAY: 1995, boxcar with 1/48-scale proportions.

EX-C7	LN-C8	Scarcity
25	30	5

17220 PENNSYLVANIA: 1996, boxcar with 1/48-scale proportions.

EX-C7	LN-C8	Scarcity
25	30	4

17221 NEW YORK CENTRAL: 1996, boxcar with 1/48-scale proportions.

EX-C7	LN-C8	Scarcity
25	30	4

17222 WESTERN PACIFIC: 1996, boxcar with 1/48-scale proportions.

EX-C7	LN-C8	Scarcity
25	30	4

[17223] MILWAUKEE ROAD: 1996, double-door boxcar with 1/48-scale proportions.

EX-C7	LN-C8	Scarcity
25	30	4

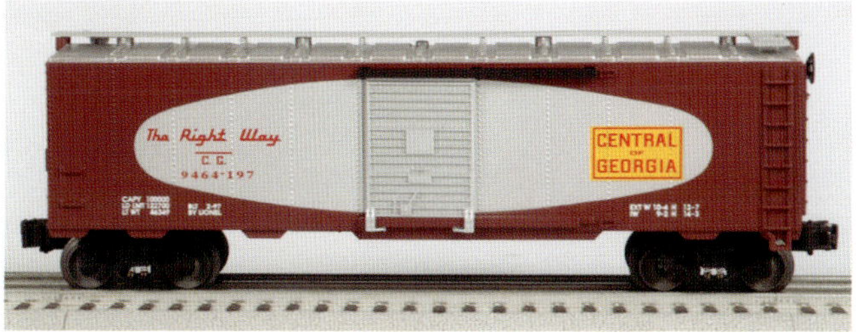

[17224] CENTRAL OF GEORGIA: 1997, boxcar numbered "9464-197" with 1/48-scale proportions.

EX-C7	LN-C8	Scarcity
15	20	4

[17225] PENN CENTRAL: 1997, boxcar numbered "9464-297" with 1/48-scale proportions.

EX-C7	LN-C8	Scarcity
15	20	4

[17226] MILWAUKEE ROAD: 1997, boxcar numbered "9464-397" with 1/48-scale proportions.

EX-C7	LN-C8	Scarcity
25	30	4

[17227] UNION PACIFIC: 1997, double-door boxcar numbered "9200" with 1/48-scale proportions.

EX-C7	LN-C8	Scarcity
25	30	4

[17231] WISCONSIN CENTRAL: 1998, double-door boxcar with Auto Frames numbered "9200" with 1/48-scale proportions.

EX-C7	LN-C8	Scarcity
25	30	4

[17232] SOUTHERN PACIFIC/UNION PACIFIC: 1998, Merger double-door boxcar numbered "9200" with 1/48-scale proportions.

EX-C7	LN-C8	Scarcity
25	30	4

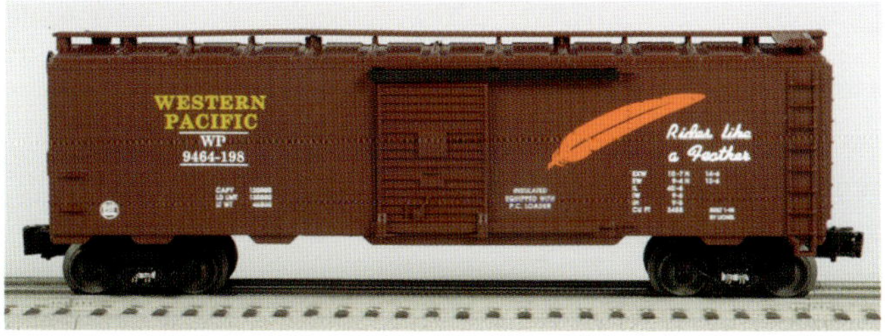

[17233] WESTERN PACIFIC: 1998, "9464-198" boxcar with 1/48-scale proportions.

EX-C7	LN-C8	Scarcity
15	20	4

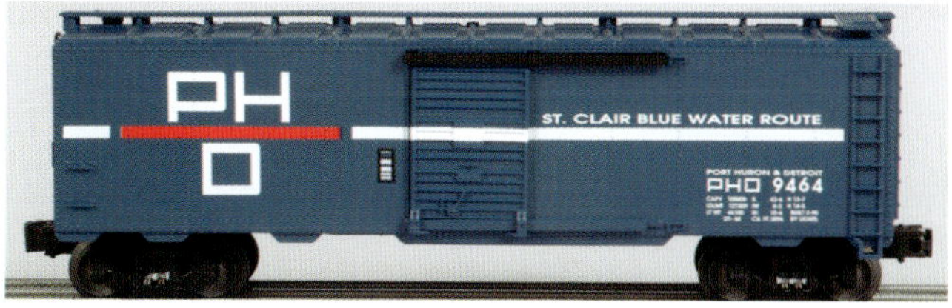

17234 PORT HURON & DETROIT (Type I): 1998, boxcar numbered "9464-298" with 1/48-scale proportions.

EX-C7	LN-C8	Scarcity
25	30	4

17234 PORT HURON & DETROIT (Type II): 1999, numbered "9464-298," LCCA/LOTS boxcar with 1/48-scale proportions.

EX-C7	LN-C8	Scarcity
35	45	6

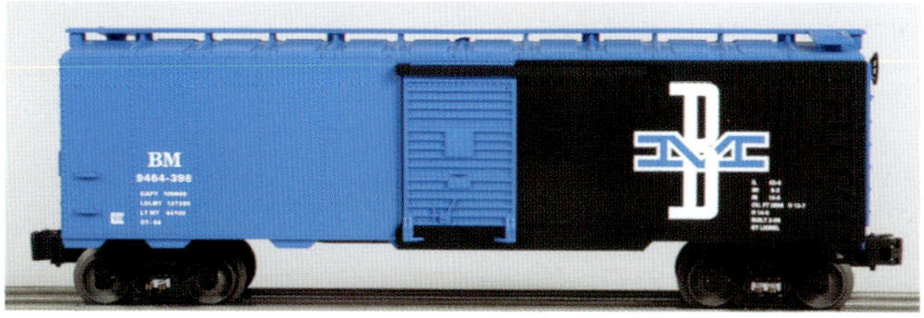

[17235] BOSTON AND MAINE: 1998, numbered "9464-398," boxcar with 1/48-scale proportions.

EX-C7	LN-C8	Scarcity
25	30	4

[17239] SANTA FE: 1997, numbered "9464-1," Texas Chief boxcar with 1/48-scale proportions.

EX-C7	LN-C8	Scarcity
30	35	4

[17240] SANTA FE: 1997, numbered "9464-2," Super Chief boxcar with 1/48-scale proportions.

EX-C7	LN-C8	Scarcity
30	35	4

[17241] SANTA FE: 1997, numbered "9464-3," El Capitan boxcar with 1/48-scale proportions.

EX-C7	LN-C8	Scarcity
30	35	4

[17242] SANTA FE: 1997, numbered "9464-4," Grand Canyon boxcar with 1/48-scale proportions.

EX-C7	LN-C8	Scarcity
40	50	5

[17243] NORTHERN PACIFIC: 1998, boxcar, numbered "8722."

EX-C7	LN-C8	Scarcity
30	35	4

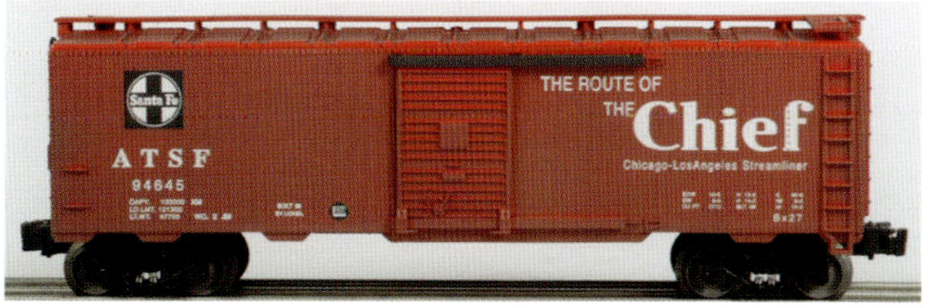

[17244] SANTA FE: 1998, Chief boxcar.

EX-C7	LN-C8	Scarcity
25	30	4

[17245] CHESAPEAKE AND OHIO: 1998, boxcar with Chessie Kitten.

EX-C7	LN-C8	Scarcity
30	35	4

[17246] NEW YORK CENTRAL: 1998, Pacemaker Rolling Stock, four-pack.

EX-C7	LN-C8	Scarcity
160	180	4

[17247] NEW YORK CENTRAL: 1998, numbered "174940," 9464 boxcar with 1/48-scale proportions.

EX-C7	LN-C8	Scarcity
80	90	4

[17248] NEW YORK CENTRAL: 1998, numbered "174945," 9464 boxcar with 1/48-scale proportions.

EX-C7	LN-C8	Scarcity
80	90	4

[17249] NEW YORK CENTRAL: 1998, numbered "174949," 9464 boxcar with 1/48-scale proportions.

EX-C7	LN-C8	Scarcity
80	90	4

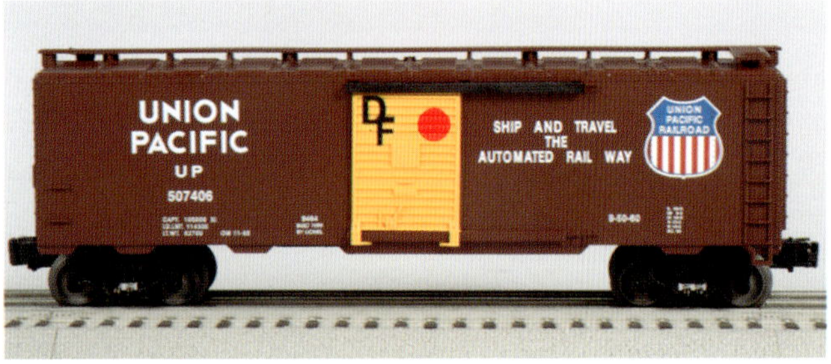

[17250] UNION PACIFIC: 1999, numbered "507406," boxcar with 1/48-scale proportions.

EX-C7	LN-C8	Scarcity
30	35	4

[17251] BNSF: 1999, numbered "103277," boxcar with 1/48-scale proportions.

EX-C7	LN-C8	Scarcity
25	30	4

[17252] NORFOLK SOUTHERN: 1999, numbered "564824," boxcar with 1/48-scale proportions.

EX-C7	LN-C8	Scarcity
25	30	4

[17253] CSX: 1999, numbered "141756," boxcar with 1/48-scale proportions.

EX-C7	LN-C8	Scarcity
25	30	4

[17254] UNION PACIFIC: 1999, boxcar numbered "551967" with 1/48-scale proportions.

EX-C7	LN-C8	Scarcity
30	35	4

[17255] CHEVROLET: 1999, double-door boxcar numbered "9200" with 1/48-scale proportions.

EX-C7	LN-C8	Scarcity
30	35	4

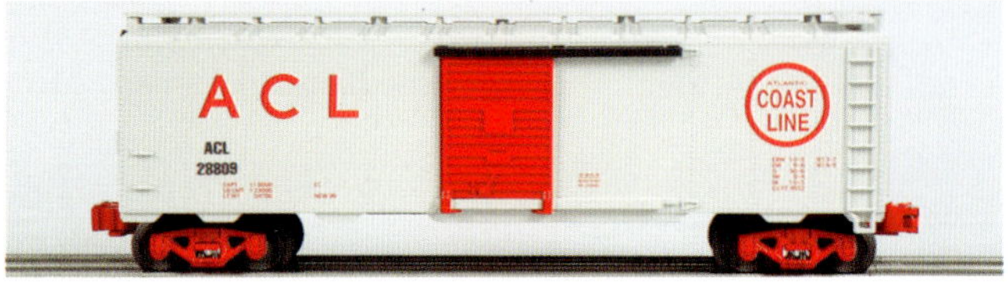

[17257] ATLANTIC COAST LINE: 1999, 9464 boxcar numbered "28809" with 1/48-scale proportions.

EX-C7	LN-C8	Scarcity
25	30	4

[17258] DELAWARE AND HUDSON: 1999, 9464 boxcar numbered "29055" with 1/48-scale proportions.

EX-C7	LN-C8	Scarcity
30	35	4

[17259] MISSOURI-KANSAS-TEXAS: 1999, 9464 boxcar numbered "1422" with 1/48-scale proportions.

EX-C7	LN-C8	Scarcity
30	35	4

[17260] CP RAIL: 2000, 9464 boxcar numbered "286138" with 1/48-scale proportions.

EX-C7	LN-C8	Scarcity
30	35	4

[17261] CP RAIL: 2000, 9464 green boxcar numbered "85154" with 1/48-scale proportions.

EX-C7	LN-C8	Scarcity
30	35	4

[17262] CP RAIL: 2000, 9464 red boxcar numbered "56776" with 1/48-scale proportions.

EX-C7	LN-C8	Scarcity
30	35	4

[17263] NEW YORK CENTRAL: 2000, modern boxcar numbered "45725" with 1/48-scale proportions.

EX-C7	LN-C8	Scarcity
25	30	4

[17264] CHESAPEAKE AND OHIO: 2000, modern boxcar numbered "6054" with 1/48-scale proportions.

EX-C7	LN-C8	Scarcity
25	30	4

[17265] U.S. ARMY: 2000, boxcar, with 1/48-scale proportions.

EX-C7	LN-C8	Scarcity
25	30	4

[17266] MONON: 2000, boxcar numbered "911" with 1/48-scale proportions.

EX-C7	LN-C8	Scarcity
25	30	4

17300 CANADIAN PACIFIC: 1989, refrigerator car with 1/48-scale proportions.

EX-C7	LN-C8	Scarcity
25	30	4

17301 CONRAIL: 1987, refrigerator car with 1/48-scale proportions.

EX-C7	LN-C8	Scarcity
25	30	4

17302 SANTA FE: 1990, refrigerator car with end of train device (ETD) with 1/48-scale proportions.

EX-C7	LN-C8	Scarcity
30	35	4

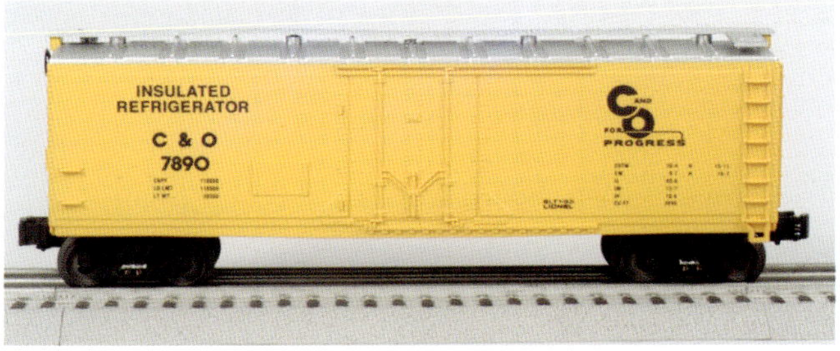

[17303] CHESAPEAKE & OHIO: 1993, refrigerator car numbered "7890" with 1/48-scale proportions.

EX-C7	LN-C8	Scarcity
25	30	4

[17304] WABASH: 1994, refrigerator car numbered "26269" with 1/48-scale proportions.

EX-C7	LN-C8	Scarcity
25	30	4

[17305] PACIFIC FRUIT EXPRESS: 1994, refrigerator car numbered "459400" with 1/48-scale proportions.

EX-C7	LN-C8	Scarcity
25	30	4

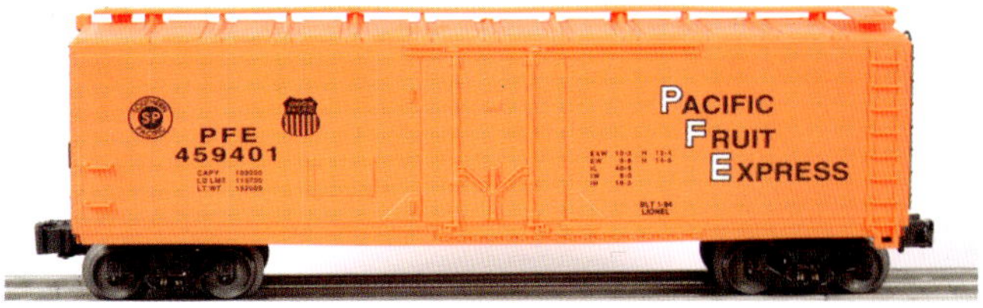

[17306] PACIFIC FRUIT EXPRESS: 1994, refrigerator car numbered "459401" with 1/48-scale proportions.

EX-C7	LN-C8	Scarcity
20	25	4

[17307] TROPICANA: 1995, refrigerator car numbered "300" with 1/48-scale proportions.

EX-C7	LN-C8	Scarcity
25	30	4

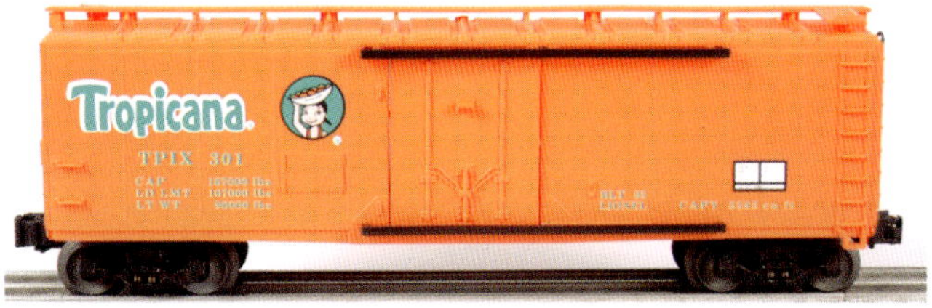

[17308] TROPICANA: 1995, refrigerator car numbered "301" with 1/48-scale proportions.

EX-C7	LN-C8	Scarcity
25	30	4

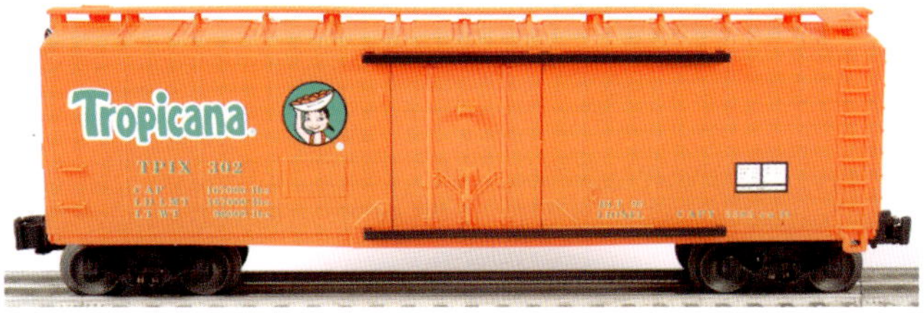

[17309] TROPICANA: 1995, refrigerator car numbered "302" with 1/48-scale proportions.

EX-C7	LN-C8	Scarcity
25	30	4

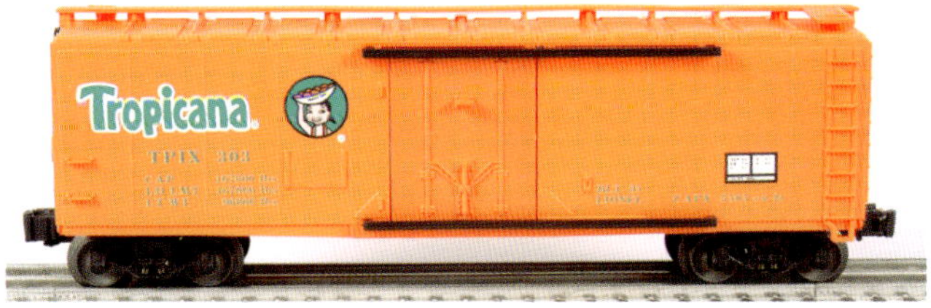

[17310] TROPICANA: 1995, refrigerator car numbered "303" with 1/48-scale proportions.

EX-C7	LN-C8	Scarcity
25	30	4

17311 RAILWAY EXPRESS AGENCY: 1996, refrigerator car with 1/48-scale proportions.

EX-C7	LN-C8	Scarcity
25	30	4

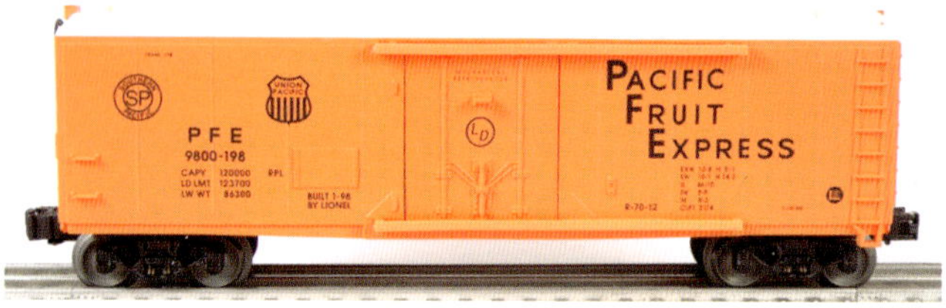

[17314] PACIFIC FRUIT EXPRESS: 1998, numbered "9800-198," refrigerator car with 1/48-scale proportions.

EX-C7	LN-C8	Scarcity
25	30	4

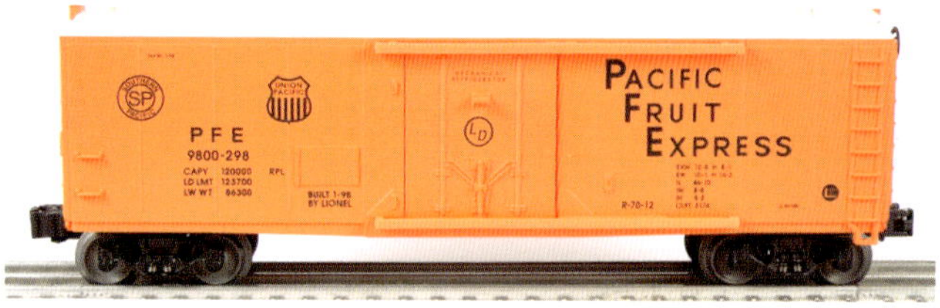

[17315] PACIFIC FRUIT EXPRESS: 1998, numbered "9800-298," refrigerator car with 1/48-scale proportions.

EX-C7	LN-C8	Scarcity
25	30	4

[17316] NORTHERN PACIFIC: 1998, numbered "98583," refrigerator car with 1/48-scale proportions.

EX-C7	LN-C8	Scarcity
35	40	4

[17317] PENNSYLVANIA: 1996, FGE numbered "91904," refrigerator car with 1/48-scale proportions.

EX-C7	LN-C8	Scarcity
30	35	4

[17318] UNION PACIFIC: 1999, numbered "170650," refrigerator car with 1/48-scale proportions.

EX-C7	LN-C8	Scarcity
40	45	4

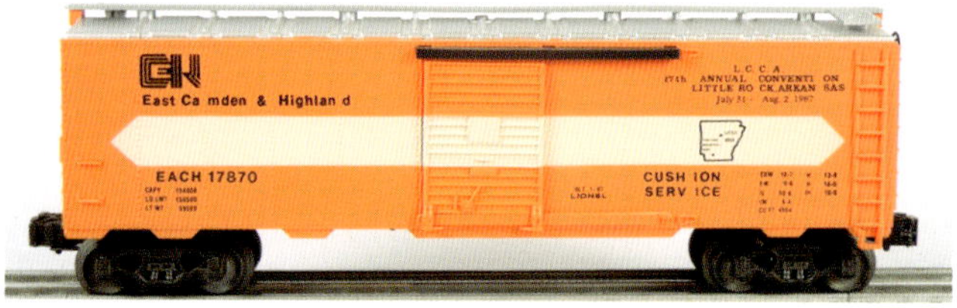

17870 EAST CAMDEN & HIGHLAND: 1987, uncataloged LCCA boxcar with 1/48-scale proportions.

EX-C7	LN-C8	Scarcity
30	35	4

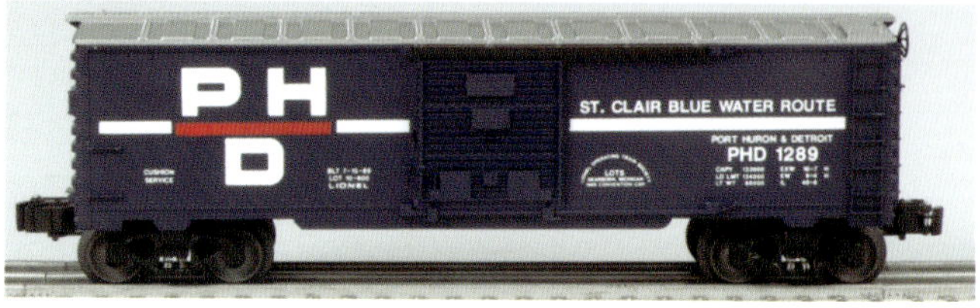

[17875] PHD: 1989, uncataloged LOTS boxcar numbered "1289."

EX-C7	LN-C8	Scarcity
45	55	6

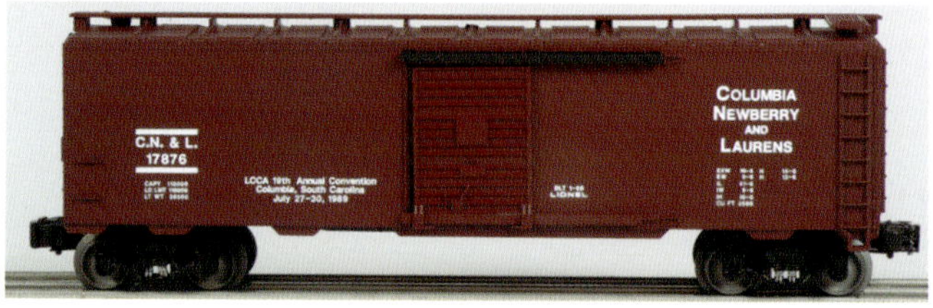

17876 COLUMBIA NEWBERRY & LAURENS: 1989, uncataloged LCCA boxcar with 1/48-scale proportions.

EX-C7	LN-C8	Scarcity
30	35	6

[17882] BALTIMORE & OHIO: 1990, uncataloged LOTS double-door boxcar with end of train device (ETD) numbered "298011."

EX-C7	LN-C8	Scarcity
45	55	6

17884 COLUMBUS & DAYTON TERMINAL: 1990, uncataloged TTOS boxcar with 1/48-scale proportions.

EX-C7	LN-C8	Scarcity
30	40	6

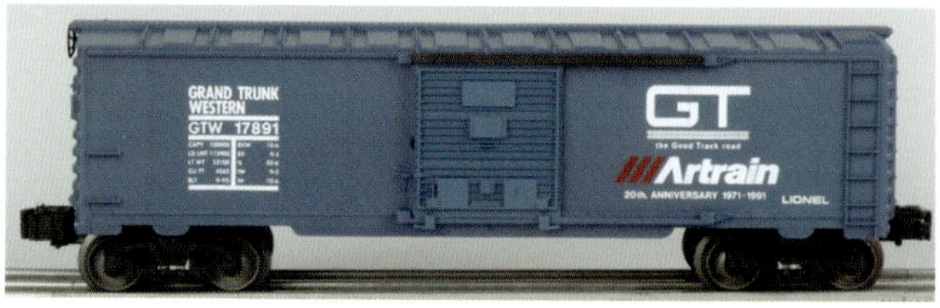

17891 GRAND TRUNK: 1991, uncataloged Artrain boxcar.

EX-C7	LN-C8	Scarcity
80	100	6

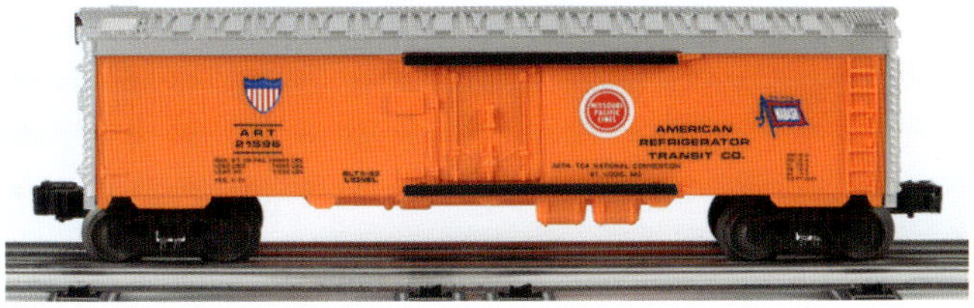

[17898] WABASH: 1992, uncataloged TCA refrigerator car numbered "21596."

EX-C7	LN-C8	Scarcity
35	40	6

[18189] ARMY OF POTOMOC: 1999, operating stock car.

EX-C7	LN-C8	Scarcity
25	30	4

[18190] MCNEIL'S RANGERS: 1999, operating stock car numbered "2."

EX-C7	LN-C8	Scarcity
25	30	4

[18556] CHICAGO & ILLINOIS MIDLAND: 1992, uncataloged Sears caboose and freight car set.

EX-C7	LN-C8	Scarcity
75	100	6

19200 TIDEWATER SOUTHERN: 1987, boxcar.

EX-C7	LN-C8	Scarcity
10	15	4

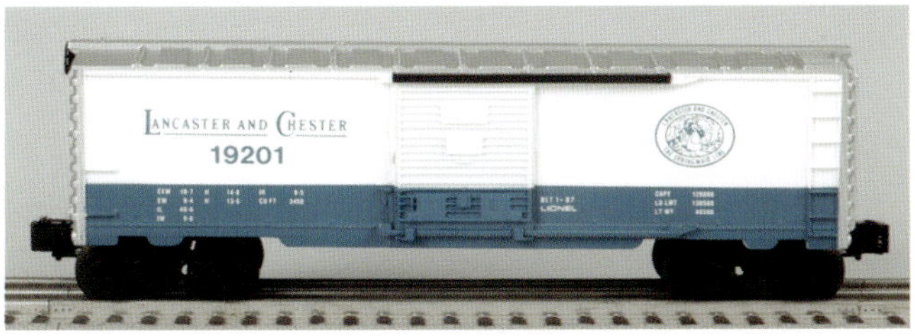

19201 LANCASTER AND CHESTER: 1987, boxcar.

EX-C7	LN-C8	Scarcity
35	30	4

19202 PENNSYLVANIA: 1987, boxcar.

EX-C7	LN-C8	Scarcity
15	20	4

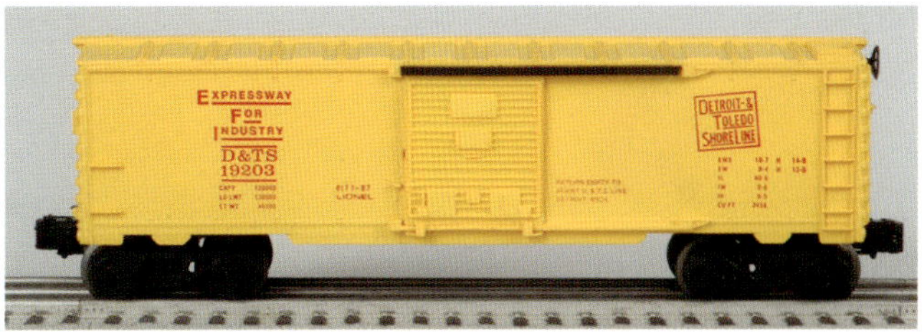

19203 D & TS: 1987, boxcar.

EX-C7	LN-C8	Scarcity
10	15	4

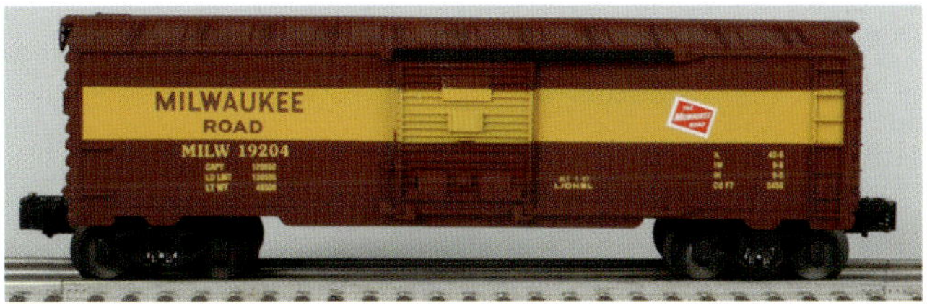

19204 MILWAUKEE ROAD: 1987, boxcar, Fallen Flags number two.

EX-C7	LN-C8	Scarcity
20	25	5

19205 GREAT NORTHERN: 1988, double-door boxcar, Fallen Flags number three.

EX-C7	LN-C8	Scarcity
15	20	5

19206 SEABOARD SYSTEM: 1988, boxcar.

EX-C7	LN-C8	Scarcity
10	15	4

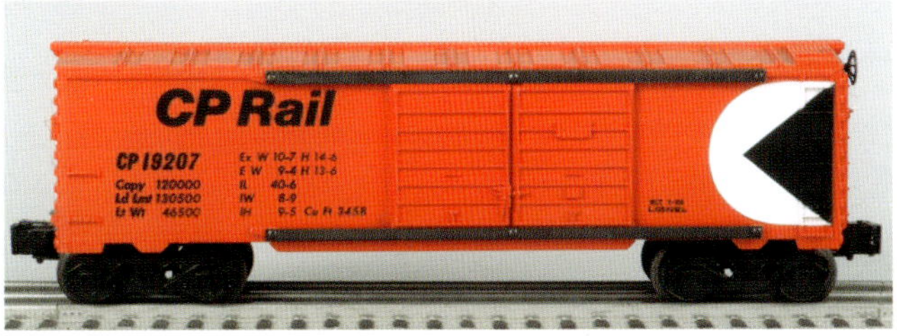

19207 CP RAIL: 1988, double-door boxcar.

EX-C7	LN-C8	Scarcity
10	15	4

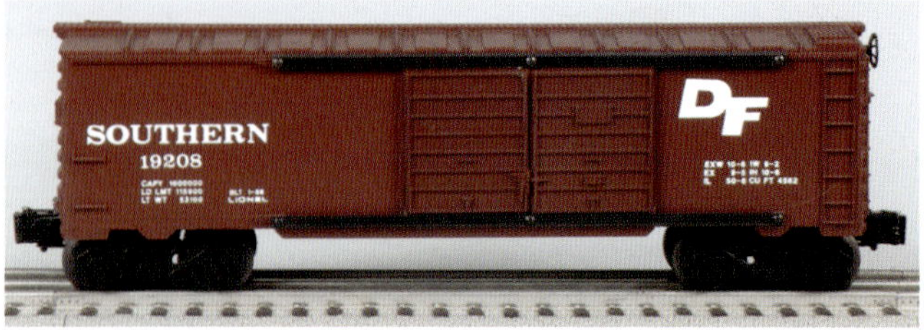

19208 SOUTHERN: 1989, double-door boxcar.

EX-C7	LN-C8	Scarcity
10	15	4

19209 FLORIDA EAST COAST: 1988, boxcar.

EX-C7	LN-C8	Scarcity
10	15	4

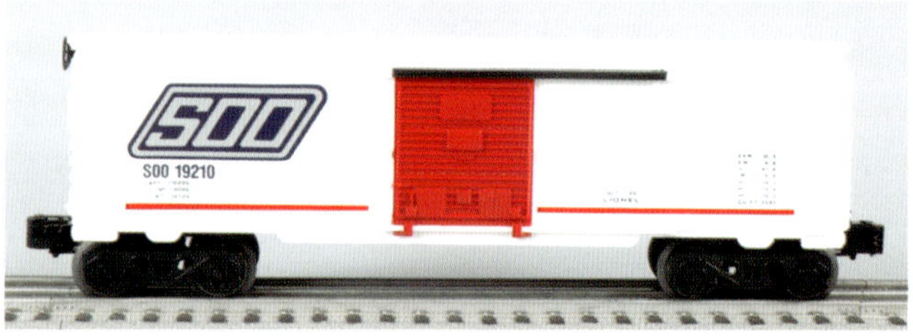

19210 SOO LINE: 1989, boxcar.

EX-C7	LN-C8	Scarcity
10	15	4

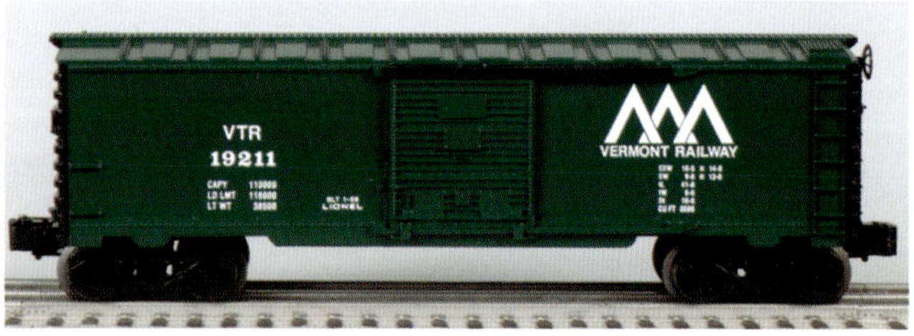

19211 VERMONT RAILWAY: 1989, boxcar.

EX-C7	LN-C8	Scarcity
15	20	4

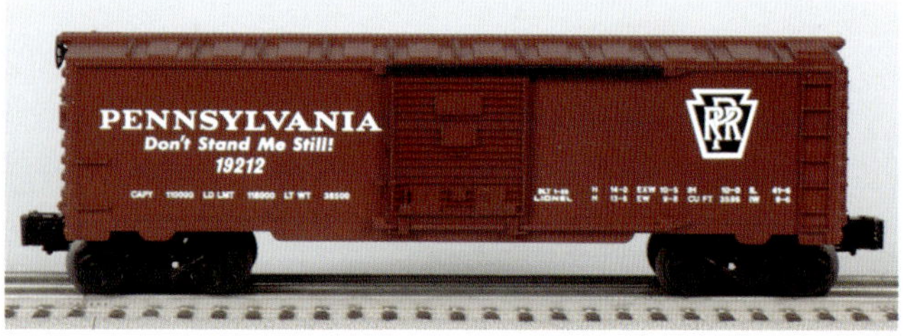

19212 PENNSYLVANIA: 1989, boxcar.

EX-C7	LN-C8	Scarcity
15	20	4

19213 SPOKANE, PORTLAND & SEATTLE: 1989, double-door boxcar.

EX-C7	LN-C8	Scarcity
10	15	4

19214 WESTERN MARYLAND: 1989, boxcar, Fallen Flags number four.

EX-C7	LN-C8	Scarcity
15	20	4

19215 UNION PACIFIC: 1990, double-door boxcar.

EX-C7	LN-C8	Scarcity
10	15	4

19216 SANTA FE: 1990, boxcar.

EX-C7	LN-C8	Scarcity
10	15	4

19217 BURLINGTON NORTHERN: 1990, boxcar.

EX-C7	LN-C8	Scarcity
10	15	4

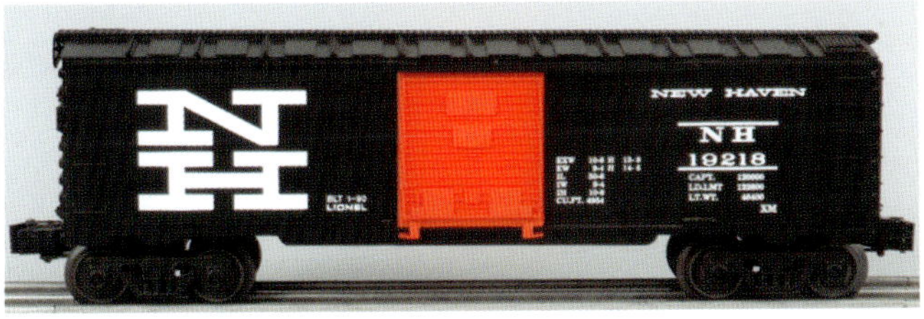

19218 NEW HAVEN: 2000, boxcar.

EX-C7	LN-C8	Scarcity
10	15	4

19219 LIONEL LINES: 2000, 1900-1906 boxcar with diesel RailSounds.

EX-C7	LN-C8	Scarcity
100	125	4

19220 LIONEL LINES: 2000, 1926-1934 boxcar.

EX-C7	LN-C8	Scarcity
20	25	4

19221 LIONEL LINES: 2000, 1935-1937 boxcar.

EX-C7	LN-C8	Scarcity
20	25	4

19222 LIONEL LINES: 2000, 1948-1950 boxcar.

EX-C7	LN-C8	Scarcity
20	25	4

19223 LIONEL LINES: 2000, 1979-1989 boxcar.

EX-C7	LN-C8	Scarcity
20	25	4

19228 COTTON BELT: 1991, boxcar.

EX-C7	LN-C8	Scarcity
10	15	4

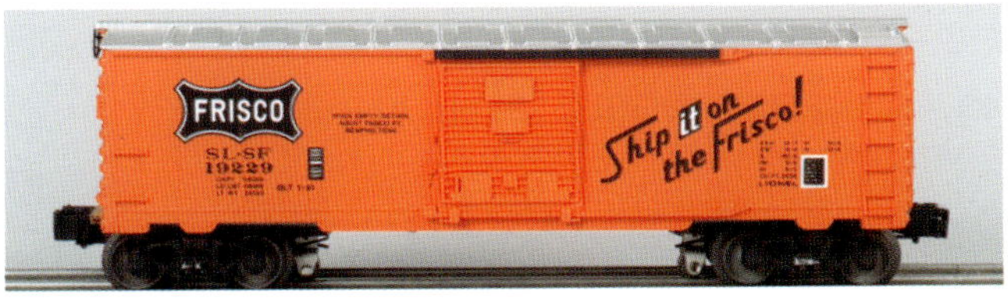

19229 FRISCO: 1991, boxcar with diesel RailSounds, Fallen Flags number five.

EX-C7	LN-C8	Scarcity
60	75	5

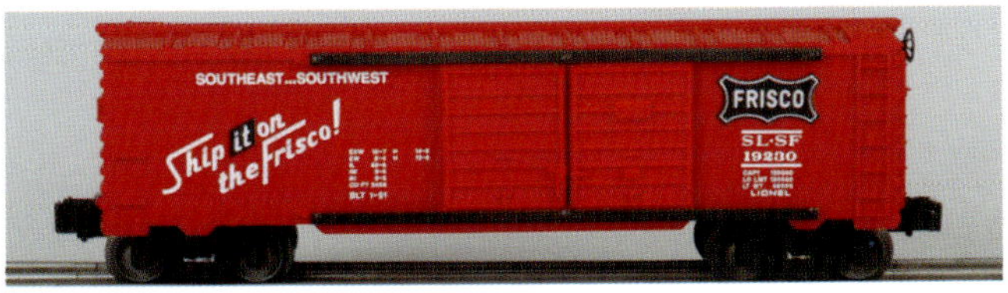

19230 FRISCO: 1991, double-door boxcar, Fallen Flags number five.

EX-C7	LN-C8	Scarcity
20	25	5

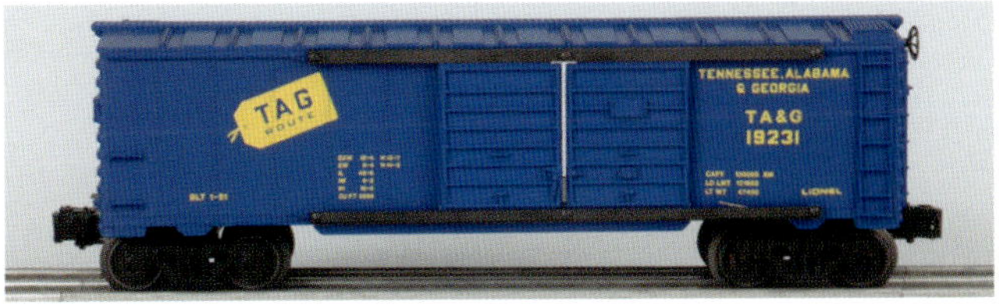

19231 TA & G: 1991, double-door boxcar.

EX-C7	LN-C8	Scarcity
10	15	4

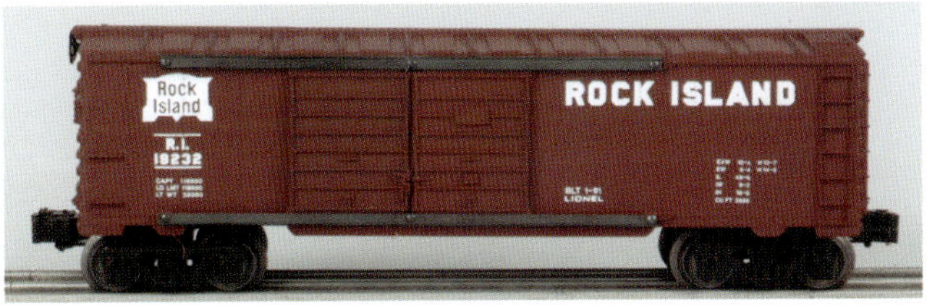

19232 ROCK ISLAND: 1991, double-door boxcar.

EX-C7	LN-C8	Scarcity
10	15	4

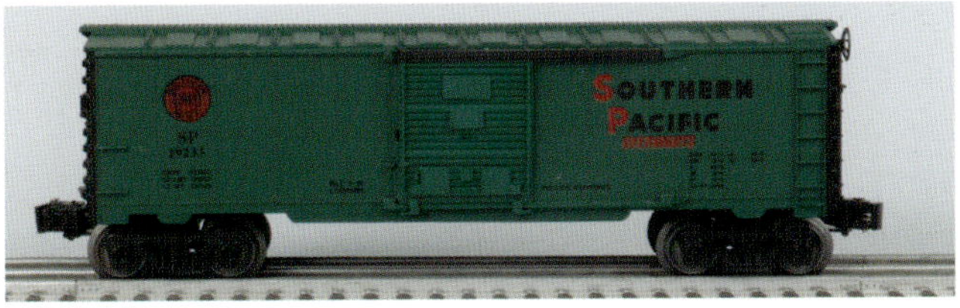

19233 SOUTHERN PACIFIC: 1991, boxcar.

EX-C7	LN-C8	Scarcity
10	15	4

19234 NEW YORK CENTRAL: 1991, boxcar.

EX-C7	LN-C8	Scarcity
60	70	5

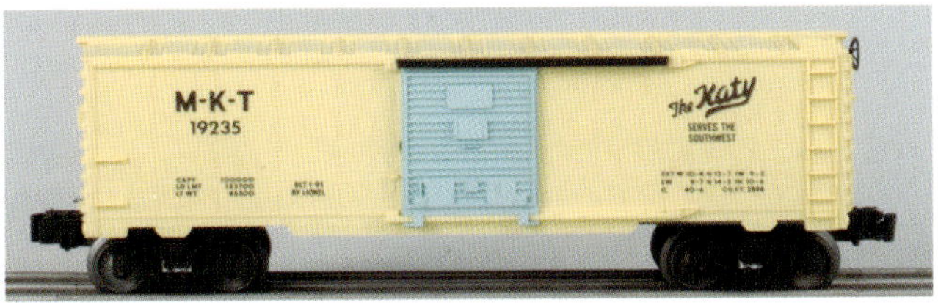

19235 MISSOURI-KANSAS-TEXAS: 1991, boxcar.

EX-C7	LN-C8	Scarcity
60	70	5

19236 NICKEL PLATE ROAD: 1992, double-door boxcar, Fallen Flags number six.

EX-C7	LN-C8	Scarcity
15	20	5

19237 CHICAGO & ILLINOIS MIDLAND: 1992, boxcar.

EX-C7	LN-C8	Scarcity
10	15	4

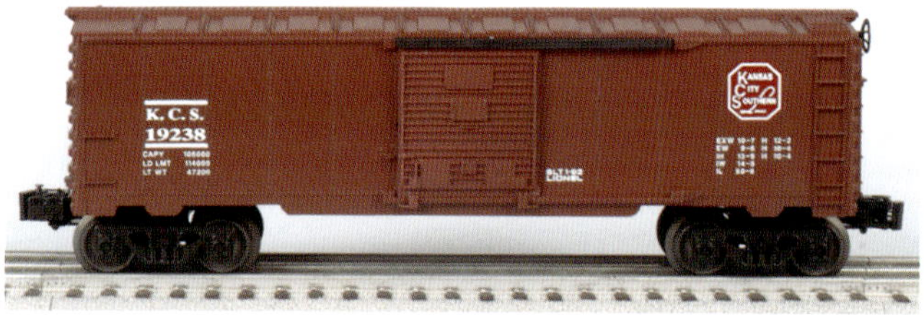

19238 KANSAS CITY SOUTHERN: 1992, boxcar.

EX-C7	LN-C8	Scarcity
15	20	4

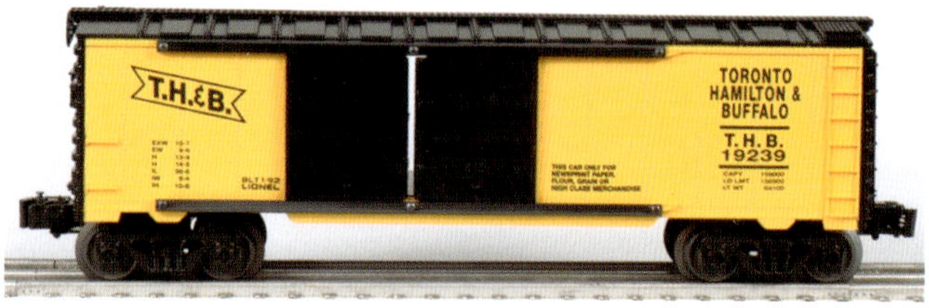

19239 TORONTO, HAMILTON & BUFFALO: 1992, double-door boxcar.

EX-C7	LN-C8	Scarcity
10	15	4

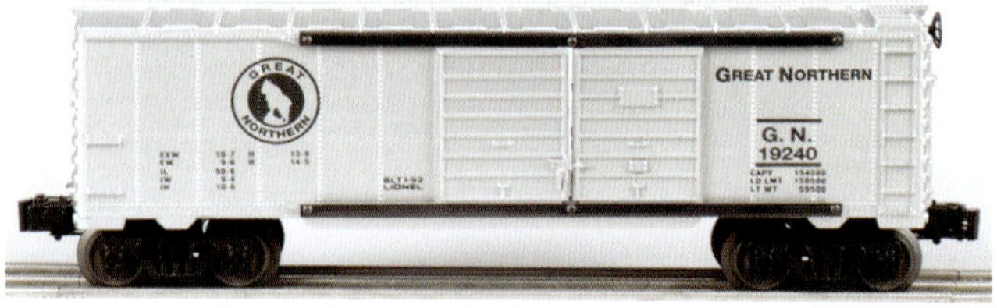

19240 GREAT NORTHERN: 1992, double-door boxcar.

EX-C7	LN-C8	Scarcity
10	15	4

19241 MICKEY MOUSE 60TH ANNIVERSARY: 1991, uncataloged High-Cube boxcar.

EX-C7	LN-C8	Scarcity
125	175	5

19242 DONALD DUCK 50TH ANNIVERSARY: 1991, uncataloged High-Cube boxcar.

EX-C7	LN-C8	Scarcity
100	125	5

[19243] CLINCHFIELD: 1991, uncataloged boxcar numbered "9790."

EX-C7	LN-C8	Scarcity
20	25	4

[19244] LOUISVILLE AND NASHVILLE: 1992, boxcar numbered "9791."

EX-C7	LN-C8	Scarcity
20	25	4

19245 MICKEY'S WORLD TOUR: 1992, uncataloged High-Cube boxcar.

EX-C7	LN-C8	Scarcity
30	40	5

19246 DISNEY WORLD 20TH ANNIVERSARY: 1992, uncataloged High-Cube boxcar.

EX-C7	LN-C8	Scarcity
30	40	5

[19247] 6464: 1993, series boxcars, First Edition, set of three.

EX-C7	LN-C8	Scarcity
325	375	5

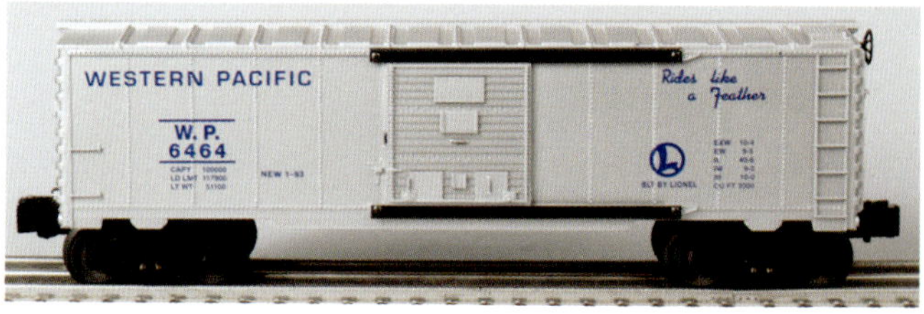

[19248] WESTERN PACIFIC: 1993, boxcar numbered "6464."

EX-C7	LN-C8	Scarcity
60	75	5

[19249] GREAT NORTHERN: 1993, boxcar numbered "6464."

EX-C7	LN-C8	Scarcity
60	75	5

[19250] MINNEAPOLIS & ST. LOUIS: 1993, boxcar numbered "6464."

EX-C7	LN-C8	Scarcity
60	75	5

[19251] MONTANA RAIL LINK: 1993, double-door boxcar numbered "10001."

EX-C7	LN-C8	Scarcity
15	20	4

19254 ERIE: 1993, boxcar, Fallen Flags number seven.

EX-C7	LN-C8	Scarcity
20	25	5

19255 ERIE: 1993, double-door boxcar, Fallen Flags number seven.

EX-C7	LN-C8	Scarcity
20	25	5

19256 GOOFY: 1993, High-Cube boxcar.

EX-C7	LN-C8	Scarcity
25	30	5

[19257] 6464: 1994, series boxcars, Second Edition, set of three.

EX-C7	LN-C8	Scarcity
110	125	5

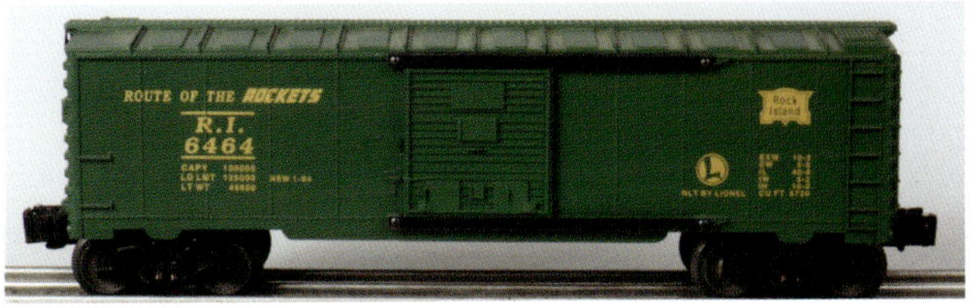

[19258] ROCK ISLAND: 1994, boxcar numbered "6464."

EX-C7	LN-C8	Scarcity
25	30	5

[19259] WESTERN PACIFIC: 1994, boxcar numbered "6464100."

EX-C7	LN-C8	Scarcity
25	30	5

[19260] WESTERN PACIFIC: 1994, boxcar numbered "6464100."

EX-C7	LN-C8	Scarcity
25	30	5

19261 PERILS OF MICKEY: 1993, High-Cube boxcar, I.

EX-C7	LN-C8	Scarcity
20	25	4

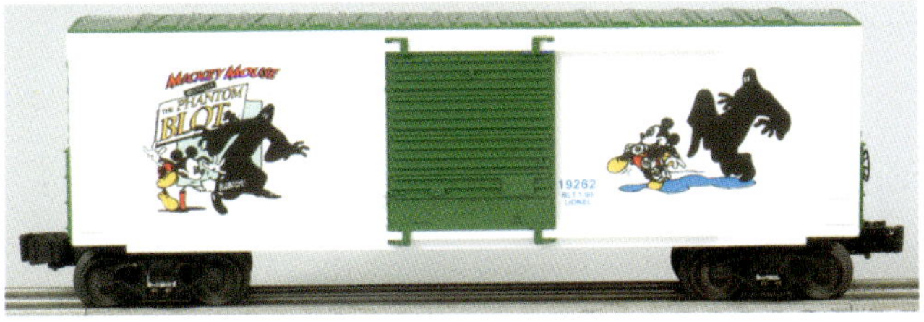

19262 PERILS OF MICKEY: 1993, High-Cube boxcar, II.

EX-C7	LN-C8	Scarcity
20	25	4

19263 NEW YORK CENTRAL: 1994, double-door boxcar, Service Station Special item.

EX-C7	LN-C8	Scarcity
25	30	5

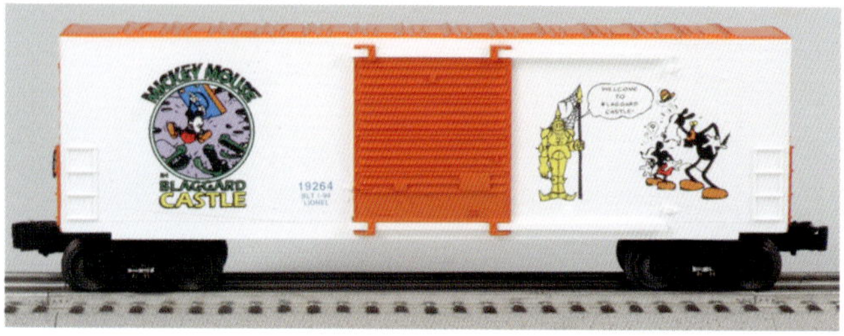

19264 PERILS OF MICKEY: 1994, High-Cube boxcar, III.

EX-C7	LN-C8	Scarcity
20	25	4

19265 MICKEY MOUSE 65TH ANNIVERSARY: 1994, High-Cube boxcar.

EX-C7	LN-C8	Scarcity
25	30	4

[19266] 6464: 1995 series boxcars, Third Edition, set of three.

EX-C7	LN-C8	Scarcity
65	80	4

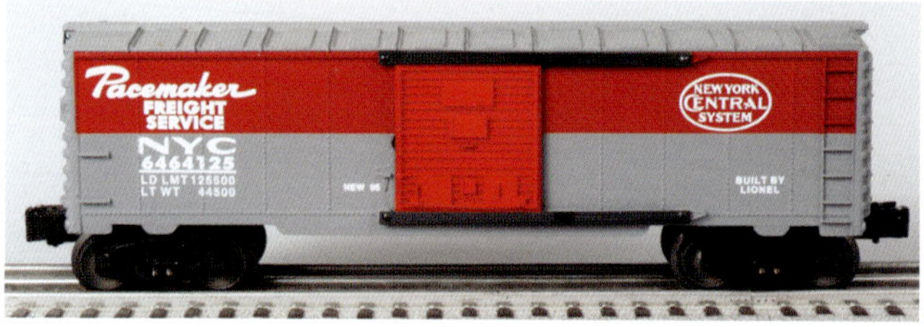

[19267] NEW YORK CENTRAL: 1995, "Pacemaker" boxcar numbered "6464125."

EX-C7	LN-C8	Scarcity
25	30	4

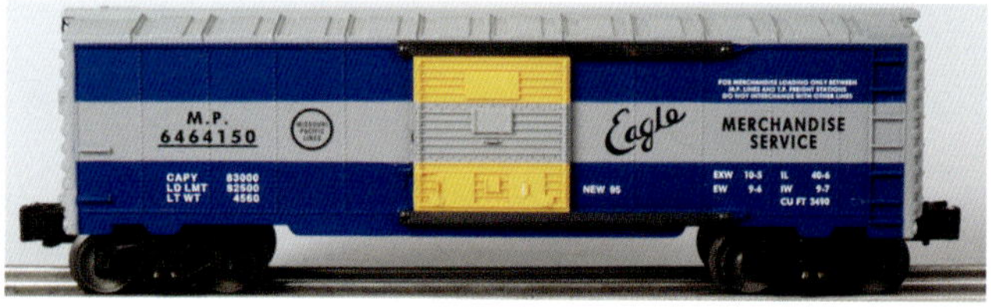

[19268] MISSOURI PACIFIC: 1995, boxcar numbered "6464150."

EX-C7	LN-C8	Scarcity
25	30	4

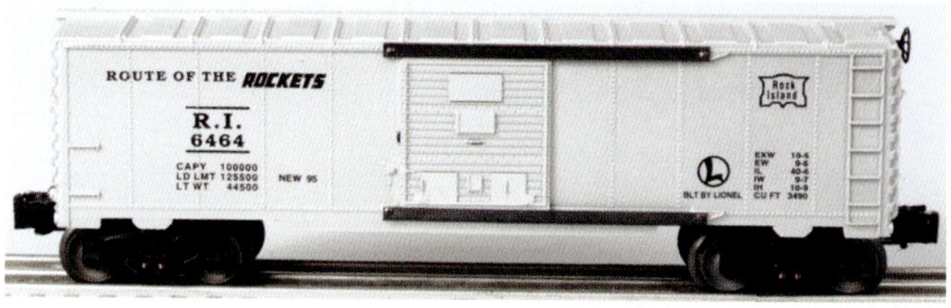

[19269] ROCK ISLAND: 1995, boxcar numbered "6464."

EX-C7	LN-C8	Scarcity
25	30	4

19270 DONALD DUCK 60TH ANNIVERSARY: 1995, High-Cube boxcar.

EX-C7	LN-C8	Scarcity
25	30	4

19271 MINNIE MOUSE: 1995, High-Cube boxcar.

EX-C7	LN-C8	Scarcity
30	35	4

[19272] 6464: 1996, series boxcars, Fourth Edition, set of three.

EX-C7	LN-C8	Scarcity
75	100	4

[19273] BANGOR AND AROOSTOOK: 1996, "State of Maine" boxcar numbered "6464275."

EX-C7	LN-C8	Scarcity
25	35	4

[19274] SOUTHERN PACIFIC: 1996, "Overnight" boxcar numbered "6464225."

EX-C7	LN-C8	Scarcity
25	35	4

19234 NEW YORK CENTRAL (Exists in 2 different shades.)

[19275] PENNSYLVANIA: 1996, boxcar numbered "6464."

EX-C7	LN-C8	Scarcity
25	35	4

[19276] 6464: 1996, series boxcar, (Series V), numbered "19277-79."

EX-C7	LN-C8	Scarcity
75	100	4

[19277] RUTLAND: 1996, boxcar numbered "6464-300," (Series V).

EX-C7	LN-C8	Scarcity
25	35	4

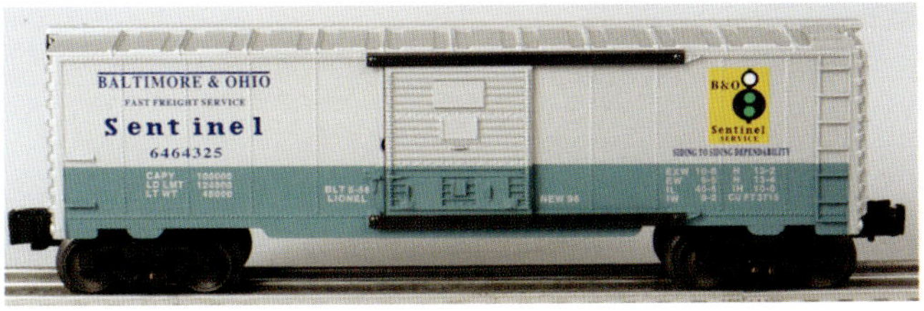

[19278] BALTIMORE & OHIO: 1996, boxcar numbered "6464-325," (Series V).

EX-C7	LN-C8	Scarcity
25	35	4

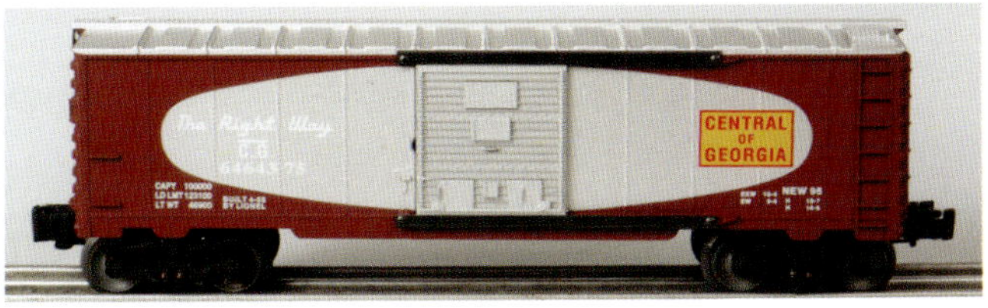

[19279] CENTRAL OF GEORGIA: 1996, numbered "6464-375," (Series V).

EX-C7	LN-C8	Scarcity
25	35	4

[19280] MICKEY'S WHEAT: 1996, High-Cube boxcar.

EX-C7	LN-C8	Scarcity
20	25	3

[19281] MICKEY'S CARROTS: 1996, High-Cube boxcar.

EX-C7	LN-C8	Scarcity
20	25	3

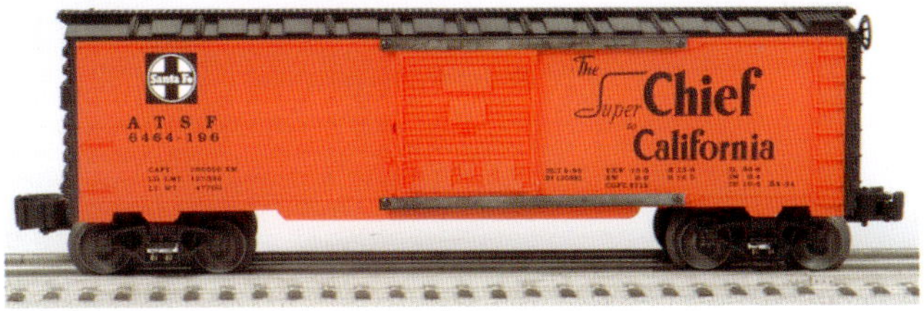

[19282] SANTA FE: 1996, "Super Chief" boxcar numbered "6464-196."

EX-C7	LN-C8	Scarcity
20	25	4

[19283] ERIE: 1996, boxcar numbered "6464-296."

EX-C7	LN-C8	Scarcity
20	25	4

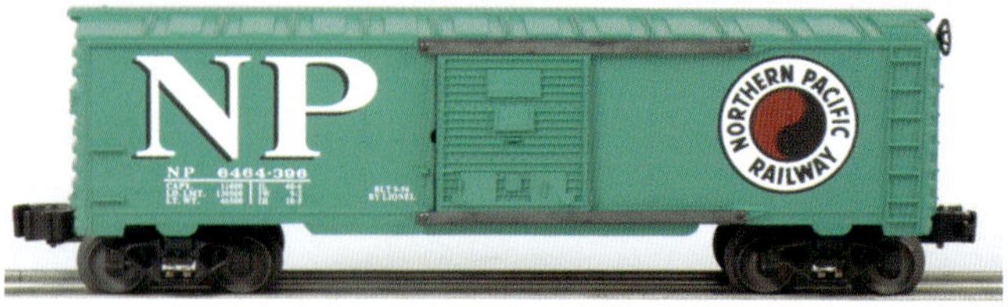

[19284] NORTHERN PACIFIC: 1996, boxcar numbered "6464-396."

EX-C7	LN-C8	Scarcity
20	25	4

[19285] BANGOR AND AROOSTOOK: 1996, "State of Maine" boxcar numbered "6464275," solid red door.

EX-C7	LN-C8	Scarcity
20	25	4

[19286] WARNER BROS: 1996, "All Abirrrrd" boxcar.

EX-C7	LN-C8	Scarcity
30	35	4

[19287] NEW YORK CENTRAL/PENN CENTRAL: 1997, Merger boxcar numbered "6464-125X," Service Station Special item.

EX-C7	LN-C8	Scarcity
35	40	5

[19288] PENNSYLVANIA/CONRAIL: 1997, Merger boxcar numbered "6464-200X," Service Station Special item.

EX-C7	LN-C8	Scarcity
35	40	5

[19289] MONON: 1997, "Hoosier Line" boxcar numbered "6464."

EX-C7	LN-C8	Scarcity
15	20	4

[19290] SEABOARD: 1997, "Silver Valley Meteor" boxcar numbered "6464."

EX-C7	LN-C8	Scarcity
15	20	4

[19291] GREAT NORTHERN: 1997, boxcar numbered "6464-397," dark green.

EX-C7	LN-C8	Scarcity
15	20	4

[19292] 6464: 1997, series boxcar, (Series VI).

EX-C7	LN-C8	Scarcity
75	90	4

[19293] MISSOURI-KANSAS-TEXAS: 1997, boxcar numbered "6464-350," (Series VI).

EX-C7	LN-C8	Scarcity
25	30	4

[19294] BALTIMORE & OHIO: 1997, boxcar numbered "6464-400," (Series VI).

EX-C7	LN-C8	Scarcity
25	30	4

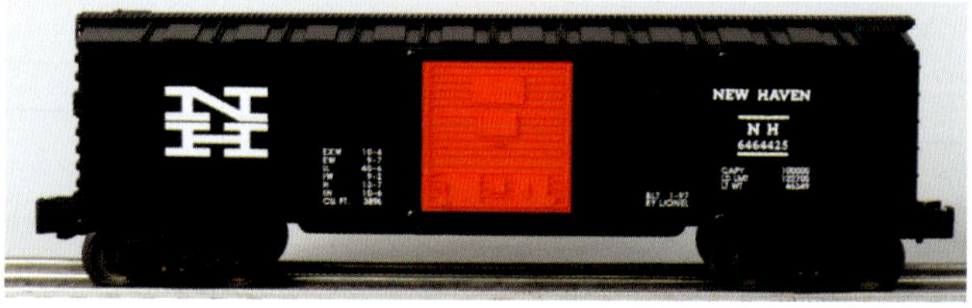

[19295] NEW HAVEN: 1997, boxcar numbered "6464-425," (Series VI).

EX-C7	LN-C8	Scarcity
25	30	4

19406 WEST POINT: 1991, uncataloged mint car.

EX-C7	LN-C8	Scarcity
50	60	5

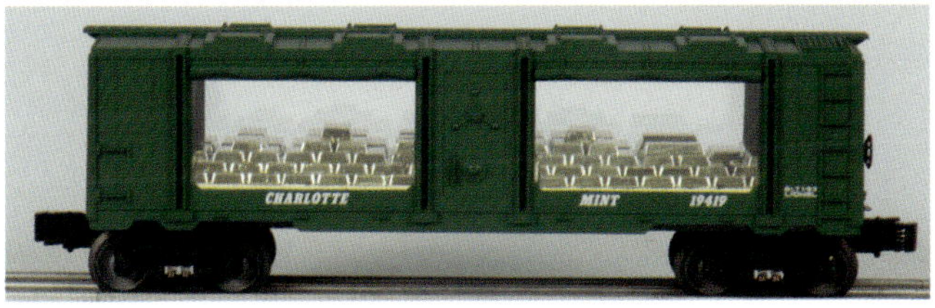

19419 CHARLOTTE: 1993, mint car.

EX-C7	LN-C8	Scarcity
20	25	4

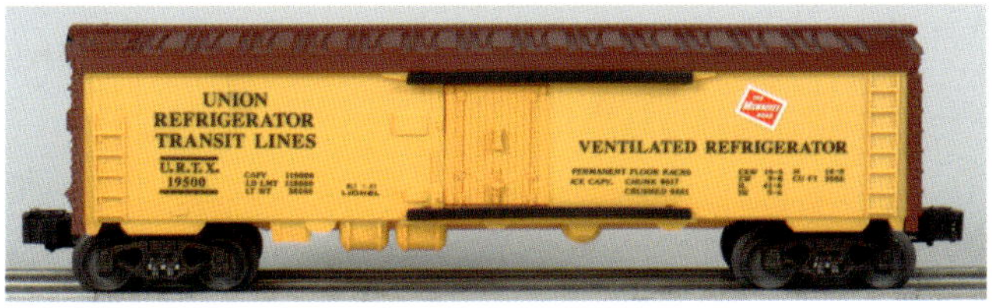

19500 MILWAUKEE ROAD: 1987, refrigerator car, Fallen Flags number two.

EX-C7	LN-C8	Scarcity
30	35	4

19502 CHICAGO & NORTHWESTERN: 1987, refrigerator car.

EX-C7	LN-C8	Scarcity
20	25	4

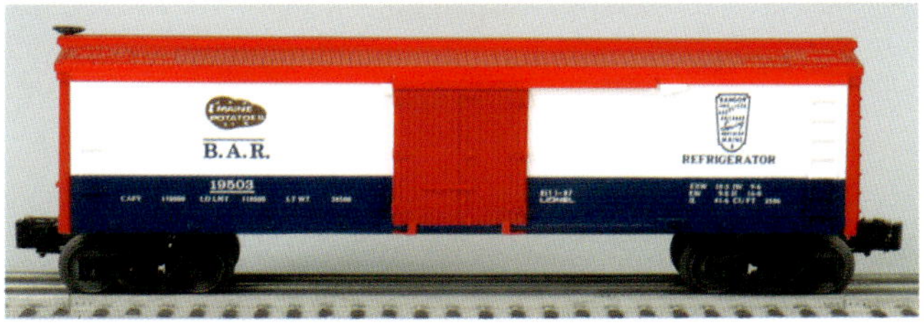

19503 BANGOR AND AROOSTOOK: 1987, refrigerator car.

EX-C7	LN-C8	Scarcity
20	25	4

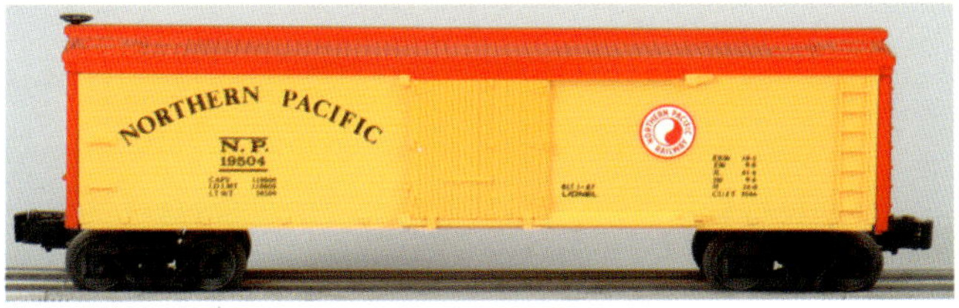

19504 NORTHERN PACIFIC: 1987, refrigerator car.

EX-C7	LN-C8	Scarcity
15	20	3

19505 GREAT NORTHERN: 1988, refrigerator car, Fallen Flags number three.

EX-C7	LN-C8	Scarcity
20	25	5

19506 THOMAS NEWCOMEN: 1988, refrigerator car.

EX-C7	LN-C8	Scarcity
15	20	3

19507 THOMAS EDISON: 1988, refrigerator car.

EX-C7	LN-C8	Scarcity
15	20	3

19508 LEONARDO DA VINCI: 1989, refrigerator car.

EX-C7	LN-C8	Scarcity
15	20	3

19509 ALEXANDER GRAHAM BELL: 1989, refrigerator car.

EX-C7	LN-C8	Scarcity
15	20	3

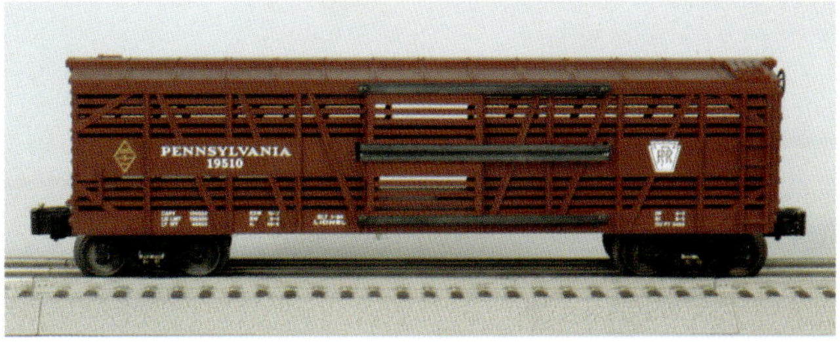

19510 PENNSYLVANIA: 1989, uncataloged stock car, Fallen Flags number five.

EX-C7	LN-C8	Scarcity
20	25	5

19511 WESTERN MARYLAND: 1989, refrigerator car, Fallen Flags number four.

EX-C7	LN-C8	Scarcity
20	25	5

19512 WRIGHT BROTHERS: 1990, refrigerator car.

EX-C7	LN-C8	Scarcity
15	20	3

19513 BEN FRANKLIN: 1990, refrigerator car.

EX-C7	LN-C8	Scarcity
15	20	3

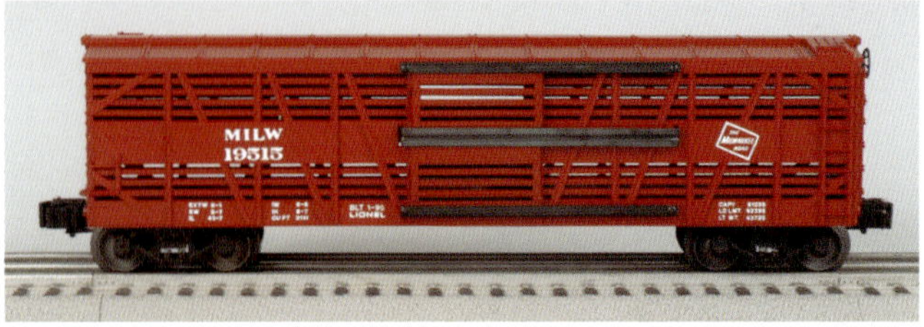

19515 MILWAUKEE ROAD: 1990, uncataloged stock car, Fallen Flags number two.

EX-C7	LN-C8	Scarcity
25	30	5

19516 GEORGE WASHINGTON: Uncataloged in 1989, cataloged in 1991, refrigerator car.

EX-C7	LN-C8	Scarcity
15	20	3

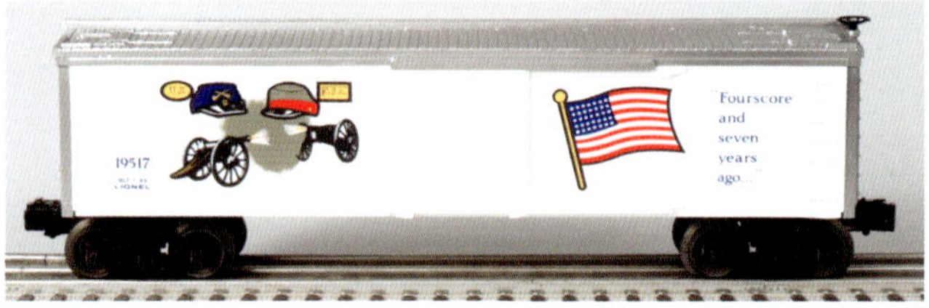

19517 CIVIL WAR: Uncataloged in 1989, cataloged in 1991, refrigerator car.

EX-C7	LN-C8	Scarcity
15	20	3

19518 MAN ON THE MOON: 1989 uncataloged, 1991 refrigerator car.

EX-C7	LN-C8	Scarcity
15	20	3

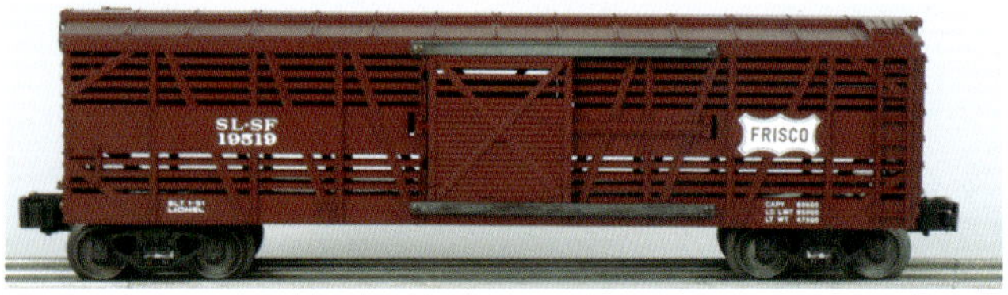

19519 FRISCO: 1991, stock car, Fallen Flags number five.

EX-C7	LN-C8	Scarcity
20	25	5

19520 CSX: 1991, refrigerator car.

EX-C7	LN-C8	Scarcity
15	20	3

19522 GUGLIELMO MARCONI: 1991, refrigerator car.

EX-C7	LN-C8	Scarcity
15	20	3

19523 DR. ROBERT GODDARD: 1991, refrigerator car.

EX-C7	LN-C8	Scarcity
15	20	3

19524 DELAWARE & HUDSON: 1991, refrigerator car, Service Station Special item.

EX-C7	LN-C8	Scarcity
20	25	5

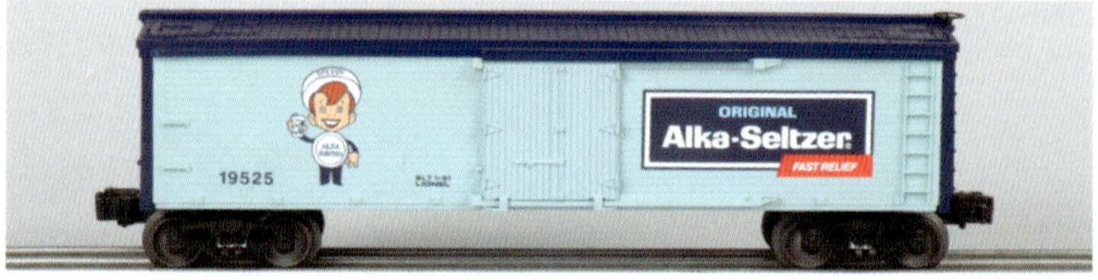

19525 SPEEDY ALKA SELTZER: 1991, uncataloged refrigerator car.

EX-C7	LN-C8	Scarcity
30	35	5

19526 JOLLY GREEN GIANT: 1991, uncataloged refrigerator car.

EX-C7	LN-C8	Scarcity
25	30	5

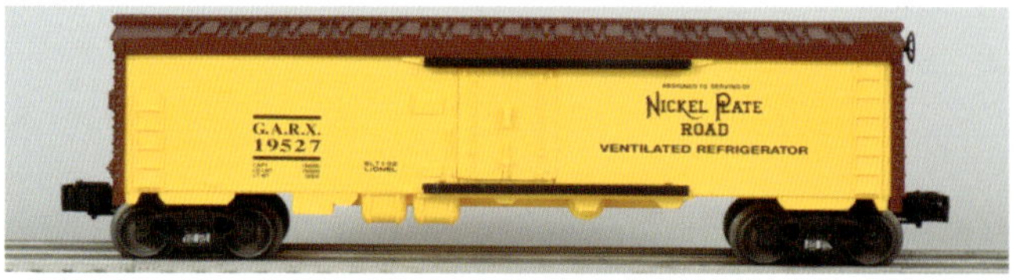

19527 NICKEL PLATE ROAD: 1992, refrigerator car, Fallen Flags number six.

EX-C7	LN-C8	Scarcity
25	30	5

19528 JOSHUA L. COWEN: 1992, refrigerator car.

EX-C7	LN-C8	Scarcity
20	25	4

19529 A.C. GILBERT: 1992, refrigerator car.

EX-C7	LN-C8	Scarcity
20	25	4

19530 ROCK ISLAND: 1992, uncataloged stock car.

EX-C7	LN-C8	Scarcity
25	30	5

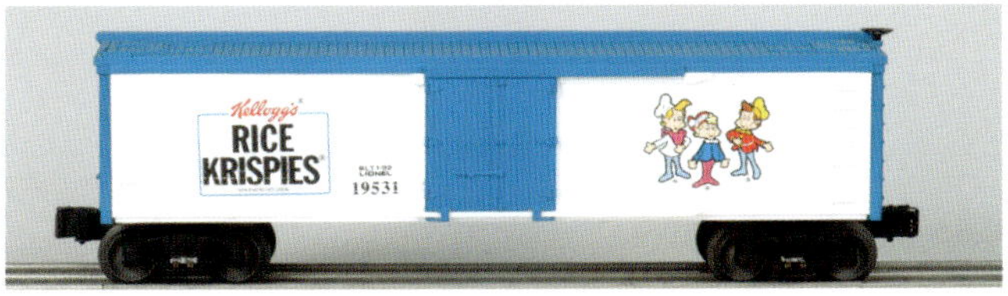

19531 RICE KRISPIES: 1992, uncataloged refrigerator car.

EX-C7	LN-C8	Scarcity
20	25	4

[19532] HORMEL: 1992, uncataloged refrigerator car, numbered "901."

EX-C7	LN-C8	Scarcity
20	25	4

19535 ERIE: 1993, refrigerator car, Fallen Flags number seven.

EX-C7	LN-C8	Scarcity
20	25	5

19536 SOO LINE REA: 1993, refrigerator car, Service Station Special item.

EX-C7	LN-C8	Scarcity
20	25	5

19537 KELLOGG'S CORN FLAKES: 1993, refrigerator car.

EX-C7	LN-C8	Scarcity
Cataloged, but not produced.		

[19538] HORMEL: 1994, refrigerator car numbered "102."

EX-C7	LN-C8	Scarcity
20	25	4

19539 HEINZ: 1994, refrigerator car.

EX-C7	LN-C8	Scarcity
20	25	4

[19540] BROKEN ARROW RANCH: 1997, stock car numbered "3356."

EX-C7	LN-C8	Scarcity
20	25	4

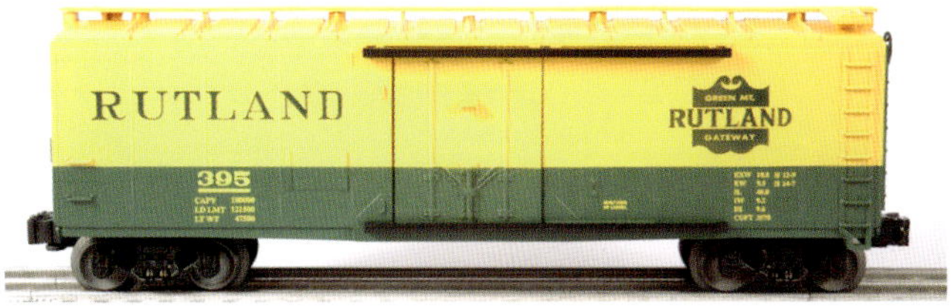

[19552] RUTLAND: 2000, refrigerator car numbered "395" with 1/48-scale proportions.

EX-C7	LN-C8	Scarcity
25	30	4

[19553] SANTA FE: 2000, stock car numbered "23003."

EX-C7	LN-C8	Scarcity
25	30	4

[19554]: 2000, milk car numbered "36621."

EX-C7	LN-C8	Scarcity
80	110	4

[19557] CIRCUS: 2000, stock car numbered "6376."

EX-C7	LN-C8	Scarcity
25	30	4

[19599] OLD GLORY: Uncataloged in 1989, cataloged in 1991, refrigerator car, set of three.

EX-C7	LN-C8	Scarcity
35	40	5

19651 SANTA FE: 1987, tool car.

EX-C7	LN-C8	Scarcity
20	25	4

19652 JERSEY CENTRAL: 1988, bunk car.

EX-C7	LN-C8	Scarcity
15	20	4

19653 JERSEY CENTRAL: 1988, tool car.

EX-C7	LN-C8	Scarcity
15	20	4

19654 AMTRAK: 1989, bunk car.

EX-C7	LN-C8	Scarcity
15	20	4

19655 AMTRAK: 1990-91, tool car.

EX-C7	LN-C8	Scarcity
15	20	4

19656 MILWAUKEE ROAD: 1990, bunk car with smoke.

EX-C7	LN-C8	Scarcity
35	40	4

19657 WABASH: 1991-92, bunk car with smoke.

EX-C7	LN-C8	Scarcity
25	30	4

19658 NORFOLK AND WESTERN: 1991, tool car.

EX-C7	LN-C8	Scarcity
20	25	4

[19660] LIONEL: 1998, mint car.

EX-C7	LN-C8	Scarcity
35	40	4

[19663] PRATT'S HOLLOW: 1999, bunk car numbered "5717."

EX-C7	LN-C8	Scarcity
30	35	5

[19664] AMBASSADOR: 1999, uncataloged bunk car numbered "1998," (Bronze) Award.

EX-C7	LN-C8	Scarcity
325	375	6

[19665] AMBASSADOR: 1999, uncataloged Engineer bunk car numbered "1998" (Silver).

EX-C7	LN-C8	Scarcity
375	450	6

[19666] AMBASSADOR: 1999, uncataloged Cowen bunk car numbered "1998" (Gold).

EX-C7	LN-C8	Scarcity
375	600	7

[19667] WELLSPRING: 1999, bullion car.

EX-C7	LN-C8	Scarcity
40	45	5

[19669] KING TUT MUSEUM: 1999, numbered "9660."

EX-C7	LN-C8	Scarcity
45	50	4

[19670] NY FEDERAL RESERVE: 2000, bullion car numbered "6445."

EX-C7	LN-C8	Scarcity
35	40	4

[19671] LIONEL MODEL SHOP: 1999-2000, display car numbered "6445-01."

EX-C7	LN-C8	Scarcity
40	45	4

[19672] LIONEL MINES: 2000, uncataloged mint car.

EX-C7	LN-C8	Scarcity
200	225	5

19673 WELLSPRING CAPITAL MANAGEMENT: 1999, uncataloged mint car.

EX-C7	LN-C8	Scarcity
150	175	5

19674 LIONEL LINES: 2000, platinum car.

EX-C7	LN-C8	Scarcity
30	35	4

19675 FT. KNOX: 2000 mint car numbered "6445."

EX-C7	LN-C8	Scarcity
30	35	4

19775 LIONEL RAILROADER CLUB: 1999, stock car.

EX-C7	LN-C8	Scarcity
25	30	5

19800 CIRCLE L RANCH: 1988, operating cattle car.

EX-C7	LN-C8	Scarcity
75	100	4

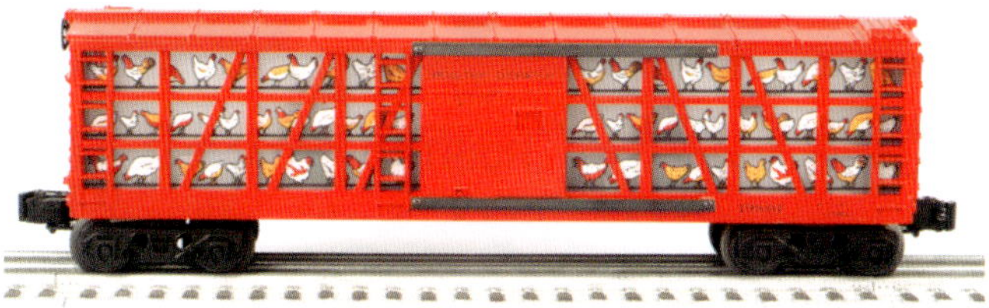

19801 POULTRY DISPATCH: 1987, chicken car.

EX-C7	LN-C8	Scarcity
20	25	4

19802 CARNATION: 1987, milk car.

EX-C7	LN-C8	Scarcity
75	100	4

19803 READING: 1987, ice car.

EX-C7	LN-C8	Scarcity
20	25	4

19805 SANTA FE: 1987, operating boxcar.

EX-C7	LN-C8	Scarcity
15	20	4

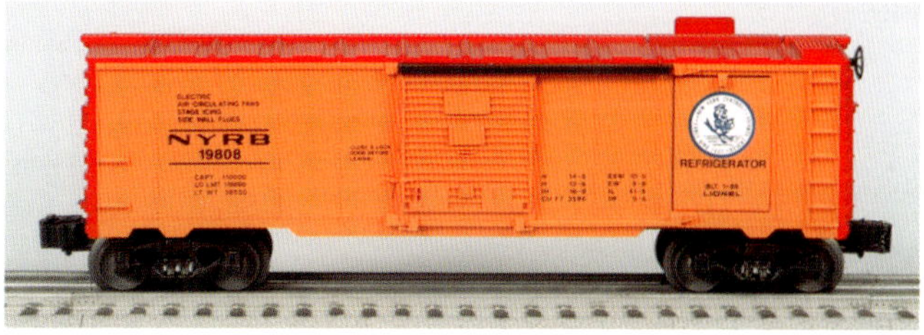

19808 NEW YORK CENTRAL: 1988, ice car.

EX-C7	LN-C8	Scarcity
25	30	4

19809 ERIE-LACKAWANNA: 1988, operating boxcar.

EX-C7	LN-C8	Scarcity
15	20	4

19810 BOSCO: 1988, milk car.

EX-C7	LN-C8	Scarcity
75	100	4

19811 MONON: 1990, operating brakeman car.

EX-C7	LN-C8	Scarcity
25	30	4

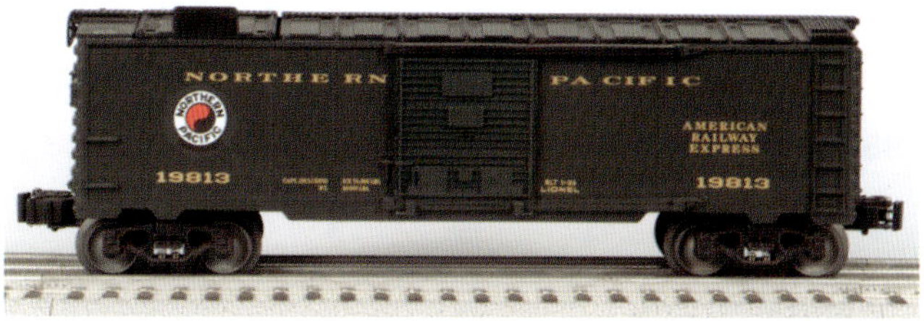

19813 NORTHERN PACIFIC: 1989, uncataloged ice car.

EX-C7	LN-C8	Scarcity
25	30	4

19815 DELAWARE AND HUDSON: 1992, operating brakeman car.

EX-C7	LN-C8	Scarcity
25	30	4

[19816] MADISON HARDWARE: 1991, uncataloged operating boxcar numbered "190991."

EX-C7	LN-C8	Scarcity
100	125	5

19907 TOY FAIR: 1989, uncataloged boxcar.

EX-C7	LN-C8	Scarcity
60	75	6

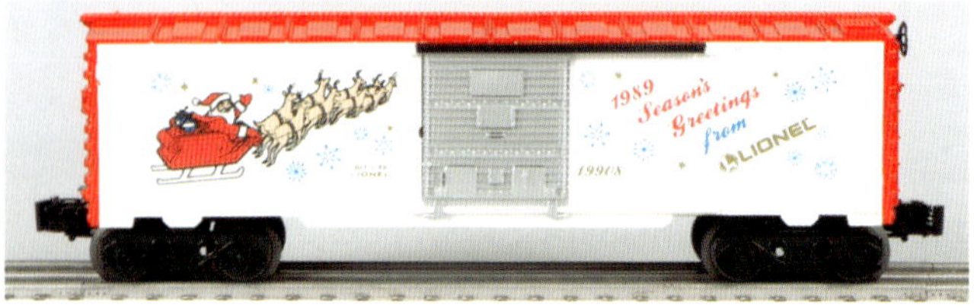

19908 CHRISTMAS: 1989, uncataloged boxcar.

EX-C7	LN-C8	Scarcity
30	35	5

19909 "I LOVE NEW JERSEY": 1990, boxcar.

EX-C7	LN-C8	Scarcity
15	18	4

19910 CHRISTMAS: 1990, uncataloged boxcar.

EX-C7	LN-C8	Scarcity
20	25	4

19911 TOY FAIR: 1990, uncataloged boxcar.

EX-C7	LN-C8	Scarcity
60	75	6

19912 "I LOVE OHIO": 1991, boxcar.

EX-C7	LN-C8	Scarcity
15	18	4

[19913] CHRISTMAS: 1991, regular issue.

EX-C7	LN-C8	Scarcity
25	30	4

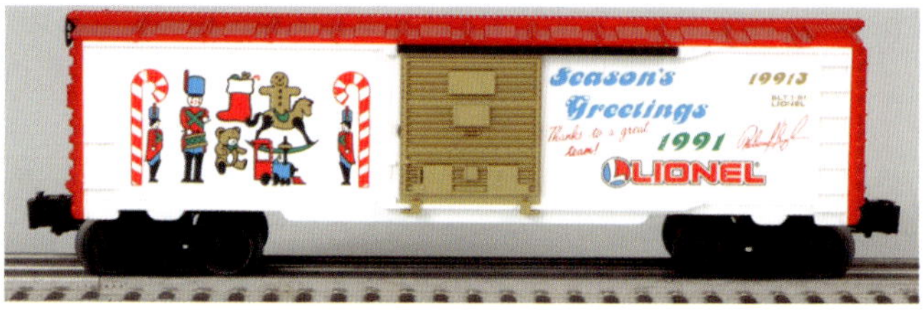

[19913] CHRISTMAS: 1991, uncataloged boxcar for Lionel employees.

EX-C7	LN-C8	Scarcity
160	180	6

19914 TOY FAIR: 1991, uncataloged boxcar.

EX-C7	LN-C8	Scarcity
60	75	6

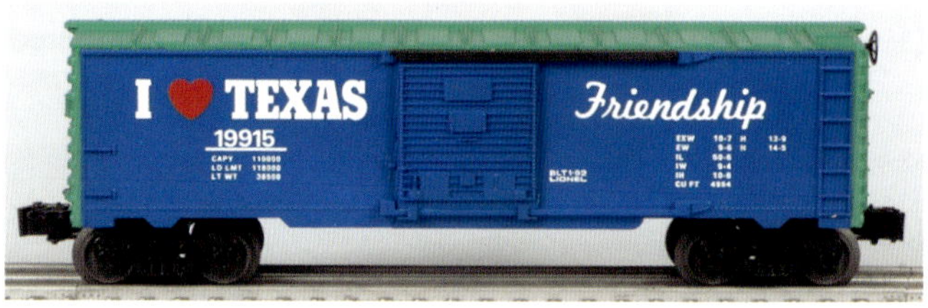

19915 "I LOVE TEXAS": 1992, boxcar.

EX-C7	LN-C8	Scarcity
20	25	4

19916 CHRISTMAS: 1992, uncataloged boxcar for Lionel employees.

EX-C7	LN-C8	Scarcity
250	300	6

19917 TOY FAIR: 1992, uncataloged boxcar.

EX-C7	LN-C8	Scarcity
60	75	6

19918 CHRISTMAS: 1992, uncataloged boxcar.

EX-C7	LN-C8	Scarcity
60	75	6

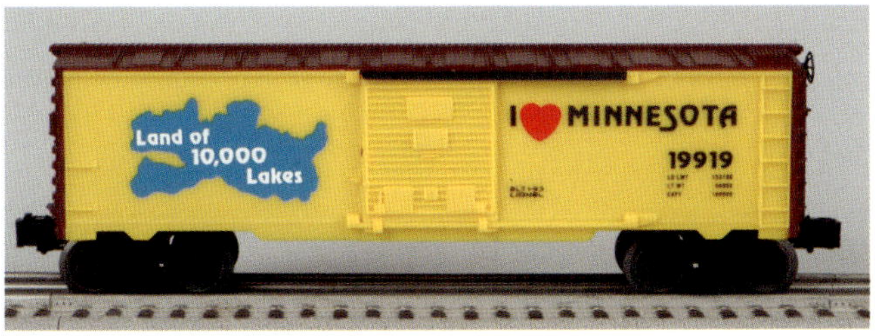

19919 "I LOVE MINNESOTA": 1993, boxcar.

EX-C7	LN-C8	Scarcity
20	30	5

[19920] LIONEL VISITOR'S CENTER (Type I): 1992, uncataloged boxcar. Without barcodes, but it does have a painted door.

EX-C7	LN-C8	Scarcity
25	30	5

[19920] LIONEL VISITOR'S CENTER (Type II): 1992, uncataloged boxcar. The packaging of other cars have barcodes, but an unpainted door.

EX-C7	LN-C8	Scarcity
25	30	5

19921 CHRISTMAS: 1993, uncataloged boxcar for Lionel employees.

EX-C7	LN-C8	Scarcity
175	200	6

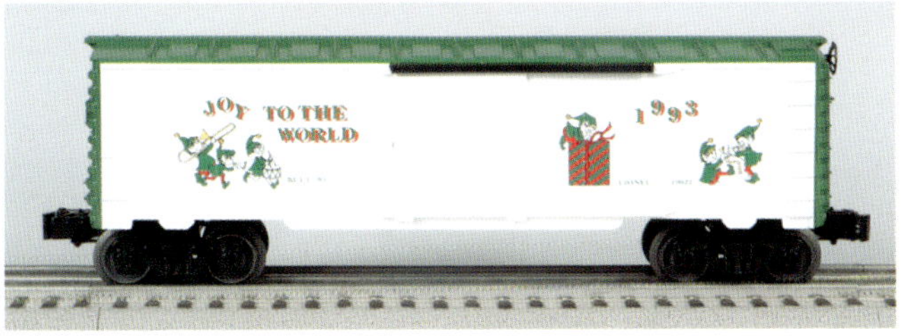

19922 CHRISTMAS: 1993, boxcar.

EX-C7	LN-C8	Scarcity
25	30	4

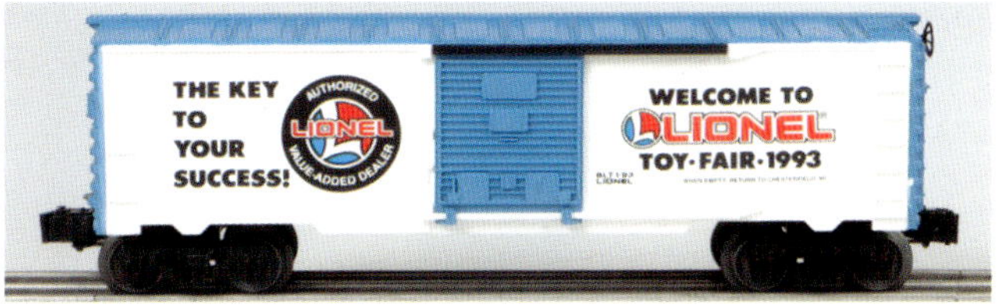

19923 TOY FAIR: 1993, uncataloged boxcar.

EX-C7	LN-C8	Scarcity
60	75	6

19924 LIONEL RAILROADER CLUB: 1993, uncataloged boxcar.

EX-C7	LN-C8	Scarcity
20	25	5

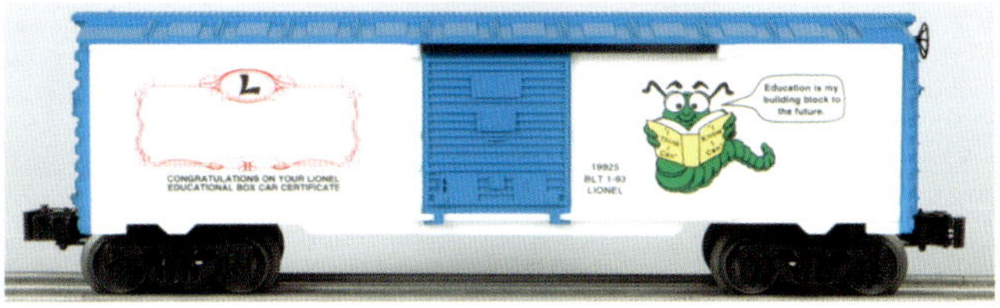

19925 LEARNING CENTER: 1993, uncataloged boxcar for Lionel employees.

EX-C7	LN-C8	Scarcity
100	125	6

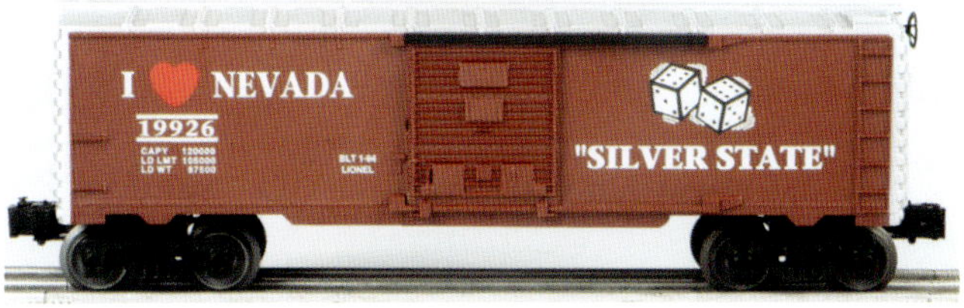

19926 "I LOVE NEVADA": 1994, boxcar.

EX-C7	LN-C8	Scarcity
15	20	4

[19927] LIONEL VISITOR'S CENTER: 1993, uncataloged boxcar numbered "1993."

EX-C7	LN-C8	Scarcity
25	30	5

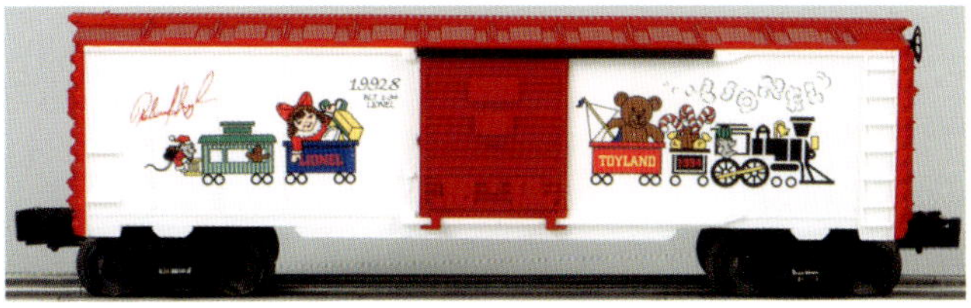

19928 CHRISTMAS: 1994, uncataloged boxcar for Lionel employees.

EX-C7	LN-C8	Scarcity
300	325	6

19929 CHRISTMAS: 1994, boxcar.

EX-C7	LN-C8	Scarcity
15	20	4

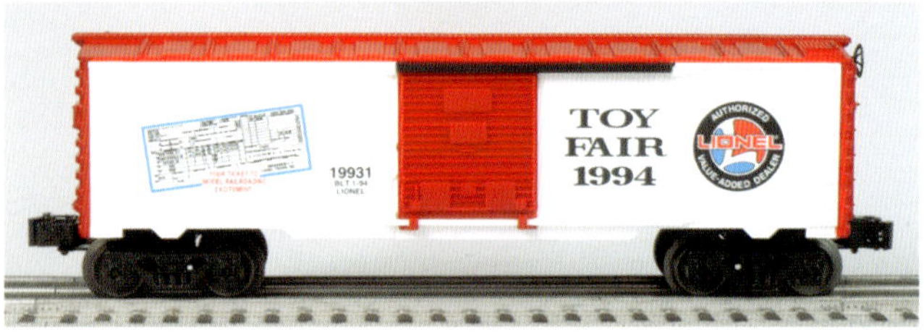

19931 TOY FAIR: 1994, uncataloged boxcar.

EX-C7	LN-C8	Scarcity
70	90	6

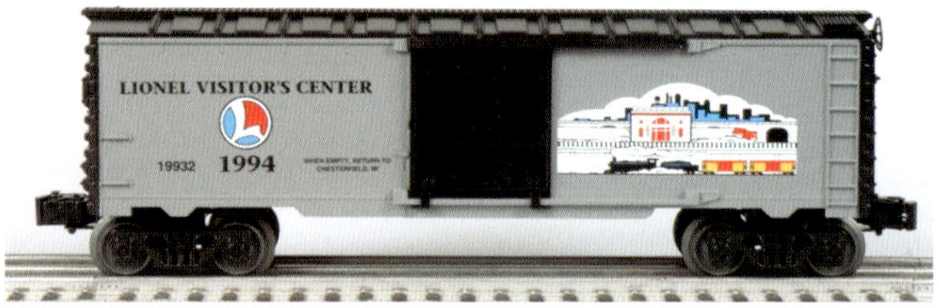

19932 LIONEL VISITOR'S CENTER: 1994, uncataloged boxcar.

EX-C7	LN-C8	Scarcity
30	35	5

19933 "I LOVE ILLINOIS": 1995, boxcar.

EX-C7	LN-C8	Scarcity
15	20	4

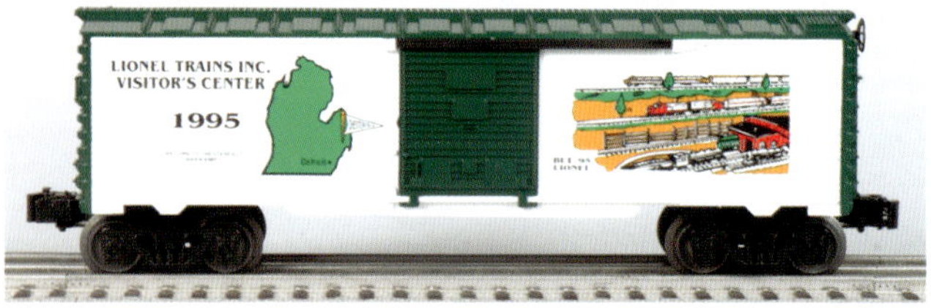

[19934] LIONEL VISITOR'S CENTER: 1995, uncataloged boxcar numbered "1995."

EX-C7	LN-C8	Scarcity
25	30	5

19937 TOY FAIR: 1995, uncataloged boxcar.

EX-C7	LN-C8	Scarcity
50	60	6

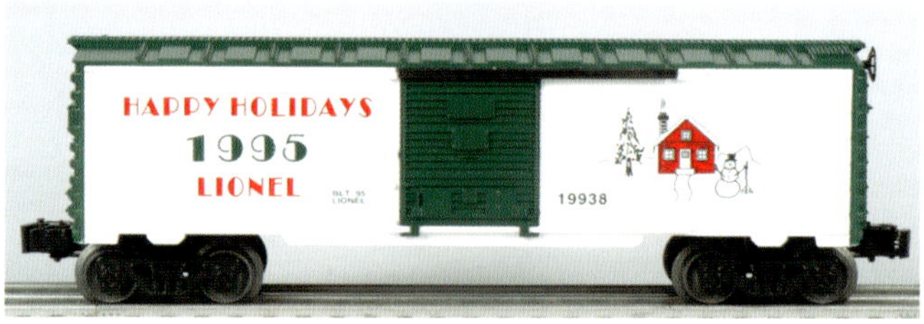

19938 CHRISTMAS: 1995, boxcar.

EX-C7	LN-C8	Scarcity
30	35	5

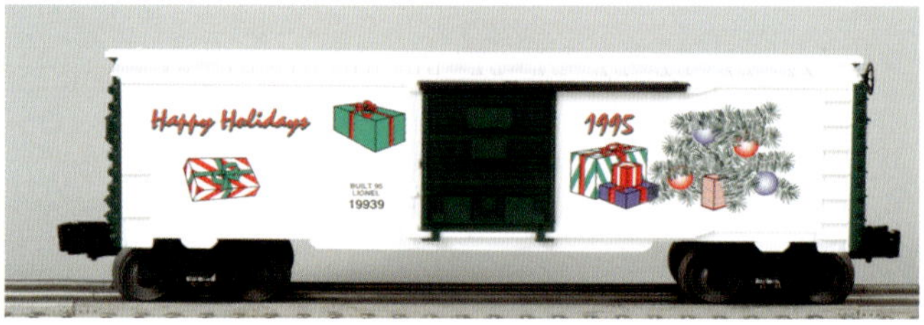

19939 CHRISTMAS: 1995, uncataloged boxcar for Lionel employees.

EX-C7	LN-C8	Scarcity
325	375	6

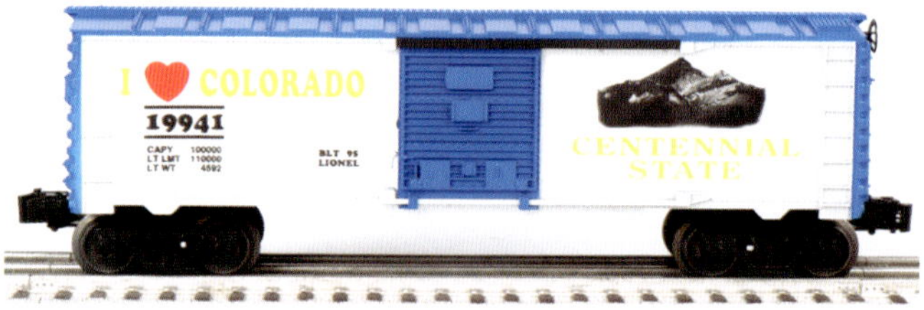

19941 "I LOVE COLORADO": 1995, boxcar.

EX-C7	LN-C8	Scarcity
15	20	4

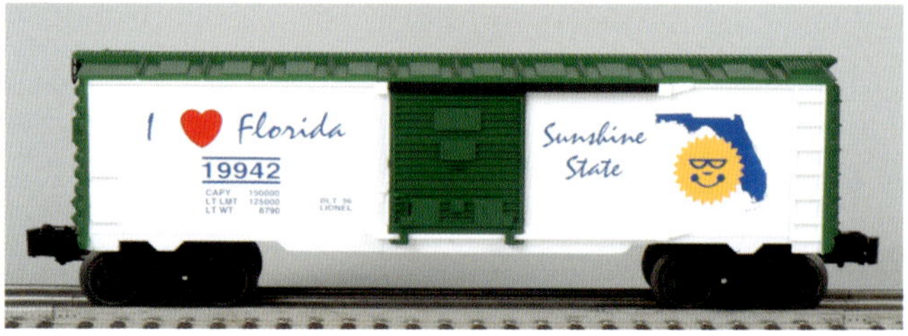

19942 "I LOVE FLORIDA": 1996, boxcar.

EX-C7	LN-C8	Scarcity
15	20	4

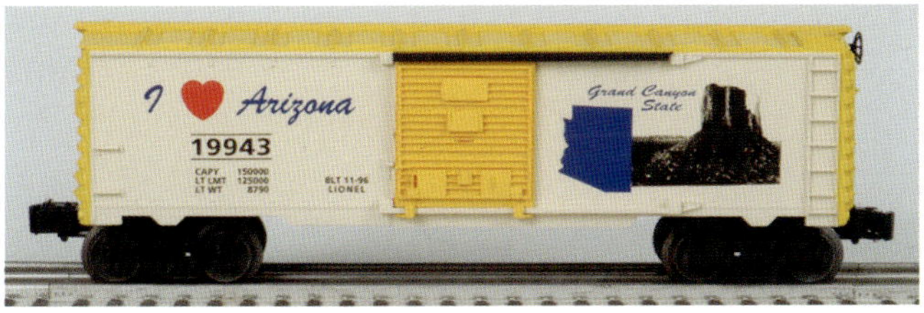

[19943] "I LOVE ARIZONA": 1996, boxcar.

EX-C7	LN-C8	Scarcity
15	20	4

[19945] HOLIDAY: 1996, boxcar.

EX-C7	LN-C8	Scarcity
25	30	4

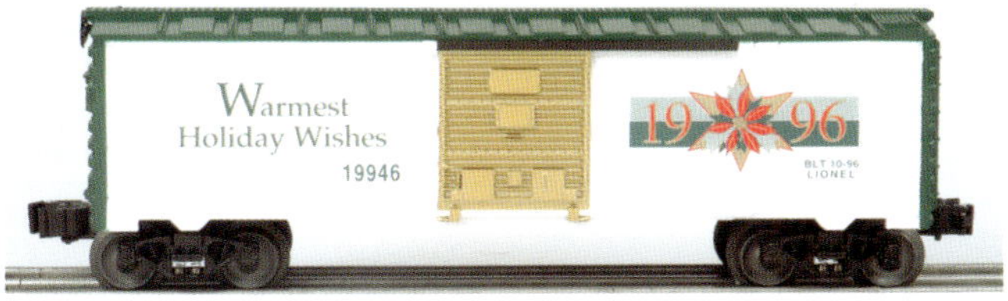

[19946] CHRISTMAS: 1996, uncataloged boxcar for Lionel employees.

EX-C7	LN-C8	Scarcity
200	225	6

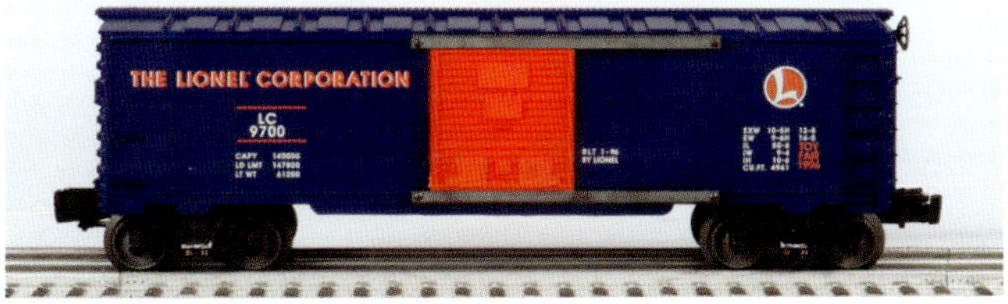

[19947] LIONEL CORPORATION: 1996, uncataloged Toy Fair boxcar numbered "9700."

EX-C7	LN-C8	Scarcity
100	150	6

[19949] "I LOVE NY": 1997, boxcar numbered "9700."

EX-C7	LN-C8	Scarcity
25	30	4

[19950] "I LOVE MONTANA": 1997, boxcar numbered "9700."

EX-C7	LN-C8	Scarcity
15	20	4

[19951] "I LOVE MASSACHUSETTS": 1998, boxcar numbered "9700."

EX-C7	LN-C8	Scarcity
15	20	4

[19952] "I LOVE INDIANA": 1998, boxcar numbered "9700."

EX-C7	LN-C8	Scarcity
15	20	4

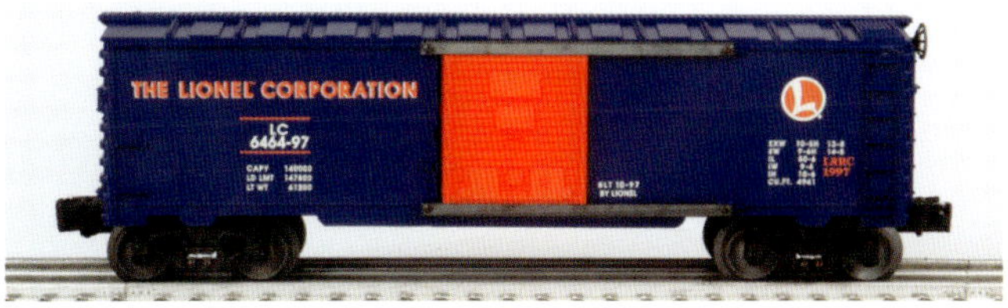

[19953] LIONEL RAILROADER CLUB: 1997, uncataloged boxcar.

EX-C7	LN-C8	Scarcity
35	40	5

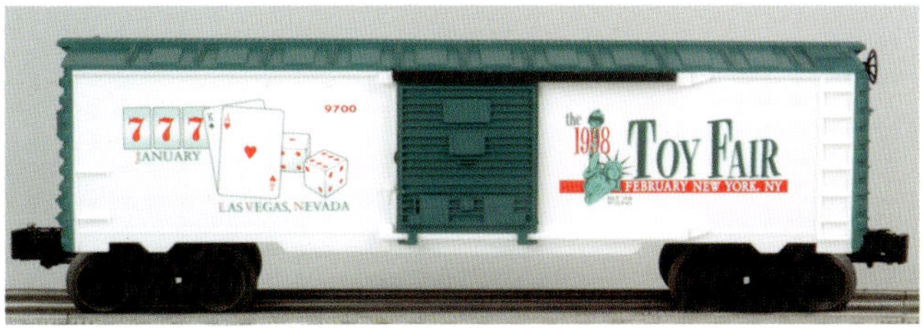

[19956] TOY FAIR: 1998, uncataloged boxcar numbered "777."

EX-C7	LN-C8	Scarcity
50	60	6

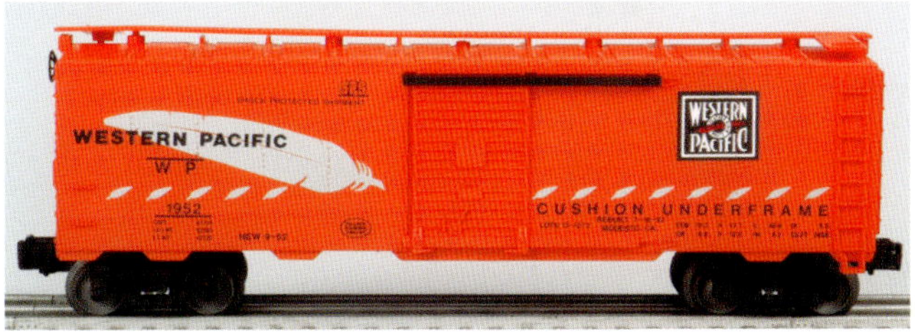

[19960] WESTERN PACIFIC: 1992, uncataloged LOTS boxcar numbered "1952" with 1/48-scale proportions.

EX-C7	LN-C8	Scarcity
40	50	6

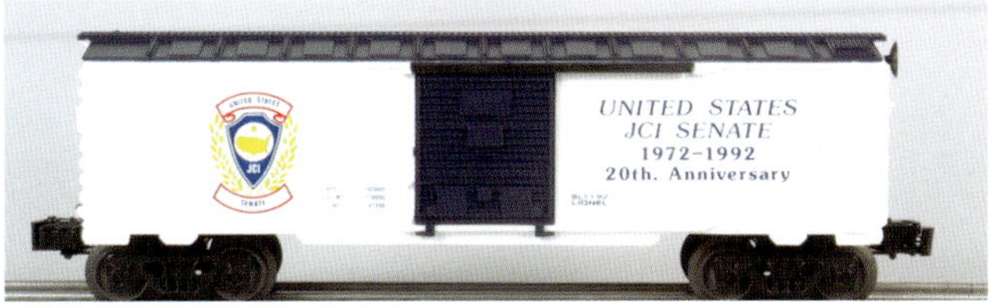

[19964] U.S. JCI SENATE: 1992, uncataloged boxcar.

EX-C7	LN-C8	Scarcity
60	70	6

[19965] LIONEL RAILROADER CLUB: 1999, uncataloged aquarium car numbered "3435."

EX-C7	LN-C8	Scarcity
45	55	5

[19968] "I LOVE MAINE": 1999, boxcar numbered "9700."

EX-C7	LN-C8	Scarcity
15	20	4

[19969] "I LOVE VERMONT": 1999, boxcar numbered "9700."

EX-C7	LN-C8	Scarcity
15	20	4

[19970] "I LOVE NEW HAMPSHIRE": 1999, boxcar numbered "9700."

EX-C7	LN-C8	Scarcity
15	20	4

[19971] "I LOVE RHODE ISLAND": 1999, boxcar numbered "9700."

EX-C7	LN-C8	Scarcity
15	20	4

[19976] HOLIDAY: 1999, uncataloged Lionel employee boxcar numbered "1999."

EX-C7	LN-C8	Scarcity
150	175	6

[19977] TOY FAIR: 1999, uncataloged boxcar numbered "9700."

EX-C7	LN-C8	Scarcity
60	75	6

[19978] "GOLD": 1999-2000, boxcar numbered "1900-2000."

EX-C7	LN-C8	Scarcity
50	60	6

[19981] LIONEL CENTENNIAL: 1999, boxcar numbered "1998-1."

EX-C7	LN-C8	Scarcity
20	25	4

[19982] LIONEL CENTENNIAL: 1999, boxcar numbered "1998-2."

EX-C7	LN-C8	Scarcity
20	25	4

[19983] LIONEL CENTENNIAL: 1999, boxcar numbered "1998-3."

EX-C7	LN-C8	Scarcity
20	25	4

[19984] LIONEL CENTENNIAL: 1999, boxcar numbered "1998-4."

EX-C7	LN-C8	Scarcity
20	25	4

[19985] "I LOVE GEORGIA": 1999-2000, boxcar numbered "9700."

EX-C7	LN-C8	Scarcity
15	20	4

[19986] "I LOVE NORTH CAROLINA": 1999-2000, boxcar numbered "9700."

EX-C7	LN-C8	Scarcity
15	20	4

[19987] "I LOVE SOUTH CAROLINA": 1999-2000, boxcar numbered "9700."

EX-C7	LN-C8	Scarcity
15	20	4

[19988] "I LOVE TENNESSEE": 1999-2000, boxcar numbered "9700."

EX-C7	LN-C8	Scarcity
20	25	4

[19989] TOY FAIR: 2000, uncataloged boxcar.

EX-C7	LN-C8	Scarcity
50	60	6

[19991] LIONEL RAILROADER CLUB: 2000, uncataloged Gold Club boxcar.

EX-C7	LN-C8	Scarcity
50	60	6

[19992] LIONEL RAILROADER CLUB: 2000, uncataloged Western Union Tel. tool car numbered "3550."

EX-C7	LN-C8	Scarcity
40	50	5

[21750] NICKEL PLATE ROAD: 1998, rolling stock, four-pack.

EX-C7	LN-C8	Scarcity
100	125	4

[21751] PENNSYLVANIA: 1998, rolling stock, four-pack.

EX-C7	LN-C8	Scarcity
125	150	4

[21756]: 1998, overstamped 6464-style boxcars, two-pack.

EX-C7	LN-C8	Scarcity
35	45	4

[21757] UNION PACIFIC: 1998, freight car set.

EX-C7	LN-C8	Scarcity
125	150	4

[21761] BOSTON AND MAINE: 1999, boxcar set, four-pack.

EX-C7	LN-C8	Scarcity
125	150	4

[21766] ATLANTIC COAST LINE: 1999, passenger car set, two-pack.

EX-C7	LN-C8	Scarcity
200	225	4

[21770] NEW YORK CENTRAL: 1999, refrigerator car set, four-pack.

EX-C7	LN-C8	Scarcity
150	175	4

[21771] DENVER & RIO GRANDE WESTERN: 1999, stock car set, four-pack.

EX-C7	LN-C8	Scarcity
200	225	4

[21774] CUSTOM SERIES: 1999, Consist One three-pack numbered "6424."

EX-C7	LN-C8	Scarcity
100	125	4

[21778] SEABOARD: 1999, freight car set.

EX-C7	LN-C8	Scarcity
175	200	4

[26108] LIONEL VISITOR'S CENTER: 2000, uncataloged refrigerator car numbered "206482."

EX-C7	LN-C8	Scarcity
20	25	4

[26126] CHEERIOS: 1998, boxcar.

EX-C7	LN-C8	Scarcity
20	25	4

[26200] NORTHERN PACIFIC: 1998, boxcar numbered "18211."

EX-C7	LN-C8	Scarcity
20	25	4

[26201] OPERATION LIFESAVER: 1998, boxcar.

EX-C7	LN-C8	Scarcity
20	25	4

[26203] DELAWARE AND HUDSON: 1998, boxcar numbered "1829."

EX-C7	LN-C8	Scarcity
20	25	4

[26204] ALASKA RAILROAD: 1998-99, boxcar numbered "10806."

EX-C7	LN-C8	Scarcity
20	25	4

[26205] ROCKY & BULLWINKLE: 1999, boxcar numbered "9700."

EX-C7	LN-C8	Scarcity
20	25	4

[26206] CURIOUS GEORGE: 1999, boxcar numbered "9700."

EX-C7	LN-C8	Scarcity
20	25	4

[26208] VAPOR RECORDS: 1998, boxcar number two.

EX-C7	LN-C8	Scarcity
15	20	4

[26214] CELEBRATE THE CENTURY STAMP: 1998, uncataloged boxcar.

EX-C7	LN-C8	Scarcity
75	100	5

[26215] AEC: 1998, Glow-in-the-Dark boxcar.

EX-C7	LN-C8	Scarcity
60	70	4

[26216] CHEERIOS: 1998, uncataloged boxcar numbered "9700."

EX-C7	LN-C8	Scarcity
60	70	4

[26218] QUAKER OATS: 1998, uncataloged boxcar.

EX-C7	LN-C8	Scarcity
275	300	6

[26219] ACE HARDWARE: 1998, uncataloged boxcar.

EX-C7	LN-C8	Scarcity
Too rarely traded to establish accurate pricing.		

[26220] SMUCKERS: 1998, uncataloged boxcar numbered "9700."

EX-C7	LN-C8	Scarcity
60	70	4

[26222] PENN CENTRAL: 1999, boxcar numbered "125962."

EX-C7	LN-C8	Scarcity
20	25	4

[26223] FLORIDA EAST COAST: 1999, boxcar numbered "5027."

EX-C7	LN-C8	Scarcity
20	25	4

[26224] DELAWARE AND HUDSON: 1999, boxcar numbered "9700."

EX-C7	LN-C8	Scarcity
20	25	4

[26228] VAPOR RECORDS: 1999, uncataloged holiday boxcar numbered "9700."

EX-C7	LN-C8	Scarcity
50	60	5

[26230] AEC: 1999, Glow-in-the-Dark boxcar II numbered "9700."

EX-C7	LN-C8	Scarcity
20	25	4

[26232] MARTIN GUITAR LUMBER: 1999, boxcar numbered "9823."

EX-C7	LN-C8	Scarcity
20	25	4

[26234] NEW YORK CENTRAL: 1999, boxcar numbered "9700."

EX-C7	LN-C8	Scarcity
20	25	4

[26235] VALENTINE: 1999, boxcar numbered "9700."

EX-C7	LN-C8	Scarcity
20	25	4

[26236] AIRCRAFT: 1999, boxcar numbered "9700."

EX-C7	LN-C8	Scarcity
20	25	4

[26237] BOY SCOUT: 1999, boxcar numbered "9700."

EX-C7	LN-C8	Scarcity
60	70	5

[26238] DETROIT HISTORICAL MUSEUM: 1999, boxcar numbered "9700."

EX-C7	LN-C8	Scarcity
25	30	5

[26239] M.A.D.D.: 1999, boxcar numbered "9700."

EX-C7	LN-C8	Scarcity
20	25	4

[26240] STARTER SET RAILBOX: 1999-2000, boxcar numbered "9700."

EX-C7	LN-C8	Scarcity
20	25	4

[26241] NORFOLK AND WESTERN: 1999-2000, Starter set boxcar numbered "9700."

EX-C7	LN-C8	Scarcity
10	15	3

[26242] D.A.R.E.: 1999, boxcar numbered "9700."

EX-C7	LN-C8	Scarcity
20	25	4

[26243] CHRISTMAS: 1999, boxcar numbered "9700."

EX-C7	LN-C8	Scarcity
20	25	4

[26244] WOODY WOODPECKER: 1999, boxcar numbered "9700."

EX-C7	LN-C8	Scarcity
25	30	4

[26247] LIONEL LINES: 1999, boxcar numbered "9700."

EX-C7	LN-C8	Scarcity
25	30	4

[26253] ACME EXPLOSIVES: 1999, uncataloged boxcar numbered "9700."

EX-C7	LN-C8	Scarcity
Too rarely traded to establish accurate pricing.		

[26254] KEEBLER: 1999, uncataloged boxcar numbered "9700."

EX-C7	LN-C8	Scarcity
Too rarely traded to establish accurate pricing.		

[26255] NEW YORK CENTRAL: 1999, uncataloged boxcar numbered "200495."

EX-C7	LN-C8	Scarcity
20	25	4

[26256] SALVATION ARMY: 1999, boxcar numbered "9700."

EX-C7	LN-C8	Scarcity
20	25	4

[26257] WHEATIES: 1999, boxcar numbered "9700."

EX-C7	LN-C8	Scarcity
50	60	5

[26264] LIONEL STATION: 1999, boxcar.

EX-C7	LN-C8	Scarcity
25	30	4

[26265] NEW YORK CENTRAL: 2000, Pacemaker boxcar numbered "9700."

EX-C7	LN-C8	Scarcity
20	25	4

[26271] AEC: 1999, Glow-in-the-Dark boxcar numbered "9700-glo."

EX-C7	LN-C8	Scarcity
25	30	4

[26272] CHRISTMAS: 2000, boxcar.

EX-C7	LN-C8	Scarcity
25	30	4

[26275] BOY SCOUT: 2000, boxcar numbered "9700."

EX-C7	LN-C8	Scarcity
40	45	4

[26276] CHESAPEAKE AND OHIO: 1999-2000, 9700 boxcar numbered "23296."

EX-C7	LN-C8	Scarcity
15	20	3

[26277] UNION PACIFIC: 2000, boxcar numbered "491050."

EX-C7	LN-C8	Scarcity
15	20	3

[26278] CAP'N CRUNCH CHRISTMAS: 1999, boxcar.

EX-C7	LN-C8	Scarcity
450	500	5

[26280] TINSEL TOWN EXPRESS: 2000, boxcar with music.

EX-C7	LN-C8	Scarcity
30	40	4

[26284] NY TOY FAIR: 1999, uncataloged preview boxcar.

EX-C7	LN-C8	Scarcity
600	650	6

[26285] NEW YORK CENTRAL: 2000, Pacemaker boxcar numbered "9700."

EX-C7	LN-C8	Scarcity
20	25	4

[26288] AEC: 1999, Glow-in-Dark boxcar numbered "9700."

EX-C7	LN-C8	Scarcity
20	25	4

[26290] SOUTHERN PACIFIC: 2000, boxcar.

EX-C7	LN-C8	Scarcity
15	20	3

[26291] PENNSYLVANIA: 2000, boxcar "47158."

EX-C7	LN-C8	Scarcity
15	20	3

[26292] FRISCO: 2000, boxcar "22015."

EX-C7	LN-C8	Scarcity
15	20	3

[26293] BURLINGTON: 2000, boxcar.

EX-C7	LN-C8	Scarcity
15	20	3

[26294] CENTENNIAL EXPRESS: 2000, boxcar.

EX-C7	LN-C8	Scarcity
Too rarely traded to establish accurate pricing.		

[26295] TRAINMASTER: 1999, uncataloged boxcar.

EX-C7	LN-C8	Scarcity
35	40	6

[26296] SERVICE STATION LTD.: 2000, boxcar set, Service Station Special item.

EX-C7	LN-C8	Scarcity
80	100	4

[26298] TAZ BOBBING: 2000, boxcar.

EX-C7	LN-C8	Scarcity
30	35	4

[26706] CHRISTMAS: 2000, lighted boxcar.

EX-C7	LN-C8	Scarcity
25	30	4

[26710] SOUTHERN: 1999, carsounds stock car.

EX-C7	LN-C8	Scarcity
60	70	4

[26712] CHURCHILL DOWNS: 1999-2000, horse car numbered "6473."

EX-C7	LN-C8	Scarcity
25	30	4

[26717] ORION STAR: 2000, boxcar.

EX-C7	LN-C8	Scarcity
20	25	4

[26718] CHRISTMAS: 2000, RailSounds boxcar.

EX-C7	LN-C8	Scarcity
115	125	5

[26719] BOBBING GHOST HALLOWEEN: 2000, boxcar numbered "9700."

EX-C7	LN-C8	Scarcity
20	25	4

[26724] VETERANS DAY: 2000, boxcar "9700."

EX-C7	LN-C8	Scarcity
45	55	5

[26725] NEW YORK CENTRAL: 2000, jumping hobo boxcar numbered "88160."

EX-C7	LN-C8	Scarcity
35	40	4

[26726] T. REX: 2000, bobbing boxcar numbered "9700."

EX-C7	LN-C8	Scarcity
25	30	4

[26727] SAN FRANCISCO CITY LIGHTS: 2000, boxcar.

EX-C7	LN-C8	Scarcity
35	40	4

[26739] SANTA & SNOWMAN: 2000, boxcar.

EX-C7	LN-C8	Scarcity
30	35	4

[26740] REINDEER: 2000, car.

EX-C7	LN-C8	Scarcity
30	35	4

[26741] SANTA: 2000, operating boxcar.

EX-C7	LN-C8	Scarcity
30	35	4

[26750] CARNEGIE SCIENCE CENTER: 1999, boxcar numbered "9200."

EX-C7	LN-C8	Scarcity
60	75	5

26776 U.S. ARMY: 2000, operating boxcar numbered "26413."

EX-C7	LN-C8	Scarcity
25	30	4

[26938] NEW YORK CENTRAL: 1999, refrigerator car.

EX-C7	LN-C8	Scarcity
50	65	4

[26940] DENVER & RIO GRANDE WESTERN: 1999, stock car numbered "37710."

EX-C7	LN-C8	Scarcity
50	65	4

[26992] NEW YORK CENTRAL: 1999, refrigerator car.

EX-C7	LN-C8	Scarcity
60	70	4

[26993] NEW YORK CENTRAL: 1999, refrigerator car.

EX-C7	LN-C8	Scarcity
60	70	4

[26994] NEW YORK CENTRAL: 1999, refrigerator car.

EX-C7	LN-C8	Scarcity
60	70	4

[26995] DENVER & RIO GRANDE WESTERN: 1999, stock car numbered "37714."

EX-C7	LN-C8	Scarcity
60	70	4

[26996] DENVER & RIO GRANDE WESTERN: 1999, stock car numbered "37715."

EX-C7	LN-C8	Scarcity
60	70	4

[26997] DENVER & RIO GRANDE WESTERN: 1999, stock car numbered "37716."

EX-C7	LN-C8	Scarcity
60	70	4

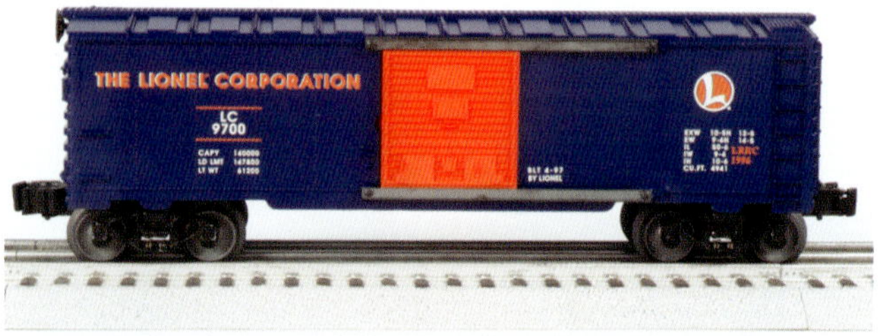

[29200] LIONEL RAILROADER CLUB: 1998, uncataloged boxcar numbered "9700."

EX-C7	LN-C8	Scarcity
35	40	5

[29202] SANTA FE: 1997, uncataloged Map boxcar numbered "6464."

EX-C7	LN-C8	Scarcity
45	50	5

[29203] MAINE CENTRAL: 1997, uncataloged boxcar numbered "6464-597."

EX-C7	LN-C8	Scarcity
25	30	5

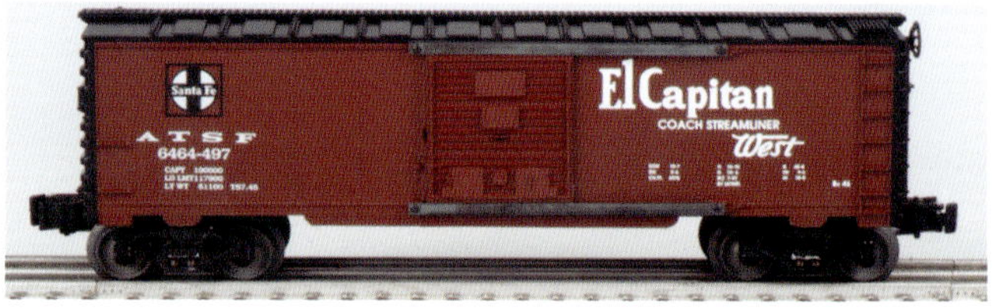

[29204] CENTURY CLUB: 1997, uncataloged boxcar numbered "1900-2000."

EX-C7	LN-C8	Scarcity
450	500	6

[29205] MM RAILROAD: 1997, High-Cube boxcar numbered "9555."

EX-C7	LN-C8	Scarcity
35	40	4

[29206] VAPOR RECORDS: 1997 boxcar, First Edition.

EX-C7	LN-C8	Scarcity
Too rarely traded to establish accurate pricing.		

[29209] 6464: 1998, boxcar series VII, three-pack.

EX-C7	LN-C8	Scarcity
75	90	4

[29210] GREAT NORTHERN: 1998, boxcar numbered "6464-450."

EX-C7	LN-C8	Scarcity
25	30	4

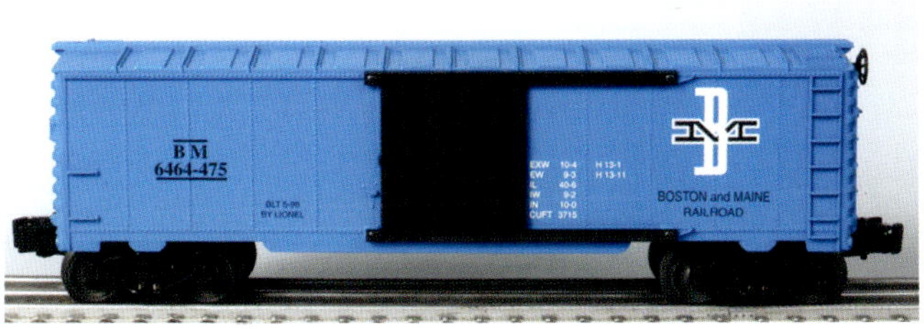

[29211] BOSTON AND MAINE: 1998, boxcar numbered "6464-475."

EX-C7	LN-C8	Scarcity
25	30	4

[29212] TIMKEN: 1998, boxcar numbered "6464-500."

EX-C7	LN-C8	Scarcity
25	30	4

[29213] SANTA FE: 1998, Grand Canyon Route 6464 boxcar numbered "6464-198."

EX-C7	LN-C8	Scarcity
15	20	4

[29214] SOUTHERN: 1998, Railway 6464 boxcar numbered "6464-298."

EX-C7	LN-C8	Scarcity
15	20	4

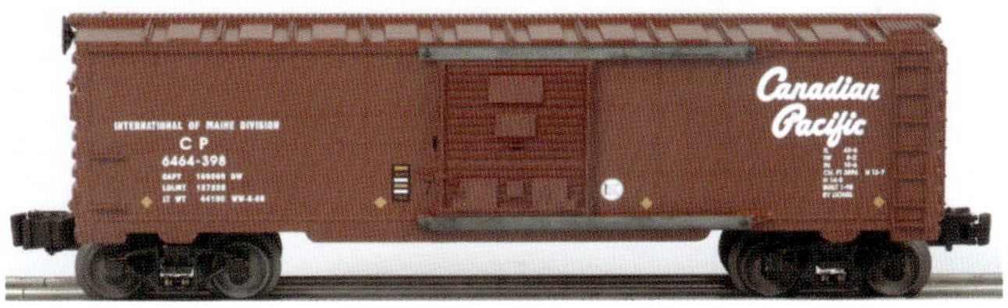

[29215] CANADIAN PACIFIC: 1998, 6464 boxcar numbered "6464-398."

EX-C7	LN-C8	Scarcity
15	20	4

[29217] AIREX: 1997, uncataloged boxcar.

EX-C7	LN-C8	Scarcity
50	65	5

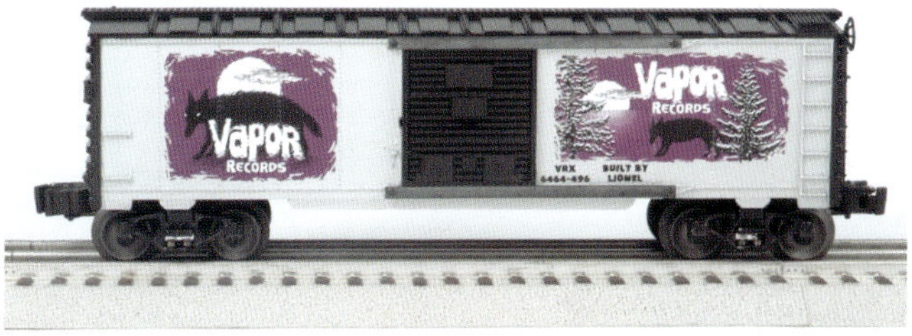

[29218] VAPOR RECORDS: 1997, uncataloged boxcar numbered "6464-496."

EX-C7	LN-C8	Scarcity
100	125	5

[29220] 1997 LIONEL CENTENNIAL SERIES: 1998, High-Cube boxcar, four-car set.

EX-C7	LN-C8	Scarcity
80	100	4

[29221] 1997 CENTENNIAL SERIES: 1998, High-Cube boxcar numbered "9697-1."

EX-C7	LN-C8	Scarcity
20	25	4

[29222] 1997 CENTENNIAL SERIES: 1998, High-Cube boxcar numbered "9697-2."

EX-C7	LN-C8	Scarcity
20	25	4

[29223] 1997 CENTENNIAL SERIES: 1998, High-Cube boxcar numbered "9697-3."

EX-C7	LN-C8	Scarcity
20	25	4

[29224] 1997 CENTENNIAL SERIES: 1998, High-Cube boxcar numbered "9697-4."

EX-C7	LN-C8	Scarcity
20	25	4

[29225] H.O.R.D.E. MUSIC FESTIVAL: 1997, boxcar.

EX-C7	LN-C8	Scarcity
30	35	4

[29226] CENTURY CLUB BERKSHIRE: 1997, uncataloged boxcar.

EX-C7	LN-C8	Scarcity
200	225	6

[29227] CENTURY CLUB GG1: 1998, uncataloged GG 1 boxcar.

EX-C7	LN-C8	Scarcity
60	75	5

[29228] CENTURY CLUB TURBINE: 1999, uncataloged boxcar numbered "671."

EX-C7	LN-C8	Scarcity
60	75	5

[29229] VAPOR RECORDS: 1998, Holiday car.

EX-C7	LN-C8	Scarcity
60	75	4

[29231] ANIMATED HALLOWEEN: 1998, boxcar.

EX-C7	LN-C8	Scarcity
20	25	4

[29232] LENNY THE LION: 1998, High-Cube.

EX-C7	LN-C8	Scarcity
35	45	4

[29233] CONRAIL: 1998, overstamped PC boxcar numbered "6464-598."

EX-C7	LN-C8	Scarcity
35	40	4

[29234] CONRAIL: 1998, overstamped Erie boxcar numbered "6464-698."

EX-C7	LN-C8	Scarcity
35	40	4

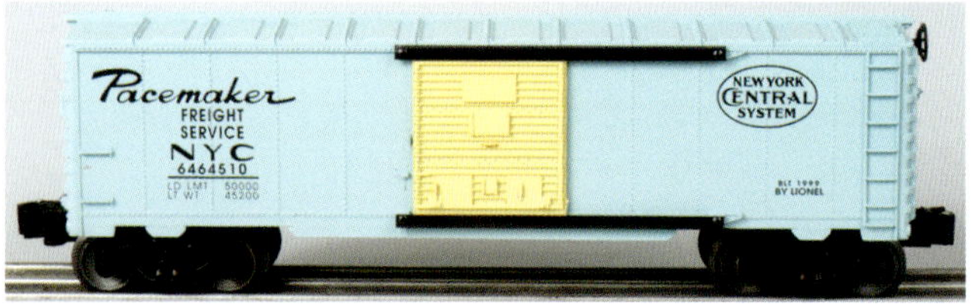

[29235] NEW YORK CENTRAL: 1999, boxcar numbered "6464-510."

EX-C7	LN-C8	Scarcity
25	30	4

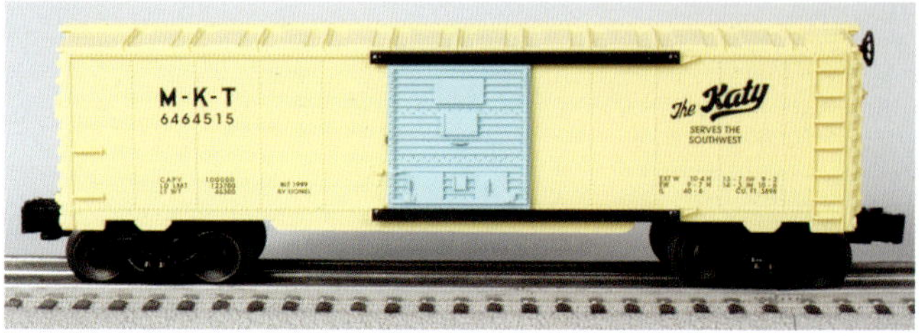

[29236] KATY: 1999, boxcar numbered "6464-515."

EX-C7	LN-C8	Scarcity
25	30	4

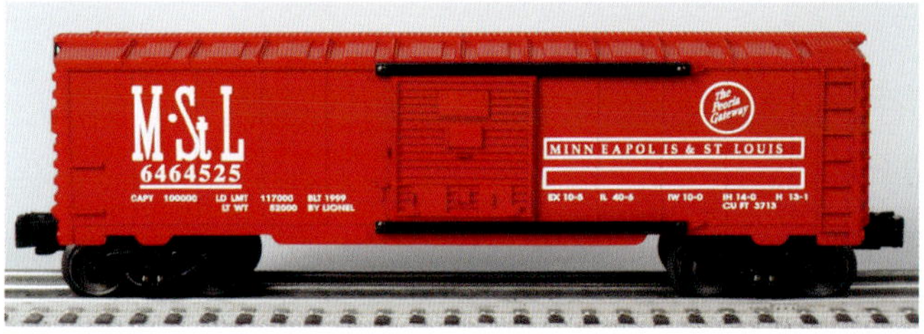

[29237] MINNEAPOLIS & ST. LOUIS: 1999, boxcar numbered "6464-525."

EX-C7	LN-C8	Scarcity
25	30	4

[29248] CENTURY CLUB F-3: 1999, uncataloged boxcar numbered "2333."

EX-C7	LN-C8	Scarcity
60	75	5

[29250] PHOEBE SNOW: 1999, boxcar numbered "6464-199."

EX-C7	LN-C8	Scarcity
25	30	4

[29251] BURLINGTON: 1999, boxcar numbered "6464-299."

EX-C7	LN-C8	Scarcity
25	30	4

[29252] CANADIAN PACIFIC: 1999, boxcar numbered "6464-399."

EX-C7	LN-C8	Scarcity
25	30	4

[29253] BOSTON AND MAINE: 1999, 6565 boxcar numbered "76032."

EX-C7	LN-C8	Scarcity
30	35	4

[29254] BOSTON AND MAINE: 1999, 6565 boxcar numbered "76033."

EX-C7	LN-C8	Scarcity
30	35	4

[29255] BOSTON AND MAINE: 1999, 6565 boxcar numbered "76034."

EX-C7	LN-C8	Scarcity
30	35	4

[29256] BOSTON AND MAINE: 1999, 6565 boxcar numbered "76035."

EX-C7	LN-C8	Scarcity
30	35	4

[29257] SOUTHERN: 1999, boxcar numbered "9464-199."

EX-C7	LN-C8	Scarcity
25	30	4

[29258] READING: 1999, boxcar numbered "9464-299."

EX-C7	LN-C8	Scarcity
25	30	4

[29259] NORTHERN PACIFIC: 1999, Bicentennial boxcar numbered "9464-399."

EX-C7	LN-C8	Scarcity
25	30	4

[29265] MAINE CENTRAL: 1999, 6565 boxcar numbered "8661."

EX-C7	LN-C8	Scarcity
25	30	4

[29266] FRISCO: 1999, 6565 boxcar numbered "8722."

EX-C7	LN-C8	Scarcity
25	30	4

[29267] 6464: 1999, series boxcar VIII, three-pack.

EX-C7	LN-C8	Scarcity
70	90	4

[29268] DENVER & RIO GRANDE WESTERN: 1999, 6565 boxcar numbered "63067."

EX-C7	LN-C8	Scarcity
25	30	4

[29279] JC/CR: 1999, boxcar numbered "6464-28X."

EX-C7	LN-C8	Scarcity
30	35	4

[29280] LEHIGH VALLEY/CR: 1999, boxcar numbered "6464-31X."

EX-C7	LN-C8	Scarcity
30	35	4

[29281] POST-MERGER BOXCAR SET; JERSEY CENTRAL & LEHIGH VALLEY OVERSTAMPED CONRAIL: 1999, two-pack set.

EX-C7	LN-C8	Scarcity
60	70	4

[29282]: 1999, archive three-pack numbered "6464."

EX-C7	LN-C8	Scarcity
80	90	4

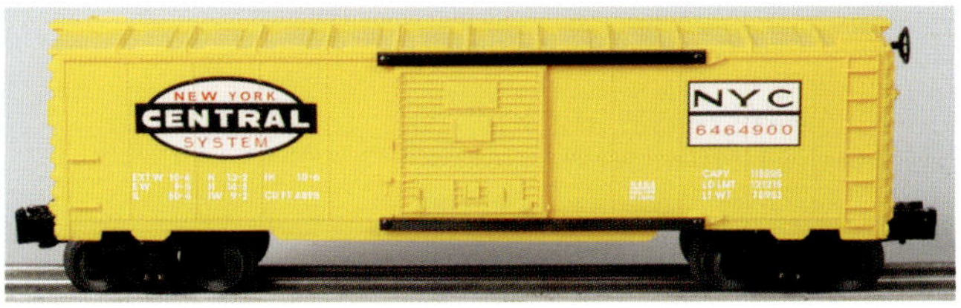

[29283] NEW YORK CENTRAL: 1999, boxcar numbered "6464-900."

EX-C7	LN-C8	Scarcity
25	30	4

[29284] GREAT NORTHERN: 1999, boxcar numbered "6464/0000."

EX-C7	LN-C8	Scarcity
25	30	4

[29285] SEABOARD: 1999, boxcar.

EX-C7	LN-C8	Scarcity
25	30	4

[29286] OVERSTAMPED: 1999, boxcar, two-pack.

EX-C7	LN-C8	Scarcity
50	60	4

[29287] NEW HAVEN/PC: 1999, boxcar numbered "6464-29X."

EX-C7	LN-C8	Scarcity
25	30	4

[29288] RDG/CR: 1999, boxcar numbered "6464-32X."

EX-C7	LN-C8	Scarcity
25	30	4

[29289] 6464: 1999-2000, series boxcar IX, three-pack.

EX-C7	LN-C8	Scarcity
60	80	4

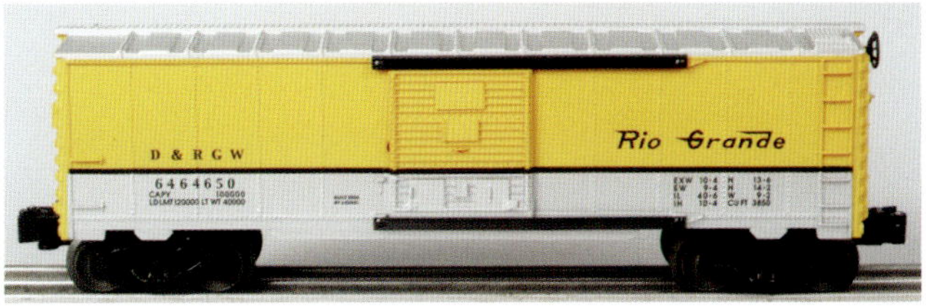

[29290] DENVER & RIO GRANDE WESTERN: 2000, boxcar numbered "6464-650."

EX-C7	LN-C8	Scarcity
20	25	4

[29291] SANTA FE: 2000, boxcar numbered "6464-700."

EX-C7	LN-C8	Scarcity
20	25	4

[29292] NEW HAVEN: 2000, boxcar numbered "6464-725."

EX-C7	LN-C8	Scarcity
20	25	4

[29293] NEW HAVEN: 1999, boxcar numbered "6464-425."

EX-C7	LN-C8	Scarcity
75	100	5

[29294] HELLGATE BRIDGE: 1999, uncataloged boxcar numbered "1900-2000."

EX-C7	LN-C8	Scarcity
75	80	5

[29295] PENNSYLVANIA 6565: 1999-2000, "Don't Stand Me Still" boxcar numbered "24018."

EX-C7	LN-C8	Scarcity
30	35	4

[29296] PENNSYLVANIA 6565: 1999-2000, "Merchandise" boxcar numbered "29296."

EX-C7	LN-C8	Scarcity
30	35	4

[29297] PENNSYLVANIA 6565: 1999-2000, "No Damage" boxcar numbered "47158."

EX-C7	LN-C8	Scarcity
30	35	4

[29298] LIONEL: 2000, boxcar numbered "6464-2000."

EX-C7	LN-C8	Scarcity
30	35	4

[36200] QUAKER LIFE CEREAL: 2000, boxcar.

EX-C7	LN-C8	Scarcity
400	450	6

[36202] MINIATURE RAILROAD & VILLAGE: 2000, uncataloged 80th Anniversary boxcar.

EX-C7	LN-C8	Scarcity
80	100	6

[36203] WHIRLPOOL: 2000, uncataloged boxcar.

EX-C7	LN-C8	Scarcity
80	100	6

[36205] EBAY: 2000, boxcar.

EX-C7	LN-C8	Scarcity
125	150	6

[36206] FATHER'S DAY: 2000, boxcar.

EX-C7	LN-C8	Scarcity
20	25	4

[36207] LIONEL EMPLOYEE CHRISTMAS: 2000, uncataloged boxcar.

EX-C7	LN-C8	Scarcity
350	375	6

[36213] VAPOR RECORDS CHRISTMAS: 2000, boxcar.

EX-C7	LN-C8	Scarcity
25	30	4

[36215] TRAIN STATION 25TH ANNIVERSARY: 2000, uncataloged boxcar.

EX-C7	LN-C8	Scarcity
40	50	5

[36218] SNAP-ON: 2000, uncataloged boxcar.

EX-C7	LN-C8	Scarcity
70	80	6

[36220] PIONEER SEED: 2000, uncataloged boxcar.

EX-C7	LN-C8	Scarcity
Too rarely traded to establish accurate pricing.		

[36227] MONOPOLY COMMUNITY CHEST: 2000, uncataloged boxcar.

EX-C7	LN-C8	Scarcity
40	50	6

[36245] LIONEL 20TH CENTURY: 2000, uncataloged boxcar numbered "1900-1925."

EX-C7	LN-C8	Scarcity
25	30	5

[36246] LIONEL 20TH CENTURY: 2000, uncataloged boxcar numbered "1926-1950."

EX-C7	LN-C8	Scarcity
25	30	5

[36247] LIONEL 20TH CENTURY: 2000, uncataloged boxcar numbered "1951-1975."

EX-C7	LN-C8	Scarcity
25	30	5

[36248] LIONEL 20TH CENTURY: 2000, uncataloged boxcar numbered "1976-2000."

EX-C7	LN-C8	Scarcity
25	30	5

[36305] EBAY: 2000, uncataloged boxcar numbered "9700."

EX-C7	LN-C8	Scarcity
75	100	5

[36703] LIONEL POSTWAR CIRCUS: 3366 horse car and corral.

EX-C7	LN-C8	Scarcity
80	90	4

[39200] HELLGATE BRIDGE: 2000, uncataloged boxcar II numbered "1900-2000."

EX-C7	LN-C8	Scarcity
65	75	6

[39201] CENTURY CLUB HUDSON: 2000, uncataloged boxcar numbered "773."

EX-C7	LN-C8	Scarcity
40	50	5

[39202] LIONEL CENTENNIAL: 2000, boxcar numbered "1900-2000."

EX-C7	LN-C8	Scarcity
40	50	5

[39203] 6464: 2001, series X boxcar, three-pack, included for continuity.

EX-C7	LN-C8	Scarcity
70	80	4

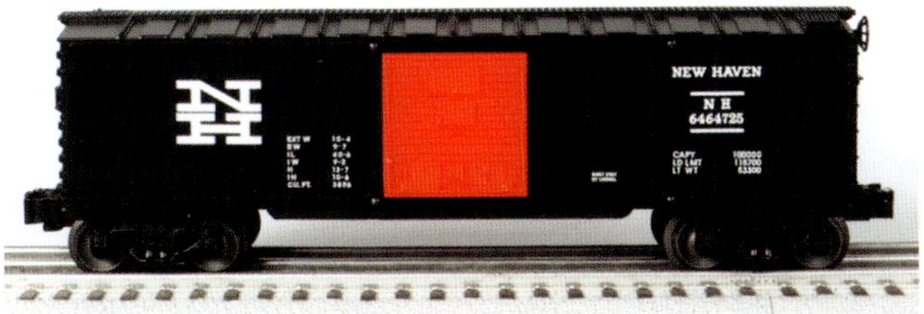

[39204] NEW HAVEN: 2001, boxcar numbered "6464-725," included for continuity.

EX-C7	LN-C8	Scarcity
25	30	4

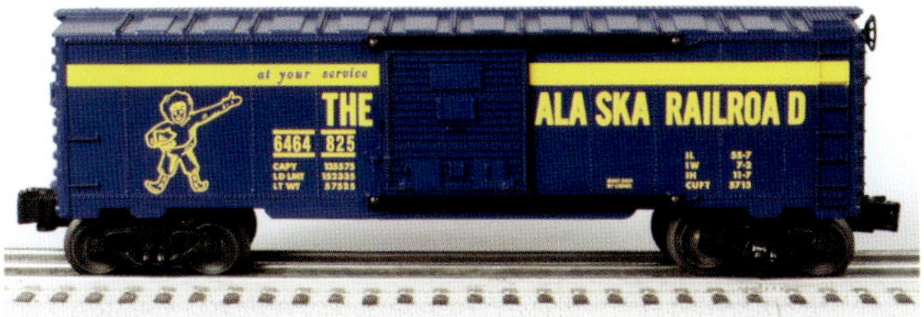

[39205] ALASKA RAILROAD: 2001, boxcar numbered "6464-825," included for continuity.

EX-C7	LN-C8	Scarcity
25	30	4

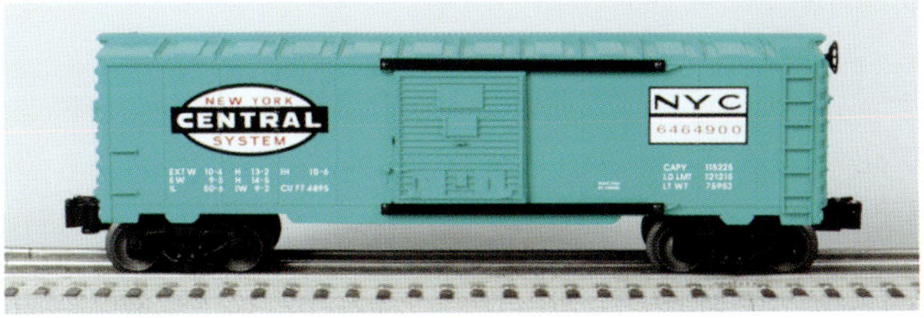

[39206] NEW YORK CENTRAL: 2001, boxcar numbered "6464-900," included for continuity.

EX-C7	LN-C8	Scarcity
25	30	4

39207 UNION PACIFIC: 2000, 6565 boxcar numbered "508500," red.

EX-C7	LN-C8	Scarcity
30	35	4

39208 UNION PACIFIC: 2000, 6565 boxcar numbered "903658," silver.

EX-C7	LN-C8	Scarcity
30	35	4

39209 UNION PACIFIC: 2000, 6565 boxcar numbered "500200," yellow.

EX-C7	LN-C8	Scarcity
30	35	4

[39210] 6530: 2000, Fire Fighting car.

EX-C7	LN-C8	Scarcity
25	30	4

[39211] 6464: 2000, Archive 2 boxcar, three-pack.

EX-C7	LN-C8	Scarcity
65	75	4

[39217] LCC II: 2000, uncataloged Member boxcar.

EX-C7	LN-C8	Scarcity
50	60	5

[51007] LCC II UNION PACIFIC: 2000, uncataloged M-10000 set.

EX-C7	LN-C8	Scarcity
700	850	5

[51301] LACKAWANNA: 1992, semi-scale refrigerator car numbered "7000."

EX-C7	LN-C8	Scarcity
200	250	5

[51401] PENNSYLVANIA: 1991, semi-scale boxcar numbered "100800."

EX-C7	LN-C8	Scarcity
100	125	5

[51402] CHESAPEAKE & OHIO: 1992, semi-scale stock car numbered "95250."

EX-C7	LN-C8	Scarcity
150	175	5

[52006] CANADIAN PACIFIC: 1993, uncataloged Lionel Collectors Association of Canada boxcar numbered "930016" with 1/48-scale proportions.

EX-C7	LN-C8	Scarcity
90	100	6

[52009] WESTERN PACIFIC: 1993, uncataloged Sacramento Valley TTOS boxcar numbered "64641993."

EX-C7	LN-C8	Scarcity
35	40	6

[52010] WEYERHAEUSER: 1993, uncataloged TTOS double-door boxcar numbered "838593" with 1/48-scale proportions.

EX-C7	LN-C8	Scarcity
40	45	6

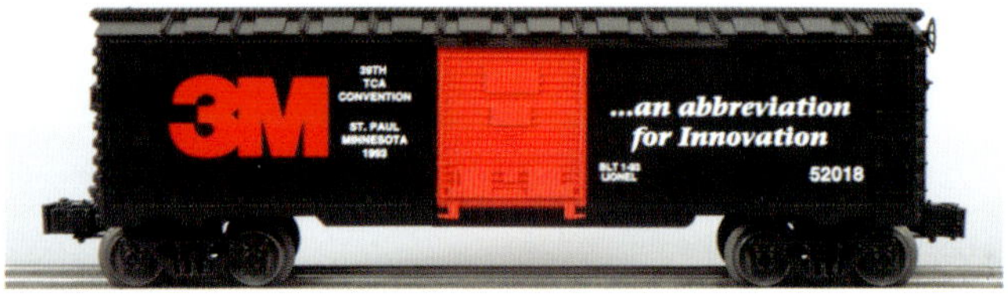

52018 3M: 1993, uncataloged Lakes & Pines TCA boxcar.

EX-C7	LN-C8	Scarcity
350	400	6

[52019] LONG ISLAND NLOE: 1993, uncataloged boxcar numbered "8393."

EX-C7	LN-C8	Scarcity
30	40	6

52022 UNION PACIFIC: 1993, uncataloged TTOS boxcar.

EX-C7	LN-C8	Scarcity
250	300	6

[52043] LL BEAN: 1994, uncataloged New England Division of Train Collectors Association boxcar numbered "1994."

EX-C7	LN-C8	Scarcity
90	125	6

[52045] PENN DUTCH: 1994, uncataloged TCA milk car numbered "61052."

EX-C7	LN-C8	Scarcity
75	80	6

[52046] ATLANTIC COAST LINE: 1994, uncataloged TTOS boxcar numbered "16247."

EX-C7	LN-C8	Scarcity
75	80	6

[52051] BALTIMORE & OHIO: 1995, uncataloged TCA "Sentinel" boxcar numbered "6464095."

EX-C7	LN-C8	Scarcity
40	45	6

[52052] TCA 40TH ANNIVERSARY: 1994, uncataloged boxcar.

EX-C7	LN-C8	Scarcity
60	70	6

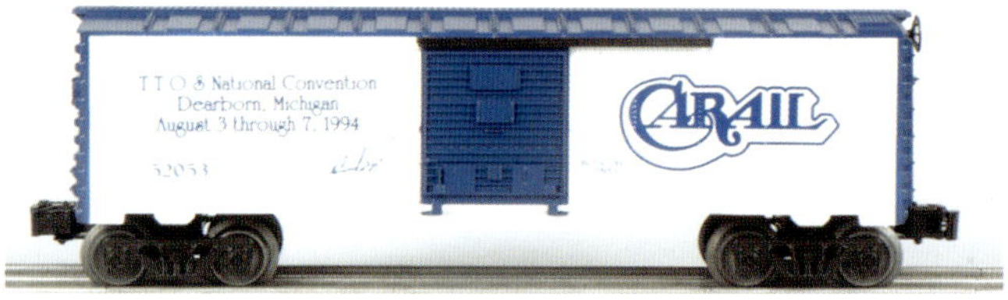

52053 CARAIL: 1994, uncataloged TTOS boxcar.

EX-C7	LN-C8	Scarcity
40	45	6

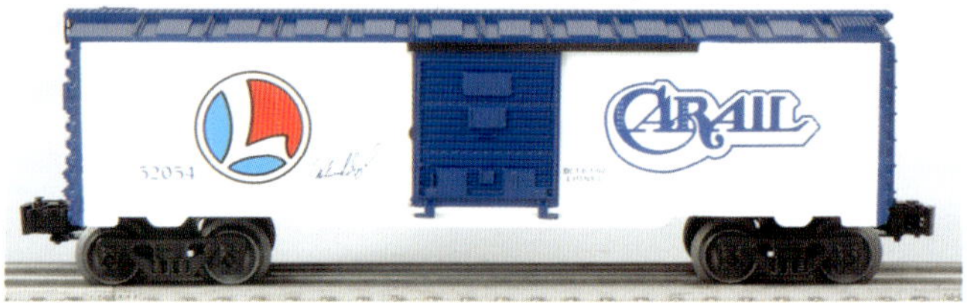

52054 CARAIL: 1994, uncataloged boxcar.

EX-C7	LN-C8	Scarcity
400	450	6

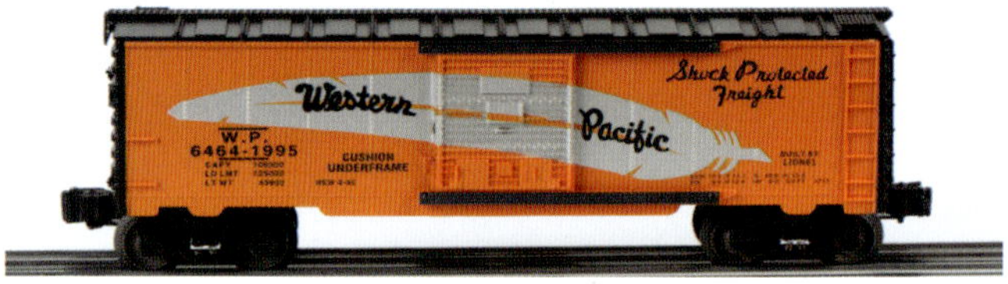

[52057] WESTERN PACIFIC: 1995, uncataloged TTOS boxcar numbered "64641995."

EX-C7	LN-C8	Scarcity
40	45	6

[52058] SANTA FE: 1995, uncataloged Central California TTOS boxcar numbered "64641895."

EX-C7	LN-C8	Scarcity
40	45	6

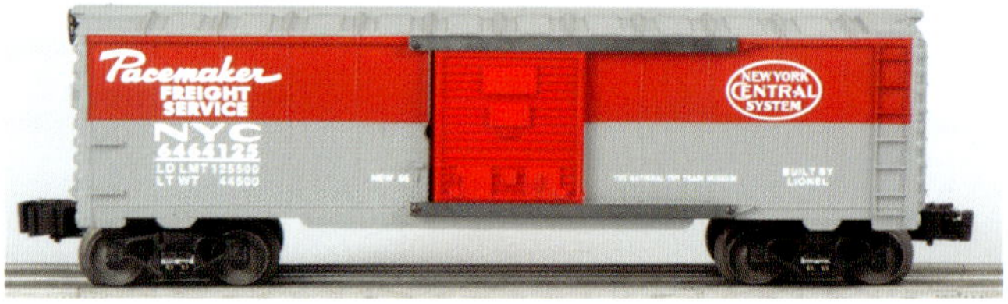

[52063] NEW YORK CENTRAL: 1995, uncataloged TCA "Pacemaker" boxcar numbered "6464125."

EX-C7	LN-C8	Scarcity
225	325	6

[52064] MISSOURI PACIFIC: 1995, uncataloged TCA boxcar numbered "6464150."

EX-C7	LN-C8	Scarcity
225	325	6

[52065] PENN-DUTCH GRAIN: 1996, uncataloged operating boxcar numbered "9028."

EX-C7	LN-C8	Scarcity
80	100	6

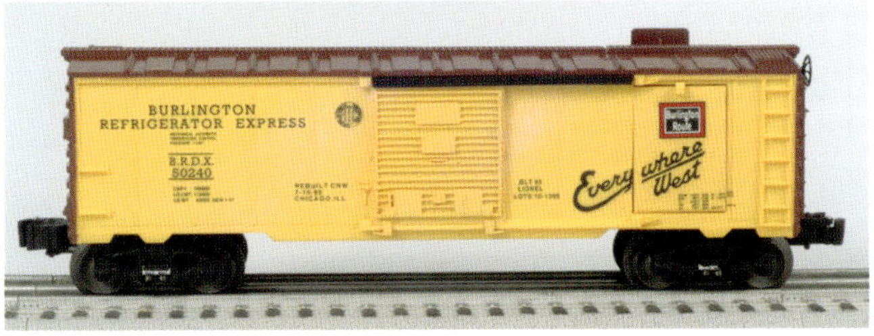

[52067] BURLINGTON: 1995, uncataloged LOTS ice car numbered "50240."

EX-C7	LN-C8	Scarcity
35	40	6

[52068] CONTADINA: 1994, uncataloged Toy Train Parade TTOS boxcar numbered "16245."

EX-C7	LN-C8	Scarcity
40	45	6

52070 KNOEBEL'S: 1995, uncataloged boxcar.

EX-C7	LN-C8	Scarcity
45	50	6

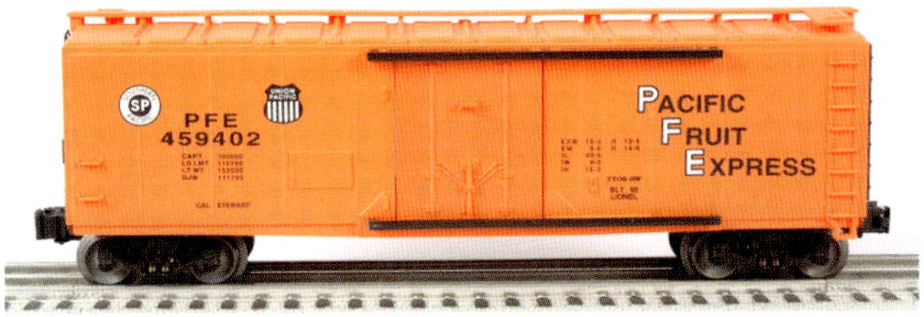

[52073] PACIFIC FRUIT EXPRESS: 1995, uncataloged Southwest TTOS refrigerator car numbered "459402" with 1/48-scale proportions.

EX-C7	LN-C8	Scarcity
45	50	6

[52074] IOWA BEEF PACKERS: 1995, uncataloged LCCA refrigerator car numbered "197095" with 1/48-scale proportions.

EX-C7	LN-C8	Scarcity
25	30	6

52075 UNITED AUTO WORKERS: 1995, uncataloged boxcar.

EX-C7	LN-C8	Scarcity
50	60	6

[52076] NLOE LONG ISLAND: 1996, uncataloged observation car numbered "8396."

EX-C7	LN-C8	Scarcity
250	300	6

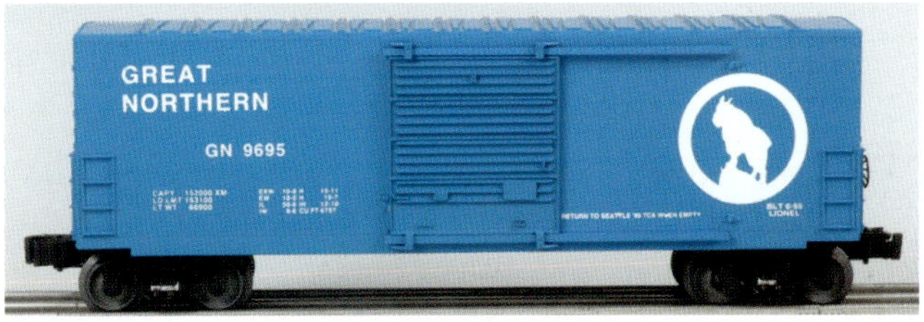

[52077] GREAT NORTHERN: 1995, uncataloged Pacific Northwest TCA High-Cube boxcar numbered "9695."

EX-C7	LN-C8	Scarcity
350	400	6

[52081] CHICAGO & NORTHWESTERN: 1996, uncataloged boxcar numbered "6464555."

EX-C7	LN-C8	Scarcity
45	55	6

52082 STEAMTOWN LACKAWANNA: 1995, uncataloged boxcar.

EX-C7	LN-C8	Scarcity
70	80	6

[52086] PACIFIC GREAT EASTERN: 1996, uncataloged Canadian TTOS boxcar numbered "6464-1972."

EX-C7	LN-C8	Scarcity
40	50	6

[52087] NEW MEXICO CENTRAL: 1996, uncataloged TTOS boxcar numbered "6464-1996."

EX-C7	LN-C8	Scarcity
40	50	6

[52090] PERE MARQUETTE: 1996, uncataloged LCCA double-door boxcar with 1/48-scale proportions.

EX-C7	LN-C8	Scarcity
30	35	6

[52093] LONE STAR TCA: 1996, uncataloged boxcar numbered "6464696."

EX-C7	LN-C8	Scarcity
45	50	6

[52096] DEPT. 56 SNOW VILLAGE: 1995, uncataloged boxcar numbered "9756."

EX-C7	LN-C8	Scarcity
55	65	6

52097 CHESSIE SYSTEM: 1995, uncataloged Artrain refrigerator car.

EX-C7	LN-C8	Scarcity
65	75	6

[52098] NATIONAL BUREAU OF STANDARDS: 1996, uncataloged boxcar with 1/48-scale proportions.

EX-C7	LN-C8	Scarcity
55	65	6

[52110] CSPM & O: 1997, uncataloged boxcar.

EX-C7	LN-C8	Scarcity
35	40	6

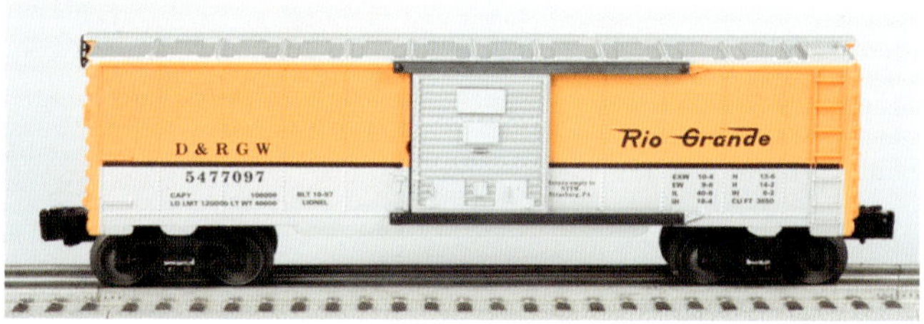

[52118] DENVER & RIO GRANDE WESTERN: 1997, uncataloged TCA boxcar numbered "5477097."

EX-C7	LN-C8	Scarcity
45	50	5

[52119] TCA MUSEUM 20TH ANNIVERSARY: 1997, uncataloged boxcar.

EX-C7	LN-C8	Scarcity
Too rarely traded to establish accurate pricing.		

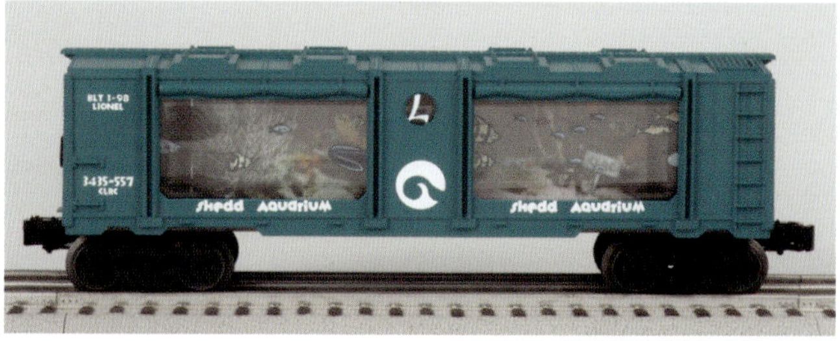

[52120] SHEDD AQUARIUM: 1998, uncataloged car numbered "3435-557."

EX-C7	LN-C8	Scarcity
60	70	6

[52126] MILWAUKEE ROAD: 1997, uncataloged boxcar with CTT logo numbered "21027."

EX-C7	LN-C8	Scarcity
45	50	5

[52128] PENNSYLVANIA DUTCH: 1997, uncataloged TCA boxcar numbered "91653."

EX-C7	LN-C8	Scarcity
55	60	6

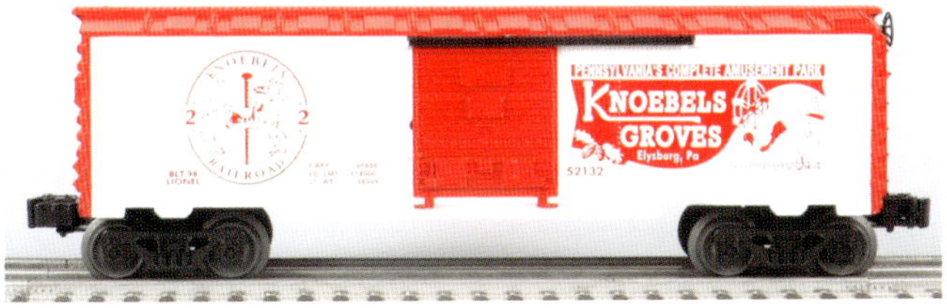

[52132] KNOEBELS: 1999, uncataloged boxcar.

EX-C7	LN-C8	Scarcity
55	60	6

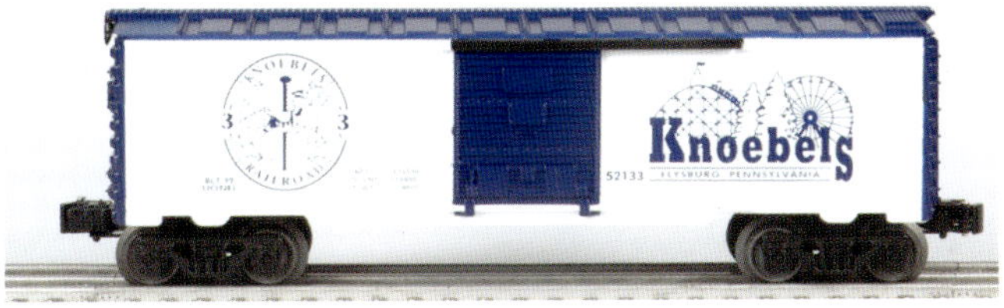

[52133] KNOEBELS: 1998, uncataloged boxcar.

EX-C7	LN-C8	Scarcity
55	60	6

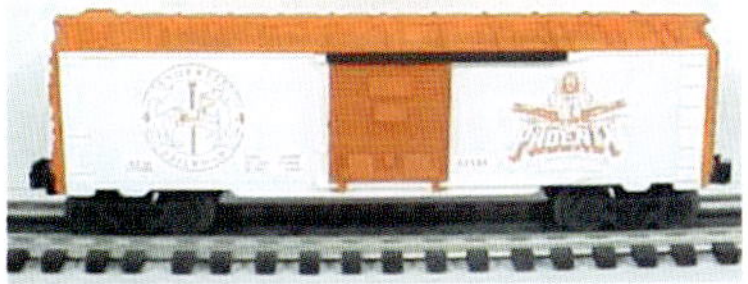

[52134] KNOEBELS PHOENIX: 2000, uncataloged number four boxcar.

EX-C7	LN-C8	Scarcity
55	60	6

[52135] SANTA FE: 1998, uncataloged refrigerator car numbered "22739."

EX-C7	LN-C8	Scarcity
35	40	6

[52140] UNION PACIFIC: 1997, uncataloged Artrain bunk car.

EX-C7	LN-C8	Scarcity
80	100	6

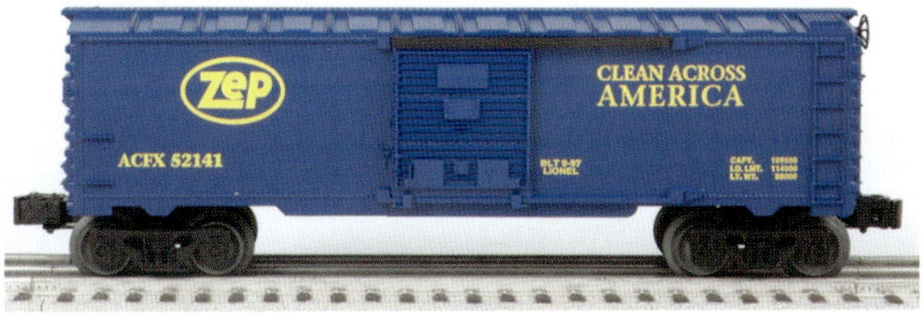

[52141] ZEP: 1996, boxcar.

EX-C7	LN-C8	Scarcity
60	70	6

[52146] OCEAN SPRAY PLUG DOOR: 1997, refrigerator car numbered "OSCX1998."

EX-C7	LN-C8	Scarcity
80	100	6

[52148] REA/SANTA FE: 1999, uncataloged operating boxcar numbered "52148-558."

EX-C7	LN-C8	Scarcity
55	60	6

[52151] AMTRAK: 1998, uncataloged Express baggage car boxcar numbered "71998" with 1/48-scale proportions.

EX-C7	LN-C8	Scarcity
45	55	6

[52152] BEN FRANKLIN PHILADELPHIA WOODSIDE: 1998, uncataloged refrigerator car.

EX-C7	LN-C8	Scarcity
80	100	6

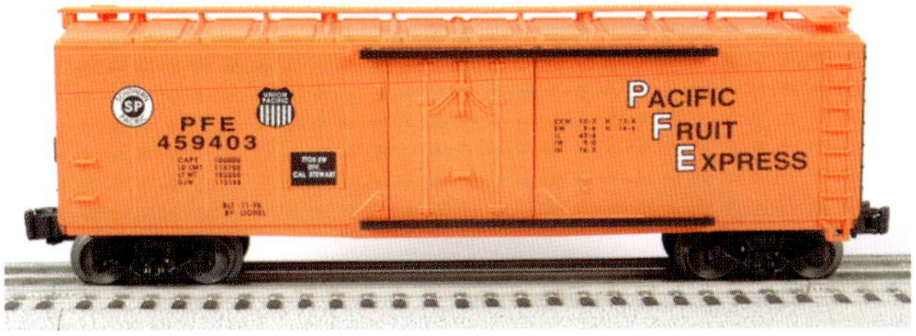

[52154] PACIFIC FRUIT EXPRESS: 1998, uncataloged refrigerator car numbered "459403" with 1/48-scale proportions.

EX-C7	LN-C8	Scarcity
55	60	6

[52155] TCA "CITY OF SAN FRANCISCO": 1999, uncataloged baggage car numbered "1999."

EX-C7	LN-C8	Scarcity
100	125	6

[52158] MONOPOLY: 1998, mint car numbered "M-0539."

EX-C7	LN-C8	Scarcity
175	200	6

[52162] GULF, MOBILE & OHIO: 1999, uncataloged LOTS double-door boxcar numbered "24580."

EX-C7	LN-C8	Scarcity
40	50	6

[52163] MILWAUKEE ROAD: 1999, uncataloged Milwaukee LRC double-door boxcar "194798."

EX-C7	LN-C8	Scarcity
40	50	6

[52170] SOUTHERN PACIFIC: 1999, uncataloged CLRC operating boxcar.

EX-C7	LN-C8	Scarcity
50	60	6

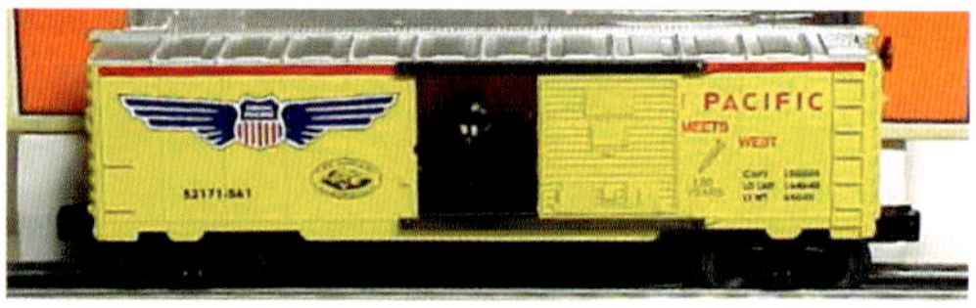

[52171] UNION PACIFIC: 1999, uncataloged CLRC operating boxcar.

EX-C7	LN-C8	Scarcity
50	60	6

[52172] LOUISVILLE & NASHVILLE: 1999, uncataloged boxcar.

EX-C7	LN-C8	Scarcity
50	60	6

[52176] FORT WORTH & DENVER: 1999, uncataloged 1/48-scale proportioned boxcar numbered "8277."

EX-C7	LN-C8	Scarcity
35	40	6

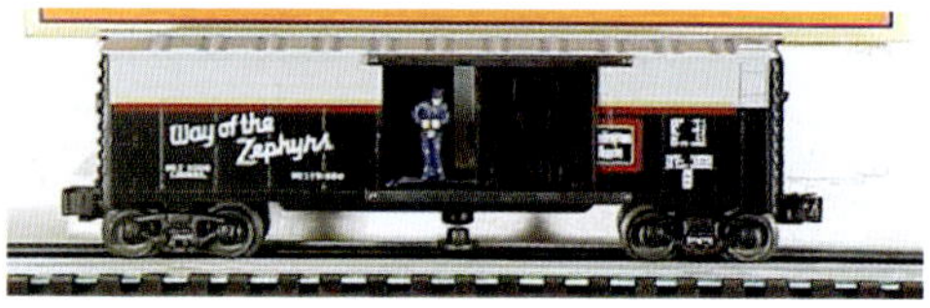

[52178] BURLINGTON ROUTE: 2000, uncataloged CLRC operating boxcar.

EX-C7	LN-C8	Scarcity
45	55	6

[52179] ATLANTIC COAST LINE: 2000, uncataloged CLRC operating boxcar.

EX-C7	LN-C8	Scarcity
45	55	6

[52181] MONOPOLY SET 2: 1999, four-pack of freight cars: two boxcars, flat with autos, and gondola.

EX-C7	LN-C8	Scarcity
275	325	6

[52182] MONOPOLY RAILROADS: 1999, uncataloged boxcar numbered "M0636."

EX-C7	LN-C8	Scarcity
80	100	6

[52183] MONOPOLY JAIL: 1999, car numbered "M-1131."

EX-C7	LN-C8	Scarcity
60	75	6

[52186] GRUCCI FIREWORKS: 2000, uncataloged boxcar numbered "2000."

EX-C7	LN-C8	Scarcity
60	75	6

[52188] CARAIL AQUARIUM: 1999, with two antique automobiles, 25th Anniversary car.

EX-C7	LN-C8	Scarcity
60	75	6

[52198] FRISCO: 2000, uncataloged boxcar numbered "5477000."

EX-C7	LN-C8	Scarcity
30	40	6

[52205] SOUTHERN PACIFIC: 2000, uncataloged Overnight Merchandise Service boxcar, five-pack numbered "6464-2000."

EX-C7	LN-C8	Scarcity
175	200	5

[52212] BERKSHIRE BREWING: 2000, uncataloged refrigerator car.

EX-C7	LN-C8	Scarcity
125	150	6

52223 SANTA FE REA: 2000, uncataloged CLRC operating boxcar.

EX-C7	LN-C8	Scarcity
35	40	6

[80948] MICHIGAN CENTRAL: 1982, uncataloged LOTS boxcar.

EX-C7	LN-C8	Scarcity
125	175	6

[86009] CANADIAN NATIONAL: 1986, uncataloged Lionel Collectors Association of Canada bunk car.

EX-C7	LN-C8	Scarcity
60	80	6

[87010] CANADIAN NATIONAL: 1987, uncataloged Lionel Collectors Association of Canada Express refrigerator car.

EX-C7	LN-C8	Scarcity
60	80	6

[99008] MICKEY'S MERRY CHRISTMAS: 1999, uncataloged boxcar numbered "9700."

EX-C7	LN-C8	Scarcity
Too rarely traded to establish accurate pricing.		

[99015] CASE CUTLERY: 2000, uncataloged boxcar numbered "1889."

EX-C7	LN-C8	Scarcity
Too rarely traded to establish accurate pricing.		

[99018] CASE CUTLERY: 2000, uncataloged rolling stock, three-pack.

EX-C7	LN-C8	Scarcity
175	200	6

[121315] PENNSYLVANIA: 1984, uncataloged LOTS High-Cube boxcar.

EX-C7	LN-C8	Scarcity
75	125	6

[830005] CANADIAN NATIONAL: 1983, uncataloged Lionel Collectors Association of Canada boxcar.

EX-C7	LN-C8	Scarcity
225	250	6

CHAPTER 12

TANK AND VAT CARS

Tank Cars

One of the first and, according to some scholars, thee first cars produced in the modern era were the 9250 Waterpoxy tank cars. This car was based on the postwar 6415-type triple-dome tank car, with the earliest production even riding on surplus postwar bar-end trucks.

The Waterpoxy car was joined by the 9150 Gulf, also entering production in 1970, and also based on a postwar design—in this case the 6315 single-dome "chemical" tank car. The third type of tank car produced in 1970 was also a single-dome car, and also based on a postwar design. The "Scout-type" 027 6015 tank car body was used as the basis for the 9050 Sunoco tanker.

The mainstay of the postwar era tank cars, the 6465-style two-dome cars, was not revived until 1983, when it returned wearing the Shell logo. At that time the car was a "stripped down" version similar to that produced in the late postwar era. In 1987, the wire handrails returned to this car.

In 1990, an all-new tank car was added to the Lionel lineup. Riding on the premium "Standard 0" sprung trucks, these cars were styled along the lines of the GATX Unibody tank cars typical of those found on railroads today. The following year Lionel turned the clock in the other direction, reviving the scale-detailed prewar 715 tank car, now numbering it "51300." Since 1991, these two car types (Unibody and 715) have dominated tank car production.

Vat Cars

In 1974, Lionel reintroduced the postwar 6475 vat car, now numbered "9128" and riding on the typical MPC Symington-Wayne trucks. Few versions of this odd-looking car have been produced, and many of them have been uncataloged and promotional items.

[303] STAUFFER CHEMICAL: 1985, uncataloged LOTS, single-dome.

EX-C7	LN-C8	Scarcity
40	75	5

0782 LIONEL RAILROADER CLUB: 1985, uncataloged, single-dome.

EX-C7	LN-C8	Scarcity
20	30	5

[1982] IETCA: 1982, uncataloged, triple-dome.

EX-C7	LN-C8	Scarcity
5	15	6

[1983] TTOS: 1983, uncataloged Phoenix, triple-dome.

EX-C7	LN-C8	Scarcity
25	75	6

6300 CORN PRODUCTS: 1981-82, triple-dome.

EX-C7	LN-C8	Scarcity
10	15	3

6301 GULF: 1981, single-dome.

EX-C7	LN-C8	Scarcity
10	15	3

6302 QUAKER STATE: 1981, triple-dome.

EX-C7	LN-C8	Scarcity
20	25	3

6304 GREAT NORTHERN: 1981, single-dome, Famous American Railroads number three.

EX-C7	LN-C8	Scarcity
20	25	5

6305 BRITISH COLUMBIA: 1981, single-dome.

EX-C7	LN-C8	Scarcity
25	30	5

6306 SOUTHERN: 1983, single-dome, Famous American Railroads number four.

EX-C7	LN-C8	Scarcity
25	30	5

6307 PENNSYLVANIA: 1983, single-dome, Famous American Railroads number five.

EX-C7	LN-C8	Scarcity
30	35	5

6308 ALASKA RAILROAD: 1982-83, single-dome in the traditional 027/Scout size.

EX-C7	LN-C8	Scarcity
20	25	4

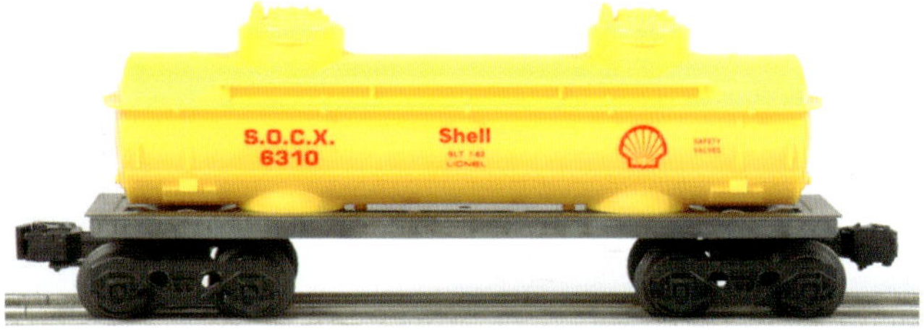

6310 SHELL: 1983-84, double-dome in the traditional 027/Scout size.

EX-C7	LN-C8	Scarcity
15	20	3

6312 CHESAPEAKE AND OHIO: 1984-85, double-dome in the traditional 027/Scout size.

EX-C7	LN-C8	Scarcity
15	25	4

6313 LIONEL LINES: 1984, uncataloged, single-dome.

EX-C7	LN-C8	Scarcity
20	25	5

6314 BALTIMORE AND OHIO: 1986, triple-dome.

EX-C7	LN-C8	Scarcity
15	25	4

6315 TCA PITTSBURGH: 1972, uncataloged, single-dome.

EX-C7	LN-C8	Scarcity
25	35	6

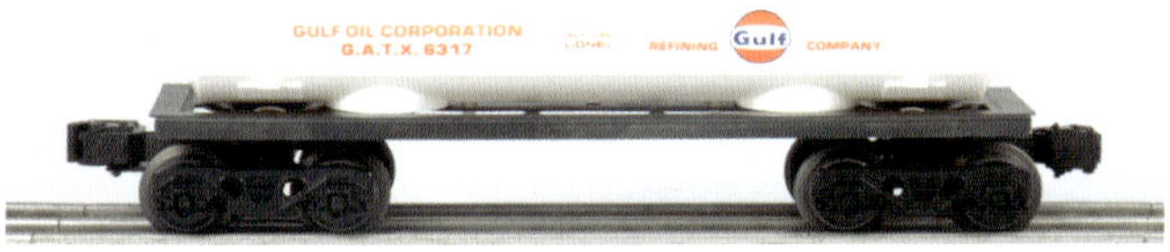

6317 GULF: 1984-85, double-dome in the traditional 027/Scout size.

EX-C7	LN-C8	Scarcity
10	18	4

6323 VIRGINIA CHEMICAL: 1986, uncataloged LCCA single-dome.

EX-C7	LN-C8	Scarcity
25	35	6

6357 FRISCO: 1983, single-dome.

EX-C7	LN-C8	Scarcity
25	35	6

[7684] VITRACO OIL: 1984, uncataloged Virginia Train Collectors, triple-dome.

EX-C7	LN-C8	Scarcity
15	20	5

8392 LONG ISLAND: 1992, uncataloged NLOE, single-dome.

EX-C7	LN-C8	Scarcity
30	45	6

9036 MOBILGAS: 1978-82, white single-dome in the traditional 027/Scout size.

9036 MOBILGAS (Type I): As described above.

EX-C7	LN-C8	Scarcity
5	10	2

9036 MOBILGAS (Type II): From 1978-79, some cars were overstamped to create uncataloged LCCA meet cars.

EX-C7	LN-C8	Scarcity
15	20	6

9039 MOBILGAS: Uncataloged in 1978, cataloged in 1980, single-dome in the traditional 027/Scout size.

EX-C7	LN-C8	Scarcity
10	15	1

9050 SUNOCO: 1970-71, single-dome in the traditional 027/Scout size. Produced in various shades of yellow.

EX-C7	LN-C8	Scarcity
10	15	2

9051 FIRESTONE: 1974-75, 1978, white single-dome in the traditional 027/Scout size.

9051 FIRESTONE (Type I): Some cars had unpainted white tanks.

EX-C7	LN-C8	Scarcity
10	15	2

9051 FIRESTONE (Type II): On other cars the tanks were painted white.

EX-C7	LN-C8	Scarcity
10	15	2

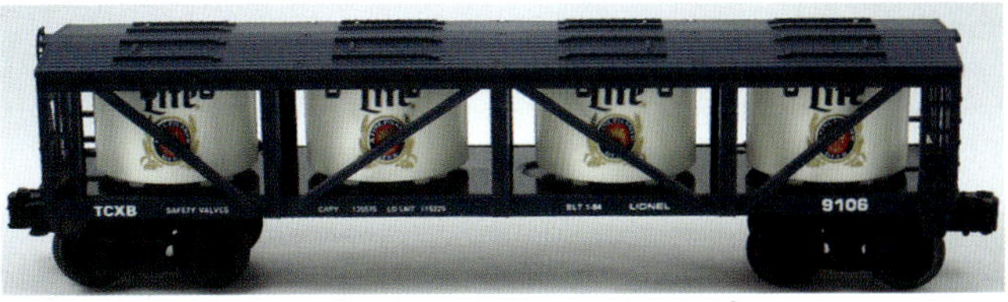

9106 MILLER: 1984-85, vat car.

EX-C7	LN-C8	Scarcity
20	25	4

9106 NABISCO EASY CHEESE: Vat car.

EX-C7	LN-C8	Scarcity
Too rarely traded to establish accurate pricing.		

9107 DR PEPPER: 1986-87, vat car.

EX-C7	LN-C8	Scarcity
15	20	4

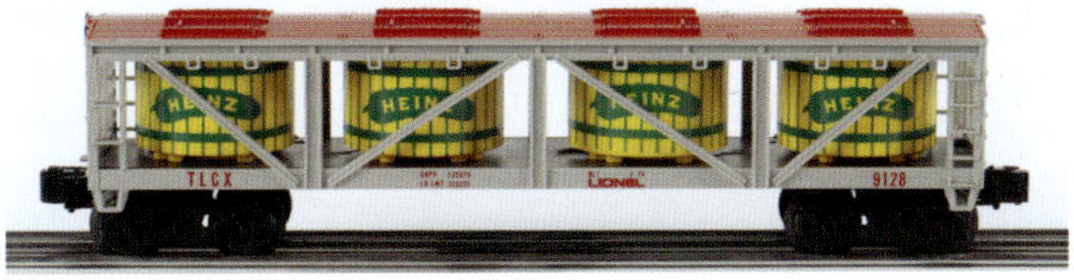

9128 HEINZ: 1974-76, vat car.

EX-C7	LN-C8	Scarcity
18	25	4

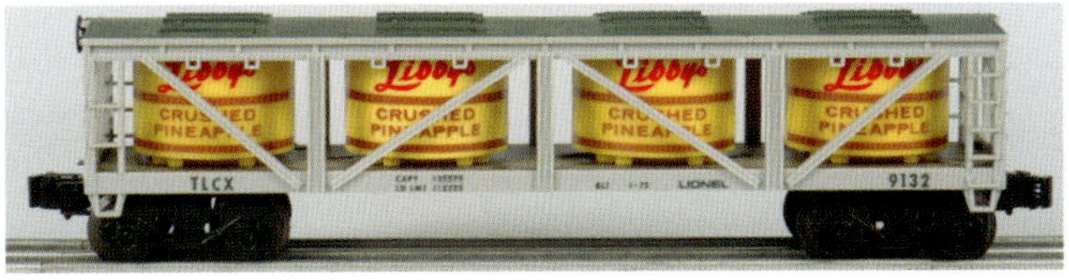

9132 LIBBY'S: 1975-77, vat car, Service Station Special item.

EX-C7	LN-C8	Scarcity
18	25	4

9138 SUNOCO: 1978, triple-dome, Service Station Special item.

EX-C7	LN-C8	Scarcity
25	30	6

9146 MOGEN DAVID: 1977-81, vat car.

EX-C7	LN-C8	Scarcity
15	20	4

9147 TEXACO: 1977-78, single-dome.

EX-C7	LN-C8	Scarcity
20	30	4

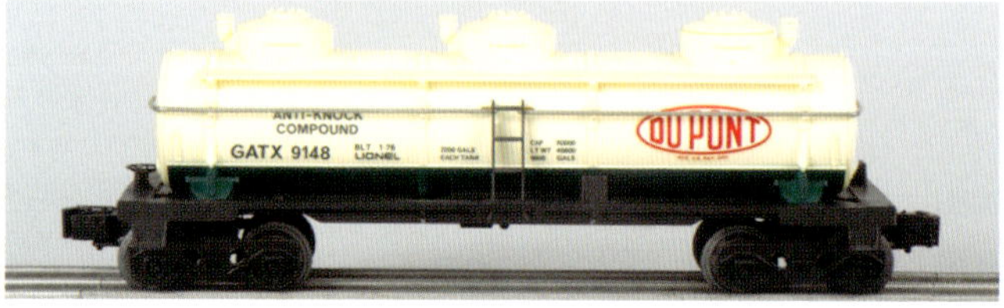

9148 DU PONT: 1977-81, triple-dome.

EX-C7	LN-C8	Scarcity
15	20	4

9150 GULF: Uncataloged in 1970, cataloged in 1971, single-dome.

EX-C7	LN-C8	Scarcity
15	20	5

9151 SHELL: 1972, single-dome.

EX-C7	LN-C8	Scarcity
20	25	4

9152 SHELL: 1973-76, single-dome.

EX-C7	LN-C8	Scarcity
20	25	4

9153 CHEVRON: 1974-76, single-dome.

EX-C7	LN-C8	Scarcity
20	25	4

9154 BORDEN: 1975-76, single-dome.

EX-C7	LN-C8	Scarcity
25	35	5

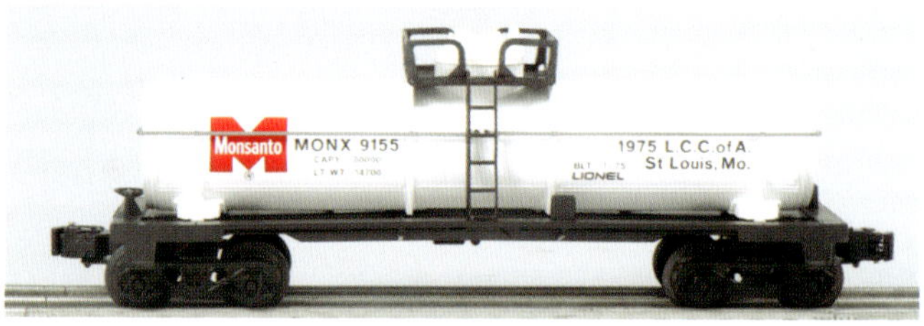

9155 MONSANTO: 1975, uncataloged LCCA, single-dome.

EX-C7	LN-C8	Scarcity
35	45	6

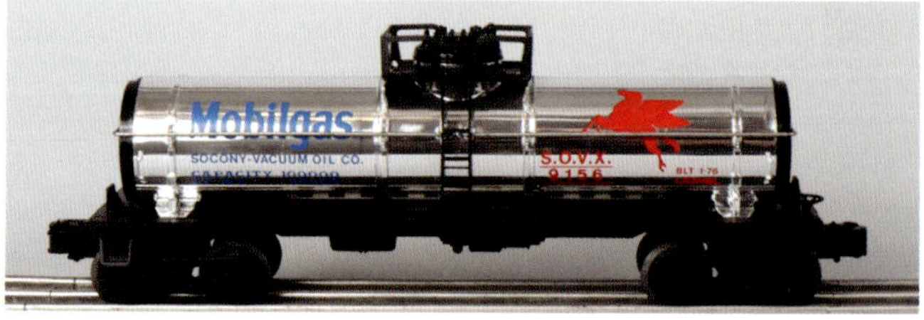

9156 MOBILGAS: 1976-77, single-dome.

EX-C7	LN-C8	Scarcity
20	25	4

9159 SUNOCO: 1976, single-dome.

EX-C7	LN-C8	Scarcity
30	40	4

9189 GULF: 1977, single-dome.

EX-C7	LN-C8	Scarcity
15	20	4

9193 BUDWEISER (Type I): 1983-84, vat car.

EX-C7	LN-C8	Scarcity
50	75	6

9193 BUDWEISER (Type II): 1984, uncataloged Atlantic TCA vat car.

EX-C7	LN-C8	Scarcity
50	75	6

9193 GARDEN COUNTRY: 1984, uncataloged vat car.

EX-C7	LN-C8	Scarcity
Too rarely traded to establish accurate pricing.		

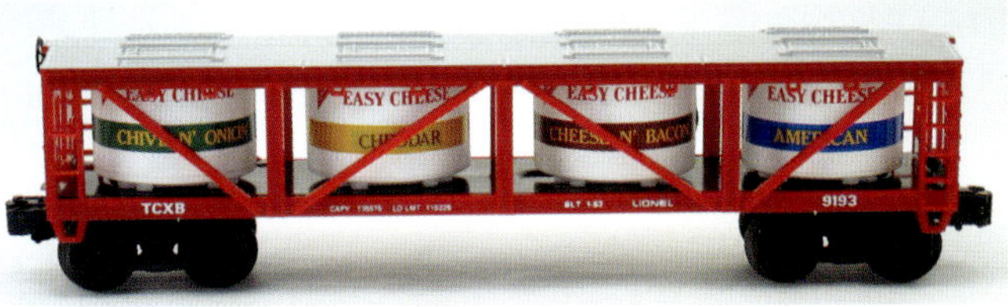

9193 NABISCO EASY CHEESE: Uncataloged vat car.

EX-C7	LN-C8	Scarcity
Too rarely traded to establish accurate pricing.		

9250 WATERPOXY: 1970-71, triple-dome.

9250 WATERPOXY (Type I): Initial production cars were equipped with postwar bar-end trucks and had tall brakewheels.

EX-C7	LN-C8	Scarcity
30	50	6

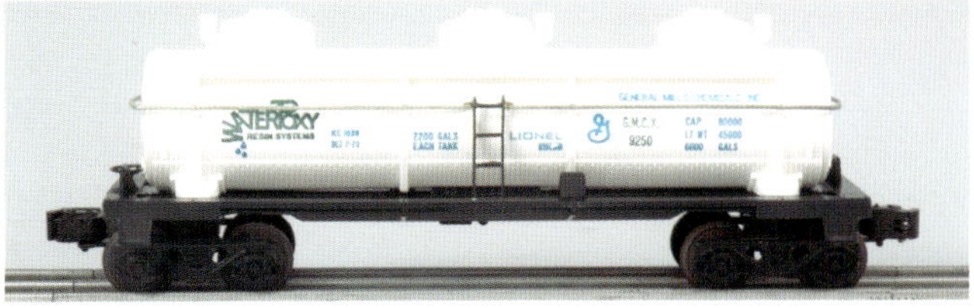

9250 WATERPOXY (Type II): Later production cars had short brakewheels and rode on Symington-Wayne trucks.

EX-C7	LN-C8	Scarcity
15	20	4

9277 CITIES SERVICE: 1978, single-dome.

EX-C7	LN-C8	Scarcity
25	30	5

9278 LIFE SAVERS: 1978-79, single-dome.

EX-C7	LN-C8	Scarcity
75	125	6

9279 MAGNOLIA: 1978-79, uncataloged triple-dome.

EX-C7	LN-C8	Scarcity
15	20	4

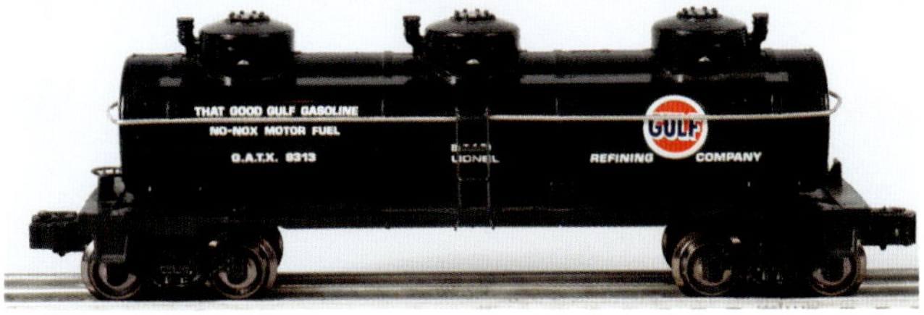

9313 GULF: 1979, uncataloged triple-dome.

EX-C7	LN-C8	Scarcity
25	30	4

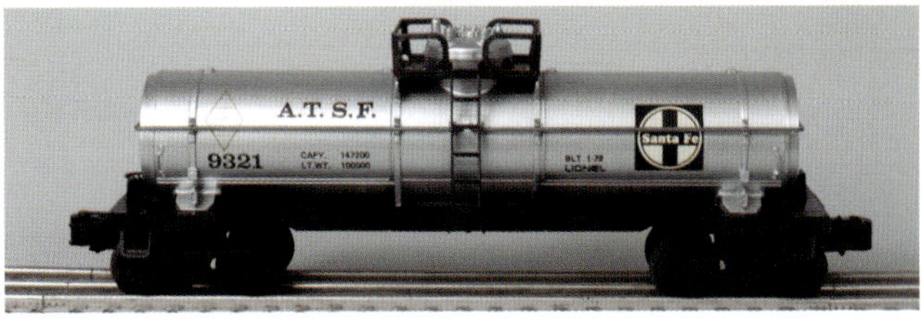

9321 SANTA FE: 1979, single-dome, Famous American Railroads number one.

EX-C7	LN-C8	Scarcity
15	20	5

9324 TOOTSIE ROLL: 1979-81, single-dome.

EX-C7	LN-C8	Scarcity
30	40	5

9327 BAKELITE: 1980, triple-dome.

EX-C7	LN-C8	Scarcity
15	20	4

9331 UNION 76: 1979, single-dome.

EX-C7	LN-C8	Scarcity
25	30	5

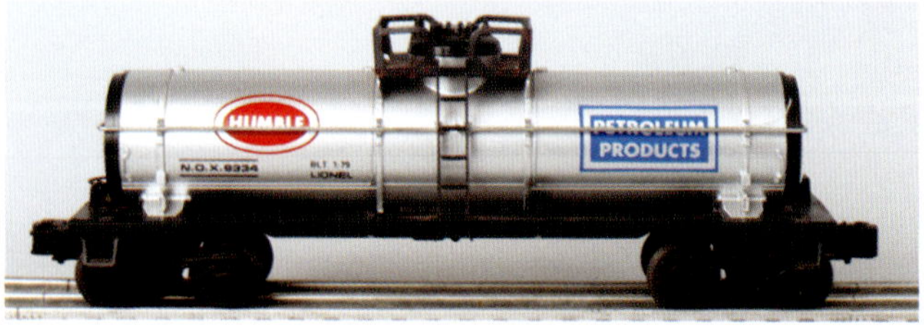

9334 HUMBLE: 1979, single-dome.

EX-C7	LN-C8	Scarcity
10	15	4

9344 CITGO: 1980, triple-dome.

EX-C7	LN-C8	Scarcity
20	25	4

9347 NIAGARA FALLS: 1979, uncataloged TTOS triple-dome.

EX-C7	LN-C8	Scarcity
30	40	6

9353 CRYSTAL LINE: 1980, triple-dome.

EX-C7	LN-C8	Scarcity
10	15	4

9354 PENNZOIL: 1980-81, uncataloged single-dome.

EX-C7	LN-C8	Scarcity
25	30	4

9356 LIFE SAVERS STIK-O-PEP: 1980, single-dome.

EX-C7	LN-C8	Scarcity
Cataloged, but not produced.		

9367 UNION PACIFIC: 1980, single-dome, Famous American Railroads number two.

9367 UNION PACIFIC (Type I): Initially, the UP herald was applied with a decal.

EX-C7	LN-C8	Scarcity
15	20	4

9367 UNION PACIFIC (Type II): On later cars the UP herald was an electrocal.

EX-C7	LN-C8	Scarcity
15	20	4

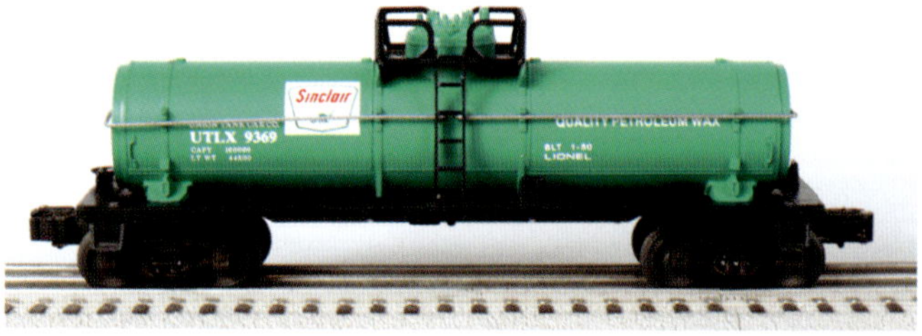

9369 SINCLAIR: 1980, single-dome.

EX-C7	LN-C8	Scarcity
30	35	5

9373 GETTY: Cataloged from 1980-81, uncataloged in 1983, single-dome.

EX-C7	LN-C8	Scarcity
20	40	5

9386 PURE OIL: 1981, single-dome.

EX-C7	LN-C8	Scarcity
25	30	5

16102 SOUTHERN: 1987, triple-dome, Service Station Special item.

EX-C7	LN-C8	Scarcity
20	25	5

16103 LEHIGH VALLEY: 1988, double-dome in the traditional 027/Scout size.

EX-C7	LN-C8	Scarcity
15	20	4

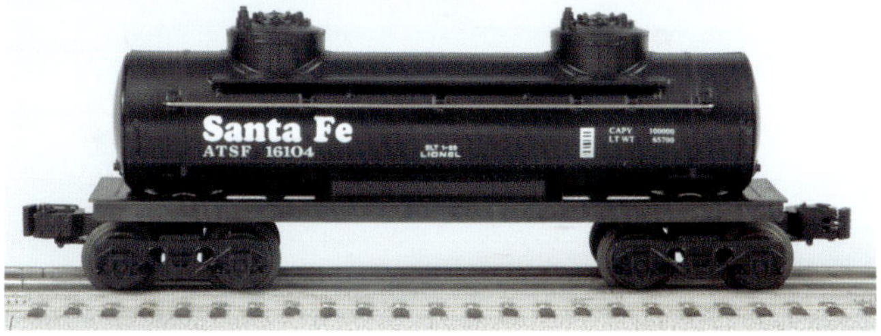

16104 SANTA FE: 1989, double-dome in the traditional 027/Scout size.

EX-C7	LN-C8	Scarcity
10	15	4

16105 DENVER & RIO GRANDE WESTERN: 1989, triple-dome, Service Station Special item.

EX-C7	LN-C8	Scarcity
35	40	5

[16106] MOPAR EXPRESS: 1988, uncataloged triple-dome.

EX-C7	LN-C8	Scarcity
70	100	6

16107 SUNOCO: 1990, double-dome in the traditional 027/Scout size.

EX-C7	LN-C8	Scarcity
10	15	4

[16108] RACING FUEL: 1989 and 1992, uncataloged single-dome numbered "6108" in the traditional 027/Scout size.

EX-C7	LN-C8	Scarcity
5	10	3

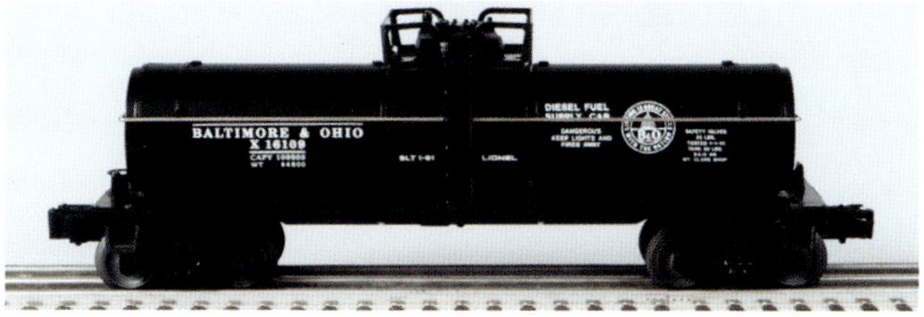

16109 BALTIMORE & OHIO: 1991, single-dome, Service Station Special item.

EX-C7	LN-C8	Scarcity
20	25	4

16111 ALASKA RAILROAD: 1990-91, single-dome in the traditional 027/Scout size.

16111 ALASKA RAILROAD (Type I): The earliest production of this car featured black lettering and Symington-Wayne trucks.

EX-C7	LN-C8	Scarcity
15	20	4

16111 ALASKA RAILROAD (Type II): Later examples of the car were lettered in dark blue, and rode on ASF trucks.

EX-C7	LN-C8	Scarcity
15	20	4

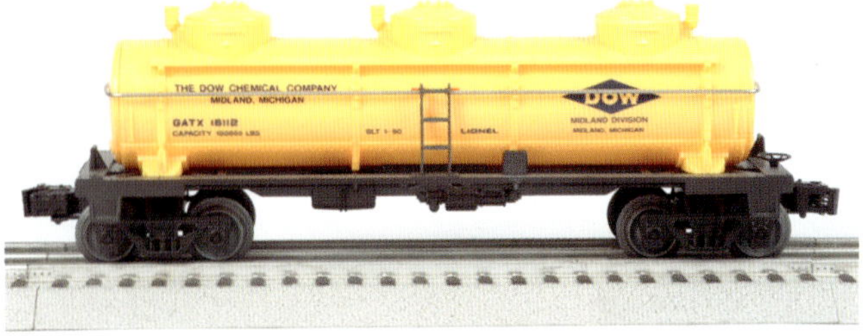

16112 DOW CHEMICAL: 1990, triple-dome.

EX-C7	LN-C8	Scarcity
15	20	4

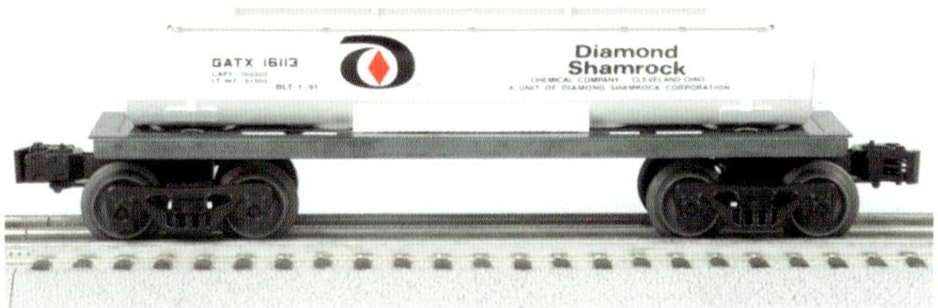

16113 DIAMOND SHAMROCK: 1991, double-dome in the traditional 027/Scout size.

EX-C7	LN-C8	Scarcity
15	20	4

16114 HOOKER CHEMICALS: 1991, single-dome in the traditional 027/Scout size.

EX-C7	LN-C8	Scarcity
10	15	4

16115 MISSOURI-KANSAS-TEXAS: 1992, triple-dome.

EX-C7	LN-C8	Scarcity
15	20	4

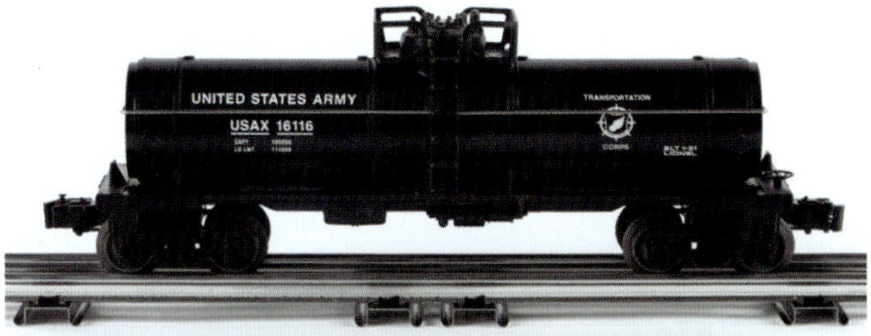

16116 U.S. ARMY: 1991, uncataloged single-dome.

EX-C7	LN-C8	Scarcity
30	40	5

16119 MISSOURI-KANSAS-TEXAS: Cataloged in 1992, uncataloged in 1993, double-dome in the traditional 027/Scout size.

EX-C7	LN-C8	Scarcity
10	15	4

16123 UNION PACIFIC: 1993-95, triple-dome.

EX-C7	LN-C8	Scarcity
10	15	4

16124 PENN SALT: 1993, triple-dome.

EX-C7	LN-C8	Scarcity
10	15	4

16126 JEFFERSON LAKE: 1993, triple-dome.

EX-C7	LN-C8	Scarcity
10	15	4

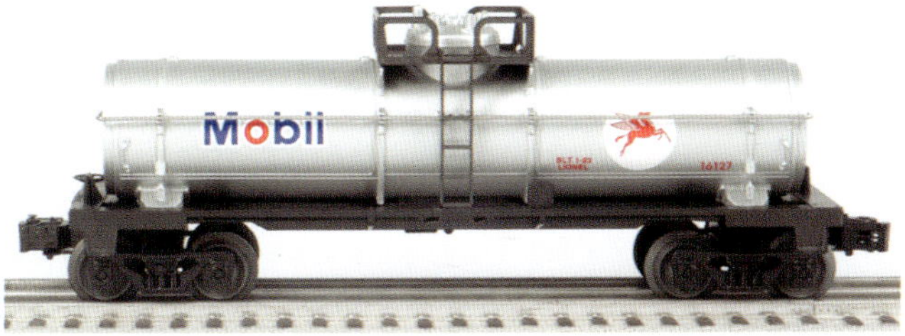

16127 MOBIL: 1993, single-dome.

EX-C7	LN-C8	Scarcity
20	25	4

16128 ALASKA RAILROAD: 1994, single-dome.

EX-C7	LN-C8	Scarcity
15	20	4

16129 ALASKA RAILROAD: Uncataloged in 1993, cataloged in 1994, single-dome in the traditional 027/Scout size.

EX-C7	LN-C8	Scarcity
15	20	4

16132 DEEP ROCK: 1994, triple-dome.

EX-C7	LN-C8	Scarcity
20	25	4

16136 BALTIMORE & OHIO: 1994, single-dome.

EX-C7	LN-C8	Scarcity
20	25	4

16137 FORD: 1994, uncataloged single-dome numbered "12."

EX-C7	LN-C8	Scarcity
25	30	6

16138 GOODYEAR: 1995, single-dome.

EX-C7	LN-C8	Scarcity
20	25	4

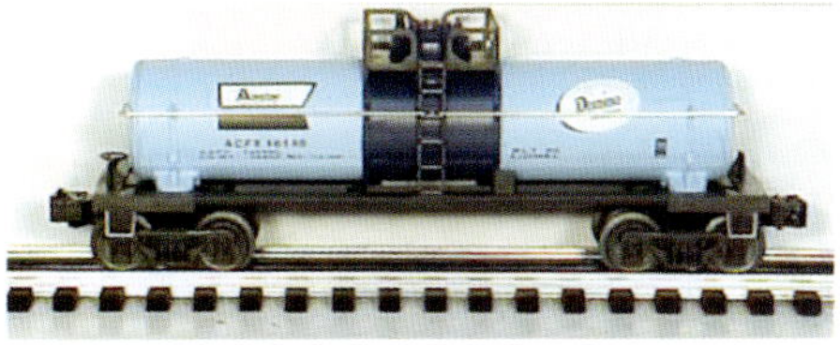

16140 DOMINO SUGAR: 1995, single-dome.

EX-C7	LN-C8	Scarcity
20	25	4

16142 SANTA FE: 1995, single-dome.

EX-C7	LN-C8	Scarcity
20	25	4

16144 SAN ANGELO: 1995, triple-dome.

EX-C7	LN-C8	Scarcity
15	20	4

[16147] CLEARLY CANADIAN: 1994, uncataloged single-dome in the traditional 027/Scout size.

EX-C7	LN-C8	Scarcity
60	75	6

16149 ZEP CHEMICAL: 1995, uncataloged single-dome in the traditional 027/Scout size.

EX-C7	LN-C8	Scarcity
60	75	6

[16150] SUNOCO: 1997, single-dome numbered "6315."

EX-C7	LN-C8	Scarcity
20	25	4

[16152] SUNOCO: 1997, triple-dome numbered "6415."

EX-C7	LN-C8	Scarcity
15	20	4

[16153] ATOMIC ENERGY COMMISSION: 1997, reactor fluid, numbered "6315-1" single-dome.

EX-C7	LN-C8	Scarcity
60	75	5

[16154] ATOMIC ENERGY COMMISSION: 1997, reactor fluid, numbered "6315-2" single-dome.

EX-C7	LN-C8	Scarcity
60	75	5

[16155] ATOMIC ENERGY COMMISSION: 1997, reactor fluid, numbered "6315-3" single-dome.

EX-C7	LN-C8	Scarcity
60	75	5

[16157] GATORADE: 1997, uncataloged Little League Baseball single-dome numbered "6315."

EX-C7	LN-C8	Scarcity
30	35	6

[16160] ATOMIC ENERGY COMMISSION: 1998, with reactor fluid, numbered "6515."

EX-C7	LN-C8	Scarcity
35	40	5

[16162] HOOKER CHEMICAL: 1997, single-dome numbered "6315-1."

EX-C7	LN-C8	Scarcity
30	40	4

[16163] HOOKER CHEMICAL: 1997, single-dome numbered "6315-2."

EX-C7	LN-C8	Scarcity
30	40	4

[16164] HOOKER CHEMICAL: 1997, single-dome numbered "6315-3."

EX-C7	LN-C8	Scarcity
30	40	4

[16165] MOBILFUEL: 1997, uncataloged triple-dome numbered "6415."

EX-C7	LN-C8	Scarcity
30	40	4

[16171] ALASKA RAILROAD: 1998-99, single-dome numbered "6171."

EX-C7	LN-C8	Scarcity
15	20	3

[16180] TABASCO: 1998, single-dome.

EX-C7	LN-C8	Scarcity
40	50	4

[16181] BIOHAZARD: 1998, with lights.

EX-C7	LN-C8	Scarcity
40	50	4

[16182] GATORADE: 1998, uncataloged single-dome numbered "6315."

EX-C7	LN-C8	Scarcity
30	40	5

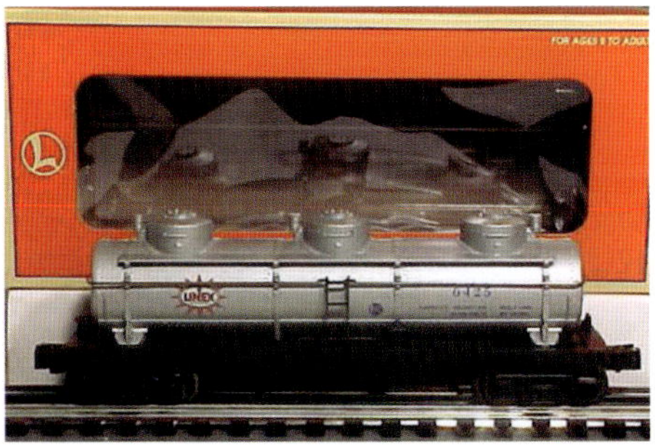

[16187] LINEX: 1999, triple-dome numbered "6425."

EX-C7	LN-C8	Scarcity
15	20	4

[16188] KODAK: 1999, single-dome numbered "6515."

EX-C7	LN-C8	Scarcity
60	80	5

[16196] LAVA LITE: 1999, single-dome numbered "9968."

EX-C7	LN-C8	Scarcity
Cataloged, but not produced.		

[16199] UNION PACIFIC: 1999-2000, single-dome numbered "6035."

EX-C7	LN-C8	Scarcity
15	20	3

16225 BUDWEISER: 1990-91, uncataloged vat car.

EX-C7	LN-C8	Scarcity
100	125	5

16390 LIONEL: 1994, flatcar with water tank.

EX-C7	LN-C8	Scarcity
15	20	4

[16817] AMBASSADOR: 2000, uncataloged single-dome numbered "1999."

EX-C7	LN-C8	Scarcity
60	70	6

[16818] ENGINEER AWARD: 2000, uncataloged.

EX-C7	LN-C8	Scarcity
400	500	7

[16819] JLC AWARD: 2000, uncataloged.

EX-C7	LN-C8	Scarcity
500	800	8

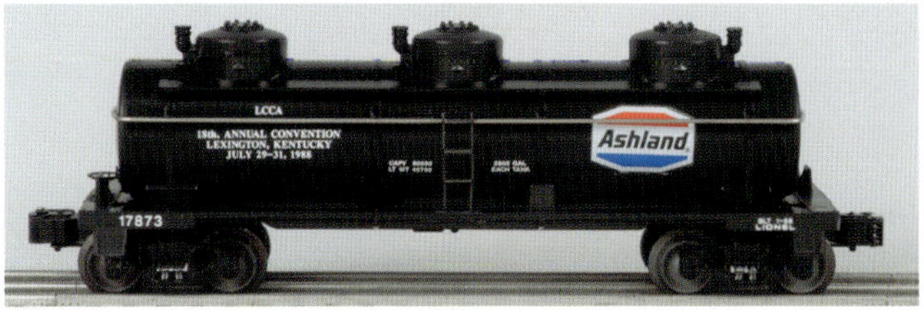

17873 ASHLAND OIL: 1988, uncataloged LCCA, triple-dome.

17873 ASHLAND OIL (Type I): Initially, the cars were painted flat black, but this caused adhesion problems for the large Ashland decal.

EX-C7	LN-C8	Scarcity
60	70	6

17873 ASHLAND OIL (Type II): Once this problem was discovered, the cars were painted glossy black, and it is in this form that the bulk of the cars were produced.

EX-C7	LN-C8	Scarcity
40	50	6

[17877] MISSOURI-KANSAS-TEXAS: 1989, uncataloged TTOS single-dome numbered "3739469."

EX-C7	LN-C8	Scarcity
45	55	6

17885 ARTRAIN: 1990, uncataloged single-dome.

EX-C7	LN-C8	Scarcity
60	70	6

[17893] BAOC: 1991, uncataloged Lionel Collectors Association of Canada single-dome numbered "914."

EX-C7	LN-C8	Scarcity
40	50	6

[17899] NASA: 1992, uncataloged LCCA Uni-body numbered "190" with 1/48-scale proportions.

EX-C7	LN-C8	Scarcity
50	60	6

17900 SANTA FE: 1990, uni-body with 1/48-scale proportions.

EX-C7	LN-C8	Scarcity
30	35	4

17901 CHEVRON: 1990, uni-body with 1/48-scale proportions.

EX-C7	LN-C8	Scarcity
30	35	4

17902 NJ ZINC: 1991, uni-body with 1/48-scale proportions.

EX-C7	LN-C8	Scarcity
30	35	4

17903 CONOCO: 1991, uni-body with 1/48-scale proportions.

EX-C7	LN-C8	Scarcity
30	35	4

17904 TEXACO: 1992, uni-body with 1/48-scale proportions.

EX-C7	LN-C8	Scarcity
30	35	4

17905 ARCHER DANIELS MIDLAND: 1992, uni-body with 1/48-scale proportions.

EX-C7	LN-C8	Scarcity
30	35	4

[17906] SCM: 1993, uni-body numbered "78286" with 1/48-scale proportions.

EX-C7	LN-C8	Scarcity
30	35	4

17908 MARATHON OIL: 1995, uni-body numbered with 1/48-scale proportions.

EX-C7	LN-C8	Scarcity
30	60	5

17909 HOOKER CHEMICALS: 1996, uni-body with 1/48-scale proportions.

EX-C7	LN-C8	Scarcity
30	35	4

[17910] SUNOCO: 1997, uni-body numbered "7900" with 1/48-scale proportions.

EX-C7	LN-C8	Scarcity
30	35	4

[17913] J.M. HUBER: 1998, with 1/48-scale proportions.

EX-C7	LN-C8	Scarcity
25	30	4

[17914] ENGLEHARD: 1998, with 1/48-scale proportions.

EX-C7	LN-C8	Scarcity
25	30	4

[17915] GULF: 2000, uni-body numbered "8438" with 1/48-scale proportions.

EX-C7	LN-C8	Scarcity
25	30	4

[17916] BURLINGTON NORTHERN: 2000, uni-body numbered "130000" with 1/48-scale proportions.

EX-C7	LN-C8	Scarcity
25	30	4

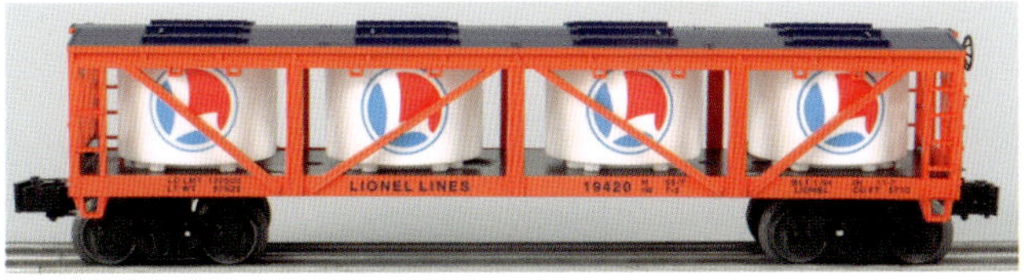

19420 LIONEL LINES: 1994, vat car.

EX-C7	LN-C8	Scarcity
20	25	4

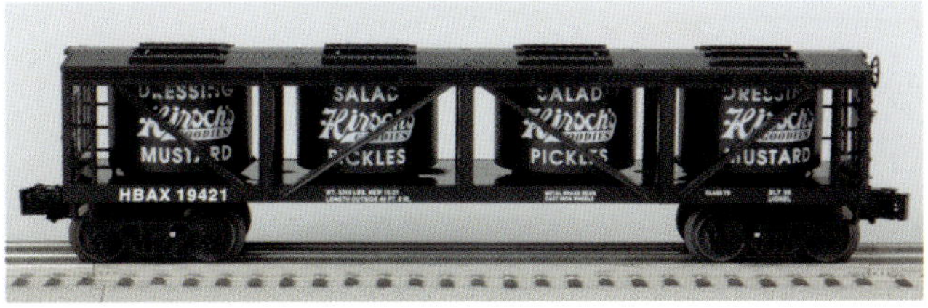

19421 HIRSCH BROTHERS: 1995, vat car.

EX-C7	LN-C8	Scarcity
20	25	4

[19441]: 1998, lobster vat car.

EX-C7	LN-C8	Scarcity
20	25	4

[19442] LIONEL CORPORATION: 1998, water supply flatcar with tank, Service Station Special item.

EX-C7	LN-C8	Scarcity
20	25	5

[19445] BORDEN MILK: 1999, numbered "520."

EX-C7	LN-C8	Scarcity
25	30	4

[19446] PITTSBURGH PAINT: 1999, vat car.

EX-C7	LN-C8	Scarcity
25	30	4

[19447] MAMA'S BAKED BEANS: 1999, vat car.

EX-C7	LN-C8	Scarcity
20	25	4

[19449] LIQUEFIED GAS: 1999, tank mounted on flatcar numbered "6469."

EX-C7	LN-C8	Scarcity
20	25	4

[19472] MOBIL: 2000, uncataloged bulkhead flatcar with tank.

EX-C7	LN-C8	Scarcity
35	45	4

[19480] VALENTINE'S: 1999-2000, vat car numbered "6475."

EX-C7	LN-C8	Scarcity
20	25	4

[19481] EASTER: 1999-2000, vat car numbered "2000."

EX-C7	LN-C8	Scarcity
20	25	4

19600 MILWAUKEE ROAD: 1987, single-dome, Fallen Flags number two.

EX-C7	LN-C8	Scarcity
35	40	5

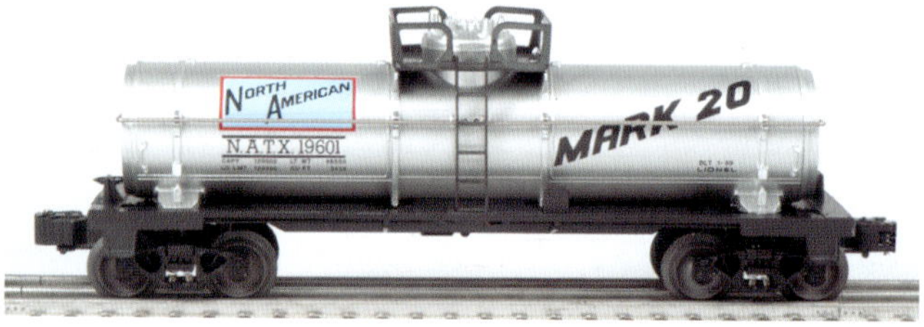

19601 NORTH AMERICAN: 1989, single-dome, Fallen Flags number four.

EX-C7	LN-C8	Scarcity
20	25	5

19602 JOHNSON: 1991, single-dome, Fallen Flags number five.

EX-C7	LN-C8	Scarcity
20	25	5

19603 GATX: 1992, single-dome, Fallen Flags number six.

EX-C7	LN-C8	Scarcity
30	35	6

19604 GOODYEAR: 1993, single-dome, Service Station Special item.

EX-C7	LN-C8	Scarcity
20	25	5

19605 HUDSON'S BAY: 1994, single-dome, Service Station Special item.

EX-C7	LN-C8	Scarcity
20	25	5

[19607] SUNOCO: 1996, single-dome numbered "6315."

EX-C7	LN-C8	Scarcity
20	25	4

[19608] SUNOCO: 1997, Aviation Services single-dome numbered "6315," Service Station Special item.

EX-C7	LN-C8	Scarcity
25	30	5

[19611] GULF: 1998, oil single-dome numbered "6315."

EX-C7	LN-C8	Scarcity
20	25	4

[19612] GULF OIL: 1998, triple-dome numbered "6425."

EX-C7	LN-C8	Scarcity
20	25	4

[19614] BASF: 1999-2000, single-dome numbered "UTLX 78252." This is a new molding of an 8,000-gallon riveted car. it is 1/48 scale sized.

EX-C7	LN-C8	Scarcity
15	50	4

[19615] VULCAN CHEMICALS: 1999-2000, single-dome. This is a new molding of an 8,000-gallon riveted car. it is 1/48 scale sized.

EX-C7	LN-C8	Scarcity
15	50	4

[19621] CENTENNIAL: 1999, single-dome numbered "6015-1."

EX-C7	LN-C8	Scarcity
30	35	5

[19622] CENTENNIAL: 1999, single-dome numbered "6015-2."

EX-C7	LN-C8	Scarcity
30	35	5

[19623] CENTENNIAL: 1999, single-dome numbered "6015-3."

EX-C7	LN-C8	Scarcity
30	35	5

[19624] CENTENNIAL: 1999, single-dome numbered "6015-4."

EX-C7	LN-C8	Scarcity
30	35	5

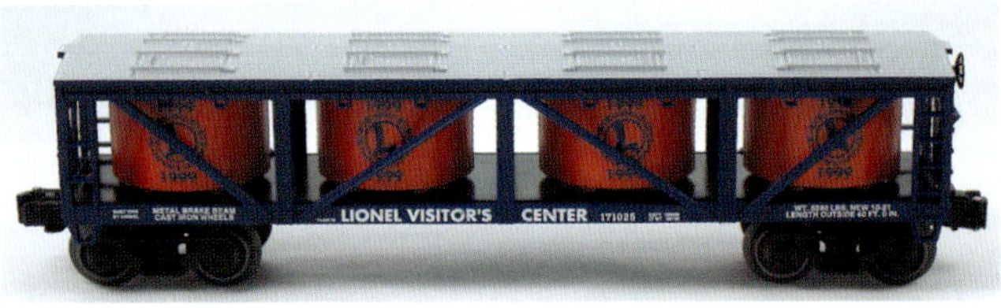

[19772] LIONEL VISITOR'S CENTER: 1999, uncataloged vat car.

EX-C7	LN-C8	Scarcity
30	35	5

[19935] LIONEL RAILROADER CLUB: 1995, uncataloged single-dome numbered "1995."

EX-C7	LN-C8	Scarcity
25	30	5

[19940] LIONEL RAILROAD: 1996, uncataloged vat car.

EX-C7	LN-C8	Scarcity
15	20	5

[19944] LIONEL VISITOR'S CENTER: 1996, uncataloged tank car.

EX-C7	LN-C8	Scarcity
30	35	5

[21769] CENTENNIAL: 1999, single-dome set, four-pack.

EX-C7	LN-C8	Scarcity
125	150	4

[26100] PENNSYLVANIA: 2000, single-dome.

EX-C7	LN-C8	Scarcity
15	20	4

[26101] LENOIL: 2000, single-dome numbered "6015."

EX-C7	LN-C8	Scarcity
20	25	4

[26102] AEC: 2000, Glow-in-the-Dark single-dome.

EX-C7	LN-C8	Scarcity
20	25	4

[26103] GATX TANK TRAIN: 2000, single-dome numbered "44588."

EX-C7	LN-C8	Scarcity
20	25	4

[26107] BP PETROLEUM: 2000, uncataloged triple-dome.

EX-C7	LN-C8	Scarcity
60	70	4

[26109] NEW YORK CENTRAL/P&LE: 2000, single-dome.

EX-C7	LN-C8	Scarcity
25	30	4

[26110] SOUTHERN PACIFIC: 2000, single-dome numbered "6415."

EX-C7	LN-C8	Scarcity
Too rarely traded to establish accurate pricing.		

[26110] SOUTHERN PACIFIC: 2000-01, triple-dome numbered "6415."

EX-C7	LN-C8	Scarcity
10	15	4

[26111] FRISCO: 2000.

EX-C7	LN-C8	Scarcity
15	20	4

[26112] GULF OIL: 2000.

EX-C7	LN-C8	Scarcity
15	20	4

[26113] U.S. ARMY: 2000.

EX-C7	LN-C8	Scarcity
15	20	4

[26114] SERVICE STATION LTD.: 2000, single-dome, Service Station Special item.

EX-C7	LN-C8	Scarcity
20	25	5

[26115] LIONEL CELEBRATION: 2000, uncataloged single-dome.

EX-C7	LN-C8	Scarcity
50	60	5

[26116] PEPE LA PEW: 2000, uncataloged single-dome.

EX-C7	LN-C8	Scarcity
50	60	5

26119 PROTEX: 2000, three-dome numbered "1054."

EX-C7	LN-C8	Scarcity
15	20	4

26120 KANSAS CITY SOUTHERN: 2000, numbered "1229."

EX-C7	LN-C8	Scarcity
15	20	4

[26122] PIONEER SEED: 2000, uncataloged.

EX-C7	LN-C8	Scarcity
Too rarely traded to establish accurate pricing.		

26127 WELLSPRING CAPITAL MANAGEMENT: 2000, uncataloged clear single-dome with confetti.

EX-C7	LN-C8	Scarcity
175	200	6

26934 PHILLIPS PETROLEUM: 1998, die-cast.

EX-C7	LN-C8	Scarcity
40	45	4

[26936]: 1998, die-cast, four-pack.

EX-C7	LN-C8	Scarcity
300	325	4

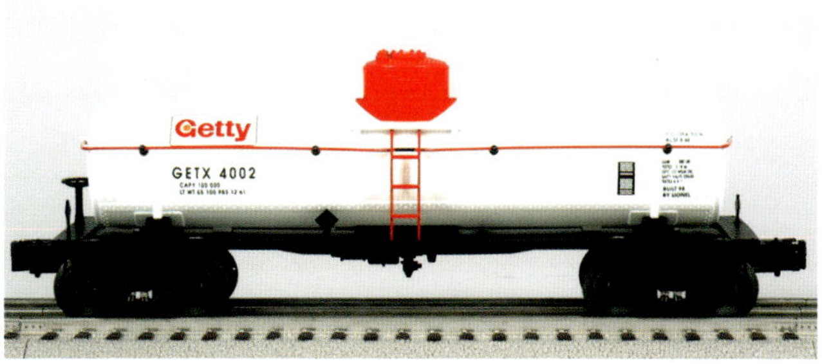

[26941] GETTY OIL: 1998, die-cast, numbered "4002."

EX-C7	LN-C8	Scarcity
60	75	4

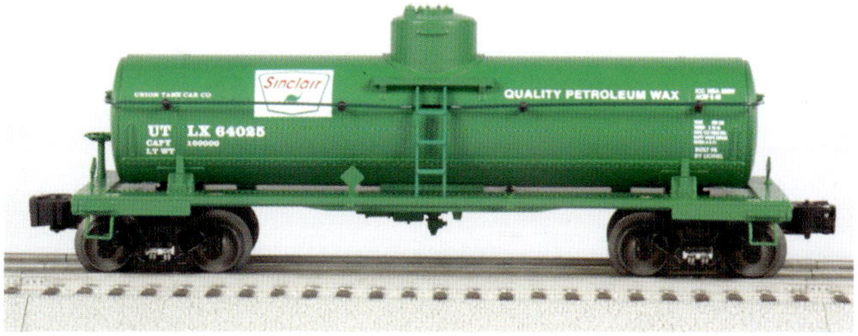

26942 SINCLAIR: 1998, die-cast, numbered "64025."

EX-C7	LN-C8	Scarcity
60	75	4

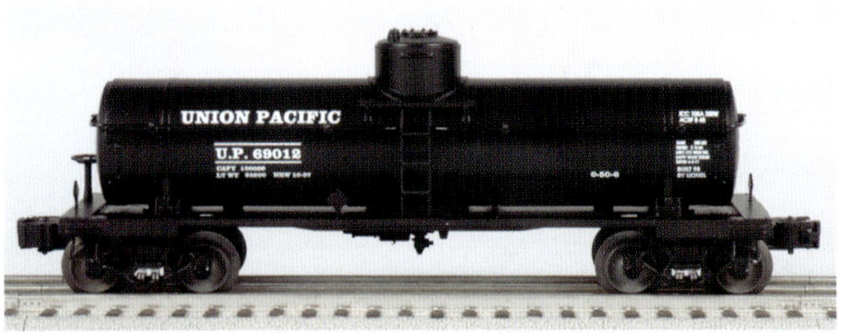

26943 UNION PACIFIC: 1998, die-cast, numbered "69012."

EX-C7	LN-C8	Scarcity
60	75	4

[26947] GULF: 1998, die-cast, numbered "5010."

EX-C7	LN-C8	Scarcity
70	80	4

[26973] GETTY: 1998, die-cast, three-pack.

EX-C7	LN-C8	Scarcity
200	225	4

[26974] GETTY: 1998, die-cast single-dome numbered "4003."

EX-C7	LN-C8	Scarcity
60	75	4

[26975] GETTY: 1998, die-cast single-dome numbered "4004."

EX-C7	LN-C8	Scarcity
60	75	4

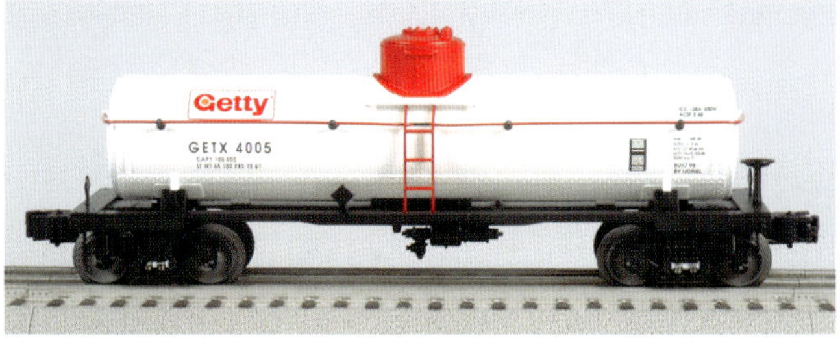

[26976] GETTY: 1998, die-cast single-dome numbered "4005."

EX-C7	LN-C8	Scarcity
60	75	4

[26977] SINCLAIR: 1998, die-cast, three-pack.

EX-C7	LN-C8	Scarcity
225	250	4

[26978] SINCLAIR: 1998, UTLX, numbered "64026."

EX-C7	LN-C8	Scarcity
65	80	4

[26979] SINCLAIR: 1998, UTLX, numbered "64027."

EX-C7	LN-C8	Scarcity
65	80	4

[26980] SINCLAIR: 1998, UTLX, numbered "64028."

EX-C7	LN-C8	Scarcity
65	80	4

[26981] GULF: 1999, die-cast, two-pack.

EX-C7	LN-C8	Scarcity
100	125	4

[36913] ALLIED CHEMICAL: 2000, single-dome, two-pack.

EX-C7	LN-C8	Scarcity
100	125	4

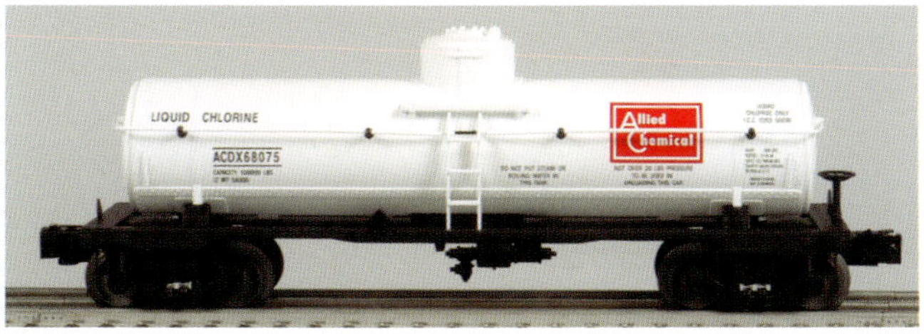

[36914] ALLIED CHEMICAL: 2000, single-dome die-cast, white, numbered "ACDX 68075."

EX-C7	LN-C8	Scarcity
50	65	4

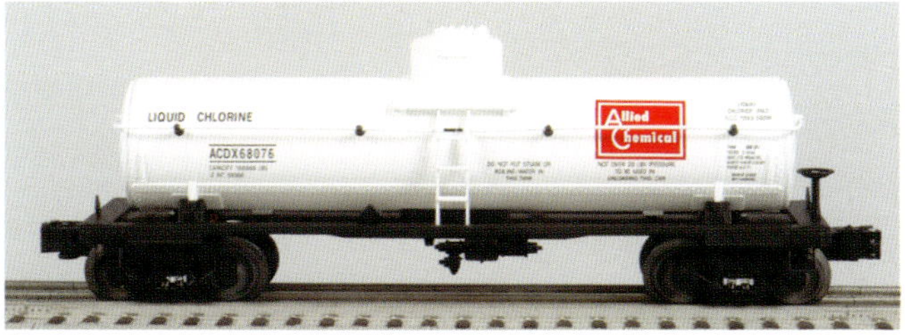

[36915] ALLIED CHEMICAL: 2000, single-dome die-cast, white, numbered "ACDX 68076."

EX-C7	LN-C8	Scarcity
50	65	4

[36916] ALLIED CHEMICAL: 2000, single-dome, two-pack.

EX-C7	LN-C8	Scarcity
100	125	4

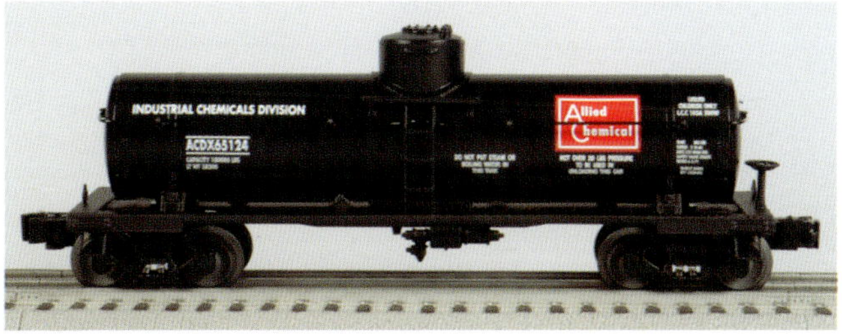

[36917] ALLIED CHEMICAL: 2000, single-dome die-cast, black, numbered "ACDX 65124."

EX-C7	LN-C8	Scarcity
50	65	4

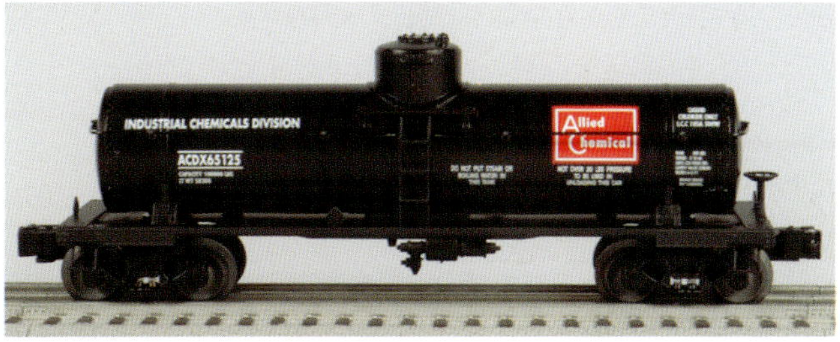

[36918] ALLIED CHEMICAL: 2000, single-dome die-cast, black, numbered "ACDX 65125."

EX-C7	LN-C8	Scarcity
50	65	4

[38356] DOW CHEMICAL: 1987, uncataloged LOTS, triple-dome.

EX-C7	LN-C8	Scarcity
70	90	6

51300 SHELL: 1991, semi-scale single-dome numbered "8124."

EX-C7	LN-C8	Scarcity
100	125	5

[52137] RED WING SHOES

[52029] FORD: 1994, uncataloged TTOS single-dome numbered "12" in the traditional 027/Scout size.

EX-C7	LN-C8	Scarcity
30	35	6

[52032] FORD: 1994, uncataloged TTOS single-dome numbered "14" in the traditional 027/Scout size with Kughn inscription.

EX-C7	LN-C8	Scarcity
60	80	6

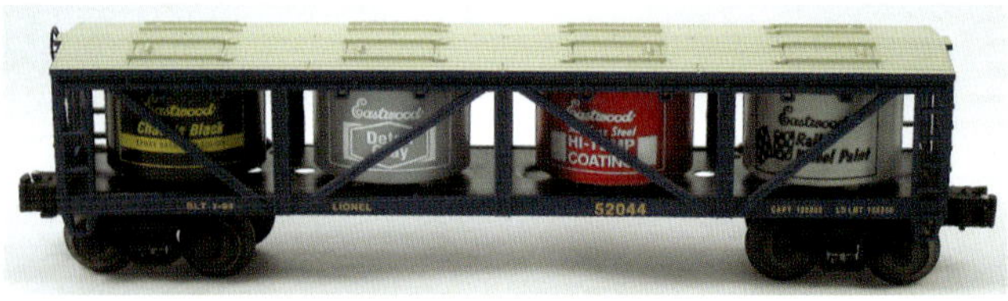

[52044] EASTWOOD: 1995, uncataloged vat car.

EX-C7	LN-C8	Scarcity
35	40	6

[52061] STERN'S PICKLE PRODUCTS: 1995, uncataloged NLOE Long Island vat car numbered "8395."

EX-C7	LN-C8	Scarcity
100	125	6

[52121] MOBILGAS: 1997, uncataloged single-dome numbered "238" with 1/48-scale proportions.

EX-C7	LN-C8	Scarcity
45	55	6

[52122] MEENAN OIL: 1997, uncataloged, numbered "9883"; 1998, uncataloged NLOE single-dome numbered "8397."

EX-C7	LN-C8	Scarcity
45	55	6

[52137] RED WING SHOES: 1998, Boot Oil.

EX-C7	LN-C8	Scarcity
35	40	6

[52157] HOLLY BROTHERS: 1998, uncataloged triple-dome numbered "6156."

EX-C7	LN-C8	Scarcity
55	60	6

[52160] MONOPOLY WATER WORKS: 1998.

EX-C7	LN-C8	Scarcity
80	100	6

[52228] MILWAUKEE ROAD: 2000, uncataloged single-dome.

EX-C7	LN-C8	Scarcity
Too rarely traded to establish accurate pricing.		

[52229] MILWAUKEE ROAD: 2000, uncataloged single-dome.

EX-C7	LN-C8	Scarcity
Too rarely traded to establish accurate pricing.		

[52230] MILWAUKEE ROAD: 2000, uncataloged single-dome, two-pack.

EX-C7	LN-C8	Scarcity
Too rarely traded to establish accurate pricing.		

[52231] BRITISH COLUMBIA RR: 2000, uncataloged single-dome.

EX-C7	LN-C8	Scarcity
Too rarely traded to establish accurate pricing.		

97330 AIRCO: 1979, uncataloged LCCA, assembled from components of the 9733 boxcar.

EX-C7	LN-C8	Scarcity
35	45	6

[99007] SMUCKERS FUDGE: 1999, uncataloged single-dome.

EX-C7	LN-C8	Scarcity
60	80	6

[99013] CASE CUTLERY: 2000, uncataloged numbered "1889."

EX-C7	LN-C8	Scarcity
Too rarely traded to establish accurate pricing.		

Chapter 13

PASSENGER CARS

The modern era was devoid of passenger cars until 1973, at which time two types entered production. The harder to find car was the first three small streamlined cars produced for the TCA commemorating the Nation's bicentennial. These cars, which were based on the postwar 2400-series cars, were issued on car per year over three years. After this brief run this style of car would remain dormant until a cheapened version was introduced in 1976.

More significantly, in 1973, an entirely new passenger car was introduced. Known as the "9500 series," these cars were representations of the "heavyweight" passenger cars that dominated American rail travel prior to WWII. The term "heavyweight" was coined by real railroaders when streamlined passenger cars with their welded, and often stainless steel sides, were introduced. The new cars weighed much less than their predecessors, and the term "heavyweight" was born. The styling of Lionel's new car was similar to that of the "Madison" cars coveted by pre and postwar Lionel collectors, although the 9500 series cars are significantly shorter and lighter than the Madisons. The appearance of these cars was enhanced in 1978 when six-wheel die-cast trucks replaced the four-wheel trucks with plastic side frames used previously.

In 1978, Lionel also revived the turn of the 20th Century style passenger cars produced in the postwar era. These cars, once again, were paired with a 4-4-0 American "General" steam locomotive.

The following year saw the return of the extruded aluminum passenger car. Also a classic from the postwar era, these cars were first produced in the same body styles as their predecessors—albeit somewhat shinier. Soon additional body styles were produced as well. Starting in 1981, Lionel produced these cars with brightly painted decoration, if appropriate for the railroad depicted. In 1983, a new variation of these cars was produced with smooth sides and roofs replacing the fluting previously found. Since that time cars have been produced smooth or fluted, painted or unpainted, as required.

In 1991, Lionel reintroduced its famed "Madison" cars. Whereas oftentimes Lionel simply removes the original 40- to 60-year-old tooling from storage, cleans it up and places an item in production—that was not the case here. The original Madison tooling had long since vanished, and all-new tooling had to be created.

Despite being significantly larger than the 9500 series cars, the Madison cars were nonetheless substantially smaller than a true 1/48-scale passenger car. Actual passenger cars typically are about 80 feet long. With the increased emphasis on scale appearance that became prevalent in Lionel's offerings of the '90s, it is not surprising that in 1996 Lionel began to offer even larger, scale sized "heavyweight" passenger cars.

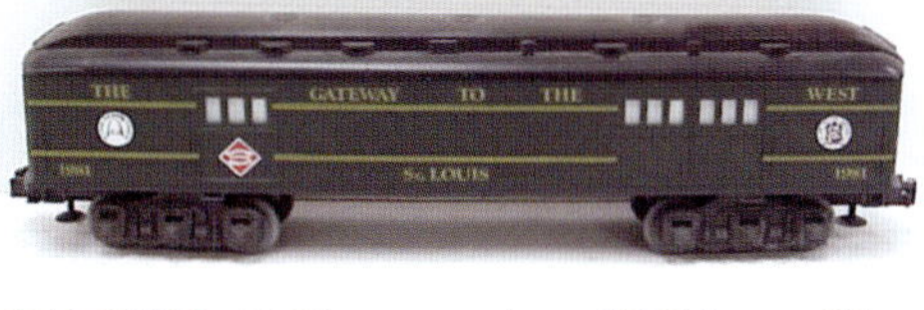

[0511] ST. LOUIS: 1981, uncataloged TCA small heavyweight baggage car, "THE GATEWAY TO THE WEST – 1981."

EX-C7	LN-C8	Scarcity
25	40	5

1973 TCA BICENTENNIAL: 1976, uncataloged observation car in the traditional 2400-series passenger car size.

EX-C7	LN-C8	Scarcity
25	45	7

1974 TCA BICENTENNIAL: 1976, uncataloged in the traditional 2400-series passenger car size.

EX-C7	LN-C8	Scarcity
25	45	7

1975 TCA BICENTENNIAL: 1976, uncataloged in the traditional 2400-series passenger car size.

EX-C7	LN-C8	Scarcity
25	45	7

6403 AMTRAK: 1976-77, Vista Dome car in the traditional 2400-series passenger car size.

EX-C7	LN-C8	Scarcity
10	15	4

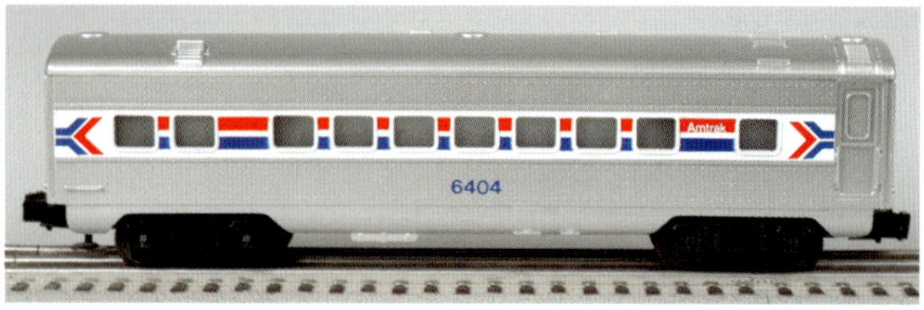

6404 AMTRAK: 1976-77, in the traditional 2400-series passenger car size.

EX-C7	LN-C8	Scarcity
10	15	4

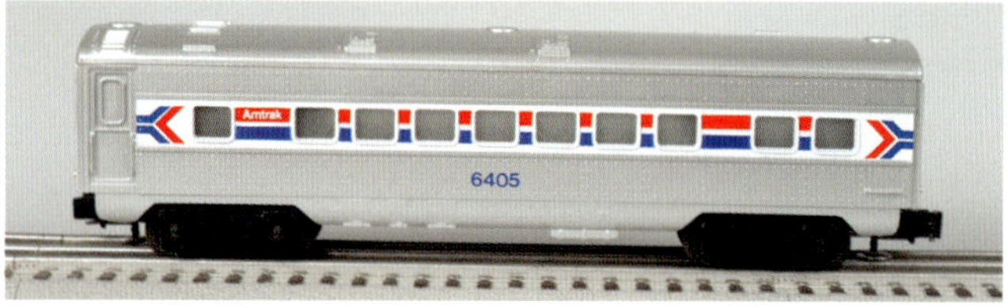

6405 AMTRAK: 1976-77, in the traditional 2400-series passenger car size.

EX-C7	LN-C8	Scarcity
10	15	4

6406 AMTRAK: 1976-77, observation car in the traditional 2400-series passenger car size.

EX-C7	LN-C8	Scarcity
10	15	4

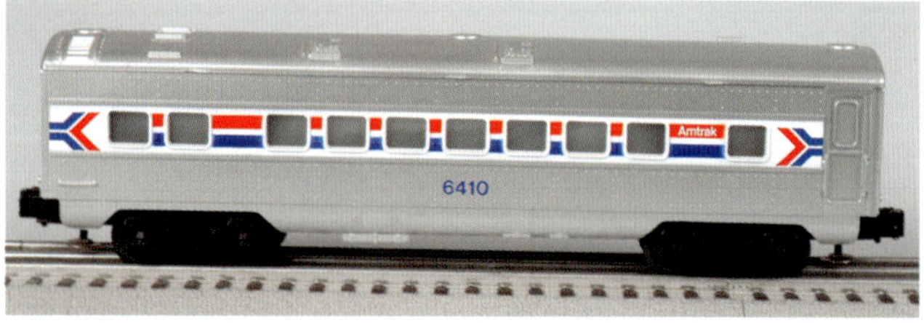

6410 AMTRAK: 1977, in the traditional 2400-series passenger car size.

EX-C7	LN-C8	Scarcity
10	15	4

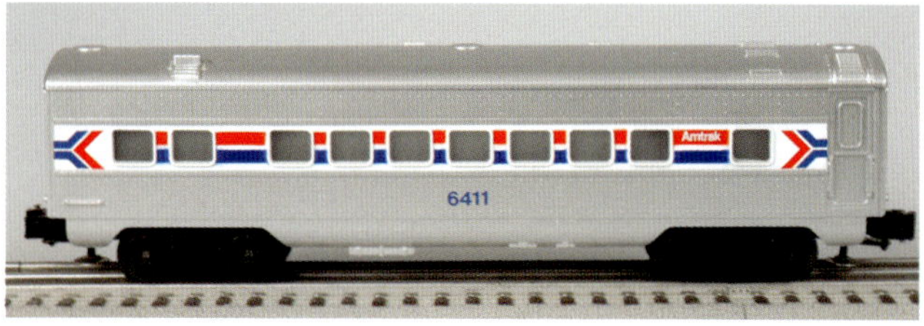

6411 AMTRAK: 1977, in the traditional 2400-series passenger car size.

EX-C7	LN-C8	Scarcity
10	15	4

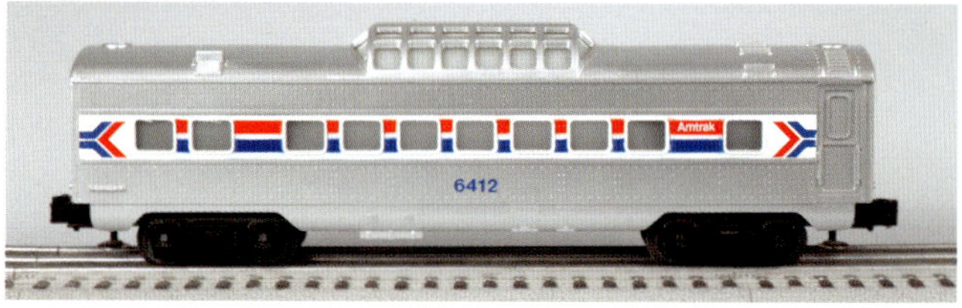

6412 AMTRAK: 1977, Vista Dome car in the traditional 2400-series passenger car size.

EX-C7	LN-C8	Scarcity
10	15	4

7200 QUICKSILVER: 1982-83, in the traditional 2400-series passenger car size.

EX-C7	LN-C8	Scarcity
15	20	3

7201 QUICKSILVER: 1982-83, in the traditional 2400-series passenger car size.

EX-C7	LN-C8	Scarcity
15	20	3

7202 QUICKSILVER: 1982-83, observation car in the traditional 2400-series passenger car size.

EX-C7	LN-C8	Scarcity
15	20	3

[7203] NORFOLK AND WESTERN: 1982, uncataloged fluted aluminum dining car numbered "491."

EX-C7	LN-C8	Scarcity
100	150	5

[7204] SOUTHERN PACIFIC: 1982, uncataloged fluted aluminum dining car.

EX-C7	LN-C8	Scarcity
125	175	5

[7205] DENVER: 1982, uncataloged TCA small heavyweight combination car, "THE ROCKY MOUNTAIN ROUTE – 1982."

EX-C7	LN-C8	Scarcity
20	25	5

[7206] LOUISVILLE: 1983, uncataloged TCA small heavyweight passenger car, "GREAT LAKES LIMITED – 1983."

EX-C7	LN-C8	Scarcity
20	25	5

7207 NEW YORK CENTRAL: 1983, uncataloged dining car.

EX-C7	LN-C8	Scarcity
80	120	5

[7208] PENNSYLVANIA: 1983, uncataloged dining car.

EX-C7	LN-C8	Scarcity
60	100	5

7210 UNION PACIFIC: 1984, dining car.

EX-C7	LN-C8	Scarcity
60	90	3

[7211] SOUTHERN PACIFIC: 1983, uncataloged Vista Dome car.

EX-C7	LN-C8	Scarcity
100	150	5

[7212] CITY OF PITTSBURGH: 1984, uncataloged TCA small heavyweight passenger car, "FORT PITT LIMITED – 1984."

EX-C7	LN-C8	Scarcity
20	25	5

7215 BALTIMORE AND OHIO: 1983-84, small heavyweight car.

EX-C7	LN-C8	Scarcity
20	25	4

7216 BALTIMORE AND OHIO: 1983-84, small heavyweight car.

EX-C7	LN-C8	Scarcity
20	25	4

7217 BALTIMORE AND OHIO: 1983-84, small heavyweight baggage car.

EX-C7	LN-C8	Scarcity
20	25	4

7220 ILLINOIS CENTRAL: 1985 and 1987, small heavyweight baggage car.

EX-C7	LN-C8	Scarcity
60	90	3

7221 ILLINOIS CENTRAL: 1985 and 1987, small heavyweight combination.

EX-C7	LN-C8	Scarcity
40	50	5

7222 ILLINOIS CENTRAL: 1985 and 1987, small heavyweight car.

EX-C7	LN-C8	Scarcity
40	50	5

7223 ILLINOIS CENTRAL: 1985 and 1987, small heavyweight car.

EX-C7	LN-C8	Scarcity
40	50	5

7224 ILLINOIS CENTRAL: 1985 and 1987, small heavyweight dining car.

EX-C7	LN-C8	Scarcity
40	50	5

7225 ILLINOIS CENTRAL: 1985 and 1987, small heavyweight observation car.

EX-C7	LN-C8	Scarcity
40	50	5

7227 WABASH: 1986-87, small heavyweight dining car, Fallen Flags number one.

EX-C7	LN-C8	Scarcity
40	50	5

7228 WABASH: 1986-87, small heavyweight baggage car, Fallen Flags number one.

EX-C7	LN-C8	Scarcity
40	50	5

7229 WABASH: 1986-87, small heavyweight combination, Fallen Flags number one.

EX-C7	LN-C8	Scarcity
40	50	5

7230 WABASH: 1986-87, small heavyweight car, Fallen Flags number one.

EX-C7	LN-C8	Scarcity
40	50	5

7231 WABASH: 1986-87, small heavyweight car, Fallen Flags number one.

EX-C7	LN-C8	Scarcity
40	50	5

7232 WABASH: 1986-87, small heavyweight observation car, Fallen Flags number one.

EX-C7	LN-C8	Scarcity
35	40	5

7241 W & ARR: 1986, uncataloged small heavyweight car.

EX-C7	LN-C8	Scarcity
20	30	5

7242 W & ARR: 1986, uncataloged small heavyweight baggage car.

EX-C7	LN-C8	Scarcity
20	30	5

[7692-1] VIRGINIA TRAIN COLLECTORS: 1992, uncataloged baggage car in the traditional 2400-series passenger car size.

EX-C7	LN-C8	Scarcity
20	25	5

[7692-2] VIRGINIA TRAIN COLLECTORS: 1992, uncataloged combination in the traditional 2400-series passenger car size.

EX-C7	LN-C8	Scarcity
20	25	5

[7692-3] VIRGINIA TRAIN COLLECTORS: 1992, uncataloged dining car in the traditional 2400-series passenger car size.

EX-C7	LN-C8	Scarcity
20	25	5

[7692-4] VIRGINIA TRAIN COLLECTORS: 1992, uncataloged in the traditional 2400-series passenger car size.

EX-C7	LN-C8	Scarcity
20	25	5

[7692-5] VIRGINIA TRAIN COLLECTORS: 1992, uncataloged Vista Dome car in the traditional 2400-series passenger car size.

EX-C7	LN-C8	Scarcity
20	25	5

[7692-6] VIRGINIA TRAIN COLLECTORS: 1992, uncataloged in the traditional 2400-series passenger car size.

EX-C7	LN-C8	Scarcity
20	25	5

[7692-7] VIRGINIA TRAIN COLLECTORS: 1992, uncataloged observation car in the traditional 2400-series passenger car size.

EX-C7	LN-C8	Scarcity
20	25	5

8764 BALTIMORE AND OHIO: 1977, Budd RDC Passenger Service Station Special item.

EX-C7	LN-C8	Scarcity
60	90	5

8765 BALTIMORE AND OHIO: 1977, Budd RDC baggage car, dummy Service Station Special item.

EX-C7	LN-C8	Scarcity
40	60	4

8766 BALTIMORE AND OHIO: 1977, Budd RDC baggage car, Service Station Special item.

EX-C7	LN-C8	Scarcity
125	175	5

8767 BALTIMORE AND OHIO: 1977, Budd RDC Passenger, dummy Service Station Special item.

EX-C7	LN-C8	Scarcity
40	60	4

8768 BALTIMORE AND OHIO: 1977, Budd RDC Passenger, dummy Service Station Special item.

EX-C7	LN-C8	Scarcity
40	60	4

8868 AMTRAK: 1978 and 1980, Budd RDC baggage car.

EX-C7	LN-C8	Scarcity
70	90	4

8869 AMTRAK: 1978 and 1980, dummy Budd RDC Passenger.

EX-C7	LN-C8	Scarcity
40	50	4

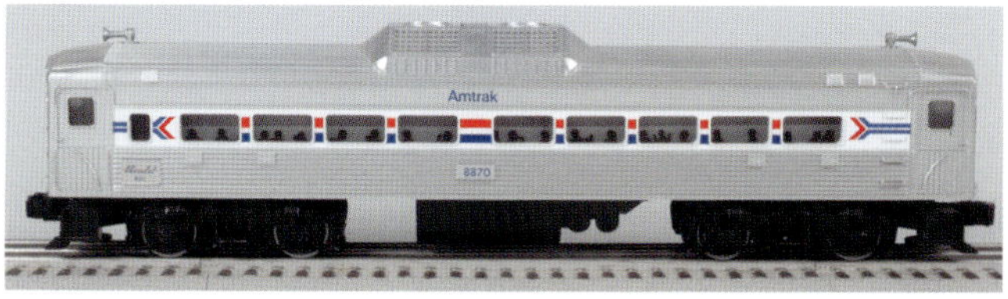

8870 AMTRAK: 1978 and 1980, dummy Budd RDC Passenger.

EX-C7	LN-C8	Scarcity
50	60	4

8871 AMTRAK: 1978 and 1980, dummy Budd RDC baggage car.

EX-C7	LN-C8	Scarcity
40	50	4

9500 MILWAUKEE ROAD: 1973, small heavyweight car.

EX-C7	LN-C8	Scarcity
20	30	4

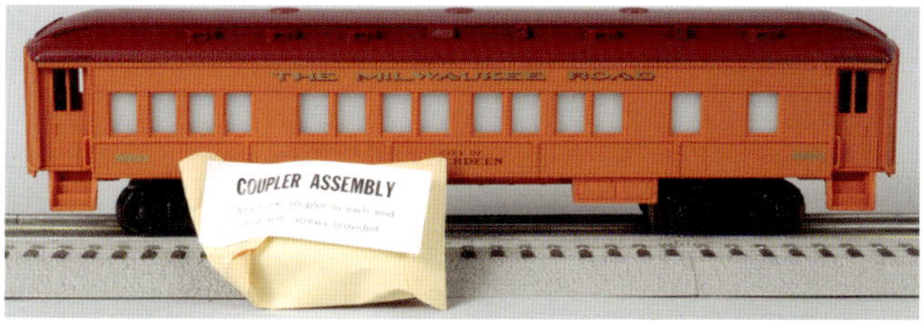

9501 MILWAUKEE ROAD: Uncataloged in 1973, cataloged from 1974-76, small heavyweight "Aberdeen" car.

EX-C7	LN-C8	Scarcity
15	20	4

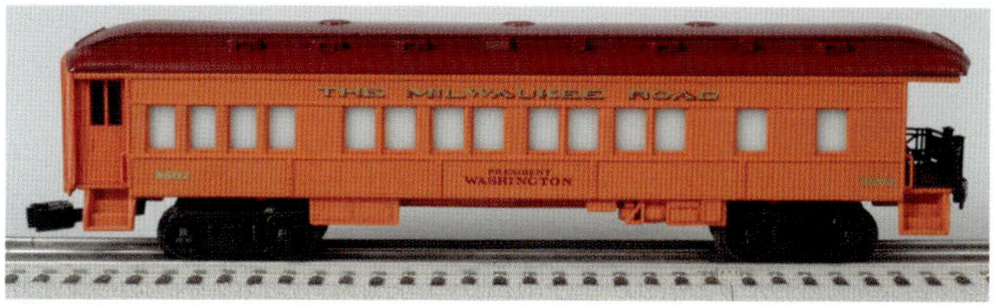

9502 MILWAUKEE ROAD: 1973, small heavyweight "President Washington" observation car.

EX-C7	LN-C8	Scarcity
18	25	4

9503 MILWAUKEE ROAD: 1973, small heavyweight Chicago car.

EX-C7	LN-C8	Scarcity
18	25	4

9504 MILWAUKEE ROAD: Uncataloged in 1973, cataloged from 1974-76, small heavyweight "City of Tacoma" car.

EX-C7	LN-C8	Scarcity
18	25	4

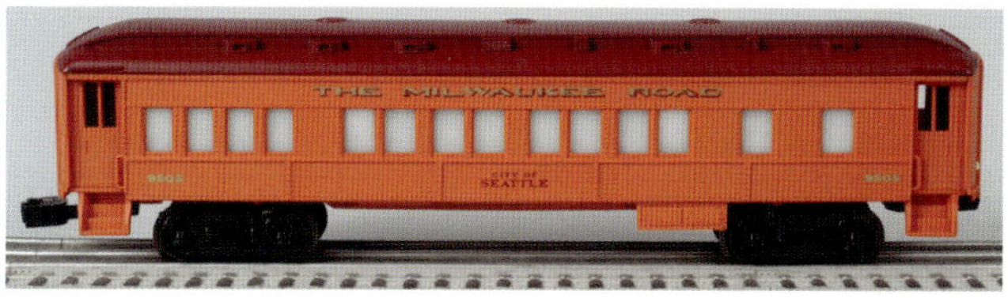

9505 MILWAUKEE ROAD: Uncataloged in 1973, cataloged from 1974-76, small heavyweight "City of Seattle" car.

EX-C7	LN-C8	Scarcity
18	25	4

9506 MILWAUKEE ROAD: Uncataloged in 1973, cataloged from 1975-76, small heavyweight combination car.

EX-C7	LN-C8	Scarcity
18	25	4

9507 PENNSYLVANIA: 1974-75, "City of Manhattan" small heavyweight car.

EX-C7	LN-C8	Scarcity
25	30	4

9508 PENNSYLVANIA: 1974-75, "City of Philadelphia" small heavyweight car.

EX-C7	LN-C8	Scarcity
25	30	4

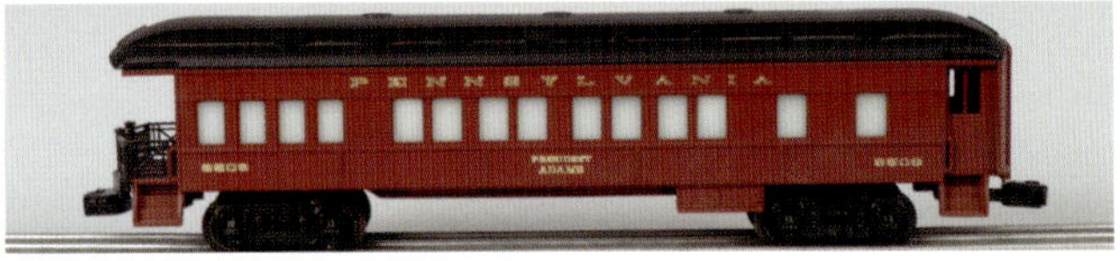

9509 PENNSYLVANIA: 1974-75, "President Adams" small heavyweight observation car.

EX-C7	LN-C8	Scarcity
25	30	4

9510 PENNSYLVANIA: Uncataloged in 1973, cataloged from 1975-76, small heavyweight combination car.

EX-C7	LN-C8	Scarcity
18	25	4

9511 MILWAUKEE ROAD: 1974, uncataloged "City of Minneapolis" small heavyweight car.

EX-C7	LN-C8	Scarcity
25	30	4

9512 TOY TRAIN OPERATING SOCIETY: 1974, uncataloged Summerdale Junction small heavyweight car.

EX-C7	LN-C8	Scarcity
25	30	6

9513 PENNSYLVANIA: 1975-76, "Penn Square" small heavyweight car.

EX-C7	LN-C8	Scarcity
18	25	4

9514 PENNSYLVANIA: 1975-76, "Times Square" small heavyweight car.

EX-C7	LN-C8	Scarcity
18	25	4

9515 PENNSYLVANIA: 1975-76, "Washington Circle" small heavyweight car.

EX-C7	LN-C8	Scarcity
18	25	4

9516 BALTIMORE AND OHIO: 1976, "Mountain Top" small heavyweight car.

EX-C7	LN-C8	Scarcity
18	25	4

9517 BALTIMORE AND OHIO: 1975, "Capital City" small heavyweight car.

EX-C7	LN-C8	Scarcity
25	30	4

9518 BALTIMORE AND OHIO: 1975, "National View" small heavyweight observation car.

EX-C7	LN-C8	Scarcity
25	30	4

9519 BALTIMORE AND OHIO: 1975, RPO small heavyweight combination car.

EX-C7	LN-C8	Scarcity
30	40	4

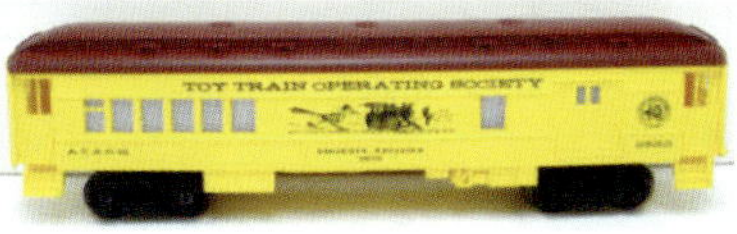

9520 TOY TRAIN OPERATING SOCIETY: 1975, uncataloged Phoenix small heavyweight combination car.

EX-C7	LN-C8	Scarcity
18	25	6

9521 PENNSYLVANIA: Uncataloged in 1975, cataloged in 1976, small heavyweight baggage car.

EX-C7	LN-C8	Scarcity
30	40	4

9522 MILWAUKEE ROAD: Uncataloged in 1975, cataloged in 1976, small heavyweight baggage car.

EX-C7	LN-C8	Scarcity
30	40	4

9523 BALTIMORE AND OHIO: Uncataloged in 1975, cataloged in 1976, small heavyweight baggage car.

EX-C7	LN-C8	Scarcity
30	40	4

9524 BALTIMORE AND OHIO: 1976, "Margaret Corbin" small heavyweight car.

EX-C7	LN-C8	Scarcity
18	25	4

9525 BALTIMORE AND OHIO: 1976, "Emerald Brook" small heavyweight car.

EX-C7	LN-C8	Scarcity
18	25	4

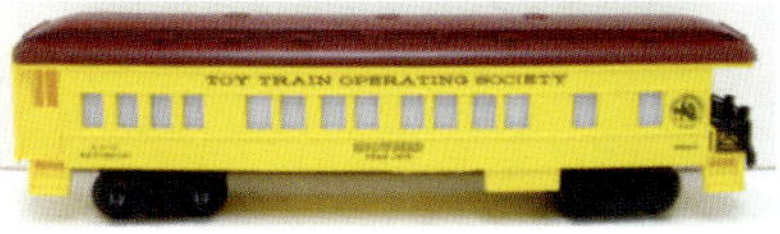

9526 TOY TRAIN OPERATING SOCIETY: 1976, uncataloged Snowbird small heavyweight observation car.

EX-C7	LN-C8	Scarcity
18	25	6

[9527] MILWAUKEE ROAD: 1976, uncataloged campaign small heavyweight observation car.

EX-C7	LN-C8	Scarcity
50	75	4

[9528] PENNSYLVANIA: 1976, uncataloged campaign small heavyweight observation car.

EX-C7	LN-C8	Scarcity
30	40	4

[9529] BALTIMORE AND OHIO: 1976, uncataloged campaign small heavyweight observation car.

EX-C7	LN-C8	Scarcity
30	40	4

9530 SOUTHERN: 1977-78, "Joel Chandler Harris" small heavyweight baggage car.

EX-C7	LN-C8	Scarcity
30	40	4

9531 SOUTHERN: 1977-78, "Andrew Pickens" small heavyweight combination.

EX-C7	LN-C8	Scarcity
30	40	4

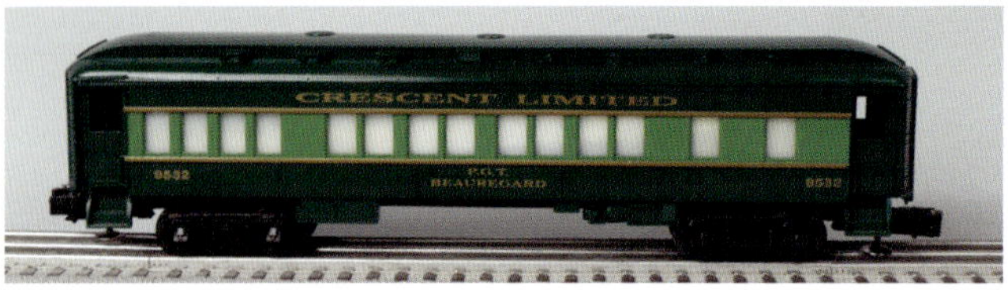

9532 SOUTHERN: 1977-78, "P.G.T Beauregard" small heavyweight car.

EX-C7	LN-C8	Scarcity
30	40	4

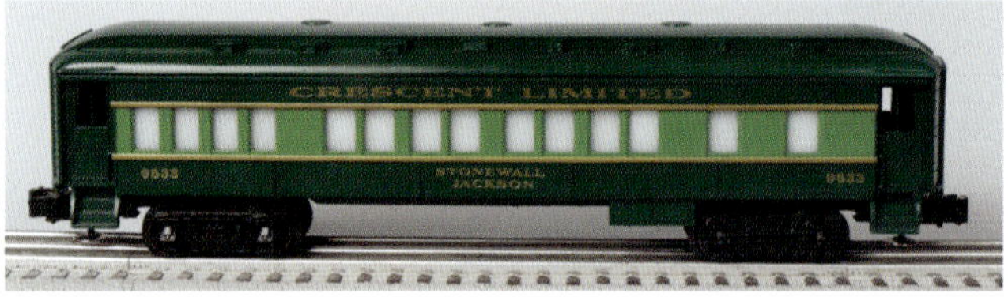

9533 SOUTHERN: 1977-78, "Stonewall Jackson" small heavyweight car.

EX-C7	LN-C8	Scarcity
30	40	4

9534 SOUTHERN: 1977-78, "Robert E. Lee" small heavyweight observation car.

EX-C7	LN-C8	Scarcity
30	40	4

9535 TOY TRAIN OPERATING SOCIETY: 1977, uncataloged "Columbus" small heavyweight baggage car.

EX-C7	LN-C8	Scarcity
20	25	6

9536 JERSEY CENTRAL BLUE COMET: 1978-80, "Barnard" small heavyweight baggage car.

EX-C7	LN-C8	Scarcity
25	30	4

9537 JERSEY CENTRAL BLUE COMET: 1978-80, "Halley" small heavyweight combination car.

EX-C7	LN-C8	Scarcity
25	30	4

9538 JERSEY CENTRAL BLUE COMET: 1978-80, "Faye" small heavyweight car.

EX-C7	LN-C8	Scarcity
25	30	4

9539 JERSEY CENTRAL BLUE COMET: 1978-80, "Westphal" small heavyweight car.

EX-C7	LN-C8	Scarcity
25	30	4

9540 JERSEY CENTRAL BLUE COMET: 1978-80, "Tempel" small heavyweight observation car.

EX-C7	LN-C8	Scarcity
25	30	4

9541 SANTA FE: 1980-82, baggage small heavyweight car.

EX-C7	LN-C8	Scarcity
15	20	4

[9544] CHICAGO: 1980, uncataloged TCA small heavyweight observation car, "LAND OF LINCOLN – 1980."

EX-C7	LN-C8	Scarcity
30	40	6

9545 UNION PACIFIC: 1984, smooth-side aluminum baggage car.

EX-C7	LN-C8	Scarcity
70	90	5

9546 UNION PACIFIC: 1984, smooth-side aluminum combination car.

EX-C7	LN-C8	Scarcity
70	90	5

9547 UNION PACIFIC: 1984, smooth-side aluminum observation car.

EX-C7	LN-C8	Scarcity
70	90	5

[9548] UNION PACIFIC: 1984, "Placid Bay," smooth-side aluminum car.

EX-C7	LN-C8	Scarcity
70	90	5

[9549] UNION PACIFIC: 1984, "Ocean Sunset," smooth-side aluminum car.

EX-C7	LN-C8	Scarcity
70	90	5

9551 W. & A.R.R.: Uncataloged in 1977, cataloged from 1978-80, baggage car.

EX-C7	LN-C8	Scarcity
25	30	4

9552 W. & A.R.R.: Uncataloged in 1977, cataloged from 1978-80.

EX-C7	LN-C8	Scarcity
25	30	4

[9554] CHICAGO AND ALTON: 1981, "Armstrong" small heavyweight baggage car.

EX-C7	LN-C8	Scarcity
30	40	4

[9555] CHICAGO AND ALTON: 1981, "Missouri" small heavyweight combination car.

EX-C7	LN-C8	Scarcity
30	40	4

[9556] CHICAGO AND ALTON: 1981, "Wilson" small heavyweight car.

EX-C7	LN-C8	Scarcity
30	40	4

[9557] CHICAGO AND ALTON: 1981, "Webster Groves" small heavyweight car.

EX-C7	LN-C8	Scarcity
30	40	4

[9558] CHICAGO AND ALTON: 1981, "Chicago" small heavyweight observation car.

EX-C7	LN-C8	Scarcity
30	40	4

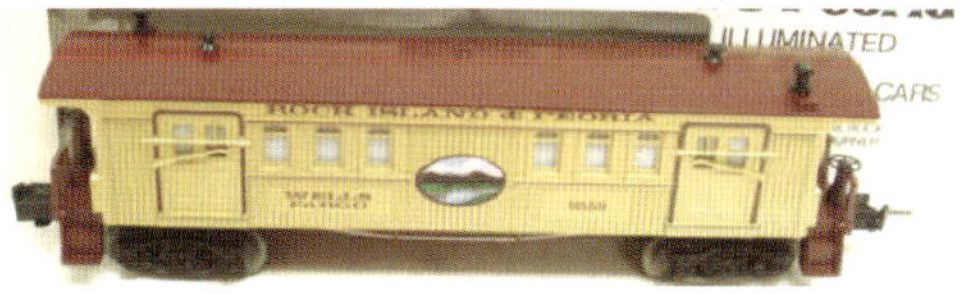

9559 ROCK ISLAND: 1981-82, baggage car.

EX-C7	LN-C8	Scarcity
20	25	4

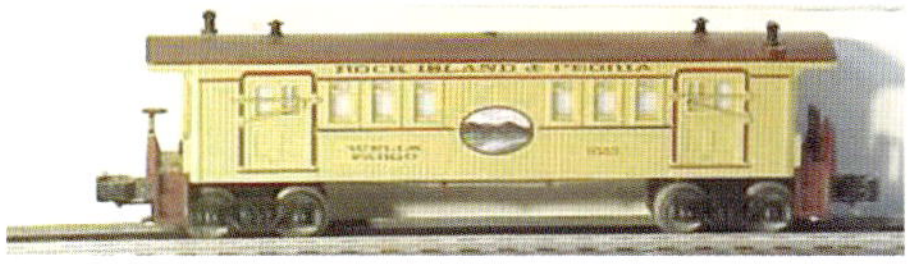

9560 ROCK ISLAND: 1981-82.

EX-C7	LN-C8	Scarcity
20	25	4

9561 ROCK ISLAND: 1981-82.

EX-C7	LN-C8	Scarcity
20	25	4

[9562] NORFOLK AND WESTERN: 1981, fluted aluminum baggage car numbered "577."

EX-C7	LN-C8	Scarcity
70	90	5

[9563] NORFOLK AND WESTERN: 1981, fluted aluminum combination car numbered "578."

EX-C7	LN-C8	Scarcity
70	90	5

[9564] NORFOLK AND WESTERN: 1981, fluted aluminum car numbered "579."

EX-C7	LN-C8	Scarcity
70	90	5

[9565] NORFOLK AND WESTERN: 1981 fluted aluminum car numbered "580."

EX-C7	LN-C8	Scarcity
70	90	5

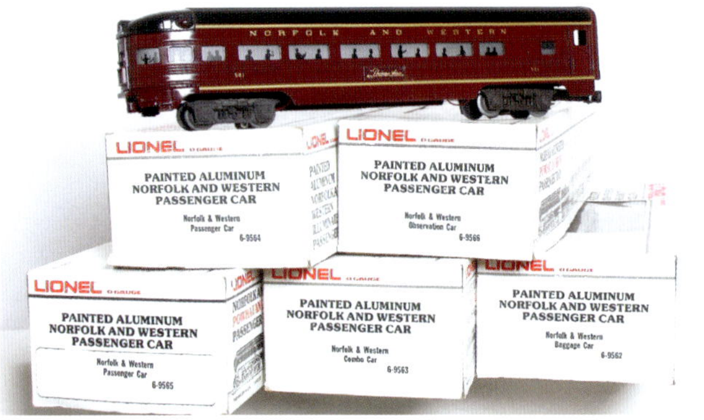

[9566] NORFOLK AND WESTERN: 1981, fluted aluminum observation car numbered "581."

EX-C7	LN-C8	Scarcity
70	90	5

[9567] NORFOLK AND WESTERN: 1981, uncataloged fluted aluminum Vista Dome car numbered "582."

EX-C7	LN-C8	Scarcity
150	225	6

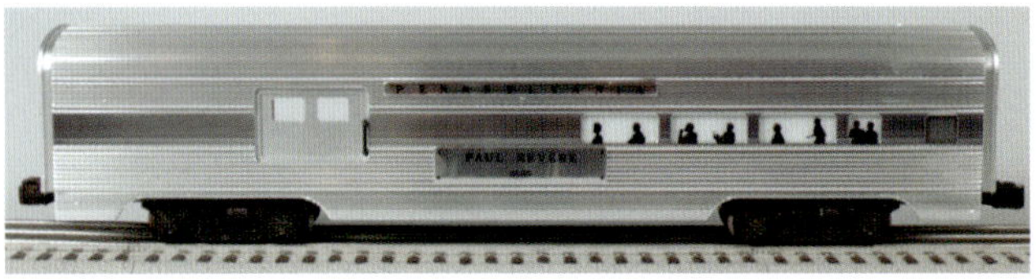

9569 PENNSYLVANIA: 1981, uncataloged fluted aluminum combination.

EX-C7	LN-C8	Scarcity
100	140	6

9570 PENNSYLVANIA: 1979, fluted aluminum baggage car.

EX-C7	LN-C8	Scarcity
70	90	5

9571 PENNSYLVANIA: 1979, fluted aluminum car.

EX-C7	LN-C8	Scarcity
70	90	5

9572 PENNSYLVANIA: 1979, fluted aluminum car.

EX-C7	LN-C8	Scarcity
70	90	5

9573 PENNSYLVANIA: 1979, fluted aluminum Vista Dome car.

EX-C7	LN-C8	Scarcity
70	90	5

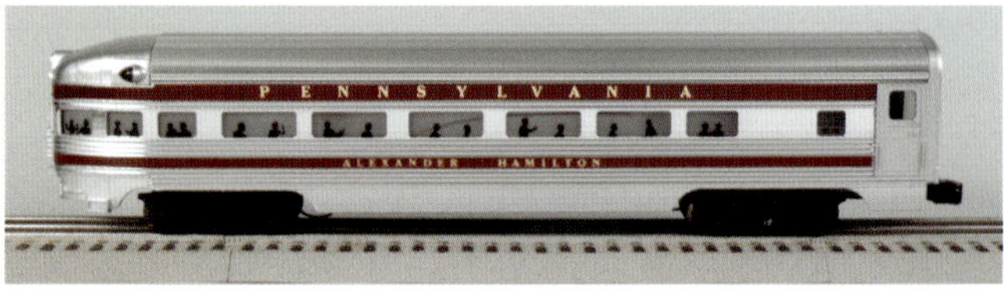

9574 PENNSYLVANIA: 1979, fluted aluminum observation car.

EX-C7	LN-C8	Scarcity
70	90	5

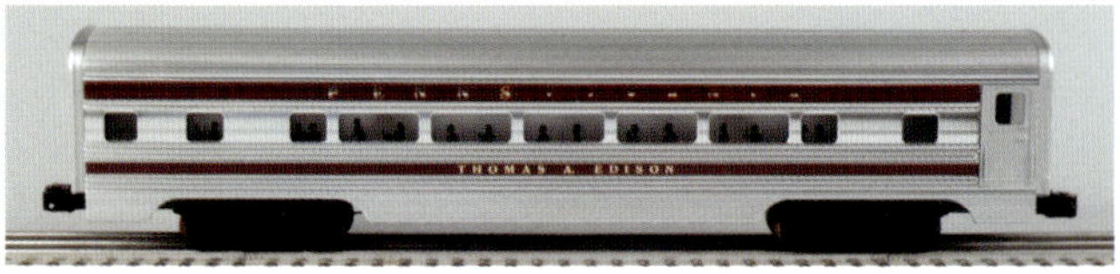

9575 PENNSYLVANIA: 1979-80, uncataloged fluted aluminum car.

EX-C7	LN-C8	Scarcity
70	90	5

9576 BURLINGTON: 1980, fluted aluminum baggage car.

EX-C7	LN-C8	Scarcity
70	90	5

9577 BURLINGTON: 1980, fluted aluminum car.

EX-C7	LN-C8	Scarcity
70	90	5

9578 BURLINGTON: 1980, fluted aluminum car.

EX-C7	LN-C8	Scarcity
70	90	5

9579 BURLINGTON: 1980, fluted aluminum Vista Dome car.

EX-C7	LN-C8	Scarcity
70	90	5

9580 BURLINGTON: 1980, fluted aluminum observation car.

EX-C7	LN-C8	Scarcity
70	90	5

9581 CHESSIE SYSTEM: 1980, small heavyweight baggage car.

EX-C7	LN-C8	Scarcity
25	30	5

9582 CHESSIE SYSTEM: 1980, combination car.

EX-C7	LN-C8	Scarcity
25	30	5

9583 CHESSIE SYSTEM: 1980, small heavyweight car.

EX-C7	LN-C8	Scarcity
25	30	5

9584 CHESSIE SYSTEM: 1980, small heavyweight car.

EX-C7	LN-C8	Scarcity
25	30	5

9585 CHESSIE SYSTEM: 1980, small heavyweight observation car.

EX-C7	LN-C8	Scarcity
25	30	5

9586 CHESSIE SYSTEM: 1986, uncataloged small heavyweight dining car.

EX-C7	LN-C8	Scarcity
60	75	6

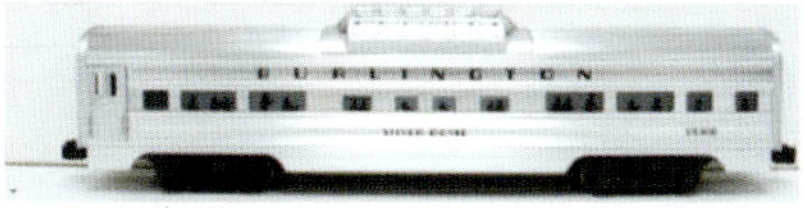

9588 BURLINGTON: 1980, uncataloged fluted aluminum Vista Dome car.

EX-C7	LN-C8	Scarcity
80	100	6

[9589] SOUTHERN PACIFIC: 1982-83, fluted aluminum baggage car.

EX-C7	LN-C8	Scarcity
80	100	5

[9590] SOUTHERN PACIFIC: 1982-83, fluted aluminum combination.

EX-C7	LN-C8	Scarcity
80	100	5

[9591] SOUTHERN PACIFIC: 1982-83, "Pullman" fluted aluminum car.

EX-C7	LN-C8	Scarcity
80	100	5

[9592] SOUTHERN PACIFIC: 1982-83, "Chair" fluted aluminum car.

EX-C7	LN-C8	Scarcity
80	100	5

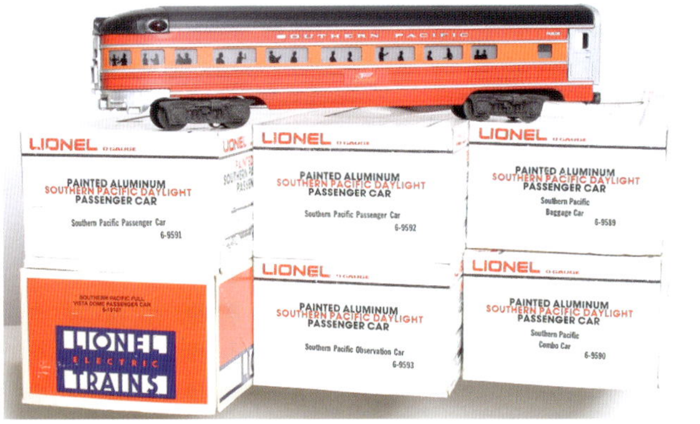

[9593] SOUTHERN PACIFIC: 1982-83, fluted aluminum observation car.

EX-C7	LN-C8	Scarcity
80	100	5

9594 NEW YORK CENTRAL: 1983-84, smooth-side aluminum baggage car.

EX-C7	LN-C8	Scarcity
70	90	5

9595 NEW YORK CENTRAL: 1983-84, smooth-side aluminum combination car.

EX-C7	LN-C8	Scarcity
70	90	5

[9596] NEW YORK CENTRAL: 1983-84, "Wayne County" smooth-side aluminum car.

EX-C7	LN-C8	Scarcity
70	90	5

[9597] NEW YORK CENTRAL: 1983-84, "Hudson River" smooth-side aluminum car.

EX-C7	LN-C8	Scarcity
70	90	5

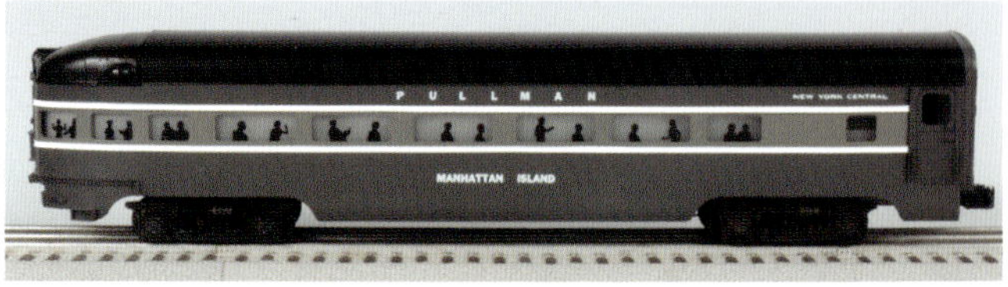

[9598] NEW YORK CENTRAL: 1983-84, smooth-side aluminum observation car.

EX-C7	LN-C8	Scarcity
70	90	5

[9599] CHICAGO AND ALTON: 1986, uncataloged small heavyweight dining car, "Bloomington."

EX-C7	LN-C8	Scarcity
60	75	6

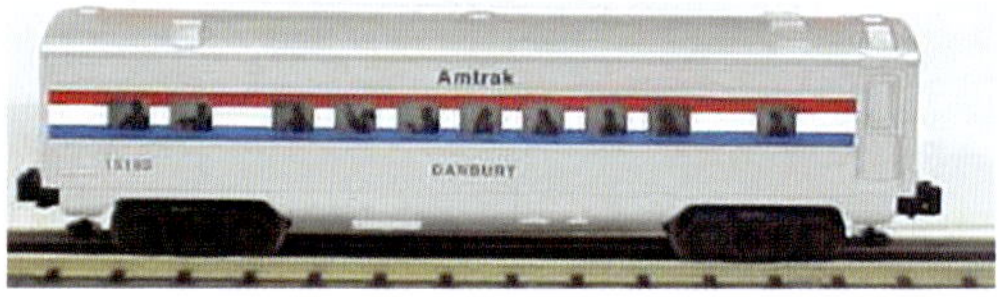

[15100] AMTRAK: 1995-97, in the traditional 2400-series passenger car size.

EX-C7	LN-C8	Scarcity
15	20	4

15101 READING: 1996, baggage car in the traditional 2400-series passenger car size.

EX-C7	LN-C8	Scarcity
15	20	4

15102 READING: 1996, combination in the traditional 2400-series passenger car size.

EX-C7	LN-C8	Scarcity
15	20	4

15103 READING: 1996, in the traditional 2400-series passenger car size.

EX-C7	LN-C8	Scarcity
15	20	4

15104 READING: 1996, Vista Dome car in the traditional 2400-series passenger car size.

EX-C7	LN-C8	Scarcity
15	20	4

15105 READING: 1996, full-length Vista Dome car in the traditional 2400-series passenger car size.

EX-C7	LN-C8	Scarcity
15	20	4

15106 READING: 1996, observation car in the traditional 2400-series passenger car size.

EX-C7	LN-C8	Scarcity
15	20	4

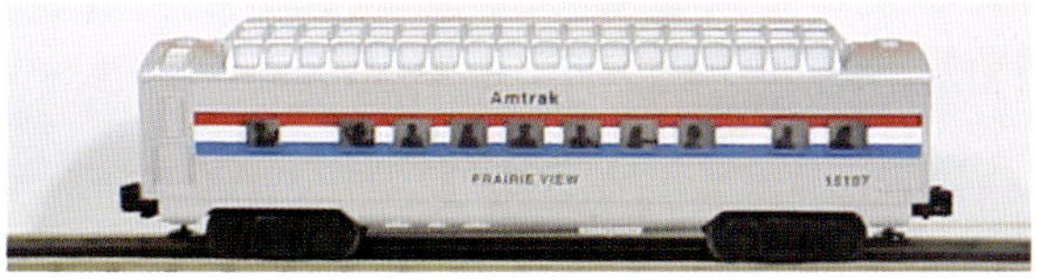

[15107] AMTRAK: 1996, full-length Vista Dome car in the traditional 2400-series passenger car size.

EX-C7	LN-C8	Scarcity
20	25	4

[15108] NORTHERN PACIFIC: 1996, full-length Vista Dome car in the traditional 2400-series passenger car size.

EX-C7	LN-C8	Scarcity
20	25	4

[15109] SANTA FE: 1997, combination car "Thoreau," numbered "2407" in the traditional 2400-series passenger car size.

EX-C7	LN-C8	Scarcity
20	25	4

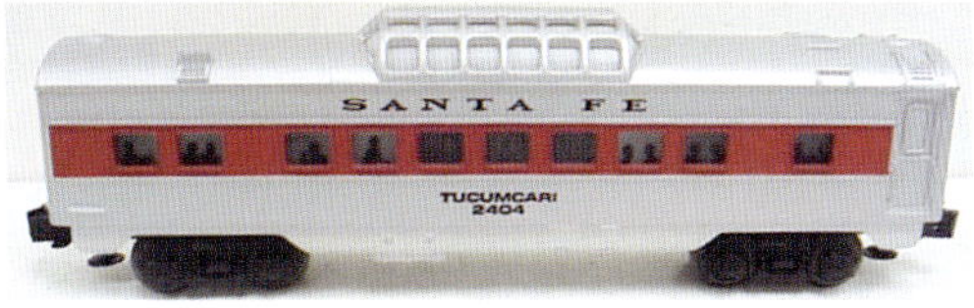

[15110] SANTA FE: 1997, Vista Dome car "Tucumcari," numbered "2404" in the traditional 2400-series passenger car size.

EX-C7	LN-C8	Scarcity
20	25	4

[15111] SANTA FE: 1997, observation car "Tehachapi," numbered "2406" in the traditional 2400-series passenger car size.

EX-C7	LN-C8	Scarcity
20	25	4

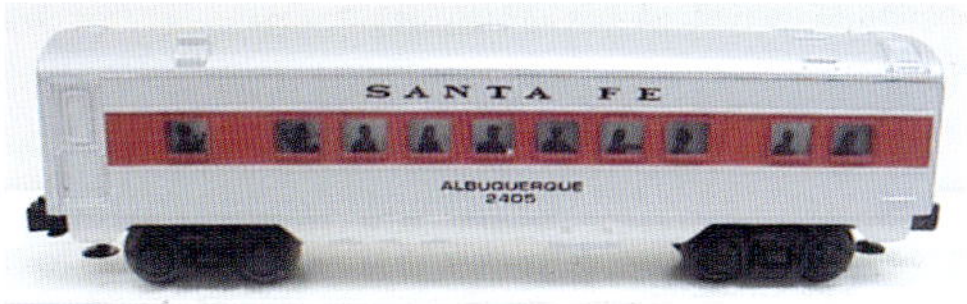

[15112] SANTA FE: 1997, coach "Albuquerque," numbered "2405" in the traditional 2400-series passenger car size.

EX-C7	LN-C8	Scarcity
20	25	4

[15113] SANTA FE: 1997, Vista Dome "Culebra," numbered "2404" in the traditional 2400-series passenger car size.

EX-C7	LN-C8	Scarcity
20	25	4

[15114] NEW JERSEY TRANSIT: 1996, uncataloged coach numbered "5610" in the traditional 2400-series passenger car size.

EX-C7	LN-C8	Scarcity
30	40	5

[15115] NEW JERSEY TRANSIT: 1996, uncataloged coach numbered "5611" in the traditional 2400-series passenger car size.

EX-C7	LN-C8	Scarcity
30	40	5

[15116] NEW JERSEY TRANSIT: 1996, uncataloged coach numbered "5612" in the traditional 2400-series passenger car size.

EX-C7	LN-C8	Scarcity
30	40	5

[15117] ANNIE PASSENGER: 1997, coach with surprised face, goes with "Thomas the Tank Engine."

EX-C7	LN-C8	Scarcity
15	20	4

[15118] CLARABEL PASSENGER: 1997, coach with smiling face, goes with "Thomas the Tank Engine."

EX-C7	LN-C8	Scarcity
15	20	4

[15122] NEW JERSEY TRANSIT: 1997, uncataloged passenger coach numbered "5613."

EX-C7	LN-C8	Scarcity
30	40	5

[15123] NEW JERSEY TRANSIT: 1997, uncataloged passenger coach numbered "5614."

EX-C7	LN-C8	Scarcity
30	40	5

[15124] NEW JERSEY TRANSIT: 1997, uncataloged passenger coach numbered "5615."

EX-C7	LN-C8	Scarcity
30	40	5

[15125] AMTRAK: 1997, uncataloged observation car.

EX-C7	LN-C8	Scarcity
30	40	5

[15126] STARS & STRIPES GENERAL: 1999, coach, "Abraham Lincoln."

EX-C7	LN-C8	Scarcity
35	45	4

[15127] STARS & STRIPES GENERAL: 1999, coach, "Ulysses S. Grant."

EX-C7	LN-C8	Scarcity
35	45	4

15128 PRIDE OF RICHMOND GENERAL: 1999, coach, "Robert E. Lee."

EX-C7	LN-C8	Scarcity
35	45	4

15129 PRIDE OF RICHMOND GENERAL: 1999, coach, "Jefferson Davis."

EX-C7	LN-C8	Scarcity
35	45	4

[15136] CUSTOM SERIES: 1999, short observation car (blue).

EX-C7	LN-C8	Scarcity
25	35	4

[15137] CUSTOM SERIES: 1999, short observation car (red).

EX-C7	LN-C8	Scarcity
25	35	4

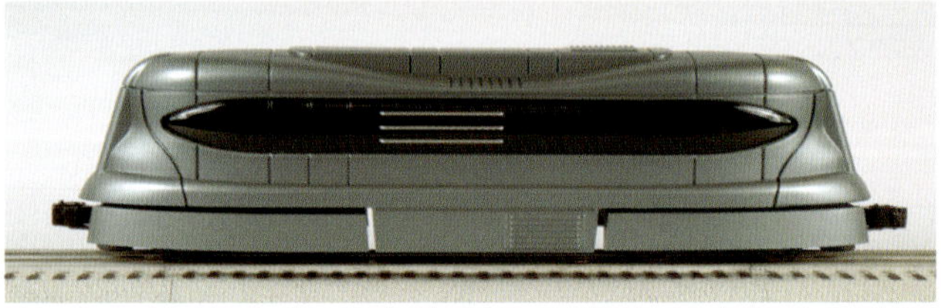

[15138] PRATT'S HOLLOW: 1998, baggage car.

EX-C7	LN-C8	Scarcity

Too rarely traded to establish accurate pricing.

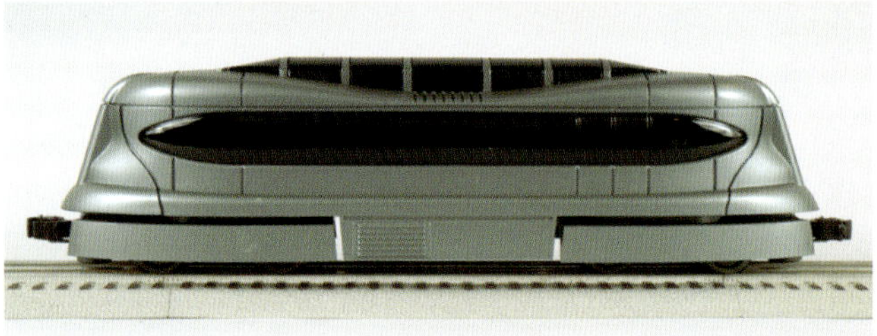

[15139] PRATT'S HOLLOW: 1998, Vista Dome.

EX-C7	LN-C8	Scarcity

Too rarely traded to establish accurate pricing.

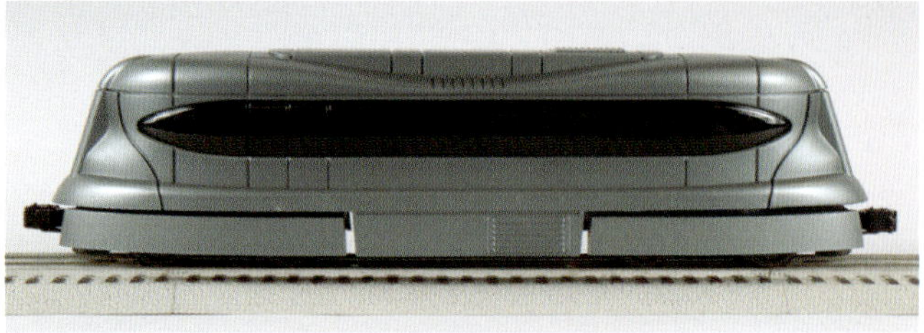

[15140] PRATT'S HOLLOW: 1998, coach.

EX-C7	LN-C8	Scarcity

Too rarely traded to establish accurate pricing.

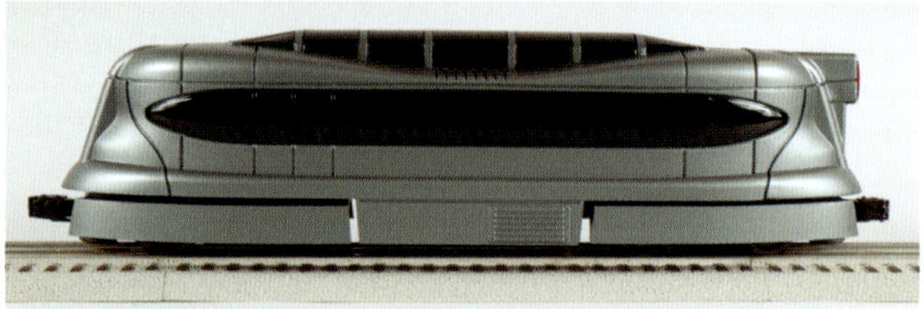

[15141] PRATT'S HOLLOW: 1998, observation car.

EX-C7	LN-C8	Scarcity

Too rarely traded to establish accurate pricing.

[15142] U.S. ARMY: 2000, small heavyweight coach.

EX-C7	LN-C8	Scarcity
35	40	4

[15143] U.S. ARMY: 2000, small heavyweight coach.

EX-C7	LN-C8	Scarcity
35	40	4

16000 PENNSYLVANIA: 1987-88, Vista Dome car in the traditional 2400-series passenger car size.

EX-C7	LN-C8	Scarcity
25	30	4

16001 PENNSYLVANIA: 1987-88, in the traditional 2400-series passenger car size.

EX-C7	LN-C8	Scarcity
25	30	4

16002 PENNSYLVANIA: 1987-88, in the traditional 2400-series passenger car size.

EX-C7	LN-C8	Scarcity
20	25	4

16003 PENNSYLVANIA: 1987-88, observation car in the traditional 2400-series passenger car size.

EX-C7	LN-C8	Scarcity
20	25	4

16009 PENNSYLVANIA: 1988, combination in the traditional 2400-series passenger car size.

EX-C7	LN-C8	Scarcity
25	30	4

16010 VIRGINIA AND TRUCKEE: 1988, Service Station Special item.

16010 VIRGINIA AND TRUCKEE (Type I): Standard-sized "Virgina and Truckee" lettering above windows.

EX-C7	LN-C8	Scarcity
25	30	5

16010 VIRGINIA AND TRUCKEE (Type II): Large "Virgina and Truckee" lettering above windows.

EX-C7	LN-C8	Scarcity
25	30	5

16011 VIRGINIA AND TRUCKEE: 1988, Service Station Special item.

EX-C7	LN-C8	Scarcity
25	30	5

16012 VIRGINIA AND TRUCKEE: 1988, baggage car, Service Station Special item.

EX-C7	LN-C8	Scarcity
25	30	5

16013 AMTRAK: 1988-89, combination in the traditional 2400-series passenger car size.

EX-C7	LN-C8	Scarcity
20	25	4

16014 AMTRAK: 1988-89, Vista Dome car in the traditional 2400-series passenger car size.

EX-C7	LN-C8	Scarcity
20	25	4

16015 AMTRAK: 1988-89, observation car in the traditional 2400-series passenger car size.

EX-C7	LN-C8	Scarcity
20	25	4

16016 NEW YORK CENTRAL: 1989, baggage car in the traditional 2400-series passenger car size.

EX-C7	LN-C8	Scarcity
25	30	4

16017 NEW YORK CENTRAL: 1989, combination in the traditional 2400-series passenger car size.

EX-C7	LN-C8	Scarcity
20	25	4

16018 NEW YORK CENTRAL: 1989 in the traditional 2400-series passenger car size.

EX-C7	LN-C8	Scarcity
20	25	4

16019 NEW YORK CENTRAL: 1989, Vista Dome car in the traditional 2400-series passenger car size.

EX-C7	LN-C8	Scarcity
20	25	4

16020 NEW YORK CENTRAL: 1989, in the traditional 2400-series passenger car size.

EX-C7	LN-C8	Scarcity
20	25	4

16021 NEW YORK CENTRAL: 1989, observation car in the traditional 2400-series passenger car size.

EX-C7	LN-C8	Scarcity
20	25	4

16022 PENNSYLVANIA: 1989, baggage car in the traditional 2400-series passenger car size.

EX-C7	LN-C8	Scarcity
20	25	4

16023 AMTRAK: 1989, in the traditional 2400-series passenger car size.

EX-C7	LN-C8	Scarcity
20	25	4

16024 NORTHERN PACIFIC: 1992, dining car in the traditional 2400-series passenger car size.

EX-C7	LN-C8	Scarcity
30	35	5

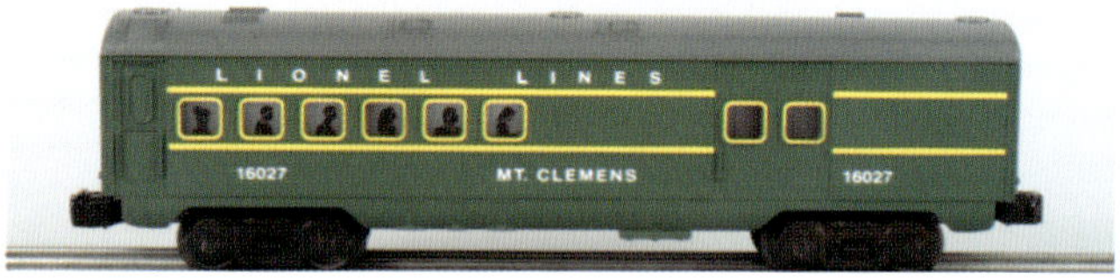

16027 LIONEL LINES: 1990, combination in the traditional 2400-series passenger car size, Service Station Special item.

EX-C7	LN-C8	Scarcity
30	35	5

16028 LIONEL LINES: 1990, "Detroit" car in the traditional 2400-series passenger car size, Service Station Special item.

EX-C7	LN-C8	Scarcity
30	35	5

16029 LIONEL LINES: 1990, "Lansing" car in the traditional 2400-series passenger car size, Service Station Special item.

EX-C7	LN-C8	Scarcity
30	35	5

16030 LIONEL LINES: 1990, "Chesterfield" observation car in the traditional 2400-series passenger car size, Service Station Special item.

EX-C7	LN-C8	Scarcity
30	35	5

16031 PENNSYLVANIA: 1990, dining car in the traditional 2400-series passenger car size.

EX-C7	LN-C8	Scarcity
25	30	4

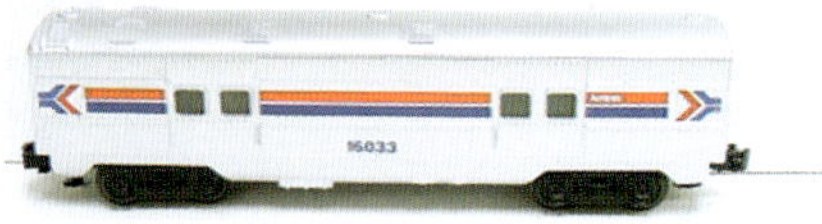

16033 AMTRAK: 1990, baggage car in the traditional 2400-series passenger car size.

EX-C7	LN-C8	Scarcity
25	30	4

16034 NORTHERN PACIFIC: 1990-91, baggage car in the traditional 2400-series passenger car size.

EX-C7	LN-C8	Scarcity
20	25	4

16035 NORTHERN PACIFIC: 1990-91, combination in the traditional 2400-series passenger car size.

EX-C7	LN-C8	Scarcity
20	25	4

16036 NORTHERN PACIFIC: 1990-91, in the traditional 2400-series passenger car size.

EX-C7	LN-C8	Scarcity
20	25	4

16037 NORTHERN PACIFIC: 1990-91, Vista Dome Car in the traditional 2400-series passenger car size.

EX-C7	LN-C8	Scarcity
20	25	4

16038 NORTHERN PACIFIC: 1990-91, in the traditional 2400-series passenger car size.

EX-C7	LN-C8	Scarcity
20	25	4

16039 NORTHERN PACIFIC: 1990-91, observation car in the traditional 2400-series passenger car size.

EX-C7	LN-C8	Scarcity
20	25	4

16040 SOUTHERN PACIFIC: 1990-91, payroll/baggage car.

EX-C7	LN-C8	Scarcity
20	25	4

16041 NEW YORK CENTRAL: 1991, dining car in the traditional 2400-series passenger car size.

EX-C7	LN-C8	Scarcity
35	40	5

16042 ILLINOIS CENTRAL: 1991, baggage car in the traditional 2400-series passenger car size.

EX-C7	LN-C8	Scarcity
20	25	4

16043 ILLINOIS CENTRAL: 1991, combination in the traditional 2400-series passenger car size.

EX-C7	LN-C8	Scarcity
20	25	4

16044 ILLINOIS CENTRAL: 1991, in the traditional 2400-series passenger car size.

EX-C7	LN-C8	Scarcity
20	25	4

16045 ILLINOIS CENTRAL: 1991, Vista Dome car in the traditional 2400-series passenger car size.

EX-C7	LN-C8	Scarcity
20	25	4

16046 ILLINOIS CENTRAL: 1991, in the traditional 2400-series passenger car size.

EX-C7	LN-C8	Scarcity
20	25	4

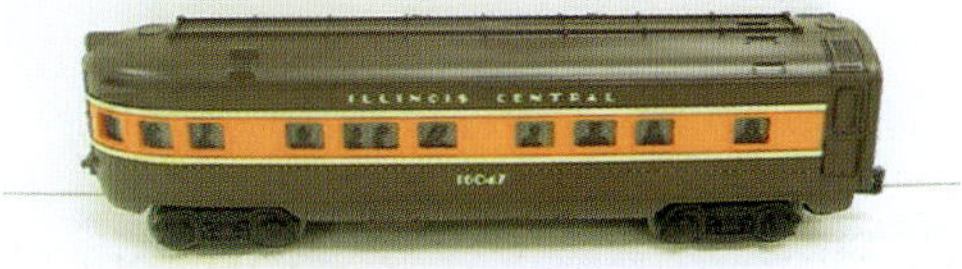

16047 ILLINOIS CENTRAL: 1991, observation car in the traditional 2400-series passenger car size.

EX-C7	LN-C8	Scarcity
20	25	4

16048 AMTRAK: 1991-92, dining car in the traditional 2400-series passenger car size.

EX-C7	LN-C8	Scarcity
20	25	4

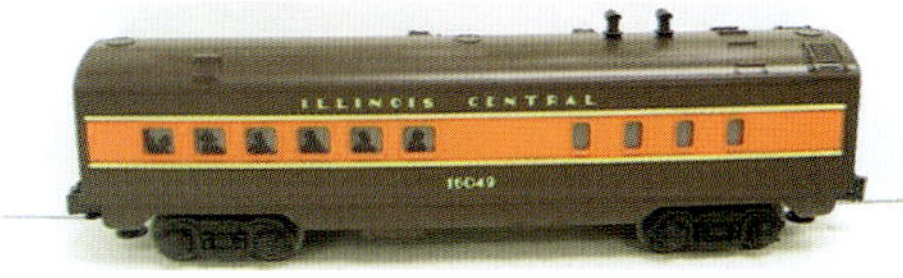

16049 ILLINOIS CENTRAL: 1992, dining car in the traditional 2400-series passenger car size.

EX-C7	LN-C8	Scarcity
20	25	4

[16050] CHICAGO & NORTHWESTERN: 1993, small heavyweight baggage car, numbered "6620."

EX-C7	LN-C8	Scarcity
35	40	5

[16051] CHICAGO & NORTHWESTERN: 1993, small heavyweight combination car, numbered "6630."

EX-C7	LN-C8	Scarcity
35	40	5

[16052] CHICAGO & NORTHWESTERN: 1993, small heavyweight "Lake Geneva" car numbered "6616."

EX-C7	LN-C8	Scarcity
35	40	5

[16053] CHICAGO & NORTHWESTERN: 1993, small heavyweight "Evanston" car numbered "6602."

EX-C7	LN-C8	Scarcity
35	40	5

[16054] CHICAGO & NORTHWESTERN: 1993, small heavyweight "Mt. Faraker" observation car numbered "6603."

EX-C7	LN-C8	Scarcity
35	40	5

16055 SANTA FE: 1993-94, in the traditional 2400-series passenger car size.

EX-C7	LN-C8	Scarcity
20	25	4

16056 SANTA FE: 1993-94, Vista Dome car in the traditional 2400-series passenger car size.

EX-C7	LN-C8	Scarcity
20	25	4

16057 SANTA FE: 1993-94, in the traditional 2400-series passenger car size.

EX-C7	LN-C8	Scarcity
20	25	4

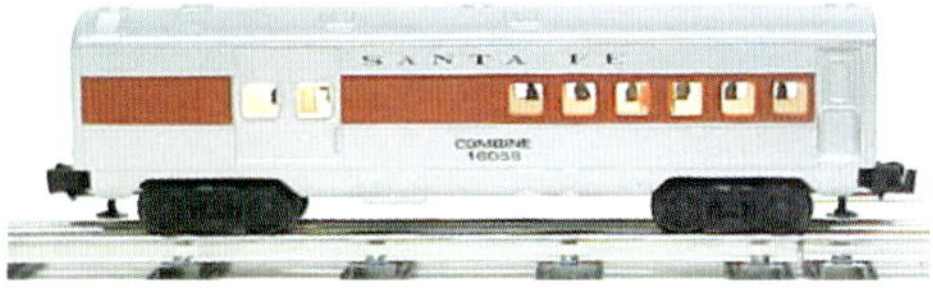

16058 SANTA FE: 1993-94, combination in the traditional 2400-series passenger car size.

EX-C7	LN-C8	Scarcity
20	25	4

16059 SANTA FE: 1993-94, Vista Dome car in the traditional 2400-series passenger car size.

EX-C7	LN-C8	Scarcity
20	25	4

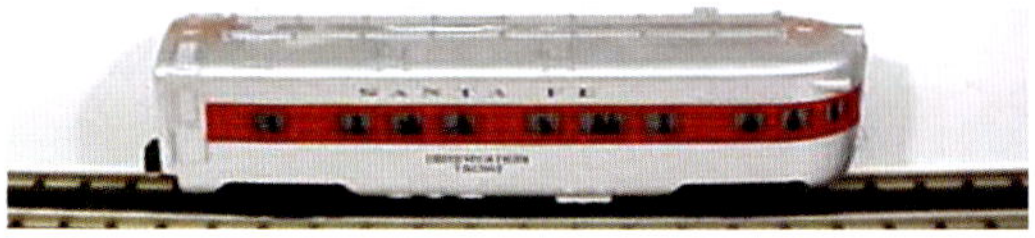

16060 SANTA FE: 1993-94, observation car in the traditional 2400-series passenger car size.

EX-C7	LN-C8	Scarcity
20	25	4

[16061] NORFOLK AND WESTERN: 1994, small heavyweight baggage car, "Plum Run," numbered "6061."

EX-C7	LN-C8	Scarcity
35	40	5

[16062] NORFOLK AND WESTERN: 1994, small heavy-weight combination car, "High Bridge," numbered "6062."

EX-C7	LN-C8	Scarcity
35	40	5

[16063] NORFOLK AND WESTERN: 1994, small heavyweight car, "Max Meadows," numbered "6063."

EX-C7	LN-C8	Scarcity
35	40	5

[16064] NORFOLK AND WESTERN: 1994, "High Hill" small heavyweight car numbered "6064."

EX-C7	LN-C8	Scarcity
35	40	5

[16065] NORFOLK AND WESTERN: 1994, "Hanging Rock" small heavyweight observation car numbered "6065."

EX-C7	LN-C8	Scarcity
35	40	5

[16066] NEW YORK CENTRAL: 1994, small heavyweight combination numbered "6066," Service Station Special item.

EX-C7	LN-C8	Scarcity
35	45	5

[16067] NEW YORK CENTRAL: 1994, small heavyweight car numbered "6067," Service Station Special item.

EX-C7	LN-C8	Scarcity
35	45	5

[16068] UNION PACIFIC: 1994, baggage car numbered "6068" in the traditional 2400-series passenger car size.

EX-C7	LN-C8	Scarcity
30	35	4

[16069] UNION PACIFIC: 1994, combination numbered "6069" in the traditional 2400-series passenger car size.

EX-C7	LN-C8	Scarcity
30	35	4

[16070] UNION PACIFIC: 1994, numbered "6070" in the traditional 2400-series passenger car size.

EX-C7	LN-C8	Scarcity
30	35	4

[16071] UNION PACIFIC: 1994, dining car numbered "6071" in the traditional 2400-series passenger car size.

EX-C7	LN-C8	Scarcity
30	35	4

[16072] UNION PACIFIC: 1994, Vista Dome car numbered "6072" in the traditional 2400-series passenger car size.

EX-C7	LN-C8	Scarcity
30	35	4

[16073] UNION PACIFIC: 1994, numbered "6073" in the traditional 2400-series passenger car size.

EX-C7	LN-C8	Scarcity
30	35	4

[16074] UNION PACIFIC: 1994, observation car numbered "6074" in the traditional 2400-series passenger car size.

EX-C7	LN-C8	Scarcity
30	35	4

[16075] MISSOURI PACIFIC: 1995, small heavyweight baggage car numbered "6620."

EX-C7	LN-C8	Scarcity
30	35	4

[16076] MISSOURI PACIFIC: 1995, small heavyweight combination car numbered "6630."

EX-C7	LN-C8	Scarcity
30	35	4

[16077] MISSOURI PACIFIC: 1995, small heavyweight car numbered "6616."

EX-C7	LN-C8	Scarcity
30	35	4

[16078] MISSOURI PACIFIC: 1995, small heavyweight car numbered "7805."

EX-C7	LN-C8	Scarcity
30	35	4

[16079] MISSOURI PACIFIC: 1995, small heavyweight observation car numbered "6609."

EX-C7	LN-C8	Scarcity
30	35	4

[16080] NEW HAVEN: 1995, baggage car numbered "6080" in the traditional 2400-series passenger car size.

EX-C7	LN-C8	Scarcity
25	30	4

[16081] NEW HAVEN: 1995, combination numbered "6081" in the traditional 2400-series passenger car size.

EX-C7	LN-C8	Scarcity
25	30	4

[16082] NEW HAVEN: 1995, numbered "6082" in the traditional 2400-series passenger car size.

EX-C7	LN-C8	Scarcity
25	30	4

[16083] NEW HAVEN: 1995, Vista Dome car numbered "6083" in the traditional 2400-series passenger car size.

EX-C7	LN-C8	Scarcity
25	30	4

[16084] NEW HAVEN: 1995, full Vista Dome car numbered "6084" in the traditional 2400-series passenger car size.

EX-C7	LN-C8	Scarcity
25	30	4

[16086] NEW HAVEN: 1995, observation car numbered "6086" in the traditional 2400-series passenger car size.

EX-C7	LN-C8	Scarcity
25	30	4

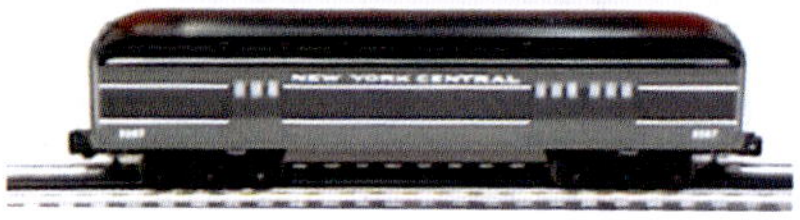

[16087] NEW YORK CENTRAL: 1995, small heavyweight baggage car numbered "6087," Service Station Special item.

EX-C7	LN-C8	Scarcity
35	45	5

[16088] NEW YORK CENTRAL: 1995, "Licking River" small heavyweight car numbered "6088," Service Station Special item.

EX-C7	LN-C8	Scarcity
35	45	5

[16089] NEW YORK CENTRAL: 1995, "Rippling Stream" small heavyweight dining car numbered "6089," Service Station Special item.

EX-C7	LN-C8	Scarcity
35	45	5

[16090] NEW YORK CENTRAL: 1995, "Babbling Brook" small heavyweight observation car numbered "6090," Service Station Special item.

EX-C7	LN-C8	Scarcity
35	45	5

[16091] NEW YORK CENTRAL: 1995, set of four small heavyweight cars, Service Station Special item.

EX-C7	LN-C8	Scarcity
135	175	5

16092 SANTA FE: 1995, full Vista Dome car in the traditional 2400-series passenger car size.

EX-C7	LN-C8	Scarcity
25	30	4

16093 ILLINOIS CENTRAL: 1995, full Vista Dome car in the traditional 2400-series passenger car size.

EX-C7	LN-C8	Scarcity
25	30	4

16094 PENNSYLVANIA: 1995, full Vista Dome car in the traditional 2400-series passenger car size.

EX-C7	LN-C8	Scarcity
25	30	4

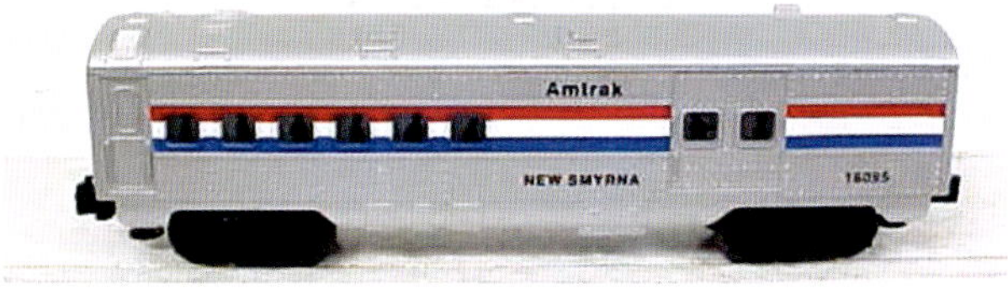

16095 AMTRAK: 1995, "New Smyrna" combination car in the traditional 2400-series passenger car size.

EX-C7	LN-C8	Scarcity
15	20	4

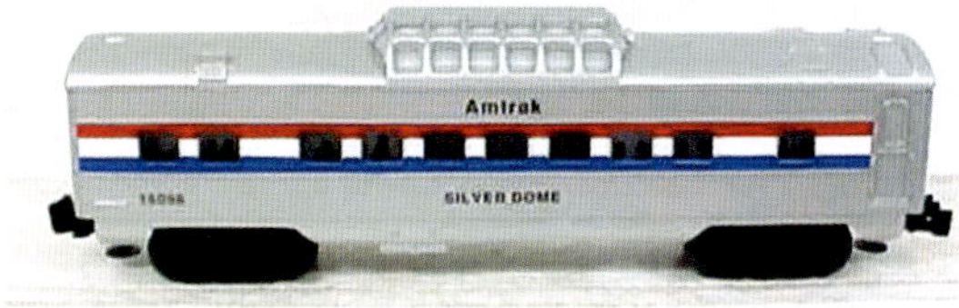

16096 AMTRAK: 1995, "Silver Dome" Vista Dome car in the traditional 2400-series passenger car size.

EX-C7	LN-C8	Scarcity
15	20	4

16097 AMTRAK: 1995, "Lake Worth" observation car in the traditional 2400-series passenger car size.

EX-C7	LN-C8	Scarcity
15	20	4

[16098] AMTRAK: 1995-97, "Temple" car in the traditional 2400-series passenger car size.

EX-C7	LN-C8	Scarcity
15	20	4

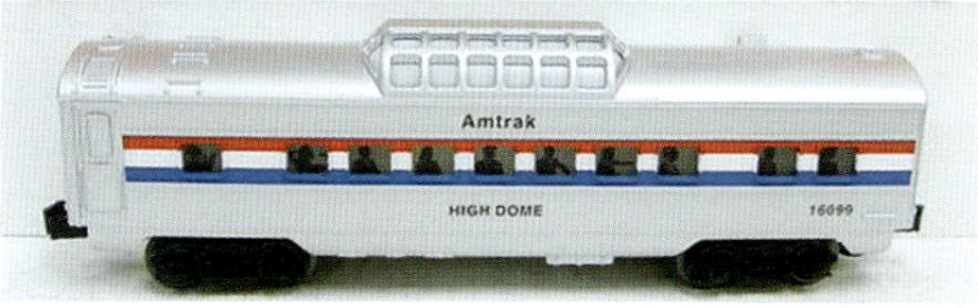

[16099] AMTRAK: 1995-97, "High Dome" Vista Dome car in the traditional 2400-series passenger car size.

EX-C7	LN-C8	Scarcity
15	20	4

[17879] VALLEY FORGE: 1989, uncataloged TCA dining car "Pennsylvania Limited," numbered "1989."

EX-C7	LN-C8	Scarcity
45	55	6

[17883) NEW GEORGIA RR: 1990, uncataloged TCA car numbered "1990."

EX-C7	LN-C8	Scarcity
40	50	6

[17897] VIRGINIA TRAIN COLLECTORS: See 7692.

[18304] LACKAWANNA: 1991, MU car set, powered and dummy, numbered "2401" and "2402."

EX-C7	LN-C8	Scarcity
225	275	4

[18305] LACKAWANNA: 1992, MU car set, pair of dummies numbered "2400" and "2403."

EX-C7	LN-C8	Scarcity
125	150	4

[18306] PENNSYLVANIA: 1992, MU car set, powered and dummy, numbered "4574" and "483."

EX-C7	LN-C8	Scarcity
150	175	4

[18310] PENNSYLVANIA: 1993, MU car set, dummies numbered "484" and "485."

EX-C7	LN-C8	Scarcity
150	175	4

[18328] NEW HAVEN: 2000, MU Commuter set, numbered "4082" and "4083," command control-equipped.

EX-C7	LN-C8	Scarcity
300	350	4

[18331] READING: 2000, MU Commuter set, numbered "9109" and "9110," command control-equipped.

EX-C7	LN-C8	Scarcity
300	350	4

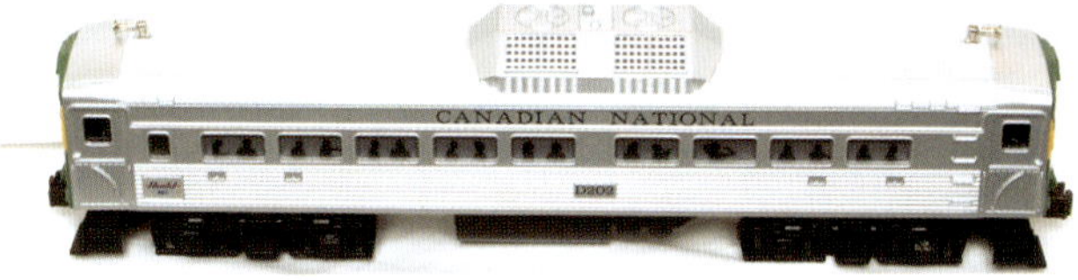

[18506] CANADIAN NATIONAL: 1992, Budd RDC powered and dummy set numbered "D202" and "D203."

EX-C7	LN-C8	Scarcity
100	125	4

[18507] CANADIAN NATIONAL: 1992, Budd RDC baggage car, powered, numbered "D202."

EX-C7	LN-C8	Scarcity
50	75	4

[18508] CANADIAN NATIONAL: 1992, Budd RDC Passenger dummy, numbered "D203."

EX-C7	LN-C8	Scarcity
125	150	4

[18510] CANADIAN NATIONAL: Budd RDC Passenger dummy, numbered "D200."

EX-C7	LN-C8	Scarcity
50	75	4

[18511] CANADIAN NATIONAL: Budd RDC Passenger dummy, numbered "D250."

EX-C7	LN-C8	Scarcity
50	75	4

[18512] CANADIAN NATIONAL: 1993, Budd RDC Dummies set numbered "D200" and "D250."

EX-C7	LN-C8	Scarcity
125	200	4

19000 JERSEY CENTRAL BLUE COMET: 1987, uncataloged "Giacobini" dining car.

EX-C7	LN-C8	Scarcity
40	45	5

19001 SOUTHERN: 1987, uncataloged dining car.

EX-C7	LN-C8	Scarcity
40	45	5

19002 PENNSYLVANIA: 1988, uncataloged dining car.

EX-C7	LN-C8	Scarcity
30	40	5

19003 MILWAUKEE ROAD: 1988, uncataloged dining car.

EX-C7	LN-C8	Scarcity
30	40	5

19010 BALTIMORE AND OHIO: 1989, uncataloged dining car.

EX-C7	LN-C8	Scarcity
30	40	5

[19011] LIONEL LINES: 1993, Manhattan-sized baggage car numbered "9011."

EX-C7	LN-C8	Scarcity
175	225	4

[19015] LIONEL LINES: 1991, "Irvington" car numbered "9015."

EX-C7	LN-C8	Scarcity
60	75	4

[19016] LIONEL LINES: 1991, "Madison" car numbered "9016."

EX-C7	LN-C8	Scarcity
60	75	4

[19017] LIONEL LINES: 1991, "Manhattan" car numbered "9017."

EX-C7	LN-C8	Scarcity
60	75	4

[19018] LIONEL LINES: 1991, "Sager Place" observation car numbered "9018."

EX-C7	LN-C8	Scarcity
60	75	4

[19019] SOUTHERN PACIFIC: 1993, baggage car numbered "9019."

EX-C7	LN-C8	Scarcity
80	100	4

[19023] SOUTHERN PACIFIC: 1992, "Arcata Bay" car numbered "9023."

EX-C7	LN-C8	Scarcity
80	100	4

[19024] SOUTHERN PACIFIC: 1992, "Half Moon Bay" car numbered "9024."

EX-C7	LN-C8	Scarcity
80	100	4

[19025] SOUTHERN PACIFIC: 1992, "Drakes Bay" car numbered "9025."

EX-C7	LN-C8	Scarcity
80	100	4

[19026] SOUTHERN PACIFIC: 1992, observation car numbered "9026."

EX-C7	LN-C8	Scarcity
80	100	4

[19027] READING: 1992, baggage car numbered "9027."

EX-C7	LN-C8	Scarcity
Cataloged, but not produced.		

[19031] READING: 1992, numbered "9031."

EX-C7	LN-C8	Scarcity
Cataloged, but not produced.		

[19032] READING: 1992, numbered "9032."

EX-C7	LN-C8	Scarcity
Cataloged, but not produced.		

[19033] READING: 1992, observation car numbered "9033."

EX-C7	LN-C8	Scarcity
Cataloged, but not produced.		

[19038] ADOLPHUS BUSCH: 1992-93, uncataloged small heavyweight observation car.

EX-C7	LN-C8	Scarcity
60	75	6

[19039] PERE MARQUETTE: 1993, baggage car.

EX-C7	LN-C8	Scarcity
40	50	4

[19040] PERE MARQUETTE: 1993, numbered "1115."

EX-C7	LN-C8	Scarcity
40	50	4

[19041] PERE MARQUETTE: 1993, numbered "1116."

EX-C7	LN-C8	Scarcity
40	50	4

[19042] PERE MARQUETTE: 1993, observation car numbered "36."

EX-C7	LN-C8	Scarcity
40	50	4

[19047] BALTIMORE AND OHIO: 1996, combination numbered "9047."

EX-C7	LN-C8	Scarcity
25	30	4

[19048] BALTIMORE AND OHIO: 1996, numbered "9048."

EX-C7	LN-C8	Scarcity
25	30	4

[19049] BALTIMORE AND OHIO: 1996, dining car numbered "9049."

EX-C7	LN-C8	Scarcity
25	30	4

[19050] BALTIMORE AND OHIO: 1996, observation car numbered "9050."

EX-C7	LN-C8	Scarcity
25	30	4

[19056] NEW YORK CENTRAL: 1996, heavyweight baggage car.

EX-C7	LN-C8	Scarcity
65	80	4

[19057] NEW YORK CENTRAL: 1996, heavyweight "Willow Run" coach.

EX-C7	LN-C8	Scarcity
65	80	4

[19058] NEW YORK CENTRAL: 1996, heavyweight "Willow Trail" coach.

EX-C7	LN-C8	Scarcity
65	80	4

[19059] NEW YORK CENTRAL: 1996, heavyweight "Seneca Valley" observation car.

EX-C7	LN-C8	Scarcity
65	80	4

[19060] NEW YORK CENTRAL: 1996, heavyweight set.

EX-C7	LN-C8	Scarcity
250	300	4

[19061] WABASH: 1997.

EX-C7	LN-C8	Scarcity
225	250	5

[19062] WABASH: 1997, "City of Columbia" numbered "2361."

EX-C7	LN-C8	Scarcity
60	70	5

[19063] WABASH: 1997, "City of Danville" numbered "2362."

EX-C7	LN-C8	Scarcity
60	70	5

[19064] WABASH: 1997, REA baggage car numbered "2360."

EX-C7	LN-C8	Scarcity
60	70	5

[19065] WABASH: 1997, "Windy City" observation car numbered "2363."

EX-C7	LN-C8	Scarcity
60	70	5

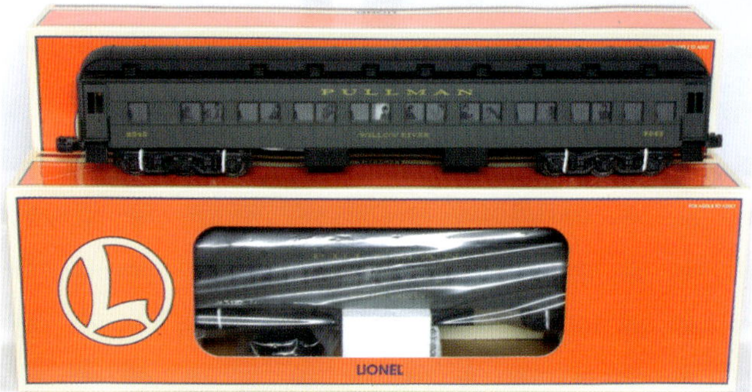

[19066] NEW YORK CENTRAL: 1997, Pullman heavyweight two-pack.

EX-C7	LN-C8	Scarcity
125	150	4

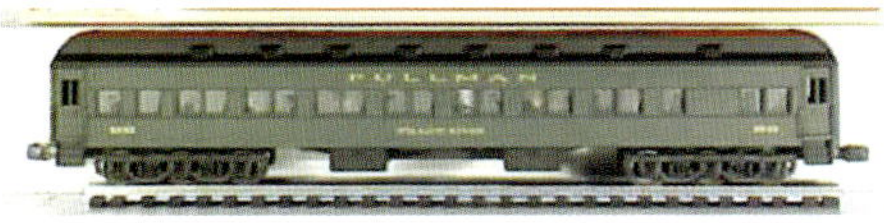

[19067] NEW YORK CENTRAL: 1997, "Willow River" heavyweight Pullman numbered "2543."

EX-C7	LN-C8	Scarcity
65	80	4

[19068] NEW YORK CENTRAL: 1997, Willow "Valley" heavyweight Pullman numbered "2544."

EX-C7	LN-C8	Scarcity
65	80	4

[19069] PULLMAN: 1997, Madison set numbered "9500" through "9502."

EX-C7	LN-C8	Scarcity
100	125	4

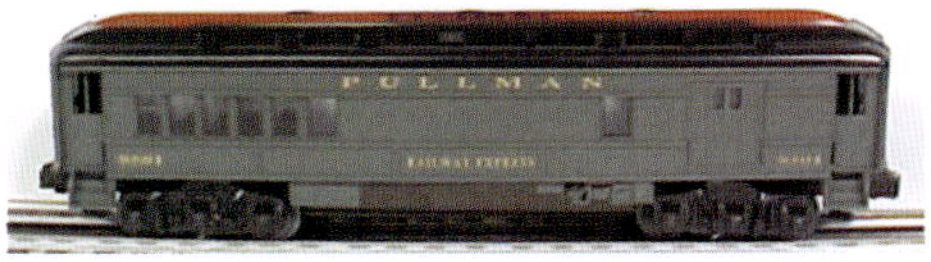

[19070] PULLMAN: 1997, REA/Combination numbered "9501."

EX-C7	LN-C8	Scarcity
30	35	4

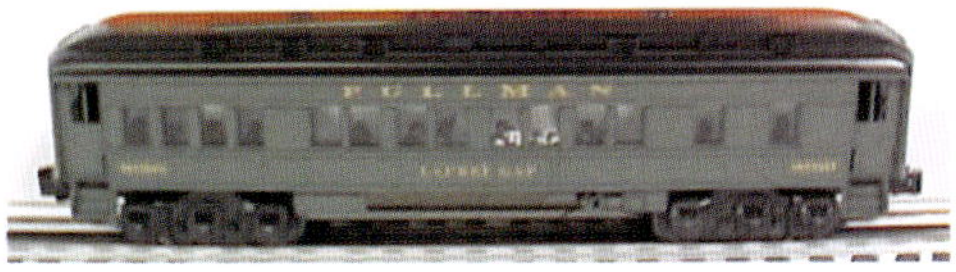

[19071] PULLMAN: 1997, "Laurel Gap," small heavyweight Pullman.

EX-C7	LN-C8	Scarcity
30	35	4

[19072] PULLMAN: 1997, "Laurel Summit," small heavyweight Pullman.

EX-C7	LN-C8	Scarcity
30	35	4

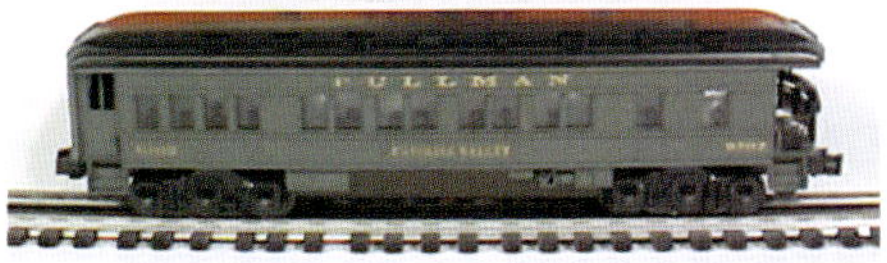

[19073] PULLMAN: 1997, small heavyweight "Catskill Valley" observation car numbered "9502."

EX-C7	LN-C8	Scarcity
30	35	4

[19074] LIONEL LINES: 1997, "Legends of Lionel" Madison set.

EX-C7	LN-C8	Scarcity
275	300	4

[19075] LIONEL LINES: 1997, "Mazzone" coach numbered "2621."

EX-C7	LN-C8	Scarcity
70	80	4

[19076] LIONEL LINES: 1997, "Caruso" coach numbered "2624."

EX-C7	LN-C8	Scarcity
70	80	4

[19077] LIONEL LINES: 1997, "Raphael" coach numbered "2652."

EX-C7	LN-C8	Scarcity
70	80	4

[19078] LIONEL LINES: 1997, "Cowen" observation car numbered "2600."

EX-C7	LN-C8	Scarcity
70	80	4

[19079] NEW YORK CENTRAL: 1997, heavyweight set.

EX-C7	LN-C8	Scarcity
275	300	4

[19080] NEW YORK CENTRAL: 1997, heavyweight REA baggage car numbered "2564."

EX-C7	LN-C8	Scarcity
75	85	4

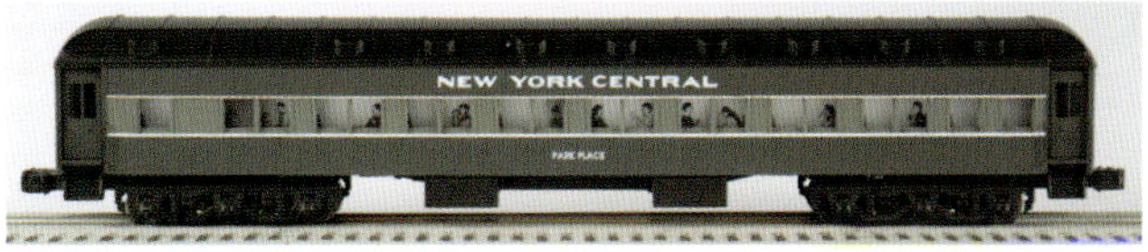

[19081] NEW YORK CENTRAL: 1997, heavyweight "Park Place" coach numbered "2565."

EX-C7	LN-C8	Scarcity
75	85	4

[19082] NEW YORK CENTRAL: 1997, heavyweight "Star Beam" coach numbered "2566."

EX-C7	LN-C8	Scarcity
75	85	4

[19083] NEW YORK CENTRAL: 1997, heavyweight "Hudson Valley" observation car numbered "2566."

EX-C7	LN-C8	Scarcity
75	85	4

[19087] CHESAPEAKE AND OHIO: 1997, heavyweight car, four-pack numbered "2571" through "2574."

EX-C7	LN-C8	Scarcity
275	300	4

[19088] CHESAPEAKE AND OHIO: 1997, heavyweight baggage car numbered "2571."

EX-C7	LN-C8	Scarcity
75	85	4

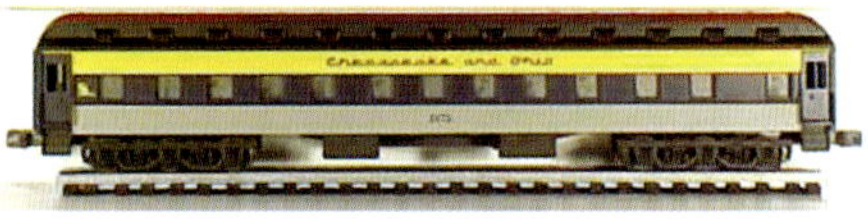

[19089] CHESAPEAKE AND OHIO: 1997, heavyweight sleeping car numbered "2572."

EX-C7	LN-C8	Scarcity
75	85	4

[19090] CHESAPEAKE AND OHIO: 1997, heavyweight dining car numbered "2573."

EX-C7	LN-C8	Scarcity
75	85	4

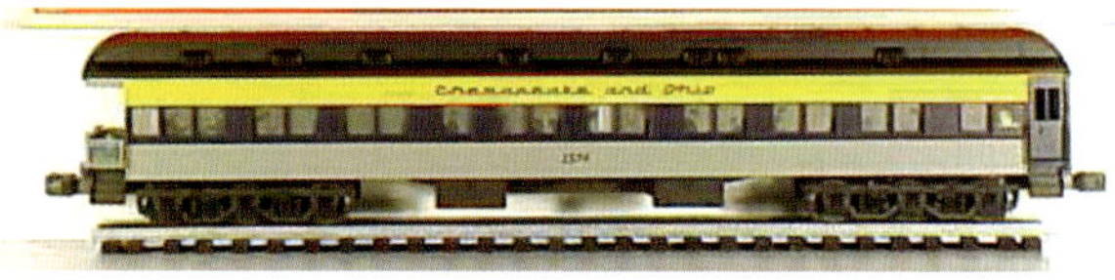

[19091] CHESAPEAKE AND OHIO: 1997, heavyweight observation car numbered "2574."

EX-C7	LN-C8	Scarcity
75	85	4

[19093] NEW YORK CENTRAL: 1998, heavyweight sleeping cars, two-pack.

EX-C7	LN-C8	Scarcity
100	125	4

[19094] NEW YORK CENTRAL: 1998, "Niagara Falls" Pullman.

EX-C7	LN-C8	Scarcity
55	65	4

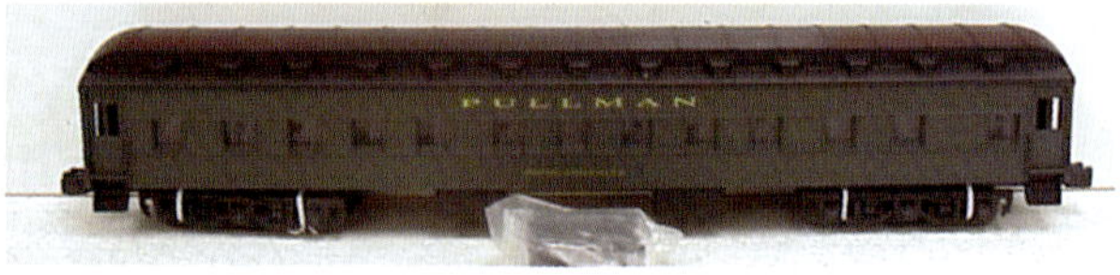

[19095] NEW YORK CENTRAL: 1998, "Highland Falls" Pullman.

EX-C7	LN-C8	Scarcity
55	65	4

[19096] LIONEL LINES: 1998, Legends of Lionel Madison cars, two-pack.

EX-C7	LN-C8	Scarcity
125	150	4

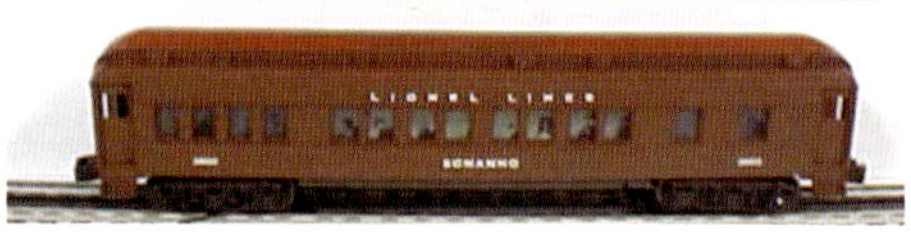

[19097] LIONEL LINES: 1998, Legends of Lionel "Bonnano" coach numbered "2653."

EX-C7	LN-C8	Scarcity
65	75	4

[19098] LIONEL LINES: 1998, Legends of Lionel "Pagano" coach numbered "2654."

EX-C7	LN-C8	Scarcity
65	75	4

[19099] PENNSYLVANIA: 1999, "Liberty Gap" baggage car numbered "2623."

EX-C7	LN-C8	Scarcity
55	65	4

[19100] AMTRAK: 1989, baggage car numbered "9100."

EX-C7	LN-C8	Scarcity
55	65	4

[19101] AMTRAK: 1989, combination numbered "9101."

EX-C7	LN-C8	Scarcity
55	65	4

[19102] AMTRAK: 1989, numbered "9102."

EX-C7	LN-C8	Scarcity
55	65	4

[19103] AMTRAK: 1989, Vista Dome car numbered "9103."

EX-C7	LN-C8	Scarcity
55	65	4

[19104] AMTRAK: 1989, dining car numbered "9104."

EX-C7	LN-C8	Scarcity
55	65	4

[19105] AMTRAK: 1989, uncataloged full Vista Dome car numbered "9105."

EX-C7	LN-C8	Scarcity
55	65	4

[19106] AMTRAK: 1989, observation car numbered "9106."

EX-C7	LN-C8	Scarcity
55	65	4

[19107] SOUTHERN PACIFIC: 1990, uncataloged full Vista Dome car.

EX-C7	LN-C8	Scarcity
55	65	4

[19108] NORFOLK AND WESTERN: 1991, uncataloged full Vista Dome car numbered "576."

EX-C7	LN-C8	Scarcity
60	80	5

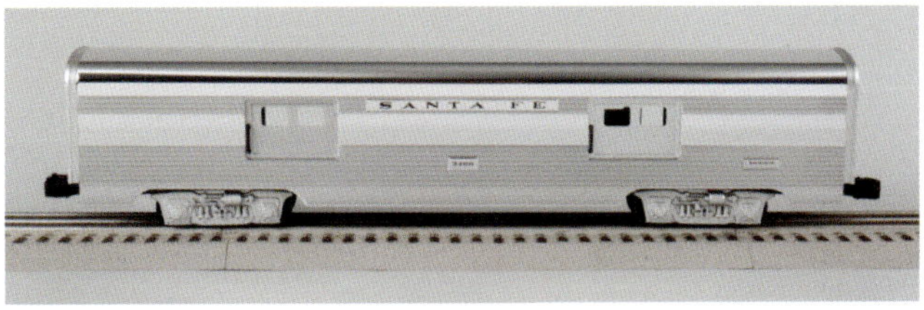

[19109] SANTA FE: 1991, baggage car numbered "3400."

EX-C7	LN-C8	Scarcity
100	125	4

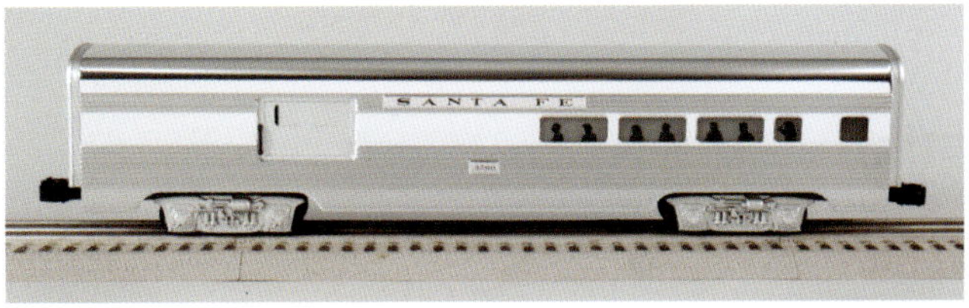

[19110] SANTA FE: 1991, combination numbered "3500."

EX-C7	LN-C8	Scarcity
100	125	4

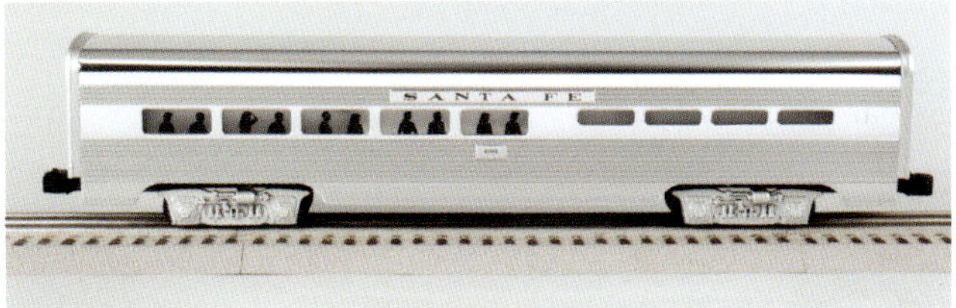

[19111] SANTA FE: 1991, dining car numbered "601."

EX-C7	LN-C8	Scarcity
100	125	4

[19112] SANTA FE: 1991.

EX-C7	LN-C8	Scarcity
100	125	4

[19113] SANTA FE: 1991, dome-observation car.

EX-C7	LN-C8	Scarcity
100	125	4

[19116] GREAT NORTHERN: 1992, baggage car numbered "1200."

EX-C7	LN-C8	Scarcity
65	80	4

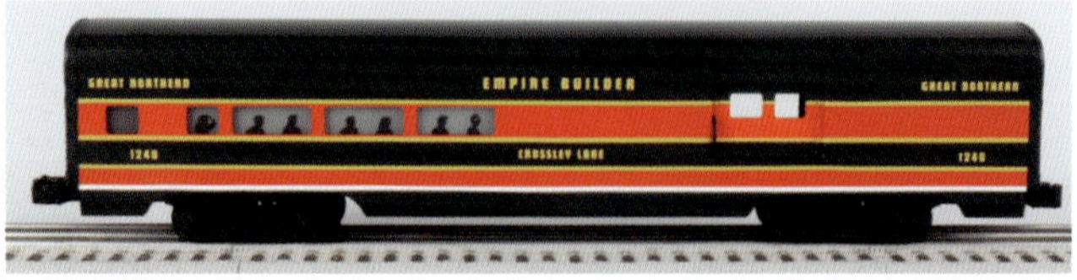

[19117] GREAT NORTHERN: 1992, combination numbered "1240."

EX-C7	LN-C8	Scarcity
65	80	4

[19118] GREAT NORTHERN: 1992, numbered "1212."

EX-C7	LN-C8	Scarcity
65	80	4

[19119] GREAT NORTHERN: 1992, Vista Dome car numbered "1322."

EX-C7	LN-C8	Scarcity
65	80	4

[19120] GREAT NORTHERN: 1992, observation car numbered "1192."

EX-C7	LN-C8	Scarcity
65	80	4

[19121] UNION PACIFIC: 1992, uncataloged Vista Dome car numbered "9121."

EX-C7	LN-C8	Scarcity
75	95	5

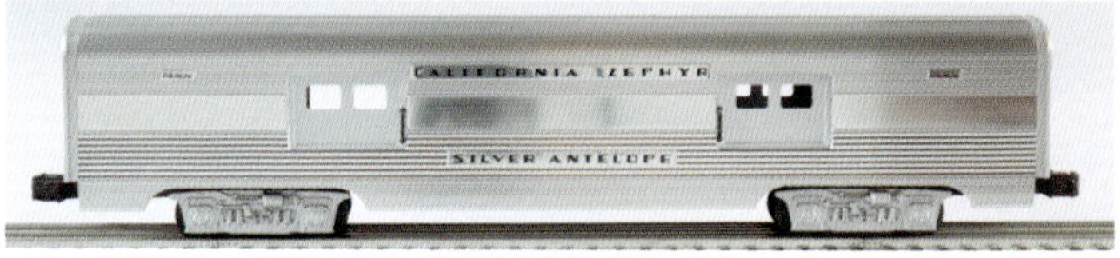

[19122] DENVER & RIO GRANDE WESTERN: 1993, California Zephyr baggage car.

EX-C7	LN-C8	Scarcity
80	100	4

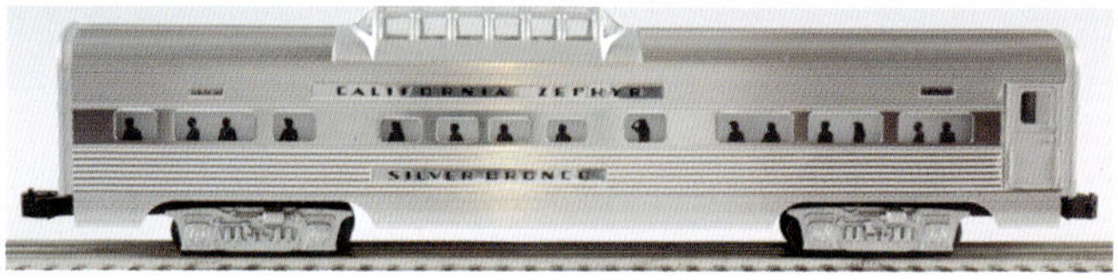

[19123] DENVER & RIO GRANDE WESTERN: 1993, California Zephyr "Silver Bronco" Vista Dome car.

EX-C7	LN-C8	Scarcity
80	100	4

[19124] DENVER & RIO GRANDE WESTERN: 1993, California Zephyr "Silver Colt" Vista Dome car.

EX-C7	LN-C8	Scarcity
80	100	4

[19125] DENVER & RIO GRANDE WESTERN: 1993, California Zephyr "Silver Mustang" Vista Dome car.

EX-C7	LN-C8	Scarcity
80	100	4

[19126] DENVER & RIO GRANDE WESTERN: 1993, California Zephyr "Silver Pony" Vista Dome car.

EX-C7	LN-C8	Scarcity
80	100	4

[19127] DENVER & RIO GRANDE WESTERN: 1993, California Zephyr dome-observation car.

EX-C7	LN-C8	Scarcity
80	100	4

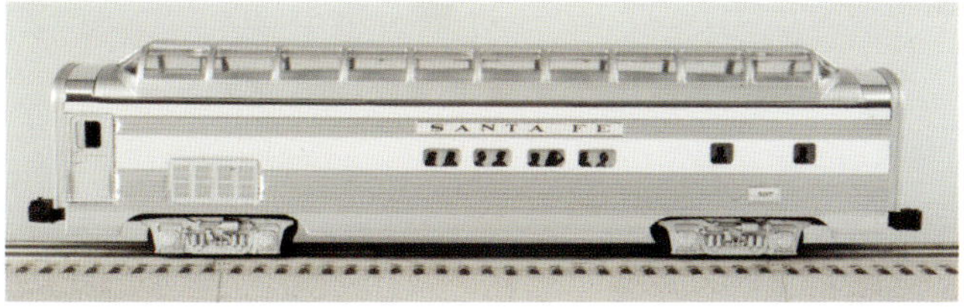

[19128] SANTA FE: 1992, uncataloged full Vista Dome car numbered "507."

EX-C7	LN-C8	Scarcity
125	150	5

[19129] ILLINOIS CENTRAL: 1993, full Vista Dome car numbered "9129."

EX-C7	LN-C8	Scarcity
60	75	4

[19130] LACKAWANNA: 1994, passenger cars, set of four.

EX-C7	LN-C8	Scarcity
300	350	4

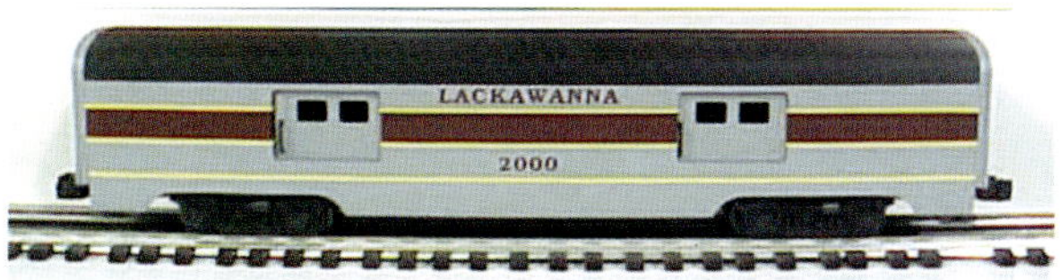

[19131] LACKAWANNA: Baggage car numbered "2000" (see 19130).

EX-C7	LN-C8	Scarcity
75	90	4

[19132] LACKAWANNA: Dining car numbered "469" (see 19130).

EX-C7	LN-C8	Scarcity
75	90	4

[19133] LACKAWANNA: Numbered "260" (see 19130).

EX-C7	LN-C8	Scarcity
75	90	4

[19134] LACKAWANNA: Observation car numbered "789" (see 19130).

EX-C7	LN-C8	Scarcity
75	90	4

[19135] LACKAWANNA: 1994, combination numbered "425."

EX-C7	LN-C8	Scarcity
75	90	4

[19136] LACKAWANNA: 1994, numbered "211."

EX-C7	LN-C8	Scarcity
75	90	4

[19137] NEW YORK CENTRAL: 1995, roomette car.

EX-C7	LN-C8	Scarcity
75	90	4

[19138] SANTA FE: 1995, roomette car.

EX-C7	LN-C8	Scarcity
75	90	4

[19139] NORFOLK AND WESTERN: 1995, baggage car numbered "577."

EX-C7	LN-C8	Scarcity
70	85	4

[19140] NORFOLK AND WESTERN: 1995, combination numbered "494."

EX-C7	LN-C8	Scarcity
70	85	4

[19141] NORFOLK AND WESTERN: 1995, dining car numbered "495."

EX-C7	LN-C8	Scarcity
85	100	4

[19142] NORFOLK AND WESTERN: 1995, numbered "538."

EX-C7	LN-C8	Scarcity
70	85	4

[19143] NORFOLK AND WESTERN: 1995, numbered "537."

EX-C7	LN-C8	Scarcity
70	85	4

[19144] NORFOLK AND WESTERN: 1995, observation car numbered "582."

EX-C7	LN-C8	Scarcity
70	85	4

[19145] CHESAPEAKE AND OHIO: 1996, combination numbered "1403."

EX-C7	LN-C8	Scarcity
60	70	4

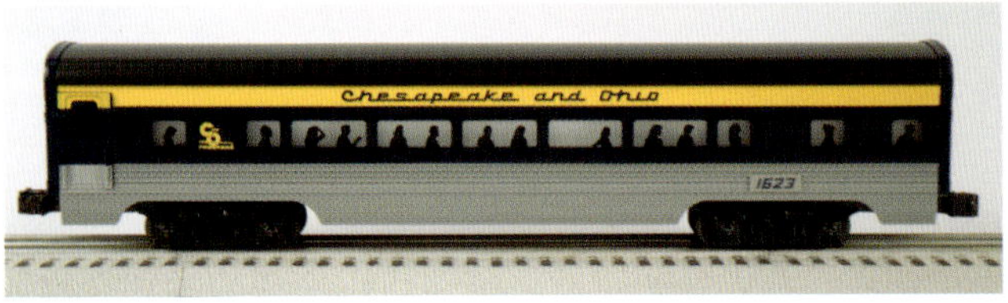

[19146] CHESAPEAKE AND OHIO: 1996, numbered "1623."

EX-C7	LN-C8	Scarcity
60	70	4

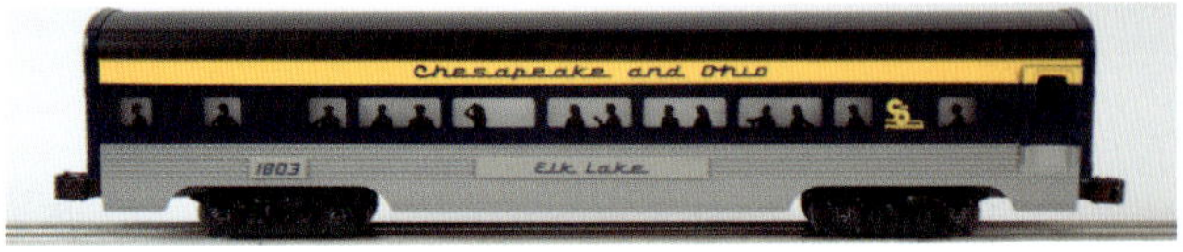

[19147] CHESAPEAKE AND OHIO: 1988, "Elk Lake" car numbered "1803."

EX-C7	LN-C8	Scarcity
60	70	4

[19148] CHESAPEAKE AND OHIO: 1996, "Chessie Club" coach numbered "1903."

EX-C7	LN-C8	Scarcity
60	70	4

[19149] CHESAPEAKE AND OHIO: 1996, "Gadsby Kitchen" dining car numbered "1950."

EX-C7	LN-C8	Scarcity
60	70	4

[19150] CHESAPEAKE AND OHIO: 1996, observation car numbered "2503."

EX-C7	LN-C8	Scarcity
60	70	4

[19151] NORFOLK AND WESTERN: 1996, "Sussex County" Duplex roomette car.

EX-C7	LN-C8	Scarcity
60	70	4

[19152] UNION PACIFIC: 1996, Duplex roomette car.

EX-C7	LN-C8	Scarcity
50	60	4

[19153] CHESAPEAKE AND OHIO: 1996, passenger cars, set of four.

EX-C7	LN-C8	Scarcity
225	275	4

[19154] ATLANTIC COAST LINE: 1996, passenger cars set.

EX-C7	LN-C8	Scarcity
250	275	5

[19155] ATLANTIC COAST LINE: 1996, Passenger/Combo numbered "101."

EX-C7	LN-C8	Scarcity
60	75	5

[19156] ATLANTIC COAST LINE: 1996, "Talladega" dining car.

EX-C7	LN-C8	Scarcity
60	75	5

[19157] ATLANTIC COAST LINE: 1996, "Moultrie" coach.

EX-C7	LN-C8	Scarcity
60	75	5

[19158] ATLANTIC COAST LINE: 1996, observation car numbered "256."

EX-C7	LN-C8	Scarcity
60	75	5

[19159] NORFOLK AND WESTERN: 1995, uncataloged passenger cars, set of four.

EX-C7	LN-C8	Scarcity
275	350	4

[19160] SANTA FE: 1996, Super Chief REA baggage car.

EX-C7	LN-C8	Scarcity
60	70	4

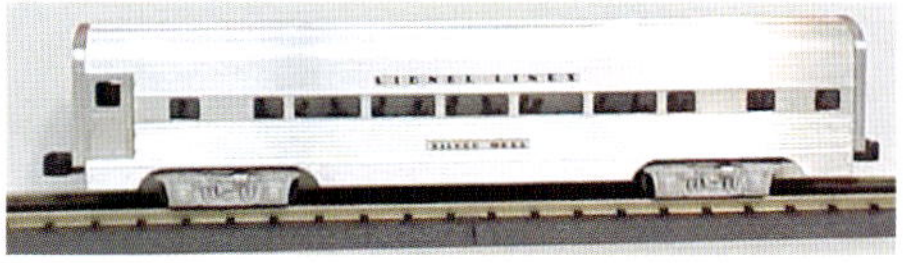

[19161] SANTA FE: 1996, Super Chief Silver Sky coach.

EX-C7	LN-C8	Scarcity
60	70	4

[19162] SANTA FE: 1996, Super Chief "Silver Mesa" Vista Dome.

EX-C7	LN-C8	Scarcity
60	70	4

[19163] SANTA FE: 1996, Super Chief "Silver Rail" observation car.

EX-C7	LN-C8	Scarcity
60	70	4

[19164] CHESAPEAKE AND OHIO: 1996.

EX-C7	LN-C8	Scarcity
100	125	4

[19165] SANTA FE: 1996, Super Chief set.

EX-C7	LN-C8	Scarcity
225	275	4

[19166] NORTHERN PACIFIC: 1997, full-length Vista Dome set in the traditional 2400-series passenger car size.

EX-C7	LN-C8	Scarcity
200	250	4

[19167] NORTHERN PACIFIC: 1997, full-length Vista Dome numbered "2571" in the traditional 2400-series passenger car size.

EX-C7	LN-C8	Scarcity
65	80	4

[19168] NORTHERN PACIFIC: 1997, full-length Vista Dome numbered "2571" in the traditional 2400-series passenger car size.

EX-C7	LN-C8	Scarcity
65	80	4

[19169] NORTHERN PACIFIC: 1997, full-length Vista Dome numbered "2570" in the traditional 2400-series passenger car size.

EX-C7	LN-C8	Scarcity
65	80	4

[19170] NORTHERN PACIFIC: 1997, full-length Vista Dome numbered "2571" in the traditional 2400-series passenger car size.

EX-C7	LN-C8	Scarcity
65	80	4

[19171] NEW YORK CENTRAL: 1997, Streamlined Passenger set numbered "2570-2575."

EX-C7	LN-C8	Scarcity
250	300	4

[19172] NEW YORK CENTRAL: 1997, smooth-sided aluminum baggage car numbered "2570."

EX-C7	LN-C8	Scarcity
65	80	4

[19173] NEW YORK CENTRAL: 1997, smooth-sided aluminum dining car, "Manhattan Island."

EX-C7	LN-C8	Scarcity
65	80	4

[19174] NEW YORK CENTRAL: 1997, smooth-sided aluminum coach, "Queensboro Bridge."

EX-C7	LN-C8	Scarcity
65	80	4

[19175] NEW YORK CENTRAL: 1997, smooth-sided aluminum observation car, "Windgate Brook."

EX-C7	LN-C8	Scarcity
65	80	4

[19176] SANTA FE: 1997, "Indian Arrow" fluted aluminum dining car numbered "2572."

EX-C7	LN-C8	Scarcity
65	80	4

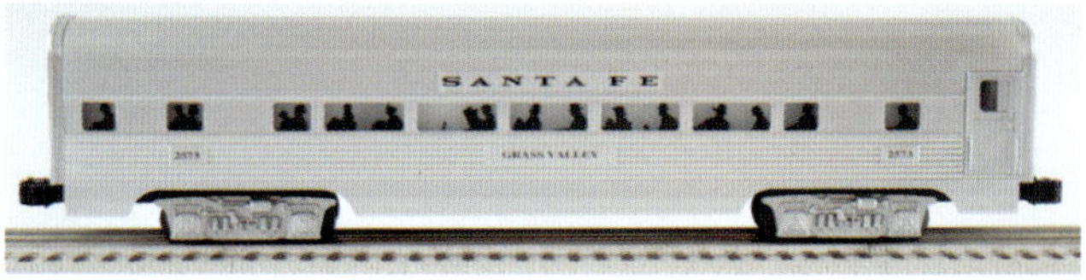

[19177] SANTA FE: 1997, "Grass Valley" fluted aluminum car numbered "2573."

EX-C7	LN-C8	Scarcity
65	80	4

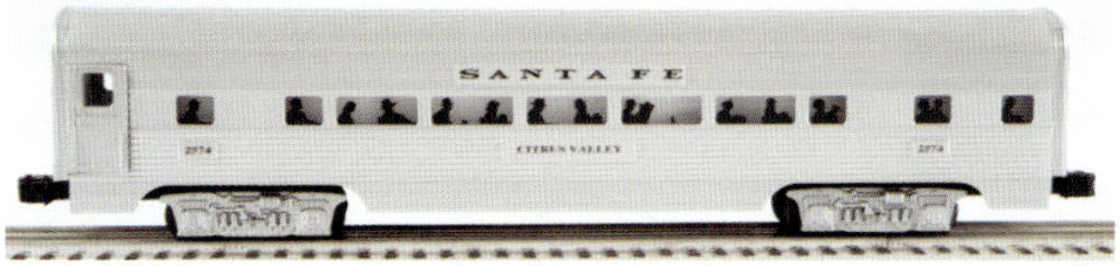

[19178] SANTA FE: 1997, "Citrus Valley" fluted aluminum car numbered "2574."

EX-C7	LN-C8	Scarcity
65	80	4

[19179] SANTA FE: 1997, "Vista Heights" fluted aluminum car numbered "2575."

EX-C7	LN-C8	Scarcity
65	80	4

[19180] SANTA FE: 1997, Surfliner aluminum car from the passenger set numbered "2572" through "2575."

EX-C7	LN-C8	Scarcity
275	325	4

[19181] GREAT NORTHERN: 1998, smooth-sided aluminum Empire Builder, "Prairie View," full Vista Dome.

EX-C7	LN-C8	Scarcity
50	60	4

[19182] GREAT NORTHERN: 1998, smooth-sided aluminum Empire Builder, "River View," full Vista Dome.

EX-C7	LN-C8	Scarcity
50	60	4

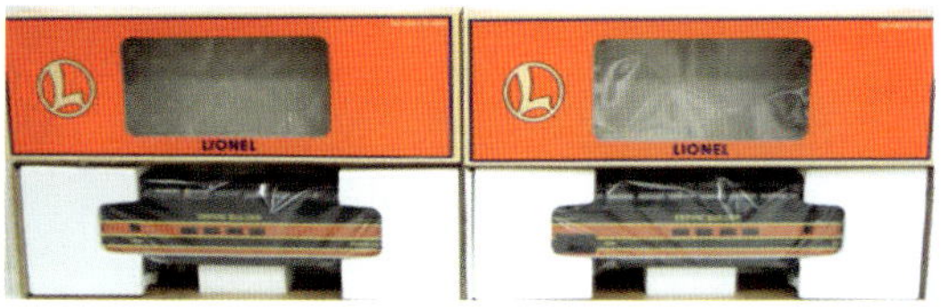

[19183] GREAT NORTHERN: 1998, smooth-sided aluminum Empire Builder Vista Dome cars, two-pack.

EX-C7	LN-C8	Scarcity
100	125	4

[19184] MILWAUKEE ROAD: 1999, smooth-sided aluminum Passenger set, four-pack.

EX-C7	LN-C8	Scarcity
325	375	4

[19185] MILWAUKEE ROAD: 1999, smooth-sided aluminum car, "194 Red River Valley."

EX-C7	LN-C8	Scarcity
75	100	4

[19186] MILWAUKEE ROAD: 1999, smooth-sided aluminum dining car numbered "170."

EX-C7	LN-C8	Scarcity
75	100	4

[19187] MILWAUKEE ROAD: 1999, smooth-sided aluminum "Sky Top" observation car, "186 Cedar Rapids."

EX-C7	LN-C8	Scarcity
75	100	4

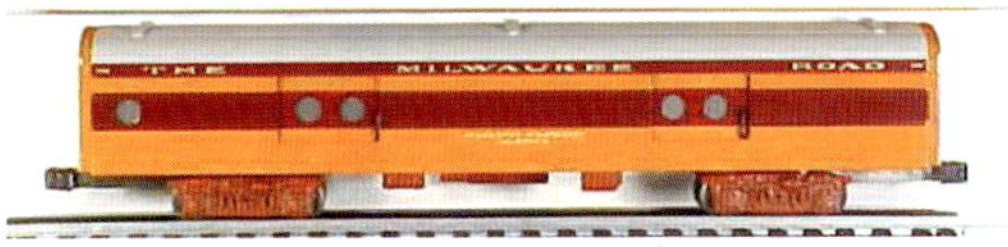

[19188] MILWAUKEE ROAD: 1999, smooth-sided aluminum baggage car numbered "1336" REA.

EX-C7	LN-C8	Scarcity
75	100	4

[19194] KANSAS CITY SOUTHERN: 2000, aluminum car, four-pack.

EX-C7	LN-C8	Scarcity
325	350	4

[21779] NEW YORK CENTRAL: 1999, aluminum car set, two-pack.

EX-C7	LN-C8	Scarcity
125	150	4

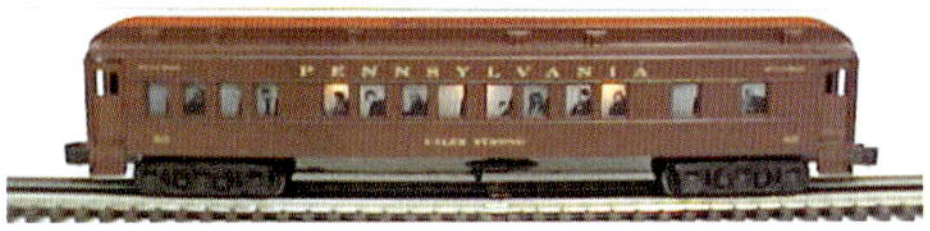

[29000] PENNSYLVANIA: 1999, Madison coach, "2622 Caleb Strong."

EX-C7	LN-C8	Scarcity
40	55	4

[29001] PENNSYLVANIA: 1999, Madison coach, "2621 Villa Royal."

EX-C7	LN-C8	Scarcity
40	55	4

[29002] PENNSYLVANIA: 1999, Madison coach, "2624 Philadelphia."

EX-C7	LN-C8	Scarcity
40	55	4

[29003] PENNSYLVANIA: 1998, Madison cars, four-pack.

EX-C7	LN-C8	Scarcity
150	225	4

[29004] NEW YORK CENTRAL: 1999, heavyweight Passenger set, two-pack.

EX-C7	LN-C8	Scarcity
125	150	4

[29007] NEW YORK CENTRAL: 1998, uncataloged Pullman car, two-pack.

EX-C7	LN-C8	Scarcity
65	75	4

[29008] NEW YORK CENTRAL: 1998, heavyweight dining car numbered "383."

EX-C7	LN-C8	Scarcity
65	75	4

[29009] NEW YORK CENTRAL: 1998, heavyweight combination, "Van Twiller."

EX-C7	LN-C8	Scarcity
65	75	4

[29010] CHESAPEAKE AND OHIO: 1999, heavyweight Passenger set, two-pack.

EX-C7	LN-C8	Scarcity
100	125	4

[29011] CHESAPEAKE AND OHIO: 1999, heavyweight car (part of 29010).

EX-C7	LN-C8	Scarcity
50	65	4

[29012] CHESAPEAKE AND OHIO: 1999, heavyweight car (part of 29010).

EX-C7	LN-C8	Scarcity
50	65	4

[29039] LIONEL LINES RECOVERY: 1999, small heavyweight combination numbered "9501."

EX-C7	LN-C8	Scarcity
Too rarely traded to establish accurate pricing.		

[29041] ALASKA RAILROAD: 1999-2000, Streamlined Passenger, four-pack.

EX-C7	LN-C8	Scarcity
175	200	4

[29042] ALASKA RAILROAD: 1999-2000, streamlined baggage car numbered "6310."

EX-C7	LN-C8	Scarcity
45	50	4

[29043] ALASKA RAILROAD: 1999-2000, Streamlined coach numbered "5408."

EX-C7	LN-C8	Scarcity
45	50	4

[29044] ALASKA RAILROAD: 1999-2000, Streamlined Vista Dome numbered "7014."

EX-C7	LN-C8	Scarcity
45	50	4

[29046] BALTIMORE AND OHIO: 1999-2000, Streamlined Passenger, four-pack.

EX-C7	LN-C8	Scarcity
125	150	4

[29047] BALTIMORE AND OHIO: 1999-2000, streamlined baggage car.

EX-C7	LN-C8	Scarcity
35	40	4

[29048] BALTIMORE AND OHIO: 1999-2000, Streamlined coach.

EX-C7	LN-C8	Scarcity
35	40	4

[29049] BALTIMORE AND OHIO: 1999-2000, Streamlined Vista Dome.

EX-C7	LN-C8	Scarcity
35	40	4

[29050] BALTIMORE AND OHIO: 1999-2000, streamlined observation car.

EX-C7	LN-C8	Scarcity
35	40	4

[29051] SANTA FE: 1999-2000, Streamlined Passenger, four-pack.

EX-C7	LN-C8	Scarcity
150	175	4

[29052] SANTA FE: 1999-2000, streamlined baggage car.

EX-C7	LN-C8	Scarcity
40	45	4

[29053] SANTA FE: 1999-2000, Streamlined coach.

EX-C7	LN-C8	Scarcity
40	45	4

[29054] SANTA FE: 1999-2000, Streamlined Vista Dome.

EX-C7	LN-C8	Scarcity
40	45	4

[29055] SANTA FE: 1999-2000, Streamlined observation.

EX-C7	LN-C8	Scarcity
40	45	4

[29056] NEW YORK CENTRAL: 1999-2000, Streamlined Passenger, four-pack.

EX-C7	LN-C8	Scarcity
150	175	4

[29057] NEW YORK CENTRAL: 1999-2000, streamlined baggage car.

EX-C7	LN-C8	Scarcity
40	45	4

[29058] NEW YORK CENTRAL: 1999-2000, Streamlined coach.

EX-C7	LN-C8	Scarcity
40	45	4

[29059] NEW YORK CENTRAL: 1999-2000, Streamlined Vista Dome.

EX-C7	LN-C8	Scarcity
40	45	4

[29060] NEW YORK CENTRAL: 1999-2000, streamlined observation car.

EX-C7	LN-C8	Scarcity
40	45	4

[29061] PENNSYLVANIA: 1999-2000, Madison Passenger, four-pack.

EX-C7	LN-C8	Scarcity
150	175	4

[29062] PENNSYLVANIA: 1999-2000, Madison baggage car, "Indian Point."

EX-C7	LN-C8	Scarcity
35	45	4

[29063] PENNSYLVANIA: 1999-2000, Madison coach, "Christopher Columbus."

EX-C7	LN-C8	Scarcity
35	45	4

[29064] PENNSYLVANIA: 1999-2000, Madison coach, "Andrew Jackson."

EX-C7	LN-C8	Scarcity
35	45	4

[29065] PENNSYLVANIA: 1999-2000, Madison observation, "Broussard."

EX-C7	LN-C8	Scarcity
35	45	4

[29066] JERSEY CENTRAL: 1999-2000, Madison Passenger, four-pack.

EX-C7	LN-C8	Scarcity
150	175	4

[29067] JERSEY CENTRAL: 1999-2000, Madison baggage car numbered "420."

EX-C7	LN-C8	Scarcity
35	45	4

[29068] JERSEY CENTRAL: 1999-2000, Madison coach, "Beachcomber."

EX-C7	LN-C8	Scarcity
35	45	4

[29069] JERSEY CENTRAL: 1999-2000, Madison coach, "Echo Lake."

EX-C7	LN-C8	Scarcity
35	45	4

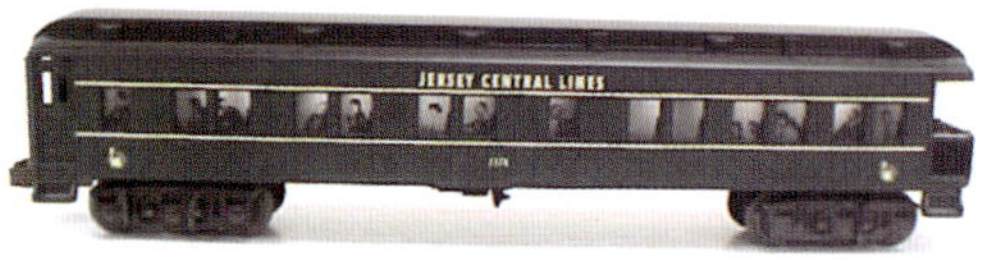

[29070] JERSEY CENTRAL: 1999-2000, Madison observation car numbered "1178."

EX-C7	LN-C8	Scarcity
35	45	4

[29071] NEW YORK CENTRAL: 2000, Madison, four-pack.

EX-C7	LN-C8	Scarcity
100	125	4

[29072) NEW YORK CENTRAL: 2000, Madison baggage car numbered "1001."

EX-C7	LN-C8	Scarcity
25	30	4

[29073] NEW YORK CENTRAL: 2000, Madison coach numbered "1005."

EX-C7	LN-C8	Scarcity
25	30	4

[29074] NEW YORK CENTRAL: 2000, Madison coach numbered "1006."

EX-C7	LN-C8	Scarcity
25	30	4

[29075] NEW YORK CENTRAL: 2000, Madison observation car, "1019 Detroit."

EX-C7	LN-C8	Scarcity
25	30	4

[29076] SOUTHERN: 2000, Madison, four-pack.

EX-C7	LN-C8	Scarcity
100	125	4

[29077] SOUTHERN: 2000, Madison baggage car, "702 Delaware."

EX-C7	LN-C8	Scarcity
25	30	4

[29078] SOUTHERN: 2000, Madison coach, "800 North Carolina."

EX-C7	LN-C8	Scarcity
25	30	4

[29079] SOUTHERN: 2000, Madison coach, "801 Maryland."

EX-C7	LN-C8	Scarcity
25	30	4

[29080] SOUTHERN: 2000, Madison observation car, "1100."

EX-C7	LN-C8	Scarcity
25	30	4

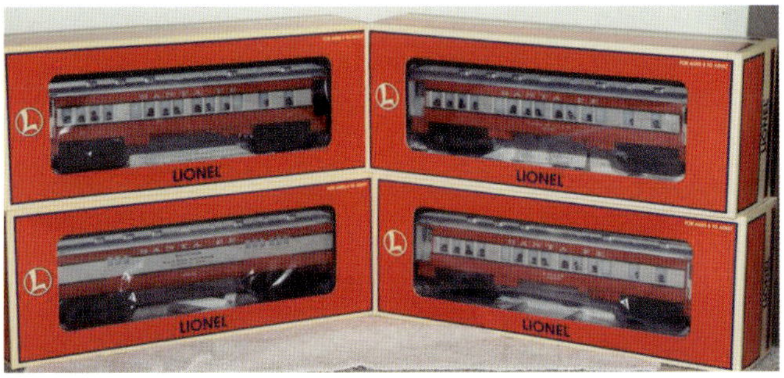

[29081] SANTA FE: 2000, small heavyweight, four-pack.

EX-C7	LN-C8	Scarcity
100	125	4

[29082] SANTA FE: 2000, small heavyweight baggage car, RPO, "1765."

EX-C7	LN-C8	Scarcity
25	30	4

[29083] SANTA FE: 2000, small heavyweight coach chair numbered "3040."

EX-C7	LN-C8	Scarcity
25	30	4

[29084] SANTA FE: 2000, small heavyweight coach, "1535 coach Club."

EX-C7	LN-C8	Scarcity
25	30	4

[29085] SANTA FE: 2000, small heavyweight observation car numbered "10."

EX-C7	LN-C8	Scarcity
25	30	4

[29086] LIONEL LINES: 1999, Madison set, three-pack.

EX-C7	LN-C8	Scarcity
225	250	4

[29090] LIONEL LINES: 1999, Lionel Liontech Madison Car numbered "2656."

EX-C7	LN-C8	Scarcity
55	65	4

[29091] LIONEL LINES: 1999-2000, Cowen Legends Madison Passenger numbered "2657."

EX-C7	LN-C8	Scarcity
55	65	4

[29123] ERIE-LACKAWANNA: 1999, smooth-sided aluminum baggage car numbered "203."

EX-C7	LN-C8	Scarcity
60	80	4

[29124] ERIE-LACKAWANNA: 1999, smooth-sided aluminum dining car numbered "770."

EX-C7	LN-C8	Scarcity
60	80	4

[29125] ERIE-LACKAWANNA: 1999, smooth-sided aluminum coach, "Eleanor Lord."

EX-C7	LN-C8	Scarcity
60	80	4

[29126] ERIE-LACKAWANNA: 1999, smooth-sided aluminum observation, "789 Tavern Lounge."

EX-C7	LN-C8	Scarcity
60	80	4

[29127] ATLANTIC COAST LINE: 1999, fluted aluminum baggage car numbered "152."

EX-C7	LN-C8	Scarcity
60	80	4

[29128] ATLANTIC COAST LINE: 1999, fluted aluminum coach, "North Hampton."

EX-C7	LN-C8	Scarcity
60	80	4

[29129]TEXAS SPECIAL: 1999, fluted aluminum Passenger set, four-pack.

EX-C7	LN-C8	Scarcity
550	600	5

[29130] TEXAS SPECIAL: 1999, fluted aluminum, "1200 Edward Burleson."

EX-C7	LN-C8	Scarcity
125	150	5

[29131] TEXAS SPECIAL: 1999, fluted aluminum, "1201 David G. Burnett."

EX-C7	LN-C8	Scarcity
125	150	5

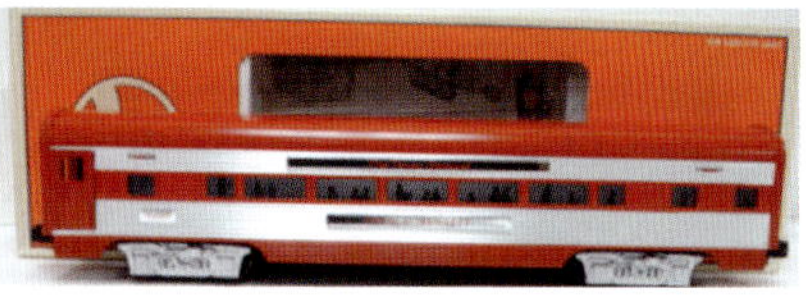

[29132] TEXAS SPECIAL: 1999, fluted aluminum, "1202 J. Pinckney Henderson."

EX-C7	LN-C8	Scarcity
125	150	5

[29133] TEXAS SPECIAL: 1999, fluted aluminum car numbered "1203."

EX-C7	LN-C8	Scarcity
125	150	5

[29134] WESTERN PACIFIC: 1999, fluted aluminum Passenger set, four-pack.

EX-C7	LN-C8	Scarcity
500	600	4

[29135] WESTERN PACIFIC: 1999, fluted aluminum California Zephyr Vista Dome, "Silver Poplar."

EX-C7	LN-C8	Scarcity
125	150	4

[29136] WESTERN PACIFIC: 1999, fluted aluminum California Zephyr Vista Dome, "Silver Palm."

EX-C7	LN-C8	Scarcity
125	150	4

[29137] WESTERN PACIFIC: 1999, fluted aluminum California Zephyr Vista Dome, "Silver Tavern."

EX-C7	LN-C8	Scarcity
125	150	4

[29138] WESTERN PACIFIC: 1999, fluted aluminum California Zephyr dome observation, "Silver Planet."

EX-C7	LN-C8	Scarcity
125	150	4

[29139] LIONEL LINES: 1999, Kughn Madison Car numbered "2655."

EX-C7	LN-C8	Scarcity
65	75	5

[29140] NEW YORK CENTRAL: 1999, aluminum Sleeper, "Castleton Bridge."

EX-C7	LN-C8	Scarcity
80	100	4

[29141] NEW YORK CENTRAL: 1999, aluminum Combine, "Martin Van Buren."

EX-C7	LN-C8	Scarcity
80	100	4

[29142] CANADIAN PACIFIC: 1999, fluted aluminum Vista Dome, "Skyline 596."

EX-C7	LN-C8	Scarcity
80	100	4

[28143] CANADIAN PACIFIC: 1999, fluted aluminum observation car, "Banff Park."

EX-C7	LN-C8	Scarcity
80	100	4

[39008] PENNSYLVANIA: 2000, heavyweight Passenger set, four-pack.

EX-C7	LN-C8	Scarcity
175	200	4

[39009] PENNSYLVANIA: 2000, heavyweight Passenger combination, "Indian Rock."

EX-C7	LN-C8	Scarcity
45	50	4

[39010] PENNSYLVANIA: 2000, heavyweight Passenger coach, "Andrew Carnegie."

EX-C7	LN-C8	Scarcity
45	50	4

[39011] PENNSYLVANIA: 2000, heavyweight Passenger coach, "Salmon P. Chase."

EX-C7	LN-C8	Scarcity
45	50	4

[39012] PENNSYLVANIA: 2000, heavyweight Passenger observation car, "Skyline View."

EX-C7	LN-C8	Scarcity
45	50	4

[39013] BALTIMORE AND OHIO: 2000, heavyweight Passenger, four-pack.

EX-C7	LN-C8	Scarcity
350	375	4

[39017] BALTIMORE AND OHIO: 2000, heavyweight Passenger combination, "Harper's Ferry."

EX-C7	LN-C8	Scarcity
85	95	4

[39018] BALTIMORE AND OHIO: 2000, heavyweight Passenger coach, "Youngstown."

EX-C7	LN-C8	Scarcity
85	95	4

[39019] BALTIMORE AND OHIO: 2000, heavyweight Passenger coach, "New Castle."

EX-C7	LN-C8	Scarcity
85	95	4

[39020] BALTIMORE AND OHIO: 2000, heavyweight Passenger observation car, "Chicago."

EX-C7	LN-C8	Scarcity
85	95	4

[39028] LIONEL LINES: 2000, Madison Passenger, three-pack.

EX-C7	LN-C8	Scarcity
125	150	4

[39029] LIONEL LINES: 2000, Madison Passenger coach, "Irvington 2625."

EX-C7	LN-C8	Scarcity
40	50	4

[39030] LIONEL LINES: 2000, Madison Passenger coach, "Madison 2627."

EX-C7	LN-C8	Scarcity
40	50	4

[39031] LIONEL LINES: 2000, Madison Passenger coach, "Manhattan 2628."

EX-C7	LN-C8	Scarcity
40	50	4

[39032] UNION PACIFIC: 2000 Madison car, four-pack.

EX-C7	LN-C8	Scarcity
175	200	4

[39042] NORFOLK AND WESTERN: 2000, heavyweight car, four-pack.

EX-C7	LN-C8	Scarcity
250	275	4

[39100] PENNSYLVANIA: 2000, Congressional set fluted aluminum "William Penn" coach.

EX-C7	LN-C8	Scarcity
70	80	4

[39101] PENNSYLVANIA: 2000, Congressional set fluted aluminum "Molly Pitcher" coach.

EX-C7	LN-C8	Scarcity
70	80	4

[39102] PENNSYLVANIA: 2000, Congressional set fluted aluminum "Betsy Ross" Vista Dome.

EX-C7	LN-C8	Scarcity
70	80	4

[39103] PENNSYLVANIA: 2000, Congressional set fluted aluminum "Alexander Hamilton" observation car.

EX-C7	LN-C8	Scarcity
70	80	4

[39104] ERIE LACKAWANNA: 1999, smooth-sided aluminum "Pocono" Station Sounds car.

EX-C7	LN-C8	Scarcity
175	200	5

[39105] MILWAUKEE ROAD: 1999, smooth-sided aluminum Hiawatha "Spring Valley" Station Sounds car.

EX-C7	LN-C8	Scarcity
150	175	4

[39106] CANADIAN PACIFIC: 2000, fluted aluminum car two-pack.

EX-C7	LN-C8	Scarcity
150	175	4

[39107] CANADIAN PACIFIC: 2000, fluted aluminum coach, "Blair Manor 2553."

EX-C7	LN-C8	Scarcity
Too rarely traded to establish accurate pricing.		

[39108] CANADIAN PACIFIC: 2000, fluted aluminum coach, "Craig Manor 2554."

EX-C7	LN-C8	Scarcity
Too rarely traded to establish accurate pricing.		

[39109] SPIRIT OF CENTURY: 1999, smooth-sided aluminum car, four-pack.

EX-C7	LN-C8	Scarcity
350	375	4

[39110] SPIRIT OF THE CENTURY: 1999-2000, smooth-sided aluminum full Vista Dome car.

EX-C7	LN-C8	Scarcity
85	95	4

[39111] SPIRIT OF THE CENTURY: 1999-2000, smooth-sided aluminum full Vista Dome car.

EX-C7	LN-C8	Scarcity
85	95	4

[39112] SPIRIT OF THE CENTURY: 1999-2000, smooth-sided aluminum full Vista Dome car.

EX-C7	LN-C8	Scarcity
85	95	4

[39113] SPIRIT OF THE CENTURY: 1999-2000, smooth-sided aluminum Skytop observation car.

EX-C7	LN-C8	Scarcity
85	95	4

[39118] TEXAS SPECIAL: 1999-2000, Station Sounds Aluminum Pass numbered "1203," "Garland."

EX-C7	LN-C8	Scarcity
200	250	4

[39119] SOUTHERN: 2000, fluted aluminum car, four-pack.

EX-C7	LN-C8	Scarcity
275	300	4

[39120] SOUTHERN: 2000, fluted aluminum baggage car, "Grand Junction 1701."

EX-C7	LN-C8	Scarcity
65	75	4

[39121] SOUTHERN: 2000, fluted aluminum coach, "Charlottesville 812."

EX-C7	LN-C8	Scarcity
65	75	4

[39122] SOUTHERN: 2000, fluted aluminum coach, "Roanoke 814."

EX-C7	LN-C8	Scarcity
65	75	4

[39123] SOUTHERN: 2000, fluted aluminum observation car, "Memphis 1152."

EX-C7	LN-C8	Scarcity
65	75	4

[51201] LIONEL LINES: 1990, Rail Chief Passenger set.

EX-C7	LN-C8	Scarcity
350	400	4

[51220] NEW YORK CENTRAL: 1993, uncataloged "Imperial Castle" car.

EX-C7	LN-C8	Scarcity
375	500	7

[51221] NEW YORK CENTRAL: 1993, uncataloged "Niagara County" car.

EX-C7	LN-C8	Scarcity
375	500	7

[51222] NEW YORK CENTRAL: 1993, uncataloged "Cascade Glory" car.

EX-C7	LN-C8	Scarcity
375	500	7

[51223] NEW YORK CENTRAL: 1993, uncataloged "City of Detroit" car.

EX-C7	LN-C8	Scarcity
375	500	7

[51224] NEW YORK CENTRAL: 1993, uncataloged "Imperial Falls" car.

EX-C7	LN-C8	Scarcity
375	500	7

[51225] NEW YORK CENTRAL: 1993, uncataloged "Westchester County" car.

EX-C7	LN-C8	Scarcity
375	500	7

[51226] NEW YORK CENTRAL: 1993, uncataloged "Cascade Grotto" car.

EX-C7	LN-C8	Scarcity
375	500	7

[51227] NEW YORK CENTRAL: 1993, uncataloged "City of Indianapolis" car.

EX-C7	LN-C8	Scarcity
375	500	7

[51228] NEW YORK CENTRAL: 1993, uncataloged "Manhattan Island" observation car.

EX-C7	LN-C8	Scarcity
375	500	7

[51229] NEW YORK CENTRAL: 1993, uncataloged dining car numbered "680."

EX-C7	LN-C8	Scarcity
375	500	7

[51230] NEW YORK CENTRAL: 1993, uncataloged baggage car numbered "5017."

EX-C7	LN-C8	Scarcity
375	500	7

[51231] NEW YORK CENTRAL: 1993, uncataloged "Century Club" car.

EX-C7	LN-C8	Scarcity
375	500	7

[51232] NEW YORK CENTRAL: 1993, uncataloged "Thousand Islands" observation car.

EX-C7	LN-C8	Scarcity
375	500	7

[51233] NEW YORK CENTRAL: 1993, uncataloged dining car numbered "684."

EX-C7	LN-C8	Scarcity
375	500	7

[51234] NEW YORK CENTRAL: 1993, uncataloged baggage car numbered "5020."

EX-C7	LN-C8	Scarcity
375	500	7

[51235] NEW YORK CENTRAL: 1993, uncataloged "Century Tavern" car.

EX-C7	LN-C8	Scarcity
375	500	7

[51236] NEW YORK CENTRAL: 1993, uncataloged "City of Toledo" car.

EX-C7	LN-C8	Scarcity
375	500	7

[51237] NEW YORK CENTRAL: 1993, uncataloged "Imperial Mansion" car.

EX-C7	LN-C8	Scarcity
375	500	7

[51238] NEW YORK CENTRAL: 1993, uncataloged "Imperial Palace" car.

EX-C7	LN-C8	Scarcity
375	500	7

[51239] NEW YORK CENTRAL: 1993, uncataloged "Cascade Spirit" car.

EX-C7	LN-C8	Scarcity
375	500	7

[51240] NEW YORK CENTRAL: 1993, uncataloged dining car numbered "681."

EX-C7	LN-C8	Scarcity
375	500	7

[51241] NEW YORK CENTRAL: 1993, uncataloged "City of Chicago" car.

EX-C7	LN-C8	Scarcity
375	500	7

[51242] NEW YORK CENTRAL: 1993, uncataloged "Imperial Garden" car.

EX-C7	LN-C8	Scarcity
375	500	7

[51243] NEW YORK CENTRAL: 1993, uncataloged "Imperial Fountain" car.

EX-C7	LN-C8	Scarcity
375	500	7

[51244] NEW YORK CENTRAL: 1993, uncataloged "Cascade Valley" car.

EX-C7	LN-C8	Scarcity
375	500	7

[51245] NEW YORK CENTRAL: 1993, uncataloged dining car numbered "685."

EX-C7	LN-C8	Scarcity
375	500	7

51249 UNION PACIFIC: Overland Sleeper, additional car for M10000.

EX-C7	LN-C8	Scarcity
80	120	6

[52002] VIRGINIA TRAIN COLLECTORS: See 7692.

[52062] TCA "SKYTOP": 1995, uncataloged observation car numbered "1995."

EX-C7	LN-C8	Scarcity
225	325	6

[52085] TCA: 1996, uncataloged full Vista Dome Car numbered "1996."

EX-C7	LN-C8	Scarcity
80	100	6

[52106] TCA "CITY OF PHOENIX": 1997, uncataloged dining car numbered "1997."

EX-C7	LN-C8	Scarcity
70	80	6

[52112] LIRR: 1997, uncataloged NLOE aluminum car numbered "9733."

EX-C7	LN-C8	Scarcity
225	250	6

[52123] LONG ISLAND: 1997, uncataloged "Ronkonkoma" full Vista Dome numbered "9783."

EX-C7	LN-C8	Scarcity
225	250	6

[52123] LONG ISLAND: 1998, uncataloged "Hicksville" dining car numbered "9883."

EX-C7	LN-C8	Scarcity
225	250	6

[52143] TCA: 1998, uncataloged "City of Providence" coach numbered "1998."

EX-C7	LN-C8	Scarcity
80	100	6

[52145] LONG ISLAND: 1999, uncataloged coach "Jamaica" numbered "99831."

EX-C7	LN-C8	Scarcity
225	250	6

[52145] LONG ISLAND: 1999, uncataloged "Penn Station" coach numbered "99832."

EX-C7	LN-C8	Scarcity
225	250	6

[52174] REA: 2000, uncataloged baggage car numbered "0083."

EX-C7	LN-C8	Scarcity
Too rarely traded to establish accurate pricing.		

[52191] TCA: 2000, uncataloged "City of Grand Rapids" sleeper/roomette car numbered "2000."

EX-C7	LN-C8	Scarcity
80	100	6

Chapter 14
CATALOGS

Throughout the prewar "Golden Age," and much of the postwar era, Lionel's catalogs were the envy of many merchandisers. By the 1960s, the catalogs, like the firm, entered into a downward spiral. The infusion of money from General Mills beginning in 1970 revived the annual consumer catalog and, by the mid-1980s, the number of catalogs, their size, and an ever-increasing number of individual brochures dwarfed the efforts of the "glory days" of the Lionel Corp.

Advance catalogs had been a part of Lionel's marketing efforts to dealers and wholesalers since before WWII—and such catalogs were carried over into the modern era as well. These catalogs differ from the consumer catalogs—sometimes substantially—and have long been coveted by collectors of Lionel paper.

Supplemental pamphlets—ranging from single-page flyers to eight-page brochures announced additions to the product line beyond the regular consumer catalog. These too have become sought-after collectibles—again in part due to their low print run as compared to the regular catalog.

As with everything in the modern era, the volume of this material produced is staggering. Due to space consideration, the following listings include only the larger of these brochures, as well as the regular consumer catalogs and the highly collectible advance or "Toy Fair" catalogs.

1970 TOY FAIR CATALOG: 8-1/2 x 11-inch, eight-page color catalog.

EX-C7	LN-C8	Scarcity
20	25	6

1970 CONSUMER CATALOG: 8-1/2 x 11-inch, eight-page color catalog.

EX-C7	LN-C8	Scarcity
8	10	5

1971 TOY FAIR CATALOG: 8-1/2 x 11-inch, 12-page color catalog.

EX-C7	LN-C8	Scarcity
10	15	6

1971 CONSUMER CATALOG: 8-1/2 x 11-inch, 12-page color catalog.

EX-C7	LN-C8	Scarcity
5	8	4

1971 CANADIAN CONSUMER CATALOG: 8-1/2 x 11-inch, eight-page color catalog.

EX-C7	LN-C8	Scarcity
8	10	5

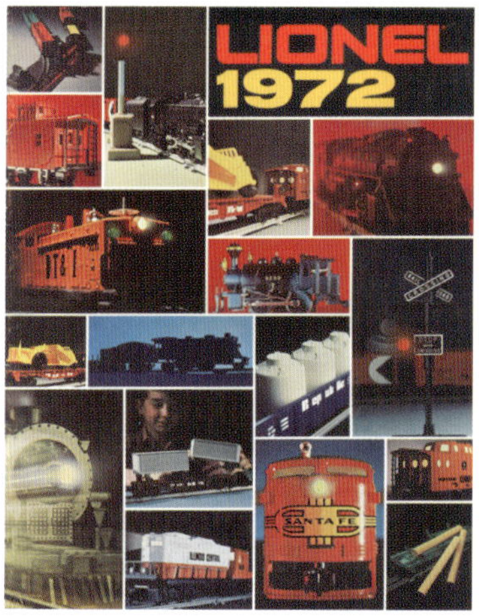

1972 TOY FAIR CATALOG: 8-1/2 x 11-inch, 16-page color catalog without price on cover.

EX-C7	LN-C8	Scarcity
10	15	6

1972 CONSUMER CATALOG: 8-1/2 x 11-inch, 16-page color catalog preprinted with a cover price of 50 cents.

EX-C7	LN-C8	Scarcity
5	8	4

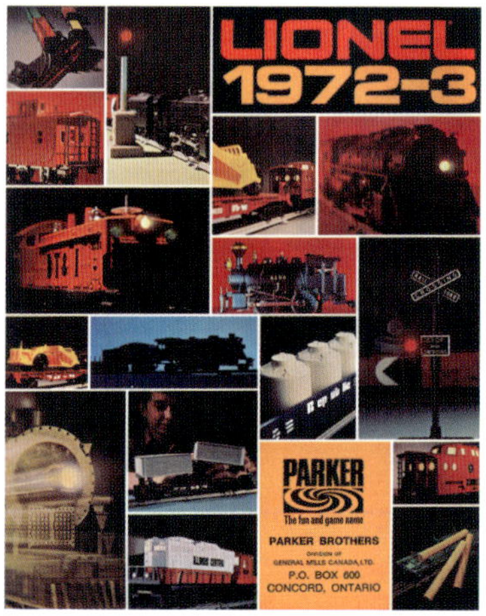

1972 CANADIAN CONSUMER CATALOG: 8-1/2 x 11-inch, eight-page color catalog dated 1972-73 on cover.

EX-C7	LN-C8	Scarcity
8	10	5

1973 ADVANCE CATALOG: 8-1/2 x 11-inch, 16-page black and white catalog with black and white covers.

EX-C7	LN-C8	Scarcity
10	15	6

1973 CONSUMER CATALOG: 8-1/2 x 11-inch, 16-page color catalog.

EX-C7	LN-C8	Scarcity
5	8	4

1974 CONSUMER CATALOG: 8-1/2 x 11-inch, 20-page color catalog.

EX-C7	LN-C8	Scarcity
3	5	3

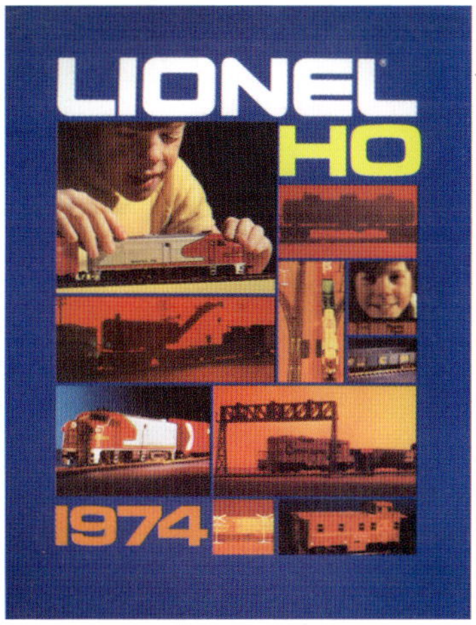

1974 CONSUMER HO CATALOG: 8-3/8 x 11-inch, eight-page color catalog.

EX-C7	LN-C8	Scarcity
3	5	3

1975 CONSUMER CATALOG: 8-1/2 x 11-inch, 24-page color catalog.

EX-C7	LN-C8	Scarcity
3	5	3

1975 CONSUMER HO CATALOG: 8-1/2 x 11-inch, 12-page color catalog.

EX-C7	LN-C8	Scarcity
3	5	3

1976 CONSUMER CATALOG: 8-1/2 x 11-inch, 24-page color catalog.

EX-C7	LN-C8	Scarcity
3	5	3

1976 CONSUMER HO CATALOG: 8-1/2 x 11-inch, 12-page color catalog.

EX-C7	LN-C8	Scarcity
3	5	3

1977 CONSUMER CATALOG: 8-1/2 x 11-inch, 24-page color catalog.

EX-C7	LN-C8	Scarcity
3	5	3

1977 CONSUMER HO CATALOG: 8-1/2 x 11-inch, 12-page color catalog.

EX-C7	LN-C8	Scarcity
3	5	3

1978 CONSUMER CATALOG: 8-1/2 x 11-inch, 24-page color catalog preprinted with a one-dollar cover price.

EX-C7	LN-C8	Scarcity
3	5	3

1979 TOY FAIR CATALOG: 8-1/2 x 11-inch, 68-page color catalog including all "Fundimensions" offerings.

EX-C7	LN-C8	Scarcity
30	40	6

1979 CONSUMER CATALOG: 8-1/2 x 11-inch, 24-page color catalog preprinted with a one-dollar cover price.

EX-C7	LN-C8	Scarcity
3	5	3

1980 CONSUMER CATALOG: 8-1/2 x 11-inch, 28-page color catalog preprinted with a one-dollar cover price.

EX-C7	LN-C8	Scarcity
3	5	3

1981 TOY FAIR CATALOG: 8-1/2 x 11-inch, 98-page color catalog including all "Fundimensions" offerings.

EX-C7	LN-C8	Scarcity
30	40	6

1981 CONSUMER CATALOG: Small 5-1/2 x 7-inch, 32-page color catalog preprinted with a one-dollar cover price.

EX-C7	LN-C8	Scarcity
3	5	3

1982 TRADITIONAL SERIES CONSUMER CATALOG: 8-1/2 x 11-inch, 20-page color catalog.

EX-C7	LN-C8	Scarcity
3	5	3

1982 COLLECTOR SERIES CONSUMER CATALOG: 8-1/2 x 11-inch, 12-page color catalog.

EX-C7	LN-C8	Scarcity
3	5	3

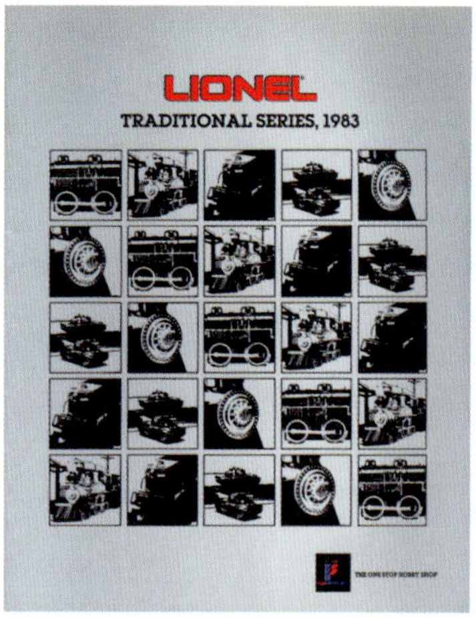

1983 TRADITIONAL SERIES CONSUMER CATALOG: 8-1/2 x 11-inch, 20-page color catalog.

EX-C7	LN-C8	Scarcity
3	5	3

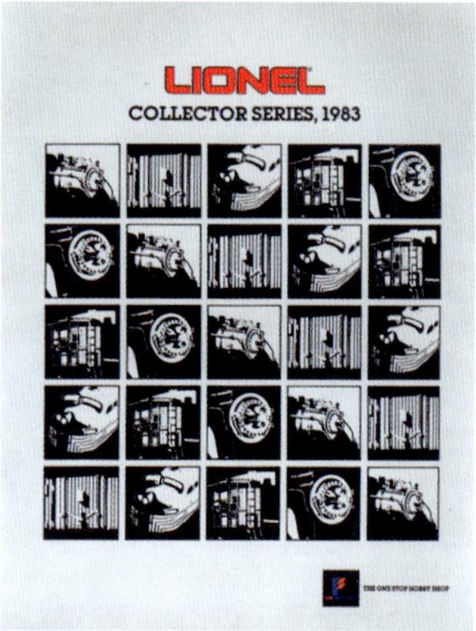

1983 COLLECTOR SERIES CONSUMER CATALOG: 8-1/2 x 11-inch, 16-page color catalog.

EX-C7	LN-C8	Scarcity
3	5	3

1984 TRADITIONAL SERIES CONSUMER CATALOG: 8-1/2 x 11-inch, 20-page color catalog.

EX-C7	LN-C8	Scarcity
3	5	3

1984 COLLECTOR SERIES CONSUMER CATALOG: 8-1/2 x 11-inch, 16-page color catalog.

EX-C7	LN-C8	Scarcity
3	5	3

1985 TRADITIONAL SERIES CONSUMER CATALOG: 8-1/2 x 11-inch, 20-page color catalog.

EX-C7	LN-C8	Scarcity
3	5	3

1985 COLLECTOR SERIES CONSUMER CATALOG: 8-1/2 x 11-inch, 12-page color catalog.

EX-C7	LN-C8	Scarcity
3	5	3

1986 TRADITIONAL SERIES CONSUMER CATALOG: 8-1/2 x 11-inch, 16-page color catalog.

EX-C7	LN-C8	Scarcity
3	5	3

1986 COLLECTOR SERIES CONSUMER CATALOG: 8-1/2 x 11-inch, 16-page color catalog.

EX-C7	LN-C8	Scarcity
3	5	3

1986 DIRECT ORDER BROCHURE: 8-1/2 x 11-inch, tri-folded, four-page color direct-to-consumer sales brochure for 784 B & A scale Hudson and seven Standard 0 series freight cars.

EX-C7	LN-C8	Scarcity
10	15	6

1986 STOCKING STUFFER: 8-1/2 x 11-inch, four-page, full-color sales brochure.

EX-C7	LN-C8	Scarcity
2	4	5

1987 SPRING PREVIEW: 8-1/2 x 11-inch, eight-page, full-color sales brochure.

EX-C7	LN-C8	Scarcity
2	4	5

1987 CONSUMER CATALOG: 8-1/2 x 11-inch, 40-page color catalog.

EX-C7	LN-C8	Scarcity
3	5	3

1987 HAPPY HOLIDAYS: 8-1/2 x 11-inch, four-page, full-color sales brochure.

EX-C7	LN-C8	Scarcity
2	4	5

1987 SIDE TRACKS: 8-1/2 x 11-inch, four-page, full-color sales brochure promoting non-train Lionel souvenirs.

EX-C7	LN-C8	Scarcity
2	4	5

1988 SPRING PREVIEW: 8-1/2 x 11-inch, 16-page, full-color sales brochure.

EX-C7	LN-C8	Scarcity
2	4	5

1988 CONSUMER CATALOG: 8-1/2 x 11-inch, 40-page color catalog.

EX-C7	LN-C8	Scarcity
3	5	3

1988 LARGE SCALE CONSUMER CATALOG: 8-1/2 x 11-inch, 16-page, full-color catalog.

EX-C7	LN-C8	Scarcity
3	5	4

1988 RAILSCOPE: 8 x 10-inch, four-page, full-color sales brochure.

EX-C7	LN-C8	Scarcity
2	4	5

1988 DOUBLE CROSSING: 8-1/2 x 11-inch, four-page, full-color sales brochure promoting Lionel board game.

EX-C7	LN-C8	Scarcity
2	4	5

1988 LIONEL CLASSICS: 8-1/2 x 11-inch, four-page, full-color sales brochure promoting reproductions of prewar Standard-Gauge items.

EX-C7	LN-C8	Scarcity
2	4	5

1988 HIAWATHA: 8-1/2 x 11-inch, four-page, full-color sales brochure promoting Hiawatha "Classic" passenger set.

EX-C7	LN-C8	Scarcity
2	4	5

1988-89 SIDETRACKS: 8-1/2 x 11-inch, four-page, full-color sales brochure promoting non-train Lionel souvenirs.

EX-C7	LN-C8	Scarcity
2	4	5

1989 PRE-TOY FAIR CONSUMER CATALOG: 8-1/2 x 11-inch, 20-page, full-color catalog.

EX-C7	LN-C8	Scarcity
2	4	5

1989 PRE-TOY FAIR LIONEL CLASSICS: 8-1/2 x 11-inch, four-page, full-color sales brochure promoting reproductions of prewar items.

EX-C7	LN-C8	Scarcity
2	4	5

1989 CONSUMER CATALOG: 8-1/2 x 11-inch, 28-page color catalog with cover reading "Toy Fair Edition 1989."

EX-C7	LN-C8	Scarcity
3	5	3

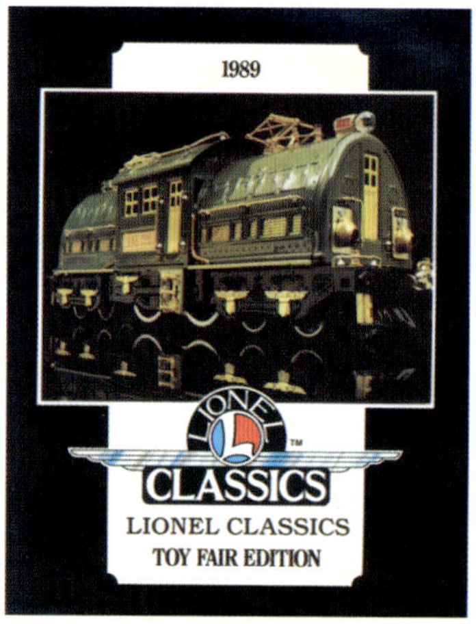

1989 LIONEL CLASSICS: 8-1/2 x 11-inch, four-page, full-color sales brochure promoting reproductions of prewar items. Cover reads "1989 Lionel Classics Toy Fair Edition."

EX-C7	LN-C8	Scarcity
2	4	5

1989 LARGE SCALE CONSUMER CATALOG: 8-1/2 x 11-inch, 28-page color catalog with cover reading "Large Scale Toy Fair Edition 1989."

EX-C7	LN-C8	Scarcity
3	5	3

1989 HOLIDAY COLLECTION: 8-1/2 x 11-inch, four-page, full-color sales brochure.

EX-C7	LN-C8	Scarcity
3	5	3

1990 "BOOK ONE" CONSUMER CATALOG: 8-1/2 x 11-inch, 20-page color catalog.

EX-C7	LN-C8	Scarcity
3	5	3

1990 "BOOK TWO" CONSUMER CATALOG: 8-1/2 x 11-inch, 36-page color catalog.

EX-C7	LN-C8	Scarcity
3	5	3

1990 LARGE SCALE CONSUMER CATALOG: 8-1/2 x 11-inch, 16-page color catalog.

EX-C7	LN-C8	Scarcity
3	5	3

1990 STOCKING STUFFER: 8-1/2 x 11-inch, four-page, full-color sales brochure.

EX-C7	LN-C8	Scarcity
2	4	5

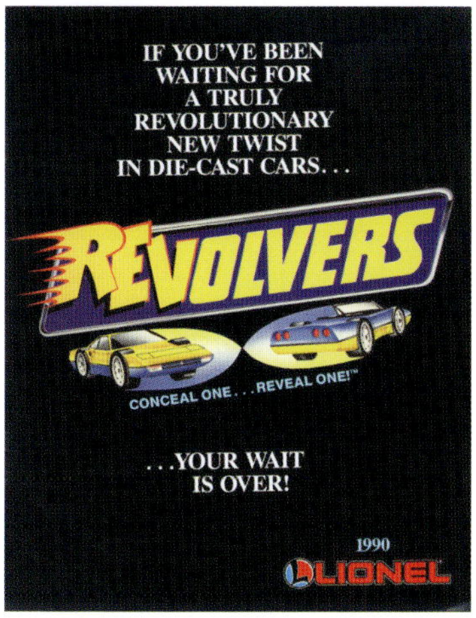

1990 REVOLVERS: 8-1/2 x 11-inch, eight-page, full-color brochure promoting Lionel's die-cast toy cars.

EX-C7	LN-C8	Scarcity
2	4	5

1991 "BOOK ONE" CONSUMER CATALOG: 8-1/2 x 11-inch, 24-page color catalog.

EX-C7	LN-C8	Scarcity
3	5	3

1991 "BOOK TWO" CONSUMER CATALOG: 8-1/2 x 11-inch, 58-page color catalog.

EX-C7	LN-C8	Scarcity
3	5	3

1992 "BOOK ONE" CONSUMER CATALOG: 8-1/2 x 11-inch, 30-page color catalog.

EX-C7	LN-C8	Scarcity
3	5	3

1992 "BOOK TWO" CONSUMER CATALOG: 8-1/2 x 11-inch, 48-page color catalog.

EX-C7	LN-C8	Scarcity
3	5	3

1992 STOCKING STUFFER: 8-1/2 x 11-inch, eight-page, full-color sales brochure.

EX-C7	LN-C8	Scarcity
2	4	5

1993 "BOOK ONE" CONSUMER CATALOG: 8-1/2 x 11-inch, 32-page color catalog.

EX-C7	LN-C8	Scarcity
3	5	3

1993 "BOOK TWO" CONSUMER CATALOG: 8-1/2 x 11-inch, 52-page color catalog.

EX-C7	LN-C8	Scarcity
3	5	3

1993 CONSUMER PAMPHLET: Small 5-3/8 x 7-1/4-inch, 24-page, full-color pamphlet showing a broad range of Lionel items.

EX-C7	LN-C8	Scarcity
2	4	5

1993 STOCKING STUFFER/SPRING RELEASES: 8-1/2 x 11-inch, 28-page, full-color catalog.

EX-C7	LN-C8	Scarcity
2	4	5

1994 CONSUMER CATALOG: 8-1/2 x 11-inch, 64-page color catalog.

EX-C7	LN-C8	Scarcity
3	5	3

1994 LIONEL TRAINMASTER: 8-1/2 x 11-inch, eight-page, full-color sales brochure.

EX-C7	LN-C8	Scarcity
2	4	5

1994 STOCKING STUFFER/1995 SPRING RELEASES: 8-1/2 x 11-inch, 32-page, full-color catalog.

EX-C7	LN-C8	Scarcity
2	4	5

1995 CONSUMER CATALOG: 8-1/2 x 11-inch, 87-page, full-color catalog.

EX-C7	LN-C8	Scarcity
3	5	3

1995 STOCKING STUFFER/1996 SPRING RELEASES: 8-1/2 x 11-inch, 32-page, full-color catalog.

EX-C7	LN-C8	Scarcity
3	5	3

1996 LIONEL CONSUMER CATALOG: 8-1/2 x 11-inch, 24-page color catalog.

EX-C7	LN-C8	Scarcity
3	5	3

1996 LIONEL CORPORATION CONSUMER CATALOG: 8-1/2 x 11-inch, 22-page color catalog.

EX-C7	LN-C8	Scarcity
3	5	3

1997 LIONEL HERITAGE BOOK 1: 8-1/2 x 11-inch, 12-page color catalog.

EX-C7	LN-C8	Scarcity
3	5	3

1997 LIONEL CLASSIC BOOK 1: 8-1/2 x 11-inch, 24-page color catalog.

EX-C7	LN-C8	Scarcity
3	5	3

1997 LIONEL CLASSIC BOOK 2: 8-1/2 x 11-inch, 36-page color catalog.

EX-C7	LN-C8	Scarcity
3	5	3

1997 LIONEL HERITAGE BOOK 2: 8-1/2 x 11-inch, 12-page color catalog.

EX-C7	LN-C8	Scarcity
3	5	3

1997 STOCKING STUFFER: 8-1/2 x 11-inch, four-page, full-color sales brochure.

EX-C7	LN-C8	Scarcity
2	4	5

1998 LIONEL HERITAGE: 8-1/2 x 11-inch, 24-page color catalog.

EX-C7	LN-C8	Scarcity
3	5	3

1998 LIONEL CLASSIC VOLUME 1: 8-1/2 x 9-inch, 62-page color catalog.

EX-C7	LN-C8	Scarcity
3	5	3

1998 LIONEL CLASSIC VOLUME 2: 8-1/2 x 11-inch, 62-page color catalog.

EX-C7	LN-C8	Scarcity
3	5	3

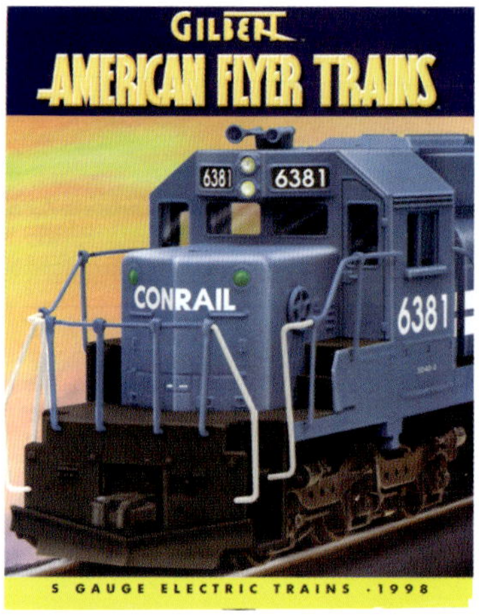

1998 AMERICAN FLYER: 8-1/2 x 11-inch, four-page, full-color sales brochure.

EX-C7	LN-C8	Scarcity
2	4	5

1999 LIONEL HERITAGE: 8-1/2 x 11-inch, 26-page color catalog.

EX-C7	LN-C8	Scarcity
3	5	3

1999 LIONEL CLASSIC VOLUME 3: 8-1/2 x 11-inch, 58-page color catalog.

EX-C7	LN-C8	Scarcity
3	5	3

1999 LIONEL CLASSIC VOLUME 1: 8-1/2 x 11-inch, 62-page color catalog.

EX-C7	LN-C8	Scarcity
3	5	3

2000 LIONEL CLASSIC VOLUME 1: 8-1/2 x 11-inch, 110-page color catalog.

EX-C7	LN-C8	Scarcity
3	5	3

1999 LIONEL CLASSIC VOLUME 2: 8-1/2 x 11-inch, 46-page color catalog.

EX-C7	LN-C8	Scarcity
3	5	3

2000 LIONEL CLASSIC VOLUME 2: 8-1/2 x 11-inch, 86-page color catalog.

EX-C7	LN-C8	Scarcity
3	5	3